Heritage Auction Galleries proudly presents

SEPTEMBER LONG BEACH SIGNATURE AUCTION #446

The Beau Clerc Collection
The Mario Eller Collection, Part One
The Diemer L. Fife Collection
The Laguna Niguel Collection, Part Two
The #3 PCGS 'Mile High' Registry Set of Carson City Morgan Dollars
The Jim O'Neal Collection of Indian Half Eagles
The Arnold & Harriet Collection, Part Two

Main Exhibition of Lots

Long Beach Convention Center • 100 S. Pine Ave • Long Beach, CA 90802

Tuesday, September 25	11:00 AM PT – 7:00 PM PT	Room 104A
Wednesday, September 26	11:00 AM PT – 7:00 PM PT	Booth 400
Thursday, September 27	8:00 AM PT – 7:00 PM PT	Booth 400
Friday, September 28	8:00 AM PT – 7:00 PM PT	Booth 400

Live, Internet, and Mail Bid Auction #446

Long Beach Convention Center • 100 S. Pine Ave • Room 103B • Long Beach, CA 90802

Session 1	Thursday, September 27	1:00 PM PT	Lot 1-836
Session 2	Thursday, September 27	7:00 PM PT	Lot 837-1992
Session 3	Friday, September 28	9:30 AM PT	Lot 1993-2297
Session 4	Friday, September 28	1:00 PM PT	Lot 2298-3003
Session 5	Friday, September 28	6:30 PM PT	Lot 3004-4167

ots are sold at the approximate rate of
00 per hour, but it is not uncommon to
ell 150 lots or 300 lots per hour. Please
lan accordingly so that you don't miss
e items you are bidding on.

his auction is subject to a 15% Buyer's Premium.

The World's #1 Numismatic Auctioneer

HERITAGE HA.com
Auction Galleries

3500 Maple Avenue, 17th Floor, Dallas, Texas 75219
214-528-3500 • 800-US COINS (872-6467)

Direct Client Service Line: Toll Free 1-866-835-3243 • e-mail: Bid@HA.com
View full-color images at HA.com/Coins

LOT SETTLEMENT AND PICKUP
Booth 400

Friday	10 AM – 1 PM PT
Saturday	9 AM – 12 PM PT

THIS AUCTION IS CATALOGED AND PRESENTED BY HERITAGE NUMISMATIC AUCTIONS, INC.

Auctioneer: Samuel W. Foose California 3S 3062 16 65
Heritage Numismatic Auctions Inc. Licensed by the State of California 3S 3062 16 63

Cataloged by Mark Van Winkle, Chief Cataloger;
Brian Koller, Catalog Production Manager; Mark Borckardt, Senior Cataloger;
Jon Amato, John Beety, John Salyer, Dennis Tarrant

Photography and Imaging by Jody Garver, Deign Rook, Joel Gonzales, Piper Crawley,
Colleen McInerney, Tony Webb, Jason Young, Lucas Garritson, Lori McKay, Leticia Crawford

Production and design by Cindy Brenner, Kelley Norwine, Michael Puttonen, Carl Watson

Operations by Cristina Gonzalez, Alma Villa, Miguel Reynaga Sr., Edna Lopez, Celeste Robertson, Maria Flores

FAX BIDS TO
214-443-8425

FAX DEADLINE
Wednesday, Sept. 26
Noon CT

NTERNET BIDDING
Closes at 10 PM CT
the day before
the session

LIVE TELEPHONE
BIDDING
Client Services:
1-866-835-3243
Must be arranged
on or before Wed.,
Sept. 26, by Noon CT

AUCTION RESULTS
Available Immediately
at HA.com/Coins

7426

THE BEAU CLERC COLLECTION

THE MARIO ELLER COLLECTION, PART ONE

THE DIEMER L. FIFE COLLECTION

THE LAGUNA NIGUEL COLLECTION, PART TWO

THE #3 PCGS 'MILE HIGH' REGISTRY SET OF CARSON CITY MORGAN DOLLARS

THE JIM O'NEAL COLLECTION OF INDIAN HALF EAGLES

THE ARNOLD & HARRIET COLLECTION, PART TWO

Dear Bidder,

Welcome to Heritage's September 2007 Long Beach Signature Auction, the Official Auction of the Long Beach Coin Expo and our 61st Official Auction at Long Beach. If you can join us at the Long Beach Convention Center, you will also be able to view more than 8,000 U.S. coin lots, with additional Signature Auctions of world coins and currency in Long Beach, plus a special Tokens and Medals catalog. Final Sessions for U.S. coins, Currency, and World Coins can be viewed in Long Beach before being auctioned the following week at HA.com. Imagine – nearly 20,000 lots of numismatic treasures will be available for your inspection and bidding in Long Beach. What a treat!

With so many lots spread over the seven catalogs, you will want to start selecting your most promising finds as soon as possible. Once you have begun selecting coins and notes, your research is easy in Heritage's free *Permanent Auction Archives* at HA.com. Just be careful not to be mesmerized by so many incredible images and descriptions from a decade of past auctions – you need to concentrate on the lots now available in Long Beach! I understand that it's easy to wander for hours among the 1.2 million items listed therein, but the most attractive lot should always be the one you have a chance of winning!

Our Long Beach anchor consignors have fascinating stories about their collecting interests and experiences. However you personally decide to collect is certainly your business, but I can tell you that the happiest consignors I meet are those who shared their passion with friends and family. Something to think about.

THE BEAU CLERC COLLECTION

The wonderful Beau Clerc Collection was assembled by a dedicated numismatist over more than four decades. He started working and collecting at the age of seven, when he was given permission to replace the older coins from the cash register in the family hardware store; there were weeks when he took his entire salary in silver and better-date coins! There were also occasional bonuses, such as when some old-timer would pay with well-worn gold. He was able to fill many of his blue folders while developing a deep love for his coins and the thrill of the hunt. During the early 1980s, he had to sell his collection to fund his new business, but he promised himself that when financial success came, he would "repay" his hobby. He also adopted new goals: one non-gold coin of each date, and then working on the Branch Mints as well. While he didn't complete his goal of owning one example of every mint from every year, he is thrilled to have come this far. From Colonials to Trade dollars, there are magnificent coins in Mint State and proof; there are also more than one hundred examples of Seated coinage, three dozen of them high quality proofs. A lifelong collector, he is now deciding what his next numismatic challenge will be.

THE MARIO ELLER COLLECTION, PART ONE

Mr. Eller started collecting rare coins about a decade ago – although he had been fascinated by them since childhood. A change in his circumstance gave him the freedom to pursue what he had desired when young but simply couldn't afford then. This belated opportunity resulted in enthusiastic buying across many denominations, and the completion of several series (including Morgan dollars, Peace dollars, and $2.50 Indians).

After ten years of pure fun, Mr. Eller decided the time was right to sell, and he sincerely wishes that their new owners enjoy the chase and pride of ownership as much as he did.

THE DIEMER L. FIFE COLLECTION

Diemer L. Fife was a Texan, through and through. Born in Houston in October 1909; died in Houston in May 1994; and lived most of his life in Hempstead, near Houston. A landowner, he leased out farm and ranch lands, and in 1945 he started a business clearing land and bulldozing lakes (or "stock tanks" as they're known in Texas). After selling his business in the 1960s, his interest in the operations of the town bank soon led to his becoming the CEO. During his retirement years, he also served on the Waller County Appraisal Board.

Mr. Fife began collecting circulated coins when he was 11 or 12, and he was collecting or buying more valuable coins by 1926. He enjoyed showing his treasures to family members or anyone who visited and showed even a mild interest! Due to his contagious enthusiasm, he quickly got them engaged in his passion. He introduced his children to the art of collecting, and his daughter recalls him "teaching us what to look for and how to research value. Probably his favorite coins – the ones of which he was most proud – were the Panama-Pacific issues." Throughout his life, Mr. Fife continued to invest in both gold and land (preferably acreage with the mineral interest intact), believing that they were lasting investments.

THE LAGUNA NIGUEL COLLECTION, PART TWO

The Laguna Niguel Collection was formed by a husband and wife collector team that spent many fun-filled and rewarding decades pursuing numismatic treasures and travel memories. The husband, who died in 2001, started collecting coins as a boy in Yugoslavia, often finding old coins along the coast. His interest continued through his years in France, and thence to America. A real estate investor, he also carefully considered the investment potential of his coins over five decades of pursuing quality. His wife helped with his grading, buying decisions, and record-keeping, while collecting coins of the world (which will be offered in the accompanying World coins Signature Auction). In words that many collectors' wives will understand, she reports that "Next to me, coins were his first love!" Part One was sold in our 2007 Milwaukee ANA Signature Auction.

THE #3 PCGS 'MILE HIGH' REGISTRY SET OF CARSON CITY MORGAN DOLLARS

The Mile High Registry Set of Carson City Dollars is rated as the #3 Current Finest, and is the seventh Finest Set of All-Time. This is an astonishing achievement when one considers the numbers of dollar collectors who are active, and the number of them that love the CC productions! The thirteen Carson City issues were minted from 1878 through 1885, and from 1889 through 1893, and the series contains both common dates and great rarities, especially in Registry quality. Their incredible eye appeal, combined with the thrill of chasing the finest examples of these pieces of western history, led the collector to focus on the CC mint, and from the beginning his intention was to seek the best. A half decade of pure joy followed as the collector "scooped up" every better example he could find in a constant process of upgrading. Occasionally, he was able to obtain the finest certified, and those would be occasions of pure joy. He now hopes that their new owners find the thrill of the hunt the same fun process that he did.

THE JIM O'NEAL #1 REGISTRY COLLECTION OF INDIAN HALF EAGLES

It is with great pleasure that Heritage is offering another exquisite collection assembled by numismatist extraordinaire Jim O'Neal. Mr. O'Neal, the former president and chief executive officer of Frito-Lay International, spent many years carefully assembling fine collections of coins and currency. Mr. O'Neal sold his magnificent collection of rare currency types with Heritage in 2005, and was so pleased with the results that he has once again entrusted us with one of his beloved collections. His complete collection of Indian half eagles, the Current #1 Set on the PCGS Registry, contains every rarity in stunning condition. Like his collections, everything about Jim O'Neal is synonymous with quality – it shows in his career, and in his personal life. The landmark O'Neal pedigree will stand for quality for many new generations of collectors.

THE ARNOLD & HARRIET COLLECTION, PART TWO

Arnold Stein's interest in rare coins started as a young man, attempting to fill all of the holes in his blue Whitman folder. A father in retailing meant a constant flow of new coins through the cash register, although the elusive S-VDB never appeared during his years of searching. Mr. Stein began the more serious pursuit of significant numismatic rarities during the 1990s, and he and his wife Harriet worked with several leading numismatists while assembling several important numismatic collections. He followed a basic buying philosophy of looking for the nicest coin and the best value for the grade. Mr. Stein, a graduate aeronautical engineer, also enjoys collecting machines of intricate functionality, including exotic mechanical watches, exotic racing cars, and exotic firearms. Part One was sold in our 2007 Milwaukee ANA Signature Auction.

****

Again, welcome to Heritage's September Long Beach event. We appreciate your participation, and wish you the very best of bidding luck. Auction is a wonderful way to obtain the coins that you want at the price that you are willing to pay. Plus, you get to participate in some of the most important events in our hobby. It just doesn't get any better. If you cannot join us in Long Beach, you'll still find bidding participation easy with Heritage's exclusive Interactive Internet™ bidding system. We have made bidding online the next best thing to being there! However you participate, we want you to have an enjoyable bidding experience – and there is no denying the excitement of being the winning bidder!

I hope that you can join us in Long Beach – and if so, please visit me at the Heritage tables. I look forward to meeting you.

Sincerely,

Greg Rohan
President

Mail Bidding at Auction

Mail bidding at auction is fun and easy and only requires a few simple steps.

1. Look through the catalog, and determine the lots of interest.

2. Research their market value by checking price lists and other price guidelines.

3. Fill out your bid sheet, entering your maximum bid on each lot using your price research and your desire to own the lot.

4. Verify your bids!

5. Mail Early. Preference is given to the first bids received in case of a tie. When bidding by mail, you frequently purchase items at less than your maximum bid.

Bidding is opened at the published increment above the second highest mail or Internet bid; we act on your behalf as the highest mail bidder. If bidding proceeds, we act as your agent, bidding in increments over the previous bid. This process is continued until you are awarded the lot or you are outbid.

An example of this procedure: You submit a bid of $100, and the second highest mail bid is at $50. Bidding starts at $55 on your behalf. If no other bids are placed, you purchase the lot for $55. If other bids are placed, we bid for you in the posted increments until we reach your maximum bid of $100. If bidding passes your maximum: if you are bidding through the Internet, we will contact you by e-mail; if you bid by mail, we take no other action. Bidding continues until the final bidder wins.

Mail Bidding Instructions

1. **Name, Address, City, State, Zip**
   Your address is needed to mail your purchases. We need your telephone number to communicate any problems or changes that may affect your bids.

2. **References**
   If you have not established credit with us from previous auctions, you must send a 25% deposit, or list dealers with whom you have credit established.

3. **Lot Numbers and Bids**
   List all lots you desire to purchase. On the reverse are additional columns; you may also use another sheet. Under "Amount" enter the maximum you would pay for that lot (whole dollar amounts only). We will purchase the lot(s) for you as much below your bids as possible.

4. **Total Bid Sheet**
   Add up all bids and list that total in the appropriate box.

5. **Sign Your Bid Sheet**
   By signing the bid sheet, you have agreed to abide by the Terms of Auction listed in the auction catalog.

The official prices realized list that accompanies our auction catalogs is reserved for bidders and consignors only. We are happy to mail one to others upon receipt of $1.00. Written requests should be directed to Customer Service.

6. **Fax Your Bid Sheet**
   When time is short submit a Mail Bid Sheet on our exclusive Fax Hotline. There's no faster method to get your bids to us *instantly*. Simply use the **Heritage Fax Hotline number: 214-443-8425.**

   When you send us your original after faxing, mark it "Confirmation of Fax" (preferably in red!)

7. **Bidding Increments**
   To facilitate bidding, please consult the Bidding Increments chart in the Terms & Conditions. Bids will be accepted on the increments or on the half increments.

Interactive Internet™ Bidding

You can now bid with Heritage's exclusive *Interactive Internet™* program, available only at our web site: HA.com. It's fun, and it's easy!

1. Register online at: **HA.com**

2. View the full-color photography of every single lot in the online catalog!

3. Construct your own personal catalog for preview.

4. View the current opening bids on lots you want; review the prices realized archive.

5. Bid and receive immediate notification if you are the top bidder; later, if someone else bids higher, you will be notified automatically by e-mail.

6. The *Interactive Internet™* program opens the lot on the floor at one increment over the second highest bid. As the high bidder, your secret maximum bid will compete for you during the floor auction, and it is possible that you may be outbid on the floor after Internet bidding closes. Bid early, as the earliest bird wins in the event of a tie bid.

7. After the sale, you will be notified of your success. It's that easy!

Bid Live using *HERITAGE LIVE*

This auction is **"HA.com/Live Enabled"** and has continuous bidding from the time the auction is posted on our site through the live event. **When normal Internet bidding ends, visit HA.com/Live and continue to place Live Proxy bids.** When the item hits the auction block, you can continue to bid live against the floor and other live bidders.

Interactive Internet™ Bidding Instructions

1. Log Onto Website

Log onto **HA.com** and chose the portal you're interested in (i.e., coins, comics, movie posters, fine arts, etc.).

2. Search for Lots

Search or browse for the lot you are interested in. You can do this from the home page, from the Auctions home page, or from the home page for the particular auction in which you wish to participate.

3. Select Lots

Click on the link or the photo icon for the lot you want to bid on.

4. Enter Bid

At the top of the page, next to a small picture of the item, is a box outlining the current bid. Enter the amount of your secret maximum bid in the textbox next to "Secret Maximum Bid." The secret maximum bid is the maximum amount you are willing to pay for the item you are bidding on (for more information about bidding and bid increments, please see the section labeled "Bidding Increments" elsewhere in this catalog). Click on the button marked "Place Absentee Bid." A new area on the same page will open up for you to enter your username (or e-mail address) and password. Enter these, then click "Place Absentee Bid" again.

5. Confirm Absentee Bid

You are taken to a page labeled, "Please Confirm Your Bid." This page shows you the name of the item you're bidding on, the current bid, and the maximum bid. When you are satisfied that all the information shown is correct, click on the button labeled, "Confirm Bid."

6. Bidding Status Notification

One of two pages is now displayed.

a. If your bid is the current high bid, you will be notified and given additional information as to what might happen to affect your high bidder status over the course of the remainder of the auction. You will also receive a Bid Confirmation notice via email.

b. If your bid is not the current high bid, you will be notified of that fact and given the opportunity to increase your bid.

TERMS AND CONDITIONS OF AUCTION

Auctioneer and Auction:

1. This Auction is presented by Heritage Auction Galleries, a d/b/a/ of Heritage Auctions, Inc., or their affiliates Heritage Numismatic Auctions, Inc. or Currency Auctions of America, Inc., d/b/a as identified with the applicable licensing information on the title page of the catalog or on the HA.com Internet site (the "Auctioneer"). The Auction is conducted under these Terms and Conditions of Auction and applicable state and local law. Announcements and corrections from the podium and those made through the Terms and Conditions of Auctions appearing on the Internet at HA.com supersede those in the printed catalog.

Buyer's Premium:

2. On bids placed through Heritage, a Buyer's Premium of fifteen percent (15%) will be added to the successful hammer price bid on lots in Coin and Currency auctions, or nineteen and one-half percent (19.5%) on lots in all other auctions. If your bid is placed through eBay Live, a Buyer's Premium equal to the normal Buyer's Premium plus an additional five percent (5%) of the hammer price will be added to the successful bid up to a maximum Buyer's Premium of Twenty Two and one-half percent (22.5%). There is a minimum Buyer's Premium of $9.00 per lot. In Gallery Auctions (sealed bid auctions of mostly bulk numismatic material) only, the Buyer's Premium is 19.5%.

Auction Venues:

3. The following Auctions are conducted solely on the Internet: Heritage Weekly Internet Coin, Currency, Comics, and Vintage Movie Poster Auctions; Heritage Monthly Internet Sports and Marketplace Auctions; Final Sessions. Signature Auctions and Grand Format Auctions accept bids on the Internet first, followed by a floor bidding session; bids may be placed prior to the floor bidding session by Internet, telephone, fax, or mail.

Bidders:

4. Any person participating or registering for the Auction agrees to be bound by and accepts these Terms and Conditions of Auction ("Bidder(s)").
5. All Bidders must meet Auctioneer's qualifications to bid. Any Bidder who is not a customer in good standing of the Auctioneer may be disqualified at Auctioneer's sole option and will not be awarded lots. Such determination may be made by Auctioneer in its sole and unlimited discretion, at any time prior to, during, or even after the close of the Auction. Auctioneer reserves the right to exclude any person it deems in its sole opinion is disruptive to the Auction or is otherwise commercially unsuitable.
6. If an entity places a bid, then the person executing the bid on behalf of the entity agrees to personally guarantee payment for any successful bid.

Credit References:

7. Bidders who have not established credit with the Auctioneer must either furnish satisfactory credit information (including two collectibles-related business references) well in advance of the Auction or supply valid credit card information. Bids placed through our Interactive Internet program will only be accepted from pre-registered Bidders; Bidders who are not members of HA.com or affiliates should pre-register at least two business days before the first session to allow adequate time to contact references.

Bidding Options:

8. Bids in Signature Auctions or Grand Format Auctions may be placed as set forth in the printed catalog section entitled "Choose your bidding method." For auctions held solely on the Internet, see the alternatives on HA.com. Review at HA.com/common/howtobid.php.
9. Presentment of Bids: Non-Internet bids (including but not limited to podium, fax, phone and mail bids) are treated similar to floor bids in that they must be on-increment or at a half increment (called a cut bid). Any podium, fax, phone, or mail bids that do not conform to a full or half increment will be rounded up or down to the nearest full or half increment and this revised amount will be considered your high bid.
10. Auctioneer's Execution of Certain Bids. Auctioneer cannot be responsible for your errors in bidding, so carefully check that every bid is entered correctly. When identical mail or FAX bids are submitted, preference is given to the first received. To ensure the greatest accuracy, your written bids should be entered on the standard printed bid sheet and be received at Auctioneer's place of business at least two business days before the Auction start. Auctioneer is not responsible for executing mail bids or FAX bids received on or after the day the first lot is sold, nor Internet bids submitted after the published closing time; nor is Auctioneer responsible for proper execution of bids submitted by telephone, mail, FAX, e-mail, Internet, or in person once the Auction begins. Internet bids may not be withdrawn until your written request is received and acknowledged by Auctioneer (FAX: 214-443-8425); such requests must state the reason, and may constitute grounds for withdrawal of bidding privileges. Lots won by mail Bidders will not be delivered at the Auction unless prearranged.
11. Caveat as to Bid Increments. Bid increments (over the current bid level) determine the lowest amount you may bid on a particular lot. Bids greater than one increment over the current bid can be any whole dollar amount. It is possible under several circumstances for winning bids to be between increments, sometimes only $1 above the previous increment. Please see: "How can I lose by less than an increment?" on our website.

The following chart governs current bidding increments.
Please note the changes in our bid increments effective immediately.

Current Bid	Bid Increment	Current Bid	Bid Increment
< $10	$1	$20,000 - $29,999	$2,000
$10 - $29	$2	$30,000 - $49,999	$2,500
$30 - $49	$3	$50,000 - $99,999	$5,000
$50 - $99	$5	$100,000 - $199,999	$10,000
$100 - $199	$10	$200,000 - $299,999	$20,000
$200 - $299	$20	$300,000 - $499,999	$25,000
$300 - $499	$25	$500,000 - $999,999	$50,000
$500 - $999	$50	$1,000,000 - $1,999,999	$100,000
$1,000 - $1,999	$100	$2,000,000 - $2,999,999	$200,000
$2,000 - $2,999	$200	$3,000,000 - $4,999,999	$250,000
$3,000 - $4,999	$250	$5,000,000 - $9,999,999	$500,000
$5,000 - $9,999	$500	> $10,000,000	$1,000,000
$10,000 - $19,999	$1,000		

12. If Auctioneer calls for a full increment, a floor/phone bidder may request Auctioneer to accept a bid at half of the increment ("Cut Bid") which will be that bidders final bid; if the Auctioneer solicits bids other the expected increment, they will not be considered Cut Bids, and bidders accepting such increments may continue to participate.

Conducting the Auction:

13. Notice of the consignor's liberty to place reserve bids on his lots in the Auction is hereby made in accordance with Article 2 of the Texas Uniform Commercial Code. A reserve is an amount below which the lot will not sell. THE CONSIGNOR OF PROPERTY MAY PLACE WRITTEN RESERVE BIDS ON HIS LOTS IN ADVANCE OF THE AUCTION; ON SUCH LOTS, IF THE HAMMER PRICE DOES NOT MEET THE RESERVE, THE CONSIGNOR MAY PAY A REDUCED COMMISSION ON THOSE LOTS. Reserves are generally posted online several days prior to the Auction closing. Any successful bid placed by a consignor on his Property on the Auction floor or by telephone during the live session, or after the reserves for an Auction have been posted, will be considered an Unqualified Bid, and in such instances the consignor agrees to pay full Buyer's Premium and Seller's Commissions on any lot so repurchased.
14. The highest qualified Bidder shall be the buyer. In the event of any dispute between floor Bidders at a Signature Auction, Auctioneer may at his sole discretion reoffer the lot. Auctioneer's decision and declaration of the winning Bidder shall be final and binding upon all Bidders.
15. Auctioneer reserves the right to refuse to honor any bid or to limit the amount of any bid which, in his sole discretion, is not submitted in "Good Faith," or is not supported by satisfactory credit, numismatic references, or otherwise. A bid is considered not made in "Good Faith" when an insolvent or irresponsible person, or a person under the age of eighteen makes it. Regardless of the disclosure of his identity, any bid by a consignor or his agent on a lot consigned by him is deemed to be made in "Good Faith." Any person apparently appearing on the OFAC list is not eligible to bid.
16. Nominal Bids. The Auctioneer in its sole discretion may reject nominal bids, small opening bids, or very nominal advances. If a lot bearing estimates fails to open for 40 –60% of the low estimate, the Auctioneer may pass the item or may place a protective bid on behalf of the consignor.
17. Lots bearing bidding estimates shall open at Auctioneer's discretion (approximately 50% of the low estimate). In the event that no bid meets or exceeds that opening amount, the lot shall pass as unsold.
18. All items are to be purchased per lot as numerically indicated and no lots will be broken. Bids will be accepted in whole dollar amounts only. No "buy" or "unlimited" bids will be accepted. Off-increment bids may be accepted by the Auctioneer at Signature Auctions and Grand Format Auctions. Auctioneer reserves the right to withdraw, prior to the close, any lots from the Auction.
19. Auctioneer reserves the right to rescind the sale in the event of nonpayment, breach of a warranty, disputed ownership, auctioneer's clerical error or omission in exercising bids and reserves, or otherwise.
20. Auctioneer occasionally experiences Internet and/or Server service outages during which Bidders cannot participate or place bids. If such outage occurs, we may at our discretion extend bidding for the auction. This policy applies only to widespread outages and not to isolated problems that occur in various parts of the country from time to time. Auctioneer periodically schedules system downtime for maintenance and other purposes, which may be covered by the Outage Policy. Bidders unable to place their Bids through the Internet are directed to bid through Client Services at 1-800-872-6467.
21. The Auctioneer or its affiliates may consign items to be sold in the Auction, and may bid on those lots or any other lots. Auctioneer or affiliates expressly reserve the right to modify any such bids at any time prior to the hammer based upon data made known to the Auctioneer or its affiliates. The Auctioneer may extend advances, guarantees, or loans to certain consignors, and may extend financing or other credits at varying rates to certain Bidders in the auction.
22. The Auctioneer has the right to sell certain unsold items after the close of the Auction; Such lots shall be considered sold during the Auction and all these Terms and Conditions shall apply to such sales including but not limited to the Buyer's Premium, return rights, and disclaimers.

Payment:

23. All sales are strictly for cash in United States dollars. Cash includes: U.S. currency, bank wire, cashier checks, travelers checks, and bank money orders, all subject to reporting requirements. Checks may be subject to clearing before delivery of the purchases. Heritage reserves the right to determine if a check constitutes "good funds" when drawn on a U.S. bank for ten days, and thirty days when drawn on an international bank. Credit Card (Visa or Master Card only) and PayPal payments may be accepted up to $1,000 from non-dealers at the sole discretion of the auctioneer, subject to the following limitations: a) sales are only to the cardholder, b) purchases are shipped to the cardholder's registered and verified address, c) Auctioneer may pre-approve the cardholder's credit line, d) a credit card transaction may not be used in conjunction with any other financing or extended terms offered by the Auctioneer, and must transact immediately upon invoice presentation, e) rights of return are governed by these Terms and Conditions, which supersede those conditions promulgated by the card issuer, f) floor Bidders must present their card.
24. Payment is due upon closing of the Auction session, or upon presentment of an invoice. Auctioneer reserves the right to void an invoice if payment in full is not received within 7 days after the close of the Auction.
25. Lots delivered in the States of Texas, California, or other states where the Auction may be held, are subject to all applicable state and local taxes, unless appropriate permits are on file with us. Bidder agrees to pay Auctioneer the actual amount of tax due in the event that sales tax is not properly collected due to: 1) an expired, inaccurate, inappropriate tax certificate or declaration, 2) an incorrect interpretation of the applicable statute, 3) or any other reason. The appropriate form or certificate must be on file at and verified by Heritage five days prior to Auction or tax must be paid; only if such form or certificate is received by Heritage within 14 days of the Auction can a tax refund be made. Lots from different Auctions may not be aggregated for sales tax purposes.

26. In the event that a Bidder's payment is dishonored upon presentment(s), Bidder shall pay the maximum statutory processing fee set by applicable state law.
27. If any Auction invoice submitted by Auctioneer is not paid in full when due, the unpaid balance will bear interest at the highest rate permitted by law from the date of invoice until paid. If the Auctioneer refers any invoice to an attorney for collection, the buyer agrees to pay attorney's fees, court costs, and other collection costs incurred by Auctioneer. If Auctioneer assigns collection to its in-house legal staff, such attorney's time expended on the matter shall be compensated at a rate comparable to the hourly rate of independent attorneys.
28. In the event a successful Bidder fails to pay all amounts due, Auctioneer reserves the right to resell the merchandise, and such Bidder agrees to pay for the reasonable costs of resale, including a 10% seller's commission, and also to pay any difference between the resale price and the price of the previously successful bid.
29. Auctioneer reserves the right to require payment in full in good funds before delivery of the merchandise.
30. Auctioneer shall have a lien against the merchandise purchased by the buyer to secure payment of the Auction invoice. Auctioneer is further granted a lien and the right to retain possession of any other property of the buyer then held by the Auctioneer or its affiliates to secure payment of any Auction invoice or any other amounts due the Auctioneer or affiliates from the buyer. With respect to these lien rights, Auctioneer shall have all the rights of a secured creditor under Article 9 of the Texas Uniform Commercial Code, including but not limited to the right of sale. In addition, with respect to payment of the Auction invoice(s), the buyer waives any and all rights of offset he might otherwise have against the Auctioneer and the consignor of the merchandise included on the invoice. If a Bidder owes Auctioneer or its affiliates on any account, Auctioneer and its affiliates shall have the right to offset such unpaid account by any credit balance due Bidder, and it may secure by possessory lien any unpaid amount by any of the Bidder's property in their possession.
31. Title shall not pass to the successful Bidder until all invoices are paid in full. It is the responsibility of the buyer to provide adequate insurance coverage for the items once they have been delivered.

Delivery; Shipping and Handling Charges:

32. Shipping and handling charges will be added to invoices. Please refer to Auctioneer's website www.HA.com/common/shipping.php for the latest charges or call Auctioneer. Auctioneer is unable to combine purchases from other auctions or affiliates into one package for shipping purposes. Lots won will be shipped in a commercially reasonable time after payment in good funds is received or credit extended, except when third-party shipment occurs.
33. Successful overseas Bidders shall provide written shipping instructions, including specified customs declarations, to the Auctioneer for any lots to be delivered outside of the United States. NOTE: Declaration value shall be the item(s) hammer price together with its buyer's premium.
34. All shipping charges will be borne by the successful Bidder. Any risk of loss during shipment will be borne by the buyer following Auctioneer's delivery to the designated common carrier or third-party shipper, regardless of domestic or foreign shipment.
35. Due to the nature of some items sold, it shall be the responsibility for the successful bidder to arrange pick-up and shipping through third-parties; as to such items Auctioneer shall have no liability.
36. Any request for shipping verification for undelivered packages must be made within 30 days of shipment by Auctioneer.

Cataloging, Warranties and Disclaimers:

37. NO WARRANTY, WHETHER EXPRESSED OR IMPLIED, IS MADE WITH RESPECT TO ANY DESCRIPTION CONTAINED IN THIS AUCTION OR ANY SECOND OPINE. Any description of the items or second opine contained in this Auction is for the sole purpose of identifying the items for those Bidders who do not have the opportunity to view the lots prior to bidding, and no description of items has been made part of the basis of the bargain or has created any express warranty that the goods would conform to any description made by Auctioneer. Color variations can be expected in any electronic or printed imaging, and are not grounds for the return of any lot.
38. Auctioneer is selling only such right or title to the items being sold as Auctioneer may have by virtue of consignment agreements on the date of auction and disclaims any warranty of title to the Property. Auctioneer disclaims any warranty of merchantability or fitness for any particular purposes.
39. Translations of foreign language documents may be provided as a convenience to interested parties. Heritage makes no representation as to the accuracy of those translations and will not be held responsible for errors in bidding arising from inaccuracies in translation.
40. Auctioneer disclaims all liability for damages, consequential or otherwise, arising out of or in connection with the sale of any Property by Auctioneer to Bidder. No third party may rely on any benefit of these Terms and Conditions and any rights, if any, established hereunder are personal to the Bidder and may not be assigned. Any statement made by the Auctioneer is an opinion and does not constitute a warranty or representation. No employee of Auctioneer may alter these Terms and Conditions, and, unless signed by a principal of Auctioneer, any such alteration is null and void.
41. Auctioneer shall not be liable for breakage of glass or damage to frames (patent or latent); such defects, in any event, shall not be a basis for any claim for return or reduction in purchase price.

Release:

42. In consideration of participation in the Auction and the placing of a bid, Bidder expressly releases Auctioneer, its officers, directors and employees, its affiliates, and its outside experts that provide second opines, from any and all claims, cause of action, chose of action, whether at law or equity or any arbitration or mediation rights existing under the rules of any professional society or affiliation based upon the assigned description, or a derivative theory, breach of warranty express or implied, representation or other matter set forth within these Terms and Conditions of Auction or otherwise. In the event of a claim, Bidder agrees that such rights and privileges conferred therein are strictly construed as specifically declared herein; e.g., authenticity, typographical error, etc. and are the exclusive remedy. Bidder, by non-compliance to these express terms of a granted remedy, shall waive any claim against Auctioneer.

Dispute Resolution and Arbitration Provision:

43. By placing a bid or otherwise participating in the auction, Bidder accepts these Terms and Conditions of Auction, and specifically agrees to the alternative dispute resolution provided herein. Arbitration replaces the right to go to court, including the right to a jury trial.
44. Auctioneer in no event shall be responsible for consequential damages, incidental damages, compensatory damages, or other damages arising from the auction of any lot. In the event that Auctioneer cannot deliver the lot or subsequently it is established that the lot lacks title, provenance, authenticity, or other transfer or condition issue is claimed, Auctioneer's liability shall be limited to rescission of sale and refund of purchase price; in no case shall Auctioneer's maximum liability exceed the high bid on that lot, which bid shall be deemed for all purposes the value of the lot. After one year has elapsed, Auctioneer's maximum liability shall be limited to any commissions and fees Auctioneer earned on that lot.
45. In the event of an attribution error, Auctioneer may at its sole discretion, correct the error on the Internet, or, if discovered at a later date, to refund the buyer's purchase price without further obligation.
46. If any dispute arises regarding payment, authenticity, grading, description, provenance, or any other matter pertaining to the Auction, the Bidder or a participant in the Auction and/or the Auctioneer agree that the dispute shall be submitted, if otherwise mutually unresolved, to binding arbitration in accordance with the commercial rules of the American Arbitration Association (A.A.A.). A.A.A. arbitration shall be conducted under the provisions of the Federal Arbitration Act with locale in Dallas, Texas. Any claim made by a Bidder has to be presented within one (1) year or it is barred. The prevailing party may be awarded his reasonable attorney's fees and costs. An award granted in arbitration is enforceable in any court of competent jurisdiction. No claims of any kind (except for reasons of authenticity) can be considered after the settlements have been made with the consignors. Any dispute after the settlement date is strictly between the Bidder and consignor without involvement or responsibility of the Auctioneer.
47. In consideration of their participation in or application for the Auction, a person or entity (whether the successful Bidder, a Bidder, a purchaser and/or other Auction participant or registrant) agrees that all disputes in any way relating to, arising under, connected with, or incidental to these Terms and Conditions and purchases, or default in payment thereof, shall be arbitrated pursuant to the arbitration provision. In the event that any matter including actions to compel arbitration, construe the agreement, actions in aid or arbitration or otherwise needs to be litigated, such litigation shall be exclusively in the Courts of the State of Texas, in Dallas County, Texas, and if necessary the corresponding appellate courts. The successful Bidder, purchaser, or Auction participant also expressly submits himself to the personal jurisdiction of the State of Texas.
48. These Terms & Conditions provide specific remedies for occurrences in the auction and delivery process. Where such remedies are afforded, they shall be interpreted strictly. Bidder agrees that any claim shall utilize such remedies; Bidder making a claim in excess of those remedies provided in these Terms and Conditions agrees that in no case whatsoever shall Auctioneer's maximum liability exceed the high bid on that lot, which bid shall be deemed for all purposes the value of the lot.

Miscellaneous:

49. Agreements between Bidders and consignors to effectuate a non-sale of an item at Auction, inhibit bidding on a consigned item to enter into a private sale agreement for said item, or to utilize the Auctioneer's Auction to obtain sales for non-selling consigned items subsequent to the Auction, are strictly prohibited. If a subsequent sale of a previously consigned item occurs in violation of this provision, Auctioneer reserves the right to charge Bidder the applicable Buyer's Premium and consignor a Seller's Commission as determined for each auction venue and by the terms of the seller's agreement.
50. Acceptance of these Terms and Conditions qualifies Bidder as a Heritage customer who has consented to be contacted by Heritage in the future. In conformity with "do-not-call" regulations promulgated by the Federal or State regulatory agencies, participation by the Bidder is affirmative consent to being contacted at the phone number shown in his application and this consent shall remain in effect until it is revoked in writing. Heritage may from time to time contact Bidder concerning sale, purchase, and auction opportunities available through Heritage and its affiliates and subsidiaries.

State Notices:

Notice as to an Auction in California. Auctioneer has in compliance with Title 2.95 of the California Civil Code as amended October 11, 1993 Sec. 1812.600, posted with the California Secretary of State its bonds for it and its employees, and the auction is being conducted in compliance with Sec. 2338 of the Commercial Code and Sec. 535 of the Penal Code.

Notice as to an Auction in New York City. These Terms and Conditions are designed to conform to the applicable sections of the New York City Department of Consumer Affairs Rules and Regulations as Amended. This is a Public Auction Sale conducted by Auctioneer. The New York City licensed Auctioneers are Kathleen Guzman, No.0762165-Day, and Samuel W. Foose, No.0952360-Day, No.0952361-Night, who will conduct the Auction on behalf of Heritage Auctions, Inc. ("Auctioneer"). All lots are subject to: the consignor's right to bid thereon in accord with these Terms and Conditions of Auction, consignor's option to receive advances on their consignments, and Auctioneer, in its sole discretion, may offer limited extended financing to registered bidders, in accord with Auctioneer's internal credit standards. A registered bidder may inquire whether a lot is subject to an advance or reserve. Auctioneer has made advances to various consignors in this sale.

Notice as to an Auction in Texas. In compliance with TDLR rule 67.100(c)(1), notice is hereby provided that this auction is covered by a Recovery Fund administered by the Texas Department of Licensing and Regulation, P.O. Box 12157, Austin, Texas 78711 (512) 463-6599. Any complaints may be directed to the same address.

Additional Terms & Conditions:
COINS AND CURRENCY AUCTIONS

COINS and CURRENCY TERM A: Signature Auctions are not on approval. No certified material may be returned because of possible differences of opinion with respect to the grade offered by any third-party organization, dealer, or service. No guarantee of grade is offered for uncertified Property sold and subsequently submitted to a third-party grading service. There are absolutely no exceptions to this policy. Under extremely limited circumstances, (e.g. gross cataloging error) a purchaser, who did not bid from the floor, may request Auctioneer to evaluate voiding a sale: such request must be made in writing detailing the alleged gross error; submission of the lot to the Auctioneer must be pre-approved by the Auctioneer; and bidder must notify Ron Brackemyre (1-800-872-6467 ext. 312) in writing of such request within three (3) days of the non-floor bidder's receipt of the lot. Any lot that is to be evaluated must be in our offices within 30 days after Auction. Grading or method of manufacture do not qualify for this evaluation process nor do such complaints constitute a basis to challenge the authenticity of a lot. AFTER THAT 30-DAY PERIOD, NO LOTS MAY BE RETURNED FOR REASONS OTHER THAN AUTHENTICITY. Lots returned must be housed intact in their original holder. No lots purchased by floor Bidders may be returned (including those Bidders acting as agents for others) except for authenticity. Late remittance for purchases may be considered just cause to revoke all return privileges.

COINS and CURRENCY TERM B: Auctions conducted solely on the Internet THREE (3) DAY RETURN POLICY: Certified Coin and Uncertified Currency lots paid for within seven days of the Auction closing are sold with a three (3) day return privilege. Third party graded notes are not returnable for any reason whatsoever. You may return lots under the following conditions: Within three days of receipt of the lot, you must first notify Auctioneer by contacting Client Service by phone (1-800-872-6467) or e-mail (Bid@HA.com), and immediately ship the lot(s) fully insured to the attention of Returns, Heritage, 3500 Maple Avenue, 17th Floor, Dallas TX 75219-3941. Lots must be housed intact in their original holder and condition. You are responsible for the insured, safe delivery of any lots. A non-negotiable return fee of 5% of the purchase price ($10 per lot minimum) will be deducted from the refund for each returned lot or billed directly. Postage and handling fees are not refunded. After the three-day period (from receipt), no items may be returned for any reason. Late remittance for purchases revokes these Return privileges.

COINS and CURRENCY TERM C: Bidders who have inspected the lots prior to any Auction will not be granted any return privileges, except for reasons of authenticity.

COINS and CURRENCY TERM D: Coins sold referencing a third-party grading service are sold "as is" without any express or implied warranty, except for a guarantee by Auctioneer that they are genuine. Certain warranties may be available from the grading services and the Bidder is referred to them for further details: ANACS, P.O. Box 182141, Columbus, Ohio 43218-2141; Numismatic Guaranty Corporation (NGC), P.O. Box 4776, Sarasota, FL 34230; Professional Coin Grading Service (PCGS), PO Box 9458, Newport Beach, CA 92658; and Independent Coin Grading Co. (ICG), 7901 East Belleview Ave., Suite 50, Englewood, CO 80111.

COINS and CURRENCY TERM E: Notes sold referencing a third-party grading service are sold "as is" without any express or implied warranty, except for guarantee by Auctioneer that they are genuine. Grading, condition or other attributes of any lot may have a material effect on its value, and the opinion of others, including third-party grading services such as PCGS Currency, PMG, and CGA may differ with that of Auctioneer. Auctioneer shall not be bound by any prior or subsequent opinion, determination, or certification by any grading service. Bidder specifically waives any claim to right of return of any item because of the opinion, determination, or certification, or lack thereof, by any grading service. Certain warranties may be available from the grading services and the Bidder is referred to them for further details: Paper Money Guaranty (PMG), PO Box 4711, Sarasota FL 34230; PCGS Currency, PO Box 9458, Newport Beach, CA 92658; Currency Grading & Authentication (CGA), PO Box 418, Three Bridges, NJ 08887. Third party graded notes are not returnable for any reason whatsoever.

COINS and CURRENCY TERM F: Since we cannot examine encapsulated coins or notes, they are sold "as is" without our grading opinion, and may not be returned for any reason. Auctioneer shall not be liable for any patent or latent defect or controversy pertaining to or arising from any encapsulated collectible. In any such instance, purchaser's remedy, if any, shall be solely against the service certifying the collectible.

COINS and CURRENCY TERM G: Due to changing grading standards over time, differing interpretations, and to possible mishandling of items by subsequent owners, Auctioneer reserves the right to grade items differently than shown on certificates from any grading service that accompany the items. Auctioneer also reserves the right to grade items differently than the grades shown in the prior catalog should such items be reconsigned to any future auction.

COINS and CURRENCY TERM H: Although consensus grading is employed by most grading services, it should be noted as aforesaid that grading is not an exact science. In fact, it is entirely possible that if a lot is broken out of a plastic holder and resubmitted to another grading service or even to the same service, the lot could come back with a different grade assigned.

COINS and CURRENCY TERM I: Certification does not guarantee protection against the normal risks associated with potentially volatile markets. The degree of liquidity for certified coins and collectibles will vary according to general market conditions and the particular lot involved. For some lots there may be no active market at all at certain points in time.

COINS and CURRENCY TERM J: All non-certified coins and currency are guaranteed genuine, but are not guaranteed as to grade, since grading is a matter of opinion, an art and not a science, and therefore the opinion rendered by the Auctioneer or any third party grading service may not agree with the opinion of others (including trained experts), and the same expert may not grade the same item with the same grade at two different times. Auctioneer has graded the non-certified numismatic items, in the Auctioneer's opinion, to their current interpretation of the American Numismatic Association's standards as of the date the catalog was prepared. There is no guarantee or warranty implied or expressed that the grading standards utilized by the Auctioneer will meet the standards of any grading service at any time in the future.

COINS and CURRENCY TERM K: Storage of purchased coins and currency: Purchasers are advised that certain types of plastic may react with a coin's metal or transfer plasticizer to notes and may cause damage. Caution should be used to avoid storage in materials that are not inert.

COINS and CURRENCY TERM L: NOTE: Purchasers of rare coins or currency through Heritage have available the option of arbitration by the Professional Numismatists Guild (PNG); if an election is not made within ten (10) days of an unresolved dispute, Auctioneer may elect either PNG or A.A.A. Arbitration.

COINS and CURRENCY TERM M: For more information regarding Canadian lots attributed to the Charlton reference guides, please contact : Charlton International, PO Box 820, Station Willowdale B, North York, Ontario M2K 2R1 Canada.

WIRING INSTRUCTIONS:
Bank Information: JP Morgan Chase Bank, N.A., 270 Park Avenue, New York, NY 10017
Account Name: HERITAGE NUMISMATIC AUCTIONS MASTER ACCOUNT
ABA Number: 021000021
Account Number: 1884827674
Swift Code: CHASUS33

Heritage Auction Galleries Staff

Steve Ivy - Co-Chairman and CEO

Steve Ivy began collecting and studying rare coins in his youth, and as a teenager in 1963 began advertising coins for sale in national publications. Seven years later, at the age of twenty, he opened Steve Ivy Rare Coins in downtown Dallas, and in 1976, Steve Ivy Numismatic Auctions was incorporated. Steve managed the business as well as serving as chief numismatist, buying and selling hundreds of millions of dollars of coins during the 1970s and early 1980s. In early 1983, James Halperin became a full partner, and the name of the corporation was changed to Heritage Rare Coin Galleries. Steve's primary responsibilities now include management of the marketing and selling efforts of the company, the formation of corporate policy for long-term growth, and corporate relations with financial institutions. He remains intimately involved in numismatics, attending all major national shows. Steve engages in daily discourse with industry leaders on all aspects of the rare coin/currency business, and his views on grading, market trends and hobby developments are respected throughout the industry. He serves on the Board of Directors of the Professional Numismatists Guild (and was immediate past president), is the current Chairman of The Industry Council for Tangible Assets, and is a member of most leading numismatic organizations. Steve's keen appreciation of history is reflected in his active participation in other organizations, including past or present board positions on the Texas Historical Foundation and the Dallas Historical Society (where he also served as Exhibits Chairman). Steve is an avid collector of Texas books, manuscripts, and national currency, and he owns one of the largest and finest collections in private hands. He is also a past Board Chair of Dallas Challenge, and is currently the Finance Chair of the Phoenix House of Texas.

James Halperin - Co-Chairman

Jim Halperin and the traders under his supervision have transacted billions of dollars in rare coin business, and have outsold all other numismatic firms every year for over two decades. Born in Boston in 1952, Jim attended Middlesex School in Concord from 1966 to 1970. At the age of 15, he formed a part-time rare coin business after discovering that he had a knack (along with a nearly photographic memory) for coins. Jim scored a perfect 800 on his math SATs and received early acceptance to Harvard College, but after attending three semesters, he took a permanent leave of absence to pursue his full-time numismatic career. In 1975, Jim personally supervised the protocols for the first mainframe computer system in the numismatic business, which would catapult New England Rare Coin Galleries to the top of the industry in less than four years. In 1983, Jim merged with his friend and former archrival Steve Ivy, whom Jim had long admired. Their partnership has become the world's largest and most successful numismatic company, as well as the third-largest auctioneer in America. Jim remains arguably the best "eye" in the coin business today (he won the professional division of the PCGS World Series of Grading). In the mid-1980s, he authored "How to Grade U.S. Coins" (now posted on the web at www.CoinGrading.com), a highly-acclaimed text upon which the NGC and PCGS grading standards would ultimately be based. Jim is a bit of a Renaissance man, as a well-known futurist, an active collector of EC comics and early 20th-century American art (visit www.jhalpe.com), venture capital investor, philanthropist (he endows a multimillion-dollar health education foundation), and part-time novelist. His first fictional novel, "The Truth Machine," was published in 1996 and became an international science fiction bestseller, and was optioned for movie development by Warner Brothers. Jim's second novel, "The First Immortal," was published in early 1998 and immediately optioned as a Hallmark Hall of Fame television miniseries. Jim is married to Gayle Ziaks, and they have two sons, David and Michael. In 1996, with funding from Jim and Gayle's foundation, Gayle founded Dallas' Dance for the Planet, which has grown to become the largest free dance festival in the world.

Greg Rohan - President

At the age of eight, Greg Rohan started collecting coins as well as buying them for resale to his schoolmates. By 1971, at the age of ten, he was already buying and selling coins from a dealer's table at trade shows in his hometown of Seattle. His business grew rapidly, and by 1985 he had offices in both Seattle and Minneapolis. He joined Heritage in 1987 as Executive Vice-President and Manager of the firm's rare coin business. Today, as an owner and as President of Heritage, his responsibilities include overseeing the firm's private client group and working with top collectors in every field in which Heritage is active. Greg has been involved with many of the rarest items and most important collections handled by the firm, including the purchase and/or sale of the Ed Trompeter Collection (the world's largest numismatic purchase according to the Guinness Book of World Records), the legendary 1894 San Francisco Dime, the 1838 New Orleans Half Dollar, and the 1804 Silver Dollar. During his career, Greg has handled more than $1 billion of rare coins, collectibles and art, and provided expert consultation concerning the authenticity and grade condition of coins for the Professional Coin Grading Service (PCGS). He has provided expert testimony for the United States Attorneys in San Francisco, Dallas, and Philadelphia, and for the Federal Trade Commission (FTC). He has worked with collectors, consignors, and their advisors regarding significant collections of books, manuscripts, comics, currency, jewelry, vintage movie posters, sports and entertainment memorabilia, decorative arts, and fine art. Additionally, Greg is a Sage Society member of the American Numismatic Society, and a member/life member of the PNG, ANA, and most other leading numismatic organizations. Greg is also Chapter Chairman for North Texas of the Young Presidents' Organization (YPO), and is an active supporter of the arts. Greg co-authored "The Collectors Estate Handbook," winner of the NLG's Robert Friedberg Award for numismatic book of the year. Mr. Rohan currently serves on the seven-person Advisory Board to the Federal Reserve Bank of Dallas, in his second appointed term. He and his wife, Lysa, are avid collectors of rare wine, Native American artifacts, and American art.

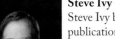

Paul Minshull - Chief Operating Officer

As Chief Operating Officer, Paul Minshull's managerial responsibilities include integrating sales, personnel, inventory, security and MIS for Heritage. His major accomplishments include overseeing the hardware migration from mainframe to PC, the software migration of all inventory and sales systems, and implementation of a major Internet presence. Heritage's successful employee-suggestion program has generated 200 or more ideas each month since 1995, and has helped increase employee productivity, expand business, and improve employee retention. Paul oversees the company's highly-regarded IT department, and has been the driving force behind Heritage's web development, now a significant portion of Heritage's future plans. As the only numismatic auction house that combines traditional floor bidding with active Internet bidding, the totally interactive system has catapulted Heritage to the top rare coin website (according to Forbes Magazine's "Best of the Web"). Paul was born in Michigan and came to Heritage in 1984 after 12 years as the General Manager of a plastics manufacturing company in Ann Arbor. Since 1987, he has been a general partner in Heritage Capital Properties, Sales Manager, Vice President of Operations, and Chief Operating Officer for all Heritage companies and affiliates since 1996. Paul maintains an active interest in sports and physical fitness, and he and his wife have three children.

Todd Imhof - Vice President

Unlike most professional numismatists, Todd Imhof did not start as a coin collector. Shortly after graduating college in 1987, Todd declined an offer from a prestigious Wall Street bank to join a former high school classmate who was operating a small rare coin company in the Seattle area. The rare coin industry was then undergoing huge changes after the advent of certified grading and growing computer technologies. Being new to the industry, Todd had an easier time than most embracing the new dynamics. He soon discovered a personal passion for rare coins, and for working with high-level collectors. Through his accomplishments, Todd enjoys a reputation envied by the entire numismatic community. During his earlier tenure with Hertzberg Rare Coins, it was named by Inc. magazine as one of the nation's fastest growing private companies 1989-1991. In 1991, Todd co-founded Pinnacle Rarities, Inc., a boutique-styled firm that specialized in servicing the rare coin industry's savviest and most prominent collectors. At 25, he was among the youngest people ever accepted into the Professional Numismatists Guild, and currently serves on its Consumer Protection Committee. In 1992, he was invited to join the Board of Directors for the Industry Council for Tangible Assets, serving as its Chairman 2002-2005. Todd served as Pinnacle's President until his decision to join Heritage in 2006. In the Morse Auction, he became the only person in history to purchase two $1mm+ coins during a single auction session! Todd serves Heritage's Legacy clients, many of whom had previously sought his counsel and found his expertise and integrity to be of great value. Todd really understands what collectors are trying to accomplish, and he has an uncanny ability to identify the perfect coins at the right prices while navigating complex and difficult deals with unsurpassed professionalism.

Leo Frese - Executive VP - Numismatic Auctions

Leo has been involved in numismatics for nearly 40 years, a professional numismatist since 1971, and has been with Heritage for over 20 years. He literally worked his way up the Heritage "ladder" through dedication, hard work, and a belief that the client is the most important asset Heritage has. He worked with Bob Merrill for nearly 15 years and now is the Director of Consignments. Leo has been actively involved in assisting clients sell nearly $500,000,000 in numismatic material. Leo was recently accepted as a member of PNG, is a life member of the ANA, and holds membership in FUN, CSNS, and other numismatic organizations. He believes education is the foremost building block in numismatics. Leo encourages all collectors to broaden their horizons, be actively involved in the hobby, and donate freely to YN organizations. Leo's interests include collecting Minnesota pottery and elegant Depression glass. Although travel is an important element of his job, he relishes time with his wife Wendy, children Alicen and Adam, and son-in-law Jeff.

David Mayfield - Consignment Director

David has been collecting and trading rare coins and currency for over 35 years. A chance encounter with his father's coin collection at the age of nine led to his lifetime interest. David has been buying and selling at coin shows since the age of 10. He became a full time coin & currency dealer in the mid-80s. David's main collecting interest is in all things Texas, specializing in currency and documents from the Republic of Texas. Being a sixth generation Texan whose family fought for Texas' independence has only increased the value and meaning of these historical artifacts for him. After more than two decades of marriage, David and Tammy have two wonderful sons, Brian and Michael.

Jim Jelinski - Consignment Director

A collector since age 8, Jim has been involved in numismatics over 5 decades, progressing from humble collector to professional dealer and educator. He is a Life Member of the *American Numismatic Association*, the *American Numismatic Society,* and other state and national organizations. Starting as Buyer for Paramount International Coin Corporation in 1972, he opened Essex Numismatic Properties in 1975 in New Hampshire. Later, positions at M.B. Simmons & Associates of Narberth, Pennsylvania included Director of Sales, Director of Marketing and Advertising, and Executive Vice President. In 1979, he reorganized Essex in Connecticut and, as Essex Numismatics, Inc., worked as COO and CFO. He joined the staff at Heritage as Senior Numismatist and Consignment Coordinator. Jim has two sons, and is actively involved in his church, and community; he just completed his 20th season of coaching youth athletics, and working in Boy Scouting as a troop leader and merit badge counselor. He has been a fund raiser for Paul Newman's "Hole in the Wall Gang" camp for terminally ill children, and for Boy Scouts. His personal diversions include fly fishing, sky diving, cooking, and wine collecting.

Sam Foose - Consignment Director and Auctioneer

Sam's professional career at Heritage divides neatly into two parts. Sam joined Heritage Numismatic Auctions, Inc. in 1993 as an Auction Coordinator. Over the next five years, Sam ran the day-to-day auction operations, ultimately rising to Assistant Auction Director, and began calling auctions. After serving as a Senior Manager and Consignment Director in other collectible fields outside of numismatics, Sam returned to Heritage in 2002 as a Consignment Director in time to help Heritage's expansion into other collectibles. Sam travels the country assisting clients who wish to liquidate their collections of coins, paper money, decorative arts, and sports collectibles. To Sam, helping consignors make the best decisions to maximize their returns from auctioning their properties is the most rewarding part of his job. Sam holds auction licenses in several jurisdictions, and has hammered in excess of $250 million in collectibles as one of Heritage's primary auctioneers. During his free time, Sam enjoys his wife (Heather) and two children (Jackson and Caroline), gardening, golf, grilling, and sports.

David Lisot - Consignment Director

David Lisot is in his fourth decade as a numismatist, writer, researcher, publisher, cataloger, public speaker, and website creator. His expertise includes US & world coins and paper money, gemstones, jewelry, stamps, pocket watches, art, postcards, cigar label art, and antique advertising. David is Director of Heritage's Coin Club Outreach program and a Consignment Director. An accomplished videographer and television producer, David produced the award-winning documentaries, *Money, History in Your Hands, Era of Hometown Bank Notes* for the Higgins Money Museum, and video productions for Heritage. He has videotaped over 750 lectures and presentations about coins and collecting as seen on Coinvideo.com. David was featured in the PBS series, *Money Moves* with Jack Gallagher, as a reporter for FNN, and as founder of CoinTelevision.com. David served as an ANA Governor and is a member of many numismatic organizations. He is a Philosophy graduate of the University of Colorado in Boulder, and a Graduate Gemologist from the GIA. David is married with two children, and enjoys travel, history, exercise, and religious studies.

Bob Marino - Consignment Director & Senior Numismatist

Bob started collecting coins in his youth, and started selling through eBay as the Internet became a serious collector resource. He joined Heritage in 1999, managing and developing Internet coin sales, and building Heritage's client base through eBay and other Internet auction websites. He has successfully concluded more than 40,000 transactions on eBay, selling millions of dollars of rare coins to satisfied clients. Many collectors were first introduced to Heritage through Bob's efforts, and he takes pride in dealing with each client on a personal level. Bob is now a Consignment Director, assisting consignors in placing their coins and collectibles in the best of the many Heritage venues – in short, maximizing their return on many of the coins that he sold to them previously! Bob and his family moved to the DFW area from the Bitterroot Valley in Western Montana. He enjoys spending time with his family, woodworking (building furniture), and remodeling his house.

Charles Clifford - Consignment Director

Charles has been involved with collectibles for over 35 years. His first venture with coins began in the 1970s when he drove to banks all over North Texas buying bags of half dollars to search for the 40% silver clad coins. He has worked as a bullion trader, a rare coin buyer, worked in both wholesale and retail sales, served as a cataloger, and has traveled to hundreds of coin and sports card conventions across the country. Charles also has the distinction of working with Steve Ivy over four decades! Currently he is assisting clients obtain top dollar for the items they have for sale, either by direct purchase or by placing their material in auction. He appreciates Heritage's total commitment to "World Class Client Service" and the "Can Do - Nothing is Impossible" attitude of management and each and every employee. He enjoys collecting hand-blown Depression glass and antique aquarium statues.

Mike Sadler - Consignment Director

Mike Sadler joined the Heritage team in September 2003. Mike attended the United States Air Force Academy, earning a degree in civil engineering and pinned on his silver wings in June 1985. After seven years flying various aircraft, he joined American Airlines where he still pilots. More than once, Mike has surprised Heritage employees serving as their pilot while they flew to shows, conventions, and to visit clients. Like so many of our clients, Mike started putting together sets of coins from circulation when he was a small boy, and that collection grew to go to the auction block with Heritage in January 2004. Before coming to Heritage, his unlimited access to air travel enabled him to attend coin shows all around the country. He gained a tremendous knowledge of rare coins and developed an outstanding eye for quality. He is a trusted friend and colleague to many of today's most active collectors. Having been a collector for so long, and a Heritage consignor himself, Mike understands the needs of the collector and what Heritage can offer. Mike is married, has three children, and enjoys coaching and playing lacrosse

David Lewis - Consignment Director

David Lewis joined Heritage in 2005 as a numismatist, with an extensive numismatic background in wholesale, retail, and internet sales. David's current duties are focused on Heritage's website features, especially "Ask an Expert" and "Coins and Currency Questions", as well as telephone consignments and purchases of rare coins and collections. David is a 22-year veteran of the United States Air Force, and has more than 5000 hours of flight-time as an Airborne Mission Supervisor and Hebrew linguist. David is the winner of the Numismatic Guarantee Corporation's 2004 and 2005 Best Presented Registry Set Awards, and is an avid collector of Washington Quarters and quarter varieties. He holds membership in the ANA, CSNS, and the Barber Coin Collectors Society, among other organizations. David's interests include flying, world travel, history, and collecting Art Deco ceramics and antiques.

Katherine Kurachek - Consignment Director

Katherine grew up in Sarasota, Florida, graduated from the University of Mississippi in 1993 as an art major, and then resided in Colorado (where she opened a pizzeria!) before moving to Dallas. Acting on a suggestion from her father, an avid collector of type coins and a client of Steve Ivy for more than two decades, Katherine came to Heritage in January 2003. She worked alongside Leo Frese for several years, honing her experience in dealing with the numismatic wholesale trade. Taking care of the needs of our dealer-consignors includes soliciting the consignments, inputting the material into our computer systems, and ensuring the smooth flow of the consignment through the many production processes. Katherine is now frequently traveling to coin shows to represent Heritage and service her dealer accounts.In her spare time, she enjoys gardening, golf, hiking, fly-fishing, and walking her two Akitas (Moses and April). Katherine has finally inherited her father's love of these pieces of history, and currently collects love tokens and counterstamps.

Harvey Gamer - Consignment Director

Harv Gamer has been collecting coins since the mid-1950s, but unlike most young collectors then, he pursued world coins. Selling his first coin for a profit in 1958, he began dealing as a California teenager. After high school, Harvey joined the USAF in 1967. After his service, he started on the coin show circuit, traveling regularly around the U.S. and Canada. In more recent years, Harv operated his own coin store in Canada. When his wife was offered a job transfer to Dallas, Harv joined the Heritage team. He just celebrated his 25th ANA anniversary, and is also a member of CNA, CNS, AINA, TAMS, and NTCA. Harv has been a Contributor to the *Standard Catalog of United States Tokens 1700-1900* by Russ Rulau and *American and Canadian Countermarked Coins* by Dr. Gregory Brunk.

Jason Friedman - Consignment Director

Jason's interest in rare coins began at the age of twelve when he discovered a bag of Wheat cents and Liberty nickels in his garage. His collecting interest expanded to Morgans and dealing in various coinage. Jason's numismatic business allowed him to pay for most of his college tuition while working part time and attending classes full time. Jason earned his degree in business from the University of North Texas in 2005. Shortly after, he joined Heritage and was able to turn his passion for numismatics into a career. His computer skills and coordinator background are invaluable tools in accessing all levels of expertise at Heritage. Jason enjoys interacting with clients and assisting them in every aspect of the auction process. Apart from his director position, Jason finds it particularly gratifying phone bidding on clients' behalf. He is a member of the American Numismatic Association (ANA) and Florida United Numismatists (FUN).

Doug Nyholm - Consignment Director

Doug has been collecting coins since the age of ten and fondly recalls spending Morgan silver dollars to purchase candy as a boy. He worked in the IT industry for 28 years with Unisys, 3Com and Sun Microsystems before joining Heritage. Doug's expertise includes all U.S. coins and varieties. He is also well acquainted with U.S. Federal currency and obsoletes. Doug has a special interest in territorials, and in 2004 he wrote and published *The History of Mormon Currency* and has authored many articles on Kirtland currency, scrip and related Utah items. He is currently writing several additional books including one on Utah National Banknotes. Doug is married, has two daughters, and enjoys mountain climbing and hiking. Doug was the President of the Utah Numismatic Society for 2006-07. His current collecting interests include Capped Bust & Seated half dollars, U.S. Type, and Mormon coins & currency.

Mark Van Winkle - Chief Cataloger

Mark has worked for Heritage (and Steve Ivy) since 1979. He has been Chief Cataloger since 1990, and has handled some of the premier numismatic rarities sold at public auction. Mark's literary achievements are considerable. He was editor of *Legacy* magazine, won the 1989 NLG award for Best U.S. Commercial Magazine, and the next year won another NLG award for Best Article with his "Interview With John Ford." In 1996 he was awarded the NLG's Best Numismatic Article "Changing Concepts of Liberty," and was accorded a third place Heath Literary Award that same year. He has done extensive research and published his findings on Branch Mint Proof Morgan Dollars, in addition to writing numerous articles for *Coin World* and *Numismatic News*. Mark has also contributed to past editions of the *Red Book*, and helped with the Standard Silver series in Andrew Pollock's *United States Patterns and Related Issues*. He was also a contributor to *The Guide Book of Double Eagle Gold Coins*.

Mark Borckardt - Senior Cataloger

Mark started attending coin shows and conventions as a dealer in 1970, and has been a full-time professional numismatist since 1980. He received the Early American Coppers Literary Award, and the Numismatic Literary Guild's Book of the Year Award, for the *Encyclopedia of Early United States Cents, 1793-1814*, published in 2000. He serves as a contributor to *A Guide Book of United States Coins*, and has contributed to many references, including the Harry W. Bass, Jr. Sylloge, and the *Encyclopedia of Silver Dollars and Trade Dollars of the United States*. Most recently, he was Senior Numismatist with Bowers and Merena Galleries, serving as a major contributor to all of that firm's landmark auctions. Mark is a life member of the A. N. A., and an active member of numerous organizations. He is an avid collector of numismatic literature, holding several thousand volumes in his library, as well as related postcards and ephemera. He is an avid bowler, carrying an 200+ average, and with seven perfect 300 games. Mark is a graduate of the University of Findlay (Ohio) with a Bachelors Degree in Mathematics. Mark and his wife have a 20-something year old son, and twin daughters who are enrolled at Baylor.

Brian Koller - Cataloger & Catalog Production Manager

Brian's attention to detail ensures that every catalog, printed and on-line, is as error free as technology and human activity allows. In addition to his coin cataloging duties, he also helps with consignor promises and client service issues. Brian has been a Heritage cataloger since 2001, and before that he worked as a telecom software engineer for 16 years. He is a graduate of Iowa State University with a Bachelor's degree in Computer Engineering, and is an avid collector of U.S. gold coins. Brian's numismatic footnote is as discoverer of a 1944-D half dollar variety that has the designer's monogram engraved by hand onto a working die. In addition to describing many thousands of coins in Heritage catalogs, Brian has written more than one thousand reviews of classic movies, which can be found on his website, filmsgraded.com.

John Salyer - Cataloger

John has been a numismatist and coin cataloger with Heritage since 2002. He began collecting Lincoln Cents, Jefferson Nickels, Mercury and Roosevelt Dimes, and Franklin Halves at the age of eleven, as a sixth-grader in Fort Worth; his best friend was also a collector, and his dad would drive them to coin shops and flea markets in search of numismatic treasures. The two youngsters even mowed lawns together in order to purchase their coins, which were always transferred into Whitman folders. John graduated from the University of Texas with a bachelor's degree in English. Prior to his numismatic employment, he worked primarily within the federal government and for several major airlines. His hobbies include playing guitar and collecting antique postcards; an avid golfer, he also enjoys spending time on the links. John has enjoyed making his former hobby his current occupation, and he still actively collects coins.

Jon Amato - Cataloger

Jon has been with Heritage since 2004. He was previously a Program Manager in the NY State Dept. of Economic Development, and an Adjunct Professor at the State University of New York at Albany, where he taught economic geography, natural disasters assessment, and environmental management. Jon is currently writing a monograph on the draped bust, small eagle half dollars of 1796-1797; his research included surveying more than 4,000 auction catalogs, recording the descriptions, grades, and photos of 1796-1797 halves. He published an article entitled "Surviving 1796-1797 Draped Bust Half Dollars and their Grade Distribution," in the *John Reich Journal*, February 2005, and also wrote "An Analysis of 1796-1797 Draped Bust Half Dollars," in *The Numismatist*, Sept. 2001. Jon belongs to many numismatic organizations, including the ANA, ANS, John Reich Collectors Society, and the Liberty Seated Collectors Club, and has made several presentations at ANA Numismatic Theaters. He earned a bachelor's degree from Arizona State University, an M.A. from the S. U. N. Y. at Buffalo, and a Ph. D. from the University of Toronto.

Greg Lauderdale - Cataloger

Greg grew up in Dallas, and began working in a coin shop there in 1979. His interest in numismatics and his trading skills blossomed, and he became a Life Member of the ANA only two years later in 1981. During the 1980s, he conducted several coin auctions in the Dallas Area, including several for the Dallas Coin Club show. He first contracted with Heritage to help write the 1985 Baltimore ANA catalog. He joined Heritage full-time in September of 1985, working as a cataloger and a coin buyer. Greg "left" Heritage in 1988 to develop his personal rare coin company, but has continued to split his time between cataloging for Heritage and trading on eBay from his new home in Maui. Greg has also developed into quite a 'presence' in the world of rare and early Hawaiian postcards. For bidders who attend Heritage's auctions, Greg can often be seen working at the front table – one of the few catalogers in America who is actively involved in the selling process!

John Beety - Cataloger

John grew up in Logansport, Indiana, a small town associated with several numismatic luminaries. Highlights as a Young Numismatist include attending Pittman III, four ANA Summer Seminars (thanks to various YN scholarships), and placing third in the 2001 World Series of Numismatics with Eric Li Cheung. He accepted a position with Heritage as a cataloger immediately after graduation from Rose-Hulman Institute of Technology, after serving an internship at Heritage during the summer of 2004. In addition to his numismatic interests, he enjoys many types of games, with two state junior titles in chess and an appearance in the Top 20 Juniors list of the World Blitz Chess Association.

Steven R. Roach, J.D. - Director, Trusts and Estates

As both a licensed attorney and a seasoned numismatist, Steve is in a unique position to help heirs, nonprofit institutions, attorneys, and advisors with their collectible assets. In his more than 15 years in the coin industry, he has worked with many of the best, including positions at Heritage as a senior grader and numismatist, ANACS as a grader, and stints with Christie's and Spink-America in New York, and PCGS in Los Angeles. Steve writes the popular "Inside Collecting" column in Coin World, and has received two Numismatic Literary Guild (NLG) awards. He received his JD from The Ohio State University Moritz College of Law. He was a judicial extern to United States District Court Judge Gregory Frost, and a summer research fellow for the American Bar Association Section on Dispute Resolution in Washington, D.C. Steve received his BA with high honors from the University of Michigan with a dual degree in the History of Art and Organizational Studies, receiving the Tappan award for outstanding performance in the History of Art program, and studied in Florence, Italy. He is a life member of the American Numismatic Association, and a member of the American Bar Association, the Dallas Bar Association, the Dallas Association of Young Lawyers, and the Dallas Estate Planning Council.

Norma L. Gonzalez - VP of Operations - Numismatic Auctions

Born in Dallas, Texas, Norma joined the U.S. Navy in August of 1993. During her five-year enlistment, she received her Bachelor's Degree in Resource Management and traveled to Japan, Singapore, Thailand and lived in Cuba for three years. After her enlistment, she moved back to Dallas where her family resides. Norma joined Heritage in 1998; always ready for a challenge, she spent her days at Heritage and her nights pursuing an M. B. A. She was promoted to Vice President in 2003. She currently manages the operations departments, including Coins, Currency, World & Ancient Coins, Sportscards & Memorabilia, Comics, Movie Posters, Pop Culture and Political Memorabilia. Norma enjoys running, biking and spending time with her family. In February 2004 she ran a 26.2-mile marathon in Austin, Texas and later, in March she accomplished a 100-mile bike ride in California.

Kelley Norwine - VP - Marketing

Born and raised in South Carolina, Kelley pursued a double major at Southern Wesleyan University, earning a BA in Music Education and a BS in Business Management. A contestant in the Miss South Carolina pageant, Kelley was later Regional Manager & Director of Training at Bank of Travelers Rest in South Carolina. Relocating to Los Angeles, Kelley became the Regional Manager and Client Services Director for NAS-McCann World Group, an international Advertising & Communications Agency where she was responsible for running one of the largest offices in the country. During her years with NAS Kelley was the recipient of numerous awards including Regional Manager of the Quarter and the NAS Courage and Dedication award. After relocating to Dallas, Kelley took a job as Director of Client Services for TMP/Monster Worldwide and joined Heritage in 2005 as Director of Client Development. She was named VP of Marketing for Heritage in 2007. A cancer survivor, Kelley is an often-requested motivational speaker for the American Cancer Society. In her spare time, she writes music, sings, and plays the piano.

John Petty - Director - Media Relations

John Petty joined Heritage in 2001 as the first employee of the newly-formed Heritage Comics division, anxious to join the exciting auction industry. A passionate collector, comics historian, and Overstreet advisor, John had a life-long interest in comics. In 2004, John became the Director of Media Relations, and now handles public relations, copywriting, and media affairs for Heritage Auction Galleries. He also works on special assignments such as magazine articles, book projects, and TV productions. John is also one of Heritage's popular auctioneers, and can frequently be seen calling Movie Poster, Entertainment, and Fine & Decorative Art auctions. Currently, John co-writes monthly columns for both *The Comics Buyers Guide* and *Big Reel Magazine*. Originally from the New York area, John now lives in Texas with Judy, his significant other, two dogs, and three cats. He holds a Bachelor of Music degree in Voice from Baldwin-Wallace College in Berea, Ohio. In his spare time, John enjoys leather carving, silent movies, and Celtic music.

Marti Korver - Manager - Credit/Collections

Marti has been working in numismatics for more than three decades. She was recruited out of the banking profession by Jim Ruddy, and she worked with Paul Rynearson, Karl Stephens, and Judy Cahn on ancients and world coins at Bowers & Ruddy Galleries, in Hollywood, CA. She migrated into the coin auction business, running the bid books for such memorable sales as the Garrett Collection and representing bidders as agent at B&R auctions for 10 years. She also worked as a research assistant for Q. David Bowers for several years. Memorable events included such clients (and friends) as Richard Lobel, John Ford, Harry Bass, and John J. Pittman. She is married to noted professional numismatist and writer, Robert Korver, (who is sometimes seen auctioneering at coin shows) and they migrated to Heritage in Dallas in 1996. She has an RN daughter (who worked her way through college showing lots for Heritage) and a son (who is currently a college student and sometimes a Heritage employee) and a type set of dogs (one black and one white). She currently collects kitschy English teapots and compliments.

DENOMINATION INDEX

SESSION ONE

Live, Internet, and Mail Bid Signature Auction #446
Thursday, September 27, 2007, 1:00 PM PT, Lots 1-836
Long Beach, California

A 15% Buyer's Premium ($9 minimum) Will Be Added To All Lots

Visit HA.com to view full-color images and bid.

COLONIALS

Choice XF Noe-29 Oak Tree Twopence

1 **1662 Oak Tree Twopence XF45 NGC.** Small 2 in date. Crosby 1-A2, Noe-29, R.6. 11.8 gns. This mark-free twopence has surprising sharpness on the tree, since every branch is distinct. The silver-gray legends and motifs contrast with the deep cream-gray to ebony fields. The obverse is well centered, while the reverse is misaligned several degrees toward 5:30. Listed on page 36 of the 2008 *Guide Book*. (#17)

Choice XF Noe-10 Pine Tree Shilling

2 **1652 Pine Tree Shilling, Large Planchet XF45 PCGS.** No pellets at trunk. Crosby 1a-C, Noe-10, R.3. This evenly struck and well centered silver shilling is toned deep dove-gray. All legends are complete except for the M on each side, affected by a slender mint-made clip. The absence of marks further ensures the eye appeal. Listed on page 37 of the 2008 *Guide Book*.
From The Diemer L. Fife Collection. (#23)

3 **(1694) London Elephant Token, Thick Planchet VF30 NGC.** Breen-186. A nicely detailed medium brown representative. The obverse border at 4:30 is moderately granular, and the reverse has a couple of minor mint-made planchet flaws. Listed on page 44 of the 2008 *Guide Book*. (#55)

4 **1723 Rosa Americana Halfpenny, Crown AU55 PCGS.** Breen-140. Crowned Rose. No stop after 3. Deep mahogany-brown surfaces with only a hint of rub on the highest points. Portions of the rims show roller marks from the planchet, as made. Listed on page 41 of the 2008 *Guide Book*. (#119)

Gem Silver 1723 Hibernia Farthing

5 **1723 Hibernia Pattern Farthing, Silver MS65 PCGS.** Breen-173, which he considered "very rare." Per Breen, "about 20 pieces showed up in England, 1971." This sharply struck Gem has prooflike fields and medium lavender and sea-green toning. Careful rotation fails to locate any noticeable marks. Exceptional eye appeal for this impressive yet collectible William Wood variety. PCGS has certified only 20 silver 1723 Hibernia farthings, but six of those are in circulated grades, which suggests that examples may have circulated as a "bit" in Britain or its colonies. Listed on page 42 of the 2008 *Guide Book*. Population: 3 in 65, 0 finer (8/07). (#179)

Choice XF 1766 Pitt Halfpenny

Choice AU 1786 New Jersey Copper

6 **1766 Pitt Halfpenny XF45 NGC.** Breen-251. This chocolate-brown medal has traces of satin luster in protected regions. Marks are limited to a solitary thin line on the vest. The obverse is essentially carbon-free, while the reverse has two tiny and inconspicuous spots. Listed on page 48 of the 2008 *Guide Book*. (#236)

7 **1766 Pitt Halfpenny, Silvered VF20 PCGS.** Breen-251. A silvered example, although the majority of the silver plate has worn through and the piece is now mostly tan-brown in color. The legends are generally clear. The chin has a pair of wispy abrasions, otherwise problem-free for the grade. Listed on page 48 of the 2008 *Guide Book*. (#239)

8 **1773 Virginia Halfpenny, Period MS62 Brown PCGS.** Seven harp strings. Newman 22-S. Substantial brick-red luster clings to the reverse arms. The obverse field is moderately abraded. Listed on page 43 of the 2008 *Guide Book*. (#240)

9 **1773 Virginia Halfpenny, Period MS62 Brown NGC.** Newman 27-J. A satiny chocolate-brown halfpenny with deeper steel-gray toning on the portrait and glimpses of the initial mint red near protected reverse regions. Listed on page 43 of the 2008 *Guide Book*. (#240)

10 **1773 Virginia Halfpenny, Period MS63 Red and Brown NGC.** Newman 27-J. The A in VIRGINIA shows clear repunching. While the surfaces of this attractive Select colonial show areas of mahogany, regions of the shields are pumpkin-orange as well. A pleasing representative of this interesting issue, listed on page 43 of the 2008 *Guide Book*.
From The Beau Clerc Collection. (#241)

11 **1773 Virginia Halfpenny, Period MS64 Red and Brown PCGS.** Newman 27-J. The obverse is more than 50% red, and the obverse has ample orange luster within the legends and the King's hair. Mark-free if slightly granular on the obverse near 7 o'clock. Housed in a green label holder. (#241)

12 **1773 Virginia Halfpenny, Period MS64 Red and Brown PCGS.** Variety 25-M. Glowing gold luster dominates the legends and shield. The king's cheek and neck have toned brown, but marks are minimal. Listed on page 43 of the 2008 *Guide Book*. (#241)

13 **1760 Hibernia-Voce Populi Halfpenny XF40 PCGS.** Z. 6-C, N.9. A glossy chocolate-brown Voce Populi with generally smooth fields and minor buildup near design recesses. The dies are rotated but well centered. Listed on page 47 of the 2007 *Guide Book*. (#262)

14 **1786 Connecticut Copper, Small Head Right VF20 PCGS.** Miller 1-A, High R.4. The scarcer "Double Chin" variety of the ETLIB INDE subtype. A well centered medium brown piece with bold legends and a few small areas of minor granularity. Listed on page 58 of the 2007 *Guide Book*. Population: 2 in 20, 6 finer (7/07). (#325)

15 **1787 Connecticut Copper, Mailed Bust Left XF45 NGC.** Miller 4-L, R.1. This is the well-known "Horned Bust" variety, but an early die state without the die break or "horn" on the lower left obverse field. Well centered with a full, bold date. Dark brown and granular with medium brown highpoints and some wispy marks near the UC in AUCTORI. Listed on page 59 of the 2008 *Guide Book*. (#349)

16 **1786 New Jersey Copper, Straight Beam, Narrow Shield AU55 PCGS.** Maris 14-J, R.1. A remarkably unabraded first-year New Jersey copper with exceptionally attractive olive-brown surfaces. Light wear on the base of the horse is typical for the grade. Listed on page 66 of the 2008 *Guide Book*. Population: 5 in 55, 7 finer (8/07). (#496)

17 **1786 New Jersey Copper, Bridle VF35 PCGS.** Maris 18-M. The "bridle" is a vertical die crack between the snout and the right truncation of the horse. A medium-brown representative with smooth surfaces and the expected moderate incompleteness of strike at the centers. Listed on page 66 of the 2008 *Guide Book*. Population: 3 in 35, 11 finer (8/07). (#501)

18 **1787 New Jersey Copper, Outlined Shield VF30 PCGS.** Maris 48-g. A walnut-brown representative with lighter brown devices. All legends are clear, and the fields lack verdigris. Minor planchet flaking is of mint origin. Listed on page 66 of the 2007 *Guide Book*. (#503)

19 **1787 New Jersey Copper, Outlined Shield AU50 NGC.** Maris 48-g, R.1. The familiar variety with a heavy diagonal die crack across the shield. Glimpses of luster emerge from the golden-tan and medium brown surfaces. Struck on a planchet with myriad small flaws, as made. Listed on page 66 of the 2008 *Guide Book*. (#503)

20 **1787 New Jersey Copper, Small Planchet, Plain Shield XF45 PCGS.** Maris 46-e, R.1. A walnut-brown Choice XF example, charming despite a couple of small gray spots. The obverse is boldly clashed and misaligned toward 10:30. Listed on page 66 of the 2008 *Guide Book*. (#506)

21 **1787 New Jersey Copper, Large Planchet, Plain Shield XF45 NGC.** Maris 64-t, R.1. The centers display the rough planchet surface, but the borders are sharply struck. Dark brown with minor reverse edge nicks at 8 o'clock. The obverse is misaligned toward 12 o'clock, and a small curved clip is present at 5 o'clock. Listed on page 66 of the 2008 *Guide Book*. (#509)

22 **1788 Vermont Copper, Bust Right VF20 PCGS.** RR-25, Bressett 16-U, High R.2. This circulated piece has light brown color in the centers and moderately deeper brown toning toward the borders. A few small planchet flaws are present on the obverse, but both sides are surprisingly unabraded. The obverse is somewhat uncentered toward 2:30, but all legends are intact. Listed on page 68 of the 2008 *Guide Book*.
From The Beau Clerc Collection. (#563)

23 **1788 Vermont Copper, Bust Right AU50 PCGS.** Ex: Ford. RR-16, Bressett 15-S, R.1. This unabraded golden-brown example features steel-gray device highpoints. The centers are softly struck, as usual for Ryder-16, and the surfaces are moderately granular. Listed on page 68 of the 2008 *Guide Book*. Population: 6 in 50, 3 finer (8/07).
Ex: H.C. Whipple Collection (Elder, 2/1921), lot 445; Hillyer Ryder; F.C.C. Boyd; John J. Ford Jr. Collection, Part One (Stack's, 10/2003), lot 44. (#563)

24 **1783 Nova Constellatio Copper, Pointed Rays, Large US XF40 NGC.** Crosby 1-A, R.3. A lightly circulated, minimally marked piece that exhibits this issue's typical softness at the central devices and the date. A die break extends from the second O in CONSTELLATIO into the rays. Listed on page 52 of the 2008 *Guide Book*. (#804)

Choice AU 1785 Nova Constellatio
Elusive Crosby 4-D Variety

25 **1785 Nova Constellatio Copper, Pointed Rays AU55 PCGS.** Crosby 4-D, R.4. A pleasing medium brown Choice AU copper. The strike is precise, the centering is exact, and no abrasions are evident despite a thorough perusal. Breen believed this series should be referred to as "Constellatio Nova," and it probably would be if NOVA was inverted relative to the viewer. Listed on page 52 of the 2008 *Guide Book*. (#813)

Select 1785 Nova Constellatio Copper

26 **1785 Nova Constellatio Copper, Pointed Rays MS63 Brown NGC.** Crosby 4-D, R.4. This satiny Nova Constellatio has consistent medium brown toning, and is well centered, evenly struck, and unabraded. Struck from a clashed obverse die. A charming example of this scarcer die pairing. Listed on page 52 of the 2008 *Guide Book*. (#813)

Very Fine 1787 Fugio Cent
Important No Cinquefoils Newman 1-L

27 **1787 Fugio Cent, STATES UNITED, No Cinquefoils VF20 PCGS.** Newman 1-L, R.6. A rare *Guide Book* variety with a cross after the date instead of the usual cinquefoil, paired with a normal STATES UNITED reverse. A search of Heritage Signature auction records indicates two prior appearances this decade. The walnut-brown surfaces are surprisingly unabraded, although a few trivial planchet flaws are present in addition to a whisper of reverse granularity. Listed on page 83 of the 2008 *Guide Book*. Population: 2 in 20, 9 finer (8/07). (#874)

28 **1787 Fugio Cent, STATES UNITED, Cinquefoils VF25 PCGS.** Newman 7-T, R.5. A moderately circulated nutmeg-brown example of this elusive Fugio cent variety, distinguished by an irregular punching of BUSINESS that puts the N close to the Y and O of YOUR. Mildly marked overall, though a significant planchet void is noted near 7 o'clock at the reverse rim. Listed on page 83 of the 2008 *Guide Book*.
From The Beau Clerc Collection. (#883)

29 **1787 Fugio Cent, STATES UNITED, Cinquefoils XF40 NGC.** Newman 8-X, R.1. The late die state with a heavy obverse die break or cud at 6 o'clock. Sharply defined for the grade, and the chocolate-brown surfaces are smooth save for two thin marks on the right obverse field. Listed on page 83 of the 2008 *Guide Book*. (#883)

30 **1787 Fugio Cent, STATES UNITED, Cinquefoils AU55 PCGS.** Newman 11-X, R.4. This golden-brown Fugio Cent has impressive sharpness on the sun, sundial, and reverse legends. Completely problem-free aside from brief circulation wear. The right-side obverse margin is boldly clashed. In a green label holder, and listed on page 83 of the 2008 *Guide Book*. (#883)

31 **1787 Fugio Cent, STATES UNITED, Cinquefoils—Corroded—ANACS. MS60 Details.** Newman 13-X, R.1. Lustrous and mark-free with apple-green and pink-red toning. Each side has a couple of thin planchet flaws, and a russet spot encroaches upon the right border of the sundial. Struck from clashed dies.
From The Diemer L. Fife Collection. (#883)

Pleasing MS62 Brown 1787 Fugio Cent with Clip

32 **1787 Fugio Cent, STATES UNITED, No Cinquefoils—Clip—MS62 Brown ANACS.** Newman 13-X, R.1. The vertical die crack at 6 o'clock on the reverse, and the clash marks from the chain links along the obverse margin, help to confirm this popular Bank of New York hoard variety. This MS62 example displays hints of underlying red. Well centered design elements are nicely defined. A small planchet clip is located between 10 and 11 o'clock (referenced to the obverse), and a planchet flaw occurs at 10 o'clock on the reverse. (#883)

33 **1787 Fugio Cent, UNITED STATES, Cinquefoils VF35 PCGS.** Newman 16-H.1, R.5. A very scarce variety that has only appeared once in a Heritage auction this decade. UNITED STATES Fugios are nearly always Newman 8-B. An evenly circulated light to medium brown piece with a heavy vertical die crack on the reverse at 6 o'clock. Listed on page 83 of the 2007 *Guide Book.* (#889)

34 **1787 Fugio Cent, UNITED STATES, Cinquefoils—Damaged— ANACS. XF40 Details.** Newman 18-H.1, R.6. A rare die pairing noteworthy for its bold obverse clash marks and a die crack through the I in MIND. The reverse die is misaligned toward 10 o'clock. A cut affects the O in YOUR and the N in BUSINESS, and the reverse has a rim bruise at 8 o'clock and a couple of moderate scrapes on the rings. Listed on page 83 of the 2008 *Guide Book.* (#889)

Delightful Choice 1787 Fugio Cent

35 **1787 Fugio Cent, UNITED STATES, Cinquefoils MS64 Brown PCGS.** Newman 8-B, R.3. Traces of mellowed orange color cling to the devices. Spectacular die clashing as almost invariably found, with the sun's face visible on the lower reverse. This more obtainable die marriage can be readily identified by the high I in FUGIO and the A over O in WE ARE ONE. Listed on page 83 of the 2008 *Guide Book.* (#889)

36 **1787 Fugio Cent, STATES UNITED, Eight-Pointed Star XF40 PCGS.** Newman 15-Y, R.3. The diagnostic die break extends from the sundial to the obverse border at about 4 o'clock. The numerals on the sundial and the letters on the reverse label are well defined, except for weakness in the lower right portion of the former and the lower part of the latter device. The letters in WE ARE ONE are relatively bold, as is the eight-pointed star at the top of the label. Indeed, most of the design elements on this milk-chocolate brown specimen are nicely defined, and are also well centered on the planchet. The semi-gloss surfaces reveal just a few light contact marks and planchet flaws, and appear to be a tad smoother on the obverse. Overall, this is an exceptional piece for an XF Fugio cent. Listed on page 83 of the 2008 *Guide Book.* Population: 14 in 40, 15 finer (8/07). (#898)

37 **1787 Fugio Cent, Club Rays, Rounded Ends VF30 PCGS.** Newman 3-D, R.3. The I in MIND is entered high, and the label border below UNITED STATES is greatly attenuated from die polish. The scarcer of only two Club Rays, Rounded Ends varieties. This chestnut-brown example shows a couple of notable planchet flakes on each side. Struck from clashed dies. Listed on page 84 of the 2008 *Guide Book.* (#904)

38 **1787 Fugio Cent, New Haven Restrike, Copper MS63 Brown PCGS.** Newman 104-FF. A charming golden-brown example with glimpses of russet buildup within the rings. Reverse right-side die rust confirms this popular 19th century Fugio "restrike." Listed on page 84 of the 2008 *Guide Book.* Population: 21 in 63 Brown, 16 finer (8/07). (#916)

Choice Brass Rhode Island Ship Token

39 **(1778-1779) Rhode Island Ship Token, Wreath Below, Brass MS64 PCGS.** Breen-1141. Betts-563. This impressive example retains its initial brassy green-gold iridescence within the letters and ship's rigging, while the open fields have toned cream-gray. Well preserved aside from a hair-thin mark between the upper two flags. Listed on page 48 of the 2008 *Guide Book.* Population: 2 in 64, 0 finer (8/07). (#587)

40 **1789 Mott Token, Thick Planchet, Plain Edge MS62 Brown NGC.** Breen-1020. A charming medium brown Mott token, pleasing despite some crimping on the obverse rim at 9:30. Late dies with flowlined borders and a large break from the upper left corner of the clock. Listed on page 70 of the 2008 *Guide Book.* (#603)

41 **(1792-94) Kentucky Token, Plain Edge AU50 PCGS.** Breen-1155. This luminous, lightly circulated token is predominantly nutmeg-brown with a few areas of deeper color. Highpoint softness is noted on the obverse, with the word CAUSE nearly missing from the scroll. Listed on page 71 of the 2008 *Guide Book.* *From The Beau Clerc Collection.* (#614)

Full Red MS66 1794 Talbot, Allum & Lee Cent

42 **1794 Talbot, Allum & Lee Cent, NEW YORK MS66 Red PCGS.** Breen-1029. This is the most extraordinary TAL Cent we have ever seen. This is the only full red example graded by either service in any grade. The surfaces are bright and show uniform, unmellowed color over both sides with sparkling, semi-prooflikeness. Sharply struck throughout. Per the consignor, this is the single highest graded Colonial coin, using the PCGS Registry system of awarding points. (#636)

Choice 1795 Talbot, Allum & Lee Cent

43 **1795 Talbot, Allum & Lee Cent MS64 Red and Brown PCGS.** Breen-1035. Pink-red iridescence is particularly extensive on the reverse, although both sides have mellowed in gunmetal-gray shades. Nearly immaculate aside from a hair-thin mark on the left reverse field. Encapsulated in a green label holder, and listed on page 72 of the 2008 *Guide Book*.
From The Beau Clerc Collection. (#641)

1820 North West Company Token

44 **1820 North West Company VG8 PCGS.** Breen-1083, "rare." Holed at 12 o'clock, as issued. All legends are clear, and the beaver and bust are nicely defined for this invariably low grade token. The fields have faint pitting and verdigris, as is customary for the issue, since most survivors were recovered from the ground. Listed on page 74 of the 2008 *Guide Book.* (#662)

Very Rare Copper 1820 North West Token

45 **1820 North West Company, Copper Fine 15 NGC.** Breen-1084. Although any North West Company token is rare, the brass examples are more collectible, courtesy of a small hoard of pieces excavated circa 1976 near the Umpqua River Valley in present-day Oregon. Breen believed copper pieces to be extremely rare. In his 1988 Encyclopedia, he was able to list only seven copper examples. "North West token man" George Eggimann estimates that only about 10% of surviving tokens are copper. As of (8/07), PCGS has certified nine brass tokens, but no copper tokens. Regardless of alloy, those tokens were issued holed to trappers and company trading posts.
Nearly all North West Company tokens have corrosion, and copper pieces are particularly susceptible. The present example is finely granular, but the legends are bold aside from COMPANY, which remains legible. Void of relevant marks, and listed on page 74 of the 2008 *Guide Book.*

46 **1783 Washington Unity States Cent XF45 PCGS.** Baker-1. The deep walnut-brown surfaces show faint skeins of orange in the obverse fields. Lightly circulated with strong central detail and great visual appeal, though the peripheral elements show softness. Listed on page 76 of the 2008 *Guide Book.*
From The Beau Clerc Collection. (#689)

47 **1795 Washington Grate Halfpenny, Large Buttons, Reeded Edge AU53 PCGS.** Baker-29AA. Hints of reddish-orange enliven the dusky brown surfaces of this modestly circulated Halfpenny Grate piece. The token's reeded edge is visible, even through the holder. Minimally marked and pleasing. Listed on page 79 of the 2008 *Guide Book.*
From The Beau Clerc Collection. (#746)

48 1795 Washington Grate Halfpenny, Large Buttons, Reeded Edge MS62 Brown PCGS. Baker-29AA. An unworn and attractive chocolate-brown piece that displays faint, scattered abrasions. The upper obverse and upper right reverse legends are cut off. Listed on page 79 of the 2008 *Guide Book*. Population: 31 in 62 Brown, 63 finer (8/07).
From The Beau Clerc Collection. (#746)

MS62 Brown Liberty & Security Penny

49 Undated Washington Liberty & Security Penny MS62 Brown PCGS. Baker-30. Although designated as brown by PCGS, ample orange-red iridescence outlines design elements. The obverse field and portrait are toned olive-brown. Nicely struck and devoid of mentionable contact. Listed on page 80 of the 2008 *Guide Book*. Population: 9 in 62 Brown, 33 finer (8/07). (#767)

Large Size Washington Success Medal AU55

50 Undated Washington Success Medal, Large Size, Reeded Edge AU55 PCGS. Baker-266, brass. From a different obverse die than the familiar variety with a die crack from Washington's nose. The eye of providence is incompletely defined, as always throughout the Success Medal series, but the remainder of the design is sharp. The deep olive-brown surfaces are pleasing aside from a few thin marks near TO. Listed on page 80 of the 2007 Guide Book. (#780)

MS63 Brown Liberty And Security Token Rare Corded Rim Variety

51 Undated Washington Liberty And Security Penny, Corded Rim MS63 Brown PCGS. Baker-30E. Much scarcer than its Plain Rims counterpart, the Corded Rim is identified by the teeth-like pattern throughout both rims. Rulau (1999) stated, "12 specimens known," up slightly from the 1988 Breen estimate of "8-10 known." This sharply struck Select representative has smooth and prooflike cherry-wood fields. Essentially void of marks, although a thin, diagonal planchet flaw through the D in AND will identify the present specimen in any future auction appearances. Listed on page 80 of the 2008 *Guide Book*. Population: 2 in 63, 1 finer (8/07). (#784)

HALF CENTS

52 **1793—Corroded—ANACS. Fair 2 Details.** C-1, B-1, High R.3. The close 17 in the date identifies the obverse, and the location of the leaf near the first A in AMERICA ensures the attribution. Liberty is nicely outlined and the date is clear, but the reverse and LIBERTY are heavily worn. A granular piece with two thin parallel marks near 12 o'clock. EAC 1. (#1000)

53 **1793 AG3 PCGS.** C-1, B-1, High R.3. HALF CENT is worn smooth, but the remaining legends are discernible. The date is clear, and Liberty's eye is visible. Only mildly granular for the grade. Encased in an old green label holder. EAC 2. (#1000)

VF25 1794 Half Cent, C-9

54 **1794 VF25 PCGS.** C-9, B-9, R.2. Breen Die State IV with a die crack atop most letters in LIBERTY and a prominent crack through the cap. A mahogany-brown cent that has clear types and legends. The reverse field has unimportant marks near each S in STATES and on the wreath near the F in HALF. EAC 15. *From The Laguna Niguel Collection, Part Two.* (#1003)

55 **1794—Corroded—ANACS. XF40 Details.** C-2a, B-2b, High R.2. A sharply defined half cent that clearly shows the characteristic C-2 clash marks beneath the chin and along the profile. The dark brown fields are only moderately granular, save for a slender reverse streak from 3:30 to 5:30. EAC 20. (#1003)

56 **1794—Corroded, Whizzed—ANACS. XF40 Details.** C-4a, B-6b, R.3. All legends are bold and the types are clear, but the lavender-brown surfaces are pitted, and the surfaces have been whizzed to remove verdigris. EAC 12. (#1003)

Sharply Detailed 1794 C-9 Half Cent, AU Details

57 **1794—Improperly Cleaned—NCS. AU Details.** C-9, B-9, R.2. This is the High Relief head style used for Cohen-7, 8, and 9. This head style is entirely unlike any other 1794 half cent variety, and it is considered by some to be a separate design for type collectors. The surfaces are faintly rough with deep steel and chocolate color, although there are no appreciable signs of actual wear. A few tiny marks are visible on the highest point of the hear left of Liberty's ear. Although considered the most common variety of 1794, higher grade examples infrequently cross the auction block. EAC 40. (#1003)

Glossy 1795 C-1 Lettered Edge Half Cent, VF30

58 **1795 Lettered Edge VF30 PCGS.** C-1, B-1, R.2. Quickly attributed by the letter I in the date instead of a 1 and the small die scratch after AMERICA. A glossy mahogany-brown example that displays balanced wear in spite of series of jagged planchet cracks on the obverse. Some old reddish corrosion is inconsequential. EAC 12. *From The Beau Clerc Collection.* (#1009)

Key-Date 1796 With Pole Half Cent. C-2, Fine Details

59 **1796 With Pole—Corroded—ANACS. Fine 12 Details.** C-2, B-2, High R.4. The 1796 is a key date that ranks high on the want lists of most early copper collectors. This darkly toned and consistently granular example has clear types, and all legends are bold except HALF. Examination with a loupe reveals a few pinscratches across the central reverse. EAC 4 *From The Beau Clerc Collection.* (#1027)

60 **1797 Plain Edge Fine 12 ANACS.** C-2, B-2, R.3. Lilac-tan legends and devices rise above the finely granular dark brown fields. Patience is required to locate a faint vertical mark beneath the cap, and there are no other abrasions. EAC 8. (#1036)

Popular 1797 C-1 Half Cent, VF25

61 **1797 1 Above 1 VF25 PCGS.** C-1, B-1, R.2. The popular 1 over 1 variety is easily recognized at a glance, with a complete digit 1 between the bust and final date position. PCGS assigned the wrong coin number to this piece, identifying it as a "Plain Edge" variety, that description usually reserved for examples of the C-2 die marriage. The surface have faint evidence of corrosion on the reverse. Attractive steel-brown color is intermingled with olive and reddish-tan. EAC 12. *From The Beau Clerc Collection.* (#1042)

62　**1797 1 Above 1—Corroded—ANACS. VF30 Details.** C-1, B-1, R.2. The distinctive and striking "1 over 1" variety, which shows a plain extra digit below the 1 in the date. This moderately worn chocolate-brown example shows areas of corrosion in both the obverse and reverse fields, particularly at the margins. Only the first half of LIBERTY is visible. EAC 10. (#1042)

63　**1800—Obverse Scratched—NCS. Unc. Details.** C-1, B-1, R.1. A curved, intermittent mark travels from the obverse rim at 10 o'clock to the central hair ribbon. Liberty's eye has a round indentation. The reverse field and left obverse border are minutely granular. Still a lustrous and well defined powder-blue and tan example. EAC 50. (#1051)

Well Defined 1803 Half Cent, VF20 Details, C-4

64　**1803—Corroded—ANACS. VF20 Details.** B-4, C-4, R.3. The footless T in LIBERTY and the six berries on the left wreath branch confirm the variety. The reverse is rotated nearly 180 degrees on this example. Brown surfaces reveal light to moderate porosity, nevertheless, the design elements are quite clear, except for the weakly struck LF in HALF. EAC 5. (#1060)
From The Diemer L. Fife Collection. (#1060)

65　**1804 Plain 4, No Stems MS62 Brown ANACS.** C-13, B-10, R.1. This attractive Mint State example displays rich reddish-brown coloration over lustrous surfaces. The design features are generally well struck, except for the O in OF, the leaves nearby, and some of the dentils. A handful of tiny contact marks are noted, along with a few minuscule carbon flecks. EAC 55. (#1063)

66　**1804 Crosslet 4, Stems AU58 PCGS.** C-10, B-9, R.1. Generally well struck, if slightly off-center, with minor counterclockwise reverse die rotation noted on the order of 20 to 25 degrees. The medium-brown surfaces reveal darker undertones across the center of the reverse. Faint highpoint wear is observed on Liberty's hair detail; surface marks are minimal. EAC 45.
From The Arnold & Harriet Collection, Part Two. (#1069)

67　**1804 Crosslet 4, No Stems MS62 Brown NGC.** C-12, B-11, R.2. Though the surfaces of this attractive half cent are predominantly nutmeg-brown, both sides display significant undercurrents of reddish-orange. Pleasingly detailed with a grade-defining vertical abrasion to the right of the Y in LIBERTY. EAC 60.
From The Beau Clerc Collection. (#1072)

68　**1833 MS63 Brown PCGS.** B-1, C-1, R.1. A lovely and carefully preserved half cent, golden-brown save for blushes of deeper steel-blue hues at 1 o'clock on the obverse and 5 o'clock on the reverse. This Classic Head piece is housed in a prior-generation holder. EAC 55.
From The Beau Clerc Collection. (#1162)

69　**1851 MS61 Red and Brown NGC.** C-1, B-1, R.1. The base of an errant 1 is punched far to the right of the date. Softly struck but fully lustrous with fiery red color and moderate scattered carbon on each side. A wispy pinscratch is noted near the reverse center. EAC 60.
From The Beau Clerc Collection. (#1225)

70　**1855 MS63 Red NGC.** C-1, B-1, R.1. A fine Select Mint State representative of this late half-cent issue. Intense luster illuminates the fire-red surfaces, that show crisply struck devices and the absence of any coin-to-coin marks or planchet irregularities. Moderate scattered carbon flecks limit the grade. EAC 64.
From The Laguna Niguel Collection, Part Two. (#1235)

LARGE CENTS

1793 Chain Cent, AMERICA, AG Details, S-3, B-4

71　**1793 Chain AMERICA—Obverse Planchet Flaw—NCS. AG Details.** S-3, B-4, Low R.3. Medium tan surfaces display most of the central obverse device, including Liberty's eye, and all of the chain, ONE CENT, and the fraction. The date and LIBERTY are weak, and all of AMERICA shows. A linear planchet flaw is visible in the upper right obverse field. EAC 3. (#1341)

Desirable 1793 S-3 Chain Cent, Fine Details

72　**1793 Chain AMERICA—Corroded—ANACS. Fine 15 Details.** S-3, B-4, Low R.3. Straight bust line with a large and high R in LIBERTY. The reverse has AMERICA spelled in its entirety. A combination of minor surface marks, original planchet marks, and later corrosion are combined on the surfaces, yet this desirable piece still retains excellent eye appeal. Some lighter reddish-tan suggests it may have been recolored. EAC 10.
From The Beau Clerc Collection. (#1341)

VG10 S-6 1793 Wreath Cent

73　**1793 Wreath Cent—Vine and Bars—VG10 PCGS.** S-6, B-7, R.3. All legends are bold, as are the berries and Liberty's eye. The dark brown surfaces are moderately granular, with some pitting near the profile. A worthy example of this coveted single-year, first-year cent type. Certified in an old green label holder. EAC 5. (#1347)

Fine Details 1793 S-8 Wreath Cent

74 **1793 Wreath Cent—Vine and Bars, Scratched—NCS. Fine Details.** S-8, B-13, R.3. This medium brown cent has clear legends, and all berries are distinct. The back of Liberty's head has much hair detail. The left obverse border is granular, and the obverse has a number of wispy pinscratches. The central reverse displays an X. A planchet cutter mark is noted between 5 and 9 o'clock on the reverse. EAC 5. (#1347)

Sharply Detailed VF20 1793 S-8 Wreath Cent

75 **1793 Wreath Cent—Vine and Bars— VF20 PCGS.** S-8, B-13, R.3. Horizontal stem parallel to the date. The bow is high and triangular. The existing detail reveals a sharpness grade of XF40, with light, evenly distributed porosity on both sides. Dark steel and greenish-brown color is accompanied by lighter brown on certain highpoints of the design. The EAC and PCGS grades of this specimen are comparable. EAC 20. (#1347)

XF Details S-8 1793 Wreath Cent

76 **1793 Wreath Cent—Vine and Bars, Corroded—NCS. XF Details.** S-8, B-13, R.3. A well defined representative of this coveted single-year design type. The dark brown fields and lilac-brown devices are surprisingly unabraded, although the obverse border is minutely porous and the reverse has a number of small, roundish pits. EAC 15.
From The Laguna Niguel Collection, Part Two. (#1347)

77 **1793 Wreath Cent—Lettered Edge, Corroded—NCS. Fine Details.** S-11b, B-16b, R.4. All legends are fully legible on this Wreath cent. S-11b, with two leaves on the edge, is scarcer than S-11c, which has a single edge leaf. Mahogany-brown with lighter highpoints. The granular surfaces exhibit fine pinscratches from verdigris removal. EAC 4. (#1350)

Well Defined 1793 Liberty Cap Cent
Fine Details, S-13, B-20

78 **1793 Liberty Cap—Scratched—NCS. Fine Details.** S-13, B-20, Low R.4. The variety is confirmed by two beads over the I in LIBERTY, and a triple leaf under the O of OF. Medium brown surfaces reveal ancient shallow scratches. All of the design elements display sharp detail for the grade. EAC 6. (#1359)

79 **1794 Head of 1794 VF20 ANACS.** S-57, B-55, R.1. The "Pyramidal Head" was the fanciful sobriquet Maris gave to this available variety. This moderately worn representative, ebony with glints of chocolate-brown, offers pleasing surfaces overall, though a number of faint rim bumps and light abrasions are present on each side. EAC 10. (#901374)

80 **1794 Head of 1794—Corroded—NCS. VF Details.** S-60, B-52, R.3. A moderately granular lavender-brown representative with a pit on the cheekbone and a rough area near the E in LIBERTY. Liberty's hair and the wreath provide impressive definition. EAC 10. (#901374)

81 **1794 Head of 1794—Corroded—ANACS. VF20 Details.** S-65, B-51, R.1. The heavy vertical die crack at 12 o'clock on the reverse aids the attribution. A lavender-brown example with consistently granular surfaces. Design elements are bold, save for the final letters in AMERICA. The obverse die is slightly misaligned toward 1:30. EAC 8. (#901374)

82 **1794 Head of 1794—Corroded—ANACS. XF40 Details.** S-55, B-47, R.2. Medium brown with blushes of lilac. The obverse field is irregularly pitted, although the reverse is relatively smooth aside from several small pits at 5:30. Splendidly detailed and collectible. EAC 12. (#901374)

Finest Known 1795 NC-3 Cent

83   **1795 Plain Edge—Corroded-ANACS. Good 6 Details.** NC-3, High R.7. This is only the fifth example of the 1795 NC-3 die variety known, and it is clearly the finest. Every other known example is low quality, grading either Fair 2 or Basal State (Poor) 1 by Noyes. The obverse has a complete outline of Liberty with the lower hair strands visible. The date is weak and LIBERTY is absent. The reverse has ONE CENT and most of the wreath boldly outlined, with UNITED complete and parts of STATES and AMERICA visible. Olive and tan surfaces are lightly corroded.

This reverse die is known only on this variety, and the low grade of survivors has not permitted a complete description. ONE CENT is central within the wreath, with CENT low. The leaf tip left of C is nearly level with the top of that letter. The leaf point left of O is above the center of that letter. A leaf pair inside the right branch at T in CENT has both leaves below or touching that letter, similar to S-78 but no others. The leaf pair right of ONE nearly touches the right top of T below and ends opposite the lower serif of E. The left branch has just three berries, all inside. This is the only 1795 reverse that does not have an outer left berry. The left terminal leaf bends sharply upward.

This is an incredible opportunity to obtain the finest known of just five examples. We sold the previous finest known example of the 1795 NC-3 in our January 2005 sale of the Rasmussen sale for $4,600, and that coin graded just Fair 2. This one is twice as nice. EAC 4. (#1380)

84   **1795 Plain Edge—Rim Damaged—ANACS. XF45 Details.** S-78, B-8, R.1. Satiny luster shimmers across the legends and devices of this medium brown Liberty Cap type coin. The right rims are irregular from abrasions, as is the reverse rim between 9 and 11 o'clock. EAC 20.
From The Laguna Niguel Collection, Part Two. (#1380)

Well Defined 1796 Draped Bust Cent
XF Details, S-93, Breen Die State 9

85   **1796 Draped Bust, Reverse of 1795—Obverse Damage—NCS. XF Details.** S-93, B-34, R.3. Breen Die State 9. The rough spot below the knot, and the joining of AM of AMERICA confirm the variety, and the cracks at ERICA affirm the late die state. Medium tan surfaces exhibit golden and faint blue undertones, and sharply defined design elements. Some minute marks are visible on the obverse, a few of which resemble tiny punches, which NCS may be referring to as "damage." At any rate, all of these marks are minor and do not significantly detract. EAC 30 (#1401)

Well Struck 1796 Draped Bust Cent
Reverse of 1797, MS62 Brown, S-119

86   **1796 Draped Bust, Reverse of 1797 MS62 Brown PCGS.** S-119, B-40, R.3. The PCGS insert says "Reverse of 1796," when in fact this variety is the Reverse of 1797, confirmed by the following: the top of the 6 in the date is buried in the drapery, there is a double leaf under the last S in STATES and another under the D of UNITED, there is an outside berry under the stand of E, and a crack travels from the rim through the bottom of the curls and 17 of the date, with another crack below the 6. Pretty chestnut brown color graces both sides of this generally well struck, semi-gloss example. Some light marks on Liberty's portrait and a few more on the lower right reverse limit the grade. EAC 60. (#1407)

87   **1797 Reverse of 1797, Stems—Corroded—NCS. XF Details.** S-140, B-22, R.1. This sharply delineated example is consistently and moderately granular. The forehead and drapery are abraded, and the obverse rim is nicked at 3 o'clock. The reverse is doubled, the result of a double strike with slight reverse die rotation between blows. EAC 15. (#1422)

Rotated Double Struck 1798 Cent AU53
Scarce S-158 First Hair Style Variety

88   1798 First Hair Style—Double Struck, Second Strike Rotated—AU53 NGC. S-158, B-17, R.4. Breen Die State II with a heavy die crack near the T in UNITED. Medium brown and steel-blue with glimpses of golden-brown. Both strikes are independently normal, but the second strike is rotated 90 degrees CCW from the initial strike. Likely, the piece was struck, then inadvertently fed between the dies a second time. Even if this cent were not a significant mint error, it would still be important as a sharp, lightly abraded, nearly carbon-free, and partly lustrous representative of this scarce First Hair Style variety. EAC 30. (#1431)

89   1798 Second Hair Style VF30 ANACS. S-186, B-39, R.2. Die cracks on the upper right obverse and the lower right reverse provide ready attribution. The die break on the denominator is well advanced. A generally smooth medium brown cent with occasional glimpses of peripheral granularity. EAC 15. (#1434)

1799/8 Key Date Cent, VG Details, S-188

90   1799/8—Damaged—NCS. VG Details. S-188, B-2, R.4. Light to medium brown patination bathes both sides of this key-date large cent. The design elements display sharp detail, especially those in the centers. Some of the light marks scattered over each side appear purposely made. (#1446)

91   1799—Corroded, Scratched—ANACS. Fair 2 Details. S-189, B-3, R.2. Nearly all of the 99 in the date is evident once the piece is bathed in light. This dark brown example is expectedly granular, and has a minor pinscratch on the field near the chin and a small obverse rim ding at 9:30. EAC 2. (#1443)

Key Date 1799 Cent, Fair 2, S-189

92   1799 Fair 2 ANACS. S-189, B-3, R.2. Just about all of the 1799 shows clearly, and most of the Liberty motif is raised above the field, and displays a slight bit of internal detail. LIBERTY is worn away, as are most of the reverse design elements. Attractive medium brown color graces both sides, and there are no significant abrasions to report. Generally speaking, this key date example illustrates just honest wear. EAC 2. (#1443)

93   1799—Damaged—ANACS. Fair 2 Details. S-189, B-3, R.2. Heavily worn, yet easily attributable by the close 99 in the date. This chocolate-brown example displays a pair of sizable rim bruises, one at 3 o'clock on the obverse and the other at 9 o'clock on the reverse, that account for the net grade. EAC 1.
From The Beau Clerc Collection. (#1443)

94 **1800 VF25 PCGS.** S-212, B-20, R.3. Attributed by the sagging die break between the two 0s in the date. A sharply defined cent with iridescent sea-green toning and several pinscratches on each side. Housed in a green label holder. EAC 10. (#1449)

95 **1800—Rim Damaged—ANACS. XF40 Details.** S-212, B-20, R.3. The chocolate-brown and steel-gray surfaces are virtually void of verdigris, but the obverse rim is nicked at 10:30, and a few other obverse marks are here and there. EAC 20. (#1449)

96 **1802—Corroded—ANACS. MS60 Details.** S-232, B-12, R.1. An interesting variety that has a T in LIBERTY cut over a Y, and a set of denticles clashed onto the reverse between the wreath and a recut R in AMERICA. Although designated as "Corroded" by ANACS, this attractive deep golden-brown cent in fact shows little granularity, and is a find for the dedicated specialist. Liberty's curls are well struck. EAC 50.
From The Laguna Niguel Collection, Part Two. (#1470)

97 **1804—Corroded, Tooled—ANACS. AG3 Details.** S-266, B-1, R.2. The date is faded but the digits are legible, and the die rotation (0 in the date opposite the O in OF) provides a further diagnostic. From early dies without any rim cuds. The upper right reverse field is pinscratched, and the dark brown surfaces are glossy from burnishing. Liberty's chin has a small roundish dig. The legends are approximately 60% readable. EAC 2. (#1504)

98 **1804 AG3 ANACS.** S-266, B-1, R.2. The central devices are outlined, and contain just a modicum of internal detail, and the date shows, albeit weakly. ONE CENT is relatively strong. The light to medium brown surfaces show just honest wear. All in all, quite pleasing for the grade. EAC 3. (#1504)

99 **1804—Damaged, Corroded—ANACS. Good 4 Details.** S-266, B-1, R.2. From late dies with the familiar rim breaks over RTY and MERIC. Liberty's forehead has a relatively large depression, which slightly bends the flan and flattens the ribbon knot opposite. Moderately granular near the profile, denomination, and hair ribbon. STATES OF is worn smooth. EAC 2. (#1504)

100 **1808—Corroded—NCS. AU Details.** S-278, B-2, R.3. This variety is easily identified by the leaf tips aligned with the second S of STATES. This walnut-brown example shows little actual wear and great detail for a Classic Head cent, though the obverse shows noticeable areas of corrosion and the reverse exhibits small pockets as well. EAC 20. (#1543)

The Finest Available 1812 S-290 Cent, MS65 Red and Brown

101 **1812 Small Date MS65 Red and Brown PCGS.** S-290, B-2, R.1. Less than 10 Mint State examples of S-290 appear in the major large cent census listings. Del Bland records exactly 10 pieces, although he has only seen eight of the ten pieces. Bill Noyes considers just six examples as full Mint State, and two of those have not been seen for 30 years. This specimen has a 34 year pedigree, and is tied for the finest known according to both Bland and Noyes. The piece it is tied with belongs to the British Museum in London, where it has resided for more than 140 years. Therefore, this example is the single finest 1812 S-290 large cent available to collectors today.

Sheldon-290 is identified by the needle-like die scratch beneath the obverse center dot. The variety is plentiful in dark, worn grades, but is very rare with noticeable remaining mint red. An extraordinary coin from a technical perspective, unabraded and unspotted, although the dies are flowlined, particularly along the right borders. Both sides have frosty cartwheel luster with olive-brown color. A tiny dark toning spot is trapped between stars 11 and 12, identifying the pedigree. Splashes of original red mint color appear on the obverse, with considerably more on the reverse. While this example is an excellent piece to represent the Classic Head design type, it is most likely destined to be a part of the finest variety cabinet of these cents. As noted by the cataloger for American Numismatic Rarities when this cent last appeared on the market: "Both Noyes and Bland grade this coin 'EAC' MS65, a true feat for a coin that is not full red and a great testament to this coin's eye appeal and originality."

Although not cracked, this example represents the latest known die state with heavy flowlines, especially on the reverse, and prominent lapping lines also on the reverse. STATES OF AME have the tops of these letters merged with the border. In an article that appeared in *America's Copper Coinage, 1783-1857*, published by the ANS after the 1984 Coinage of the Americas Conference, Pete Smith described the flowlines that often appear on the Classic Head cents.

> "In the striking process the metal of the planchet is compressed between the two dies. It is also forced outward from the center. This lateral movement may have a cumulative effect upon the dies. The effect can be observed as radial lines across the surface of the coin. Some of these radial lines are a natural product of the metal stretching. However, when they appear in the same place and pattern on many coins, it is apparent that the lines are transferred from the surface of the die. These lines can also be observed at the points of greatest resistance. Often the points of the stars on the obverse or the letters of the reverse legend become connected to the rims because of this effect."

Population: 2 in 65 Red and Brown, 0 finer (7/07). EAC 65. *Discovered at a 1973 coin show by Malcolm Varner; A-Mark Coin Co. (3/1973), lot 244; Douglas M. McHenry; Superior Galleries (9/1986), lot 429; Anthony Terranova; R.E. Naftzger, Jr. (2/23/1992); Eric Streiner; Jay Parrino (The Mint); Superior (2/1999), lot 2157; Alan Kollar; Superior (5/2005), lot 1040; American Numismatic Rarities (9/2005), lot 52. (#1562)*

102 **1817 15 Stars AU55 NGC.** N-16, High R.1. The only 15 Stars variety for the year, as only one reverse die was paired with the distinctive obverse. The rose-tinged chocolate-brown surfaces have excellent visual appeal and strong central detail, though the lower left stars are soft. EAC 45. (#1597)

103 **1820 Large Date MS64 Red and Brown PCGS.** N-13, R.1. This exquisite near-Gem is delightfully free from marks, and the satin luster is comprehensive. Brick-red iridescence fills design recesses, with gunmetal-gray present on the portrait and fields. EAC 62. (#1616)

104 **1820 Large Date MS65 Red and Brown PCGS.** N-13, R.1. Orange-gold outlines the stars and legends, while the highpoints and open fields are steel-gray. Carbon is surprisingly minimal for this Randall Hoard example. Encapsulated in a first generation holder. EAC 63. (#1616)

Gem 1823 Restrike Cent

105 **1823 Restrike MS65 Brown NGC.** An impressive piece with exceptional quality and also a late die state, representing the terminal state of the dies. We know this because the original dies for the 1823 Restrike still exist, and are on loan to the ANA Museum from the Jules Reiver family. Both sides have reflective chocolate surfaces with hints of original red. A delightful example. EAC 60. (#1627)

106 **1824/2 XF40 PCGS.** N-1, High R.1. A late die state with a die crack throughout most of the reverse peripheral legends. Medium brown and dark olive toning. AMERICA and the lower portion of the wreath are granular, and a subtle spot is present above the N in ONE. EAC 20. (#1639)

Scintillating 1825 Cent MS64, N-10

107 **1825 MS64 Brown NGC.** N-10, High R.3. Noyes Die State C with a die break or "cud" above star 7. A lustrous chocolate-brown to medium brown Matron Head example. Crisply struck save for the left-side stars. Slightly bright near star 5, and a few unimportant marks are noted above the E in CENT. EAC 62. (#1642)

1839 N-9 Silly Head Cent, MS65

108 **1839 Silly Head MS65 Brown NGC.** N-9, R.2. The die crack is diagnostic with additional rim breaks along the upper obverse margin. Hints of red and violet are visible on the medium-brown surfaces, which are well-preserved and appealing. EAC 60. Census: 8 in 65 Brown, 9 finer (8/07). *From The Beau Clerc Collection.* (#1748)

109 **1839 Booby Head—Scratched—ANACS. MS60 Details.** N-11, R.1. The most available of the Booby Head variants. While the obverse of this rosewood and walnut-brown piece presents beautifully, the reverse shows a number of scratches around the word CENT within the wreath. EAC 50. *From The Beau Clerc Collection.* (#1751)

MS66 Census Level 1840 N-5 Cent

110 **1840 Large Date MS66 Brown PCGS.** N-5, R.1. Grellman Die State a-b. The recutting over the digit 0 and the die lines over RICA are all visible, although they are blurred by flowlines. Although a few stars are weak, all remaining details are boldly evident. The surfaces have full cartwheel luster with even brown color accented by hints of original red. While our EAC grade seems a little conservative, we consider this cent to be a Census level example. EAC 62. Population: 2 in 66 Brown, 0 finer (8/07). *Ex: Superior (5/2004), lot 165; Tom Reynolds.* (#1820)

111 **1841 MS62 Brown NGC.** N-6, R.1. Grellman state b. Bold die lines behind the hair bun and in front of the neck help identify the variety. Deep brown toning offers hints of rose and sea-green color. A couple of faint fingerprints are noted on the borders, and a strike-through (as made) weakens the first S in STATES. A tick on the nose and a few even smaller marks near the jaw will identify future appearances. Scarce in Mint State grades with pleasing surfaces. EAC 40. *From The Beau Clerc Collection.* (#1832)

Census Level MS66 Red and Brown 1848 N-9 Cent

112 **1848 MS66 Red and Brown PCGS.** N-9, R.1. Grellman Die State b, cracked over AM but without rim breaks at the top of the reverse. Both sides have rich bluish-brown color with considerable original red mint luster, and pristine surfaces. Previously certified MS67 RB by NGC, this piece is the finest red and brown 1848 cent certified by either service. EAC 64. (#1884)

113 **1850 MS65 Red and Brown NGC.** N-7, R.2. Generally fire-red, although the cheek and neck show glimpses of steel-gray. Satiny and nearly free from marks. Certified in a former generation holder. EAC 63. (#1890)

114 **1851 MS66 Brown NGC.** N-2, R.1. A lustrous and attentively struck medium brown Premium Gem that retains some mint orange luster across portions of the left reverse. A smooth and impressive type coin. EAC 60. (#1892)

Superb Red and Brown 1851 N-10 Cent

115 **1851 MS67 Red and Brown NGC.** N-10, R.1. Grellman Die State b. Bob Grellman writes "in latest state, this die has no useful attribution points" in his discussion of the reverse. The fields on both sides are covered with flowlines. Frosty red mint luster is subdued by attractive light blue toning on both sides. This piece ranks in the top 10 for the variety. EAC 63. (#1893)

116 **1851/81 MS63 Red and Brown NGC.** N-3, R.1. A luminous Select representative of this popular repunched date variety, which has the date punched upside-down first and later corrected. This well-defined example has a striking appearance. While most of the obverse and the entirety of the reverse are cherry-red, the lower left third of the obverse is mint-green, and a dollop of gold graces the date. EAC 60. (#1896)

117 **1853 MS66 Brown PCGS.** N-24, R.2. Steel-blue and plum accents grace this solidly struck large cent. The surfaces offer both excellent visual appeal and exquisite preservation. EAC 60. (#1901)

118 **1853 MS64 Red PCGS.** N-13, R.1. The most prevalent of the die varieties for 1853, particularly in Mint State, due to a hoard. This copper-orange and peach piece offers pleasing central detail and minimal carbon, though the stars are soft. A mark is present on the bridge of Liberty's nose. EAC 65. (#1903)

Outstanding 1855 Upright 5s Cent, MS67 Brown

119 **1855 Upright 5s MS67 Brown NGC.** N-4, R.1. A pair of die lumps show below Liberty's earlobe and a pair of faint die lines are within the N in CENT, these being used to confirm the Newcomb variety. Although designated as Brown, there is a considerable amount of orange-red luster on each side. An attentive strike brings out bold detail on the design elements, with only a few star centers showing softness. Both faces are impeccably preserved, further enhancing the coin's outstanding eye appeal. EAC 63. Census: 4 in 67 Brown, 0 finer (8/07). (#1907)

Gem Mint State 1855 N-9 Knob on Ear Cent

120 **1855 Knob on Ear MS65 Red and Brown PCGS.** N-9, R.1. Grellman state d. An earlier die state of this popular variety, with the knob still in its developing stages. Cracks have outlined the knob between Liberty's ear and the letter T, and this break is beginning to rise above the surface of the hair strands, but has not yet expanded over to the Y of LIBERTY. Grellman state d. Deep orange mint color is visible on both sides, a shade or two lighter on the reverse. At least 50% of the original color remains, although this is so nicely and attractively blended with light brown toning that it is difficult to pinpoint an exact percentage of red color. Exceptional surfaces with full cartwheel luster. EAC 63. Population: 1 in 65, 0 finer (8/07). *Ex: Del Bland (7/19/1969); Jules Reiver (Heritage, 1/2006), lot 20620.* (#1914)

121 **1856 Upright 5 MS65 Red and Brown NGC.** N-12, High R.1. Fully struck with intense luster and dappled fire-red and steel-gray coloration. A small lint mark (as struck) pierces the lower, outer edge of Liberty's ear. A faint fingerprint is noted on the obverse, but abrasions are not found on either side of this attractive Gem. EAC 63. (#1920)

Census Level 1856 N-21 Cent, MS66

122 **1856 Slanted 5 MS66 Brown PCGS.** N-21, R.2. Although it is considered a common variety today, the N-21 die combination was not known to Newcomb before his reference was posthumously published. This example is well within the Census for the variety, probably ranking among the four finest known pieces. Incredible luster and gorgeous blue-brown color accompanies splashes of original frosty mint red. EAC 63. Population: 1 in 66, 0 finer (8/07). (#1922)

Broadstruck N-1 1857 Large Cent, VF-35

123 **1857 Large Date—Broadstruck—PCGS. VF35.** N-1, R.1. This piece was struck out of the collar, resulting in exceptionally wide borders and an increased diameter of nearly 29 mm. Pleasing light brown surfaces have the usual minor circulation marks that are expected for the grade. EAC 15.
From The Beau Clerc Collection. (#1928)

PROOF LARGE CENT

Red and Brown PR66 1854 Large Cent

124 **1854 PR66 Red and Brown NGC.** N-12. Probably High R.5 as a proof. This is an excellent example with considerable light orange that is accented by sea-green toning on each side. The reverse has additional hints of gold color. A small rim flaw is located on the obverse border between stars 1 and 2, permanently marking the pedigree of this piece. There are no other marks of any significance on either side of this Premium Gem proof. A few faint hairlines can only be seen with magnification, and these in no way affect the eye appeal or overall quality of this proof. EAC PR62. (#1992)

FLYING EAGLE CENTS

Rare Snow-5 1856 Flying Eagle Cent, MS62

125 **1856 MS62 PCGS.** Snow-5, R.6. A rare die pairing of this immensely popular and historic issue. Early small cent expert Rick Snow believes that Snow-5 is a proof-only variety, and the needle-sharp strike and moderately reflective fields of the present well-made example support his classification. PCGS has certified this coin as a business strike, probably because the obverse die differs from the usual proof variety, Snow-9. Snow-5 is about forty times scarcer than Snow-9, and approximately ten times scarcer than the business strike Snow-3 marriage.

    The current lot has attractive straw-gold and salmon-pink toning. Both carbon and contact are unimportant relative to the conservatively assessed grade. Minor retained laminations at 7:30 and 9 o'clock on the reverse serve to identify this important piece. *From The Beau Clerc Collection.* (#2013)

126 **1857 MS63 NGC.** An attractive Select example of the short-lived Flying Eagle design, well-defined with warm orange and mushroom-brown surfaces. Slight streakiness is noted on the obverse, which is surprisingly mark-free. (#2016)

127 **1857 MS63 NGC.** Both sides show some grade-limiting weakness of strike, especially on TED STATES, the eagle's head and tail, and the reverse wreath leaves. Intense satin luster and warm champagne-tan coloration improves the eye appeal, however. An appealing Select Mint State example overall. (#2016)

128 **1857 MS64 PCGS.** Luminous salmon and orange surfaces with few marks are the primary attraction for this pleasing near-Gem. While the eagle has strong detail overall, the tailfeathers are a touch soft, and weakness is noted at parts of the wreath. A lovely example of the first circulation-strike small cent issue. (#2016)

129 **1857 MS64 PCGS.** In contrast to the large cent of the same year, which had a mintage of just over one-third of a million pieces, the 1857 Flying Eagle cent had a total production of 17.45 million circulation strikes, a staggering total for the time. This well-defined and carefully preserved example's mahogany surfaces show delicate, delightful orange-blossom accents. (#2016)

130 **1857 MS64 PCGS.** This shimmering, dusky, tan-brown near-Gem is remarkably void of contact, and would surely receive a higher grade were it not for a typical strike on the tail feathers and bow knot. (#2016)

131 **1857 MS64 PCGS.** This near-Gem Flying Eagle cent is richly toned and highly lustrous, yielding considerable eye appeal. Interesting die cracks extend through the eagle's left (facing) wing, and the reverse has a series of interesting, mint-made laminations. An attractive and abrasion-free example of this brief type. *From The Arnold & Harriet Collection, Part Two.* (#2016)

132 **1857 MS64 PCGS.** A well struck example from the first circulation-strike small cent issue, predominantly salmon with a few areas of deeper color. Few flaws are present on the devices, though a handful of wispy abrasions are noted in the fields. (#2016)

133 **1857 Doubled Die Obverse MS63 NGC.** VP-001, FS-002, Snow-4. Wide die doubling on the first S in STATES is a pick-up point for this popular *Cherrypickers'* variety. This boldly impressed tan-gold cent is smooth aside from a luster graze above the left (facing) wing. VP-001 Census: 8 in 63, 13 finer (7/07). (#2017)

134 **1858 Large Letters MS63 PCGS.** High Leaves, Closed E in ONE. A lustrous and nearly unabraded small cent with minor obverse carbon and a few small strike-throughs near the denomination. Encased in a green label holder. (#2019)

135 **1858 Large Letters MS64 NGC.** Low Leaves, Closed E in ONE. This decisively struck tan-gold near-Gem has a well preserved obverse and a few inconsequential ticks on the central reverse. The final year for the briefly produced introductory small cent type. (#2019)

136 **1858 Large Letters MS64 PCGS.** High Leaves, Closed E in ONE. A dusky olive-green near-Gem with glimpses of orange in selected areas. Crisply struck aside from the lower right cotton leaf. (#2019)

Beautiful Gem 1858 Large Letters Cent

137 **1858 Large Letters MS65 NGC.** High Leaves, Closed E in ONE. The overall strike is precise, although due to a slight die misalignment, OF and the right ribbon end are incompletely brought up. The date and cotton leaves are razor-sharp. The lustrous fields are straw-gold and remarkably carbon-free. (#2019)

138 **1858 Small Letters MS64 NGC.** Low Leaves, Open E in ONE. An unabraded sun-gold near-Gem. A good strike despite minor softness on the eagle's tail and the right-side cotton leaves. The E in AMERICA is faint due to a strike-through. (#2020)

139 **1858 Small Letters MS64 PCGS.** Low Leaves, Closed E in ONE. A beautiful and lustrous type coin, well struck save for a hint of incompleteness on the eagle's breast. The obverse is rose-gold with a blush of yellow-gold, and the reverse is light pumpkin-gold. (#2020)

PROOF FLYING EAGLE CENT

Impaired Proof 1856 Flying Eagle Cent, Very Fine Details

140   **1856—Whizzed—NCS. Proof, Very Fine Details.** Snow-9. The surfaces show overbrightness and the fine metal movement characteristic of whizzing. The 1 and 8 in the date show minor damage on each digit, but the all-important 5 and 6 are bold. This piece likely saw light circulation some time before its "improvement," but much detail remains, making this piece an affordable choice to complete that last key date in the Indian and Flying Eagle collection. (#2037)

INDIAN CENTS

141   **1859 MS64 NGC.** This is a visually enchanting near-Gem example of the first Indian cent issue. In addition to its status as a first-year issue, the piece also represents the unique Laurel Wreath reverse type, which was only produced in 1859. This example is boldly struck, showing the usual softness of definition on the tips of the headdress feathers. Lustrous with even tan coloration and minimal contact marks.
From The Laguna Niguel Collection, Part Two. (#2052)

142   **1859 MS64 PCGS.** A luminous salmon representative of this popular one-year type, well struck with pleasingly preserved surfaces. A hint of lighter orange is present within the plain laurel wreath. (#2052)

Appealing Gem 1859 Indian Cent

143   **1859 MS65 PCGS.** An appealing Gem from this abundant mintage in excess of 36 million pieces. The surfaces are reddish-tan, with a good amount of luster. This piece shows a decent strike, with some typical softness on the feather tips. Surface abrasions are minimal and consistent with the Gem grade. PCGS has certified only 15 pieces finer (8/07). (#2052)

Scarce 1860 Pointed Bust Cent, MS65

144   **1860 Pointed Bust MS65 PCGS.** Richard Snow, in his Flying Eagle and Indian Head cents guidebook writes of the 1860 Pointed Bust: "These are presently quite scarce in Mint State grades, with premiums rising from three to six times the price of a Broad Bust example." Beautiful light tan color resides on highly lustrous surfaces that exhibit sharply struck design elements. A minute planchet flake occurs between the IC of AMERICA. Population: 27 in 65, 5 finer (8/07). (#2056)

Lovely MS66 1860 Indian Cent

145   **1860 MS66 PCGS.** Commonly called the Type Two Obverse, the bust is on this hub type is broader. This change and the deeper sinking of the central head of the Indian in the hub were undoubtedly done to improve the striking details of the coins. Better struck on the reverse than the obverse, the surfaces have a pebbly finish and are highly lustrous. The copper-nickel alloy has taken on an attractive purplish patina on the obverse, while the reverse is a lovely reddish-brown. As one would expect from the grade, there are no obvious marks on either side. Population: 31 in 66, 7 finer (8/07). (#2058)

146   **1861 MS65 PCGS.** Warm salmon and peach surfaces enhance the visual appeal of this well-defined copper-nickel Indian cent. Isolated carbon is noted at the obverse and reverse margins. (#2061)

147   **1861 MS65 PCGS.** Ex: Chiro Collection. Eagle Eye Photo Seal, card not included. This is a lustrous piece with lovely chestnut-gold coloration and attractive reddish accents on the obverse. The design elements are quite sharp, with minimal weakness noted on the feather tips of Liberty's headdress. A couple of nicks on Liberty's cheek are insignificant. (#2061)

Iridescently Toned 1861 Cent, MS66

148 **1861 MS66 PCGS.** Sharply defined throughout with no mentionable or observable marks. The original "white" color of the copper-nickel alloy has taken on a beautiful iridescence. The same colors are present on each side, but they are differently located. The mint luster shows a spectrum of colors from pale whitish-purple to rose to bright golden. A beautiful copper-nickel cent and seldom seen in this grade. (#2061)

149 **1862 MS66 PCGS.** This honey-gold representative is sharply struck down to the tips of the feathers in Liberty's headdress. A die crack is noted at 3 o'clock on the reverse from the wreath to the rim. A delightful, satiny representative of this copper-nickel issue, available in most grades but very scarce as a Gem or better. PCGS has graded just seven finer representatives (7/07). (#2064)

150 **1864 Copper-Nickel MS65 PCGS.** Approximately 25% of the Indian cents dated 1864 were struck in copper-nickel; the remainder were produced in bronze. This Gem example is well struck and lustrous, with subtly variegated coloration on both sides. The surfaces are blemish-free with minimal flyspecks. Only the upper feather tips of Liberty's headdress are softly struck. Certified in a first-generation PCGS holder. (#2070)

Crisply Struck 1864 Copper-Nickel Cent, MS66

151 **1864 Copper-Nickel MS66 NGC.** This Premium Gem 1864 copper-nickel cent has uncharacteristically orange-red luster, that at first glance makes one think that this coin might in fact be bronze. Upon examination by several catalogers, however, we believe the piece to indeed be copper-nickel. We weighed the encapsulated coin on a gram scale, comparing its weight to an NGC-holdered Mint State bronze Indian cent, and found the former heavier than the latter. Also, the feathers in the headdress of the copper-nickel coins appear to be slightly narrower than those of the bronze cent. The strike leaves crisp definition on the devices, and both sides are nicely preserved. Census: 14 in 66, 0 finer (8/07). (#2070)

152 **1864 Bronze No L MS66 Red NGC.** Blazing mint red color is seen over each side of this first year of production of bronze alloy cents. Sharply struck and die clashed on each side. Rarely encountered with full red color. Census: 23 in 66, 2 finer (8/07). (#2078)

153 **1864 L On Ribbon MS64 Red NGC.** This is an attractive near-Gem cent with considerable numismatic appeal. It is a first-year example of the bronze Indian cent; a first-year representative with the L (for designer Longacre) on the ribbon at the bottom of Liberty's headdress; and it shows broad doubling on 18 in the date. Well struck, lustrous, and blemish-free, only light flyspecks limit the grade. (#2081)

154 **1865 Plain 5 MS65 Red and Brown NGC.** Fully struck with intense, shimmering luster and beautifully deep golden-bronze and purple-violet coloration. A pair of small die lumps are noted on Liberty's neck. Both side of the piece are free of grade-limiting distractions. Census: 3 in 65 Red and Brown, 0 finer (8/07). (#92083)

155 **1866 MS65 Brown PCGS.** This lovely olive-brown and mahogany Gem is one of nearly 10 million example struck in this early post-Civil War year. A well-defined and attractive piece with carefully preserved fields. Population: 9 in 65 Brown, 1 finer (8/07). (#2085)

156 **1866 MS64 Red and Brown PCGS.** An attentively struck and gently shimmering near-Gem whose unabraded fields and devices ensure the eye appeal. The reverse has minor carbon at 4 and 10 o'clock. Encapsulated in a green label holder. (#2086)

157 **1866 MS65 Red and Brown PCGS.** This early bronze issue's mintage of under 10 million pieces was a steep drop from the production of the previous two years. This predominantly pumpkin-orange Gem shows just a few small hints of mahogany, though these are enough to preclude a Red designation. PCGS has graded just one finer Red and Brown example (8/07). (#2086)

Full Red MS65 1866 Indian Cent

158 **1866 MS65 Red PCGS.** Unusually for an Indian cent, some obverse clash marks are visible before the Indian's face from the area around the wreath and the O in the denomination on the reverse. Orange-gold, pleasing surfaces are well struck, save for a couple of the diamonds in the ribbon. In a green-label holder. Population: 23 in 65, 5 finer (8/07). (#2087)

159 **1868 MS64 Red and Brown PCGS.** This yellow-orange Choice Indian cent approaches a full red designation, and no marks are consequential. Well struck save for softness on the shield. The reverse rim has a small lamination at 7 o'clock. (#2092)

Scarce MS65 Red 1868 Cent

160 **1868 MS65 Red PCGS.** One of the characteristics of 1868 cents is weakness around the rims, legends, and shield. This piece shows some softness in those areas, but in reality it is probably not something that the casual viewer would notice. The Gem surfaces display a rich overlay of reddish patina with an undertone of original orange-red luster. A couple of small specks of carbon on the reverse prevent an even higher grade. Population: 30 in 65, 3 finer (8/07). (#2093)

Brown (With Some Red) MS66 1869 Cent

161 1869 MS66 Brown PCGS. This coin has a surprise waiting for anyone who views it: how much red is present on a coin that has been certified as Brown. Deep cherry-red outlines the margin on each side and the devices on the reverse. Otherwise, steel-gray and brown color is seen over the remainder of the glossy surfaces. Fully struck. Population: 3 in 66, 0 finer (8/07). (#2094)

162 1869 MS63 Red and Brown PCGS. The vibrant reddish-orange surfaces of this Select post-war piece mellow slightly at the center of the obverse. An attractive example kept from a finer grade by faint abrasions on and around the well-defined portrait. (#2095)

163 1869 MS64 Red and Brown PCGS. Eagle Eye Photo Seal, card not included. This semi-prooflike near-Gem is beautifully patinated orange-red and aquamarine. Void of marks, and worthy of specialist attention. (#2095)

164 1869/69 MS64 Red and Brown ANACS. Snow-3a, FS-008.3. The 69 is repunched north, with the greater spread on the 9. Ample initial orange-gold cedes to medium brown across the portrait and open fields. (#2095)

165 1870 MS64 Red and Brown PCGS. Bold N. Snow-6 with a lightly repunched date. Lime-green and rose-red adorn this lustrous and nicely struck near-Gem. A few carbon flecks are of little concern. (#2098)

166 1870 MS64 Red and Brown PCGS. The obverse has a blend of dusky reddish-orange and cinnamon, while the reverse has a lighter, more vibrant copper-orange appearance. Well struck with few marks and solid visual appeal. (#2098)

167 1870 MS66 Red and Brown PCGS. Shallow N. This exquisite Premium Gem has vibrant luster and a crisp strike. Orange and plum-red dominate the reverse, while the obverse has gold legends and a gunmetal-blue field and portrait. (#2098)

168 1870 MS64 Red PCGS. Shallow N. Lustrous and mark-free with a suitable strike and distributed minor carbon. Encased in a first generation holder. (#2099)

Pleasing 1871 Cent, MS66 Brown
Tied for Finest Certified

169 1871 MS66 Brown NGC. Bold N in ONE. Ample hints of honey-brown color peer from beneath the lilac-brown fields. An exquisitely struck Premium Gem that has impressive surfaces. The C in CENT has multiple clash marks that are as produced. This is one of the two MS66 Brown cents certified by either major service, with none finer (8/07). (#2100)

170 1871 MS64 Red and Brown PCGS. This well-defined Choice representative has four clear diamonds on the ribbon. The smooth surfaces are predominantly reddish-orange with zones of mahogany and walnut. (#2101)

171 1871 MS64 Red and Brown NGC. Snow-1c. Bold N in ONE. Struck from clashed dies, and housed in an older generation holder. An exactingly struck and satiny near-Gem with dusky gold and lilac shadings. (#2101)

172 1871 MS64 Red and Brown PCGS. Bold N. This low mintage cent has an exacting strike and satiny luster. Faded red-gold outlines design elements. A glass reveals minor contact on the cheek. (#2101)

173 1872 MS64 Red and Brown PCGS. A pleasing, predominantly copper-orange example that shows faint speckles of nutmeg-brown on each side. A well-defined and attractive survivor from a mintage of just over 4 million pieces. (#2104)

174 1872 MS64 Red and Brown PCGS. Bold N in ONE. A well preserved and satiny near-Gem with consistent mellowed red-gold color. A small mint-made strike-through is noted near the base of the ME in AMERICA. (#2104)

175 1872 MS64 Red and Brown PCGS. Both sides exhibit a blend of reddish-orange and copper, while the right obverse periphery shows a measure of chocolate-brown as well. Well-defined with a small area of grade-defining abrasions to the left of the portrait. (#2104)

176 1872 MS64 Red and Brown PCGS. Copper-gold surfaces show splashes of tan on the reverse. Generally well struck for the issue, though softness shows in a couple of the diamonds and in the upper right corner of the shield. Richard Snow (2006) states that: "Aside from the 1877, this is the toughest date to find today." He also indicates: "Many are missing detail ... due to machine oil or water resting on the planchet or on the dies." (#2104)

Lustrous Red and Brown 1872 Cent, MS65

177 1872 MS65 Red and Brown PCGS. In addition to having a lower mintage, the 1872 was also melted. These two factors created a semi-key among early Indian cents. This upper-end Gem shows bright surfaces that are mellowed just a bit with significant portions of the original red luster remaining. Sharply struck with slight softness at the top of the feathers in the headdress. (#2104)

Near-Gem 1872 Cent, MS64 Red

178 1872 MS64 Red PCGS. The reverse has slight peripheral weakness as often seen on this date. The surfaces are brilliant with faint mellowing of the red mint luster. Examples of this issue are infrequently encountered in the marketplace, and most of those that do make an appearance are lower quality. An extremely important opportunity for the advanced collector. Population: 45 in 64 Red, 15 finer (8/07). (#2105)

179 **1873 Open 3 MS65 Red and Brown PCGS.** A solidly struck example coined later in the year, ruby and orange at the margins with elements of amethyst and plum at the centers. Gorgeous with excellent surface quality. PCGS has graded only three finer Red and Brown examples. (#2107)

180 **1873 Open 3 MS65 Red and Brown PCGS.** Bold N in ONE. A handsome Gem with medium brown centers and lighter gold margins. Satiny and exquisitely struck. Essentially void of contact, although a faint fingerprint fragment is found at 7 o'clock. (#2107)

Scarce Closed 3 1873 Indian Cent
MS65 Red and Brown

181 **1873 Closed 3 MS65 Red and Brown PCGS.** Most of the Closed 3 Indian cents struck in 1873 show streaky surfaces from improperly mixed bronze alloy. Thus, Full Red Closed 3 cents are very elusive. Overall, the Closed 3 coins are approximately twice as scarce as their Open 3 counterparts. This is a fully struck example with generous portions of mint red remaining. Population: 21 in 65, 1 finer (8/07). (#2110)

182 **1874 MS64 Red PCGS.** Boldly impressed with shining copper-orange surfaces that show only the slightest evidence of mellowing. A great example for the discerning date collector. PCGS has graded 33 finer Red representatives (8/07). (#2120)

183 **1877 Good 4 ANACS.** The obverse shows slightly uneven wear which is a bit heavier on the upper right side. The reverse shows even wear. Chocolate-brown coloration is seen across both sides. Third-party authentication is always a good idea when purchasing an example of this rare key date. (#2127)

184 **1877 Good 6 ANACS.** This well circulated key date example displays light olive-brown coloration and moderate even wear across both sides. A small puncture mark is noted on Liberty's lower cheek. (#2127)

185 **1877—Improperly Cleaned—NCS. VG Details.** Subdued gunmetal-blue and rose-red toning. Mildly granular near ONE CENT, and the obverse has scattered tiny marks. (#2127)

186 **1877—Cleaned—ANACS. VG10 Details.** The olive and lilac toning is perhaps enhanced, but this key date cent is otherwise problem-free for the VG10 grade. Longacre's initial is bold, as are several of the vertical shield lines. (#2127)

187 **1877 Fine 12 NGC.** Highly appealing despite significant wear, this minimally marked and appealing Fine piece has an excellent appearance. Elements of ruby and orange add color to the walnut-brown surfaces of this Indian key. (#2127)

188 **1877—Corroded—ANACS. VF30 Details.** This key date cent has little actual wear, but the reverse is corroded from environmental exposure. The obverse has been cleaned and darkened, but deposits are limited to protected areas. The portrait has a thin vertical mark. (#2127)

Pleasing Choice XF 1877 Cent

189 **1877 XF45 NGC.** This Choice XF key-date representative displays light to medium tan patina and soft gold undertones. Strong definition is visible on the design elements, save for light wear on the highpoints. Remarkably clean surfaces add to the desirability of this pleasing specimen. (#2127)

Highly Sought Out AU58 1877 Cent

190 **1877 AU58 PCGS.** Struck from misaligned dies, the right side of the obverse and right side of the reverse are weakly impressed as a result. The surfaces otherwise are sharp and the medium brown patina shows a significant outline of red around the devices. A popular grade for this key Indian cent. (#2127)

Elegant 1877 Cent, MS63 Red and Brown

191 **1877 MS63 Red and Brown NGC.** An unworn and visually appealing example, pleasingly detailed with reddish-orange and walnut-brown surfaces. Shallow depressions on Liberty's neck and in the fields to the left account for the grade. A noteworthy and highly desirable representative of this prominent Indian cent key, one far less available than its stated mintage of 852,500 pieces might suggest. (#2128)

Desirable 1877 Cent, MS64 Red and Brown

192 **1877 MS64 Red and Brown PCGS.** The 1877 has always held a favored position as the key issue in the Indian cent series. Its low mintage of only 852,500 pieces explains its scarcity in all grades. It is especially difficult to locate in Mint condition and with remnants of original mint color. This is an attractive coin that is well defined. Most of the original mint red is still evident beneath the woodgrain pattern of brown that overlies each side. The only trace of carbon we see is a tiny spot beneath the ribbon end on the lower reverse. An exceptionally good value and sure to be of interest to a wide range of collectors. (#2128)

Pleasing 1878 Cent, MS65 Red

193 **1878 MS65 Red PCGS.** A colorful Gem, bright copper-orange with a touch of jade at the obverse periphery and russet-violet accents elsewhere on the surfaces. The strike is relatively sharp, with clarity on all four diamonds. A few light flecks are noted over each side, but these do not significantly detract from the overall eye appeal. Housed in a green-label holder. Population: 45 in 65, 13 finer (7/07). (#2132)

Premium Gem Red 1883 Cent

194 **1883 MS66 Red NGC.** A lustrous cherry-red Premium Gem with remarkably uniform color and a carbon-free appearance. Minor contact on the cheek denies technical perfection. A common date, but uncommon in such exemplary quality. Certified in a prior generation holder. Census: 18 in 66 Red, 3 finer (8/07). (#2147)

195 **1884 MS66 Red and Brown NGC.** One would be hard pressed to point out the brown on this Red and Brown coin. There is a significant presence of pale olive, but that really does not qualify as Brown in our book. Sharply struck and pleasing throughout. If the successful bidder can get this coin at a slight premium over the Red and Brown price, that would be a great buy. (#2149)

Gorgeous MS66 Red 1884 Cent

196 **1884 MS66 Red PCGS.** Snow-PR1. The lower loop of the first 8 is repunched. This highly lustrous and sharply struck Premium Gem is mostly butter-gold, although each side has a blush of cherry-red. Elusive in carbon-free full red preservation. Population: 12 in 66 Red, 3 finer (8/07). (#2150)

197 **1886 Type One MS66 Red and Brown PCGS.** The obverse of this Type One piece has rose and salmon tints, while the reverse displays just enough mellowing to preclude a full Red designation. Carefully preserved with excellent eye appeal. Population: 2 in 66 Red and Brown, 0 finer (8/07). (#2155)

198 **1886 Type Two MS64 Red and Brown PCGS.** The later variety, which shows the lowest feather pointing below the C in AMERICA. The obverse is reddish-orange with hints of lemon in the center, while the reverse is predominantly olive with rosewood tints. Well-preserved with above-average detail. (#92155)

199 **1888 MS64 Red PCGS.** Boldly struck, if slightly weak on the feather tips and Liberty's hair detail. Pleasing olive-orange and terra cotta toning adorns both sides. Lustrous and nearly blemish-free, a lovely near-Gem representative of this mid-date issue. Population: 45 in 64 Red, 42 finer (8/07). (#2168)

200 **1894 MS64 Red NGC.** Sharply struck and lustrous with rich red-orange coloration across the blemish-free surfaces. A relatively modest number of scattered flyspecks, located mostly on the obverse, seemingly prevent a Gem grade designation. Census: 42 in 64 Red, 38 finer (8/07). (#2189)

Flaming Red 1895 Cent, MS66

201 **1895 MS66 Red PCGS.** An outstanding example of this popular date from the 1890s. The surfaces show rich, even, cherry-red color over each side with no trace of mellowing or spotting. Sharply defined throughout with four diamonds on the ribbon (which is not always the case). Population: 30 in 66, 2 finer (8/07). (#2192)

Beautiful 1895 Cent, MS66 Red

202 **1895 MS66 Red NGC.** Ex: Maine Roll. Beautiful orange-gold luster embraces both sides of this Premium Gem Red Indian cent. A well executed strike brings out sharp definition on the design features, and both sides have been well cared for. Census: 32 in 66 Red, 7 finer (8/07). (#2192)

Pleasing 1895 Red Premium Gem Cent

203 **1895 MS66 Red PCGS.** The 1895 cent is widely available in lower grades. Even Mint State examples are available in the various color designations through MS65. The PCGS/NGC certified population takes a significant drop in MS66 Red (about 60 Red Premium Gems graded, and fewer than 10 finer). This bright orange example displays pleasing luster and sharply struck design elements. A few minute obverse marks are consistent with the numerical grade designation. Population: 30 in 66 Red, 2 finer (8/07). (#2192)

204 **1899 MS66 Red NGC.** An attractive example, well-defined despite die erosion evident in the fields on both sides. The carefully preserved surfaces are predominantly orange with elements of salmon and peach. NGC has graded just eight finer Red representatives (7/07). (#2204)

205 **1899 MS66 Red PCGS.** An uncommonly vibrant representative of this later Indian cent issue, predominantly copper-orange with effusive rose accents in the centers. PCGS has graded only nine finer Red representatives (8/07). (#2204)

206 **1900 MS66 Red PCGS.** A superior type coin. Both sides show even, orange-red color and thick mint frost. There is a touch of softness at the end of the upper feathers of the headdress, but the remainder of the coin is fully detailed. A wonderful turn-of-the-century type coin. Population: 56 in 66, 6 finer (8/07). (#2207)

Conditionally Scarce Premium Gem 1901 Indian Cent

207 **1901 MS66 Red PCGS.** Highly lustrous and generally well struck, with the usual minor softness on the upper feather tips, this Premium Gem is one of the relatively few examples to survive in such a lofty state of preservation. After all, more than 79.5 million pieces were struck, but a mere 77 coins have been graded at MS66 Red, by NGC and PCGS combined, and only four finer. PCGS Population: 49 in 66, 2 finer (8/07). (#2210)

208 **1902 MS66 Red PCGS.** Ex: Larry Shapiro. One of the frequently encountered post-1900 dates in the Indian cent series. This piece is well, but not quite fully struck. Each side shows an intermingling of orange and cherry-red color and there are no mentionable abrasions. Population: 44 in 66, 8 finer (8/07). (#2213)

209 **1905 MS66 Red PCGS.** The shining surfaces of this well-defined piece are predominantly copper-orange with faint salmon accents. Beautifully preserved with only tiny luster grazes and minimal carbon. PCGS has graded no finer Red representatives (8/07). (#2222)

Gorgeous, Condition Rarity 1909 Indian Cent, MS67 Red

210 **1909 MS67 Red PCGS.** In his *Buyer's and Enthusiast's Guide to Flying Eagle and Indian Cents*, David Bowers writes that the 1909 is one of the most plentiful Mint State Indian cents despite its somewhat low mintage (14,368,470 business strikes). Bowers says: "Bright red specimens are among the most common issues, although this date has sometimes been called 'scarce' in this regard, no doubt by catalogers who look at the mintage figure and consider little else."

A perusal of the population data indicate that more than 2,000 Mint State 1909 full Red Indian cents have been certified by PCGS and NGC, primarily in MS64 and MS65 grades, confirming the availability of this issue in high grade. In Superb Gem Red, however, the classification of the coin in this lot, the 1909 is anything but common. The two services have seen only six such coins, and none finer.

Gorgeous yellow-gold surfaces radiate glowing luster, and an attentive strike imparts excellent delineation to the design elements. All four diamonds are crisp, though the feather tips exhibit the usual softness. Impeccably preserved surfaces are devoid of mentionable abrasions or spots. Population: 4 in 67 Red, 0 finer (8/07). (#2237)

211 **1909-S MS64 Red and Brown NGC.** This copper-orange example shows areas of deeper red, mahogany, and chocolate-brown, largely on the obverse. Luminous and well-preserved, a pleasing representative of this mintmarked Indian key. (#2239)

212 **1909-S MS64 Red and Brown PCGS.** While predominantly copper-orange, this mintmarked key's surfaces range from lemon-gold to mahogany. This pleasingly detailed near-Gem displays four intact diamonds on the ribbon. (#2239)

Sharply Struck 1909-S Indian Cent, MS64 Red

213 **1909-S MS64 Red NGC.** Lustrous surfaces give off pleasing orange coloration, and exhibit sharply struck design elements, except for the usual softness in the feather tips. A few tiny flecks on each side just barely keep this piece from full Gem classification. All in all, a pleasing key branch-mint issue. (#2240)

Red Gem 1909-S Indian Cent

214 **1909-S MS65 Red PCGS.** This Gem Mint State example rich orange luster blended with pale orange color on each side. It is typical of the issue with slightly weak definition at the feather tips. The final Indian cent issue had a limited mintage of just 309,000 coins, the lowest mintage of any Indian cent issue by a large margin. The next lowest mintage was the key-date 1877 cent, with more than double the production. Only a dozen finer examples of this date have been certified by PCGS (7/07). (#2240)

Exceptional Key Date Gem 1909-S Indian Cent

215 **1909-S MS65 Red PCGS.** This is an exceptional Gem example of the key date 1909-S Indian cent. This issue is known to be somewhat softly struck on the feather tips of Liberty's headdress, and this piece is no exception; but the coin's overall quality is remarkable. The rich coppery-red and lime-green toning is highlighted by vibrant luster, and surface marks are virtually nonexistent. (#2240)

PROOF INDIAN CENTS

216 **1860 PR64 PCGS.** Fully detailed, as one would expect from a proof. The surfaces are uncommonly red for a copper-nickel product. A pleasing, problem-free example. (#2253)

Impressive 1861 Cent, PR66 ★
Finest NGC-Certified

217 **1861 PR66 ★ NGC.** The 1861 proof cent is the key date in the proof series, partly due to low mintage (est. 1,000 pieces), low survivability, poor quality of the dies, and poor striking quality (Richard Snow, 2006). The Premium Gem proof with Star can thus be considered a special offering. Its razor-sharp and lightly frosted design elements stand amidst reflective fields, and yield noticeable contrast when the coin is tilted under a light source. A couple of as-made unobtrusive planchet indentations on the neck do not detract in the least. Census: 1 in 66 ★, 0 finer with or without star(8/07). (#2256)

218 **1862 PR65 PCGS.** Decisively struck with vibrant reddish-orange surfaces. This carefully preserved copper-nickel Gem proof displays a few tiny dots of haze in the obverse fields. One of just 550 specimens coined. (#2259)

219 **1863 PR63 NGC.** A needle-sharp cent with moderately mirrored fields and consistent rose-gold toning. The reverse is well preserved, while the left obverse field has a few faint hairlines. (#2262)

220 **1864 Copper-Nickel PR64 PCGS.** A dusky copper-orange representative of this challenging transition-year issue, one of only 370 specimens coined. Faint hairlines appear in the fields, though the crisply struck devices are well-preserved. Housed in a first-generation holder. (#2265)

221 **1864 Bronze No L PR66 Brown NGC.** Sharply struck except for softness on the upper feather tips of the headdress. This gorgeous proof specimen shows deep mirrors and variegated steel-blue, tobacco-brown, and gold toning. Expertly preserved and free of grade-limiting marks or hairlines. Census: 10 in 66 Brown, 2 finer (8/07). (#2276)

222 **1865 PR64 Red and Brown PCGS.** Sharply struck with deep layers of violet-red toning over both sides. The fields are highly reflective, and free of contact marks or bothersome hairlines. From an original proof mintage of just 500 pieces. Population: 60 in 64, 25 finer (7/07). (#2283)

223 **1866 PR64 Red and Brown ICG.** A decisively struck representative of this Reconstruction-era proof issue, predominantly copper-orange with areas of mahogany on the obverse. Faint hairlines are noted in the fields. (#2286)

224 **1866 PR64 Red and Brown PCGS.** While the obverse is vibrant copper-gold, the reverse of this boldly impressed Choice proof has mellowed to mahogany. A touch of haze and small, isolated hairlines are the only minor detractions from this coin's otherwise strong visual appeal. (#2286)

Brilliant Proof 1866 Cent, PR65 Red Cameo

225 **1866 PR65 Red Cameo PCGS.** This Gem example has brilliant and vibrant olive-red color on both sides with excellent contrast between the lustrous devices and fully mirrored fields. Traces of darker toning hug the devices, especially on the reverse. Population: 7 in 65 Red Cameo, 3 finer (8/07). (#82287)

226 **1867 PR65 Red and Brown PCGS.** This exquisitely struck straw-gold and olive Gem is close to full red, although the obverse has a few pinpoint carbon flecks. Encased in a green label holder. Just 625+ proofs were struck. (#2289)

227 **1867 PR65 Red and Brown NGC.** Deeply toned in layers of fire-red, sunset-orange, and royal-blue over both sides. This outstanding Gem proof specimen is fully struck on all of the design elements. Contact marks are nonexistent, and carbon specks are minimal in number. Census: 38 in 65 Red and Brown, 9 finer (7/07). (#2289)

228 **1868 PR65 Red and Brown PCGS.** Fully struck, with the reverse rotated nearly 180 degrees from the obverse. A pleasing woodgrain finish appears on each side. A tiny contact mark, on Liberty's cheekbone, is the only such mark on either obverse or reverse. Population: 35 in 65, 4 finer (7/07). (#2292)

Stunning 1868 Red Gem Proof Cent

229 **1868 PR65 Red PCGS.** Beautiful copper-gold color exhibits lime-green and rose accents in the fields, which along with their mirrors yield a noticeable contrast with the motifs, especially when the coin is tilted under a light source. Exquisitely struck throughout. The reverse is inverted nearly 180 degrees. A few tiny obverse flecks do not detract in the least. Population: 7 in 65 Red, 2 finer (8/07). (#2293)

230 **1869 PR64 Red Cameo PCGS.** The strike is strong, and there are no outwardly distracting blemishes on this straw-orange near-Gem. A small swirl of rose-red is noted on the reverse near 9 o'clock. An unusual and attractive specimen. (#82296)

231 **1870 PR64 Red PCGS.** Shallow N. A needle-sharp and glossy Choice specimen with lovely fire-red and yellow-gold color. Minor carbon above the bust tip is unimportant for the grade. Housed in a first generation holder. Population: 30 in 64 Red, 27 finer (8/07). (#2299)

Incredible Proof 1870 Indian, PR66 Red

232 **1870 PR66 Red NGC.** Fully brilliant red proof surfaces and sharp design features ensure that this example ranks among the finest proof 1870 cents ever certified. Just nine similar examples have been graded by NGC and PCGS with none finer. Census: 5 in 66 Red, 0 finer (8/07). (#2299)

233 **1870 PR64 Cameo NGC.** All of the design elements are fully struck, with intense reflectivity noted in the fields, and mild mint frost on the devices. A lovely cameo effect is created on both sides. Well preserved from harmful contact, with scattered carbon specks that prevent an even higher grade assessment. (#82299)

234 **1871 PR66 Brown NGC.** Shallow N in ONE. A remarkably preserved and originally toned example of this better date in the proof Indian cent series. The design elements reveal razor-sharp details throughout, including the feather tips of the headdress. Contact marks and hairlines are nonexistent. Census: 2 in 66 Brown, 0 finer (7/07). (#2300)

235 **1871 PR65 Red and Brown NGC.** Shallow N in ONE. The olive-green centers are framed by glimpses of rose-gold near the rims. An intricately struck Gem of this low mintage date. Certified in a prior generation holder. (#2301)

Remarkable 1872 Cent, PR66 Red and Brown

236 **1872 PR66 Red and Brown PCGS.** A remarkable Gem proof example with nearly full red color on both sides, only beginning to fade to light brown. A few minuscule specks are all that keep this out of the Superb Gem category. It is sharply struck, and the fields are fully reflective although not deeply mirrored. Tied for the finest Red and Brown proof example certified by PCGS. Population: 7 in 66, 0 finer (8/07). (#2304)

1872 Indian Cent PR65 Red and Brown Cameo

237 **1872 PR65 Red and Brown Cameo NGC.** Sharply struck with glassy fields and mildly frosted devices. Neither side displays any troublesome contact marks or grade-limiting hairlines. A few flyspecks are noted, but only with the assistance of a magnifier. Census: 1 in 65 Red and Brown Cameo, 1 finer in 65 Red Cameo (8/07). (#2304)

238 **1873 Closed 3 PR66 Brown NGC.** Deep purple-rose, electric-blue, and amber coloration covers the surfaces of this Premium Gem. Sharply struck and trouble-free. All proofs from 1873 are of the so-called "Closed 3" variety. Census: 2 in 66 Brown, 0 finer (7/07). (#2306)

1873 Closed 3 Indian Cent PR64 Red and Brown Cameo

239 **1873 Closed 3 PR64 Red and Brown Cameo NGC.** Sharply struck with deeply reflective fields and minimal carbon on both sides. This is the only proof 1873 Indian cent graded both Red and Brown and Cameo by NGC. Just two pieces have been certified finer by the same service: one apiece at MS64 and MS65 Red Cameo (8/07). (#2307)

Brilliant Proof 1874 Cent, PR65 Red Cameo

240 **1874 PR65 Red Cameo PCGS.** A gorgeous specimen that displays lovely light orange color with hints of iridescence on each side. It is sharply struck and the cameo contrast readily obvious. Minor date doubling is visible, with the diagonal of the digit 4 extending below the left end of the crossbar. (#82311)

241 **1875 PR64 Red and Brown Cameo NGC.** A radiant near-Gem with salmon-pink and sky-blue toning. Exactingly struck and essentially carbon-free. The reverse rim has a small strike-through at 9 o'clock. (#2313)

242 **1876 PR65 Red and Brown PCGS.** Warm mahogany and copper-orange patina graces the well-preserved surfaces of this appealing Gem. A sharply struck proof from the centennial year. Population: 37 in 65 Red and Brown, 8 finer (7/07). (#2316)

Coveted Gem Proof 1877 Indian Cent

243 **1877 PR65 Red and Brown PCGS.** This Gem proof Indian cent displays moderately reflective surfaces with variegated sunset-orange, purple-rose, and deep-blue toning across both sides. Free from troubling carbon spots, with just a couple of small ones noted on the lower obverse. A highly coveted key date in this immensely popular series. Population: 57 in 65 Red and Brown, 5 finer (7/07). (#2319)

Sharp Key Issue 1877 Indian Cent PR65 Red

244 **1877 PR65 Red PCGS.** The rarity and desirability of the 1877 business strike issue makes the current Gem proof specimen much more challenging than it otherwise would be, in comparison to other proof Indian cents of the 1870s and 1880s. This example is sharply struck throughout, with reflective fields and essentially pristine surfaces. Golden-tan and sea-green toning adorns the obverse, while a mixture of red-orange and lime-green coloration is distributed across the reverse. A more attractive proof representative of this key date is hard to imagine. Population: 19 in 65 Red, 13 finer (8/07). (#2320)

245 **1878 PR66 Red PCGS.** A glittering Gem example with unfathomably deep mirrors and a fully original, coppery-red color. A virtually carbon-free specimen, however, a couple of microscopic nicks on the obverse can be seen under magnification. Population: 8 in 66 Red, 1 finer (7/07). (#2323)

246 **1879 PR66 Brown PCGS.** Bold magenta and violet suffusions characterize the vibrant obverse, while the reverse has similar, slightly softer colors with dabs of orange at the top and bottom. Crisply struck and pleasing. Population: 2 in 66 Brown, 2 finer (7/07). (#2324)

247 **1879 PR64 Red and Brown PCGS.** Copper-orange fields and magenta-accented devices are the rule on both sides of this Indian proof, though the reverse has mellowed a bit too much for this coin to qualify as full Red. Decisively struck with only a handful of faint hairlines. (#2325)

248 **1879 PR65 Red and Brown NGC.** Snow-PR1. The date is lightly repunched. Rick Snow states, "One of the few collectable proof die varieties." Most of the mint red still remains on this nicely mirrored Gem. Intricately struck and beautiful. (#2325)

249 **1879 PR65 Red and Brown PCGS.** Eagle Eye Photo Seal, Card included. Beautiful orange, rose, gold, and aquamarine endow the obverse. The pumpkin-gold reverse is full red. Razor-sharp and exquisite. (#2325)

250 **1879 PR66 Red PCGS.** Boldly impressed with rich reddish-orange surfaces that show few flaws, even under a loupe. A lovely specimen with grand visual appeal. Population: 25 in 66 Red, 10 finer (8/07). (#2326)

251 **1880 PR65 Red PCGS.** Rich toning and a splendid strike are hallmarks of this Gem proof Indian cent. The watery fields are unmarked and only show minor carbon. Housed in a green label PCGS holder. Population: 61 in 65 Red, 25 finer (8/07). (#2329)

252 **1880 PR66 Red PCGS.** The surfaces of this lovely Premium Gem proof are predominantly yellow-orange with blushes of rose at the upper obverse and lower reverse. Boldly impressed and gleaming with a tiny planchet flaw on the cheek. An attractive example of this mid-date issue. Population: 16 in 66 Red, 9 finer (8/07). (#2329)

253 **1881 PR66 Brown NGC.** Lavish original toning adorns the well preserved surfaces of this impressive Premium Gem. All of the design elements are fully struck, and both sides of the piece are distraction-free. Census: 10 in 66 Brown, 3 finer (7/07). (#2330)

254 **1881 PR66 Red and Brown PCGS.** The margins of this mid-date proof cent are predominantly copper-orange. More dramatic patina is noted at the centers, with magenta, lemon-gold, and green among the myriad colors. (#2331)

Pleasing 1882 Cent, PR67 Brown

255 **1882 PR67 Brown PCGS.** Fully struck and pristine, with lovely purple-lilac and satin-brown toning. Magnificently preserved with outstanding eye appeal. A recent article in *Coin World* by Dave Bowers pointed out the good value represented by iridescently toned Brown Indian cents. An interesting concept and worthy of consideration by those who are contrarians. Population: 5 in 67 Brown, 0 finer (8/07). (#2333)

256 **1884 PR66 Brown NGC.** Fully struck and unabraded, with satiny fields and lovely tan and lime-green toning. Carbon-free proofs, such as the present specimen, are more difficult to locate than the mintage would suggest. (#2339)

257 **1884 PR66 Brown NGC.** Fully struck with a pleasing mixture of lime-green and golden-brown coloration over each side. The fields are highly reflective, and the carefully preserved surfaces are virtually pristine. A lovely Premium Gem proof Indian cent. Census: 29 in 66 Brown, 5 finer (7/07). (#2339)

258 **1884 PR66 Red PCGS.** After 1877, a low-mintage year for both business strikes and proofs, production figures for the latter never fell below 1,000 pieces for the rest of the series, and the record continues to the present day. Of the 3,942 examples coined for 1884, few remain in such exquisite condition as the present piece, which is boldly impressed and flashy with pale orange-copper surfaces. An attractive and carefully preserved specimen. Population: 31 in 66, 10 finer (8/07). (#2341)

259 **1884 PR66 Red PCGS.** Snow-PR1. The lower loops of the 8s show faint recutting. A flashy Premium Gem that benefits from a precise strike and lovely orange-gold color. A trivial retained lamination is noted beneath the C in CENT. Population: 31 in 66 Red, 10 finer (8/07). (#2341)

260 **1885 PR66 Brown PCGS.** The first 8 in the date is lightly repunched within the lower loop. Impressive mauve-violet, gold, and yellow-olive colors appear when the Cent is rotated under a light. An exquisitely struck premium Gem with surfaces that are essentially unimprovable. An Eagle Eye Photo Seal sticker appears on the holder, though the certificate is missing. Population: 40 in 66 Brown, 8 finer (7/07). (#2342)

261 **1885 PR66 Brown PCGS.** Eagle Eye Photo Seal. Pleasing surfaces with some light underlying purple and green, and the high quality expected for the grade. A gorgeous Premium Gem proof Indian cent. Population: 40 in 66, 8 finer (7/07). (#2342)

Lightly Toned 1885 Cent, PR66 Red

262 **1885 PR66 Red PCGS.** Splashes of orange, lime-green, crimson, and gold visit both sides of this Premium Gem Red proof. A well directed strike imparts good definition to the design elements, including the feather tips and the diamonds. There are no significant contact marks or unsightly spots to report. Population: 8 in 66 Red, 3 finer (7/07). (#2344)

263 **1886 Type One PR66 Brown NGC.** A fabulous mixture of deep electric-blue and purple-rose toning decorates each side of this amazing specimen. A faint planchet streak (as made) occurs beneath the N in ONE on the lower reverse. Sharply struck and free of post-striking distractions. (#2345)

264 **1886 Type One PR66 Brown NGC.** Rose-red and apple-green patina emerges when this exquisite specimen is rotated beneath a lamp. In mid-1886 the Type One obverse, with the last feather of the headdress pointing between I and C in AMERICA, was changed to the Type Two, with the last feather pointing between C and A. (#2345)

265 **1886 Type One PR66 Red and Brown NGC.** This exquisitely struck premium Gem is undisturbed by contact, and is delightfully toned in glossy rose, gold, and sea-green colors. The final year of the Type One obverse, which shows the lowest headdress feather between I and C in AMERICA. Census: 30 in 66, 4 finer (7/07). (#2346)

266 **1886 Type One PR66 Red and Brown PCGS.** Vivid crimson, violet, and golden-tan patination adheres to both sides of this Premium Gem proof. An expected well executed strike brings out excellent definition on the design features, and relatively strong field-motif contrast shows up when the piece is tilted under a light source, especially on the reverse. Exquisitely preserved throughout. (#2346)

267 **1887 PR66 Brown PCGS.** A sharply struck example of this mid-date proof issue, predominantly reddish-brown with traces of rosewood and mahogany. Carefully preserved and pleasing. Population: 10 in 66 Brown, 0 finer (7/07). (#2348)

268 **1889 PR66 Brown NGC.** Decisively struck with subtle, yet distinct blue overtones that enliven the chocolate-brown surfaces. A carefully preserved delight. Census: 18 in 66 Brown, 0 finer (8/07). (#2354)

269 **1892 PR65 Red and Brown PCGS.** Deep red-brown coloration adorns each side of this lovely Gem proof Indian cent. The design motifs are sharply struck and the fields are highly reflective. A mild cameo effect is noted on both sides. Population: 54 in 65 Red and Brown, 9 finer (8/07). (#2364)

270 **1892 PR65 Red PCGS.** Yellow-gold and peach with dashes of plum-red on the central reverse. An unmarked and well struck Gem that has only a few peripheral obverse pinpoint flecks. Encapsulated in an old green label holder. Population: 43 in 65 Red, 14 finer (8/07). (#2365)

271 **1894 PR64 Brown ANACS.** Dramatic lime-green, gold, and rose illuminate this sharply struck and flashy specimen. (#2369)

272 **1897 PR65 Brown PCGS.** Well struck with a dense layer of deep forest-green, apple-green, amber and purple-rose toning across both sides. Free of grade-limiting hairlines or contact marks. Population: 12 in 65, 11 finer (7/07). (#2378)

273 **1897 PR65 Brown PCGS.** This Gem offers carefully preserved surfaces and a sharp strike. The patina of this specimen is the real draw, however, with electric blue, violet, and azure evident on each side, all with faint copper-brown overtones. Population: 12 in 65 Brown, 11 finer (7/07). (#2378)

274 **1897 PR65 Red PCGS.** This vibrant specimen displays fiery copper-red toning on the reverse and on the left side of the obverse, with lighter greenish-tan color over the obverse center. The fields are flashy and deeply reflective. A couple of faint marks are noted on Liberty's cheekbone. Population: 11 in 65 Red, 12 finer (8/07). (#2380)

275 **1898 PR65 Red PCGS.** Decisively struck with surfaces that sport a lovely blend of carrot-orange and pumpkin. A tiny contact mark appears at the truncation, though this is consistent with the grade assigned. An attractive example of this late 19th century Indian proof issue. Population: 27 in 65 Red, 15 finer (8/07). (#2383)

276 **1898 PR65 Red PCGS.** This flashy Gem provides blended gold and fire-red fields and devices. The strike is exacting, and carbon is minimal. Tilting the coin reveals noticeable cameo contrast, undesignated by the green label holder. (#2383)

277 **1899 PR66 Brown NGC.** Sharply struck with lovely purple-rose and sky-blue toning. Free of contact marks or hairlines; an impressive Premium Gem proof from the final year of the 19th century. Census: 7 in 66 Brown, 1 finer (7/07). (#2384)

278 **1900 PR65 Red and Brown PCGS.** Solidly struck with lemon-gold and sea-green on the obverse and deeper orange and cherry-red patina on the reverse. Carbon is noted at the foot of the Y in LIBERTY and the second-lowest feather on the headdress. Population: 45 in 65 Red and Brown, 8 finer (7/07). (#2388)

279 **1900 PR65 Red PCGS.** A dazzling turn-of-the-century issue that benefits from bright, watery mirrors and appealing flashes of orange and rose peripheral color. Population: 29 in 65, 20 finer (7/07). (#2389)

280 **1900 PR65 Red PCGS.** An enticing reddish-orange Gem specimen of this turn-of-the-century issue, exquisitely struck with exemplary visual appeal. A lovely example from a mintage of 2,262 pieces. Population: 29 in 65 Red, 20 finer (8/07). (#2389)

281 **1901 PR66 Red NGC.** The fields of this 20th century Indian cent proof are copper-orange, while the portrait is mint-green. A striking and exquisitely preserved specimen. Census: 11 in 66 Red, 5 finer (8/07). (#2392)

282 **1902 PR65 Brown PCGS.** A crisply struck mushroom-brown piece that shows faint olive overtones, this 20th century Indian Gem has excellent definition and great eye appeal. One of only 2,018 specimens coined. Population: 8 in 65 Brown, 1 finer (8/07). (#2393)

283 **1902 PR66 Red and Brown PCGS.** The shining surfaces of this boldly impressed proof are predominantly cherry-red and mahogany with a touch of green to the right of the date. A delightful example of this 20th century issue. Population: 17 in 66 Red and Brown, 1 finer (7/07). (#2394)

284 **1902 PR65 Red PCGS.** Lovely rose-red and lime endow this satiny and meticulously struck Gem. The reverse field has a few minute olive flecks. Encased in an older green label holder. Population: 51 in 65 Red, 33 finer (8/07). (#2395)

285 **1903 PR66 Brown PCGS.** An electrifying piece with carefully preserved surfaces and vibrant patina. Magenta and raspberry-violet tones dominate the obverse, while the reverse has a distinctive blueberry cast. Population: 3 in 66 Brown, 0 finer (7/07). (#2396)

286 **1903 PR66 Red and Brown PCGS.** Deep crimson coloration on the obverse with a touch of original orange-red on the reverse. Deeply mirrored with no observable flaws. Population: 5 in 66 Red and Brown, 0 finer (7/07). (#2397)

287 **1903 PR66 Red NGC.** Cherry-red and sun-gold with a glimpse of apple-green on the reverse. Razor-sharp and essentially carbon-free. Census: 17 in 66 Red, 3 finer (8/07). (#2398)

288 **1903 PR66 Red PCGS.** Intricately detailed with rich cherry-red and lime-green coloration complemented by smooth, highly reflective fields. Exceptional quality. Population: 31 in 66, 11 finer (8/07). (#2398)

289 **1904 PR66 Brown PCGS.** Deep violet patina dominates the obverse fields, while the portrait has a sapphire cast. The upper two-thirds of the reverse offer similar coloration, while lighter rose-orange toning appears at the knot of the bow. Crisply struck with excellent eye appeal. Population: 1 in 66 Brown, 0 finer (7/07). (#2399)

290 **1904 PR66 Red and Brown NGC.** A splendid, deeply mirrored proof striking. The surfaces show a blend of light orange-red with lime green over each side. Essentially defect-free. Census: 7 in 66, 1 finer (8/07). (#2400)

291 **1904 PR66 Red and Brown NGC.** Eagle Eye Photo Seal, no card included. The obverse is yellow-gold with peripheral cherry-red, and on its own would surely qualify as full Red. The reverse has vivid streaks of copper-gold, lemon, violet, and electric-blue patina. A sharply struck Gem with contact-free surfaces and a minuscule carbon fleck or two. Census: 7 in 66, 1 finer (7/07). (#2400)

292 **1909 PR65 Red PCGS.** A splendidly mirrored Gem that has noticeable obverse cameo contrast, although this feature is unrecognized by the first generation holder. Light orange-gold with small dashes of sea-green on the chin and cheek. The strike is penetrating, and only a few pinpoint flecks on the left reverse limit the grade. Population: 29 in 65 Red, 16 finer (8/07). (#2416)

1907 Victor D. Brenner Lincoln Plaque and Autographed Card with V.D.B. Cent

293   1907 Brenner Lincoln Plaque and Autographed Card. Bronze, 180 mm x 240 mm x 8 mm. Victor D. Brenner's 1907 plaque was the model for the 1909 Lincoln cent. A half-length portrait of a bearded President Lincoln facing right. The plaque is backed by jade-green and ivory-gray marble that measures 215 mm x 270 mm x 13 mm. The back of the marble features a bronze stand. Nearly as made aside from a couple of unimportant toning spots.

Lot 6785 in our 2006 September Long Beach Signature included reminiscences by the consignor of a different-sized (170 mm x 230 mm) plaque. That consignor stated,

"As a mechanical engineering student at Oregon State University in late 1954, I was selected to present a paper at a conference of ASME in Pittsburgh after winning the regional competition in San Francisco a short time before. My host in Pittsburgh was an avid small cent collector and possessed an example of the 180 mm x 240 mm plaque. It was glued (probably using shellac by the sculptor himself) to a polished green rectangle. In detail, it was precisely the same as the present example, except without the cast-in hanger. My host said that Brenner lived and worked in Pittsburgh at the time the plaque was cast.

"The next example that I saw was in the summer of 1957 and was on display at the Smithsonian as part of the Mint's regular small cent exhibit. That one was the same as the Pittsburgh specimen."

Also included with the lot is a cream-white cardboard cent holder, 85 mm x 65 mm, autographed "with compliments, V. D. Brenner" in purple ink. The holder houses an AU 1909 VDB cent. (Total: 3 pieces)

294   1909-S VDB VG8 NGC. Well detailed for the grade, and free of any distracting marks or abrasions. An affordable example of the most famous key date in the Lincoln cent series. (#2426)

295   1909-S VDB—Cleaned—ANACS. Fine 12 Details. The VDB initials are clear, as are most lines in the wheat ears, but the yellow-gold obverse is overly bright, and the lilac-olive toning on the reverse is also suspect. (#2426)

296   1909-S VDB Fine 15 NGC. Though the violet-tinged walnut-brown surfaces show significant wear, the fields and devices show few marks, and the overall eye appeal is strong for the grade. A pleasing and comparatively affordable representative of this early Lincoln key. (#2426)

297   1909-S VDB Fine 15 PCGS. Though this chocolate-brown Lincoln key shows significant wear, the surfaces show few marks, and the overall eye appeal is strong. Small areas of deeper color appear above the date and around the letters of UNITED STATES OF AMERICA on the reverse. (#2426)

298   1909-S VDB VF30 ANACS. A moderately worn, attractive example of this widely coveted Lincoln issue, mahogany and golden-brown with few marks overall. A lovely piece that would fit well in a similarly graded date set. (#2426)

299   1909-S VDB—Scratched—ANACS. VF30 Details. This tan-brown key date cent has no sign of carbon, but there are several thin cuts, mostly on the obverse, that range from minor to distracting. (#2426)

300   1909-S VDB XF40 NGC. An attractive chocolate-brown piece that maintains strong detail despite light, even wear. The fields and devices show faint, scattered ticks and delicate strawberry accents. (#2426)

301   1909-S VDB—Corroded, Cleaned—ANACS. XF45 Details. A bold key date representative with clear VDB initials. Protected areas display moderate charcoal verdigris, and the open fields are discolored and slightly glossy from a cleaning. (#2426)

302   1909-S VDB—Cleaned—ANACS. AU53 Details. A glossy key date cent with pleasing sharpness and bold VDB initials. The surfaces display streaky sea-green and orange hues. A lamination is retained from the cheekbone to the mouth with a tiny peeled section in the field above the chin. (#2426)

303   1909-S VDB—Rims Damaged—ANACS. AU55 Details. A satiny golden-brown key date cent with only a hint of wear on the cheekbone, jaw, and hair above the ear. The VDB initials are sharp. The rims show minor pitting, but this seems unworthy of a "Damaged" designation. (#2426)

304   1909-S VDB AU55 ANACS. A lightly circulated, predominantly chocolate-brown representative of this classic Lincoln key. Minimally marked for the grade assigned with hints of golden-brown at the margins and excellent overall detail. (#2426)

305   1909-S VDB AU55 ANACS. A well struck example of this prized first-year issue, predominantly copper-brown with a touch of orange at the left reverse. Light, even wear affects the highpoints of the otherwise pleasingly preserved devices. (#2426)

306   1909-S VDB—Cleaned—ANACS. AU58 Details. Extensive evaluation beneath a loupe and a glass locates a few trivial hairlines, but most collectors would be pleased to acquire this satiny key date cent. The cheekbone has only a whisper of friction, and the strike is precise. Lightly toned in olive and apricot shades. (#2426)

307   1909-S VDB AU58 NGC. The obverse is rosewood with hints of mahogany, while the reverse shows mellowed pumpkin-orange in the center. A pleasing example of this Lincoln key that shows just a touch of friction on the well-defined highpoints. (#2426)

308   1909-S VDB MS64 Brown PCGS. This needle-sharp and satiny Choice key date cent is nearly void of contact, and carbon is also minimal. Golden-brown and olive with glimpses of faded mint red near the margins. (#2426)

309   1909-S VDB MS63 Red and Brown NGC. The mellowed copper-orange surfaces of this Select piece show distinct rosewood tints in the fields. A solidly struck example of this popular Lincoln issue that shows a short horizontal abrasion on the jaw. (#2427)

310 **1909-S VDB MS63 Red and Brown ANACS.** A pleasingly detailed and unworn representative of this low-mintage issue, one of just two circulation strike Lincoln cents to have a mintage of under a million pieces. The obverse is predominantly mellowed copper-orange with mahogany elements to the right, while the reverse has an even blend of the two. (#2427)

Near-Gem 1909-S VDB Cent

311 **1909-S VDB MS64 Red and Brown PCGS.** Primarily orange-gold, but slightly mellowed in olive-tan shades. A crisply struck representative with bold VDB initials. The fields are essentially devoid of contact, although thorough evaluation locates a few pinpoint flecks. The ever-popular low mintage key date. (#2427)

Popular 1909-S VDB Cent
MS64 Red and Brown

312 **1909-S VDB MS64 Red and Brown PCGS.** Lustrous copper-gold surfaces display traces of crimson on the obverse, along with speckles of light tan patination, which is slightly more prevalent on the reverse. The design elements are well brought up, especially Lincoln's facial features and bow tie, the grains and lines in the wheat stalks, and the VDB. A few light handling marks are visible on the reverse. (#2427)

Pleasing 1909-S VDB Cent, MS65 Red and Brown

313 **1909-S VDB MS65 Red and Brown PCGS.** Generous copper-gold color stands out over both sides of this key-date Lincoln. That the planchet received an attentive strike is evident by the sharpness of Lincoln's hair and bowtie, all of the grains and lines in the wheat stalks, and in the V.D.B. Lustrous surfaces reveal no marks of consequence. Very pleasing in overall appearance! (#2427)

Pleasing 1909-S VDB Cent, Gem Red and Brown

314 **1909-S VDB MS65 Red and Brown PCGS.** Golden-orange, gold, and crimson coloration occupies the obverse, while faded orange-red runs over the reverse. Lustrous surfaces that show a modest number of scattered, tiny flyspecks, more so on the reverse. A well struck example of this key date in the Lincoln cent series that would fit nicely in a Gem set. (#2427)

Colorfully Toned 1909-S VDB Cent
MS65 Red and Brown

315 **1909-S VDB MS65 Red and Brown NGC.** Glowing luster exudes from both sides of this Gem. A medley of crimson, orange, sea-green, tan, and sky-blue patina rests over the obverse, while the reverse takes on a more golden-tan and apple-green coloration. A solid strike leaves its mark on the design features, enhancing the overall eye appeal. Well preserved. (#2427)

Full Red MS63 1909-S VDB Cent

316 **1909-S VDB MS63 Red PCGS.** Key dates within popular types remain in constant demand. To find a 1909-S VDB that is still relatively affordable yet with full red color is difficult indeed. 2009 is about 16 months away. The Lincoln cent will celebrate its 100th anniversary while Congress considers abolishing the cent forever. Perhaps the Lincoln cent will go out with a bang but the collector should purchase this key date now while it remains relatively affordable. The surfaces on this piece show a lovely yellow-gold color with booming luster and a crisp strike. Tiny flecks in the right obverse field limit the grade, but are only moderately distracting. (#2428)

Glowing 1909-S VDB Cent, Select Red

317 **1909-S VDB MS63 Red NGC.** Glowing luster radiates from the copper-orange surfaces of this Select '09-S VDB example. A well executed strike brings out sharp definition on the design features, including full separation in all of the grains and lines of both wheat stalks, and boldness on the V.D.B. elements. A few inoffensive, light toning spots are scattered about the obverse, but both sides are devoid of significant contact marks or annoying dark carbon spots. (#2428)

Breathtaking 1909-S VDB, MS64 Red

318 **1909-S VDB MS64 Red PCGS.** This is a breathtaking S-VDB example for a piece that is "only" a near-Gem. Effusive luster radiates from surfaces that possess a medley of yellow-gold, mint-green, and crimson color. A solid strike sharpens the design elements, with none revealing even a hint of weakness. A couple of unobtrusive handling marks in the right obverse field, and some tiny inoffensive flecks in the upper reverse field, might be all separating this gorgeous specimen from full Gem status. Worthy of serious consideration! (#2428)

Sharply Struck 1909-S VDB Red Near-Gem Cent

319 **1909-S VDB MS64 Red PCGS.** The results of an amazingly sharp strike immediately greet the observer of this '09-S VDB cent, as the Lincoln motif, the date and mintmark, the wheat stalks, and the V.D.B. project strong definition. Gold and yellow luster compete for territory on both sides. A few light flecks define the grade. (#2428)

Sharply Struck 1909-S VDB Cent, MS65 Red

320 **1909-S VDB MS65 Red PCGS.** Deeply lustrous apricot-golden surfaces with a hint of speckled steel-gray toning across the obverse, and a solid strike brings out excellent detail on the design features. A couple of light marks on Lincoln's portrait are within the parameters of the numerical grade. (#2428)

Gorgeous 1909-S VDB Cent, MS65 Red

321 **1909-S VDB MS65 Red PCGS.** Gorgeous orange-gold color adorns each side of this popular key date Lincoln, and wisps of pale red visit Lincoln's portrait and the upper right obverse field. A well directed strike brings out sharp definition on the design elements, including the bow tie, the V.D.B., and the lines and grains in the wheat ears. Well preserved throughout. (#2428)

Outstanding 1909-S VDB Cent, MS65 Red

322 **1909-S VDB MS65 Red PCGS.** Glowing luster emanates from coppery-gold surfaces accented with occasional whispers of crimson at the margins. A solid strike delineates the design features, including crispness on the date and mintmark and the initials VDB. There are no bothersome marks on either side to report. An ideal coin for a Mint State Lincoln collection. *From The Beau Clerc Collection.* (#2428)

Impressive 1909 Lincoln Cent, MS67 Red

323 **1909 MS67 Red PCGS.** Glowing orange-gold luster exudes from both sides of this first-year Lincoln cent, and an attentive strike translates into excellent definition on the design features. Close inspection reveals no mentionable marks or spots on its well cared for surfaces. Population: 53 in 67 Red, 0 finer (8/07). (#2431)

324 **1909-S MS65 Red and Brown PCGS.** Each side is evenly mellowed and just slightly off of full mint red. Exceptional technical quality and seemingly free from carbon. (#2433)

325 **1909-S MS65 Red PCGS.** Rich orange-gold color is imbued with traces of light blue on Lincoln's head. Sharply struck, with impeccably preserved, highly lustrous surfaces. (#2434)

326 **1910 MS66 Red PCGS.** By 1910, the Lincoln cent's novelty had faded, and upper-end Mint State examples of this second-year issue are elusive. This copper-orange Premium Gem offers carefully preserved, pale surfaces that host well-defined devices. (#2437)

327 **1910-S MS65 Red PCGS.** Well struck with scintillating mint luster and lovely golden-peach coloration across both sides. The surfaces are beautifully preserved, and perhaps the absence of carbon is the most impressive single feature of this outstanding Gem example. (#2440)

328 **1910-S MS65 Red PCGS.** Typically struck with amazingly smooth, clean surfaces. Lightly marked on the reverse, but close to pristine on the obverse. (#2440)

Exquisite 1911 Cent, MS67 Red

329 **1911 MS67 Red PCGS.** The 1911 Lincoln cent from the Philadelphia Mint, with a mintage exceeding 100 million pieces, is readily available in all grades. David Lange, in his 2005 treatise *The Complete Guide to Lincoln Cents*, writes of this issue: "... uncirculated coins of this date are more likely than previous P-mint cents to have unattractive toning or spotting. If original rolls exist, they may reflect this slightly lower quality. When gems are found, however, they more often than not have outstanding luster."

The MS67 Red example presented in this lot does indeed display outstanding luster, that seems to jump out at the observer. Exquisitely defined design elements complement this attribute, as do the immaculately preserved copper-orange surfaces. In sum, this piece looks as it did when it first came off of the press. Population: 7 in 67 Red, 1 finer (8/07). (#2443)

Sharp 1911-D Cent, MS66 Red

330 **1911-D MS66 Red PCGS.** A scarcer early Lincoln with a mintage of 12.6 million pieces. Only 18 pieces have been certified in MS66 Red by PCGS and NGC, with two coins finer (8/07). This piece shows smooth golden-orange surfaces that have been well cared for. The design elements are sharply impressed throughout, which is significant for an issue that is often weakly struck. (#2446)

331 **1911-S MS65 Red and Brown ANACS.** A lustrous and highly pleasing straw-gold Gem that approaches full red despite a blush of charcoal-gray near 11 o'clock on the reverse. In an ANA cache holder. (#2448)

332 **1912 MS66 ★ Red NGC.** Vivid copper-orange with a splash of strawberry-red on each side. Intricately struck and unabraded with only minute carbon. As of (8/07), the only 1912 cent to receive a Star designation from NGC. (#2452)

333 **1912 MS66 Red PCGS.** This lovely Gem is sharply detailed with full red color and hints of pale lilac toning in the center of the obverse. Population: 61 in 66, 7 finer (8/07). (#2452)

334 **1912-D MS64 Red PCGS.** A carrot-orange early Lincoln exemplar that shows impressive central detail, though the obverse margins show a touch of blurriness. The reverse displays a fingerprint above the left wheat ear and a measure of other spotting. (#2455)

335 **1912-S MS64 Red PCGS.** Ex: LaBute Collection. A pale peach-gold near-Gem with satin luster and a near absence of carbon. The fields are unabraded, and the strike is intricate aside from the right edge of the right wheat ear.
Ex: Long Beach Signature (Heritage, 2/02), lot 5186. (#2458)

336 **1913-D MS64 Red PCGS,** a beautiful straw-gold near-Gem early branch mint cent; and a **1927-D MS64 Red and Brown PCGS,** substantial brick-red remains, well preserved, bold save for the AM in AMERICA. (Total: 2 coins) (#2464)

337 **1913-S MS64 Red and Brown NGC.** Almost fully struck, save for minor incompleteness on URIBUS UN, and on the top of O in ONE. Deep red-brown toning covers each side of this lustrous, glossy near-Gem. Essentially mark-free with a modest amount of carbon on both sides. From an early, semi-key issue in the Lincoln cent series. (#2466)

338 **1914 MS65 Red PCGS.** This crisply struck and satiny orange and olive Gem is virtually void of marks or carbon. A slender, vertical retained lamination approaches Lincoln's chin. Housed in an old green label holder.
Ex: Kyle Patrick Collection (Heritage, 6/04), lot 5272, which realized $690. (#2470)

339 **1914-D XF45 PCGS.** A well-defined chocolate-brown Choice XF example of this D-mint key, minimally marked with light, even wear across the devices. Appealing and comparatively affordable, a wonderful choice for a similarly graded date set. (#2471)

340 **1914-D XF45 PCGS.** A pleasing example of this key date, which is recognized by many numismatists as being scarcer than the famous 1909-S VDB at most grade levels. This Choice XF piece is well detailed and mildly worn, with a few small marks on the reverse. (#2471)

341 **1914-D—Corroded, Cleaned—ANACS. AU50 Details.** Lincoln's jaw and cheekbone exhibit slight wear, and the dusky olive-green and rose-tan toning appears unnatural. Corrosion is minimal, and marks are inconsequential. (#2471)

342 **1914-D AU53 ANACS.** This briefly circulated D-mint Lincoln key offers luminous chocolate-brown surfaces with violet overtones. Well-defined with few marks and excellent overall eye appeal.
From The Laguna Niguel Collection, Part Two. (#2471)

Key Date 1914-D Cent MS64

343 **1914-D MS64 Brown PCGS.** The surfaces of this well struck near-Gem have swaths of olive and sandy-brown, as well as significant areas of slightly faded copper-orange at the reverse periphery. While this low-mintage issue did not attract much contemporary notice, collectors today avidly pursue attractive examples. Population: 40 in 64 Brown, 9 finer (7/07). (#2471)

344 **1916 MS66 Red PCGS.** Dazzling luster radiates from yellow-gold and orange surfaces that exhibit remarkable preservation. All of the design elements have benefited from a powerful strike. (#2488)

345 **1916-S MS64 Red PCGS.** An attentively struck and lovely near-Gem example of this earlier San Francisco Lincoln issue, predominantly pale salmon-orange with a touch of spotting near the left corner of the bust. PCGS has graded 22 finer Red pieces (8/07). (#2494)

346 **1918-S MS65 Red and Brown NGC.** A lovely Gem with blended olive-gold and tan shades. The satiny surfaces are essentially void of marks, and the strike is precise aside from the right edge of the right wheat ear. Encapsulated in an older holder. (#2511)

Incredible 1919 Cent, MS67 Red

347 **1919 MS67 Red PCGS.** A sharply struck and elegant representative of this early Lincoln cent issue, struck one year after Victor David Brenner's initials were placed on the truncation of Lincoln's bust. The surfaces have a lemon-gold appearance with splashes of richer orange on the reverse. Immensely appealing. Population: 55 in 67 Red, 15 finer (7/07). (#2515)

Splendid 1919 Cent, MS67 Red

348 **1919 MS67 Red PCGS.** An beautiful, fiery Gem with splendid orange-gold and mint-green coloration. Both the luster and strike of this Superb '19-P would be difficult to improve upon. Both faces are immaculately preserved. Housed in a green-label holder. Population: 55 in 67 Red, 15 finer (8/07). (#2515)

349 **1922-D Weak D AU58 PCGS.** Die Pair 1. The reverse shows the diagnostic die crack through the O in ONE on the weak reverse. The chocolate-brown surfaces show minor friction, and the upper left corner of the mintmark is visible to the unaided eye. (#3110)

350 **1922 No D Strong Reverse—Corroded, Damaged—ANACS. VF20 Details.** This chocolate-brown key date cent has a pair of minor nicks on the portrait that seem unworthy of the "Damaged" designation. The right reverse has glimpses of charcoal verdigris, but these are also minor for the VF20 level. (#3285)

351 **1922 No D Strong Reverse—Corroded, Cleaned—ANACS. VF20 Details.** FS-401. Somewhat bright for the VF20 level, and each side has a few small dark gray spots. The left obverse has a pair of parallel laminations. A nicely detailed example of this key *Guide Book* variety. (#3285)

352 **1922 No D Strong Reverse VF30 PCGS.** Die Pair #2. Despite moderate wear, the wheat ears on the reverse of this No D cent exhibit considerable detail. The chocolate-brown obverse is suitably mushy with a minor abrasion on Lincoln's forehead. (#3285)

353 **1922 No D Strong Reverse VF35 PCGS.** FS-013.2. Die Pair 2. Lovely light brown patination graces semi-glossy surfaces of this key date Lincoln cent. Generally well defined, and free of significant contact marks. (#3285)

354 **1922 No D Strong Reverse VF35 PCGS.** A medium brown Choice VF example of this elusive and popular variety. Minor carbon is relegated to the obverse at 4 o'clock and the reverse at 7 o'clock. (#3285)

1922 No D Weak Reverse Cent MS62 Red and Brown

355 **1922 No D Weak Reverse MS62 Red and Brown NGC.** The obverse is mostly red, although a glass locates distributed minor carbon. The reverse border is orange-gold, while the wheat ears and central legends are toned lilac and deep cherry-red. Attractive despite a trio of slender marks on the upper right reverse field. (#2541)

Impressive Near-Gem Red and Brown 1923-S Cent

356 **1923-S MS64 Red and Brown PCGS.** This boldly struck and satiny example is mostly orange-red, and approaches a full Red designation despite a hint of peripheral apple-green toning. The obverse field is minutely granular, as made. Pinpoint reverse carbon is all the precludes an even finer grade. (#2547)

Red Near-Gem 1924-S Cent

357 **1924-S MS64 Red NGC.** Rose-red and lime shades visit portions of this primarily orange-gold near-Gem. Sharply struck save for the AM in AMERICA. Unabraded, although a minor spot is seen beneath the B in LIBERTY. Certified in a prior generation holder. Population: 17 in 64, 1 finer (7/07). (#2557)

358 **1925 MS67 Red NGC.** A beautiful peach-red Superb Gem that boasts a sharp strike and a minimum of pinpoint carbon flecks. Neither NGC nor PCGS has certified any examples in higher grades. (#2560)

359 **1925-D MS64 Red PCGS.** This softly mellowed, yet vibrant Denver near-Gem has carrot-orange surfaces with undercurrents of brick-red. Solidly struck with a single grade-defining abrasion that crosses Lincoln's jawline. (#2563)

360 **1926-S MS64 Brown PCGS.** Deep steel-blue and cherry-red embrace this satiny and unblemished near-Gem. Struck from worn dies, and thus lacking some highpoint details. Population: 23 in 64, 3 finer (8/07). (#2573)

Sharply Defined 1926-S Cent, MS64 Red

361 **1926-S MS64 Red PCGS.** In his Lincoln Cents reference book (2005) David Lange, discussing the 1926-S cent, writes: "Mushy coins are the rule for this issue. Most seen are from worn dies revealing distorted details, particularly toward the peripheries." This near-Gem Red example does not fit the profile. Its design elements, including those at the peripheries, are sharply defined. Copper-gold luster greets the viewer. Abrasions are absent, though a few light flecks define the grade. Population: 67 in 64 Red, 1 finer (8/07). (#2575)

362 **1927-S MS64 Red and Brown NGC.** The deep reddish-bronze and purple toning of this near-Gem cent is highly attractive. Boldly struck and highly lustrous, the piece shows a pair of faint slide marks across Lincoln's temple and cheekbone. Scattered carbon flecks are noted on both sides. Census: 48 in 64 Red and Brown, 11 finer (8/07). (#2583)

363 **1928-D MS65 Red PCGS.** A lustrous Gem with a sharp strike and bright golden color. Seemingly free from abrasion, but a few trivial carbon flecks are noted. Certified in a green label holder. (#2590)

364 **1928-S MS64 Red PCGS.** This piece is well struck for the issue and shows orange-red surfaces with some light carbon. A charcoal streak is noted through the O of ONE. Seldom found in full Red, and perhaps underrated as such. (#2593)

Vibrant 1929 Cent, MS67 Red

365 **1929 MS67 Red PCGS.** Both sides of this Superb Gem are awash with vibrant luster and stunning copper-orange color, and a well executed strike imparts excellent definition to the design features, including the bow tie and the grains and lines on the wheat stalks. Impeccably preserved throughout. Population: 31 in 67 Red, 0 finer (8/07). (#2596)

366 **1930-D MS66 Red PCGS.** boldly struck and shimmering with smooth dusky orange-red surfaces; and a 1949 **MS66 Red PCGS,** flashy and nicely struck with lovely cherry-red and apple-green shades. (Total: 2 coins) (#2608)

367 **1931 MS66 Red PCGS.** A vibrant and well-defined representative of this Depression-era issue, one with a deep orange obverse and paler copper color on the reverse. PCGS has certified only 11 finer Red representatives (7/07). (#2614)

368 **1931-D MS65 Red PCGS.** Coppery-gold surfaces exhibit pleasing luster and sharply struck design elements. Each side is free of significant marks or unsightly spots. (#2617)

369 **1931-S MS65 Red PCGS.** This low mintage cent has scintillating luster, a good strike, and a few splashes of orange-red across the predominantly straw-gold fields. Encapsulated in an old green label holder. (#2620)

370 **1931-S MS65 Red PCGS.** Rich orange luster exudes from the well cared for surfaces of this fully Red Gem. Sharply struck throughout. A couple of minuscule flecks on each side are not bothersome. (#2620)

371 **1931-S MS65 Red PCGS.** Typically struck with glowing luster and variegated purple-red and yellow-gold coloration. There are just two or three small contact marks on each side of the coin. (#2620)

372 **1932-D MS66 Red PCGS.** Despite a mintage of 10.5 million pieces, only a fraction of the production survives in Mint State with original color. This decisively struck reddish-orange example has great eye appeal, though a shallow mark is noted behind Lincoln's head. PCGS has graded just six finer Red representatives (7/07). (#2626)

Gorgeous, Sharply Struck 1933-D Cent, MS67 Red

373 **1933-D MS67 Red PCGS.** David Lange, writing of the 1933-D in his Lincoln cents reference book, states that "Mint State coins are fairly common at the choice (MS63-64) level. Enough are poorly struck ... that fully struck gems are scarce." A sharp strike emboldened the design elements of this lustrous orange Superb Gem, highlighting its scarcity. Nicely preserved. Population: 19 in 67 Red, 0 finer (8/07). (#2632)

Pleasing 1944-D/S Red Gem Cent
FS-020, OMM-1

374 **1944-D/S MS65 Red PCGS.** FS-020, OMM-1, the better variety. The design elements are exquisitely struck up on this Red Gem, and the lustrous surfaces display attractive orange-gold color. A few light toning spots do not take away from the coin's overall eye appeal. Population: 18 in 65 Red, 7 finer (8/07). (#2728)

375 **1949 MS64 Red and Brown PCGS.** An attractive near-Gem Lincoln cent. The obverse boasts fire-red color, while the reverse displays golden-peach patina. Well struck and highly lustrous, with a few light toning streaks on the reverse. Population: 6 in 64, 3 finer (7/07). (#2769)

376 **1949 MS65 Red and Brown PCGS.** The surfaces of this vividly toned P-mint cent range from strawberry-red to tangerine and pale copper at the margins. A well-defined and pleasing Gem. Population: 3 in 65 Red and Brown, 0 finer (7/07). (#2769)

377 **1949-D MS64 Red PCGS.** This is a bright, highly lustrous near-Gem Lincoln cent that betrays lovely golden-peach coloration with appealing mint-green accents near the periphery. Well struck with a few small marks and several noticeable toning streaks across each side. (#2773)

378 **1949-D MS64 Red PCGS.** Intense luster is the chief hallmark of this visually arresting cent. Alluring lime-green and fire-red toning are also noted on both sides. Several spots and small contact marks on the upper right side of the obverse preclude the Gem assessment. (#2773)

379 **1949-S MS64 Red and Brown PCGS.** Boldly struck save for weakness on the upper half of O in ONE. Deep fire-red color competes with sea-green patina on each side. Satiny and highly lustrous with scattered small abrasions and a few flyspecks. (#2775)

380 **1949-S MS65 Red PCGS.** Intense fire-red, lime-green, and gold coloration decorates the bright, lustrous surfaces of this carefully preserved Gem. The design elements are boldly struck on both sides, and surface marks are minor. (#2776)

Superb, Full Red 1950 Cent

381 **1950 MS67 Red PCGS.** The fields display pronounced horizontal die polishing marks that add even more to the brightness of this piece. The strike is complete and we do not see any specks of carbon on either side. What is most important, though, is the even, unmellowed red color and the lack of any noticeable abrasions. Population: 18 in 67, 0 finer (8/07). (#2779)

382 **1955/55 Doubled Die Obverse—Whizzed—ANACS. AU50 Details.** FS-101. The pumpkin-orange surfaces of this prominently doubled cent have unnatural wire-brush luster. The well struck devices show only a touch of actual wear. A comparatively affordable example of this popular Lincoln variant. *From The Diemer L. Fife Collection.* (#2825)

383 **1955/55 Doubled Die Obverse AU53 PCGS.** FS-101. A deep brown representative of this impressive and famous doubled die. Lincoln's cheekbone has only slight wear. (#2825)

384 **1955/55 Doubled Die Obverse AU58 PCGS.** FS-101. Sharply struck with dark chocolate surfaces and nearly full satiny luster. The most visually arresting of the various Lincoln cent doubled die varieties, since the doubling is visible to the unaided eye. (#2825)

Classic Doubled Die 1955 Cent MS62

385 **1955/55 Doubled Die Obverse MS62 Brown PCGS.** A satiny and glossy example of this spectacular doubled die variety. The obverse is olive-gold and lilac-red, while the reverse is ruby-red with violet tints. Attentively struck, and post-strike contact is inconsequential for the assigned grade. (#2825)

Attractive Near-Gem 1955/55 Lincoln Cent

386 **1955/55 Doubled Die Obverse MS64 Brown PCGS.** FS-101. This dramatic overdate variety has become an important issue in the Lincoln cent series, highly coveted by collectors. This near-Gem is sharply struck and lustrous, with chocolate-brown coloration enhanced by noticeable steel-green accents on the highpoints. A few tiny contact marks limit the grade. (#2825)

387 **1956 MS67 Red NGC.** The fresh copper-orange surfaces of this Superb Gem show faint blushes of rose on either side of the portrait and minimal carbon on the wheat-ears reverse. A well-defined representative that presents beautifully. Neither NGC nor PCGS has graded a numerically finer Red example (8/07). (#2836)

388 **1960-D Small Date MS67 Red NGC.** Ex: Omaha Bank Hoard. A gorgeous sun-gold Superb Gem that lacks obvious carbon. Well struck aside from the lower central stairs of the Memorial. (#2869)

389 **1963-D MS66 Red PCGS.** An attractive example of this earlier mintmarked Lincoln Memorial cent, well-defined and gleaming with elements of lemon-gold and copper-orange. PCGS has graded no finer Red representatives (8/07). (#2887)

390 **1968-S MS67 Red PCGS.** Copper-orange and lemon-gold elements converge on this shining Superb Gem. The issue marked the acknowledged return of San Francisco to the lineup of active Mints. Population: 35 in 67, 1 finer (8/07). (#2909)

391 **1971 Doubled Die Obverse MS64 Red ANACS.** FS-101, formerly FS-031. GOD, LIBERTY, and the date are nicely die doubled. Less dramatic than the famous 1972 DDO, but still desirable, and very scarce as well. A lustrous pumpkin-gold near-Gem with minor contact on the right obverse field. (#92941)

392 **1973-S MS66 Red PCGS,** magnificent save for a minor mark west of UNUM; and a **2003-D MS69 Red PCGS,** an exemplary pumpkin-orange example of this modern conditional scarcity. (Total: 2 coins) (#2968)

393 **1980-D MS67 Red PCGS;** nearly perfect aside from minor blending of detail on STATES; and a **1984 MS68 Red PCGS;** a splendid orange-red Superb Gem with a trace of gray between the 84 in the date. (Total: 2 coins) (#3004)

394 **1982 MS68 Red PCGS.** This flawless brick-red Large Date example has tiny, telltale air bubbles beneath the plating, characteristic of copper-plated zinc examples from this transitional year. PCGS has yet to divide the 1982-dated population data by Large and Small Dates, or by copper or zinc alloy. Population: 25 in 68 Red, 0 finer (8/07). (#3047)

395 **1982-D MS68 Red PCGS.** Square Base 2. A pristine orange-gold Superb Gem. Only STATES lacks a crisp impression. Presumably copper alloy, since no bubbles are visible beneath the fields. (#3050)

396 **1983-D MS68 Red PCGS.** Bright, even, fiery red color covers each side of this superlative coin. Population: 20 in 68, 0 finer (8/07). (#3051)

397 **1984 Doubled Die Obverse MS67 Red PCGS.** This "Doubled Ear" variety has bright red color that is accented by a couple of dabs of lilac on each side. (#3062)

398 **1986 MS68 Red PCGS.** Fully struck, highly lustrous, and seemingly pristine, this is a nearly perfect Lincoln cent, with rich mint-red coloration and a very flashy overall appearance. Population: 28 in 68 Red, 0 finer (8/07). (#3124)

399 **1990 MS68 Red PCGS.** Aside from a touch of milky toning at the obverse margins, the surfaces of this Red Superb Gem retain their original, vibrant copper-orange. Attentively detailed and a significant piece for the Registry enthusiast. Population: 30 in 68 Red, 0 finer (8/07). (#3083)

400 **1991 MS68 Red PCGS.** A boldly impressed and entirely fresh copper-orange representative of this modern issue, pristine and noteworthy for the Lincoln Memorial enthusiast. Population: 28 in 68 Red, 0 finer (8/07). (#3092)

401 **1997-D MS68 Red PCGS.** Boldly impressed with lovely peach and copper-orange surfaces that are nearly flawless to the unaided eye. Despite this issue's recent vintage, neither NGC nor PCGS has certified a better representative. Population: 21 in 68 Red, 0 finer (8/07). (#3142)

402 **1999 Wide AM MS67 Red PCGS.** A wide space is visible between the AM of AMERICA, which normally is only found on proof cents of recent years, but appears on some Philadelphia Mint circulation strikes of 1998, 1999, and 2000 also. Lustrous orange surfaces are carefully preserved. (#3154)

PROOF LINCOLN CENTS

Exceptional 1913 PR65 Red Cent

403 **1913 PR65 Red PCGS.** The 1913 is considered the most "common" date in the matte proof series. "Common" must certainly be understood in the context of the series and also in the context of coins certified with fully intact red surfaces. Only 39 pieces have been so graded by PCGS in PR65 with 28 finer (8/07). This is an outstanding piece. The striking details are razor-sharp and the surfaces are rich red on the obverse with pale olive on the reverse. (#3317)

Red Gem 1936 Type One Proof Cent

404 **1936 Type One—Satin Finish PR65 Red PCGS.** Two distinct types of proof cents and nickels were coined in 1936, known as Satin and Brilliant proofs. The Satin proofs are reminiscent of the matte proof pieces coined two decades earlier. Some additional proofs seem to by hybrid issues, such as this piece, with characteristics of both styles. Brilliant mint red surfaces are moderately reflective and accented by hints of lilac and gold toning. (#3332)

Lovely Brilliant Finish 1936 Lincoln Cent PR65 Red

405 **1936 Type Two—Brilliant Finish—PR65 Red PCGS.** Uniformly brilliant with deep cherry-red coloration and fully struck design elements on each side. Nearly perfect, except for a couple of wispy, milky streaks in the upper right obverse field that are difficult to detect without magnification. The Brilliant finish was adopted on proof Lincoln cents in 1936 after Type Ones, with matte-like surfaces, proved unpopular. (#3335)

Rare Cameo 1936 Cent, PR65 Red

406 **1936 Type Two—Brilliant Finish—PR65 Red Cameo NGC.** The 1936 is even scarcer than its mintage of 5,569 pieces indicates. Two distinct finishes were used, Satin and Brilliant. Approximately equal numbers of each were struck, but collectors seek both variants for proof date sets. This is a deeply mirrored proof that shows a moderate overlay of mint frost on the devices, which of course, yields the cameo effect. Any 1936-1942 proof of any denomination is rare with a cameo contrast. Each side has deep cherry-red color with a few darker specks of color scattered about. (#83335)

407 **1950 PR67 Red Cameo NGC.** This first-year issue is rarely found with cameo contrast on any of the denominations. The fields are deeply reflective and there is just enough mint frost over the devices to give the coin contrast. Rich cherry-red color throughout. (#83359)

Highly Attractive 1951 Cent, PR66 Cameo

408 **1951 PR66 Cameo PCGS.** This brilliant proof displays splashes of highly attractive yellow-gold, orange, and coppery colors. The well struck design elements stand out on this example, offering pleasing contrast with the mirrored fields, regardless of the angle from which the coin is viewed. There are no mentionable contact marks or spots to report. Population: 31 in 66 Cameo, 6 finer (8/07). (#83362)

Marvelous 1956 Lincoln Cent PR67 Deep Cameo

409 **1956 PR67 Deep Cameo PCGS.** The mintage for this mid-1950s issue was nearly 670,000 pieces; yet only 44 examples have been graded at PR67 Deep Cameo by NGC and PCGS combined, and a mere 11 coins finer (8/07). This piece displays razor-sharp striking details and immense reflectivity in the fields. Fully brilliant and seemingly pristine, with great Deep Cameo contrast evident on each side. (#93377)

Conditionally Rare 1956 Cent PR67 Deep Cameo

410 **1956 PR67 Deep Cameo PCGS.** Beautifully struck with amazingly deep reflectivity evident in the utterly black mirror fields. The red-gold central devices are heavily frosted, and the Deep Cameo contrast is obvious on both sides. According to Tomaska (1991): "gem cameo 1956 Lincoln cents are extremely scarce ... . Ultra-heavy examples do exist, but they are quite rare." (#93377)

411 **1956 PR68 Red Ultra Cameo NGC.** An essentially perfect specimen from the year of Elvis Presley's television debut. Devoid of carbon and exactingly struck. Census: 4 in 68 Red Ultra Cameo, 2 finer (8/07). (#93377)

PR68 Deep Cameo 1960 Small Date Cent

412 **1960 Small Date PR68 Deep Cameo PCGS.** The 1960 Small Date is much scarcer than its Large Date counterpart, both in business strike and proof format. Nonetheless, Small Date proofs are obtainable, particularly if some toning or spotting is acceptable. What makes the present piece remarkable is its radiant frosted devices and exemplary, carbon-free surfaces. The orange-red color is seamless, aside from a wisp of powder-blue tint at 6 o'clock on the reverse. Population: 20 in 68 Deep Cameo, none finer (8/07). (#93392)

413 **1962 PR68 Red Deep Cameo PCGS,** a pumpkin-gold beauty with particularly pronounced cameo contrast on the reverse; and a **1963 PR69 Red Cameo PCGS,** a gorgeous fire-red specimen with exemplary preservation. (Total: 2 coins) (#93398)

414 **1970-S Small Date PR67 Red Deep Cameo PCGS.** A boldly struck and unabraded orange-gold Superb Gem. A few minute carbon flecks are noted. Population: 34 in 67 Red Deep Cameo, 21 finer (8/07). (#93426)

415 **1971-S Doubled Die Obverse PR68 Red NGC.** FS-033. IN GOD WE TRUST and LIBERTY are die doubled with a noticeable spread. *Cherrypickers'* gives this variety a "five star" interest designation, and it is also listed in the *Guide Book*. Brightly mirrored with orange-red surfaces that show a touch of haziness about the portrait. (#3434)

416 **1999-S Close AM PR68 Deep Cameo PCGS.** The Close AM, distant FG variety was intended for business strikes, but an unknown number of proof 1999-S cents of this subtype were also inadvertently produced. This variety is listed in the *Guide Book*. A pinpoint-sharp and gorgeous Superb Gem with unperturbed mirrored fields. (#38222)

TWO CENT PIECES

Gem 1864 Small Motto Two Cent

417 **1864 Small Motto MS65 Red and Brown NGC.** The two cent piece was introduced in 1864 with a mintage of nearly 20 million pieces, but the vast majority of those were the Large Motto subtype. The Small Motto is comparatively rare, and was struck only in 1864. This evenly struck and unblemished example is orange-gold and medium brown with the former color more prevalent on the reverse. (#3580)

418 **1864 Large Motto MS66 Red and Brown NGC.** KF-L8-RPD. The 18 in the date is obviously repunched. The lower central obverse has mellowed slightly in lilac-red, but the remainder of this lustrous Premium Gem is olive-gold. Well struck and unmarked with only minor carbon. (#3577)

419 **1864 Large Motto MS65 Red NGC.** This inviting Gem offers warm pumpkin-orange surfaces with reddish accents. A solidly struck first-year example of this odd-denomination series that shows minimal carbon overall. (#3578)

420 **1864 Large Motto MS65 Red NGC.** A well-defined and carefully preserved representative of this popular two cent type issue. The pumpkin-orange obverse and carrot-colored reverse show only scant evidence of mellowing. Challenging any better with Red surfaces; NGC has graded only 42 such pieces (8/07). (#3578)

421 **1864 Large Motto MS65 Red NGC.** Boldly struck and intensely lustrous, with a dazzling cartwheel sheen across the fields. Bright reddish-golden toning increases the eye appeal of the piece. Scattered flyspecks and a few minor marks are noted on each side. (#3578)

422 **1865 MS65 Red PCGS.** Plain 5. This luminous second-year Gem offers pleasing detail and considerable visual appeal. While the obverse is copper-orange, the reverse shows a measure of deeper color within the wreath. (#3584)

423 **1865 MS65 Red NGC.** Well struck with bright satiny luster and light reddish-gold toning. Both sides of the piece are minimally marked with just a few flyspecks. A lovely Gem example, housed in an early-generation NGC holder. (#3584)

424 **1868 MS65 Red and Brown NGC.** A crisply struck and attractive odd-denomination Gem that has an appealing balance of orange and umber on each side. A small chocolate-brown spot is present to the right of the date. NGC has certified just six finer Red and Brown representatives (8/07). (#3598)

425 **1870 MS64 Red and Brown PCGS.** Boldly struck save for the tops of the right-side vertical shield lines. The orange-gold obverse is close to full Red, while the reverse features dusky olive toning. Encapsulated in a green label holder. (#3607)

426 **1872 MS61 Red and Brown ANACS.** The obverse has a dusky reddish-orange appearance, while the reverse of this unworn coin offers a hue closer to mahogany. Solidly struck with only a few abrasions, a great representative of the denomination's final circulation-strike issue. (#3613)

PROOF TWO CENT PIECES

427 **1865 PR63 Brown ANACS.** Plain 5. Ice-blue, rose, and pumpkin-gold emerge when this exactingly struck proof is rotated beneath a light. The reverse has a faint fingerprint at 6 o'clock. Just 500+ proofs were struck. (#3627)

Dazzling, Full Red 1866 Two Cent Piece, PR65

428 **1866 PR65 Red PCGS.** An outstanding proof two cent piece. Even after several years of increasing prices, these type coins are still underrated when compared to type coins of other denominations. Although not designated on the insert, the devices on this coin show a light bit of frost which gives a slight but noticeable cameo effect. Light and bright and deeply mirrored with virtually flawless surfaces. Population: 32 in 65, 2 finer (8/07). (#3632)

429 **1867 PR63 Red PCGS.** This beautiful butter-gold specimen merits a finer technical grade, but the borders have subtle laminations, most prominently to the west of the date. A strike-through is right of the second S in STATES. Certified in a green label holder. (#3635)

430 **1868 PR64 Red and Brown NGC.** Cherry-red, electric-blue, and orange-gold adorn this flashy, glossy, and penetratingly struck near-Gem proof. Infrequent carbon limits the grade. Encased in an older generation holder. (#3637)

431 **1868 PR64 Red NGC.** A boldly struck copper-orange near-Gem of this mid-date issue, which has a proof mintage of only 600 pieces. The fields are deeply mirrored, and the strike is bold. Examination with a glass reveals a few toning flecks and hairlines on each side. Census: 15 in 64 Red, 18 finer (8/07). (#3638)

432 **1871 PR64 Red and Brown PCGS.** The light rose-red centers are bounded by pale olive-gold. TRUST and the right-side arrowhead are die doubled, as is diagnostic for this proof date. Encased in a green label holder. (#3646)

433 **1871 PR62 Red ANACS.** A beautiful sun-gold two cent piece. The strike is penetrating, and carbon and marks are minimal. The obverse rim at 7:30 has a small lamination, and a lintmark wanders above the N in CENT. TRUST is die doubled, as always. (#3647)

434 **1872 PR64 Red and Brown NGC.** An attractive example of the last proof two cent issue to have accompanying business strikes. The copper-orange of the obverse gives way to nutmeg and mahogany on the boldly impressed, modestly hairlined reverse. (#3649)

435 **1872 PR65 Red and Brown PCGS.** The 1872 was the penultimate proof issue for the two cent piece and the last to accompany a business strike mintage. This attractive Gem offers rich copper-orange surfaces with a splash of violet at the right obverse. One of just 950 pieces struck. (#3649)

436 **1872 PR65 Red and Brown PCGS.** While the obverse is nearly pure reddish-orange, the reverse shows areas of deeper mahogany on and within the wreath. This pleasingly preserved Gem hails from the penultimate proof two cent issue. (#3649)

Choice Red and Brown Closed 3 1873 Two Cent Proof

437 **1873 Closed 3 PR64 Red and Brown NGC.** This older holder proof-only specimen is precisely struck and offers dusky tan-gold and lime-green toning. Carbon is minimal, and the quality is impressive for the grade. The Closed 3 variety is about twice as available as its Open 3 counterpart, although both varieties are very scarce. (#3652)

1873 Closed 3 Two Cent Piece PR64 Red and Brown

438 **1873 Closed 3 PR64 Red and Brown PCGS.** This was the final year of issue for the short-lived two cent denomination, which was introduced in 1864. Only proofs were produced with the 1873 date, although the Open 3 coins were believed by Walter Breen to be restrikes, possibly from a later time period. This is a well mirrored near-Gem with rich coloration that is more red than brown. The surfaces are blemish-free. (#3652)

Gem Proof-Only 1873 Closed 3 Two Cents, Red and Brown

439 **1873 Closed 3 PR65 Red and Brown PCGS.** Rich apple-green and rose-gold adorn this well struck and nearly mark-free Gem. Carbon is limited to a tiny fleck above the right foot of the 1 in the date. A colorful and moderately mirrored example of this popular proof-only issue. Only 600 proofs were struck. (#3652)

Gem Red and Brown Proof 1873 Closed 3 Two Cent

440 **1873 Closed 3 PR65 Red and Brown PCGS.** Rich red-brown coloration with electric-blue accents near the centers, on both obverse and reverse. A highly reflective Gem, housed in a first-generation PCGS holder. Population: 76 in 65 Red and Brown, 15 finer in the same color (8/07). (#3652)

PR58 Open 3 1873 Two Cent

441 **1873 Open 3 PR58 NGC.** This medium-brown proof-only example has selected flatness on WE, the right arrow, and the obverse leaves. NGC has interpreted this flatness as cabinet friction, although an indifferent strike may also be the cause. A small spot is noted near the left arrow, and a minor lamination (as made) resides on the inner right side of the wreath.
From The Beau Clerc Collection. (#3654)

Near-Gem 1873 Open 3 Two Cent Proof

442 **1873 Open 3 PR64 Brown PCGS.** The final-year two cent date was only issued in proof format. Closed 3 pieces are considered originals, while Open 3 examples are traditionally referred to as restrikes. The "restrikes," however, may also have been struck in 1873, and sold in sets with the Open 3 Arrows proof Seated coins. A boldly defined representative with mark-free surfaces and original pumpkin-gold, aquamarine, and lilac patina. Housed in a green label holder. (#3654)

THREE CENT SILVER

443 **1851 MS66 PCGS.** A satiny and carefully preserved example of this first-year issue, pearl-gray with a touch of lavender in the centers and rich purple-red and green toning near the peripheries. PCGS has graded only 11 pieces finer (7/07). (#3664)

444 **1851 MS66 PCGS.** A flashy stone-white Premium Gem representative of this first-year trime issue, a popular selection for type collectors. Immensely appealing and challenging any finer, with just 11 such pieces graded by PCGS (8/07). (#3664)

445 **1851-O MS64 PCGS.** This issue's status as the only branch mint trime has ensured its popularity for generations. The near-Gem offered here has sky-blue and gold patina over each side, with brick-red patina of varying intensity at the reverse margins. (#3665)

446 **1851-O MS64 NGC.** A lovely near-Gem representative of this popular issue, the only trime struck outside Philadelphia. Solidly struck with few marks and soft luster beneath a layer of peach patina. (#3665)

447 **1851-O MS64 PCGS.** A satiny, softly struck Choice example of this popular mintmarked trime issue, silver-blue at the margins with a measure of canary-gold in the centers. A planchet flaw appears at the rim near the second T of STATES. (#3665)

Impressive Gem 1851-O Three Cent Silver

448 **1851-O MS65 PCGS.** Glowing luster emanates from both sides of this lovely New Orleans Mint issue. The design elements are much better impressed than often seen on the '51-O trime, and the frosty surfaces are essentially untoned. Close examination reveals no significant marks. Population: 44 in 65, 11 finer (8/07). (#3665)

449 **1852 MS65 NGC.** Well struck from lightly worn dies, with typical clash marks noted on each side. Lustrous and untoned in the center of the obverse, with a slight degree of speckled green and russet patina on each side. A highly attractive Gem.
From The Arnold & Harriet Collection, Part Two. (#3666)

Amazing 1852 Three Cent, MS67

450 **1852 MS67 PCGS.** Frosty luster adheres to silver-gray surfaces that display a blush or two of olive-green. The design elements are generally well struck, except for the usual softness in the centers. Both sides are well preserved, and clashmarks are visible on the reverse. Population: 11 in 67, 2 finer (8/07). (#3666)

451 **1854 MS64 PCGS.** Both sides of this appealing near-Gem example are boldly struck, and the reverse design elements are particularly sharp. Light champagne and lilac toning enhances the visual appeal of the piece. Five radial die cracks are counted on the obverse, and both sides display faint die clashing. (#3670)

452 **1856 MS64 PCGS.** The Type Two trimes present a challenge for type collectors, though the 1856 is one of the more available issues for the period. The surfaces of this well struck near-Gem shine beneath attractive rose and sky-blue toning. Population: 73 in 64, 23 finer (8/07). (#3672)

Nicely Toned 1856 Gem Three Cent Silver

453 **1856 MS65 NGC.** Speckled sea-green, russet, and gold coloration blankets each side of this Gem. Lustrous and nearly pristine with exquisitely struck motifs. The borders show occasional minor softness of strike. The middle date of the five-year Type Two coinage. Census: 15 in 65, 4 finer (8/07). (#3672)

454 **1861 MS65 NGC.** Though trime production in 1861 approached half a million pieces, the upswing was temporary, and mintages continued to fall until the silver denomination's discontinuation in 1873. This lovely Gem offers pillowy detail and frosty silver-white surfaces.
From The Mario Eller Collection, Part One. (#3679)

455 **1861 MS66 PCGS.** While the 1861 is a mid-date issue for trimes, it falls near the end of the readily collectible series, as post-1862 circulation-strike pieces mostly found the melting pot. This well-defined Premium Gem exhibits pleasing luster beneath rich rose and violet toning. Population: 68 in 66, 22 finer (8/07). (#3679)

456 **1863 MS64 NGC.** This gleaming, radiant near-Gem trime is essentially untoned with strong detail. An attractive example from an issue that was decimated in the denomination's mass melting in 1873. Census: 24 in 64, 32 finer (8/07). (#3682)

457 **1867 MS62 NGC.** Intermingled gold, lilac, and blue iridescence. Wisps of charcoal-gray toning can be seen at the borders. The devices are frosty and the fields are lightly reflective. Most design features are sharply defined. A great example of this less-available issue of only 4,000 pieces.
From The Beau Clerc Collection. (#3687)

458 **1870 MS64 PCGS.** Rich cerulean, blue-green, and plum toning graces both sides of this luminous near-Gem. Pleasingly detailed and a high-end survivor from this heavily melted issue of only 3,000 pieces. Population: 15 in 64, 12 finer (8/07).
From The Beau Clerc Collection. (#3691)

459 **1871 MS64 NGC.** Heavy rose-violet toning covers much of this Choice example, while the protected areas reveal metallic blue patina. Crisply struck with great eye appeal, and one of just 3,400 examples minted for this post-war issue.
From The Beau Clerc Collection. (#3692)

PROOF THREE CENT SILVER

460 **1861 PR64 NGC.** Crisply struck with strong luster beneath the gold-green and silver-gray patina that graces the fields. Faint hairlines are noted beneath the toning. This Civil War-era proof issue had a round mintage of 1,000 specimens. Census: 33 in 64, 27 finer (7/07).
From The Laguna Niguel Collection, Part Two. (#3710)

461 **1863—Improperly Cleaned—NCS. Proof.** A lightly polished specimen of this low mintage Civil War issue. Partly retoned in sea-green and gold tints. A mere 460 proofs were struck.

462 **1864 PR65 NGC.** This crisply struck Gem, one of just 470 specimens coined, has delightful blue-green, violet, and lavender patina. Modest reflectivity appears where the toning thins. Census: 34 in 65, 22 finer (8/07).
From The Beau Clerc Collection. (#3714)

Beautiful 1864 Three Cent Silver PR67

463 **1864 PR67 PCGS.** Few examples can ever hope to match the overall quality of this lovely Superb Gem proof. Fully struck with deep electric-blue and rose toning over the reverse, and multicolored iridescence on the lower obverse. Exquisitely preserved and free of imperfection. Population: 5 in 67, 0 finer (8/07). (#3714)

464 **1865 PR64 NGC.** A gleaming, essentially untoned Choice Proof trime from the year that saw the introduction of the three cent nickel, which would replace the three cent silver pieces entirely eight years later. Boldly impressed with only a few faint hairlines in the fields. (#3715)

465 **1866 PR67 PCGS.** By 1866, the trime was on its way out, though the three cent silver denomination persisted in proof format through 1873. This decisively struck Superb Gem gleams beneath rich blue-green and rose toning on the obverse and cloud-gray patina on the reverse. Population: 2 in 67, 0 finer (8/07). (#3716)

466 **1867 PR65 PCGS.** A predominantly green-gold Gem that offers elements of silver-blue on each side. The strike is crisp, and the overall eye appeal is high. A thin strike-through thread appears above the upper left arm of the star. Population: 54 in 65, 22 finer (8/07). (#3717)

Cameo PR65 1867 Three Cent Silver

467 **1867 PR65 Cameo NGC.** Icy devices and glassy fields confirm the Cameo designation. Well struck, even on the shield lines and peripheral stars. By 1867, fractional currency had driven the three cent silver from circulation. Only 625 proofs and 4,000 business strikes were issued. Census: 5 in 65 Cameo, 10 finer (7/07). (#83717)

468 **1869 PR63 ANACS.** Gold, lavender, sky-blue, and amber patina drapes the luminous surfaces of this decisively struck late-date proof trime. A number of light, scattered hairlines in the fields preclude a finer grade. One of just 600 specimens struck.
From The Beau Clerc Collection. (#3719)

469 **1869 PR64 NGC.** Faint aquamarine and cherry-red tints embrace this fully struck and flashy near-Gem. Only 600 proofs and 4,500 business strikes were coined. Housed in a older generation holder. (#3719)

Appealing 1869 Three Cent Silver, PR65 Cameo

470 **1869 PR65 Cameo NGC.** A relatively large number of 1869 proof trimes have survived from an initial mintage of 600 pieces, judging from the 350 or so coins certified by NGC and PCGS. The two services have assigned the Cameo designation to only about 30 examples, however. Pronounced field-motif contrast characterizes the Gem Cameo in this lot. A powerful strike adds to the coin's appeal, as do the impeccably preserved, essentially untoned surfaces. Census: 4 in 65 Cameo, 9 finer (8/07). (#83719)

471 **1870 PR64 NGC.** Lilac and ocean-blue intermingle across this precisely struck and flashy near-Gem proof. For the 1870, proofs and business strikes are difficult to distinguish, but both are scarce, due to a combined mintage of 4,000 pieces. (#3721)

Conditionally Scarce 1872 Three Cent Silver PR66 Cameo

472 **1872 PR66 Cameo NGC.** Sharply struck with glassy mirrored fields and mildly frosted devices that together create an attractive degree of cameo contrast on both sides. This exceptionally well preserved piece is free of marks, except for a few tiny planchet flaws on each side. Faint die striations (as struck) are noted on the reverse. A conditionally scarce offering at the current grade level. Census: 3 in 66 Cameo, 1 finer (8/07). (#83723)

Delightful Gem Cameo Proof 1873 Trime

473 **1873 PR65 Cameo PCGS.** One of the most enticing survivors from this proof-only issue of just 600 pieces, this specimen exhibits rich frost on the sharply struck devices. Both sides show excellent contrast despite a measure of cloud-gray haze that has settled over the fields. Pleasingly preserved with only a few scattered planchet flaws. Population: 5 in 65 Cameo, 2 finer (8/07).
From The Beau Clerc Collection. (#83724)

THREE CENT NICKELS

474 **1865 MS66 PCGS.** The nickel-gray surfaces display frosty luster and heavy clash marks on both sides. Crisply struck with the excellent quality demanded of the grade. A lovely first-year piece. PCGS has graded only two finer examples (8/07). (#3731)

475 **1868 MS66 PCGS.** More than 3.2 million pieces were struck of this early issue, but relatively few were set aside in lofty grades such as this. The present example has radiant luster and light tan patina which assumes a somewhat streaked appearance. The design elements are exquisitely struck, and the surfaces are devoid of mentionable marks. Population: 27 in 66, 1 finer (8/07). (#3734)

1873 Closed 3 MS66 Three Cent Nickel
One of Finest Certified

476 **1873 Closed 3 MS66 PCGS.** The Closed 3 pieces represent a distinct minority of the total annual production. Walter Breen estimated the respective mintage totals to be 390,000 Closed 3 coins and 783,000 Open 3 coins, based on quarterly delivery figures. This Premium Gem specimen is tied for the finest certified, and it is sharply detailed with frosty luster and subliminal champagne toning over pleasing light gray surfaces. Population: 8 in 66, 0 finer (8/07). (#3739)

477 **1874 MS65 PCGS.** This satiny nickel-gray Gem has surprisingly clean surfaces. While the reverse offers pleasing detail, the highpoints of the portrait show a measure of softness. Still, a lovely example of this mid-date three cent nickel issue. Population: 22 in 65, 10 finer (8/07). (#3742)

478 **1880 MS65 PCGS.** A softly lustrous example toned gold and nickel-gray, this Gem hails from an issue of only 21,000 pieces. Pleasingly detailed for the issue and carefully preserved. (#3748)

479 **1881 MS66 PCGS.** One of the truly common dates in the three cent nickel series with more than a million pieces struck. This is a bright, satiny example that has just a hint of light color over each side. A sharply struck, upper-end coin. Population: 41 in 66, 7 finer (8/07). (#3749)

480 **1885—Cleaned—ANACS. Unc. Details, Net MS60.** Satiny and sharply struck with faint gold and ivory-gray toning. Slightly subdued by a mild cleaning. Only 1,000 business strikes were coined for this date, the lowest mintage of any in the series apart from the three proof-only emissions. (#3753)

481 **1888 MS66 PCGS.** Highly lustrous and untoned, with a lovely satiny sheen, this is an impressive Premium Gem example that seems virtually pristine. The design elements are crisply struck. This penultimate year for the three cent nickel saw a low mintage of only 36,500 business strikes. Population: 55 in 66, 31 finer (7/07). (#3757)

482 **1888 MS67 PCGS.** Wonderfully detailed for the issue with gleaming, pristine silver-white surfaces. Both sides exhibit vibrant, swirling luster. A delightful exemplar that would be difficult to trump for a high-end date set. Population: 30 in 67, 1 finer (8/07). (#3757)

PROOF THREE CENT NICKELS

483 **1865 PR63 NGC.** FS-001.5. The date is repunched west, as usual for this scarce first-year proof issue. A moderately mirrored pearl-gray specimen, undisturbed aside from a small spot near the M in AMERICA. (#3761)

484 **1866 PR65 PCGS.** A crisply struck and enticing tawny-gold Gem example, this lovely piece comes from the second proof three cent nickel issue. Carefully preserved and attractive, one of only 725 specimens struck. Population: 61 in 65, 26 finer (8/07). (#3762)

485 **1866 PR64 Cameo NGC.** An attractive second-year proof that offers distinct contrast between the gleaming pink-toned fields and the frosted devices. Faint hairlines are present at the margins. Census: 15 in 64 Cameo, 29 finer (7/07). (#83762)

486 **1866 PR65 Cameo PCGS.** The obverse is essentially untoned, while the reverse has a thin curtain of dappled cloud-gray haze within the wreath. Deeply reflective and carefully preserved with rich frost on the boldly impressed devices and undeniable contrast. Population: 17 in 65 Cameo, 12 finer (7/07). (#83762)

487 **1867 PR65 Cameo PCGS.** Sharply struck except for the lower half of the central numeral "I" on the reverse. Pretty gray-green toning is augmented by light sprays of gold on some of the highpoints. A lovely cameo Gem proof three cent nickel. Population: 16 in 65 Cameo, 19 finer (7/07). (#83763)

488 **1868 PR64 NGC.** Only a few faint hairlines appear in the champagne-tinged nickel-gray fields of this Choice Proof. A solidly struck example of this early three cent nickel issue that shows a degree of streakiness on the reverse. (#3764)

489 **1868 PR66 Cameo NGC.** A lovely Premium Gem representative of this earlier three cent nickel proof issue, crisply struck with distinct contrast and reflectivity. Light layers of canary and pink grace the fields, and two dots of crimson appear at the left obverse rim. Census: 18 in 66 Cameo, 9 finer (7/07). (#83764)

Cameo PR67 1868 Three Cent Nickel

490 **1868 PR67 Cameo NGC.** The design motifs on both sides of this Superb proof are sharply detailed and they retain a significant overlay of mint frost that creates an attractive appearance in contrast with the deeply mirrored fields. Just a trace of oil-slick iridescence can be seen on each side (with magnification) on this otherwise untoned specimen. Census: 9 in 67, 0 finer (8/07). (#83764)

491 **1869 PR65 NGC.** Though later issues would have mintages in the thousands, the proof three cent nickels of 1869 amounted to approximately 600 specimens. This olive-gold and silver-gray Gem shows a splash of amethyst toning over the portrait. NGC has graded only 13 finer representatives (8/07). (#3765)

492 **1869 PR65 Cameo PCGS.** Typically well struck with bright, sparkling, virtually untoned surfaces that have a small, curly lint mark on Liberty's cheek, and some faint die striations in the reverse fields. Population: 28 in 65 Cameo, 9 finer (7/07). (#83765)

493 **1869 PR65 Deep Cameo PCGS.** Though the minor base-metal coinage of the era is not known for strong cameo effects, this nickel-white piece shows rich frost on the portrait and distinct contrast with the gleaming fields. A delightful Gem. Population: 14 in 65 Deep Cameo, 2 finer (8/07). (#93765)

494 **1869 PR65 Deep Cameo PCGS.** Both sides of this gold-washed Gem offer bold contrast, though Liberty's neck shows a few tiny luster breaks. Strongly reflective with the well-preserved surfaces required of the grade. Population: 14 in 65 Deep Cameo, 2 finer (8/07). (#93765)

495 **1869 PR66 Ultra Cameo NGC.** A boldly struck and nearly immaculate Premium Gem that boasts flashy fields and obvious white-on-black contrast. A lovely specimen of this transition-era proof issue. Census: 8 in 66 Ultra Cameo, 1 finer (8/07). (#93765)

496 **1870 PR65 Cameo NGC.** This gleaming Gem has a measure of contrast on the obverse and richer frost on the reverse devices. Well-defined with a touch of golden patina and a small planchet flaw at the hair behind the coronet. Census: 18 in 65 Cameo, 18 finer (7/07). (#83766)

497 **1870 PR65 Cameo NGC.** Soft golden tints visit the shining surfaces of this enticing Gem, well-defined with a measure of contrast on each side. The 1870 is one of the more available three cent nickel proofs and the first to have a four-figure mintage. Census: 18 in 65 Cameo, 18 finer (8/07). (#83766)

Sharply Struck 1871 Three Cent Nickel, PR67

498 **1871 PR67 NGC.** This is a solidly struck Superb Gem, which includes complete separation of the lines in the numeral III. Untoned surfaces are devoid of mentionable marks, but some greenish specks are visible on the obverse. Census: 7 in 67, 0 finer (8/07). *From The Beau Clerc Collection.* (#3767)

Cameo PR66 1871 Three Cent Nickel

499 **1871 PR66 Cameo NGC.** The three cent nickel is somewhat plentiful as a proof type, but most such pieces are dated 1879 or later. Proofs from the type's first decade are scarce, and early cameo proofs are rare. This untoned Premium Gem is immaculate and attractive with noticeable frost on the portrait and wreath. Census: 4 in 66 Cameo, 3 finer (7/07). (#83767)

500 **1872 PR65 PCGS.** Delicate golden-tan toning enhances the visual appeal of this shining Gem. Attentively detailed with carefully preserved surfaces, a delightful earlier three cent nickel proof. PCGS has graded 16 finer specimens (8/07). (#3768)

501 **1872 PR65 PCGS.** A lovely nickel-gray Gem with moderate mirrors and well-defined devices. Though a contact mark is present near Liberty's hair ribbon, the piece's overall appearance is consistent with the Gem grade. An attractive example from near the end of the transitional era. *From The Beau Clerc Collection.* (#3768)

502 **1874 PR65 NGC.** Delicate peach-gold and sky-blue toning graces both sides of this well-defined and shining Gem. This pleasing three cent nickel proof comes from the first issue in which the denomination did not have a silver counterpart. NGC has graded 24 finer specimens (8/07). (#3770)

503 **1874 PR66 NGC.** Freckles of gold-tan color appear to float over nickel-gray surfaces that exhibit nice field-motif contrast at all angles. Sharply struck, and devoid of mentionable marks. Census: 23 in 66, 1 finer (7/07). (#3770)

504 **1875 PR65 NGC.** Light peach-gold toning visits this attentively struck and satiny Gem. An interesting mint-made die chip is noted on Liberty's cheek. Just 700+ proofs were issued. Census: 64 in 65, 10 finer (8/07). (#3771)

505 **1875 PR65 PCGS.** The surfaces are uncommonly bright on each side, even though there is just a bit of light patina present. Population: 83 in 65, 13 finer (8/07). (#3771)

Outstanding 1875 Three Cent Nickel PR66 Cameo

506 **1875 PR66 Cameo PCGS.** An estimated 700 or so proof three cent nickels were produced in 1875. A goodly number have apparently survived, as PCGS and NGC have certified more than 400 examples. Only about 20 pieces have been classified as Cameos. The Premium Gem Cameo being offered in this lot displays freckles of gold color that show up under magnification, and yields stunning field-motif contrast, especially when the coin is rotated under a light source. The design elements are exquisitely defined, befitting a proof striking; all of the lines in the III are fully separated. Close inspection reveals no mentionable marks. Population: 3 in 66 Cameo, 0 finer (8/07). (#83771)

507 **1877 PR62 PCGS.** A slate-gray proof-only representative with a precise strike and a few unimportant hair-thin marks on the left obverse. Housed in a former generation holder. (#3773)

Scarce, Proof-Only 1877 Three Cent Nickel, PR64

508 **1877 PR64 NGC.** Perhaps not as widely known to the general collecting fraternity, but the proof-only 1877 three cent nickel is the key to its series, just as the 1877 Indian cent is a key to its type. Indeed, more than *1,600 times* as many 1877 cents were produced as of this issue, but of course there are many more collectors of Indian cents. This beautiful near-Gem shows shallowly mirrored fields and problem-free gray-gold surfaces.
From The Beau Clerc Collection. (#3773)

509 **1878 PR64 NGC.** A solidly struck and highly appealing Choice representative from this proof-only issue of 2,350 pieces. Golden-tan patina drapes the lightly hairlined surfaces, and a planchet flaw appears to the right of OF in the obverse legend. (#3774)

510 **1878 PR66 PCGS.** The surfaces of this nickel-blue specimen offer strong luster with a hint of satin. Exquisitely detailed with wonderful eye appeal, a great representative of this proof-only issue. PCGS has graded only 15 finer pieces (8/07). (#3774)

511 **1878 PR64 Cameo NGC.** An appealing and affordable Cameo example of this proof-only issue, pleasingly detailed with delicate golden accents and vibrant luster. Both sides exhibit a measure of contrast.
From The Beau Clerc Collection. (#83774)

512 **1878 PR65 Cameo PCGS.** The 1878, while not so elusive as the 1877, is considerably more difficult to acquire than the 1886 proof-only issue. This attractive Gem sports excellent contrast and reflectivity with a touch of gold in the fields. Population: 35 in 65 Cameo, 63 finer (8/07). (#83774)

513 **1878 PR65 Cameo NGC.** The 1877 and 1878 proof-only issues are the keys to the popular three cent nickel series, and Gem survivors experience heavy demand from both series specialists and type collectors. This coin shows bold contrast and a hint of golden patina over the well-preserved surfaces. A long, interesting, straight die line runs from the rear of Liberty's hair, just above the bun, onto her cheek. Census: 32 in 65, 50 finer (7/07). (#83774)

514 **1879 PR66 PCGS.** The 8 and 9 in the date are filled. Well struck with highly reflective fields and pleasant light toning over both sides. The surfaces are immaculately preserved. The reverse die is rotated clockwise by approximately 25 degrees. An attractive Premium Gem representative of this low mintage proof issue. In a green label holder.
From The Arnold & Harriet Collection, Part Two. (#3775)

515 **1879 PR66 PCGS.** A hint of yellow-gold patina graces both sides of this otherwise nickel-gray Premium Gem. Well-defined with a dearth of post-striking flaws, though a shallow depression is noted to the right of OF on the obverse. (#3775)

516 **1879 PR67 NGC.** Following the unusually popular proof-only issue of 1878, the 1879 three cent nickel had a total production of 3,200 specimens, the highest figure to that time. The delicate blue and violet toning that graces the carefully preserved surfaces offers subtle iridescence as well. NGC has graded six finer pieces (8/07). (#3775)

517 **1879 PR67 NGC.** Strongly reflective with a hint of golden toning at the margins. The strike is crisp, and the nickel-gray fields are carefully preserved. One of 3,200 pieces struck following the proof-only issues of 1877 and 1878. NGC has graded only six finer specimens (8/07). (#3775)

Dazzling 1879 Three Cent Nickel PR68

518 **1879 PR68 NGC.** The obverse is delicately toned ice-blue and apricot, while the reverse has light but uniform sun-gold patina. An unabraded, exquisitely struck, and virtually carbon-free specimen that has a satiny obverse and a flashy reverse. Census: 6 in 68, 0 finer (7/07). (#3775)

519 **1879 PR64 Cameo NGC.** Dappled lavender and tan patina graces both sides of this Choice proof, strongly reflective with excellent contrast. A depression is noted to the left of Liberty's nose.
From The Beau Clerc Collection. (#83775)

520 **1879 PR67 Cameo PCGS.** A sharply struck Superb Gem, fully brilliant and has virtually pristine surfaces. A splendid proof type coin that shows excellent contrast. PCGS has graded no finer Cameo specimens (7/07). (#83775)

521 **1879 PR67 Cameo PCGS.** A wonderful Superb Gem that displays boldly executed design features and freckles of milky patina in the fields. An exquisitely preserved proof with distinct contrast and undeniable visual appeal. Population: 28 in 67 Cameo, 0 finer (8/07).
From The Mario Eller Collection, Part One. (#83775)

522 **1880 PR66 NGC.** Philadelphia struck fewer than 25,000 three cent nickel pieces in 1880, and of them, 3,955 specimens were proofs. This Premium Gem offers carefully preserved, gleaming fields and satiny devices that provide noticeable contrast. Census: 15 in 66 Cameo, 3 finer (7/07). (#83776)

Superb Cameo Proof 1880 Three Cent

523 **1880 PR67 Cameo NGC.** While proofs are encountered fairly often in lower grades, Superb Gems with obvious cameo contrast are seldom seen, as the population data indicates. NGC and PCGS have combined to grade just six similar Cameo proofs with only one finer. An exquisite piece, this Superb Gem has full mint brilliance and excellent eye appeal. Census: 3 in 67 Cameo, 1 finer (8/07). (#83776)

524 **1881 PR66 PCGS.** Crisply struck with reflective fields and pristine surfaces. Essentially untoned, with pearl-gray color and faint golden highlights near the periphery. A great Premium Gem proof three cent nickel. (#3777)

525 **1881 PR67 PCGS.** This is a beautiful proof three cent nickel with fully brilliant surfaces that display intense reflectivity in the fields and substantial frost on the devices. Immaculately preserved and free of even the tiniest blemish, this Superb Gem is housed in an early PCGS holder, from before the days of the Cameo designation. (#3777)

526 **1881 PR67 PCGS.** This year's proof issue of 3,575 pieces complemented the last business-strike issue of over a million coins. This luminous Superb Gem shows lovely champagne patina overall with hints of lavender. PCGS has graded just four finer non-Cameo proofs (8/07).
From The Mario Eller Collection, Part One. (#3777)

527 **1881 PR67 PCGS.** This enticing Superb Gem is one of the best-preserved representatives from an issue of 3,575 proofs. The gleaming fields show only a hint of patina on the reverse. PCGS has graded only four finer specimens (8/07). (#3777)

528 **1881 PR67 NGC.** Though 1881 brought a resurgence in the business strike mintage for three cent nickels, proof production experienced a slight decline from the year before. This gleaming Superb Gem offers strong detail and only tiny dots of haze in the fields. Census: 45 in 67, 7 finer (8/07). (#3777)

529 **1881 PR67 Cameo NGC.** The 1881 three cent nickel proofs are among the most available pieces from the final decade of issue, though populations remain small and demand high for Superb Gems. This carefully preserved and gleaming nickel-gray Superb Gem shows significant contrast on both sides. Census: 30 in 67 Cameo, 7 finer (8/07). (#83777)

Impressive 1881 Three Cent Nickel, PR65 Deep Cameo

530 **1881 PR65 Deep Cameo PCGS.** PCGS and NGC have certified several hundred 1881 proof three cent nickels, out of a mintage of 3,575 pieces. A mere seven coins have been assigned the Deep Cameo classification, including the Gem offering in the present lot. A white-on-black appearance greets the viewer of this piece, which is further enhanced by the sharply impressed design elements. Well preserved throughout. Population: 2 in 65 Deep Cameo, 1 finer (8/07). (#93777)

531 **1883 PR66 PCGS.** While the obverse is largely untoned, the gleaming reverse of this carefully preserved Premium Gem displays lovely golden patina. Despite this issue's substantial mintage of 6,609 proofs, the 1883 is less available than proofs of certain later dates. (#3779)

532 **1883 PR66 PCGS.** Streaks of honey-gold grace each side of this sharply struck and refreshingly unmarked Premium Gem. Certified in an old green label holder. (#3779)

533 **1883 PR67 NGC.** The 1883 proof three cent nickel issue is noted as the first of several which had mintages exceeding those of the business strikes with the same date. Delicate blue-green and periwinkle patina graces both sides of this enticing Superb Gem specimen. NGC has graded only five fiver pieces (8/07). (#3779)

534 **1883 PR67 PCGS.** Gorgeous ice-blue, peach, and lilac patina graces each side of this beautifully patinated Superb Gem coin. As of (8/07), PCGS has certified only four pieces finer than the present coin. (#3779)

535 **1884 PR66 NGC.** Hints of champagne patina grace the rims of this shining Premium Gem, decisively struck with grand visual appeal. A carefully preserved and delightful representative of this later three cent nickel issue.
From The Beau Clerc Collection. (#3780)

536 **1885 PR66 NGC.** A few isolated specks of tan and milk-white patina grace the center of the obverse. This lovely proof, one of only 3,790 pieces coined, offers intense reflectivity and solid visual appeal. NGC has graded only 19 finer examples (8/07).
From The Beau Clerc Collection. (#3781)

537 **1886 PR66 Cameo NGC.** An attractive Cameo specimen from the last of three proof-only three cent nickel issues, strongly lustrous and essentially untoned with distinct contrast. Carefully preserved with excellent visual appeal. Census: 17 in 66 Cameo, 11 finer (8/07). (#83782)

538 **1887(6) PR66 PCGS.** Die-linked to the overdate, but there is no evidence of the 6 underdigit. Sharply defined, befitting a proof strike, with light golden-tan color visible under magnification. Well preserved throughout. (#3783)

539 **1887/6 PR66 NGC.** Delicate golden accents grace the shining surfaces of this overdated Premium Gem proof. The devices show attractive detail, and the fields are clean. NGC has graded only two finer representatives (8/07).
From The Beau Clerc Collection. (#3784)

Fascinating 1887/6 Three Cent Nickel, PR66 Cameo

540 **1887/6 PR66 Cameo PCGS.** A plain overdate distinguishes this interesting later three cent nickel issue, one of the few proof overdates struck by the United States. This lovely specimen offers light nickel-gray surfaces on both sides with subtle steel-blue accents. Population: 25 in 66 Cameo, 4 finer (8/07). (#83784)

541 **1888 PR65 NGC.** Sharply struck and incredibly appealing with a thin coat of bronze and shell-pink patina that offers a hint of iridescence at the margins. A distinctly reflective and carefully preserved Gem specimen of this penultimate proof three cent nickel issue. (#3785)

Spectacular 1888 Three Cent Nickel
PR66 Deep Cameo

542 1888 PR66 Deep Cameo PCGS. With the second-highest mintage for a three cent nickel proof issue and a high survival rate, the 1888 is popular with type collectors. The typical proof for the year has satiny, swirling luster with little reflectivity, and even pieces found in Cameo holders often display indifferent contrast.

This stunning exemplar offers a wonderful exception to the rule. The boldly impressed devices display rich frost, particularly the broad, untextured areas of the portrait. The design elements create excellent contrast with the gleaming, fathomless mirrors. Both sides show only a touch of patina; a smidgen of tan visits Liberty's upper hair, and a single spot of milky toning appears to the left of the III but within the wreath. A small planchet flaw to the right of the date and a tiny depression on the cheek (as made) are the only possible distractions to the unaided eye. Population: 2 in 66 Deep Cameo, 1 finer (8/07). (#93785)

543 1889 PR67 PCGS. Even golden toning graces both sides of this intricately detailed and shining Superb Gem, an excellent specimen from the final year of the denomination. PCGS has graded just one finer piece (8/07). (#3786)

544 1889 PR67 PCGS. A Superb specimen with delicate champagne patina over carefully preserved surfaces. The fields have a measure of flash, and the portrait exhibits delicate detail. PCGS has graded just one finer example (8/07). (#3786)

SHIELD NICKELS

545 1866 Rays MS65 PCGS. The surfaces of this attractive first-year Gem exhibit delicate peach and gold patina over each side. Pleasingly detailed and carefully preserved. PCGS has graded just 28 finer examples (8/07). (#3790)

Premium Gem 1866 Rays Shield Nickel

546 1866 Rays MS66 PCGS. Impressive cartwheel sheen and dusky caramel-gold toning confirm the originality of this unabraded and typically struck Premium Gem. A scarce type coin in such lofty grade, since the Rays design was used for only the initial two years of the nickel five cent piece. Population: 28 in 66, 0 finer (7/07). (#3790)

547 1867 Rays MS64 PCGS. The more challenging of the two With Rays issues, the 1867 has a mintage of just over 2 million pieces, and few such coins were saved at the time of issue. Pastel blue and nickel-gray patina graces the lustrous surfaces of this Choice example. Both the obverse and reverse margins show evidence of die buckling. PCGS has graded only 18 pieces finer (8/07). (#3791)

548 1868 MS65 PCGS. Lovely pastel colors enhance the visual appeal of this highly lustrous Gem. Sharply struck, with a couple of spidery die cracks noted on the reverse, and die clash marks apparent on the lower portion of the obverse shield. Surface marks are minimal, and nearly nonexistent. Population: 67 in 65, 25 finer (7/07). (#3795)

549 1870 MS65 NGC. A crisply struck and enticing Gem example of this earlier Shield issue, strongly lustrous beneath delicate layers of gold and sea-green patina. A thin die crack appears over the cross on the obverse. Census: 34 in 65, 6 finer (8/07). *From The Beau Clerc Collection.* (#3797)

550 1875 MS64 PCGS. A satiny and suitably struck Choice Shield nickel with pastel almond-gold and lime patina. Pleasing for the grade, and encapsulated in a green label holder. Population: 47 in 64, 28 finer (8/07). (#3804)

Appealing 1876 Nickel, MS66

551 1876 MS66 PCGS. David Bowers (2006) writes that "A properly graded MS65 or finer coin, if well struck and with good eye appeal, is a rare find indeed." This description fits the bill for this Premium Gem. Its essentially untoned surfaces exhibit sharply struck devices, that on the obverse, stand out against prooflike fields. The reverse fields exhibit heavy die polish lines, and both sides are devoid of mentionable abrasions. Great overall eye appeal! Population: 8 in 66, 0 finer (8/07). (#3805)

552 1880 VF25 PCGS. With only 16,000 business strikes coined, the 1880 has the lowest mintage for any issue intended for circulation. This moderately worn piece, turquoise-gray with hints of golden-tan at the margins, offers smooth surfaces with only a few marks. (#3810)

553 1880—Cleaned—ANACS. MS60 Details. This later Shield nickel is solidly struck with no trace of wear. The green-gold rims surround lackluster, significantly hairlined nickel-gray surfaces that account for the net grade.
From The Diemer L. Fife Collection. (#3810)

554 1882 MS66 PCGS. Blazing luster is the hallmark of this exceptional, untoned Premium Gem. Spindly die cracks are noticeable on the obverse, as usual. A planchet flaw is observed on the upper obverse border, between D and W. Surface blemishes are nearly nonexistent. Population: 68 in 66, 4 finer (7/07). (#3812)

555 1883 MS65 PCGS. Fewer than 1.5 million of the "tombstone" nickels were struck in 1883, as that year saw the arrival of the Liberty design. The surfaces of this lovely Gem have only two spots of color, a small brick-red point to the right of the date and an area of peach to the left of the 5 on the reverse. (#3813)

556 1883 MS66 NGC. A lovely, bright, untoned example of this popular, final-year issue in the Shield nickel series. The surfaces are essentially defect-free except for a couple of shallow planchet flakes on each side. (#3813)

557 1883 MS66 PCGS. A crisply struck final-year example that shows flashy luster and minimal patina. Philadelphia struck fewer than 1.5 million Shield nickels before the transition to the Liberty design. PCGS has graded just nine finer representatives (8/07). (#3813)

558 1883 MS66 NGC. In the final year for the design, Philadelphia struck fewer than 1.5 million Shield nickels before the change to Barber's Liberty-and-wreath devices. This boldly impressed Premium Gem displays lovely green-gold, peach, and champagne patina. NGC has graded 15 finer pieces (8/07). (#3813)

559 1883/2 AU55 ANACS. FS-303, formerly FS-013.2. The base of an errant 2 is unmistakable between the 83 in the date. A problem-free pearl-gray Choice AU example of this desirable and scarce overdate. (#3814)

560 1883/2 MS61 PCGS. FS-013.2. Considering that four different *Cherrypickers'* obverse varieties constitute the 1883/2, this overdate is surprisingly rare in Mint State. Blushes of chestnut-brown grace this satiny and generally smooth example. Certified in a green label holder. (#3814)

PROOF SHIELD NICKELS

561 1866 Rays PR62 NGC. A decisively struck proof example from the first year of copper-nickel five cent coinage. Delicate golden toning graces the hazy, moderately hairlined surfaces. Center dots on the obverse and reverse confirm this piece's proof status. (#3817)

Attractive 1866 Rays Shield Nickel PR64

562 1866 Rays PR64 PCGS. Unquestionably a proof, as the reverse shows a prominent center dot and recutting along the upper left edge of 5. The obverse also displays a slightly less noticeable center dot. This near-Gem is well struck, with a light coating of greenish-gray toning over both sides, and blemish-free surfaces. As usual for the type, the fields are only mildly reflective. (#3817)

Superb Proof 1866 Rays Nickel

563 1866 Rays PR67 NGC. Although a few patterns from the regular issue design were struck in 1865, the 1866 With Rays nickel represents the first year of issue, with examples available in all grades, Mint State and proof.

The first proof reverse was used to strike this example. Two reverse dies have been identified for the 1866 Rays proofs. This reverse, used only in 1866, has a prominent center dot, and the upper left vertical of the large 5 sharply doubled.

This Superb Gem proof has light gray color with subtle blue, lilac, and gold toning on each side. The fields are exquisitely preserved and fully mirrored, with light cameo contrast. Undoubtedly minted with special care as all of the design elements are boldly defined. Census: 4 in 67, 0 finer (8/07). (#3817)

First Year 1866 Rays Shield Nickel PR63 Cameo

564 1866 Rays PR63 Cameo NGC. Crisply struck, with typical minor weakness noted on the shield lines. The fields are reflective and show a modest degree of reflectivity, with several small milky spots and a couple of tiny contact marks observed near the center of the reverse. An attractive example of this popular proof issue, from the first year of the series. (#83817)

565 **1867 No Rays PR64 NGC.** One of an estimated 600 specimens coined for the more available proof variety for the year. This strongly reflective Choice proof shows a hint of milky patina on the obverse, while the faintly hairlined reverse displays softness on the upper right stars. (#3821)

Remarkable 1867 No Rays Nickel PR65 Cameo

566 **1867 No Rays PR65 Cameo PCGS.** Reverse IIa, as indicated by a reverse leaf tip pointing between A and M of AMERICA. Fully struck with lovely light toning, this remarkable specimen displays impeccably preserved surfaces that are nearly pristine. An attractive mild cameo effect is noted on both sides. Population: 26 in 65 Cameo, 7 finer (8/07). (#83821)

Appealing 1867 Nickel No Rays, PR65 Cameo

567 **1867 No Rays PR65 Cameo PCGS.** The 1867 without rays are fairly elusive, and quality can be a problem, more in the way of eye appeal than in sharp details (David Bowers, 2006). This stunning Gem Cameo is essentially untoned on the obverse, and displays speckled milky-gray color on the reverse. Boldly impressed motifs add to the eye appeal. Population: 26 in 65 Cameo, 7 finer (8/07). (#83821)

568 **1868 PR65 Cameo PCGS.** Absolutely brilliant with intense field-to-device contrast noted on both sides. The design features are crisply struck throughout. Interesting die lines (as made) are noted beneath the upper vertical shield stripes, and near the obverse periphery. Faint diagonal roller marks are likewise apparent across the reverse center. Handling marks are nonexistent. Population: 18 in 65 Cameo, 9 finer (7/07). (#83822)

569 **1872 PR65 NGC.** The obverse is obviously die doubled, with the annulet as the pick-up point. Pastel gold and sky-blue adorn this satiny and smooth Gem. Only 950+ proofs were struck. (#3826)

570 **1872 PR66 PCGS.** Brilliant throughout and moderately reflective in the fields. Fully defined in all areas. One of 950 proofs struck. (#3826)

571 **1873 Closed 3 PR65 NGC.** A canary-gold Gem specimen of this No Rays Shield nickel issue, of the Closed 3 logotype as with all representatives. Boldly impressed with pleasing reflectivity and strong eye appeal. (#3827)

572 **1876 PR65 Cameo NGC.** A gleaming, predominantly nickel-gray Cameo Gem from the centennial year, decisively struck with distinct contrast. A handful of tiny toning spots are present at the obverse margins. Census: 14 in 65 Cameo, 26 finer (8/07). (#83830)

Choice Proof-Only 1877 Nickel

573 **1877 PR64 NGC.** A satiny near-Gem with dusky caramel-gold, sky-blue, and pearl-gray toning. Crisply struck, and attractive despite a trivial obverse spot at 4 o'clock. This proof-only Shield nickel is from a tiny reported mintage of 510+ pieces. Much scarcer than its 1878 proof-only successor. Encased in a prior generation holder. (#3831)

Vibrant 1877 Nickel, PR66 Cameo

574 **1877 PR66 Cameo NGC.** Among the most challenging of the proof Shield nickel issues, the proof-only 1877 has an estimated mintage that is slightly greater than 510 pieces. This crisply detailed and carefully preserved piece offers strong reflectivity and a measure of contrast between the green-gold fields and the largely untoned devices. Census: 25 in 66 Cameo, 4 finer (8/07). *From The Beau Clerc Collection.* (#83831)

575 **1878 PR64 ANACS.** Both sides of this Choice Proof show modest reflectivity through light bronze patina, and the rims show rings of deeper reddish-orange toning. A crisply struck example of this popular proof-only issue that shows only a few scattered hairlines. (#3832)

576 **1878 PR66 PCGS.** A lovely example of this always-popular proof-only issue. The surfaces are contact-free with just the slightest bit of lilac toning present on each side. The obverse has good reflectivity, while the reverse could almost pass for a business strike save for its excellent detail. PCGS has graded 14 finer pieces (8/07). (#3832)

577 **1879 PR65 PCGS.** Dusky orange and lavender patina graces both sides of this boldly impressed and luminous Gem. An attractive representative of this later proof Shield nickel issue. (#3833)

578 **1879/8 PR65 NGC.** Breen-2514. An attractive example of this *Guide Book* overdate, an unusual error for proof coinage. The surfaces of this Gem gleam beneath hazy green-gold and lavender patina. (#3834)

579 **1879/8 PR66 PCGS.** While the overdated proof 1879 nickel has a population near that of its "normal" counterpart, the former has attracted considerably more interest over the years. Aside from a few faint, scattered planchet flaws, this peach-tinged Premium Gem appears flawless to the unaided eye. (#3834)

580 **1880 PR66 NGC.** Rich olive, green-gold, and robin's-egg-blue patina graces both sides of this luminous and decisively struck Premium Gem. An attractively toned and carefully preserved survivor from this issue of just under 4,000 pieces. (#3835)

581 **1880 PR66 Cameo NGC.** Iridescent sky-blue, gold, and rose-gray patina endows the borders of this beautifully toned Premium Gem. Hairline-free with a few subtle spots near the E in STATES. A popular low mintage date. (#83835)

582 **1881 PR66 PCGS.** Sharply struck and free of any pesky planchet irregularities or contact marks, this essentially untoned specimen has an appealing overall appearance. An impressive Premium Gem proof, housed in a green label PCGS holder.
From The Arnold & Harriet Collection, Part Two. (#3836)

Elusive 1881 Nickel, PR67 Cameo

583 **1881 PR67 Cameo NGC.** The 1881 proof nickels, with a mintage of 3,575 pieces, are readily available to collectors today, as evidenced by the several hundred examples certified by NGC and PCGS. Cameos are more elusive, especially at the PR67 level. The essentially untoned surfaces of this Superb Gem Cameo exhibit sharply struck design elements, and are impeccably preserved. Census: 21 in 67 Cameo, 1 finer (8/07). (#83836)

584 **1882 PR67 Cameo NGC.** An exquisitely preserved and undeniably appealing representative from the penultimate proof Shield nickel issue. The fields offer hints of gold and milk-white patina, though these impede neither the fields' reflectivity nor the devices' frost. Census: 21 in 67 Cameo, 0 finer (7/07). (#83837)

585 **1883 PR65 PCGS.** This precisely struck final-year Gem offers gentle tan and sky-blue tints. Unabraded with only moderate carbon. A minor retained lamination is noted near the 18 in the date. (#3838)

586 **1883 PR66 PCGS.** A lovely example of this always popular final issue of the type, seemingly struck from new dies, with fully detailed devices and exceptionally smooth fields. The reflective olive-gray tinted surfaces are undisturbed aside from a small mark on the upper part of the large number 5, on the reverse, and a minor planchet flaw (as struck) also on the reverse, located specifically between two of the left reverse stars. (#3838)

587 **1883 PR66 NGC.** A gleaming gold-toned exemplar of the final proof Shield nickel issue, crisply struck with minimal carbon and carefully preserved surfaces. NGC has graded only 43 finer specimens (8/07).
From The Beau Clerc Collection. (#3838)

588 **1883 PR66 Cameo PCGS.** A gorgeous final-year piece that displays moderate contrast and elegant golden tints. The boldly mirrored fields are carefully preserved and greatly enhance the overall visual appeal. PCGS has graded just five finer Cameo pieces (8/07). (#83838)

LIBERTY NICKELS

589 **1883 No Cents MS66 PCGS.** As is typical for a new type, the No Cents pieces were saved in considerably greater numbers, although the With Cents pieces had the higher mintage. This No Cents piece offers untoned, attractive, and lightly contrasting surfaces with radiant luster. Light die cracks are seen on each side. PCGS has graded only 15 pieces finer (7/07). (#3841)

590 **1883 No Cents MS66 PCGS.** A well-struck example of this popular, one-year type. Each side is satiny and shows pronounced rose and sea-green toning. (#3841)

591 **1883 No Cents MS67 ICG.** Both sides of this well struck, carefully preserved No Cents piece exhibit lovely steel-blue patina with faint olive accents. A wonderful example of this famous one-year type. (#3841)

592 **1883 With Cents MS65 PCGS.** Though the No Cents Liberty nickels of 1883 were saved in quantity, the With Cents pieces were not given the same attention. This delightful Gem offers excellent detail and a few dots of milky patina against the lustrous nickel-gray and champagne surfaces. (#3844)

593 **1883 With Cents MS66 NGC.** While numerous No Cents Liberty nickels of 1883 survive in high Mint State grades today, considerably fewer of the With Cents pieces are known. This strongly lustrous example, well-defined at the centers with slight softness at a few of the stars, has traces of rose, peach, and orange toning at the margins. (#3844)

594 **1884 MS65 PCGS.** This piece is well struck save for the left ear of corn, and only the slightest hint of color is present on the lustrous surfaces. A lovely example of this challenging early Liberty nickel. Population: 48 in 65, 15 finer (7/07). (#3845)

Lustrous 1885 Nickel, MS62

595 **1885 MS62 NGC.** The predominantly nickel-gray surfaces of this early Liberty key offer shining luster. Scattered dots and lines of milk-white and charcoal patina appear in the fields and on the well-defined devices. Assorted marks and abrasions are present on each side, though the overall visual appeal is better than the grade might suggest.
From The Beau Clerc Collection. (#3846)

Key Date 1885 Liberty Nickel MS63

596 **1885 MS63 NGC.** This Select Mint State example has an attractive cartwheel sheen over both sides, and natural, light olive-gray toning. The design elements are typically struck, with softness noted on three or four of the obverse stars, as well as on the reverse left ear of corn. A couple of small abrasions are observed near the center of the reverse. A coveted key date issue. (#3846)

597 **1886 MS62 PCGS.** This low mintage Liberty nickel is richly toned in blended apricot and olive hues. Marks are surprisingly few for the grade. Certified in an old green label holder. (#3847)

Key Date Gem 1886 Liberty Nickel

598 **1886 MS65 PCGS.** This intensely lustrous Gem is a great example of the 1886, a significant key date in the Liberty nickel series. Slight striking softness is noted on the reverse left ear of corn and on approximately half of the obverse stars. The sparkling surfaces are essentially untoned, except for some very faint apricot color on each side. Spidery peripheral die cracks are extensive on the reverse. (#3847)

599 **1887 MS65 NGC.** This attractive piece offers satiny, silver-gray, lustrous, and untoned surfaces. The stars are all fully struck. Fairly well struck on the reverse as well, with softness only on the left ear of corn and a couple of letters of UNITED. A couple of non-distracting, grade-consistent marks on the cheek are noted. Census: 65 in 65, 17 finer (8/07). (#3848)

600 **1891 MS65 PCGS.** Golden-gray patina rests on lustrous surfaces that exhibit sharply struck design elements. Well preserved throughout. Population: 63 in 65, 12 finer (7/07). (#3852)

601 **1892 MS65 PCGS.** This delightful Liberty Gem shows soft luster beneath lovely rose and orange patina. Crisply struck overall with excellent eye appeal for this earlier issue. PCGS has graded 13 pieces finer (8/07). (#3853)

602 **1893 MS65 PCGS.** The portrait displays excellent detail on this Gem, though some of the stars and parts of the lower wreath show softness. Gold and violet toning graces both sides. An interesting example that was struck a decade after the design's debut. PCGS has graded just 12 finer pieces (8/07). (#3854)

Untoned MS66 1893 Liberty Nickel

603 **1893 MS66 PCGS.** A splendid, high grade example. The surfaces show evidence of metal flow that gives the coin a matte-like appearance. Unusually thick mint luster is seen over each side with no evidence of any mentionable abrasions. Sharply defined on the left ear of corn, but showing some localized softness on the peripheral obverse stars. Population: 12 in 66, 0 finer (8/07). (#3854)

Conditionally Unsurpassed 1895 Liberty Nickel MS66

604 **1895 MS66 PCGS.** This is a remarkably attractive Premium Gem Liberty nickel with blazing luster and an intense cartwheel sheen across both sides. The design elements are crisply impressed, including the reverse left ear of corn. Immaculately preserved and essentially untoned, this coin seems unimprovable in terms of both technical and visual quality. Population: 10 in 66, 0 finer (8/07). (#3856)

605 **1897 MS65 PCGS.** The carefully preserved surfaces are luminous beneath vibrant gold and lavender patina. This mid-date Gem offers excellent overall detail, though the lower wreath shows a touch of softness. Population: 59 in 65, 11 finer (8/07). (#3858)

606 **1898 MS65 NGC.** This shining mid-date Liberty nickel has pleasing all-around detail, though the lowest parts of the wreath show a trace of softness. Whispers of sky-blue and apricot patina greatly enhance the overall eye appeal. Census: 61 in 65, 15 finer (8/07). (#3859)

607 **1899 MS66 PCGS.** A delightful Liberty nickel from the waning years of the 19th century. The strike is pleasing, and the shining fields exhibit delicate peach-rose and gold patina. PCGS has graded a single finer representative (8/07). (#3860)

608 **1899 MS66 PCGS.** Blazing luster and light golden toning grace this unblemished Premium Gem. Well struck save for the usual blending on the left ear of corn. (#3860)

Exceptional 1900 Superb Gem Nickel

609 **1900 MS67 NGC.** Smooth, highly lustrous surfaces are covered with a light coat of pastel apple-green, lilac, powder-blue, and golden-beige toning. The strike is exquisite, and both sides are immaculately preserved. This Superb Gem specimen does not fit the typical profile of poor quality for the date. David Bowers writes in his Shield and Liberty Head nickel book: "... most were made in a careless manner and often show light striking, granular fields, or other problems." Census: 3 in 67, 0 finer (8/07). (#3861)

610 **1903 MS66 PCGS.** Light golden toning adorns this thoroughly lustrous Premium Gem. Carefully preserved with excellent overall definition for this 20th century nickel issue. PCGS has graded only two finer examples (8/07). (#3864)

611 1903 MS66 PCGS. Still one of the great values among type coins, only 81 pieces have been certified MS66 by PCGS out of the 28 million struck of this issue. Superb mint luster with light olive and rose toning over each side. Sharply defined throughout. (#3864)

612 1903 MS66 PCGS. This impressive Premium Gem Liberty nickel displays scintillating luster and light olive-gold toning across each side. Softly struck on the first two obverse stars, and on the reverse left ear of corn; the remaining design elements are crisply produced. Population: 81 in 66, 2 finer (8/07). (#3864)

613 1904 MS65 PCGS. The obverse sports pleasing central detail, though a few scattered stars on that side show softness. Both sides are luminous beneath soft periwinkle-blue patina with a touch of peach. (#3865)

614 1907 MS66 PCGS. This Premium Gem is tied for the finest that NGC and PCGS have certified. Just 33 pieces have qualified at the MS66 grade level, including 22 at PCGS and 11 at NGC. An incredible piece with full design details on both sides, accented by hints of gold toning, slightly deeper on the reverse. (#3868)

615 1907 MS66 PCGS. Satiny and well struck over each side with even, light rose toning. A lovely type coin and a scarcer date in this grade. Population: 24 in 66, 0 finer (8/07). (#3868)

616 1908 MS65 PCGS. This satiny nickel-gray Gem displays subtle sea-green overtones in the fields. While the portrait shows strong detail, the stars and lower wreath are soft. Still, a carefully preserved example of this later Liberty issue. Population: 72 in 65, 11 finer (8/07). (#3869)

617 1908 MS65 PCGS. This later Liberty nickel is generally bold save for minor weakness on the left ear of corn in the wreath. A shining silver-gray Gem, housed in a green label holder. PCGS has graded 11 finer representatives (8/07). (#3869)

618 1909 MS65 NGC. Lightly toned and highly lustrous, with generally bold striking details except for the reverse left ear of corn. Surface marks are minimal. An attractive, high-grade type coin. Census: 34 in 65, 8 finer (8/07). (#3870)

Conditionally Rare Premium Gem 1909 Liberty Nickel

619 1909 MS66 PCGS. This conditionally rare Premium Gem displays stunning luster and remarkably well struck design elements. Essentially untoned, both sides of the piece are distraction-free, and surface marks of any kind are virtually nonexistent. Neither of the major grading services has certified an example of this late Liberty nickel issue any finer. PCGS Population: 21 in 66, 0 finer (8/07). (#3870)

620 1912-D MS65 PCGS. The "other" branch mint Liberty Head nickel, the 1912-D is not so prominent as its S-mint counterpart, yet the issue has its own charms. This subtly lustrous, well-defined example has splashes of peach patina over the fields. (#3874)

Alluring Premium Gem 1912-D Liberty Nickel

621 1912-D MS66 PCGS. A light coating of golden-gray patina delicately graces the surfaces of this typically struck and lightly abraded Premium Gem nickel. Only the obverse stars and the reverse left ear of corn are somewhat softly struck. Eye appeal such as this is only possible in the loftiest grades of preservation. Population: 27 in 66, 0 finer (8/07). (#3874)

622 1912-S XF40 ANACS. The luminous nickel-gray surfaces display a distinct olive tinge on the reverse. A well struck, lightly circulated example of the lowest-mintage official Liberty nickel issue, one of just 238,000 pieces struck. (#3875)

Satiny 1912-S Nickel MS63

623 1912-S MS63 NGC. Almond-gold and cream-gray intermingle across this satiny Select nickel. Sharply struck for the issue, with nearly full definition on the left corn ear and the forehead curls. The first San Francisco nickel five cent piece, and also a scarce low mintage issue. Certified in an older generation holder. (#3875)

Key Date 1912-S Near-Gem Five Cent

624 1912-S MS64 PCGS. The 1912-S is one of the key dates in the Liberty Head nickel series. A medley of powder-blue, golden-beige, and lilac patination adheres to both faces of this near-Gem example. A solid strike translates into sharp definition on the design features, leaving none with hints of weakness. Minute obverse marks define the grade. We also note an as-made planchet defect on the lower right part of Liberty's neck. (#3875)

Lushly Toned Gem 1912-S Nickel

625   **1912-S MS65 ANACS.** The peach centers are bounded by powder-blue and gold bands. The 1912-S has a reputation for soft strikes, but the present Gem is well defined, particularly on the left ear of corn and on the stars near the coronet tip. A lustrous and impressive example of this low mintage key date. (#3875)

PROOF LIBERTY NICKELS

626   **1883 With Cents PR66 Cameo PCGS.** The last of three proof nickel issues for the year, the 1883 also has the highest mintage of any pre-Jefferson five cent proof. This lovely type coin offers sharp detail, excellent contrast, bold reflectivity, and minimal patina. Population: 20 in 66 Cameo, 1 finer (8/07). (#83881)

627   **1884 PR66 PCGS.** Delicate orange-gold color bathes the obverse, while the reveres is nearly untoned. Exquisitely struck design features stand out against deeply mirrored fields. Impeccably preserved throughout. Population: 44 in 66, 0 finer (7/07). (#3882)

628   **1884 PR66 Cameo NGC.** FS-13.8. The 1 in the date is sharply repunched southeast. Gentle honey toning augments this exquisitely struck and satiny Premium Gem. The devices are consistently frosted, including the face and neck of Liberty. Census: 22 in 66 Cameo, 14 finer (8/07). (#83882)

629   **1885 PR63 PCGS.** This crisply struck key date nickel is attractively patinated in orange and steel-gray. Remarkably smooth for the Select level. Housed in an old green label holder. (#3883)

630   **1885 PR63 NGC.** A green-gold Select specimen of the most popular proof Liberty nickel issue, solidly struck with pleasing patina. Small dots of deeper color and light hairlines are present to the right of the portrait. (#3883)

631   **1886 PR65 PCGS.** Pastel orange, lime, and ivory-gray enrich this satiny and exactingly struck key date nickel. Void of hairlines, and only a couple of inconspicuous spots are present. Encapsulated in an old green label holder. (#3884)

632   **1886 PR66 NGC.** The obverse of this gleaming Premium Gem proof is predominantly ice-blue, while the upper part of that side and the reverse are grass-green. A decisively struck and incredibly appealing example of this popular issue. (#3884)

Desirable Superb Proof 1886 Liberty Nickel

633   **1886 PR67 NGC.** Business strikes of this date are elusive, especially in the highest grades, thus Superb Gem proof examples are highly desired as a more affordable alternative for many collectors. Sharp design details and rich proof luster are evident through a thin veil of golden toning. Census: 16 in 67, 0 finer (8/07). (#3884)

634   **1887 PR65 PCGS.** A boldly impressed and gleaming Gem, predominantly nickel-gray with glints of sky-blue and gold. A lovely specimen of this earlier proof Liberty nickel issue. PCGS has graded 45 finer examples (8/07). (#3885)

Deep Cameo PR65 1891 Nickel

635   **1891 PR65 Deep Cameo PCGS.** This razor-sharp Gem exhibits ice-white motifs, and the fields are deeply mirrored. Close to brilliant, although glimpses of sky-blue visit the reverse periphery. Most proof 1891 nickels have minimal contrast, and likely only the initial pieces struck from fresh dies are true cameos. Population: 3 in 65 Deep Cameo, 2 finer (7/07). (#93889)

636   **1896 PR66 Cameo NGC.** Crisply struck with gleaming, carefully preserved champagne-tinged surfaces. A touch of cloudy toning is present above the V on the reverse between the ends of the wreath. An attractive late 19th century nickel proof that shows considerable contrast. Census: 8 in 66 Cameo, 3 finer (8/07).
From The Mario Eller Collection, Part One. (#83894)

637   **1899 PR66 PCGS.** Ex: Eliasberg. Light streaks of tan-gold run over bright proof surfaces that are impeccably preserved. A solid strike imparts excellent definition to the design features. Population: 44 in 66, 7 finer (8/07). (#3897)

638   **1903 PR66 PCGS.** Deeply mirrored and boldly defined with just a touch of color. A nearly perfect proof type coin. Population: 58 in 66, 20 finer (8/07). (#3901)

Beautifully Toned 1903 Nickel, PR68

639   **1903 PR68 NGC.** Enticing patina graces the gleaming surfaces of this Liberty nickel proof, flawless to the unaided eye. On the obverse, the watery fields have delightful blue-green patina that surrounds the canary-gold of the portrait, while the thinner reverse patina shows a more even blend of the two hues. A top-notch survivor from this issue of only 1,790 specimens. Census: 5 in 68, 0 finer (8/07). (#3901)

640   **1904 PR66 NGC.** A scarcely toned, positively gleaming Premium Gem example of this 20th century proof Liberty nickel issue, decisively struck with great eye appeal. One of only 1,817 specimens coined. (#3902)

641   **1904 PR66 Cameo NGC.** A gleaming and essentially untoned representative of this early 20th century proof issue, solidly struck with a degree of contrast evident on each side. An excellent piece with above-average eye appeal for the issue. Census: 1 in 66 Cameo, 3 finer (7/07). (#83902)

642 **1904 PR66 Cameo PCGS.** Sharp design details and light cameo contrast are evident on this brilliant Premium Gem proof. As an early 20th century proof, the degree of actual contrast is less than seen on later 19th century proofs. This is due to attempts within the Mint to eliminate the "undesirable" cameo appearance. Population: 3 in 66 Cameo, 0 finer (8/07). (#83902)

643 **1905 PR65 Cameo PCGS.** One of just 2,152 specimens coined, decisively struck with appreciable contrast and chromelike reflectivity. While the obverse is scarcely toned, elegant champagne patina drapes the reverse. Population: 4 in 65 Cameo, 2 finer (8/07). (#83903)

644 **1906 PR66 PCGS.** A crisply struck Premium Gem proof that displays mild field-motif contrast. Faint traces of champagne color adhere to well preserved surfaces. Population: 41 in 66, 10 finer (7/07). (#3904)

645 **1907 PR65 PCGS.** A solidly struck and eminently appealing Gem specimen that offers excellent reflectivity. Layers of champagne and aqua patina are the only evidence of the passage of a century. Housed in a green label holder. (#3905)

646 **1909 PR67 NGC.** Moderately mirrored and nearly untoned with traces of lilac haze on each nearly immaculate side. An exquisite Superb Gem specimen that soon will venture into antique territory. One of 4,763 pieces coined. (#3907)

647 **1909 PR67 NGC.** Boldly struck with glittering prooflike fields and bright untoned surfaces that yield a mild cameo effect on each side. This Superb Gem offers excellent eye appeal for this later Liberty issue. NGC has graded just six finer representatives (8/07). (#3907)

648 **1909 PR67 PCGS.** This issue's unusually high mintage of 4,763 pieces makes it popular with proof type collectors. This crisply struck Superb Gem has flashy luster beneath areas of rose-gold and orange patina. PCGS has graded just two finer examples. (#3907)

Beautiful 1910 Liberty Nickel PR67 Cameo

649 **1910 PR67 Cameo PCGS.** This is a beautiful Superb Gem nickel with fully struck design elements and pristine surfaces. A small amount of champagne-russet patina appears on each side. This is a relatively available proof issue that becomes quite scarce with the Cameo designation as a part of its assigned grade, from either of the major services. Population: 19 in 67 Cameo, 2 finer (8/07). (#83908)

650 **1912 PR66 Cameo PCGS.** Green-gold patina graces both sides of this pretty Premium Gem, a strongly lustrous specimen with pleasing contrast. This piece comes from the last authorized proof Liberty nickel issue, which amounted to 2,145 coins. Population: 13 in 66 Cameo, 4 finer (8/07). (#83910)

BUFFALO NICKELS

651 **1913 Type One MS67 PCGS.** A well-defined and enticing Superb Gem representative of this popular one-year type, lightly gold-toned overall with hints of nickel-white at the margins. PCGS has graded just 11 finer examples (8/07). (#3915)

652 **1913 Type One MS67 PCGS.** A thin veneer of pastel violet-blue patina visits the lustrous surfaces. The design elements are well struck, and there are no significant marks to report. A lovely Superb Gem. (#3915)

653 **1913 Type One MS67 PCGS.** A wonderful Superb Gem representative from the original incarnation of Fraser's iconic design, boldly impressed with vibrant luster and a touch of golden toning. PCGS has graded only 11 finer pieces. (#3915)

654 **1913 Type One MS67 PCGS.** Pleasing, light rose and blue patina takes on a slightly deeper shade on the reverse, and overlays lustrous, virtually unmarked surfaces. The design elements are fully struck throughout. PCGS and NGC together have certified only 19 pieces finer (8/07). (#3915)

Remarkable Superb Gem 1913-D Type One Buffalo Nickel

655 **1913-D Type One MS67 PCGS.** Ex: ADM Collection. This is a truly marvelous Superb Gem example of the 1913-D Buffalo nickel; an immensely popular issue among type collectors. Fully struck and lightly toned, with attractive iridescent accents near the borders and pleasing matte-like surface textures. Close inspection of both sides, under low magnification, fails to reveal any surface flaws whatsoever. Population: 38 in 67, 2 finer (8/07). (#3916)

656 **1913 Type Two MS66 PCGS.** Warm golden patina graces both sides of this shining Type Two nickel, from an issue less available in higher grades than its Type One counterpart. Crisply detailed overall with only a touch of softness on the bison's shoulder. (#3921)

657 **1913 Type Two MS66 NGC.** A well-defined first-year representative from the revised design, strongly lustrous with pale nickel-white surfaces and occasional champagne accents. The Type Two pieces of 1913 are considerably less available than their Type One counterparts. Census: 62 in 66, 8 finer (7/07). (#3921)

Lightly Toned 1913-D Type Two Nickel, MS66

658 **1913-D Type Two MS66 PCGS.** Radiantly lustrous surfaces on this Premium Gem display a thin coat of pastel gold, powder-blue, and lilac patina. The design elements are sharply impressed, save for minor softness in the hair on the bison's head. Devoid of significant marks. Population: 40 in 66, 10 finer (8/07). (#3922)

1913-D Type Two Nickel, MS68
Single Finest Certified by NGC or PCGS

659 **1913-D Type Two MS68 NGC.** The Type Two 1913-D Buffalo nickel (as well as the Type Two 1913 and 1913-S) resulted from a flaw in James Earle Fraser's initial design. This is explained in an April 3, 2007 *Numismatic News* article by Paul Green:

"The James Earle Fraser design, while enormously popular, stared out with a design that had the animal standing on a mound. The denomination was placed on that mound and 1913 production began before officials discovered that upon the denomination had become the highest part of the design and might well wear off quickly."

Green goes on to say: "... officials ... were taking no chances deciding immediately to change the reverse by putting the animal on a line so the denomination could be lower in the design."

The MS68 1913-D Type Two nickel offering in this lot is the single highest graded example of this issue by either NGC or PCGS. Its radiantly lustrous surfaces are bathed in pastel violet, aqua-blue, gold, and apricot patina, and are immaculately preserved. A powerful strike imparts crisp and even definition to all of the design elements. A simply amazing coin! (#3922)

660 **1913-S Type Two AU55 ANACS.** A luminous, briefly circulated gold-gray representative of the most elusive Buffalo nickel issue for 1913, struck from significantly eroded obverse dies. Minimally marked with a thin die crack that runs from the Indian's head to the upper rim. (#3923)

661 **1913-S Type Two AU58 PCGS.** A lovely example from the most elusive of the first-year Buffalo nickel issues, richly toned with only a touch of highpoint friction. Both sides exhibit above-average definition and luminous surfaces beneath sage patina that sports violet accents. (#3923)

662 **1913-S Type Two AU58 ANACS.** A luminous and well struck near-Mint representative that shows just a trace of wear on the pink-tinged highpoints. The Type Two 1913-S Buffalo nickel is easily the most elusive issue for the first year of the design. (#3923)

663 **1913-S Type Two AU58 NGC.** Though a soft strike and eroded dies make this luminous piece appear considerably worn, in reality, only a trace of friction appears on the highpoints. The luminous surfaces have golden toning with distinct rose elements. (#3923)

664 **1913-S Type Two MS64 PCGS.** This delicately gold-tinted Choice piece shows pleasing iridescence in its patina under closer examination. A softly struck piece with quicksilver luster, this nickel was struck from heavily eroded dies and shows a "chin whiskers" die clash. (#3923)

665 **1914 MS66 PCGS.** The strike is penetrating, and the original apricot and steel-gray toning contributes further to the eye appeal. Essentially perfect aside from minor obverse carbon near 3 o'clock. (#3924)

666 **1914/3 XF40 ANACS.** FS-014.87. A moderately circulated slate-gray example of this seldom seen variety. The upper crossbar of the underdigit 3 is faintly evident. (#93924)

Scarce 1914/3 Overdate Buffalo Nickel MS63

667 **1914/3 MS63 ANACS.** FS-014.87. This is a high-end example of the scarce 1914/3 overdate variety. The *Guide Book* of Buffalo and Jefferson nickels, by Q. David Bowers, gives an estimate of 220,000 to 330,000 pieces produced for this variety, based upon the hypothesis that either two or three different obverse dies were used to make them, with an average of approximately 109,000 coins coming from each die. Well struck and carefully preserved, with strong satin luster and variegated, iridescent toning on both sides, this example would make a fine addition to the cabinet of any Buffalo nickel collector. (#93924)

Lightly Toned 1914/3 Nickel, MS64

668 **1914/3 MS64 PCGS.** FS-014.87. David Lange, in his Buffalo nickel reference book, says of the 1914/3, the first example of which was found in 1996: "... two and possibly three obverse dies have been found with the overdate feature. This suggests that the dual-dating occurred during the creation of a working hub that then transferred this feature to each working die made from it. This explains both the appearance of several working dies displaying the overdate and also the shallowness of the undertype date. As with any transfer process, the image erodes somewhat as it is copied, and the overdates seen on each coin are thus third-generation copies."

This near-Gem specimen displays a series of horizontal die scratches above the 4 in the date, perhaps the result, according to Lange, "of attempting to remove the underlying numeral 3." The design elements are sharply impressed, and lustrous surfaces exhibit light champagne color accented with rainbow toning around some of the margins. Population: 11 in 64, 4 finer (8/07). (#93924)

669 **1914-D MS65 PCGS.** A satiny Gem that sports above-average detail. Hazy red-violet patina covers most of the surfaces, while the upper obverse periphery has orange-gold toning. PCGS has graded 41 pieces finer (8/07). (#3925)

Premium Gem 1914-D Nickel

670 **1914-D MS66 PCGS.** Ex: ADM Collection. This is an impressive example, nearly the finest available. PCGS has only graded five finer pieces (8/07), including one that is recorded on the PCGS Set Registry in the Gerald Forsythe Collection. The specimen offered here has frosty light blue and pale gold toning on each side. Although falling short of a full strike, the design motifs are nicely detailed. A pleasing piece for the connoisseur. Population: 36 in 66, 5 finer (8/07). (#3925)

671 **1915 MS66 PCGS.** Pleasingly detailed and highly lustrous with waves of gold and orange patina over each side. An attractive example of this earlier issue, one that uses the original portrait on the obverse, unlike the pieces of 1916 and later. (#3927)

672 **1915 MS66 PCGS.** An enticing Premium Gem nickel that offers wonderful eye appeal. The coin's solid strike, vibrant luster, and attractive ice-blue and gold patina all contribute. A carefully preserved and delightful early Buffalo piece. (#3927)

Attractive 1915 Superb Gem Nickel

673 **1915 MS67 PCGS.** The 1915-S nickel can be located through near-Gem, but Gem-quality coins are challenging, especially in the lofty grade of MS67, the level of preservation of the coin in this lot. A melange of golden-tan, powder-blue, and lilac patina visits highly lustrous surfaces that exhibit well struck design elements. Close examination reveals no mentionable marks. Population: 36 in 67, 0 finer (7/07). (#3927)

Exceptional 1915-D Five Cent, MS66

674 **1915-D MS66 PCGS.** This Premium Gem nickel exhibits a much better strike than is normally seen for the issue. The central obverse, and the bison's head, shoulder, and tail, typically weak areas, are well defined on this specimen. Soft luster emanates from surfaces delicately toned in golden-gray and rose hues, being somewhat more extensive and deeper on the reverse. A few tiny pepper-like specks on the obverse are noted for complete accuracy. Population: 27 in 66, 2 finer (8/07). (#3928)

Captivating Superb Gem 1915-D Buffalo Nickel

675 **1915-D MS67 NGC.** While the Type One Buffalo nickels of 1913 were saved in quantity, by 1915, far fewer pieces were saved for their novelty, and Gem and better representatives of the branch mint issues for that year are challenging. Pleasing luster and delicate peach and gold patina greatly enhance the visual appeal of this noteworthy and exquisitely preserved nickel. Lange offers words of caution about the 1915-D, calling it "the first date from the Denver Mint in which weakness of strike becomes a factor." On this piece, however, the bold detail on both sides rises above all but the most petty criticism. The only Superb Gem graded by NGC, with just three such pieces across both major services and none finer at either (8/07). (#3928)

Lustrous MS66 1915-S Buffalo Nickel

676 **1915-S MS66 PCGS.** Ex: ADM Collection. One of the scarcer issues among the early Buffalo nickels. Unlike most examples seen, this piece is sharply defined on both obverse and reverse. The surfaces have a pronounced matte-like texture with an overlay of mint frost. Even golden toning completes the picture of this superior example with the slightest accent of lilac on the highpoints. Population: 28 in 66, 3 finer (8/07). (#3929)

Rare 1915-S Premium Gem Nickel

677 **1915-S MS66 PCGS.** Choice and Gem examples of the 1915-S are genuinely rare (David Lange, 2006). Light champagne-gold color dominates the highly lustrous surfaces of this attractive Premium Gem. An attentive strike leaves excellent delineation on the design elements, and both faces are nicely preserved. Population: 28 in 66, 3 finer (8/07). (#3929)

678 **1916 MS66 PCGS.** Fraser's original models for the Buffalo nickel did not last; the reverse was altered in 1913, and in 1916, the obverse underwent revision as well. This satiny and well struck piece has pleasing blue, gold, and rose patina over each side. (#3930)

679 **1916-S MS64 ANACS.** Pleasingly detailed for this early S-mint issue with vibrant amber and champagne patina over each side. Strongly lustrous beneath the toning with clean surfaces for the grade. (#3933)

Sharply Struck 1916-S Nickel, MS66

680 **1916-S MS66 PCGS.** Ex: A D M Collection. The 1916-S is difficult to locate sharply struck (David Lange, 2006). The Premium Gem in this lot is certainly an exception, as excellent definition is apparent on the design elements. A thin coat of barely discernible orange-gold color covers highly lustrous surfaces that are devoid of significant marks. Population: 28 in 66, 4 finer (8/07). (#3933)

681 **1917 MS66 PCGS.** Apricot and olive toning invigorates this lustrous and mark-free Premium Gem. Well struck save for the unavoidable minor incompleteness above the braid. Housed in a green label holder. (#3934)

Gorgeous Gem 1917-D Nickel

682 **1917-D MS65 PCGS.** An amazing Gem, this lovely piece is fully lustrous with satiny surfaces that are accented by hints of pale gold color. Although less than a full strike, the design elements are much sharper than usual for the issue. Just 14 finer examples have been certified by PCGS. An excellent candidate for the advanced Set Registry collector. (#3935)

Satiny Gem 1917-S Buffalo Nickel

683 **1917-S MS65 PCGS.** An amazing Gem with sharp details and delightful gold toning over satiny luster. The only design points that lack full detail are the bison's head and top of the front leg. This example probably ranks in the top 25% of all known pieces for the quality of its strike. Population: 84 in 65, 22 finer (8/07). (#3936)

Thickly Frosted MS66 1918 Nickel

684 **1918 MS66 PCGS.** Variability characterizes both the strike and luster on the 1918 nickel. The strike on this piece shows the usually seen softness just above the knot in the Indian's braid. What is simply outstanding on this coin is the luster. It is thick and frosted, racing around each side as the coin is tilted beneath a light. Nearly brilliant. The 1918 is deceptively difficult to locate in superior condition in spite of the mintage of more than 32 million pieces. Population: 39 in 66, 7 finer (8/07). (#3937)

685 **1918-D MS63 NGC.** Despite a touch of softness on the braid and shoulder, this luminous Select representative has above-average definition for the issue. The lightly abraded surfaces of this D-mint nickel display lovely gold and pink toning. (#3938)

Well Struck 1918-D Gem Five Cent

686 **1918-D MS65 NGC.** In his Buffalo nickel reference book (2006), David Lange writes that "Mint State coins are available with the characteristic weakness of strike. Choice and Gem pieces are rare." Iridescent rainbow toning adorns the well preserved, lustrous surfaces of the Gem example in this lot. A well executed strike leaves better-than-average definition on the design features, including sharpness on the horn and tail. Census: 22 in 65, 6 finer (8/07). (#3938)

687 **1918/7-D—Corroded—ANACS. VG Details, Net Good 4.** FS-016.5. The thick downstroke of the 7 remains evident, although the 191 are well worn. All other legends are bold. Protected areas of the reverse display dark russet and forest-green verdigris. A key to the series. (#3939)

688 **1918/7-D Good 6 PCGS.** Although this silver-gray key date nickel is well circulated, the mintmark is bold, and all four digits in the date are plain to the unaided eye. The thick horizontal and downward stroke of the 7 is evident. The bison displays a few wispy abrasions. (#3939)

689 **1918/7-D Good 6 NGC.** Rich mustard-gold toning graces the margins of this heavily circulated overdate nickel. The flat-topped 8 is plain, and on the nickel-gray reverse, the bison shows a stub of horn. (#3939)

690 **1918/7-D—Scratched—ANACS. VG8 Details.** Though heavily worn, this gold-tinged nickel-gray representative still displays the flat-topped 8 that signals this popular overdate. A circular cut that passes through LIBERTY and other peripheral obverse elements is the reason for the details grade. (#3939)

691 **1918/7-D—Cleaned—ANACS. VG8 Details.** FS-016.5. This example is moderately worn but shows few marks on the light beige-gray surfaces. An unusually satiny appearance is the result of harsh cleaning. The 1918/7 overdate has become an important key date in the Buffalo nickel series. (#3939)

692 **1918/7-D VG8 ANACS.** The underdigit is just barely visible with magnification. Probably pulled from a group of low grade Buffalo nickels, this piece is uncleaned with deeper charcoal color outlining the devices. (#3939)

693 **1918/7-D—Damaged—NCS. Fine Details.** FS-016.5. This dove-gray key date nickel shows the underdigit 7 within the lower loop of the 8 and from its upper right corner. The obverse border has circular marks, perhaps caused by a coin counter. (#3939)

694 **1918-S MS62 PCGS.** Ex: Benson. A mark-free and satiny example of this early branch mint issue. Minute carbon flecks are distributed, and the dies have an orange-peel surface from extended use. (#3940)

Select 1918-S Buffalo, MS63

695 **1918-S MS63 PCGS.** This is a lovely and affordable reddish-gold toned example with an average or typical strike that exhibits some central weakness on both sides. A small area of pale green corrosion exists below the eagle's tail along the reverse border, along with a few faint scratches. (#3940)

Sharp, Beautifully Toned MS65
1918-S Buffalo Nickel

696 **1918-S MS65 PCGS.** Ex: ADM Collection. The 1918-S has long been recognized as one of the most challenging issues in the early Buffalo nickel series. Some of the problem is absolute rarity, as coins grading VF or better are scarce. But even when high grade pieces are found, the striking details are often soft. This is not necessarily because the striking pressure was weak, but as David Lange points out in the third edition of his book on this series: "In some instances the dies were set too far apart to make a complete impression. This was done as an economy measure to reduce wear on both the dies and press and to thus extend their useful life." This particular coin is better struck than most, but of course, it still lacks complete highpoint definition above the knot in the braid. The reverse details are exceptionally sharp over the bison's head and tail. This is also a beautifully toned coin that shows rich rose centers and a slight accent of blue around the margins. Population: 29 in 65, 1 finer (8/07). (#3940)

697 **1919 MS66 PCGS.** Elegant champagne and orange patina graces most of the shining surfaces, while other areas are untoned or cornflower-blue. A crisply struck and eminently appealing example of this earlier Philadelphia issue, available as a Premium Gem but conditionally rare any finer. PCGS has graded only seven such coins (8/07). (#3941)

698 **1919-D MS60 ANACS.** The most distinctive features of this unworn Buffalo nickel are its rose-tinged tan patina, its quicksilver luster, and a small rim break near 4 o'clock on the obverse. Both sides show soft central detail, typical for this often-weak D-mint issue. (#3942)

Satiny Gem 1919-D Buffalo Nickel

699 **1919-D MS65 PCGS.** The 1919-D and 1919-S Buffalo nickels rank among condition rarities in the series. This specimen has unusually sharp design details, and a curious rim break along the left obverse border. The surfaces have satiny luster with pleasing lilac and gold color. Population: 54 in 65, 13 finer (8/07). (#3942)

700 **1919-S MS62 NGC.** Generally well-defined at the lower points, though the braid and the bison's shoulder and tail show slight softness, a typical trait for this poorly produced issue. Both sides of this minimally abraded nickel show golden patina over quicksilver luster. (#3943)

701 **1920 MS64 NGC.** Lavishly toned in rose-red, sea-green, and orange. A nicely struck near-Gem with shimmering luster and exceptional eye appeal for the grade. (#3944)

702 **1920 MS65 PCGS.** A well-defined and gleaming Gem example of this P-mint issue, essentially untoned with a touch of die erosion noted around the devices. Minimally marked for the grade and highly appealing. (#3944)

703 **1920 MS66 PCGS.** A lovely example of this postwar issue, solidly struck with swirling luster and colorful patina. Ice-blue patina graces the centers, while deeper green-gold toning is present at the margins. PCGS has graded just eight coins finer (7/07). (#3944)

704 **1920 MS66 PCGS.** The 1920 is one of the most consistently well produced early Buffalo nickels. This piece displays bright mint luster that is overlaid with blue and golden toning of varying configurations on each side. Fully struck. (#3944)

Spectacular MS67 1920 Buffalo Nickel

705 **1920 MS67 PCGS.** Ex: ADM Collection. The mintage of more than 63 million pieces gives an indication that Mint State pieces should be available of this issue. However, very few have survived in MS67 condition. PCGS has only certified eight in this grade, and NGC has graded only five. None are finer at either service. This is a spectacularly lustrous coin. While basically presenting as brilliant, there is actually just a hint of pink and lilac patina on each side. Fully struck also. (#3944)

Important 1920-D Nickel, MS65

706 **1920-D MS65 PCGS.** Ex: ADM Collection. The 1920-D continues the difficulty with strike that began with the 1918-D and continued through most of the 1920s. Otherwise, it is a median rarity in the series with more than 9 million pieces produced. The surfaces on this piece are bright and satiny with a hard, metallic sheen. An untoned example, the obverse is sharply defined but the reverse displays localized weakness over the bison's head. Population: 46 in 65, 1 finer (8/07). (#3945)

707 **1920-S MS63 PCGS.** Though the obverse of this glowing, lightly toned nickel has pleasing detail, the bison has a soft appearance. A thin abrasion crosses the Indian's hair above the braid. (#3946)

708 **1920-S MS63 PCGS.** This issue of under 10 million pieces has its roots in the depression that affected the American economy immediately after the Great War. The uncommonly lustrous Select piece offered here is lightly abraded with delicate blue and gold tints over each side. Solidly struck and pleasing. (#3946)

709 **1920-S MS63 PCGS.** Delicate rose and peach tints drape the quicksilver surfaces of this S-mint Select piece, struck from slightly worn obverse and reverse dies. Faint, scattered abrasions on and around the portrait account for the grade. (#3946)

710 **1920-S MS63 PCGS.** Nickel-gray and gold-green patina graces both sides of this luminous Select piece. Well-defined for the issue with light, scattered abrasions and quicksilver luster. (#3946)

Patinated Choice 1920-S Nickel

711 **1920-S MS64 PCGS.** Attractively toned in honey-gold, rose, and aquamarine. This lustrous better date nickel is essentially unabraded, and mintmark is needle-sharp. The centers and the tail are also crisp. The obverse border has an orange peel texture, as struck from a long-in-use die. (#3946)

712 **1921-S VF35 PCGS.** Scarce in all grades and especially challenging in VF. This piece is better detailed on the obverse than the reverse. Light gray accents on the highpoints with deeper, charcoal color around the peripheries and within the recesses. (#3948)

713 **1921-S AU58 NGC.** This bright yellow-green near-Mint semi-key nickel has shimmering luster and only a couple of subtle spots. The borders show minor weakness, but the centers are well impressed. In a former generation holder. (#3948)

Exceptional 1921-S Nickel, MS65

714 **1921-S MS65 PCGS.** The 1921-S is a challenging coin to find in desirable condition, due to it being subject to laminations and toning streaks, the result of poorly prepared planchet stock (David Lange, 2006). This radiantly lustrous specimen is devoid of these afflictions. Soft violet and gold patina rest upon each side, and the design elements are well brought up, save for softness in the hair on the bison's head. Close examination reveals no mentionable marks. Population: 53 in 65, 8 finer (8/07). (#3948)

715 **1923 MS65 NGC.** A solidly struck and luminous representative of this Philadelphia issue, struck a decade after the design's debut. Elements of green-gold haze appear over the ice-blue surfaces, with one such area evident to the right of the Indian's chin. (#3949)

716 **1923 MS66 PCGS.** The contrast between the nickel-blue and gold-green elements on the obverse intensifies on the reverse. Well-defined for this Philadelphia issue with delightful, swirling luster. PCGS has graded only nine coins finer (8/07). (#3949)

717 **1923 MS66 PCGS.** This crisply struck and enticing Premium Gem exhibits vibrant luster beneath delicate gold-orange patina with faint pink accents. A great example of this 1920s Philadelphia issue. PCGS has graded just nine finer pieces (8/07). (#3949)

718 **1923-S MS62 ANACS.** Though softly struck from eroded dies, this Roaring Twenties S-mint nickel shows no trace of wear, and the gold-orange patina that graces both sides offers subtle iridescence. Pleasing for the grade with few abrasions. (#3950)

719 **1923-S MS64 PCGS.** In some ways, this Choice Mint State nickel is typical for its issue. Both sides exhibit significant die wear and a soft strike, as well as the soft luster that characterizes so many branch mint issues of the 1920s. Yet the pale rose, gray, and gold patina of this piece allows its eye appeal to overcome such flaws. (#3950)

Well Struck, Lustrous MS65 1923-S Nickel

720 **1923-S MS65 NGC.** Better struck than many of this issue, which is one of the notorious strike rarities from the 1920s. The obverse is almost completely struck up, and the reverse shows just a bit of highpoint softness. Rich, softly frosted surfaces with no mentionable abrasions. Each side shows light golden and lilac toning. An excellent '23-S for a high grade set. (#3950)

Condition Rarity 1923-S Gem Nickel

721 **1923-S MS65 PCGS.** David Lange (2006) writes of the 1923-S nickel: "Despite its relatively low mintage (6.142 million pieces), this date is available in all grades short of gem," and "fully struck pieces are rare." Rainbow toning travels over this Gem, and the design elements are generally well struck, save for the hair on the bison's head and its tail. Lustrous surfaces are well preserved. Population: 30 in 65, 2 finer (8/07). (#3950)

722 **1924 MS65 PCGS.** This luminous Gem offers above-average definition for the issue, though softness is present on the Indian's hair. The surfaces show delicate golden patina with occasional pink accents. (#3951)

MS66 1924 Nickel, Conditionally Scarce

723 **1924 MS66 PCGS.** The 1924 is an issue that is difficult to accept as a condition rarity. After all, more than 21 million pieces were produced; so high grade, well produced pieces should be plentiful. Right? Not necessarily. Apparently many of this issue were incompletely hubbed and the result is a substandard strike for a Philadelphia coin. This particular piece is sharply defined, especially on the reverse. The luster is also bright and frosted, another trait that is not to be taken for granted on the 1924. Attractively toned also in shades of rose and lilac. Population: 63 in 66, 4 finer (8/07). (#3951)

Lustrous 1924-D Five Cent, MS65

724 **1924-D MS65 PCGS.** Fully struck coins of the 1924-D are nearly unknown (David Lange, 2006). This Gem displays some localized softness on the bison's head, but its tail is quite sharp. Lustrous surfaces show gold, rose, and powder-blue patina, and are devoid of mentionable marks. Population: 84 in 65, 1 finer (8/07). (#3952)

Bright, Lustrous MS65 1924-S Nickel
A Series Key With Only 1.4 Million Pieces Struck

725 **1924-S MS65 PCGS.** Ex: ADM Collection. Occasionally well struck 1924-S nickels can be found, but the scarcity of such coins is not directly related to poor production methods in the mint. Rather, it is related to the absolute rarity of this issue in all grades. Only 1.4 million pieces were struck, which leaves few coins extant today with a strong strike, weak strike, VF condition, MS60, or MS65 condition. This piece has a bright, satiny finish that is overlaid with rich golden-rose and lilac toning. The reverse can be termed fully struck, but there is a bit of the expected softness on the Indian's braid on the obverse. Population: 32 in 65, 1 finer (8/07). (#3953)

726 **1925 MS66 PCGS.** A remarkable and brightly lustrous high grade 1925 with frosty nickel-gray luster and faint golden and blue toning. PCGS has only certified five finer examples of this date (8/07). (#3954)

727 **1925-D MS63 PCGS.** A satiny green-gray branch mint nickel. Essentially unabraded, but the dies are long in use and exhibit a mint-made orange peel texture. (#3955)

728 **1925-D MS63 PCGS.** A mushy strike on both sides is evidence of moderate die erosion. The semi-prooflike luster highlights brassy golden toning. Neither side shows any distracting marks. A slightly uneven wire rim is noted on the reverse. (#3955)

Scarce MS65 1925-D Nickel

729 **1925-D MS65 NGC.** A beautifully toned piece with bright blue in the centers that is surrounded by golden at the rims. Widely regarded as one of the great strike rarities in the series, this piece shows the usual softness of highpoint detail. However, when compared to other '25-D nickels, this piece is far above average and actually shows good definition on the obverse. Census: 54 in 65, 8 finer (8/07). (#3955)

Sharply Defined MS65 1925-D Buffalo Nickel

730 **1925-D MS65 PCGS.** Ex: ADM Collection. This particular coin could lead one to conclude that strike is not a problem on this issue. Just the opposite is the case, as is well known to specialists. However, the reverse is unusually well defined with sharp definition on the bison's head and tail. The obverse shows just a bit of softness. Simply outstanding definition for this issue. The mint luster tends more to the frosted side than the expected satiny variant. Lightly and attractively toned. Just a lovely, problem-free piece in all regards. Population: 71 in 65, 3 finer (8/07). (#3955)

731 **1925-D MS66 NGC.** Entirely unlike the typical 1925-D Buffalo nickel, this example is sharply struck with exceptional detail. In *A Guide Book of Buffalo and Jefferson Nickels*, David Bowers writes that 3% of this issue comes with a full strike while another 20% are seen with a sharp strike. His observations are based on more than 50 years experience in the numismatic marketplace. Our own experience, over a somewhat shorter period of time, indicates that less than 1% of this issue has a full strike, and perhaps 10% have a sharp strike.

While strike plays a certain role in grading, only 11 MS66 coins have been certified by NGC and PCGS combined. With the Bowers observation that only 23% appear sharply or fully struck, only three or four pieces qualify. This example is one such coin. The date is bold, each letter of LIBERTY is fully defined without the slightest evidence of merging into the rim. The bison's tail is completely outlined but not fully detailed. Other reverse detail are essentially full and sharp. Both sides have soft, frosty luster with exceptional lilac and blue color, framed by peripheral gold toning.

About 15 years ago, we handled a small hoard (a hoardlet) of 1924-D and 1925-D Buffalo nickels that had been saved by the Connecticut State Library. While this hoard changed the overall availability of the two issues, Premium Gem pieces were not represented. This is only the third MS66 example that we have handled since 1993. Census: 8 in 66, 0 finer (8/07). (#3955)

732 **1925-S MS63 NGC.** This piece has lovely rainbow iridescence on both sides with underlying bright satiny luster. Surprisingly sharp for the date with nearly full details on both sides. (#3956)

733 **1925-S MS63 ICG.** Boldly struck with minor softness noted on 192 in the date, and on the bison's head. The cream-gray surfaces exhibit golden highlights, very few marks, and pleasing satin luster. (#3956)

Fully Lustrous 1925-S Nickel, MS64

734 **1925-S MS64 PCGS.** Fully lustrous beneath milky lilac-gray and golden patina, with a typically soft strike, especially in the hair on the bison's head. A few minute marks are undisturbing. Primarily because of the characteristic striking deficiency, Gem examples of the 1925-S are among the most difficult in the Buffalo nickel series. In this regard, PCGS has seen only 20 Gem-quality coins (8/07). (#3956)

Choice Mint State 1925-S Buffalo

735 **1925-S MS64 PCGS.** Brilliant mint frost is immediately apparent with attractive champagne toning on both sides. This example is a little unusual, as the obverse appears to have a slightly below average strike and the reverse appears to be slightly above average. A scarce date at this grade level, with just 20 finer pieces certified by PCGS (8/07). (#3956)

Sharp MS67 1926 Buffalo Nickel

736 **1926 MS67 NGC.** Bright apricot patina and pleasing luster illuminate the well-preserved surfaces. This piece is well struck on the legends and throughout the bison's head and shoulder. Only a touch of softness is present on the braid. An attractive example of this mid-date P-mint issue, nearly impossible to find any finer. Population: 12 in 67, 1 finer (7/07). (#3957)

Shimmering MS64 1926-S Nickel

737 **1926-S MS64 PCGS.** Recognized for decades as the key to the regular Buffalo nickel series, a mere 970,000 pieces were struck. This, of course, means the '26-S is scarce in all grades, and it is a notable rarity in mint condition. As a strike rarity, this issue's status is beyond comparison in the series. The coins simply did not leave the San Francisco Mint with full definition. As Lange states in his third edition: "Worn reverse dies are the norm for 1926-S. These were probably leftovers from previous years, since dateless dies could be used until they failed completely."

This piece has bright mint luster with a metallic sheen, rather than the frosted finish one might expect from a San Francisco product. Better struck than many 1926-S nickels, but of course still lacking highpoint definition. Pale iridescent toning is seen over each side. (#3959)

Splendid 1927 Nickel, MS67

738 **1927 MS67 NGC.** With a mintage approaching 38 million pieces, the 1927 five cent is common in all grades. NGC and PCGS have certified several hundred coins through the MS66 level of preservation. The certified population drops precipitously any finer. The current MS67 displays violet and greenish-gold patina on the obverse, while gold and light green dominate the reverse. Sharply struck and well preserved throughout, with outstanding luster. Census: 8 in 67, 0 finer (8/07). (#3960)

739 **1927-D MS64 PCGS.** Pink and gold toning graces both sides of this D-mint near-Gem. While the portrait and the bison's shoulder show the softness that appears on the vast majority of examples, the overall eye appeal remains above-average. (#3961)

Choice 1927-S Buffalo, MS64

740 **1927-S MS64 PCGS.** Pale gray-gold surfaces with brilliant underlying luster, and splashes of deeper gold on the obverse. While this date is not particularly difficult to locate in Choice Mint State quality, finer examples are quite rare, with just 20 Gems certified by PCGS (8/07). The strike is typical, with complete details but lacking the sharpness of a full strike. (#3962)

Satiny Near-Gem 1927-S Buffalo Nickel

741 **1927-S MS64 PCGS.** A satiny near-Gem example, exhibiting pale gray-gold color with lilac and iridescent toning on both sides. Dave Bowers described the MS64 grade as the "Optimal Collecting Grade" for the '27-S. A trademark of Whitman Publishing Company, the Optimal Collecting Grade for each issue provides an indication of the best value, after considering several factors. We hope that future editions of *A Guide Book of Buffalo and Jefferson Nickels* will actually inform the readers of the various factors that are considered. (#3962)

Gorgeous 1927-S Gem Nickel

742 **1927-S MS65 NGC.** Writing about the 1927-S Buffalo nickel in the September 16, 2003 *Numismatic News*, Paul Green says: "Its mintage of 3,430,000 suggests it is a better Buffalo nickel and it remains a better one in almost every grade. In Uncirculated the 1927-S becomes better and the higher the grade the better the 1927-S gets."

NGC and PCGS combined have certified a little more than 750 Mint State examples of this issue, most of which fall into the Select and near-Gem grade range. There is a sharp drop in numbers between MS64 and MS65, from approximately 400 of the former to about 35 of the latter. A solitary finer piece has been seen!

Bright luster adorns both sides of this lovely Gem, each of which displays pastel powder-blue, lilac, and golden-gray coloration. The strike is impressive, bringing sharp definition to all of the design elements. A couple of unobtrusive marks preclude an even higher grade. Census: 14 in 65, 1 finer (8/07). (#3962)

743 **1928 MS66 PCGS.** The well-preserved and lustrous surfaces offer faint golden patina on the obverse, while the reverse shows faint violet, pale-blue, and champagne toning. A lovely example of this Roaring Twenties P-mint issue. PCGS has graded just 12 coins finer (7/07). (#3963)

Conditionally Challenging 1928 Nickel, MS67

744 1928 MS67 PCGS. While generally considered a common date, the 1928 is conditionally rare in MS67 grade (the highest grade obtainable). Only 12 pieces have been so graded by PCGS, and another five coins have been certified in this grade by NGC (8/07). The surfaces are extraordinarily lustrous. Just the slightest hint of toning is present, the coin generally presents as brilliant. Sharply defined throughout. (#3963)

745 1928-D MS65 PCGS. An attractive Gem example, better-defined than average for this Coolidge-era D-mint issue. Thin layers of dusky blue and gold patina grace the luminous surfaces. PCGS has graded just 31 finer examples (7/07). (#3964)

746 1928-D MS65 ANACS. Boldly struck overall and lustrous, with attractive light golden color on the reverse, and well preserved surfaces that are free of distracting marks or abrasions. The bison's head, shoulder, and rear leg are typically soft. (#3964)

747 1928-D MS65 PCGS. This Gem Buffalo nickel is lustrous and well preserved, with light greenish-gray toning that yields to antique-gold and iridescent accents near the periphery. Boldly struck except on the top of the bison's head. The '28-D is readily obtainable in MS63 and MS64 condition, but becomes scarce above that level. (#3964)

Lustrous MS66 1928-D Nickel

748 1928-D MS66 PCGS. More sharply struck than most 1928-D nickels, this piece shows strong hair detail on the obverse, full hair on the bison's head, and almost a complete split in the tail. Bright mint luster, as usually seen on this issue, the surfaces are exceptionally clean and there is just the slightest hint of color on each side. Population: 31 in 66, 0 finer (8/07). (#3964)

749 1928-S MS64 NGC. A generally unrecognized strike rarity, coins with this degree of strike are seldom seen. Each side has thick mint luster that is overlaid with lime green centers and deep rose peripheral color. A couple of facial marks explain the less-than-Gem grade. (#3965)

750 1929 MS66 PCGS. Well struck with swirling luster and carefully preserved fields. This pleasing nickel-gray P-mint piece hails from the year in which the Roaring Twenties gave way to the Great Depression. PCGS has graded only two finer representatives (7/07). (#3966)

751 1929 MS66 PCGS. Ice-blue toning with sea-green accents drapes the shining surfaces of this Premium Gem, attractively detailed overall with faint highpoint softness that is typical for this issue. A delightful Philadelphia nickel. PCGS has graded just three pieces finer (8/07). (#3966)

752 1929 MS66 PCGS. Highly lustrous with just the lightest overlay of pale blue and rose toning. Sharply defined on the reverse. (#3966)

753 1929-S MS65 PCGS, lustrous and smooth with well struck borders and a few areas of dusky gray toning; and a **1930 MS66 PCGS,** lovely gold and mauve patina, unabraded, a suitable strike. (Total: 2 coins) (#3968)

754 1929-S MS66 NGC. A solidly struck and attractive example of this Depression-era Buffalo nickel, delicately gold-toned with quicksilver luster. Difficult to acquire any finer, as NGC has graded just four Superb Gems (8/07). (#3968)

755 1929-S MS66 PCGS. Ex: ADM Collection. A flashy coin with a strike that is superior to most '29-S nickels. In fact, this piece is almost completely brought up. With the luster, strong strike, and rich color combined, this is an upper-end MS66. (#3968)

756 1929-S MS66 PCGS. Gold, sunset-orange, and soft heather patina covers each side of this Premium Gem. The minimally marked surfaces have quicksilver luster. An attractive example from the year that saw the Roaring Twenties give way to the Great Depression. PCGS has graded just five pieces finer (8/07). (#3968)

Remarkable 1929-S Nickel, MS67

757 1929-S MS67 NGC. The striking details are essentially full, as is the remarkably effulgent mint luster. More remarkable still is the beautiful steel-blue and golden toning that adorns this seemingly pristine, conditionally rare Superb Gem. NGC and PCGS combined have graded a mere nine pieces at MS67, with none finer at either service (8/07). (#3968)

758 1930-S MS66 PCGS. This Depression-era S-mint piece offers above-average detail overall, though the braid and shoulder still show a degree of softness. Champagne and silver-gray patina graces the beautifully preserved quicksilver surfaces. PCGS has certified just four finer representatives (7/07). (#3970)

759 1930-S MS66 PCGS. Ex: A D M Collection. A silky chestnut-gold and steel-gray Premium Gem. Unabraded, and virtually void of carbon. The strike is exquisite save for the expected slight incompleteness above the braid. (#3970)

760 **1931-S MS66 NGC.** A delectable Premium Gem, impeccably preserved with vibrant luster beneath blushes of deep golden toning. Lesser quality Uncirculated examples of this hoarded, low-mintage issue are always around, but pieces this nice seldom surface. NGC has graded just two finer representatives (8/07). (#3971)

761 **1931-S MS66 PCGS.** Though the 1931-S nickels were saved in quantity and examples are available even in Premium Gem, PCGS has graded just one finer example (8/07). This pleasingly detailed piece offers vibrant luster and delicate sky-blue and champagne tints. (#3971)

762 **1931-S MS66 PCGS.** Delicate orange and peach patina with soft rose and lavender tints covers both sides of this lower-mintage S-mint nickel. This luminous Premium Gem is nearly impossible to top; PCGS has graded only one finer piece (8/07). (#3971)

763 **1934 MS66 PCGS.** Delicate ice-blue patina graces the shining surfaces of this Depression-era nickel. Well struck with faint evidence of carbon at the braid. PCGS has graded only 19 finer representatives (7/07). (#3972)

Gorgeous Superb Gem 1934 Buffalo Nickel

764 **1934 MS67 NGC.** Deep, beautiful mauve coloration predominates on each side, complementing the amber-gold patina at the rims. The strike is robust, although the 3 in the date is partially filled due to buildup from the die. Nonetheless, a delightful later example and among the couple of dozen finest-graded examples at both services combined. Census: 3 in 67, 0 finer (7/07). (#3972)

Sharp 1934-D Premium Gem Nickel

765 **1934-D MS66 PCGS.** Locating a sharply struck 1934-D nickel with full luster is challenging. The Premium Gem in this lot has been the recipient of a well directed strike, as the design elements are crisply defined. Just a hint of softness is seen in portions of the bison's hair. Well cared for surfaces exhibit effusive luster, and are attractively toned in iridescent rainbow hues. Population: 40 in 66, 0 finer (8/07). (#3973)

766 **1935-D/D MS66 ANACS.** A secondary mintmark appears just to the west. This pleasingly detailed and shining gold-tinged Premium Gem comes from one of the more challenging later mintmarked Buffalo nickel issues. Well-preserved overall with a faint graze on the cheekbone. (#3975)

Sharply Struck 1935-D Nickel, MS67

767 **1935-D MS67 NGC.** David Lange (2006) writes that "Fully-struck Gems are genuinely rare. Many of these coins were struck from extremely worn dies … ." An attentive strike brings out excellent definition on the Superb Gem in this lot, save for a touch of softness in the outer parts of some of the letters in LIBERTY. Impeccably preserved surfaces exhibit outstanding luster and pastel violet and gold patination. Census: 4 in 67, 0 finer (8/07). (#3975)

MS67 1935-S Nickel, RPM-1

768 **1935-S MS67 PCGS.** RPM-1. The mintmark was first punched in to the right of the final position and its remnants were not polished away. The 1935-S is a lesser strike rarity among late-date Buffalo nickels. But one would never know it from examining this piece, which is sharply defined throughout. The surfaces are bright and shimmering with a light overlay of golden-rose and lilac toning on each side. Population: 27 in 67, 0 finer (8/07). (#3976)

769 **An Uncertified roll of 1937 Buffalo Nickels.** Most pieces grade between MS63 and MS65. All are lustrous and lightly toned with minor incompleteness of strike on the hair above the braid. (Total: 40 coins) (#3980)

770 **1937-D Three-Legged Fine 12 ANACS.** FS-020.2. This famous "mint error" is well known even to non-numismatists. This steel-gray example is honestly worn with original light-gray surfaces that are only slightly abraded. (#3982)

771 **1937-D Three-Legged VF25 ANACS.** A moderately circulated representative of this popular Buffalo nickel variant, silver-gray with slightly deeper color near the devices. Minimally marked for the grade assigned and pleasing. (#3982)

772 **1937-D Three-Legged VF30 ANACS.** A moderately worn example of this popular late-date Buffalo nickel variety, predominantly cloud-gray with olive-tan accents at the margins. Minimally marked on the obverse, though an abrasion appears in the space below the bison's body. (#3982)

773 **1937-D Three-Legged VF35 ANACS.** Moderately worn silver-gray and olive surfaces characterize this Choice VF representative. A minimally marked and pleasing representative of this popular Buffalo nickel variety. (#3982)

774 **1937-D Three-Legged—Scratched—ANACS. XF40 Details.** The lower reverse has a few pinscratches from an idle hour long ago. A satiny key date nickel with subtle chestnut and ice-blue toning. (#3982)

775 **1937-D Three-Legged XF40 NGC.** Rich olive and dolphin-gray patina saturates both sides of this lightly circulated and pleasing Three-Legged nickel. Struck from significantly eroded dies, though the series of raised die lumps below the bison's body is incomplete. (#3982)

776 **1937-D Three-Legged—Corroded—ANACS. XF45 Details.** This steel-gray key date nickel has minimal marks and a full horn. A number of tiny gray spots are present, most of which are on the obverse. (#3982)

777 **1937-D Three-Legged XF45 NGC.** Dusky silver-gray toning with golden peripheral elements drapes the luminous surfaces of this Choice XF coin. Both sides offer pleasing detail for this often-weak variant. (#3982)

778 **1937-D Three-Legged—Cleaned—ANACS. AU50 Details.** This oddly luminous Three-Legged piece shows aberrant lavender and gold-gray patina over each side. Still, pleasingly detailed for this often-weak variant with only minor wear.
From The Diemer L. Fife Collection. (#3982)

779 **1937-D Three-Legged AU55 PCGS.** FS-020.2. Dusky olive and rose-red shades embrace this satiny and briefly circulated key date nickel. Unblemished fields contribute further to the charm. (#3982)

780 **1937-D Three-Legged—Scratched, Cleaned—ANACS. AU55 Details.** This bright example has light powder-blue and gold toning. The reverse has two pinscratches, one on the flank and the other beneath the beard. A popular variety. (#3982)

781 **1937-D Three-Legged AU58 NGC.** Surprisingly well-defined for the variety with quicksilver luster and a thin layer of reddish-orange patina over the margins. Minor friction on the devices is the only bar to a Mint State grade. A pleasing example of this popular Buffalo nickel. (#3982)

782 **1937-D Three-Legged AU58 NGC.** FS-020.2. This satiny pearl-gray representative has bold definition and only moderate wear on the hipbone. The reverse rim has a few faint marks. (#3982)

783 **1937-D Three-Legged—Scratched—ANACS. AU58 Details.** This lustrous example's blue-accented gold-toned fields are unaffected by the faint friction found on the highpoints. Well struck with a pair of scrapes near the bison's tail that account for the details grade. Still, a desirable example of this popular Buffalo nickel variety. (#3982)

784 **1937-D Three-Legged AU58 NGC.** FS-020.2. A thin layer of gold-tan color complements exceptionally clean surfaces that exhibit well defined motifs. This classic variety is always in demand by Buffalo nickel collectors. (#3982)

MS63 1937-D Three-Legged Nickel

785 **1937-D Three-Legged MS63 NGC.** FS-020.2. A gently shimmering example with moderate caramel-gold patina. Only inconsequential contact is detected, and the strike is crisp for the series, particularly on the Indian's braid. Long regarded as a key date, the 1937-D Three-Legged nickel ranks as one of the most famous die polishing errors in numismatics. (#3982)

Select 1937-D Three-Legged Nickel

786 **1937-D Three-Legged MS63 NGC.** FS-020.2. This satiny key date nickel has medium apricot-gold toning and bright, unabraded fields. A faint, thin, curved mark is noted near the jaw of the Native American. The diagnostic diagonal trail of minute die lumps is present beneath the bison's flank. (#3982)

Choice 1937-D Three Legged Nickel

787 **1937-D Three-Legged MS64 PCGS.** FS-020.2. A gently shimmering pearl-gray and almond-gold near-Gem of this ceaselessly popular variety. Marks are inconsequential, and carbon is also minimal. Sharply struck, including the diagnostic series of minute die lumps beneath the bison's flank. (#3982)

Near-Gem 1937-D Three-Legged Buffalo

788 **1937-D Three-Legged MS64 PCGS.** A Choice Mint State example of the ever-popular and highly desirable Three-Legged Buffalo, a variety that is considered by most to be an integral part of a complete Buffalo nickel set. Frosty luster and full mint brilliance shines through light champagne toning. (#3982)

789 **1937-S MS67 PCGS.** Sharply struck with pale blue-gray color and hints of gold toning. The surfaces are bright with a satiny texture. Population: 79 in 67, 0 finer (8/07). (#3983)

Finest Certified 1937-S Nickel, MS68 ★

790 **1937-S MS68 ★ NGC.** David Lange, writing of the 1937-S nickel (5,635,000 mintage) in the third edition (2006) of his book *The Complete Guide to Buffalo Nickels*, says "This issue is common in all grades. It is also the most available S-mint Buffalo nickel in Gem condition." The population figures bear this out. NGC and PCGS combined have graded more than 4,000 coins as MS65, nearly 2,000 in MS66, and about 120 MS67s. A single coin has been seen finer—this NGC-graded MS68 ★.

Iridescent rainbow patina gravitates to the margins of this marvelous specimen, while golden-gray, mauve, and powder-blue toning rests in the center areas. A powerful strike emboldens the design features, and radiantly lustrous surfaces are immaculately preserved. (#3983)

791 **1938-D MS67 PCGS.** A solidly struck and immensely appealing representative of this final-year type issue, one often chosen by type collectors. The rich gold, peach, and orange patina that drapes the obverse peripheries cedes to slightly softer colors on the reverse. PCGS has graded just seven finer examples (7/07). (#3984)

792 **1938-D MS68 ★ NGC.** Splashes of lemon, ruby-red, and lime-green endow this lustrous and boldly struck Superb Gem. The fields have an orange peel texture, as made from long-lived dies. A prize for the toning connoisseur. Census: 7 in 68 ★, 0 finer (8/07). (#3984)

793 **1938-D/S MS67 NGC.** OMM-2. The final-year Buffalo nickel was struck only at Denver, while the first-year Jefferson nickel was produced at all three Mint facilities. Lustrous and close to brilliant. The strike is exquisite except for the hair above the braid. Census: 60 in 67, 3 finer (8/07). (#3985)

794 **1938-D/S MS67 PCGS.** FS-020.5. OMM-1. The desirable overmintmark variety that also exhibits repunching of the Denver mintmark beneath its base. This lustrous Superb Gem features golden-brown, sky-blue, and champagne-rose patination. An above average strike only adds to the eye appeal. (#3985)

PROOF BUFFALO NICKELS

Satiny Gem Proof 1915 Nickel

795 **1915 PR65 PCGS.** At first glance, this Gem proof looks just like a business strike, but the full design features confirm its proof status. Although called a matte proof in the literature, the surfaces have brilliant satin luster, more closely resembling the 1936 satin proof nickels. Both sides are graced by light gold toning. (#3992)

Important PR67 1916 Buffalo Nickel

796 **1916 PR67 PCGS.** Just 600 matte proof nickels were struck in 1916, but further reinforcing its rarity is that an unknown number of proofs remained unsold at the end of the year and were destroyed in the Mint. Few of the survivors remain in as pristine condition as this sharply struck example. Light nickel-gray surfaces are fully lustrous, and are accented by hints of pale rose toning. Neither side of this Superb Gem has any imperfections. There is no evidence of the usual fly specks that so often plague the early proof Buffalo nickels. This is one of the finest examples on the market today, and represents an extremely important opportunity for the advanced specialist. (#3993)

Memorable 1936 Type One-Satin Finish Nickel, PR68

797 **1936 Type One—Satin Finish PR68 PCGS.** An essentially perfect Satin Finish example of this first striking variant from 1936. Pinpoint striking details characterize this proof, and each side is covered with rich golden-rose and lilac toning. A memorable Satin Finish nickel. Population: 25 in 68, 1 finer (8/07). (#3994)

798 **1937 PR66 PCGS.** Wisps of lilac and green-gold toning envelop this virtually immaculate final-year proof Buffalo nickel. The strike is sharp despite a whisper of incompleteness above the braid. Encapsulated in an old green label holder. (#3996)

799 **1937 PR66 NGC.** This exquisitely struck and gleaming specimen hails from the final proof Buffalo nickel issue, which amounted to just 5,769 pieces. Carefully preserved with just a touch of golden toning on each side. (#3996)

800 **1937 PR66 NGC.** The fields are deeply reflective and the devices seem to be just as bright with no significant frost on the devices. Most of each side retain original brilliance with a bit of reddish-golden color intermixed. (#3996)

Superb Gem Proof 1937 Nickel

801 **1937 PR67 PCGS.** Deep mirrors and sharp design elements are enhanced by light gold toning over the blue-gray surfaces of this Superb Gem proof. Both sides are remarkably well preserved with no distractions of any sort. While Superb pieces regularly appear on the market, PCGS has only certified 11 finer coins. For the connoisseur, PR67 coins are an excellent choice, combining quality and availability. (#3996)

JEFFERSON NICKELS

1938 Jefferson Nickel, MS67 Five Full Steps

802 **1938 MS67 Five Full Steps NGC.** Ex: Omaha Bank Hoard. Crisply struck design elements and untoned surfaces are illuminated by a pleasing satiny sheen. Wispy die striations are noted in the fields, adding character to the piece. A lovely and important piece from a first-year issue seldom found so well-preserved. Census: 3 in 67 Five Full Steps, 0 finer (7/07). (#84000)

803 **1938-D MS67 Full Steps PCGS.** Although the slightest merging is present, all of the steps on this example are sharp. The frosty surfaces have excellent gold and iridescent toning over shining surfaces. A delightful first-year piece. Population: 28 in 67 Full Steps, 0 finer (8/07). (#84001)

804 **1938-S MS66 Full Steps PCGS.** Light golden-gray surfaces reveal some subtle pale blue undertones. Sharply struck, with no distracting marks. Population: 46 in 66 Full Steps, 4 finer (8/07). (#84002)

805 **1939-D Reverse of 1938 MS66 Full Steps PCGS.** A well struck Premium Gem with shimmering luster and rich olive-gold and blue-gray toning. A beautiful example of this scarce low mintage issue. Population: 38 in 66 Full Steps, 4 finer (8/07). (#84005)

806 **1942-P Type Two MS68 NGC.** The 1942 Philadelphia is the only issue struck with and without the large mintmark above the dome. Proofs and business strikes are available for both subtypes, and the Type Two (mintmarked) varieties are scarcer. This spectacularly preserved olive-gold Superb Gem appears perfect save for some incompleteness on the steps. Census: 2 in 68, 0 finer (8/07). (#4016)

807 **1944-P MS67 Five Full Steps NGC.** Nearly 120 million 1944-P nickels were produced, but the issue is a strike rarity. In MS67 NGC has certified only a single piece as Six Full Steps, while just eight examples achieve the Five Full Steps level (4/07). The present Superb Gem has undisturbed fields, potent luster, and only a hint of ivory-gray toning. (#84022)

Outstanding 1944-D Nickel, MS67 ★ 5 Full Steps

808 **1944-D MS67 ★ 5 Full Steps NGC.** This is one of just four 1944-D 5 Full Steps War nickels that have been assigned the coveted Star designation by NGC. Golden-tan patina in the centers transitions to concentric circles of lavender, violet, cobalt-blue, and crimson-gold, and a powerful strike leaves excellent definition on all of the design elements, culminating in five (technically 5 3/4) full steps. Impeccably preserved. Simply outstanding technical quality and aesthetic appeal! (#84023)

809 **1945-S MS66 Full Steps PCGS.** The design elements are crisply struck, and intense, coruscating luster flashes over both sides. Only slight hints of gold color keep the piece from being fully untoned. Surface marks are minimal. Population: 80 in 66 Full Steps, 4 finer (8/07). (#84027)

810 **1949 MS63 PCGS.** A luminous and well struck Select representative of this earlier nickel issue, silver-gray with rose and orange accents on the obverse. Similar colors with a more even distribution are evident on the reverse, as is a faint fingerprint above Monticello. (#4037)

811 **1949 MS64 PCGS.** Well struck with satin luster and pleasing light toning. The surfaces reveal careful preservation and very few marks. (#4037)

812 **1949-D MS65 PCGS.** Lovely rose and apple-green toning adorns the lustrous, carefully preserved surfaces of this Denver Mint Jefferson nickel. Surprisingly few have been graded as Gems. (#4038)

813 **1949-D MS65 PCGS.** A robust blend of carrot-orange and mauve patina graces both sides of this shining Jefferson nickel Gem. Well-defined with only isolated points of incompleteness on Monticello's steps. (#4038)

814 **1949-S MS64 PCGS.** The gleaming obverse exhibits delightful sea-green and lemon-gold coloration, while the reverse displays similar colors mixed with ice-blue. A well struck example of this S-mint Jefferson issue, one of fewer than 10 million pieces coined. (#4040)

815 **1949-S MS64 PCGS.** Elegant ice-blue and yellow-green patina drapes the subtly lustrous surfaces of this Choice Jefferson nickel representative. Well struck with excellent visual appeal for the grade. (#4040)

816 **1950 MS66 Full Steps PCGS.** Sharply struck and lustrous, with a variegate toning scheme over both sides that includes elements of olive-drab, antique-gold, and rose-gray. A few trivial marks are noted under magnification. Population: 29 in 66, 2 finer (8/07). (#84041)

817 **1952 MS64 Full Steps PCGS.** The shining surfaces of this near-Gem display vibrant gold and apricot patina. A crisply struck representative of this postwar Jefferson issue that shows excellent delineation on the steps. Population: 10 in 64 Full Steps, 12 finer (8/07). (#84046)

Fully Lustrous, Lightly Toned 1952-S Nickel MS66 Full Steps

818 **1952-S MS66 Full Steps PCGS.** Fully lustrous surfaces are coated with a veil of light champagne patina, and an attentive strike brings out sharp definition on the design elements. Well preserved surfaces exhibit as-made die polish lines in the reverse fields. Population: 6 in 66 Full Steps, 0 finer (8/07). (#84048)

Appealing 1953 Gem Full Steps Nickel

819 **1953 MS65 Full Steps PCGS.** Dappled pastel toning runs over both sides of this lustrous Gem, taking on sky-blue and olive-green hues on the obverse, and olive-green on the reverse. A well directed strike imparts good definition to all of the design elements, culminating in Full Steps on Monticello. A few minute marks do not disturb. Population: 6 in 65 Full Steps, 0 finer (8/07). (#84049)

820 **1954-D MS65 Full Steps PCGS.** Delicate champagne toning graces the surfaces of this attractive Gem, solidly struck with bold luster. A faint mark on Monticello's steps does not impede their sharpness. Population: 22 in 65 Full Steps, 1 finer (8/07). (#84053)

821 **1955-D MS64 Full Steps PCGS.** A thin veil of golden toning graces the lustrous surfaces of this solidly struck piece. A couple of flecks are noted in the left obverse field, and some minuscule abrasions appear on Monticello. Still, a well-preserved representative of an issue infrequently found with Full Steps. Population: 18 in 64 Full Steps, 5 finer (8/07). (#84057)

822 **1957-D MS66 Five Full Steps NGC.** Honey toning enriches this lustrous and attentively struck Premium Gem. The 1957-D is available in Mint State, but few among those have a good strike on the steps. Census: 6 in 66 Five Full Steps, 0 finer (8/07). (#84062)

823 **1958 MS65 Five Full Steps NGC.** Gentle caramel-gold toning coats this satiny Gem. Tiny marks from the planchet prior to the strike are uneffaced, but the upper steps are unbroken. Census: 5 in 65 Five Full Steps, 2 finer (8/07). (#84063)

824 **1962-D MS65 Five Full Steps NGC.** A satiny Gem with faint green-gold toning. The 1962-D is a formidable strike rarity within the series, seldom encountered with five unbroken steps on Monticello. As of (7/07), NGC has graded just **two** examples with Five Full Steps, and none with Six Full Steps. (#84072)

825 **1962-D MS65 Five Full Steps NGC.** This brilliant and semi-prooflike piece is evenly struck and unblemished. The 1962-D is notoriously difficult to locate with full steps. Census: 2 in 65 Five Full Steps, 0 finer (8/07). (#84072)

826 **1963-D MS63 Full Steps PCGS.** Highly lustrous with subtle variations of antique-gold and olive coloration. Scattered small marks limit the grade. Some of the central design elements are softly struck, but the steps of Monticello are well defined. Population: 2 in 63 Full Steps, 11 finer (8/07). (#84074)

827 **1964 MS66 Five Full Steps NGC.** This shimmering Premium Gem has faint golden toning. Both sides are remarkably unabraded, and the steps are unusually sharp for the issue. Census: 2 in 66 Five Full Steps, 0 finer (8/07). (#84075)

Lustrous 1964-D Nickel, MS67 Five Full Steps
Tied for Finest Certified

828 **1964-D MS67 Five Full Steps NGC.** The fully lustrous surfaces of this Superb Gem are essentially untoned on the obverse, and display whispers of olive-green on the reverse. The design elements are well struck throughout, culminating in five full steps on Monticello. A couple of light reverse ticks do not distract. Census: 2 in 67, 0 finer (8/07). (#84076)

Rare 1966 Full Steps Nickel, MS65

829 **1966 MS65 Full Steps PCGS.** In spite of the massive numbers of nickels struck in 1966, very few qualify for Full Steps. Only one in 150 coins are estimated to have this degree of striking detail on the reverse. PCGS has only certified three others at the Gem level, and none are finer (8/07). This is a light golden example that has silky, satin-like mint luster. A rare opportunity for the specialist. (#84078)

SMS JEFFERSON NICKELS

830 **1965 SMS MS66 Deep Cameo PCGS.** Though the Special Mint State pieces are not true proofs, the best representatives approach the reflectivity and contrast of proofs from prior years. This faintly gold-tinged example sports excellent contrast between the thickly frosted, well struck devices and the shining fields. (#94197)

831 **1965 SMS MS66 Deep Cameo PCGS.** Quite reflective with great contrast. Close to a proof except for the strike. Slight lemon-yellow and orange peripheral patina appears on each side. In a green label holder. (#94197)

832 **1967 SMS MS67 Deep Cameo PCGS.** A Superb Gem, lightly toned in blue and gold. The brilliant fields and frosted devices are fully prooflike and truly special. A small handling mark is noted on the front of Monticello. (#94199)

PROOF JEFFERSON NICKELS

833 **1942-P Type Two PR68 ★ NGC.** Beautiful honey-gold, orange-rose, powder-blue, and lime-green shades invigorate this satiny and exactingly struck Superb Gem. The sole proof date of the billon silver alloy. (#4180)

Splendid 1942-P Type Two Nickel, PR66 Cameo

834 **1942-P Type Two PR66 Cameo NGC.** Cameo proofs of the 1936 to 1942 era are extremely elusive. The present Premium Gem Cameo proof wartime silver alloy example is untoned silver-gray throughout, and sharply struck as expected, with considerable contrast provided by frosty devices against the deeply mirrored fields. Both sides are immaculately preserved. Census: 1 in 66 Cameo, 4 finer (7/07). (#84180)

835 **1954 PR66 Deep Cameo PCGS.** Fathomless fields and strongly contrasting, moderately frosted fields are the prime draws of this essentially untoned Premium Gem. Elegantly preserved and delightful. Population: 2 in 66 Deep Cameo, 11 finer (8/07). (#94186)

836 **1956 PR67 Deep Cameo PCGS.** Strongly reflective with carefully preserved mirrors and moderately frosted devices that combine for excellent contrast. The reverse fields exhibit a faint golden aura. An attractive Philadelphia Jefferson proof. Population: 9 in 67 Deep Cameo, 4 finer (8/07). (#94188)

End of Session One

SESSION TWO

Live, Internet, and Mail Bid Signature Auction #446
Thursday, September 27, 2007, 7:00 PM PT, Lots 837-1992
Long Beach, California

A 15% Buyer's Premium ($9 minimum) Will Be Added To All Lots

Visit HA.com to view full-color images and bid.

EARLY PROOF SETS

11-Piece 1868 Proof Set With Two Patterns

837 **Partial 1868 Proof Set PR61 to PR65 NGC.** The set includes:

1868 Indian Cent PR64 Red NGC. Struck with nearly medal turn, this well struck and unabraded cent has light orange-gold color and a few minuscule flyspecks.

1868 Two Cent Piece PR65 Red and Brown NGC. A beautiful, exactingly struck Gem with pleasing rose-red and pumpkin-gold toning. Mark-free, and carbon is practically nonexistent.

1868 Three Cent Silver PR61 NGC. A needle-sharp specimen with cream-gray patina and a few faint obverse field marks. The reverse is well preserved. A low mintage date.

1868 Three Cent Nickel PR64 Cameo NGC. A flashy near-Gem with light almond-gold toning and a precise strike. Minor carbon is all that limits the grade.

1868 Three Cent Nickel Pattern, Judd-618, Pollock-687, R.4, PR63 NGC. Similar to the issued design, but modifications include a lack of ribs on the Roman numerals. Struck in nickel with a plain edge. A boldly struck pearl-gray piece with a mildly granular charcoal-gray streak to the right of the wreath bow.

1868 Shield Nickel PR64 NGC. Caramel-gold and ice-blue tints visit the mark-free and flashy fields. A minor spot is noted near the N in UNITED. The date is lightly repunched.

1868 Five Cent Pattern, Judd-633, Pollock-705, R.4, PR65 NGC. The high date Pollock variant. The design is much like the issued three cent nickel, but Liberty has a star on her coronet, the Roman numeral V dominates the reverse, and the upper reverse has the motto IN GOD WE TRUST on a scroll topped by a Maltese cross. Struck in nickel with a plain edge. Lovely lemon-gold and cherry-red toning visits the unperturbed and suitably struck surfaces.

1868 Seated Half Dime PR63 NGC. Precisely struck and flashy with variegated olive-tan toning. Attractive for the grade. A low mintage date. Only 600 proofs were struck, the same reported mintage as the other non-patterns in the present set.

1868 Seated Dime PR64 NGC. An exquisitely struck specimen that boasts good reflectivity and unabraded surfaces. Peripheral charcoal-gold toning deepens on the reverse near 4 o'clock.

1868 Seated Quarter PR64 NGC. Fully struck and nicely mirrored with dappled gunmetal-gray and olive toning. Proofs and business strikes combined for only 30,000 pieces.

1868 Seated Half Dollar PR64 Cameo NGC. A precisely struck and nearly brilliant near-Gem with radiant devices and glassy fields. High quality for the certified grade. (Total: 11 coins)

838 **Six-Piece 1903 Proof Set PR65 to PR68 NGC.** The set includes:

1903 Indian Cent PR65 Red NGC. Both sides are predominantly golden-orange in color with a typically attractive appearance for the grade. A swath of crimson iridescence is also noted near the upper right obverse rim. Census: 18 in 65 Red, 20 finer (8/07).

1903 Liberty Nickel PR66 NGC. A well mirrored specimen struck with medallic alignment and displaying a touch of milky golden patina, primarily on the obverse.

1903 Barber Dime PR66 NGC. Splendid, glassy reflectivity is further enhanced by colorful reddish-orange and cobalt-blue peripheral accents. Census: 34 in 66, 11 finer (8/07).

1903 Barber Quarter PR68 Cameo NGC. In terms of both technical merit and eye appeal, easily the darling of this well preserved set. Appreciable contrast between the glassy fields and the major device elements is substantial, all being framed in orange and blue iridescent toning. Census: 10 in 68 Cameo, 1 finer (8/07).

1903 Barber Half Dollar PR66 NGC. Another impeccable specimen, this with deep pools of mirrored brilliance in the fields and an attractive outline of violet and russet toning at the margins. Census: 41 in 66, 19 finer (8/07).

1903 Morgan Dollar PR66 NGC. A dazzling proof Morgan that benefits from ample mirrors, hairline-free fields, and just a hint of field-to-device contrast. Like the other silver issues, a hint of peripheral color is noticed on each side. Census: 34 in 66, 29 finer (8/07). (Total: 6 coins)

839 **1795—Scratched—ANACS. VF30 Details.** V-5, LM-8, R.3. Liberty's portrait has parallel and relatively deep adjustment marks, as made, although a couple of faint pinscratches are also present near the eye and on the cheek. Nonetheless, this dove-gray Flowing Hair half dime is decidedly more impressive than the ANACS grade and notations suggest.
From The Laguna Niguel Collection, Part Two. (#4251)

Choice XF 1795 Half Dime
Rare LM-5 Variety

840 **1795 XF45 NGC.** V-9, LM-5, R.6. As of (8/07), NGC has only certified three examples of this very rare variety. Since the finest of those grades MS64 and is out of reach for the non-CEO, the present Choice XF representative provides an affordable alternative. Deeply toned in lavender and peach. The eagle's wings and tail show ample feather definition. Distributed minor marks are unworthy of further description. (#4251)

Sharp LM-8 1795 Half Dime, AU58

841 **1795 AU58 NGC.** V-5, LM-8, R.3. Attributed by star 1 between curls 2 and 3, low L in LIBERTY, a die crack from the right side of Y to the bridge of the nose, three berries left and four right, but none under the wings. Pleasing golden-gray toning bathes both sides, and well centered design elements are well defined. Some light adjustment marks cross Liberty's portrait, and a minute planchet flaw is located under the eagle's neck. A sharp early half dime. (#4251)

LM-1, XF45 Details 1796 Half Dime

842 **1796—Cleaned, Damaged, Bent—ANACS. XF45 Details.** V-1, LM-1, R.3. Predominantly cream-gray, although glimpses of olive-brown are also present. This slightly wavy Draped Bust half dime has pleasing sharpness, although the reverse exergue is granular, and the obverse is abraded and has a couple of ice-blue stains.
From The Laguna Niguel Collection, Part Two. (#4254)

843 **1797 15 Stars—Environmental Damage—NCS. Fine Details.** V-2, LM-1, R.3. The only die pairing featuring the obverse with 15 stars. The obverse and the reverse devices are predominantly cloud-gray, while the lower obverse margin and the reverse fields show rich red and violet toning. A measure of pitting that affects the portrait and the nearby fields accounts for the details grade.
From The Beau Clerc Collection. (#4258)

MS62 1797 Half Dime, 16 Stars, LM-2

844 **1797 16 Stars MS62 NGC.** V-4, LM-2, R.4. This attractive example offers a melange of medium golden-gray patina with lavender, crimson and aqua-blue accents. A few light toning streaks are apparent on the lower right reverse. The design elements are well struck save for the expected softness in the centers, and nicely centered on the planchet, with virtually all of the dentilation showing. Heavy die clashing is noted in the right obverse field. As most Draped Bust Small Eagle half dime survivors are in low grades, this is an excellent opportunity to acquire a handsome Mint State example. (#4259)

845 **1800—Bent, Cleaned—ANACS. VF30 Details.** V-1, LM-1, R.3. Orange-red and forest-green enrich much of this lightly cleaned early silver type coin. A curved pinscratch is noted on the eagle's shield, and the reverse rim is depressed between 3 and 7 o'clock.
From The Laguna Niguel Collection, Part Two. (#4264)

XF Sharpness 1800 Half Dime, LM-1

846 **1800—Cleaned—ANACS. XF40 Details.** V-1, LM-1, R.3. A large die break beneath the 00 in the date confirms a later die state. Although slightly bright from a long-ago wipe, this piece has retoned in olive and pearl-gray shades. Both major devices are sharply struck for the type, with all letters in E PLURIBUS UNUM distinct. *From The Beau Clerc Collection.* (#4264)

LM-2 Very Fine 1801 Half Dime

847 **1801 VF20 PCGS.** V-1 and V-2, LM-2, R.4. 1801 is a rare date with only two known die varieties. Since LM-1 is non-collectible, date and *Guide Book* variety collectors must choose examples of LM-2. This cream-gray example is unabraded and shows pleasing detail across portions of the major devices. The strike is typical on AMERICA and the final S in STATES. Population: 3 in 20, 23 finer (8/07). *From The Beau Clerc Collection.* (#4267)

BUST HALF DIMES

848 **1829 MS63 PCGS.** V-7, LM-1, R.2. Dappled pearl-gray and tan toning adorns this satiny and decisively struck Select half dime. No marks are remotely worthy of singular mention, and the eye appeal is exemplary. (#4276)

849 **1829 MS64 PCGS.** V-13, LM-4, R.3. This is the first year of the Capped Bust design for the denomination, and there are more varieties of this issue than any other through 1837. A total of 18 die varieties are known from six obverse and 10 reverse dies. The LM-4 combination is from an obverse with the ball of the digit 9 doubled. This obverse was also used for LM-3 and LM-9. The reverse has two pale gules in the shield (each vertical shield stripe has two individual lines). The second T of STATES is higher than the adjacent letters, and this characteristic is diagnostic. Splashes of cobalt-blue alternate with gold-brown. The design elements are sharply impressed. A few minute marks on Liberty's cheek do not distract. (#4276)

850 **1830 MS63 PCGS.** V-3, LM-4, R.2. A slender die crack through the first star helps identify the variety. A die chip has not yet developed within the upper loop of the second S of STATES, suggesting LM-4.1 instead of LM-4.2. This piece has subtle gold-tan color over gently shimmering surfaces. Boldly struck and attractive. (#4277)

Lustrous 1830 Half Dime, MS66, V-7, LM-7

851 **1830 MS66 PCGS.** V-7, LM-7, R.2. A wide space between stars 6 and 7 distinguishes LM-7 from the otherwise similar LM-8, and the tip of the feather is right of the upright of 5 in the denomination. Lustrous, well preserved surfaces display whispers of peripheral golden-tan, accented in places with electric-blue. The design features are well impressed. Population: 20 in 66, 7 finer (8/07). (#4277)

852 **1831 MS63 NGC.** V-5, LM-5, R.1. The first 1 in the date is centered below the fold of drapery, and on the reverse, the center of the M is near the end of the scroll. This gleaming Select piece exhibits gleaming luster and lovely caramel patina at the obverse and reverse peripheries. (#4278)

853 **1831 MS64 PCGS.** V-5, LM-5, R.1. Blue-green, gold, azure, and silver-gray patina graces both sides of this Choice Capped Bust dime. Well-defined with subtle luster beneath the toning and excellent eye appeal. (#4278)

854 **1831 MS64 PCGS.** V-3, LM-7, R.2. This intricately impressed and pleasing Mint State example has delicate autumn-gold patina over satiny silver luster. A die crack from the obverse border about 12 o'clock extends to the top of the cap where it branches to the right and the left. (#4278)

Sharp LM-7 1831 Half Dime, MS66

855 **1831 MS66 PCGS.** V-3, LM-7, R.2. The 1s in the date are centered over denticles, and the branch stem is distant from the upper serif of the C. Whispers of olive-green visit the highly lustrous surfaces on the obverse of this Premium Gem example. An attentive strike sharpens the design elements, and there are no significant marks to report. Population: 36 in 66, 8 finer (8/07). *From The Mario Eller Collection, Part One.* (#4278)

856 **1832 MS63 NGC.** V-5, LM-8, R.3. Ocean-blue and plum-red with light golden-brown centers. Well struck and satiny with exemplary preservation aside from a small obverse mark at 9 o'clock. (#4279)

857 **1833 MS64 PCGS.** V-1, LM-10, R.1. The 83 in the date is closer at the top, and both loops of the second S in states are filled. The lustrous surfaces offer fine lavender, peach, and plum patina that is slightly deeper on the obverse. The design elements are marvelously struck throughout. A fine die crack bisects the obverse. *From The Beau Clerc Collection.* (#4280)

858 **1835 Large Date, Large MS64 PCGS.** V-3, LM-3, R.1. Block 8 in date, a faint crack from rim through base of digits 183, a crack along inside points of stars 8 through 12, and a crack from top of cap to rim. On the reverse, the tip of the feather is centered over the flag of 5. A lustrous untoned near-Gem, and relatively sharp motifs. A few light marks are noted on the cheek, and doubling occurs on the date and some stars. (#4282)

859 **1835 Small Date, Small MS63 PCGS.** V-7, LM-10, R.1. An exactly struck almond-gold representative with impressively unabraded fields and devices. Undoubtedly scarce in such quality, yet affordable for an early silver type. (#4285)

MS65 1836 Inverted 3 Half Dime

860 **1836 3/Inverted 3 MS65 PCGS.** V-4, LM-3, R.1. A popular Large variety that receives a separate Guide Book listing. The base of the U in UNITED is also nicely repunched south. This impressive Gem features dappled golden-brown, yellow-gold, mauve, and electric-blue toning. Attentively struck and satiny with exemplary preservation. *From The Beau Clerc Collection.* (#94288)

SEATED HALF DIMES

861 **1837 Small Date (Flat Top 1) MS62 NGC.** The flag of the 1 is straight and flat, a distinguishing feature for this "Small Date" variety (though the Small Date and Large Date are actually similar in size). This strongly lustrous, unworn example has a vertical arc of green-gold toning at the upper obverse and wispy marks that define the grade. (#4312)

Gem 1837 Small Date Seated Half Dime

862 **1837 Small Date (Flat Top 1) MS65 PCGS.** There is no substantial difference in size between the Small Date and Large Date, but the logotypes have little in common. The Small Date has a flat top 1, a script 8, and a relatively closed 3. The Large Date has a curved top 1, a block 8, and an open 3. Both are similar in scarcity, and in demand as an example of the No Stars subtype. This smooth and satiny cream-gray Gem is well struck and has interesting die crumbling near Liberty's knee. (#4312)

Brilliant Gem 1837 No Stars Half Dime

863 **1837 Small Date (Flat Top 1) MS65 NGC.** Incorrectly attributed as a Large Date piece on the holder. This is a brilliant Gem that displays bright, frosted mint luster and only a few faint field grazes. A solidly struck and remarkable example of the short-lived No Stars Obverse type, worthy of a strong bid. *From The Beau Clerc Collection.* (#4312)

864 **1838 Large Stars, No Drapery MS64 PCGS.** The obverse of this early Seated half dime exhibits right blue-green and golden-tan patina, while the reverse shows only wisps of caramel peripheral toning around a strongly lustrous silver-gray center. Well-defined with grand eye appeal. (#4317)

865 **1838 Large Stars, No Drapery MS65 NGC.** An exquisitely struck Gem example of this No Drapery issue. The lustrous surfaces shine beneath rich olive-gold, blue, and rose patina. An incredibly appealing and desirable selection for the type or date collector. *From The Beau Clerc Collection.* (#4317)

Gem 1839 Half Dime, V-2

866 **1839 No Drapery MS65 NGC.** V-2. A later strike that just shows the outer curve of the 9 repunched. Sharply struck, as usual, the mostly brilliant surfaces show just a hint of light golden color over each side. Superior mint luster with only the slightest field marks visible with a magnifier. Census: 32 in 65, 24 finer (8/07). (#4319)

Sharp MS63 1839-O No Drapery Half Dime

867 **1839-O No Drapery MS63 PCGS.** Medium intensity golden-gray and olive-green toning covers soft luster on this Select specimen, and a sharp strike brings out strong definition on the design elements. A toned-over hair-thin mark in the upper left obverse field and a couple of more in the upper reverse field apparently limit the grade. Population: 8 in 63, 7 finer (8/07). (#4320)

Well Struck 1839-O No Drapery Gem Half Dime

868 **1839-O No Drapery MS65 NGC.** Whispers of aqua-green and gold visit both sides of this Gem O-mint half dime. The design elements have benefited from an attentive strike, and close examination reveals no significant marks. A die crack runs from the O in OF through the left side of the bowknot, and another branches through the first T in STATES, and the 1 and 9 are recut at the base. Census: 3 in 65, 2 finer (8/07). (#4320)

869 **1840 Drapery MS64 PCGS.** A crisply struck and enticing Drapery half dime, luminous beneath delicate lilac and apricot tints. Carefully preserved for this early issue, which is exceedingly challenging any finer. Population: 19 in 64, 6 finer (8/07). *From The Beau Clerc Collection.* (#4326)

Splendid MS65 1840 Drapery Half Dime

870 **1840 Drapery MS65 NGC.** V-7. A single obverse and reverse die was used to create the Drapery half dimes for this date. The reverse is from the hub first used on the 1840-O Transitional (Large Letters), no Drapery coins. This is a bright, frosted coin with semi-prooflike fields. Well, but not fully struck. The mostly brilliant surfaces show just a hint of light golden color on each side. Splendid quality. (#4326)

Colorful Premium Gem 1841 Half Dime

871 **1841 MS66 PCGS.** Forest-green and rose-gray toning embrace this intricately struck and unabraded Premium Gem. Scarcer than expected in Mint State, given a mintage of 1.15 million pieces. Struck from moderately clashed dies, and encapsulated in a green label holder. Population: 7 in 66, 4 finer (8/07). *From The Beau Clerc Collection.* (#4328)

Premium Gem 1841-O Half Dime

872 **1841-O MS66 NGC.** Medium O mintmark. Specialists who collect the Seated Liberty half dimes recognize certain dates as major rarities, and other dates as condition rarities. A member of the second group, the 1841-O is plentiful in circulated and lower Mint State grades, but extremely rare in Gem quality.

At least five different die varieties are known, with Small O and Medium O mintmarks. At one time, Will Neil published a Large O mintmark variety, but it is now believed that his description resulted from a measurement error.

Struck from worn dies that result in a grainy appearance, this lovely piece has ivory color, frosty surfaces, and brilliant luster. Most design elements are sharp, although the obverse and reverse borders fade into the fields. Census: 2 in 66, 1 finer (8/07). *From The Beau Clerc Collection.* (#4329)

873 **1843 MS65 NGC.** A shining, enticing Gem representative of this early half dime issue, solidly struck with hints of peach and gold patina. Carefully preserved and exquisite. Census: 22 in 65, 9 finer (7/07). (#4332)

874 **1843 MS65 NGC.** Pleasingly detailed overall with a single dot of charcoal patina above Liberty's head and small fragments of similar toning nearby on the rim. The carefully preserved, shining surfaces are silver-white otherwise. A great early half dime. Census: 22 in 65, 9 finer (8/07). *From The Beau Clerc Collection.* (#4332)

875 **1844-O XF45 PCGS.** A lightly circulated example of early New Orleans minor silver, this half dime displays rose and violet peripheral toning around silver-gray centers. Well struck with excellent visual appeal for the grade. Population: 2 in 45, 21 finer (8/07). *From The Beau Clerc Collection.* (#4334)

876 **1845 MS65 PCGS.** The date is repunched west. A moderately prooflike and needle-sharp Gem with deep navy-blue and olive-gold patina. The obverse is exquisitely smooth, and the reverse field has only inconsequential contact. Population: 16 in 65, 16 finer (7/07). (#4335)

Important Gem 1848 Large Date Half Dime

877 **1848 Large Date MS65 PCGS.** FS-301. The *Cherrypickers' Guide* states it succinctly: "The digits of the date are much larger than normal. It is very obvious a 4-digit logotype punch intended for a dime was used. The digits protrude well into the rock." Luxuriously toned in sea-green, gold, and lilac shades. The reverse has a bisecting die crack. Encased in a green label holder. Population: 2 in 65, 1 finer (8/07). *From The Beau Clerc Collection.* (#4339)

878 **1848-O MS63 PCGS.** Splashes of caramel-gold and powder-blue toning grace this lustrous and conditionally scarce New Orleans half dime. The reverse is immaculate but has minor softness of strike. A hair-thin mark crosses Liberty's left (facing) wrist. Encased in an old green label holder. (#4340)

879 **1850 MS66 PCGS.** A well-defined and delectably toned Premium Gem representative of this Philadelphia half dime issue, luminous beneath layers of lavender, gold, and blue. One of fewer than a million pieces struck. Population: 16 in 66, 8 finer (8/07). (#4345)

880 **1851 MS65 PCGS.** A medley of lavender, cobalt-blue, and olive-gray toning clings to highly lustrous surfaces, and a well directed strike brings out good detail on the design features. A couple of hair-thin marks are visible in the right obverse field. (#4347)

881 **1851-O MS64 PCGS.** Delicate golden tints visit the luminous surfaces of this dainty New Orleans near-Gem. Well struck with two tiny dots of deeper toning near Liberty's feet and few flaws. Population: 14 in 64, 5 finer (8/07). *From The Beau Clerc Collection.* (#4348)

Rarely Seen 1852-O Half Dime, MS64

882 **1852-O MS64 PCGS.** The 1852-O has a deceptively high mintage of 260,000 pieces. It is deceptively high because the majority struck were melted in 1852 and early 1853 as they were worth more melted than their face value. That situation was remedied in February 1853, but for silver coins produced in the early 1850s widespread melting renders mintages largely irrelevant. Scarce in all grades, and especially challenging in mint condition, only 13 other pieces have been so graded by PCGS and NGC combined with 11 finer (8/07). The satiny surfaces of this coin are brilliant throughout and the striking details are fully detailed on each side. Light die clash marks are the only mentionable "flaws" on the obverse or reverse. (#4350)

883 **1854 Arrows MS65 PCGS.** Though the 1854 has less than half the mintage of the 1853, the former is similarly suitable for the type collector. This well struck and shining Gem is predominantly silver-white with hints of ice-blue. The large date's final two digits run into Liberty's base. Population: 39 in 65, 9 finer (8/07). (#4358)

884 **1854 Arrows MS65 PCGS.** The upper left obverse shows lovely cornflower-blue patina, while the lower obverse and parts of the reverse exhibit peach accents. A solidly struck and highly lustrous Gem example of the short-lived Arrows type. Population: 39 in 65, 9 finer (8/07). (#4358)

Toned MS66 1855 Arrows Half Dime

885 **1855 Arrows MS66 NGC.** V-1. This is a last-year issue of the Arrows at Date subtype. The arrows signified a reduced silver content, caused by the rising silver prices in terms of gold, due to the glut of Western gold coming onto the world markets. This variety shows the arrow barbs overlapping the rock base. The shield point is over the left side of the 1, and the pendant is centered over the first 5. The bold date has the first 5 open, the second 5 closed. The dentilation is weak on both sides, as made, from about 1 to 5 o'clock on each side. This lovely Premium Gem offers iridescent blue patina with amber and gold scattered about. A prize for Seated Liberty specialists. Census: 4 in 66, 5 finer (8/07). *From The Beau Clerc Collection.* (#4360)

Scarce 1855-O Arrows Gem Half Dime

886 **1855-O Arrows MS65 PCGS.** This O-mint issue is, according to Al Blythe (1992), scarce in all grades. Whispers of green and reddish-brown toning rest on pleasingly lustrous and well preserved surfaces. Sharp definition is apparent on all of the design elements. Population: 9 in 65, 2 finer (8/07). (#4361)

887 **1857 MS65 PCGS.** Both sides of this Gem half dime exhibit pleasing luster and traces of olive-gray color. A sharp strike is noted on the design elements, though the centrils in the stars along the right border are weak. Appealing despite clash marks on each side and a few scattered planchet defects to the right of Liberty. Population: 54 in 65, 19 finer (7/07). (#4365)

888 **1858 MS66 NGC.** A brilliant, sharply struck, and moderately prooflike Premium Gem, struck from clashed dies. A delightful representative of this desirable pre-war issue. NGC has graded just 21 finer examples (8/07). (#4367)

889 **1858 MS66 PCGS.** A well struck example of this Stars on Obverse half dime issue, luminous beneath rich caramel-tan and blue-green toning over the obverse and olive and violet patina over the reverse. Carefully preserved and immensely appealing. Population: 39 in 66, 13 finer (8/07). (#4367)

1858 Over Inverted Date Half Dime, MS66
Finest Certified Example

890 **1858 Over Inverted Date MS66 NGC.** VP-001. Al Blythe, in his Seated Liberty half dime book, says of this issue that "All four digits of the date were originally punched upside down and then corrected. Tops of the inverted punched numerals can be seen slightly above the middle of the corrected date." Aqua-gray patina rests on the lustrous surfaces of this well preserved Premium Gem. Generally well struck. The finest certified specimen of either NGC or PCGS. (#4368)

'Nationless' Transitional 1860 Half Dime, MS67

891 **1860 Transitional MS67 NGC.** Judd-267, Pollock-315, R.4. Considered a pattern by tradition, the Transitional half dime was actually issued by James Ross Snowden as "trade bait" to help enhance the Mint Collection. Most collectors today include it as a part of the Seated half dime series. It is believed that the Philadelphia Mint produced about 100 of these coins early in 1860. Since the obverse retained the stars of the 1838-1859 issues and the reverse was that of the 1860-1873 issues, these fascinating coins do not bear the legend UNITED STATES OF AMERICA. The stars of both the 1859 and 1860 issues are hollow. This is a wholly original example with bright silver-gray, lustrous surfaces. The strike is well above average for the issue, with most of the design elements well impressed. Only a couple of stars along the upper right obverse border reveal softness in the centers. Even the leaves on the reverse wreath display nice detail. The pristine surfaces are immaculately preserved, with no mentionable contact marks. An excellent opportunity for the advanced Seated Liberty half dime specialist, this lovely Superb Gem should command a generous bid. Census: 3 in 67, 1 finer (8/07). (#4373)

892 **1862 MS65 PCGS.** Bright luster exudes from the well preserved surfaces of this civil War era Gem. Faint yellow-tan patina rests on the obverse, while the reverse takes on deeper golden-gray hues. A solid strike leaves good definition on the design features. Light clash marks are visible on the obverse. Population: 64 in 65, 53 finer (8/07). (#4381)

893 **1867 MS65 PCGS.** One of the best-preserved survivors from an issue of just 8,000 pieces, this Gem post-war half dime displays dappled green-gold and lilac-blue tints. Crisply struck with enticing luster. Population: 8 in 65, 7 finer (8/07).
From The Beau Clerc Collection. (#4390)

894 **1868 MS64 NGC.** Dusky olive-gold patina graces the surprisingly reflective obverse of this near-Gem, while the reverse shows green-gold peripheral toning around a sapphire center. Solidly struck and attractively preserved. Census: 20 in 64, 19 finer (8/07).
From The Beau Clerc Collection. (#4392)

895 **1868-S MS64 PCGS.** An attractive example of this late-date S-mint half dime issue, perhaps underappreciated in light of its mintage of only 280,000 pieces. This well struck and frosty piece is predominantly silver-white with a hint of gold near the date. Population: 14 in 64, 12 finer (8/07). (#4393)

896 **1872 MS65 PCGS.** The lustrous silver-gray surfaces exhibit cobalt-blue and reddish-brown toning at the lower obverse. Softly struck and pleasing with a few tiny, isolated field marks that are consistent with the grade. A lovely example of this penultimate half dime issue. (#4400)

897 **1872 MS65 NGC.** A common date among late-date half dimes, and one of almost 3 million pieces produced. Apparently quite a few were set aside as novelties as the end of the series was near. This is a sharply struck example with deep blue and rose toning over each side. Census: 26 in 65, 11 finer (8/07). (#4400)

898 **1872 MS66 PCGS.** Central orange-gold toning is framed by ruby-red and ocean-blue. A lustrous high grade dime with minor incompleteness of strike on the bowknot and an upper left portion of the wreath. Population: 10 in 66, 0 finer (7/07). (#4400)

899 **1872-S Mintmark Below Bow MS65 NGC.** Well struck, except on the left side of the reverse wreath bow, with intense satiny luster and alluring creamy-beige coloration. Faint die clash marks are observed on the obverse, but abrasions seem essentially nonexistent.
From The Arnold & Harriet Collection, Part Two. (#4401)

PROOF SEATED HALF DIMES

Outstanding 1858 Gem Proof Half Dime

900 **1858 PR65 PCGS.** Ex: Eliasberg. Walter Breen in his 1988 *Encyclopedia* estimates 80 plus proof half dimes were minted in 1858, while Al Blythe, in his half dime reference book, suggests 40 to 50 proofs. In contrast to these estimates, the PCGS/NGC population data show about 130 certified examples (some of which are undoubtedly resubmissions). In any event, this exquisitely struck Gem displays strong field-device contrast when the coin is rotated under a light source. The frosty design elements are primarily grayish-mauve in color, and are further highlighted by iridescent cobalt-blue, lavender, and golden-tan in the fields. Nicely preserved throughout, and housed in a green-label holder. Population: 10 in 65, 2 finer (8/07). (#4437)

901 **1859 PR61 NGC.** From the curious and briefly used obverse subtype with hollow stars and a slightly different rendition of Liberty. The flashy fields are typically abraded. Breen reports a proof mintage of 800 pieces, "many later melted." (#4438)

Attractive 1859 Half Dime, PR65

902 **1859 PR65 PCGS.** Walter Breen (1988) says 800 1859 proof half dimes were minted, and PCGS/NGC population data indicate well over 300 examples have been certified. The Gem in this lot displays attractive medium gray surfaces with bluish accents. The strike is solid, and both sides are devoid of significant marks. Population: 22 in 65, 10 finer (8/07). (#4438)

Stunning 1859 PR65 Cameo Half Dime

903 **1859 PR65 Cameo PCGS.** Al Blythe (1992) does not give the mintage of 1859 proof half dimes, but contends that "60 to 75 remain." A little over 20 examples have been given the Cameo designation by PCGS and NGC. This PR65 Cameo exhibits white surfaces that show exceptional contrast between sharply struck, highly frosted motifs and mirrored fields. A couple of obverse lint marks are noted. Population: 2 in 65 Cameo, 1 finer (8/07). (#84438)

Outstanding 1861 Half Dime, PR65 Cameo

904 **1861 PR65 Cameo NGC.** Frosted, sharply struck motifs stand out against the deeply mirrored fields, all of which are covered in a barely discernible layer of white-champagne color. Both faces are impeccably preserved, further enhancing the coin's outstanding eye appeal. NGC and PCGS have certified only nine Cameos out of the 1,000 piece mintage. Census: 1 in 65 Cameo, 1 finer (7/07). (#84444)

905 **1863—Stained—NCS. Proof.** A boldly struck and lightly abraded representative with milky tan-brown toning. Only 18,000 business strikes and 460 proofs were struck.

906 **1864 PR64 PCGS.** A delightful, diminutive Choice proof from the Civil War years, strongly lustrous and largely untoned with a measure of contrast on each side. Boldly impressed with a few scattered hairlines in the fields. Population: 45 in 64, 24 finer (8/07). (#4447)

Outstanding 1864 PR65 Ultra Cameo Half Dime Tied for Finest Certified

907 **1864 PR65 Ultra Cameo NGC.** Proof half dimes of 1864 are more elusive than the 470-piece mintage might suggest, and in Deep Cameo they are extremely rare. NGC and PCGS have each certified a solitary 1864 proof in this classification! White-on-black contrast greets the observer of this Gem proof specimen. Crisp definition is displayed on the motifs, and untoned surfaces have been well cared for. A small planchet defect is visible in the rock above the 4 in the date. Simply outstanding overall eye appeal! (#94447)

908 **1870 PR65 Cameo NGC.** Although 1,000 proofs were struck in 1870, few have received the Cameo designation. This richly frosted, subtly gold-tinged Gem offers wonderful contrast and strong visual appeal. A touch of softness on Liberty's staff arm is a minor distraction at worst. Census: 2 in 65 Cameo, 6 finer (8/07). *From The Mario Eller Collection, Part One.* (#84453)

Impressive 1873 Half Dime, PR66 Cameo

909 **1873 PR66 Cameo NGC.** Al Blythe, writing about the 1873 proof issue in his Seated Liberty half dime reference, indicates that "Many of the 600 proofs were melted ... in July 1873. There is no estimate of the survivors." We do know, however, that fewer than 50 1873 proofs have been given the Cameo designation by NGC and PCGS combined. This Premium Gem Cameo displays a thin veneer of champagne color, and profound field-motif contrast. Crisply struck throughout, and no significant marks. Census: 4 in 66 Cameo, 4 finer (8/07). (#84456)

EARLY DIMES

910 **1796—Cleaned, Bent, Scratched, Damaged—ANACS. Fair 2 Details.** JR-1, R.3. Somewhat wavy, which causes uneven wear. All legends are partly to mostly legible. Cloudy from hairlines, and a small dig is noted on the obverse near 3 o'clock. The reverse has a few unimportant pinscratches. (#4461)

911 **1796 AG3 ANACS.** JR-6, R.3. Jade-green and lilac with an ivory-gray central obverse. Portions of AMERICA and UNITED are worn into the rim, but all legends are legible. The base of the portrait has a few thin marks, and selected areas are moderately granular. *From The Laguna Niguel Collection, Part Two.* (#4461)

VF Details 1796 Dime
Important "No Cud" JR-1 Die State

912 **1796—Corroded, Tooled—ANACS. VF20 Details.** JR-1, R.3. An early die state (as indicated on the insert) without the cud at star 1 ("No Cud" is also indicated on the holder). The still-standard reference to the series, *Early United States Dimes 1796-1837*, states "all specimens seen have die cud at S1 on obverse which increases in size until S1 obliterated." This piece is an exception, and was presumably among the first few dimes struck. In its A.N.R. appearance, that cataloger noted only one other JR-1 was known without the star 1 cud, the high-grade Jimmy Hayes-Whitney example sold in 1999.

Silver-gray surfaces display whispers of purple color, especially on the reverse, and some micro porosity, again mostly on the reverse. A few minute contact and tooling marks are noted on both sides. *Ex: Coin Galleries, 11/97, lot 2815; C.L. Lee Sale (American Numismatic Rarities, 9/05), lot 232.* (#4461)

Attractively Toned 1796 Dime, VF25, JR-1

913 **1796 VF25 NGC.** JR-1, R.3. The die cud break at star 1, the two leaf points under the left foot of the A in STATES, and the leaf point below the O in OF confirm the variety. Pleasing light to medium gray patina rests on this VF25 specimen. Well centered devices exhibit good detail. A small indentation near Liberty's shoulder might be as made. (#4461)

XF Sharpness JR-4 1796 Dime

914 **1796—Eagle Tooled, Improperly Cleaned—NCS. XF Details.** JR-4, R.4. A slate-gray example with slightly deeper toning on the stars and central reverse. The eagle has been strengthened, particularly on the wings and tail, probably because it was softly struck, although Liberty's curls have excellent and original definition. The obverse rim has a slender planchet defect from 3 to 4 o'clock. (#4461)

Rare 13-Star 1797 Dime, AU55, JR-2

915 **1797 13 Stars AU55 NGC.** JR-2, R.4. Scarcer than JR-1, the JR-2 variety is especially difficult to locate in grades above XF. This attractive example retains evidence of the original finish beneath rich copper-brown, forest-green, and lilac-gray toning. The boldly defined features are nicely centered within well defined borders. There is a large planchet lamination (as struck) on the eagle's breast, and several shallow adjustment marks are noted below Liberty's ear. Both sides are free of severe marks, but a few minor abrasions are located near the T in UNITED and along TAT in STATES, near the reverse border. The reported mintage of 25,261 dimes may have included more than 10,000 coins dated 1796, according to several numismatic authorities. At the AU55 level, only three other pieces have been so graded by NGC with one finer. PCGS has certified two coins in this grade with just two finer (7/08). *From The Beau Clerc Collection.* (#4463)

Pleasing Near-Mint 1798 Large 8 JR-4 Dime

916　**1798 Large 8 AU58 NGC.** JR-4, R.3. A middle die state with obverse die cracks to the chin and nose, but no die break is yet present near the left wingtip. Luster dominates the hair, shield, and legends. The left side stars are soft, but the major devices are bold, with slight wear on the cheek and shoulder. The left obverse field has a pair of hair-thin laminations, as made, and a short mark is concealed on the field near the forehead. (#4466)

Lovely 1798 Small 8 Dime, XF40
JR-3, R.5

917　**1798 Small 8 XF40 PCGS.** JR-3, R.5. This rare *Guide Book* variety is attributed by the large 7 in the date, the missing left foot of the digit 1, and the four berries on the branch. Violet, lilac, and golden-orange patination adheres to remarkably clean surfaces. A small indentation at the outer point of star 8 identifies this particular specimen. Well centered design elements are nicely defined, including the eagle's breast feathers. Population: 1 in 40, 4 finer (8/07). (#4467)

Smooth AU58 1798/97 16 Stars Reverse Dime, JR-1

918　**1798/97 16 Stars on Reverse AU58 NGC.** JR-1, R.3. A late die state with the dies clashed, lapped, and clashed again, especially on the obverse. It is generally believed that this variety represents the first use of the obverse die prior to production of the 13 Stars overdate variety, JR-2. The obverse die has heavy clash marks in the field near Liberty's chin, and an incuse star along Liberty's upper bust line. This die is lightly bulged, and has been heavily lapped. The lowest curl is merely a fragment, the curl near star 1 is almost entirely missing, and the hair curls on top of Liberty's head are similarly fragmented. Although the centers are typically defined, there is little evidence of actual wear on either side. Both sides have brilliant silver color with frosty mint luster. Aside from a few wispy hairlines, the surfaces are exceptional for their quality. (#4468)

Partly Lustrous Choice AU 1800 Dime, JR-1

919　**1800 AU55 PCGS.** JR-1, R.4. On this variety, the obverse shows a die dot over curl #1, another between the 1 and the 8 in the date, and the reverse displays star 12 touching the motto ribbon, but not the eagle's beak. The deliveries of dimes in 1800 were made in two deliveries; 16,760 pieces on March 25, and 5,000 coins on March 26.

　　This Choice AU example displays semi-bright silver-gray surfaces imbued with wisps of light tan, and the retention of luster in the protected areas. Nice definition graces Liberty's hair and drapery and the eagle's wing feathers. Even the often-weak breast of the eagle shows fairly good delineation. The few light marks on the obverse do not distract. Population: 3 in 55, 8 finer (8/07). *From The Beau Clerc Collection.* (#4470)

Popular AU JR-1 1801 Dime

920 **1801 AU50 PCGS.** JR-1, R.4. Mottled orange-red, apple-green, and pearl-gray embrace this attractive representative. The eagle's breast feathers and the right shield border are incomplete, but the strike is generally crisp. Marks are nonexistent, and the eye appeal is undeniable. Struck from a rusted reverse die. Only two varieties are known for the 1801 dime. Both share the same obverse, which has a repunched R in LIBERTY. JR-1 is distinguished by the arrowhead beneath the U in UNITED, which extends past the U for the rare JR-2. Population: 3 in 50, 6 finer (7/07). (#4471)

Good 1802 Dime, Rare JR-4

921 **1802 Good 6 PCGS.** JR-4, R.4. Cream-gray devices contrast slightly with lavender fields. All letters are distinct from the rim save for the CA in AMERICA. Obverse stars 10 to 12 are also partly faded, and a thin mark passes through the 18 in the date. A rare date, since PCGS and NGC combined have certified only 66 examples (8/07). *From The Beau Clerc Collection.* (#4472)

Important AU55 Details 1802 JR-4 Dime

922 **1802—Damaged, Bent—ANACS. AU55 Details.** JR-4, R.4. The JR-4 die combination is the most easily encountered of the four known 1802 varieties. A truly amazing example, this specimen has prooflike fields with only a trace of wear. Minor damage occurs only at the final digit of the date, and it appears that these marks also caused a slight bend. Attractive light blue and iridescent toning is evident on each side. Even after accounting for the minor problems, this example easily qualifies for the Condition Census of the die pair. (#4472)

923 **1803 Good 4 PCGS.** JR-3, R.4. Despite its status as the most available die pairing for the issue, the JR-3 is very scarce in its own right. Though this heavily worn seal-gray and cloud-gray piece is not Condition Census quality, it is a pleasing example of the issue nonetheless. Greatest wear is present at the upper obverse and lower reverse. Population: 1 in 4, 31 finer (8/07). (#4473)

Rare Choice VF 1803 Dime, JR-3

924 **1803 VF35 PCGS.** JR-3, R.4. The 1803 has five die varieties, and all are very scarce to rare, as can be seen by a glance at the third party population data. Gently toned in lilac and autumn-gold with impressive detail on the eagle's wings. The B in LIBERTY is softly defined, as made since the slight die rotation places it opposite the eagle's tail. Population: 4 in 35, 15 finer (8/07). *From The Beau Clerc Collection.* (#4473)

925   **1804 13 Stars on Reverse VF25 PCGS.** JR-1, R.5. Except for the half cent, 1804 is a rare date across all denominations. Although the 1804 cent gets more publicity, the dime is certainly rarer, even though two die marriages are known. These are often separately collected, as they receive separate Guide Book listings due to a different number of stars on the reverse.

The present 13 reverse stars example has medium apricot and steel-gray toning. Careful scrutiny fails to locate remotely mentionable marks. The shield lines are fully separated, and the wings retain substantial plumage. Population: 2 in 25, 8 finer (8/07).
From The Beau Clerc Collection. (#4474)

926   **1807 AU53 PCGS.** JR-1, R.2. A still-lustrous, briefly circulated silver-gray representative of the only die variety for this final Draped Bust dime issue. Well struck and important despite significant abrasions on and around the portrait. (#4480)

BUST DIMES

927   **1814 Large Date AU55 ANACS.** JR-3, R.2. Substantial luster emerges from this attractively detailed pearl-gray Capped Bust dime. The obverse field is heavily clashed, while the reverse has several slender die cracks and small die lumps within the shield.
From The Laguna Niguel Collection, Part Two. (#4488)

Charming JR-1 1814 Small Date Dime MS62

928   **1814 Small Date MS62 NGC.** JR-1, R.3. The sole Small Date variety of the year, and thus requisite for a *Guide Book* collection of the series. This satiny pearl-gray piece has unabraded surfaces and irrefutable eye appeal. Crisply struck aside from portions of the right borders. Struck from clashed dies. (#4489)

929   **1820 Medium 0 MS63 Prooflike NGC.** JR-11, R.3. A flashy and lightly toned representative that has intricate definition on the stars, curls, and plumage. Each side has a few flecks, and a curly lintmark (as made) resides near the N in UNITED. One of only three 1820 dimes certified as Prooflike by NGC (8/07). (#84492)

930   **1824/2 AU58 NGC.** JR-1, R.3. A lushly toned Borderline Uncirculated piece with an olive-green and ocean-blue obverse. Tan-gold and sky-blue embrace the lightly abraded and generally lustrous surfaces. (#4502)

Difficult Near-Gem JR-1 1825 Dime

931   **1825 MS64 PCGS.** JR-1, R.4. Olive and rose shades enrich this satiny and attractive near-Gem. Patience and a strong glass is required to locate a few nearly imperceptible slide marks on the cheek. A good strike overall, despite moderate blending of plumage detail on the eagle's neck. (#4503)

932   **1827 MS63 NGC.** JR-6, R.2. Gorgeous golden-brown, sky-blue, and lime-green shades grace this flashy and nicely struck Capped Bust type coin. (#4504)

Lustrous MS64 JR-12 1829 Dime

933 1829 Medium MS64 PCGS. JR-12, R.3. In addition to the size of the date, this variety is most easily attributed by the two pale gules on the reverse shield—a feature unique to this 1829 variety. The JR reference states that this scarce variety can be found in VF20 or better condition and it mentions that "possibly six pieces exist in MS-60 or better condition." The only finer pieces we have offered at public auction are two MS66 coins and an MS65. The surfaces are exceptionally lustrous and each side has a light coating of gray-lilac toning. A bit softly struck in the usual places for this variety: over the eye and ear and on the eagle's head. (#4511)

934 1833 MS60 NGC. JR-6, R.1. The second S in STATES is directly above the second U in PLURIBUS. Pearl-gray and autumn-gold tints enrich the margins of this boldly impressed and unblemished Capped Bust dime. (#4522)

935 1835 MS63 NGC. JR-8, R.3. Green-gold peripheral toning encircles ocean-blue centers on this lovely later Bust dime. Well-defined with shining luster and minor abrasions that account for the grade.
From The Beau Clerc Collection. (#4527)

Near-Gem JR-9 1835 Dime

936 1835 MS64 NGC. JR-9, R.2. A high A in STATES and a high 5 in the date confirm the die pairing. With uncommonly sharp striking definition that leaves no major feature undefined, this essentially abrasion-free example belongs in a high quality type set. The otherwise silver-gray surfaces exhibit golden peripheral shadings on both sides.
From The Mario Eller Collection, Part One. (#4527)

SEATED DIMES

937 1837 No Stars, Large Date AU58 PCGS. Only a hint of highpoint friction affects the shining surfaces of this silver-white dime. A delightful piece for the grade, eminently suitable for a similarly graded type or date set.
From The Beau Clerc Collection. (#4561)

Pleasing 1838 No Drapery, Large Stars Dime, MS65

938 1838 Large Stars MS65 PCGS. The Large Stars 1838 dime can be distinguished from the Small Stars variety by the fact that the latter, according to Brian Greer (1992): "Always (has) a die crack through the first six stars." This Gem possesses no such crack. Lustrous surfaces display light gold-tan color, are somewhat frosty, and are generally well preserved. Sharply struck throughout. Population: 25 in 65, 14 finer (7/07). (#4568)

Lustrous 1838 Large Stars Dime, MS66

939 1838 Large Stars MS66 NGC. Lustrous surfaces display light to medium gray patina on the obverse, joined by orange-gold on the reverse. Sharply struck on the design elements, and devoid of significant marks. Census: 25 in 66, 9 finer (8/07).
From The Beau Clerc Collection. (#4568)

Dazzling MS67 1838 Large Stars Dime

940 1838 Large Stars MS67 NGC. Fortin-105. A lustrous and precisely struck Superb Gem whose sparkling surfaces display only a hint of gold patina. Stars 9 and 13 are boldly repunched, since stars were added by hand to the working die for this issue. This dazzling coin is virtually perfect. Of interest is the metal flow that is seen around the margins on each side. (#4568)

941 **1839 No Drapery MS64 PCGS.** A wonderfully appealing example of this early Seated dime issue, sharply struck with delicate canary-gold toning over each side. Considerably more appealing than the Choice designation would suggest, and housed in a first-generation holder. Population: 28 in 64, 32 finer (8/07). *From The Beau Clerc Collection.* (#4571)

Conditionally Scarce 1840-O No Drapery Dime AU58

942 **1840-O No Drapery AU58 NGC.** Boldly struck, with considerable satin luster remaining, this coin's most noteworthy characteristic is its multicolored, speckled patina; this is deepest near the reverse periphery, where electric-green and russet shades are observed. Several wispy pinscratches occur on the upper reverse, one of which bisects the O in ONE. Conditionally scarce at this level and rare in Mint State. Census: 5 in 58, 6 finer (8/07). (#4574)

943 **1841 MS64 NGC.** A delightful Choice piece that exhibits strong luster beneath rich olive, green-gold, and juniper patina. Excellent quality for the grade with solid central detail and only a trace of softness on the last star. Census: 18 in 64, 15 finer (8/07). (#4579)

944 **1844 Fine 15 ANACS.** A significantly worn, yet pleasing representative of the "Little Orphan Annie," dolphin-gray on the devices with deeper patina in the fields. Despite the wear, the surfaces show few marks. *From The Beau Clerc Collection.* (#4585)

945 **1849-O AU58 NGC.** Greer-102, Small O. From a heavily rusted obverse die; die rust is especially noticeable on Liberty's breast. "A fairly scarce date that is very scarce in XF or better," according to Greer (1992). Minimally worn on the highpoints of the design, with a moderate layer of cobalt-blue and brownish-gray toning over both sides. *From The Beau Clerc Collection.* (#4592)

946 **1852 MS64 PCGS.** This delicately toned Seated dime exhibits swirling luster and green-gold and turquoise patina over the reverse and at the obverse margins. Crisply struck for the issue with only a few tiny marks that deny a Gem grade. Population: 33 in 64, 19 finer (8/07). (#4597)

947 **1853 Arrows MS64 NGC.** Both sides display an attractive coating of mottled olive, rose, and lilac patina which is clearly original. Boldly struck, if typically soft on the top of Liberty's head, with satiny luster and moderate clash marks on the reverse, beneath ME in DIME. Some shallow pinscratches are noted in the obverse field to the left of stars 11 and 12. In an earlier generation NGC holder. *From The Arnold & Harriet Collection, Part Two.* (#4603)

Exceptional MS67 1854 Arrows Dime

948 **1854 Arrows MS67 NGC.** Rich russet-brown and gunmetal-blue shades are particularly prominent near the margins. The centers are lightly toned. A lustrous and crisply struck Superb Gem that has virtually perfect surfaces. A memorable example of this briefly produced type. Census: 5 in 67, 1 finer (8/07). *From The Beau Clerc Collection.* (#4605)

949 **1854-O Arrows dime AU55 PCGS,** apple-green, russet, and cherry-red toning; **1883 No Cents Liberty nickel MS64 NGC,** lustrous and lightly toned with a precise strike; and an **1885 Morgan dollar MS64 ★ NGC,** beautiful bands of gold, plum-red, and blue-green adorn half the obverse. (Total: 3 coins) (#4606)

Choice 1854-O Arrows Dime

950 **1854-O Arrows MS64 PCGS.** A lustrous example of this short-lived variety that has pleasing dove-gray patina over each side. Well struck save for the lower obverse dentils, and the matte-like surfaces have only a few nearly imperceptible hairlines. Housed in an old green label holder. Population: 13 in 64, 8 finer (8/07). *From The Beau Clerc Collection.* (#4606)

951 **1855 Arrows MS64 PCGS.** Dusky silver-gray and violet shades grace the satiny surfaces of this Arrows near-Gem. Well-defined for the issue with only a few minor flaws in the fields. Population: 9 in 64, 10 finer (8/07). *From The Beau Clerc Collection.* (#4607)

952 **1856-S—Corroded—ANACS. XF40 Details.** A lightly circulated example of this lower-mintage early San Francisco issue, well struck with pleasing rose, gold, and lavender toning. The minor but distinct corrosion that appears on each side is more prevalent on the reverse. *From The Beau Clerc Collection.* (#4613)

953 **1857 MS64 PCGS.** The 1857, a popular type issue, has a mintage in excess of 5.5 million pieces, and no dime issue would match that total until 1875. This well struck near-Gem shows lavender and green-gold toning over softly lustrous surfaces. Population: 39 in 64, 21 finer (8/07). (#4614)

954 **1857 MS65 PCGS.** The stars to the left show a touch of softness, but the devices are bold. This carefully preserved and frosty silver-gray Philadelphia Gem was struck from lightly clashed dies. Population: 19 in 65, 2 finer (8/07). (#4614)

Fully Patinated 1857 Dime MS67

955 **1857 MS67 NGC.** This richly toned example displays competing swirls of deep cobalt-blue and crimson-magenta colors throughout. The features are sharply struck, and the surfaces are distraction-free. As of (7/07), this is the single finest example graded by NGC, and is tied with one other MS67 at PCGS. A perfect candidate for inclusion in an originally toned, Superb Gem quality type set. (#4614)

956 **1859-O MS64 PCGS.** This antebellum dime issue has a mintage of only 480,000 pieces, and this attractively toned near-Gem ranks among the best survivors. The coin is well struck and luminous beneath plum, pink, and peach patina. Population: 30 in 64, 20 finer (8/07). (#4620)

Pleasing 1859-O Dime, MS65

957 **1859-O MS65 NGC.** Pleasing luster radiates from the silver-gray surfaces of this O-mint Gem. The design features are well impressed, except for minor softness in some of the hair at Liberty's head. Close examination reveals no significant marks. Census: 17 in 65, 16 finer (8/07). (#4620)

958 **1862-S XF45 PCGS.** A pleasing, briefly circulated seal-gray example of this early S-mint dime, from an issue that has a surprisingly low survival rate in better grades. The richly patinated surfaces show few marks. Population: 3 in 45, 6 finer (8/07). *From The Beau Clerc Collection.* (#4636)

959 **1864-S MS62 NGC.** While the Civil War raged on the other side of the continent, the distant West Coast states of California and Oregon remained largely unaffected, and San Francisco's dime production remained consistent through those years. This well-defined, modestly abraded piece exhibits subtle luster beneath golden-brown patina. Census: 5 in 62, 12 finer (8/07). (#4640)

Rare MS63 1866-S Dime

960 **1866-S MS63 PCGS.** Like many Seated dimes of the decade, this date is rarely seen in Mint State grades, especially at higher grade levels, as indicated by the current population. Wisps of lilac and gold toning are evident on both sides over brilliant satiny luster. Population: 2 in 63, 4 finer (8/07). *From The Beau Clerc Collection.* (#4644)

Near-Gem 1870-S Seated Dime

961 **1870-S MS64 PCGS.** A remarkable coin that is seldom seen any finer, with just 17 better pieces certified by both NGC and PCGS. The surfaces are mostly brilliant with splashes of peripheral gold and iridescent toning. The lustrous surfaces have reflective fields that are nearly prooflike. Slight design weakness is limited to Liberty's head. Population: 5 in 64, 10 finer (8/07). *From The Beau Clerc Collection.* (#4652)

962 **1873 Arrows MS63 PCGS.** This lovely Select example shows strong detail and lovely luster. This captivating Arrows piece displays enticing peach, blue, and gold peripheral toning, while the centers are silver-gray. Population: 25 in 63, 42 finer (8/07). (#4665)

963 **1873 Arrows MS64 PCGS.** A hint of reflectivity visits the margins of this otherwise satiny silver-white near-Gem. Pleasingly detailed with faint, scattered marks in the fields. An excellent example of the short-lived Arrows design variant. Population: 26 in 64, 16 finer (8/07). (#4665)

964 **1873-S Arrows MS61 NGC.** Softly struck on Liberty's head and the first S in STATES. Lustrous and essentially untoned, with a few wispy hairlines in the fields, and a small scrape near the lower reverse rim, just to the left of the mintmark. A relatively scarce date with an original mintage of 455,000 pieces. *From The Beau Clerc Collection.* (#4667)

Scarce 1874-S Arrows Dime, MS64

965 **1874-S Arrows MS64 PCGS.** The 1874-S with Arrows dime, from a mintage of 240,000 pieces, is scarce in all grades. Light golden-gray patination is accented with hints of violet and blue, and rests on well preserved surfaces dancing with luster. The design elements are sharply struck, except for the usual softness on Liberty's head. Population: 10 in 64, 4 finer (8/07). (#4670)

966 **1875-CC Mintmark Above Bow MS64 PCGS.** The mintmark appears within the wreath. This solidly struck, luminous Choice piece shows rich peach, amethyst, and pink patina over both sides. A delightful example of Carson City minor silver. Population: 41 in 64, 28 finer (7/07). (#4673)

967 **1875-CC Mintmark Below Bow MS65 PCGS.** A frosty silver-gray that exhibits delicate tan accents on the obverse. The well-defined devices and luminous fields are equally clean. The Mintmark Below variant is slightly more elusive than the Mintmark Above. Population: 7 in 65, 1 finer (8/07).
From The Beau Clerc Collection. (#4674)

968 **1876 MS66 NGC.** Type One Reverse. The silver-white surfaces exhibit touches of light tan color and frosty luster. A shimmering and well-preserved Premium Gem, boldly struck save for the usual softness on a few cereal grains on the upper left wreath. A lovely type piece. Census: 22 in 66, 4 finer (7/07). (#4679)

Dynamic Superb Gem 1876 Dime

969 **1876 MS67 NGC.** Type One Reverse. A lustrous and lightly toned Superb Gem with refreshingly mark-free fields and devices. The strike is precise, even on the upper left cereal grains. A wonderful souvenir from our centennial year. Struck from prominently clashed dies. Census: 4 in 67, 0 finer (7/07). (#4679)

Low Mintage MS67 ★ 1879 Dime

970 **1879 MS67 ★ NGC.** The lower loop of the 8 is widely repunched. Golden-brown and cobalt-blue perimeters frame the brilliant fields and devices. Lustrous and nicely struck with clean surfaces. A low mintage date because of heavy Morgan dollar production. Census: 7 in 67 ★, 3 finer as MS68 without a star, and 1 finer as MS68 Prooflike ★ (8/07).
From The Beau Clerc Collection. (#4687)

971 **1882 MS65 PCGS.** Great luster blossoms through light blue patination that has admixtures of rose coloration in the centers. The design features are well struck up, and just one minute mark is noted, to the left of Liberty's head. (#4690)

972 **1882 MS65 PCGS.** The surfaces of this enticing Gem are lavender, plum, and green-gold with a silver-white center. Crisply struck with incredible quality for the grade, and housed in a first-generation holder.
From The Beau Clerc Collection. (#4690)

973 **1882 MS66 NGC.** Lustrous and exquisitely preserved, this Premium Gem Seated dime is also well struck and pleasingly toned in hues of sea-green, gold, and silver-gray. Distracting marks are nonexistent. Most of the design motifs are well defined, except for parts of the reverse wreath. (#4690)

974 **1885 MS65 PCGS.** This satiny Gem is well struck with luminous green-gold and lavender shades that drape the surfaces. Carefully preserved, as demanded of the grade, and a great example of this later Seated dime issue. Population: 39 in 65, 28 finer (8/07).
From The Beau Clerc Collection. (#4694)

Elusive 1885-S Ten Cent, AU50

975 **1885-S AU50 NGC.** Discussing the 1885-S dime in his Seated Liberty dime reference, Brian Greer says it is "The key to the San Francisco seated dimes and rarer than its mintage (43,690 pieces) indicates. Light gray patina graces both faces of this AU50 specimen, and good definition characterizes the design features. A couple of minor marks occur beneath the second 8 of the date.
From The Beau Clerc Collection. (#4695)

976 **1886 MS65 Prooflike NGC.** This Gem offers moderately reflective fields with thin layers of cloud-gray patina punctuated by occasional dabs of charcoal toning. Well-defined overall, though softness is present on Liberty's head. Census: 2 in 65 Prooflike, 1 finer (7/07).

977 **1886 MS66 PCGS.** This well struck Premium Gem exhibits vibrant luster and colorful patina. Green-gold patina graces the margins, while the centers have opaque cloud-gray toning. The reverse shows a greater proportion of the latter. Population: 29 in 66, 7 finer (8/07). (#4696)

978 **1886 MS66 PCGS.** This sharply struck Premium Gem is fully patinated in golden-brown and aquamarine shades. Exceptionally preserved, and housed in a green label holder. Population: 29 in 66, 7 finer (8/07).
Ex: November Palm Beach Signature (Heritage, 11/04), lot 6228. (#4696)

Richly Toned Superb Gem 1889 Dime

979 **1889 MS67 NGC.** Electric-blue borders encompass the orange-red centers. Highly lustrous and precisely struck. Even the aid of a loupe fails to locate any abrasions. An exceptional Superb Gem silver type coin. Struck from lightly clashed dies. Census: 6 in 67, 0 finer (8/07). (#4702)

980 **1890-S MS64 NGC.** An attractive near-Gem with sea-green, rose, and amber toning over both sides. Boldly struck and free of distracting marks. A better date in the Seated dime series, with a mintage of 1.4 million pieces. Census: 20 in 64, 20 finer (8/07). *From The Beau Clerc Collection.* (#4705)

981 **1891-O MS66 NGC.** Greer-106 obverse with repunched 189; and Greer-107 reverse with repunched mintmark. A lustrous and untoned Premium Gem example combining two different varieties. Clash marks are noticeable on the upper obverse, but post-striking marks are nonexistent on both sides.
From The Beau Clerc Collection. (#4707)

PROOF SEATED DIMES

Gem Proof 1837 No Stars Dime

982 **1837 No Stars PR65 PCGS.** Large Date. A key proof subtype, since the No Stars Liberty Seated design was only struck in proof during 1837. In his 1988 Encyclopedia, Breen states "some 30 brilliant proofs [were] struck for presentation to Treasury officials and other VIPs" on June 30, 1837. Those proofs can be identified by a die line from a denticle above the left half of the first T in STATES, and also by recutting on the base of the 7 in the date. Mark Borckardt adds that all proofs he has seen have an identical die rotation of 200 degrees, slightly clockwise from coin turn.
This lovely Gem has dusky powder-blue, yellow-green, and plum-mauve toning. The strike is penetrating, even on Liberty's hair and the dentils. Careful rotation under a light fails to locate grade-limiting imperfections. Population: 2 in 65, 1 finer (8/07). (#4718)

983 **1859 PR64 NGC.** This white near-Gem proof dime exhibits well struck design elements. A few wispy field marks visible under magnification define the grade. (#4748)

984 **1859 PR64 PCGS.** Delicate champagne tints visit the steel-gray surfaces of this Choice specimen, from the last of the official proof dime issues with stars on the obverse. Faint hairlines in the fields account for the grade.
From The Beau Clerc Collection. (#4748)

Brilliant Cameo PR66 1859 Dime

985 **1859 PR66 Cameo NGC.** The With Stars type is only really available in two years, 1858 and 1859; otherwise, it is rarely seen in earlier years. Only 800 proofs were struck, but far fewer have survived. In all grades and from both services around 200 pieces have been certified, both as Cameo and non-Cameo. This number helps confirm that numerous proofs remained unsold at year's end and were probably melted, as in 1860. This is a spectacular coin that has deeply reflective fields. The devices display a strong overlay of mint frost which gives the coin its cameo contrast. Census: 3 in 66, 5 finer (8/07). (#84748)

Superb Cameo Gem Proof 1860 Dime

986 **1860 PR67 Cameo NGC.** Brilliant surfaces, sharp design details, and excellent contrast result in a high degree of aesthetic appeal. This Superb Gem is a visual treat for the connoisseur. Only a few finer pieces have been certified over the years. Census: 3 in 67, 4 finer (8/07).
From The Beau Clerc Collection. (#84753)

987 **1863 PR62 Cameo NGC.** Ice-white devices rise above the darkly mirrored fields, with contrast that approaches an Ultra Cameo designation. Faint handling marks preclude a finer grade. Just 14,000 business strikes and 460 proofs were produced. (#4756)

988 **1864 PR64 PCGS.** A richly patinated Choice survivor from this wartime proof issue of only 470 dimes. Dusky violet, gold, and rose shades grace the luminous surfaces of this crisply struck, faintly hairlined specimen. Population: 39 in 64, 21 finer (8/07).
From The Beau Clerc Collection. (#4757)

989 **1864 PR65 NGC.** Vibrant gold and orange patina graces both sides of this carefully preserved and attractive Gem proof, boldly struck with strong reflectivity. Only 470 specimens were coined for this Civil War year. Census: 23 in 65, 17 finer (8/07). (#4757)

990 **1864 PR65 Cameo NGC.** Brilliant and well struck with pleasing contrast between the frosty devices and deep mirrored fields. Only 470 proofs were struck, and the business strikes from this date are also very elusive. Census: 7 in 65 Cameo, 10 finer (8/07). (#84757)

Brilliant PR66 Cameo 1864 Dime

991 **1864 PR66 Cameo PCGS.** An important Civil War date with a low mintage for both business strikes and proofs. Only 11,000 coins were struck for circulation purposes, and 470 proofs were produced. Undoubtedly because of the low production run of proofs, a higher percentage of the remaining population show some degree of contrast. This is a brilliant coin that has strong contrast between the deeply reflective fields and the frosted devices. Essentially defect-free except for a couple of squiggly lint marks that were struck into the obverse at the time of manufacture. Population: 5 in 66 Cameo, 2 finer (8/07). (#84757)

992 **1865 PR64 NGC.** Richly toned over both sides in layers of deep, multicolored iridescence. Sharply struck and free of bothersome marks or hairlines. From a low mintage of 500 pieces.
From The Beau Clerc Collection. (#4758)

Iridescently Toned PR68 1866 Dime

993 **1866 PR68 NGC.** This remarkable representative offers sun-gold, ruby-red, and blue-green swaths, and the reverse has similar peripheral colors that surround an untoned center. Alertly struck and unblemished. A mere 725 proofs were struck, along with only 8,000 business strikes. Census: 2 in 68, 0 finer (8/07). (#4759)

994 **1867 PR64 Cameo PCGS.** A low total mintage date with only 6,000 business strikes produced along with 625 proofs. This is a sparkling, deeply mirrored proof with significant, contrasting mint frost over the devices. Lightly and evenly toned. Population: 9 in 64 Cameo, 3 finer (8/07). (#84760)

Deep Cameo PR65 1868 Dime
Blundered Date, Breen-3345

995 **1868 PR65 Deep Cameo PCGS.** Breen-3345. Blundered Date. Discovered by Walter in 1965, the bottom of the 1 in the date was first mispunched far too high and can be seen just right of the shield point. All proofs struck from these dies show die rust in the central drapery. This is a brilliant coin that also has several stray die polishing lines in the fields. The mint frost is unbelievably thick and contrasts sharply against the illimitable depth of reflectivity in the fields. Brilliant throughout. (#94761)

Impressive 1869 Seated Dime, PR66 Cameo

996 **1869 PR66 Cameo NGC.** A borderline Ultra Cameo example, this Premium Gem proof has exceptional contrast with brilliant silver surfaces. There are no contact marks or other imperfections of any significance on either side. Census: 7 in 66, 0 finer (8/07). *From The Beau Clerc Collection.* (#84762)

997 **1872 PR66 Cameo NGC.** The gleaming fields and richly frosted, boldly struck devices of this Premium Gem contribute to its spectacular eye appeal. A minimally toned representative of this pre-metric proof dime issue. Census: 7 in 66 Cameo, 4 finer (8/07). (#84765)

998 **1873 No Arrows PR65 Cameo NGC.** An enticing Gem specimen from an issue of 1,100 pieces. This faintly hazy example sports strong contrast and the Closed 3 logotype, like all No Arrows proofs for the year. Census: 1 in 65 Cameo, 4 finer (8/07). (#84766)

999 **1873 Arrows PR63 NGC.** One of just 800 specimens struck for the initial issue of this short-lived type. Vivid blue-green and violet patina graces both sides of this lightly hairlined Select representative. Census: 20 in 63, 55 finer (8/07). (#4769)

Superb Cameo Proof 1873 Arrows Dime

1000 **1873 Arrows PR67 Cameo NGC.** Both sides of this Superb Gem proof have exceptional contrast and full mint brilliance with no indication of toning. This piece represents the first of two years that saw arrows added to the obverse design. Two examples have been graded PR67 Cameo by NGC, this piece and another that carries a ★. None have received a higher grade. (#84769)

1001 **1874 Arrows PR64 PCGS.** Dusky emerald-green and rose-gray toning drapes this suitably struck and mark-free proof type coin. Housed in a first generation holder. A mere 700 proofs were struck. (#4770)

Conditionally Scarce 1874 Arrows
Seated PR64 Cameo Dime

1002 **1874 Arrows PR64 Cameo NGC.** A relatively small number of survivors from this issue have been certified with Cameo contrast, by the two major services, from an original production of just 700 pieces. This near-Gem is boldly struck with intense reflectivity in the fields and substantial mint frost on the devices. A curiously large lint mark (as struck) resides in the left obverse field, and snakes around each side of the first S in STATES. Census: 2 in 64 Cameo, 5 finer (8/07). (#84770)

1003 **1875 PR66 NGC.** Gorgeous electric-blue, turquoise-green, and reddish-amber toning graces the exquisitely preserved surfaces of this Premium Gem proof. Sharply struck, as expected, with just a bit of typical weakness noted on Liberty's hair detail. One of only 700 proofs struck. Census: 15 in 66, 3 finer (7/07). (#4772)

1004 **1875 PR66 NGC.** The 1875 is one of the larger production dates in the Seated dime series with more than 10 million circulation strikes minted. However, only 700 proofs were struck. This is an attractively toned example that has irregular patches of deep russet and blue toning interspersed with brilliance on the obverse, while the reverse has a rich blue center that is surrounded by pale golden peripheral color. Census: 16 in 66, 3 finer (8/07). (#4772)

1005 **1875 PR64 Cameo PCGS.** Light tan-gray toning visits this precisely struck and unmarked near-Gem. The devices are evenly frosted. Only 700 proofs were struck. Population: 9 in 64 Cameo, 9 finer (7/07). (#84772)

Colorful Superb Gem Proof 1876 Dime

1006 **1876 PR67 NGC.** Type One Reverse. Fortin-103. The D and E in DIME are die doubled. This Centennial-year Superb Gem offers lavish cobalt-blue, caramel-gold, and plum-red patina. The flashy fields are unabraded, and the strike is intricate throughout. Census: 3 in 67, 1 finer (8/07). (#4773)

1007 **1878 PR65 Cameo PCGS.** Type Two Reverse. An impressive proof example with stark contrast seen between the deeply mirrored fields and thickly frosted devices. Mostly brilliant with light golden toning seen around the margins. Population: 5 in 65 Cameo, 1 finer (8/07). (#84775)

1008 **1879 PR64 PCGS.** Well struck with pleasing original toning, nicely reflective fields, and carefully preserved surfaces. The sky-blue reverse peripheral coloration is especially attractive. A near-Gem proof example of this low total mintage issue. (#4776)

1009 **1879 PR63 Deep Cameo PCGS.** Unfathomably deep mirrors in the fields. The dies were overpolished as there are certain lowpoints in the gown that are missing. Starkly contrasted between the deeply reflective fields and the heavily frosted devices. A few light contact marks account for the grade. Lightly toned. (#94776)

1010 **1880 PR65 PCGS.** Deep gold-green and dusky jade patina drapes the luminous surfaces of this attentively struck Gem. An attractive, carefully preserved exemplar of this comparatively available issue. Population: 43 in 65, 35 finer (8/07).
From The Beau Clerc Collection. (#4777)

1011 **1880 PR65 Cameo PCGS.** The practically untoned fields and richly frosted devices of this Gem create dramatic contrast. A boldly struck and wonderfully well-preserved representative of this later Seated dime issue. Population: 15 in 65 Cameo, 15 finer (8/07). (#84777)

Appealing 1881 Dime, PR66

1012 **1881 PR66 PCGS.** Golden-gray centers are framed by cobalt-blue, lavender, and yellow-gold toning at the margins. An attentive strike leaves well defined devices, enhancing the coin's eye appeal. Both faces have been well cared for. Population: 10 in 66, 4 finer (8/07).
From The Beau Clerc Collection. (#4778)

1013 **1882 PR65 Cameo NGC.** Essentially untoned with vibrant luster and exquisite contrast. The reverse of this carefully preserved later Gem shows exceptional frost on the devices. Census: 13 in 65 Cameo, 29 finer (8/07).
From The Mario Eller Collection, Part One. (#84779)

1014 **1885 PR64 Cameo PCGS.** Vibrant champagne patina with orange and rose tints graces the shining surfaces of this Choice specimen. The moderately frosted devices of this late-date piece contrast strongly with the fields despite a layer of toning. Population: 13 in 64 Cameo, 27 finer (8/07). (#84782)

Dazzling PR67 Ultra Cameo 1885 Dime

1015 **1885 PR67 Ultra Cameo NGC.** Remarkable white-on-black contrast characterizes this magnificent Superb Gem. The stone-white surfaces are unabraded, and the strike is good despite minor blending on the left-side wheat grains. A mere 930 proofs were struck. Census: 2 in 67 Ultra Cameo, 0 finer (7/07). (#94782)

Impressive PR67 1887 Dime

1016 **1887 PR67 NGC.** Struck from overpolished dies with incomplete detailing on the drapery near the shield. This is found on a minority of proof 1887 dimes. The surfaces on this piece are deeply reflective in the fields, no doubt from the overzealous repolishing, and there is a slight overlay of mint frost on the devices. The reverse is more toned than the obverse with dusky cinnamon color in the center that deepens to a bright blue at the margin. The obverse is brilliant over most of that side with a couple of thin rings of color present at the periphery. Census: 7 in 67, 0 finer (8/07). (#4784)

BARBER DIMES

1017 **1892-S MS63 PCGS.** A needle-sharp first-year Barber dime with untoned centers and light honey-gold patina near the rims. Marks are minimal, and the eye appeal is undeniable. Population: 21 in 63, 34 finer (8/07). (#4798)

1018 **1893-O MS64 PCGS.** An enticing silver-gray near-Gem, satiny with elements of violet at the margins. Unusually sharply struck for this early New Orleans issue and carefully preserved for the grade. Population: 25 in 64, 16 finer (8/07). (#4801)

Attractively Toned 1894 Dime, MS66

1019 **1894 MS66 NGC.** Invigorating luster issues from somewhat frosty surfaces of this Premium Gem dime. Delicate lilac and powder-blue patina dominates the obverse, yielding to orange-gold at the margins, while reddish-gold and lime-green accent powder-blue toning on the reverse. Well struck, with no significant marks. Census: 7 in 66, 3 finer (7/07).
From The Arnold & Harriet Collection, Part Two. (#4803)

1020 **1896 MS65 PCGS.** A crisply struck silver-white Gem that offers a hint of reflectivity in the fields. The unmarked devices show a hint of frost as well. Population: 12 in 65, 9 finer (7/07). (#4809)

Sharply Struck 1897 Dime, MS67

1021 **1897 MS67 NGC.** Whispers of cobalt-blue, rose, and apple-green bathe the obverse, while the reverse is primarily lilac and powder-blue. A powerful strike manifests itself in sharp delineation on the design elements, with no areas revealing hints of softness. Close examination shows no significant marks. This Superb Gem ranks among the finest certified. Census: 5 in 67, 0 finer (8/07). (#4812)

1022 **1903 MS65 PCGS.** Flynn RPD-002. Repunching on the 1 in the date is plain under magnification. Strongly lustrous with above-average detail. Delicate sea-green, golden-brown, and purple-red toning hugs the obverse and reverse borders, while the centers are untoned. Population: 16 in 65, 9 finer (8/07). (#4830)

1023 **1903-O MS64 PCGS.** The satiny surfaces of this New Orleans minor are largely silver-gray with elements of forest-green and sky-blue. Pleasingly detailed for the issue with only small, shallow flaws on each side. (#4831)

1024 **1904 MS65 NGC.** This lustrous and exactingly struck Gem has pearl-gray centers and sparkling sea-green borders. A carefully preserved representative of this conditionally challenging issue. Census: 8 in 65, 7 finer (8/07). (#4833)

1025 **1906-O MS66 NGC.** Uncommonly well-defined for this New Orleans issue. On this satiny representative, deep russet peripheral patina frames untoned centers. Census: 13 in 66, 7 finer (8/07). (#4840)

Lovely Gem 1907-D Barber Dime

1026 **1907-D MS65 NGC.** The '07-D is much a much scarcer issue than its mintage of more than 4 million pieces would indicate. Only 12 pieces have been certified as Gems by NGC (8/07), with another nine in higher grades. Brilliant and sharply struck with frosty, untoned surfaces. (#4843)

1027 **1908-O MS65 PCGS.** Sharply struck with intense luster and gorgeous deep red-brown and cobalt-blue peripheral toning on both sides. A few wispy slide marks are noted on Liberty's cheek and neck, but these are not obvious or distracting. (#4848)

1028 **1908-O MS66 NGC.** Consistently well-defined with radiant, frosty luster and delicate, widely scattered specks of toning about the peripheral devices. A delightful, carefully preserved representative from the waning years of the New Orleans Mint. Census: 12 in 66, 3 finer (8/07). (#4848)

1029 **1909-D MS64 PCGS.** This lovely Choice dime hails from an issue of under 1 million pieces. Amber, orange, sea-green, and cerulean peripheral toning surrounds silver-gray centers. Well-defined with few marks on the satiny obverse, though a wispy abrasion is noted within the wreath. Population: 18 in 64, 17 finer (8/07). (#4851)

Lower Mintage 1910-S Dime, MS66

1030 **1910-S MS66 PCGS.** Only 1.2 million pieces were struck of the 1910-S, thus making it a scarcer, late-date issue in the Barber dime series. It is also a challenging issue to locate in MS66 condition. This is a lovely, immaculate example that has speckled russet toning over each side that brightens to light blue at the margins. Sharply defined throughout. Population: 8 in 66, 2 finer (8/07). (#4856)

Dazzling MS67 1911 Dime

1031 **1911 MS67 NGC.** A superlative example that is essentially mark-free, with thick, snow-white mint frost—a beautiful Superb Gem representative of the Barber dime and an obvious type coin candidate. The strike is boldly defined, and the surfaces offer no hint of even the palest patina. Census: 11 in 67, 2 finer (8/07). (#4857)

1032 **1911-S MS65 PCGS.** An exceptionally pleasing, late-date Barber dime. The surfaces are nicely frosted and each side is covered with rose-gray and sea-green toning. Sharply struck. (#4859)

1033 **1911-S MS66 NGC.** Boldly struck with intense mint frost over snow-white surfaces. Some wispy marks near Liberty's mouth are only noticeable with the aid of a magnifier. An impressive and conditionally scarce Premium Gem. Census: 24 in 66, 4 finer (7/07). (#4859)

1034 **1912 MS66 PCGS.** Delicate gold and tan accents grace the margins of this frosty Premium Gem, while the centers are largely untoned. A pleasingly delineated and attractive example of this later Barber dime issue. Population: 42 in 66, 4 finer (8/07). (#4860)

Satiny MS66 1912-D Barber Dime

1035 **1912-D MS66 PCGS.** One of the more obtainable mintmarked Barber dimes, and occasionally available in high grade also—good news for the type collector. This is a remarkably clean coin that has thick, satiny mint luster. Much original brilliance remains with a swath of deep golden at the bottom of the obverse and on the lower rim of the reverse. Well struck. Population: 15 in 66, 0 finer (8/07). (#4861)

1036 **1914 MS66 NGC.** Sharply struck and highly lustrous, with attractive ivory-gold coloration and well preserved, abrasion-free surfaces. A lovely Premium Gem that seems entirely worthy of the grade. Census: 29 in 66, 1 finer (8/07). (#4865)

1037 **1916 MS65 NGC.** This lustrous Gem is sharply struck, since only a few of the upper grain kernels lack full definition. Lightly toned aside from a smattering of russet toning on the right obverse field. (#4870)

1038 **1916 MS66 PCGS.** A shining and solidly struck example of this final Barber dime issue, predominantly silver-white with a touch of champagne toning on the obverse. Beautifully preserved and undeniably appealing. Population: 35 in 66, 5 finer (7/07). (#4870)

1039 **1916 MS66 PCGS.** The shining surfaces of this predominantly silver-white Barber dime show hints of ice-blue at the margins. A well-defined and carefully preserved Premium Gem, possibly saved as a souvenir of the design's final year. Population: 36 in 66, 5 finer (8/07). (#4870)

1040 **1916 MS66 NGC.** This piece's satiny and lustrous surfaces exhibit gorgeous sky-blue and gold patina. The sharp strike is particularly noteworthy on the reverse wreath. A lovely example from the Barber design's finale. Census: 35 in 66, 7 finer (8/07). (#4870)

1041 **1916 MS66 PCGS.** The "25-year rule" laid out in 1890 largely ensured the survival of the Barber design until 1916, though Mint officials wasted little time in scrapping it once change no longer required Congressional approval. This final-year piece has vibrant luster and dappled orange and amber toning over the obverse. The reverse shows elements of magenta and cerulean as well. Population: 36 in 66, 5 finer (8/07). (#4870)

PROOF BARBER DIMES

1042 **1893 PR66 Cameo NGC.** The essentially untoned obverse shows the wonderful contrast for which early proof Barber dimes are known, while the reverse displays just a touch of milky haze within the wreath. One of just 792 specimens coined. Census: 12 in 66 Cameo, 17 finer (7/07). (#84877)

1043 **1894 PR65 Cameo NGC.** While the obverse shows layers of rich violet, blue, rose, and champagne patina, both it and the less overtly toned reverse show significant contrast. Strongly detailed with the careful preservation required of a Gem. Census: 5 in 65 Cameo, 27 finer (8/07). (#84878)

1044 **1895 PR64 PCGS.** The obverse exhibits a measure of silver-gray patina, while the reverse is gold-toned with splashes of cobalt-blue. This crisply struck early Barber proof shows a number of light hairlines that account for the grade. (#4879)

Lovely PR67 ★ Cameo 1896 Dime

1045 **1896 PR67 ★ Cameo NGC.** Gold, rose-red, and cobalt-blue enrich the peripheries of this exactingly struck Superb Gem. Icy motifs contrast with the seamless mirrored fields. As of (8/07), NGC has awarded star designations to three proof 1896 dimes, two as PR66 ★ Cameo and the present piece as the single finest. (#84880)

Ultra Cameo PR66 1896 Dime

1046 1896 PR66 Ultra Cameo NGC. A flashy and faintly toned Premium Gem with obvious contrast between the pearl-gray devices and the glassy fields. A wonderful souvenir from the year of William Jennings Bryan's famous "Cross of Gold" convention speech. A scant 762 pieces were struck. Census: 1 in 66 Ultra Cameo, 1 finer (8/07). (#94880)

1047 1897 PR66 PCGS. The dusky green-gold and turquoise patina that graces both sides of this earlier Barber proof dime is thin enough to show the coin's excellent reflectivity. Sharply struck with great eye appeal. Population: 28 in 66, 16 finer (8/07). (#4881)

1048 1901 PR66 PCGS. The depth of toning (jade green, rose-golden, and yellow) somewhat subdues the thick mint frost on the devices. But it cannot suppress the unfathomable depth of mirrored reflectivity in the fields. An exceptional, high grade proof Barber dime. Population: 21 in 66, 5 finer (8/07). (#4885)

White 1901 Dime, PR66 Cameo

1049 1901 PR66 Cameo NGC. The 1901 dime comes from a mintage of 813 pieces, a relatively large number that apparently have survived, judging from the several hundred certified by NGC and PCGS. Fewer than 50 examples have received the Cameo classification. This white Premium Gem is crisply struck and possesses well preserved surfaces. Census: 8 in 66 Cameo, 7 finer (8/07). (#84885)

Superb Gem Proof 1904 Dime

1050 1904 PR67 NGC. Beautiful ruby-red, apple-green, and gold consume the obverse. The reverse is fully toned as well, in aquamarine shades. Sharply struck save for a couple of the uppermost cereal grains. Only 670 proofs were struck, few of which have survived in such exemplary quality. Census: 8 in 67, 1 finer (8/07). (#4888)

1051 1904 PR65 Cameo NGC. A gleaming, essentially untoned proof with distinct contrast on each side, though the reverse has stronger frost on the devices. Cameo examples are far less common for 20th century Barber issues than their 19th century counterparts. Census: 2 in 65 Cameo, 8 finer (8/07). (#84888)

1052 1907 PR65 NGC. One of just 575 specimens coined. The surfaces are modestly reflective beneath moderate mauve, aqua, and orange patina. This well struck Gem is housed in a former generation holder. Census: 33 in 65, 48 finer (8/07). (#4891)

1053 1910 PR65 PCGS. Both sides show an appealing blend of blue, orange, and lavender toning. This luminous and carefully preserved Gem is housed in a first-generation PCGS holder. One of just 551 specimens struck. (#4894)

1054 1911 PR65 NGC. By 1911, collectors were largely disenchanted with the Barber design, and the proof dime issue for the year amounted to just 543 specimens. This Gem has strong reflectivity, traces of golden patina at the margins, and surprisingly heavy contrast for a piece not awarded the Cameo designation. Census: 48 in 65, 47 finer (7/07). (#4895)

1055 1914 PR66 NGC. A lovely specimen of this late-date proof Barber issue, boldly impressed with thin layers of amber-gold, violet, and tan patina. One of the most carefully preserved survivors from a mintage of only 425 pieces. Census: 18 in 66, 10 finer (8/07). (#4898)

MERCURY DIMES

MS68 ★ Full Bands 1916 Mercury Dime

1056 1916 MS68 ★ Full Bands NGC. A fully brilliant Superb Gem with invigorating cartwheel luster. Although the obverse peripheral legends are lack an absolute strike, the centers have bold definition. An attractively preserved example of this popular first-year issue. Population: 14 in 68, 0 finer (7/07). (#4905)

1057 1916-D AG3 ANACS. This example seems conservatively graded at the current grade level. The surfaces are evenly worn and lack noticeable marks. A certified example of this key date is always preferable, since many '16-Ds are counterfeit. (#4906)

1058 1916-D Good 4 PCGS. A nice, original example of this key date, with evenly worn light-gray surfaces that are abrasion-free. (#4906)

1059 1916-D—Scratched—ANACS. Good 4 Details. A cream-gray example of this enormously popular series key. A reverse pinscratch at 10:30 confirms the ANACS assessment. The reverse legends are clear despite minor fading into the rim. (#4906)

1060 1916-D Good 4 ANACS. The date and mintmark are free from the rim, although the tops of AMERICA are partly blended into the border. An ivory-gray example of this coveted collector key. (#4906)

1061 1916-D—Cleaned, Scratched—ANACS. VG8 Details. All peripheral letters are distinct from the rim. This key date dime is somewhat bright, although the piece is toned cream-gray and lilac. A hair-thin horizontal mark is noted on the upper neck. (#4906)

1062 1916-D—Corroded, Tooled, Cleaned—ANACS. XF40 Details. A sharp example of this famous key date. Selected areas have dark deposits, which were likely more extensive prior to a harsh cleaning. Granular and abraded, but very scarce above the VG level. (#4906)

1916-D Dime XF45 Details

1063 **1916-D—Whizzed—ANACS. XF45 Details.** This brilliant key date dime has bold design detail, but has a bright, granular, monochrome surface from whizzing. Given that the majority of survivors of this issue are in VG or lower grades, the present piece provides an affordable substitute to those who prefer greater design detail. (#4906)

AU50 Sharpness 1916-D Dime

1064 **1916-D—Whizzed—ANACS. AU50 Details.** A deceptively lustrous key date dime that has light gold toning and only a trace of highpoint wear. The surfaces are bright, but less granular than expected. The lowest mintage issue of the series, one-fourth that of its closest competitor, the 1921-D. (#4906)

Important Key Date MS62 1916-D Mercury Dime

1065 **1916-D MS62 ANACS.** Lustrous and boldly struck, with minor weakness on the fasces and the central reverse bands. This is still an important and conditionally scarce representative of the unquestioned key date in the Mercury dime series. Deep purple, rose, golden-brown and cobalt-blue patina adorns the reverse and the upper half of the obverse. Just one or two tiny contact marks are revealed on each side, under careful inspection. (#4906)

Lustrous 1916-D Mercury, MS62 Full Bands

1066 **1916-D MS62 Full Bands PCGS.** Wispy gold toning on the obverse does little to diminish the brilliant silver surfaces of this frosty Mint State piece. The design elements are sharp, except for the highpoints of the obverse that are slightly blunt. All reverse details, including the central bands, are crisp.

The 1916-D Mercury dime is coveted as a key date issue in all grades. This piece, near the lower end of the Mint State scale, provides an excellent opportunity for the specialist to acquire an attractive coin at a price level more reasonable than other higher grade coins. (#4907)

Brilliant 1916-D Dime
MS63 Full Bands

1067 **1916-D MS63 Full Bands NGC.** The key date to the Mercury dime series, the 1916-D dime is an issue that is in demand in AG or Mint State—and everything in between, as long as the mintmark is visible and the authenticity is certain. Recent price surges for this issue obviously reflect that ceaseless demand, and show no sign of diminution. Mint State examples are certainly difficult to locate, which is why we are pleased to offer no less than four different examples in the present sale.

This specimen has a well executed strike and satiny silver luster, with brilliant surfaces complemented by a hint of champagne toning. The all-important central bands are fully split (as are the top and bottom horizontal bands), although the lower diagonal joins the nearby olive leaf, as often seen. A couple of ticks on each band likely help determine the grade, but this piece seems high-end, and there is no doubt at all about its eye appeal. (#4907)

1068 **1917 MS66 Full Bands PCGS.** A shining and sharply struck representative of this popular second-year issue, carefully preserved with wonderful visual appeal. Though Premium Gems are available for a price, better Full Bands examples are hard to come by; PCGS has graded only 13 finer Full Bands pieces (8/07). (#4911)

1069 **1917-S MS64 Full Bands PCGS.** Delicate champagne and ice-blue tints visit the shining surfaces of this decisively struck Choice piece. While the left obverse field shows a faint luster break, the devices are clean overall. (#4915)

1070 **1917-S MS65 Full Bands PCGS.** A boldly impressed Gem representative of this early S-mint dime, predominantly silver-white with hints of gold at the right obverse and reverse. Carefully preserved and delightful. (#4915)

1071 **1917-S MS66 Full Bands PCGS.** A conditionally scarce issue in MS66 grade with only 58 pieces so graded and 10 finer (8/07). This is a dazzling, brilliant coin that has thickly frosted mint luster. A lovely example of this second-year S-mint. (#4915)

1072 **1918 MS65 Full Bands PCGS.** Well struck with just a touch of peripheral fadeaway in spots, with soft, frosty mint luster and ice-blue surfaces that show trace amounts of apricot color on each side. Surface blemishes are nonexistent. Conditionally scarce and highly attractive. (#4917)

1073 **1918 MS66 Full Bands PCGS.** A special coin that shows thick mint frost and hardly any patina. The combination of high grade and bold detail is surprisingly elusive for this early P-mint issue, and Full Bands examples remain underrated. Population: 33 in 66 Full Bands, 4 finer (7/07). (#4917)

1074 **1918 MS66 Full Bands PCGS.** This high mintage P-mint dime seems underrepresented at the MS66 grade level with only 34 coins certified by PCGS and four finer (8/07). The matte-like surfaces are mostly brilliant with just a hint of color present. The central bands are deep struck. (#4917)

1075 **1919 MS67 Full Bands NGC.** An essentially untoned, decisively struck Superb Gem example of this early Philadelphia issue. The fields and devices are exquisitely preserved. Census: 3 in 67 Full Bands, 0 finer (7/07). (#4923)

Choice Full Bands 1919-D Dime

1076 **1919-D MS64 Full Bands PCGS.** Delicate chestnut toning graces this lustrous and beautifully preserved near-Gem. Hair-thin obverse die cracks are noted at 6, 7, and 12 o'clock, but no abrasions are visible. The centers are needle-sharp. The 1919-D is a famous conditional rarity, common in circulated grades but non-collectible as a Superb Gem. Population: 65 in 64, 18 finer (8/07). (#4925)

1077 **1919-S MS66 PCGS.** The attractive surfaces combine russet with lemon-yellow and jade-green on the obverse, while the reverse offers a consistent light gold patina. An appealing example housed in a green label holder. Population: 16 in 66, 2 finer (8/07). (#4926)

Superb Gem 1920 Dime, Full Bands

1078 **1920 MS67 Full Bands PCGS.** Amazing quality with intense mint frost beneath pale green, gold, and iridescent toning. Every detail is full and sharp, especially at the centers. A remarkable example, tied for the finest certified by PCGS. Population: 12 in 67, 0 finer (8/07). (#4929)

Choice Full Bands 1920-S Dime

1079 1920-S MS64 Full Bands PCGS. This bright, satiny example is essentially untoned except for scattered pale gray obverse freckles. The 1920-S is elusive in Mint State, particularly as well preserved as the present coin. Well struck at the centers with minor spreading near the rims. Population: 79 in 64 Full Bands, 36 finer (7/07). (#4933)

1080 1921 MS62 Full Bands ANACS. The lustrous surfaces of this solidly struck example host an alluring blend of peach, rose, and amethyst patina. Light, scattered abrasions define the grade, though the eye appeal is better than the numeric designation might suggest. (#4935)

1081 1921-D XF45 NGC. Luminous and lightly circulated, this well struck semi-key has silver-blue and golden-tan toning over each side. An attractive, affordable Choice XF example, this piece is one of under 1.1 million coins minted. (#4936)

1082 1921-D—Cleaned—ANACS. AU58 Details. This low mintage semi-key dime is a bit bright from cleaning, although it is partly retoned in almond-gold shades. Boldly detailed despite minor peripheral incompleteness of strike. (#4936)

1083 1921-D MS64 NGC. The 1921-D, though largely unappreciated when minted, has since assumed a role as one of the most elusive Mercury dimes. This Choice example shows attractive luster and above-average detail with vibrant orange patina at the lower obverse and reverse margins. Census: 40 in 64, 23 finer (8/07). (#4936)

Gem Full Bands 1921-D Dime

1084 1921-D MS65 Full Bands NGC. Ex: Richmond Collection. This stone-white Gem has dazzling luster and a pristine appearance. Generally well struck, with slight incompleteness on the tops of the CA in AMERICA and the base of the 21 in the date. The central bands are separated. Other than the better-known 1916-D, the 1921-D has the lowest mintage of the series. The Richmond Collection was a remarkably extensive holding dispersed in 2004. (#4937)

1085 1924 MS66 Full Bands PCGS. Frosty and essentially untoned with an uncommonly sharp strike. Excellent all-around quality for this Roaring Twenties issue. PCGS has graded just 11 finer representatives (8/07). (#4943)

1086 1924-D MS65 Full Bands PCGS. Sharply struck with full definition on the central reverse bands and nary a trace of fadeaway on the peripheral devices. Both sides are entirely brilliant and untoned. A scarce date at the Gem level of preservation. (#4945)

1087 1924-S MS62 Full Bands PCGS. Well struck with satin luster and speckled olive, green, and lilac patina near the borders. The central reverse bands are fully detailed. Two or three tiny contact marks are noted on Liberty's face. A conditionally scarce issue in Mint State, especially with Full Bands. (#4947)

Appealing 1924-S Dime, MS64 Full Bands

1088 1924-S MS64 Full Bands PCGS. Faint traces of tan and powder-blue color residing on highly lustrous surfaces are only visible under magnification. A solid strike emboldens the design elements, culminating in full middle bands. Excellent technical quality and aesthetic appeal. Population: 92 in 64 full Bands, 16 finer (8/07). (#4947)

1089 1925-D MS63 Full Bands NGC. A crisply detailed and pleasingly toned Select example of this mid-date D-mint issue. Strongly lustrous with lightly abraded, minimally patinated centers and glints of violet and tan at the margins. (#4951)

1090 1925-D MS64 Full Bands PCGS. A shining silver-white Choice example of this D-mint Roaring Twenties issue, faintly marked in the fields with excellent central detail. A touch of milky patina appears in the left obverse field. (#4951)

1091 1925-S MS63 Full Bands PCGS. Champagne-tan patina blankets the obverse and rings the reverse periphery. Boldly impressed and uncommon as such, this Select example has a handful of grade-defining abrasions near the center of the reverse. (#4953)

Semi-Key 1926-D Dime, MS66 Full Bands

1092 1926-D MS66 Full Bands NGC. David Lange (2005) writes of the 1926-D dime: "Finding one with both full bands and a fully struck legend UNITED STATES OF AMERICA will be challenging." This Premium Gem comes very close to attaining this goal: a well executed strike transcends the Full Bands to bring strong definition to all of the design elements, with the exception of minor softness in the outer parts of the letters in AMERICA. Further enhancing this coin's eye appeal is the bright luster and well preserved, essentially untoned surfaces. Census: 7 in 66, 0 finer (8/07). (#4957)

1093 1926-S MS64 ICG. Smooth luster and delicate sky-blue and brown patina enhance the visual appeal of this near-Gem Mercury dime. Well-defined overall with above-average definition on the bands of the fasces, which frequently are found flat on this Coolidge-era issue. (#4958)

Full Bands Gem 1927-D Dime

1094 **1927-D MS65 Full Bands PCGS.** A beautiful Gem of this conditionally scarce branch mint dime. Gunmetal-gray surfaces are augmented by lime, gold, and rose-red. The centers are decisively struck, and only the left borders show any indication of incompleteness. Population: 24 in 65 Full Bands, 9 finer (7/07). (#4963)

Shimmering MS66 Full Bands 1927-D Dime

1095 **1927-D MS66 Full Bands PCGS.** One of the series keys with Full Bands and especially in high grade, the 1927-D ranks 12th out of the 77 issues in the Mercury dime series. This issue has see-sawed in value and popularity over the past 60 years. It was originally thought to be a key rarity in 1945. Then, in 1980, Rick Sear reported that the '25-D was actually scarcer in high grade than the '27-D. Since then, this has proven to not be the case and the 1927-D is once again one of the key issues for the Mercury dime collector.

This is a lovely, high-end example that has mostly brilliant surfaces with just a hint of light peripheral color. Remarkably free from abrasions. The reverse fields show evidence of die erosion that gives that side a crinkled, matte-like appearance. Population: 9 in 66, 0 finer (8/07). (#4963)

1096 **1928-D MS64 Full Bands PCGS.** Sharply struck and well preserved, this satiny near-Gem is virtually pristine. The nearly untoned light-gray surfaces reveal mere wisps of gold color on each side. If the luster were a bit stronger, this piece might have been graded as a Gem. (#4969)

1097 **1928-D MS64 Full Bands PCGS.** The shining silver-white surfaces of this late 1920s mintmarked issue show small sections of reddish-gold patina. Decisively struck with a handful of wispy marks that deny a Gem grade. (#4969)

1098 **1928-S MS67 NGC.** This is a nearly flawless, brilliant coin that has striated fields which impart even more brightness. Sharply struck on most of the design elements other than the central bands. A great example of this conditionally challenging Roaring Twenties S-mint. Census: 7 in 67, 0 finer (7/07). (#4970)

1099 **1928-S MS65 Full Bands PCGS.** Large Mintmark. Despite a mintage of 7.4 million pieces, Full Bands Gem examples of this Roaring Twenties S-mint issue remain elusive. The shining surfaces of the present piece offer an appealing blend of silver-gray and champagne patina. Boldly impressed and carefully preserved. (#4971)

1100 **1931 MS66 Full Bands PCGS.** Vibrant luster with a touch of iridescence in the fields. This boldly impressed Premium Gem has strong overall eye appeal. Population: 58 in 66 Full Bands, 10 finer (8/07). (#4983)

1101 **1931-D MS67 Full Bands NGC.** Sharply struck, essentially untoned, and frosty. This Depression-era D-mint dime has few equals, and the piece's visual appeal is impressive. Census: 10 in 67 Full Bands, 0 finer (8/07). (#4985)

Toned Gem 1931-S Mercury Dime with Full Bands

1102 **1931-S MS65 Full Bands PCGS.** Fully brilliant mint luster is enhanced by lovely light gold toning on each side of this frosty Gem. It is fully struck with sharp hair and wing details on the obverse, and crisp bands on the reverse. Our consignor particularly likes this dime, and we are sure the new owner will too. Census: 9 in 65, 5 finer (8/07). (#4987)

MS66 Full Bands 1931-S Dime

1103 **1931-S MS66 Full Bands PCGS.** Wisps of golden-brown patina embrace this highly lustrous and attentively struck Premium Gem. Only inconsequential marks are present, and the obverse field is essentially pristine. Because of the Great Depression, circulation demand for dimes was diminished. Of the 1931-S, only 1.8 million pieces were struck, and no dimes at all were produced in either 1932 or 1933. (#4987)

1104 **1935-S MS67 Full Bands PCGS.** Ex: Larry Shapiro. Lustrous with a blush of golden toning on the upper obverse and around the periphery of the reverse. Tied with several dozen others as the finest Full Bands example certified by either NGC or PCGS (8/07). (#4997)

1105 **1936-D MS67 Full Bands PCGS.** Subtle yellow-gold and salmon-pink patina graces the obverse, while dusky apple-green and plum-mauve adorn the reverse. Sharply struck and unblemished. PCGS has certified only seven pieces finer (8/07). (#5001)

1106 **1936-S MS67 Full Bands PCGS.** A gleaming, essentially untoned, and decisively struck Superb Gem exemplar of this S-mint Depression issue. Immensely appealing with only the tiniest of flaws visible, even under magnification. PCGS has graded only two finer Full Bands pieces (8/07). (#5003)

1107 **1942/1—Scratched—ANACS. AU50 Details.** FS-101, formerly FS-010.7. A partly lustrous silver-gray representative that appears problem-free at first glance, although thorough examination locates a diagonal pinscratch from the jaw into the wing. (#5036)

1108 **1942/1—Cleaned—ANACS. AU55 Details.** FS-101, formerly FS-010.7. A patch of hairlines near the profile is only visible when seen from certain angles. This well struck key date dime is primarily pearl-gray but exhibits peripheral orange patina. (#5036)

1109 **1942/1 AU55 NGC.** Plain as the overdate is, it is little wonder that this well-known Mercury dime variety was discovered in 1943, just one year after its manufacture. This briefly circulated, well struck piece shows hints of blue and gold toning, as well as a rim bruise at 12 o'clock on the obverse. (#5036)

Select Key Date 1942/1 Dime

1110 **1942/1 MS63 PCGS.** FS-101, formerly FS-010.7. A lovely representative with original pearl-gray toning that deepens slightly to russet near the rims. Only inconsequential contact is detected, and the MS63 grade appears conservative despite some incompleteness of strike on the central bands and peripheral letters. (#5036)

1111 **1942/1-D VF30 ANACS.** Golden-gray surfaces display bluish and violet accents, and retain sharp definition on the design elements. Both faces are quite clean for a coin that has seen light to moderate circulation. (#5040)

1112 **1942/1-D AU55 PCGS.** A delightful Choice AU representative of this popular Mercury dime overdate, strongly lustrous despite evidence of brief circulation on the highpoints. Subtle blue and gold tints visit the otherwise silver-white surfaces. Population: 35 in 55, 46 finer (8/07). (#5040)

1113 **1942/1-D—Scratched—ANACS. AU55 Details.** Light gray surfaces retain ample luster, and exhibit sharply struck design elements, including middle bands that are nearly completely split. A couple of shallow, short scratches on the neck account for the ANACS disclaimer. (#5040)

1114 **1944-D MS68 Full Bands PCGS.** Decisively struck with pristine surfaces and uncommonly strong luster. A tiny rim depression near 8 o'clock on the reverse is the only flaw visible without magnification. A great example of this World War II issue. Population: 67 in 68 Full Bands, 0 finer (8/07). (#5053)

1115 **1945 Dime MS68 ANACS,** beautifully toned, typical band detail; **1940 Dime PR66 PCGS,** ex: Benson, russet and cream-gray with an intricate strike; **1992-S Quarter PR70 Deep Cameo PCGS,** white-on-black perfection, **1886 Morgan dollar MS64 NGC,** brilliant, lustrous, well struck, and superior for the grade; and an **1888-O Morgan dollar MS64 NGC,** flashy and boldly struck with a wisp of tan toning. (Total: 5 coins) (#5056)

Enticing 1945 Mercury Dime, MS64 Full Bands

1116 **1945 MS64 Full Bands NGC.** The 1945 has a well-established reputation as a strike rarity, and Full Bands examples are prized with a fervor associated with few other 20th century coins. This exquisitely detailed, strongly lustrous near-Gem has few marks for the grade and rich, dappled blue-green and peach patina over both sides. An excellent choice for the discerning date collector. Census: 6 in 64 Full Bands, 11 finer (8/07). (#5057)

Full Bands MS64 1945 Dime
A Famous Strike Rarity

1117 **1945 MS64 Full Bands PCGS.** The 1945 Full Bands dime is the most famous "strike rarity" in American numismatics. Uncirculated 1945 dimes are sufficiently common that they are sometimes available by the roll. But invariably, these pieces are softly defined on the all-important central bands. The present piece is a fortunate exception to the rule. Not only are the bands fully split, but the peripheral legends are crisp at the tops of the letters. In addition, the lightly toned and lustrous surfaces are clean for the MS64 level. Encapsulated in a first generation PCGS holder. (#5057)

1945-P Dime, MS66 Full Bands
The Key Strike Rarity to the Mercury Dime Series

1118 1945 MS66 Full Bands NGC. Thirty years ago, when Harold Kritzman was on a one-man campaign to educate collectors and dealers about Full Band dimes, it came as quite a surprise to learn that the key to the Full Band series was the 1945-P. After all, with more than 159 million pieces struck how hard could it be? The intervening years have answered the question: it is extremely difficult to locate this issue in any grade with complete definition on the central bands. Of course, such a coin in MS66 is even rarer (and more valuable) with only a handful of pieces known. NGC has only certified six pieces in this grade with one finer (8/07). This is a splendid piece with thick, frosted mint luster. Just the slightest hint of toning is seen on each side with a couple of specks of deeper golden present. Essentially defect-free, the surfaces appear clean enough for an even higher grade. (#5057)

PROOF MERCURY DIMES

1119 1936 PR64 NGC. Wisps of elegant champagne patina grace the gleaming surfaces of this boldly impressed Choice proof. A faintly hairlined, yet eminently appealing example of the first proof Mercury dime issue, one of just 4,130 specimens coined. (#5071)

1120 1937 PR67 NGC. A boldly impressed blast-white representative of this popular early proof Mercury dime. Beautifully preserved with gleaming fields and incredible visual appeal. (#5072)

1121 1937 PR67 PCGS. Brilliant and pristine with razor-sharp striking details and highly reflective fields. A lovely specimen from the second year of modern proof coinage, which came after a twenty-year respite. (#5072)

Glorious PR68 1937 Dime

1122 1937 PR68 NGC. A pristine and fully struck stone-white representative of this low mintage proof issue. Time has been kind to this flashy specimen, which looks the same today as when it was struck seven decades ago. None have been certified finer by either major service (7/07). (#5072)

Outstanding 1938 Dime PR68

1123 1938 PR68 NGC. This fully brilliant Superb Gem has a needle-sharp strike, and even a lengthy perusal beneath a light and loupe fails to locate the slightest imperfection. The dies are rotated counterclockwise. Scarcer than the 1939 to 1942 dates that close the proof series. Census: 29 in 68, 1 finer (7/07). (#5073)

1124 1939 PR67 NGC. Even in 1939, the fourth of seven years for proof Mercury dimes, the mintage only reached four figures. This exquisitely detailed and essentially untoned Superb Gem offers immense reflectivity. NGC has graded 52 numerically finer specimens (8/07). (#5074)

Superb Gem 1939 Dime, PR68

1125 1939 PR68 NGC. Light cameo contrast on each side places this coin in an elite category. Although not designated as a Cameo proof, it has more contrast than usually encountered. The surfaces are entirely brilliant with no evidence of toning. Census: 52 in 68, 0 finer (8/07). (#5074)

1126 1942 PR67 PCGS. A brilliant, sparkling Superb Gem with highly reflective fields and immaculately preserved surfaces. The striking details are razor-sharp, as slight clockwise reverse die rotation is noted. A beautiful and seemingly unimprovable example of this final proof Mercury dime issue. (#5077)

1127 1942 PR67 PCGS. Beautiful lemon, russet, and sky-blue toning enlivens this satiny and intricately struck Superb Gem. A gorgeously preserved specimen from the terminal date of proof Mercury dime production. (#5077)

1128 1942 PR68 NGC. A decisively struck, gleaming, and essentially untoned representative of this final-year proof Mercury dime. Exquisitely preserved with surfaces that fall just shy of perfection. NGC has graded just one numerically finer piece (8/07). (#5077)

ROOSEVELT DIMES

1129 Set of Silver Roosevelt Dimes 1946 to 1964, MS67 NGC. A complete set of the 48 circulation-strike issues of the Roosevelt dime in 90% silver composition, without varieties, each a Superb Gem graded by NGC. The set includes: **1946**, delicate peach-gold patina over the obverse with an essentially untoned reverse; **1946-D**, thin streaks of charcoal-gray toning against a backdrop of lemon-gold; **1946-S**, frosty and essentially untoned with wonderful eye appeal; **1947**, delicate champagne accents with delightful frosty luster; **1947-D**, dappled fire-orange at the margins and on Roosevelt's neck; **1947-S**, well struck with vibrant luster and minimal patina; **1948**, delicate silver-gray patina overall with elements of charcoal at the margins; **1948-D**, frosty and beautiful with a touch of haze at the lower obverse; **1948-S**, delicate, dappled golden-brown and peach patina over both sides; **1949**, highly lustrous with a touch of reddish-tan toning on the central devices; **1949-D**, vibrant golden-brown and cherry-red patina over both sides; **1949-S**, apricot toning at the margins around sky-blue centers; **1950**, booming luster and minimal patina, a gorgeous piece; **1950-D**, frosty, well struck, and essentially untoned; **1950-S**, satiny luster beneath rich rose-violet toning; **1951**, green-gold and turquoise patina at the margins with untoned centers; **1951-D**, practically brilliant with pristine surfaces; **1951-S**, untoned with delightful mint frost; **1952**, a gorgeous silver-white example that displays powerful luster; **1952-D**, thin streaks of cherry-red at the obverse margins with a greater area of coverage at the reverse periphery; **1952-S**, well struck and essentially untoned with evidence of die erosion at the margins; **1953**, frosty with sky-blue and turquoise peripheral toning that fades to violet and pink in the centers; **1953-D**, frosty luster beneath areas of mustard-gold toning that are more prevalent on the reverse; **1953-S**, highly lustrous with small dots of tan toning in the centers; **1954**, dappled brick-red and silver-gray patina with cobalt-blue accents; **1954-D**, lemon-gold toning over much of the margins with deep crimson at the rims; **1954-S**, frosty with tan and burgundy toning that appears predominantly at the margins; **1955**, strongly lustrous with small dots of violet toning at the peripheries; **1955-D**, modestly reflective with two horizontal streaks of reddish-brown toning across Roosevelt's neck; **1955-S**, powerful luster and small splashes of golden toning near the rims; **1956**, vibrant blue-green and violet patina with minor untoned regions and faint golden accents; **1956-D**, frosty with silver-gray patina overall and tan-orange and gunmetal dots at the margins; **1957**, rich olive-green, blue, and violet toning over each side; **1957-D**, gold-orange toning in the fields with deeper patina at the reverse rims; **1958**, delicate gold and mint-green toning with a dash of red near the torch; **1958-D**, frosty with dots of gunmetal patina at the margins; **1959**, brilliant with pleasing detail and excellent eye appeal; **1959-D**, frosty with a touch of tan at the right reverse, with no finer examples certified by NGC (8/07); **1960**, swirling blue, violet, and gold patina with untoned centers; **1960-D**, goldenrod and tan toning on the obverse with slightly subdued color on the reverse; **1961**, frosty with minimal patina and patches of brilliance at the reverse margins; **1961-D**, vibrant luster and delicate golden patina overall with tiny dots of deeper color; **1962**, faint rose patina at the obverse margins with richer gold and blue near the reverse periphery; **1962-D**, delicate golden tints with elements of mustard over frosty surfaces; **1963**, consistent blue and lavender patina on the reverse with an untoned center and thin streaks of similar color on the obverse; **1963-D**, frosty with a hint of champagne patina on each side; **1964**, lemon-gold and orange toning over the obverse with elements of lavender on the reverse; and a **1964-D**, regions of warm orange and gold patina against strongly lustrous silver-gray surfaces. An attractive and interesting group. (Total: 48 coins)

1130 1949 MS65 PCGS. A strongly lustrous silver-blue Gem that offers areas of cerulean on the reverse and small dots of lead-gray patina on each side. Well-defined with solid visual appeal. (#5091)

1131 1949 MS65 PCGS. Well-defined with soft, swirling luster. This lovely early Roosevelt Gem offers elegant cloud-gray patina with regions of blue-green in the fields on both sides. (#5091)

1132 1949-D MS66 PCGS. Boldly struck and satiny, with pristine surfaces that display rich amber-red patina across the left side of the reverse, and wisps of speckled toning on the obverse. (#5092)

1133 1949-D MS66 PCGS. Crisply struck with satiny luster and speckled russet and amber-red patina over the reverse, and near the obverse periphery. An appealing Premium Gem from the fourth year of the long-lived Roosevelt dime series. (#5092)

1134 1949-S MS66 PCGS. While the centers of this pleasing Premium Gem are largely untoned, an arc of gunmetal patina appears behind Roosevelt's head, while the reverse margins offer dappled bronze toning. A lovely representative of this early S-mint issue. (#5093)

1135 1949-S MS66 PCGS. A well struck and pleasing dime with bold luster and speckled kelly-green patina across the obverse. The reverse displays a deep coating of lovely purple-rose and cobalt-blue toning. Surface blemishes are nonexistent. (#5093)

Gem Doubled Die Reverse 1964-D Dime
Elusive FS-803 Variety

1136 1964-D Doubled Die Reverse MS65 PCGS. FS-803. The reverse legends are die doubled, particularly AMERICA. Listed as URS-1 (!) in the *Cherrypickers' Guide*. Light gold toning visits this lustrous piece, which has a splendidly smooth reverse and only moderate marks on the lower left obverse. (#95129)

PROOF ROOSEVELT DIMES

Key 1950 Dime, PR67 Deep Cameo

1137 **1950 PR67 Deep Cameo PCGS.** Thickly frosted devices rise above the prominently mirrored fields. Light gold toning visits this flashy Superb Gem. Perfect save for a single pinpoint fleck behind the base of the neck. A rare issue in the Cameo dime series. Housed in a green label holder. Population: 10 in 67, 1 finer (8/07). (#95225)

1138 **1963 Doubled Die Reverse PR68 NGC.** FS-802, formerly FS-017.5. The reverse legends are die doubled, with the spread particularly wide on ONE DIME. Cobalt-blue and sun-gold toning cedes to brilliant centers. Intricately struck and unabraded. Listed in the 2008 Guide Book on page 154. (#5224)

1139 **1983 No S PR68 Deep Cameo Uncertified.** The dime is part of a five-piece 1983-S proof set from the cent through half dollar. All coins still reside within the mint-issued black plastic holder. The dime is untoned and virtually immaculate. The other four coins in the set are also Superb Gems. (Total: 5 coins) (#95265)

1140 **1983 No S PR68 Deep Cameo PCGS.** Brilliant throughout, the devices are heavily frosted and present a stark cameo contrast against the unfathomable depth of reflectivity in the fields. Made in error with no S-mintmark punched into the die. (#95265)

TWENTY CENT PIECES

Colorful Choice 1875 Twenty Cent

1141 **1875 MS64 PCGS.** Of the five circulation-strike issues of the twenty cent piece, the 1875 ranks third in population. The mintage of 36,910 pieces is far below that of the savior for type set collectors, the 1875-S. This solidly struck Choice piece shows strong luster beneath vivid gold and amber patina. Population: 62 in 64, 29 finer (8/07). (#5296)

Attractive 1875 Near-Gem Twenty Cent

1142 **1875 MS64 PCGS.** This attractive near-Gem twenty cent piece is essentially untoned on the obverse, but takes on wisps of russet, lavender, and cobalt-blue at the reverse borders. A well directed strike brings out sharp definition on the design features. A few minute handling marks on highly lustrous surfaces account for the grade. *From The Mario Eller Collection, Part One.* (#5296)

1143 **1875-S MS62 PCGS.** A well struck and strongly lustrous Mint State example of this popular odd-denomination type issue, gold-toned with deep amber spots on the obverse with a minimally patinated reverse. Wispy abrasions in the fields preclude a finer grade. (#5298)

1144 **1875-S MS62 NGC.** An unworn, solidly struck representative of this definitive twenty cents type issue. The dusky surfaces have a blend of silver-gray and tan patina with dots of deeper crimson. *From The Laguna Niguel Collection, Part Two.* (#5298)

1145 **1875-S MS63 PCGS.** MPD-004. A partial date digit, presumably the top of an 8, is present within the denticles beneath the 8 in the date. This satiny cream-gray type coin is well struck except for the two stars that bookend Liberty's head. Surprisingly mark-free for the grade. (#5298)

1146 **1876 MS63 PCGS.** Satiny silver surfaces with reflective fields and a splash of dark steel toning at the top of the obverse. *From The Beau Clerc Collection.* (#5299)

PROOF TWENTY CENT PIECES

Impressive 1875 Twenty Cent Piece PR65

1147 **1875 PR65 PCGS.** Fully struck with a dense layer of olive and rose toning across both sides. A tiny contact mark in the right obverse field seems hardly worth mentioning, and hairlines are not noticeable on either side of this impressive Gem proof. Semicircular die lines are noted on the upper obverse, beside and above Liberty's head. 1875 was the first year of the short-lived twenty cent denomination. Population: 26 in 65, 12 finer (8/07). (#5303)

1148 **1876 PR61 NGC.** A distinct if mild degree of cameo contrast is observed on each side of this attractive proof specimen. Boldly struck with a slight degree of reflectivity in the fields, where wispy hairlines are also noted. An affordable example of this proof issue. *From The Arnold & Harriet Collection, Part Two.* (#5304)

1149 **1877—Cleaned—ANACS. PR60 Details.** This brilliant and intricately struck specimen has distributed small marks, and is bright and faintly hairlined from a past wipe. Minor granularity is noted near the date. Only 350 proofs were struck for this desirable proof-only date. (#5305)

Outstanding 1877 Twenty Cent Piece, PR66

1150 **1877 PR66 PCGS.** Walter Breen, in his 1977 *Encyclopedia of United States and Colonial Proof Coins*, writes that the 1877 proof-only twenty cent is a little rarer than its 350-piece mintage would suggest. He also indicates that "Many of the survivors are cleaned, some drastically so; and I have seen several damaged and 3 or 4 circulated ones." Many were also likely melted.

This Premium Gem proof specimen displays a medley of medium intensity cobalt-blue, lavender, gold, and gray patina, that does not impede the striking field-motif contrast, especially when the coin is rotated beneath a light source. The strike is solid, imparting sharp and uniform definition to the design elements. Close inspection reveals just one trivial mark above the eagle's head, that we mention primarily because it may help in identifying this example for future catalogers. Population: 14 in 66, 0 finer (8/07). (#5305)

1151 **1878—Improperly Cleaned—NCS. Proof.** The brief four-year run of the twenty cent piece ensures that any proof is desirable as a type coin. But the series ended with two low mintage proof-only dates, which makes these particularly in demand. For the 1878, only 600 proofs were struck. The present specimen is well struck and has light pearl-gray toning. The fields are subdued but only faintly hairlined. (#5306)

Dr. Henry R. Lindeman
Director of the Mint 1873-1879

Choice AU 1796 Quarter, B-2

1152 **1796 AU55 NGC.** High 6, B-2, R.3. The 6 in the date nearly touches the bottom of the drapery, and star 15 is twice as far from the bust as it is on the B-1 Low 6 quarter. The T and Y in LIBERTY do not touch on the B-2, although they are close, while they merge on the B-1 variety. On the B-2 the digits of the date are equidistant, while on the B-1 the date is spaced 1 79 6, with the 7 and 9 too close. The tiny mintage of 6,146 pieces appears to have been rather unevenly split between the considerably rarer B-1 and the more-available B-2, both of which share a common reverse. However, the B-2 usually shows weakness on the eagle's head, while the B-1 occasionally shows perfect impressions that lack mentionable weakness.

While the year 1796 is a year replete with rarities in copper, silver, and gold denominations, the 1796 quarter occupies a unique niche as the premier first-year silver coin of that denomination, one that would not be minted again until 1804. Accordingly, while some other coin denominations minted during the year may be technically rarer, both varieties of 1796 quarter are in demand as one-year type coins, and due to their low mintage, both varieties are considered rare.

In both technical and aesthetic terms this is a simply gorgeous piece, with light pinkish-gray patina on the obverse, to which the reverse adds some iridescent steel-blue and green coloration. Considerable mint luster remains under the light patina, and the few adjustment marks through the eagle's head, the O of OF, the wreath nearby, and the lower clouds are not particularly distracting. The eagle's head is typically struck. This fine Choice AU 1796 quarter is destined to form the centerpiece of a fine and memorable collection. (#5310)

1153 1804 Fair 2 PCGS. B-1, R.4. Most of the central design details have been worn away, but the date and left side obverse stars are still apparent, as is LIBERTY. The eagle's head, the stars and clouds above, and STATES OF are readily evident on the reverse. Some faint pinscratches and adjustment marks are noted on each side. From the first year of the Heraldic Eagle design type, and one of just 6,738 pieces produced. (#5312)

Colorful B-4 XF 1805 Quarter

1154 1805 XF40 NGC. B-4, R.3. Deep orange, yellow-green, and plum-red tints emerge when this lightly abraded early quarter is rotated beneath a light. The strike on the shield and opposite curls is typically indistinct, but the wing plumage is bold and lustrous. From an early die state without the clash mark through the O in OF. (#5313)

1155 1806 VF20 ANACS. B-3, R.1. The I in LIBERTY has a defective right foot, and the 5 and C in the denomination on the reverse are clear of the central devices. Elements of blue and lavender grace the silver-gray surfaces of this moderately circulated early quarter. Minimally marked and appealing. (#5314)

1156 1806 VF25 PCGS. B-7, R.5. A much better variety, Browning-7 is identified by a slender vertical die crack through the central serif of the E in AMERICA. Rose-gray color dominates both sides of this VF25 example, and the design elements show nice detail for the grade. The surfaces are quite clean for a light to moderately circulated coin. (#5314)

Lightly Toned, Pleasing 1806 Quarter, MS62, B-3

1157 1806 MS62 PCGS. B-3, R.1. The foot of the 1 in the date and the T in LIBERTY are defective at left, and the 5 in 25 C. dose not touch the arrows. Light golden-tan patina covers lustrous surfaces that are weakly struck in the centers. A few minor obverse marks are not disturbing. Overall, a rather pleasing coin for the grade. (#5314)

BUST QUARTERS

Near-Mint 1815 Bust Quarter, B-1

1158 1815 AU58 ANACS. B-1, R.1. The A in STATES is recut. This crisply struck and attractively preserved example is richly patinated in olive-brown, gold, and steel-blue. Light rub on the forehead and claws prevents an Uncirculated assignment. Struck from lightly clashed dies.
From The Beau Clerc Collection. (#5321)

1159 1818/5 AU55 PCGS. B-1, R.2. A briefly circulated, attractively toned example of this *Guide Book* overdate, lightly marked overall with a touch of wear on the highpoints. Both sides display faint die cracks and lovely peach and blue-gray patina. The reverse is rotated approximately 20 degrees counterclockwise. Population: 2 in 55, 39 finer (8/07). (#5323)

1160 1818—Cleaned—ANACS. XF40 Details. B-8, R.3. A charcoal-gray and olive-green representative of this popular date. The fields display a few minor abrasions. Struck from prominently clashed dies. (#5322)

1161 1818—Cleaned—ANACS. XF40 Details. B-7, R.4. The rare early die state without the die crack through the left stand of the N in UNITED, which Breen and Browning agreed is always present. Our January 2006 Reiver auction (lot 22360) had a Good 6 example without the die crack. A slate-gray example of this scarcer die pairing. Slightly subdued, and a thin mark is noted in front of the arrowheads. (#5322)

1162 1818—Cleaned—ANACS. AU55 Details. B-2, R.1. Golden-brown and forest-green freckles frequent the borders, but the fields and devices are untoned. Thickly hairlined, but otherwise close to Mint State with well struck features.
From The Laguna Niguel Collection, Part Two. (#5322)

Choice AU 1820 Quarter, B-3

1163 1820 AU55 PCGS. Large 0. B-3, R.3. Listed in the updated Browning as the first variety of the year. All known examples show a die crack that connects all the stars on the left and the 1 and 8 in the date. Considered "exceedingly rare" in mint condition. At the AU55 level, this piece is tied with several others at the lower end of the Condition Census. Granted, that C.C. is out of date now, but when the Breen update was published in 1992 it was listed as (63, 60, 60, 60, 55, 55).

Softly struck over the highpoints on each side. The surfaces display brightness beneath the speckled gray-blue toning that covers both obverse and reverse. (#5329)

1164 **1821 XF45 ANACS.** B-4, R.3. An early die state with faint obverse clash marks but no indication of reverse clash marks, and no die cracks. Light ivory color on the devices and in the fields, surrounded by deeper steel toning along the borders. *From The Beau Clerc Collection.* (#5331)

Select Mint State B-1 1821 Quarter

1165 **1821 MS63 PCGS.** B-1, R.2. Emerald-green, sky-blue, and mauve toning endow this satiny and lightly abraded Bust type coin. The star centers are all needle-sharp, and only the claws lack a precise impression. Minor die rust is noted above the beak and on the reverse border at 1 o'clock and 5:30. (#5331)

Popular 1825/4/3 Quarter, VF35, B-2

1166 **1825/4/3 VF35 PCGS.** B-2, R.2. An interesting overdate quarter, one of two varieties from this year that share this common obverse. The obverse and reverse show uneven detailing with the reverse showing significantly better definition. Light, generally untoned surfaces with just a trace of golden-rose color around the devices. (#5336)

1167 **1825/4/3—Cleaned—ANACS. AU50 Details.** B-3, R.3. Liberty's curls, cheek, and drapery show slight wear, but this is a bold example with ample luster in protected regions. Subdued by a relatively mild cleaning, and retoned in powder-blue and plum-mauve shades. (#5336)

1168 **1828—Scratched—ANACS. XF40 Details.** B-1, R.1. Lightly circulated and luminous beneath layers of olive-gold and violet patina. The surfaces display a number of pinscratches and a small gouge to the right of the date, though the piece retains considerable eye appeal. (#5342)

1169 **1828—Rim Damaged—ANACS. AU55 Details.** B-1, R.1. A gunmetal-gray Capped Bust quarter with attractive surfaces despite a brief, bright obverse edge mark at 9:30. Boldly brought up except for the LU in PLURIBUS. (#5342)

1170 **1833 AU55 NGC.** B-2, R.3. Die State II with clash marks near ear. The variety without a period after the denomination, also noteworthy for only two lines (instead of the usual three) in the vertical shield stripes. A lightly abraded piece with pleasing peripheral luster and sharpness. (#5352)

1171 **1835 XF45 NGC,** B-2, R.2, identifiable by a leaf tip that extends past the C in the denomination, charcoal-gray on the obverse with lighter cloud-gray toning on the highpoints of that side and the reverse; and an **1835 AU55 NGC,** B-5, R.3, distinguished by recutting of OF AM on the reverse, well struck with few marks and dusky seal-gray patina with lighter color and the faintly worn highpoints. (Total: 2 coins) (#5354)

Delightful MS62 1836 Quarter, B-3
Dramatic Terminal Die State

1172 **1836 MS62 PCGS.** B-3, R.1. The terminal die state (Breen's VI) with a large die break on Liberty's bust truncation. Both sides display multiple lengthy bold die cracks. A satiny and unmarked Capped Bust type coin with pearl-gray centers and peripheral golden-russet toning. Well struck save for the eagle's beak and right-side stars. Population: 6 in 62, 14 finer (7/07). (#5355)

1173 **1837 XF40 ANACS.** B-5, R.5. A lightly circulated, attractive example of the second-rarest die marriage for the year, well struck with warm violet, olive, and silver-gray patina over luminous surfaces. A long, thin abrasion passes below the eagle's beak. (#5356)

Satiny B-3 1837 Quarter, MS64

1174 **1837 MS64 NGC.** B-3, R.4. In addition to the usual identifiers for this variety, the most distinctive one is an almost rim-to-rim die crack from the D in UNITED to above the E in STATES. This is the finest B-3 we have offered at public auction since we sold an MS66 (surely the finest known) in 2005. The bright, satiny mint luster on this piece is almost completely brilliant. The striking details are uncommonly sharp, one might say full, except for localized softness on several of the hair curls. A clean, upper-end coin that is suggestive of an even higher grade. (#5356)

Legendary 1827/3 Quarter Restrike, PR65

1175 1827/3 Restrike PR65 NGC. Incorrect and misleading Information regarding the celebrated 1827/3 quarter has been disseminated to collectors throughout the past century. Even the most rudimentary of specifications such as the mintage of the 1827/3 Original pieces is incorrect. For years it has been repeatedly published that 4,000 quarters were struck bearing the date of 1827. Bust quarter specialist and researcher Karl Moulton has recently offered an in-depth study on this issue to the numismatic community. Among many facts he extracted from years of researching documents in the National Archives is that the 4,000 figure that is suggested as the mintage of 1827 quarters actually represents the first delivery of 1828 B-1 quarters. In stark contrast to the previously accepted mintage of 1827/3 quarters, Moulton concludes in his dissertation on the subject that only "eight or nine" Originals were struck in 1827.

Contemporary documentation unearthed by Moulton helped to unravel the mystery of the 1827/3 quarters to some degree, although it should be known that his research should still be considered theory rather than absolute fact. Extensive examination of auction records and official Mint documentation formed the basis of his conclusion that there were five emissions of 1827/3 quarters:

1) Two Essay pieces, struck over draped bust quarters using a close collar press in 1827.

2) Eight or nine silver Originals that were created in an open collar press in 1827.

3) Nine or 10 silver Restrikes made from rusted dies in an open collar configuration in 1876.

4) Copper Restrikes, struck one year later with the same dies as the third emission. Four or five coins produced.

5) Another batch of silver strikes using rusted dies in an open collar, this time damaged on the obverse. Five or six pieces struck during the 1877 to 1878 timeframe.

The damage to the obverse die that Moulton refers to in his research is simply a light die crack from the juncture of the neck and throat and into the left obverse field. He speculates that this damage occurred after the copper Restrikes were made. If Moulton's reasoning is correct, then the current example offered in this lot is a fifth emission Restrike, thus qualifying it as being technically rarer than the Originals from the second emission. Regardless of the emission sequence, any 1827/3 quarter is a legendary coin that few numismatists will ever have the privilege of owning. The current example has the added distinction of being one of the finest pieces known, although the proof designation given by the grading services is the subject of yet another debate regarding this issue. Technically speaking, the 1827/3 quarters, both Originals and Restrikes, are simply prooflike strikes produced from freshly lapped dies. However, in terms of surface quality, the 1827/3 quarter offered here is a true Gem regardless of strike classification. This brilliantly lustrous piece exhibits beautiful aquamarine toning with slightly deeper cobalt-blue centers and mint-green coloration at the peripheries of both sides. A touch of smoke-gray toning is observed in the right obverse fields above and behind Liberty's head. Census: 3 in 65, 1 finer (8/07). (#5374)

SEATED QUARTERS

Impressive MS63 1840-O No Drapery Quarter

1176 1840-O No Drapery MS63 NGC. The 1838, 1839, and the 1840-O are the only three issues contained in the short-lived Seated quarter series that do not show extra drapery folds at Liberty's right (facing) elbow. Original autumn-brown and forest-green patina deepens toward the margins. The striking details are well defined in all areas, including the often-weak neck of the eagle. One of the most impressive 1840-O No Drapery quarters we have handled, regardless of grade. Housed in an early generation holder. Census: 5 in 63, 6 finer (8/07).
From The Beau Clerc Collection. (#5393)

Lustrous 1840-O Drapery Quarter, MS63

1177 1840-O Drapery MS63 PCGS. Briggs 2-C. The mintmark position and lower reverse die cracks are distinctive on this variety. Most of the 2-C coins are from the Meridien Hotel Hoard found in New Orleans in the early 1980s. This particular piece shows excellent mint luster and is well struck except on the left (facing) leg of the eagle. Gray-golden toning is seen over each side. Population: 6 in 63, 9 finer (8/07). (#5398)

MS62 1841 Doubled Die Reverse Quarter

1178 1841—Doubled Die Reverse—MS62 PCGS. Briggs 1-A. STATES OF is nicely die doubled toward the rim. This satiny Seated quarter has original olive-gold and gunmetal-gray toning. Evenly struck, and free from noticeable marks. For all 1841 Philadelphia quarters, only 120,000 pieces were struck. Population: 2 in 62, 12 finer (8/07).
From The Beau Clerc Collection. (#5399)

1179 1845 MS63 NGC. Though available in lower grades, the 1845 offers a significant challenge in Select and better. Sunset-orange and cornflower-blue patina covers much of this pleasingly detailed piece, which shows a number of thin abrasions in the fields. Census: 16 in 63, 20 finer (8/07). (#5408)

1180 1847-O—Cleaned—ANACS. MS60 Details. A scarce issue at all grade levels. Generally bold, except for slight softness in the usual areas, this piece displays even charcoal-gray toning imbued with slight rose and greenish accents. A few wispy marks are observed on each side. Slightly subdued after an ill-advised cleaning. (#5411)

Choice Repunched Date 1848 Quarter

1181 1848 MS64 NGC. Ex: Sweet Collection. Briggs 2-B, triple-punched 1, double-punched 8. Three serifs show on the bottom left of the 1, and the bottom of the 8 is doubled. On the so-called "Plain" reverse, the peripheral letters are large and thick, and light die cracks connect many of the letters. The silver-white surfaces are well struck and show no singular distractions, save for a couple of contact marks in the reverse field above the eagle. This is a scarce coin above Very Fine, regardless of the variety. NGC and PCGS combined have certified four coins (of both known Briggs varieties) in MS64, with three pieces finer (8/07).
Ex: Rod Sweet Collection (Bowers and Merena, 3/04), lot 1342.
From The Beau Clerc Collection. (#5412)

1182 1850-O AU58 PCGS. The 1850-O quarter is typically poorly struck, especially at the obverse periphery, including the date (Larry Briggs, 1991). This silver-gray piece contains ample luster, and is sharply struck, including in the areas mentioned above. Very scarce in AU, and rare in Uncirculated (Briggs). Population: 8 in 58, 13 finer (8/07).
From The Beau Clerc Collection. (#5416)

Difficult XF 1851-O Quarter

1183 1851-O XF40 NGC. The 1851-O quarter, with a mintage of 88,000 pieces is scarce in all grades. About 70 pieces have been certified by NGC and PCGS combined. This XF40 specimen displays dusky light gray color with light blue undertones. Relatively clean surfaces exhibit well defined design elements.
From The Beau Clerc Collection. (#5418)

1184 1852 MS63 NGC. Pumpkin-orange and plum patina graces the luminous surfaces of this pre-arrows Seated quarter. Attentively struck with faint, grade-defining abrasions scattered on each side. (#5419)

1185 **1853 Arrows and Rays MS63 PCGS.** Whispers of reddish-gold, golden-brown, and cobalt-blue toning race over lustrous surfaces. A well directed strike brings out sharpness on the design elements. An excellent type coin.
From The Beau Clerc Collection. (#5426)

1186 **1853-O Arrows and Rays AU50 PCGS.** Traces of luster reside in the protected areas of this AU Arrows and Rays specimen. It possesses light golden-gray surfaces, and is generally well detailed. Quite clean for a coin that has seen some circulation. Population: 16 in 50, 27 finer (7/07). (#5428)

1187 **1853-O Arrows and Rays AU55 NGC.** A briefly circulated, enticingly toned example of this popular one-year type. Ocean-blue and lavender toning dominates the obverse, while pumpkin-orange patina covers the reverse. A lovely O-mint example. (#5428)

Scarce 1853-O Arrows and Rays Quarter, AU58

1188 **1853-O Arrows and Rays AU58 NGC.** A still-lustrous pearl-gray example that has minor highpoint friction and faint handling marks in the fields. Appealing overall with above-average detail. Though over 1.3 million examples were coined for this issue, few were saved, as most fueled the commerce of the bustling port city. Census: 5 in 58, 14 finer (8/07).
From The Beau Clerc Collection. (#5428)

MS62 1854-O Arrows Quarter

1189 **1854-O Arrows MS62 PCGS.** A sharply detailed example of this scarce date, seldom seen in any Mint State grade. The original surfaces have full luster, but it is subdued by dusky grayish-brown toning, with a few splashes of lighter ivory. Population: 7 in 62, 16 finer (8/07).
From The Beau Clerc Collection. (#5433)

1190 **1857-O AU58 PCGS.** A scarce issue in AU, and rare in Mint State. This high-end AU example displays a better strike than usually seen, though the centrils of the stars along the left border are slightly soft. The silver-gray and lilac surfaces retain considerable luster and are remarkably clean.
From The Beau Clerc Collection. (#5443)

1191 **1859 MS63 NGC.** Rose and orange patina with blue and plum accents at the margins enhances the visual appeal of this Select Seated quarter. Attentively detailed with scattered abrasions in the fields. Census: 11 in 63, 25 finer (8/07). (#5448)

Richly Toned MS64 1859 Quarter

1192 **1859 MS64 PCGS.** The 1859 is one of the few issues in the No Motto series that is occasionally available in mint condition, as seen by the coins offered in this auction. This is a lovely example that is richly toned in shades of violet, rose, and blue with strong underlying luster. Sharply defined throughout. (#5448)

Choice Mint State 1859 Seated Quarter

1193 **1859 MS64 PCGS.** This highly lustrous piece has satiny silver surfaces with considerable reddish-gold, lilac, and blue toning on both sides. Well over 1 million examples of this No Motto issue were coined, yet few can equal or exceed the quality of this piece. Population: 20 in 64, 11 finer (8/07).
From The Beau Clerc Collection. (#5448)

Toned Gem 1859 Quarter

1194 **1859 MS65 PCGS.** A number of quarters were set aside this year out of the mintage of 1.34 million pieces. Several dozen are known today in the various grades of Uncirculated. The present coin is, of course, among the finest known. The two major services have certified 13 pieces in Gem condition and another five are finer (8/07). Thickly frosted, as usual, with rich sea-green and rose toned surfaces. There are only a few minor field marks present that prevent an even higher grade. (#5448)

Pleasing, Rare 1859-O Near-Gem Quarter

1195 1859-O MS64 NGC. Larry Briggs, in his Seated Liberty quarter book, says the 1859-O "... is fairly common in low grades and readily available up to AU grades. Unc's are quite rare ... ." Lustrous surfaces on this near-Gem are dominated by bluish-gray toning, and accented with gold and lilac. Sharply struck, except for the usual softness in the star centers. A few unobtrusive handling marks preclude full Gem classification. Census: 6 in 64, 4 finer (8/07). (#5449)

1196 1864 MS63 PCGS. Hints of light tan color show up under magnification. Sharply struck, mildly frosted design elements offer moderate contrast with partially prooflike fields that possess fairly strong die polish lines. A few light obverse handling marks preclude a higher grade. (#5459)

Attractive, Bright MS63 1870 Quarter

1197 1870 MS63 PCGS. The 1870 is a scarcer date among early With Motto issues. Most high grade examples show some trace of prooflikeness or semi-prooflikeness in the fields. This piece is brilliant and has just a trace of reflectivity on each side. The devices are sharply struck, and there are minimal abrasions present. An important offering for the Seated quarter specialist. Population: 3 in 63, 11 finer (8/07). (#5476)

1198 1873 Arrows MS62 PCGS. An unworn and enticing representative of this transitional issue, well-defined in the centers with a touch of softness on the stars. The steel-gray surfaces show a touch of lemon-yellow patina at the upper right obverse. (#5491)

1199 1873 Arrows MS63 PCGS. Though the weight change for minor silver in 1873 was not nearly so momentous as that of 1853, the Mint resumed the use of arrows to designate new-tenor pieces. This Select example offers pleasing central detail, shining silver-white surfaces, and few abrasions. Population: 26 in 63, 44 finer (7/07). (#5491)

1200 1876 MS65 PCGS. Type Two Reverse. A frosty Gem representative of this popular centennial-year issue, solidly struck with faint flecks of toning around Liberty's shield. An uncommonly well-preserved piece that would make an excellent addition to a similarly graded 19th century type set. Population: 33 in 65, 24 finer (8/07). (#5501)

Desirable Premium Gem 1876 Quarter

1201 1876 MS66 NGC. Type Two Reverse with narrow feet on the A in STATES. Lustrous, nicely struck, and unblemished with only a trace of tan toning. Areas of prooflike surface are present on the upper reverse. The Centennial year mintage was high for the type, but few have survived as Premium Gems. Census: 19 in 66, 7 finer (7/07). (#5501)

MS65 ★ 1876-CC Quarter

1202 1876-CC MS65 ★ NGC. Type Two Reverse. Cameo contrast is noticeable on both sides of this moderately prooflike Gem. A whisper of gold toning denies full brilliance. Splendidly preserved, well struck, and highly desirable. Previously certified as MS65 by PCGS, and its former PCGS insert accompanies the lot. Census: 16 in 65, 10 finer (8/07). *From The Beau Clerc Collection.* (#5502)

Lustrous MS66 1877 Quarter

1203 1877 MS66 PCGS. Type Two Reverse. Satiny with generally bold devices, save for minor softness on Liberty's head and some of the obverse stars. A mixture of light steel-gray, gold, and sky-blue toning adorns the well preserved surfaces. "Even though common, not seen as often as one would think," according to Larry Briggs (1991). (#5504)

Splendid Superb Gem 1877 Seated Quarter

1204 **1877 MS67 PCGS.** Type Two Reverse. Well struck with an intense satiny sheen, and essentially untoned silver-white surfaces that show a hint of golden color along the lower right reverse periphery. Faint clash marks are noted on both obverse and reverse. Despite a high mintage, this issue is scarcer than expected overall, and Superb Gems are rarely seen. Population: 41 in 67, 1 finer (8/07). (#5504)

1205 **1877-CC MS63 PCGS.** A pleasing example of this comparatively available Carson City minor silver issue, solidly struck with lovely blue-green and plum toning over each side. Minimally marked overall, though close inspection reveals a handful of wispy abrasions. (#5505)

1206 **1877-CC MS64 NGC.** Popular as an issue of the Carson City Mint, this date is an excellent choice for type collectors. More than 4 million of these coins were minted, and examples trade for only a modest premium over type prices. This example has satiny silver surfaces with sharp design details and pale champagne toning. (#5505)

Lustrous 1877-S/Horizontal S Quarter, MS64

1207 **1877-S Over Horizontal S MS64 NGC.** VP-001, FS-501, Briggs 4-D. The initial S mintmark was punched into the die horizontally, then corrected with an upright S mintmark. A popular and well known variety. Whispers of olive-green and tan patina race over highly lustrous surfaces, and an attentive strike brings out good definition on the design features. Some light as-made roller marks occur on portions of Liberty. Census: 7 in 64, 3 finer (8/07). (#5507)

1208 **1879 MS65 NGC.** Type Two Reverse. Both sides are pearl-gray in color and essentially untoned. A boldly struck and rather prooflike Gem that has a well preserved reverse. A scarce issue, as only 13,700 pieces were struck. (#5511)

Gorgeous 1879 Quarter, MS66

1209 **1879 MS66 NGC.** Type Two Reverse. An amazing Gem with frosty luster beneath rich heather and sea-green toning, with additional lilac color on the reverse. The 1879 quarter is a low mintage issue, with a total production of only 13,600 coins, although quite a few better grade pieces exist. Population: 26 in 66, 23 finer (8/07). *From The Beau Clerc Collection.* (#5511)

Important 1880 Seated Quarter, MS66

1210 **1880 MS66 PCGS.** An amazing coin, seldom encountered so fine, with satiny silver luster, bold design details, and pristine surfaces. The obverse is lightly toned with peripheral yellow, lilac, and blue . The reverse is similar with additional russet toning. Population: 29 in 66, 8 finer (8/07). *From The Beau Clerc Collection.* (#5512)

Brilliant Prooflike MS67 1881 Quarter

1211 **1881 MS67 Prooflike NGC.** Icy devices and legends contrast with the flashy fields. This carefully preserved high-grade example is well struck, since only the star 8 lacks crisp centrils. Only 12,000 business strikes were produced, since the Bland-Allison Act kept the Mint occupied with silver dollar coinage. *From The Beau Clerc Collection.* (#5513)

1212 **1886 MS62 NGC.** The fields are prooflike, as almost always seen, and yield sharp contrast with mildly frosted, exquisitely struck design elements. Wisps of cobalt-blue, violet, and gray-tan concentrate at the borders. Some wispy obverse marks show up under magnification. Very scarce in Mint State, from a mintage of 5,000 pieces. *From The Beau Clerc Collection.* (#5518)

1213 **1888 MS65 PCGS.** This scarce and underrated issue comes from a mintage of 10,001 circulation strikes. Bright luster adorns this lovely Gem, and occasional wisps of green and tan color visit the margins. A handful of unobtrusive obverse marks likely prevent an even higher grade. *From The Beau Clerc Collection.* (#5520)

1214 **1889 MS65 NGC.** An attentive strike brings out sharp definition, even on the star centers, that are often weak on this issue. The surfaces yield pleasing luster, light gold-beige and pastel blue-gray patina, and reveal just a couple of minute, grade-consistent marks on the obverse. *From The Beau Clerc Collection.* (#5522)

1215 **1891 MS64 NGC.** A crisply struck and enticing near-Gem from the final year of issue, strongly lustrous with vibrant rose, orange, and violet toning at the margins. A wonderful exemplar for the discerning type collector. (#5524)

PROOF SEATED QUARTERS

Rare Choice Proof 1856 Quarter

1216 1856 PR64 NGC. The mintage and survival rate of the 1856 proof quarter are unclear. Walter Breen, in his two *Encyclopedias* (1977 and 1988), gives no mintage figures, but estimates that fewer than 30 examples are known. Larry Briggs (1991) gives a mintage figure of "25+ proofs." NGC and PCGS have graded a total of 42 examples, an unknown number of which are likely resubmissions.
The near-Gem specimen in this lot displays hints of light tan-gold color at the margins, a little more so on the reverse. A solid strike leaves crisp definition on the design features. A few unobtrusive handling marks limit the grade. The nearly imperceptible "bulge" resulting from die failure (alluded to by Breen and Briggs) extends from AM through the left (right facing) wing through the field to the arrows. Census: 8 in 64, 6 finer (8/07). (#5552)

1217 1858 PR63 PCGS. Blue-green and golden-orange patina embraces both sides, with the former more prevalent on the obverse and the latter predominant on the reverse. Crisply struck with scattered hairlines on both sides and a handful of contact marks near Liberty. A great example of this earlier proof quarter. Population: 11 in 63, 14 finer (8/07). (#5554)

1218 1859 PR63 NGC. Rose-orange and violet patina graces the luminous surfaces of this decisively struck, immensely appealing Select quarter. Faint, scattered hairlines are present in the fields. One of only 800 pieces struck. Census: 33 in 63, 64 finer (8/07). (#5555)

Toned PR64 Cameo 1859 Quarter

1219 1859 PR64 Cameo NGC. Only 800 proofs were struck in 1859 and an unknown number were melted at year's end as unsold—apparently Director Snowden overestimated the collecting public's interest in proofs in the late 1850s. This piece shows noticeable frost over the devices, even through the multiple layers of toning that cover each side. The fields are also deeply reflective. An attractive proof striking of this scarcer proof quarter. Census: 3 in 64, 11 finer (8/07). (#85555)

1220 1860 PR63 PCGS. Larry Briggs (1991) writes that 458 of the 1,000 proofs made in 1860 were melted. Golden-tan and light blue patina on the obverse yields to medium intensity cobalt-blue and lavender on the reverse. Sharply struck, save for the usual softness in some of the star centers. Some unobtrusive handling marks on the obverse preclude a higher grade.
From The Beau Clerc Collection. (#5556)

Kaufman's Colorful PR66 1862 Quarter

1221 1862 PR66 NGC. Ex: P. Kaufman. Beautiful sun-gold, plum-red, and powder-blue endow this exactingly struck Premium Gem. Inspection with a loupe fails to locate either carbon or contact. A mere 550 proofs were struck for this Civil War date. Census: 9 in 66, 0 finer (8/07).
From The Beau Clerc Collection. (#5558)

1222 1863 PR63 Cameo NGC. Light almond-gold patina embraces this smooth and mildly glossy Select proof quarter. Precisely struck with noticeable white-on-black contrast.

1223 1865 PR64 NGC. A lovely white proof that projects significant field-motif contrast, and is crisply struck. An inoffensive wiping in the right obverse field limits the grade. Census: 42 in 64, 30 finer (8/07).
From The Beau Clerc Collection. (#5561)

Conditionally Rare 1866 Seated Quarter PR67

1224 1866 Motto PR67 PCGS. First year of the Motto type, and an originally toned Superb Gem example. The obverse surfaces are covered in pastel rose and electric-blue coloration. The reverse is bright and flashy, with glassy mirrored fields and deep golden-brown, rose, and cobalt-blue patina near the lower left periphery. Population: 2 in 67, 0 finer (8/07). (#5565)

1225 1867 PR64 PCGS. The mirrored fields establish notable contrast with the frosty devices, that are exquisitely struck. A thin layer of champagne color rests on both faces. Some faint handling marks just barely preclude a higher grade. Housed in a green-label holder. Population: 38 in 64, 20 finer (8/07).
From The Beau Clerc Collection. (#5566)

1226 1867 PR63 Cameo NGC. This earlier With Motto proof quarter, from an issue of just 625 specimens, exhibits strong contrast between the pale, frosted devices and the butterscotch-toned fields. Boldly impressed with scattered hairlines that preclude a finer grade. Census: 7 in 63 Cameo, 19 finer (8/07). (#85566)

1227 1868 PR62 ANACS. Deep electric-blue, purple-rose, and golden-tan coloration covers both sides of this sharply struck proof. A few minor handling marks limit the grade. (#5567)

1228 1868 PR63 PCGS. This penetratingly struck specimen provides deep mauve and powder-blue patina. A mere 600 proofs were struck, in addition to only 29,400 business strikes. (#5567)

1229 1868 PR63 NGC. One of just 600 proofs struck for the year, this elegantly toned Select specimen has ethereal tan patina over each side. Boldly impressed with strong reflectivity and minor, scattered hairlines in the fields. (#5567)

Colorful Gem Proof 1868 Quarter

1230 1868 PR65 NGC. Briggs 2-B. This obverse die, which was used exclusively for proofs of this date, displays triple punching on the first digit in the date and light recutting inside the upper loop of the final 8. There is also a die break on the scroll between the ER in LIBERTY, and a lump attached to the scroll at the bottom on the letter B. The latter two are curious features for a proof die, but, nonetheless, they make it easy for one to distinguish between proofs and business strikes of the 1868 quarter. This proof striking displays razor sharp definition in all areas with sparkling, deeply mirrored fields. Colorful cobalt-blue toning at the borders gradually changes to magenta, then deep golden-red at the central regions. Census: 12 in 65, 11 finer (8/07).
From The Beau Clerc Collection. (#5567)

1231 1869 PR64 NGC. Vivid gold-orange patina blankets most of this near-Gem, while the upper obverse shows a thin crescent of deep blue-green toning. Crisply struck with pleasing reflectivity and faint, scattered flaws in the fields. An attractive example of this Reconstruction-era issue. (#5568)

1232 1870 PR63 NGC. Although not so designated, this is a deeply toned cameo proof with excellent contrast. Both sides have dark steel toning with splashes of lighter silver color on the reverse. (#5569)

1233 1870 PR64 NGC. Small, intermittent patches of cloudy silver-gray toning dot the golden-tan surfaces of this Choice proof. Well-defined with strong reflectivity and faint hairlines in the obverse fields. One of just 1,000 examples struck. Census: 42 in 64, 25 finer (8/07). (#5569)

1234 1871 PR63 Cameo PCGS. Slivers of cobalt-blue, lavender, and golden-brown toning cling to the right margins of both obverse and reverse. Exquisitely struck, frosty design elements stand out amidst the mirrored fields. A faint and inoffensive staple scratch in the upper right obverse field precludes a higher grade. Population: 6 in 63, 6 finer (8/07).
From The Beau Clerc Collection. (#85570)

1235 1872 PR64 PCGS. Soft golden-gray patina bathes both sides of this sharply struck near-Gem proof. A well cared for example. Population: 39 in 64, 21 finer (8/07).
From The Beau Clerc Collection. (#5571)

Stunning 1872 Gem Proof Quarter

1236 1872 PR65 NGC. This deeply toned Gem proof displays electric-blue color at the margins that yields to lavender and then golden-tan in the central areas. Unlike many proofs of the 1870s that, according to Walter Breen (1977), were carelessly made and poorly struck, this example is strongly and uniformly impressed throughout, thereby adding to its stunning eye appeal. Both sides have been well cared for. Census: 28 in 65, 11 finer (8/07). (#5571)

1237 1873 Arrows PR62 PCGS. This boldly impressed Arrows proof is strongly reflective beneath layers of subdued lavender and gold-orange patina. Both sides show evidence of hairlines and contact, and the right obverse field exhibits a shallow pinscratch. One of just 540 struck. (#5574)

Attractive Toned 1873 Quarter, PR64

1238 1873 Arrows PR64 ANACS. The 1873 quarter, from a mintage of 540 pieces, becomes more difficult to acquire in near-Gem and better levels of preservation. Medium intensity cobalt-blue and lavender patina occupies the right half of the obverse and the marginal areas of the reverse on this PR64 example. Champagne-gold coloration takes over the left obverse half and the central reverse. An attentive strike brings out exquisite definition on the design elements, and a few unobtrusive handling marks prevent a higher grade. (#5574)

Toned, Deeply Mirrored PR64 1873 Arrows Quarter

1239 **1873 Arrows PR64 PCGS.** First of only two years of the Arrows type, and an important and highly collectible coin in proof format. While circulation strikes are normally found with weak details on Liberty's head, no such problem is encountered with proof strikings. This piece has several layers of gray, blue, indigo, and rose toning—enough toning to subdue much of the flash from the mirrored fields for the casual observer. However, when the coin is angled beneath a light, the full reflectivity of the proof finish flashes forcefully through the layers of color. An important proof type coin. (#5574)

Beautifully Toned PR67 1874 Arrows Quarter

1240 **1874 Arrows PR67 NGC.** The 1874 quarter is only available with arrows on each side of the date—unlike the 1873, which is available with and without the arrowheads. The curious thing about the arrows on this two-year type is that they are level on the 1873 coins and point slightly upward on the 1874s. We point this out ever so often in our catalogs, but no one has ever corresponded with us and explained why this is so.

This is a pristine proof striking. The fields are deeply reflective and glassy. The devices have a slight but noticeable overlay of mint frost, which is somewhat surprising given the toning that is present. The obverse shows olive green and rose-gold colors intermixed, while the reverse has a scarlet center that is surrounded by deep cobalt blue. Fully struck throughout. Census: 6 in 67, 1 finer (8/07). (#5575)

1241 **1875 PR64 Cameo NGC.** Type Two Reverse. One of just 700 pieces from the first proof issue following the removal of arrows from the date exergue, this Cameo near-Gem offers delightfully frosted, boldly struck devices that contrast with the faintly hairlined, highly reflective olive-gold fields. Census: 15 in 64 Cameo, 8 finer (8/07). (#85576)

1242 **1876 PR63 PCGS.** Type Two Reverse. Blushes of luminous golden-brown patina enliven this sharply struck example. The left obverse field has a few wispy hairlines, but the surfaces are otherwise clean. The base of the 6 in the date is recut. (#5577)

1243 **1877 PR64 NGC.** Type Two Reverse. Interest in proofs waned after the centennial year, and in 1877, Philadelphia struck just 510 specimen quarters, less than half the previous year's total. This exquisitely struck and strongly reflective piece exhibits faint haze over the lightly hairlined surfaces and a diagonal planchet defect just to the left of Liberty's left (facing) arm. Census: 35 in 64, 31 finer (8/07). (#5578)

1244 **1877 PR63 Cameo PCGS.** Type Two Reverse. Despite a measure of haze in the silver-gray fields, the surfaces remain reflective, and the moderately frosted, sharply struck devices present significant contrast. A lightly hairlined, yet pleasing Select example of this later Seated quarter issue. Population: 5 in 63 Cameo, 9 finer (8/07). (#85578)

1245 **1877 PR65 Cameo NGC.** After the centennial year passed, demand for proofs crashed, and the 1877 proof quarter has a mintage of only 510 specimens. This Gem exhibits moderately frosted, boldly impressed devices that contrast with the ocean-blue and onyx-silver of the fields. Census: 4 in 65 Cameo, 5 finer (8/07). (#85578)

Lightly Toned 1877 Quarter, PR66 Cameo

1246 **1877 PR66 Cameo NGC.** Type Two Reverse. This Premium Gem Cameo proof displays whispers of light tan-gold patina, most noticeable around the obverse border. Well frosted design elements stand out against deeply mirrored fields, and exhibit an attentive strike. Some minute milling marks between stars 3 and 4 serve to pedigree the coin. Census: 4 in 66, 1 finer (8/07). (#85578)

Eliasberg's 1879 Quarter PR66

1247 **1879 PR66 PCGS.** Type Two Reverse. Ex: Eliasberg. Original golden-brown toning is bounded by electric-blue and ruby-red along the rims. The reverse appears immaculate, while the obverse field has only trivial imperfections. A precisely struck Premium Gem with an outstanding pedigree. Housed in a green label holder. *Ex: Louis E. Eliasberg, Sr. Collection (Bowers and Merena, 4/97), lot 1528.* (#5580)

1248 **1880 PR64 NGC.** Type One Reverse, diagnostic for proofs. This date has a combined proof and business strike mintage of fewer than 15,000 pieces. A well struck specimen with a peach and sky-blue obverse and a variegated sea-green and rose-gold reverse. Certified in a prior generation holder. (#5581)

1249 **1880 PR64 PCGS.** An impressive cameo proof, although it carries no designation. Both sides have bright silver color at the centers, surrounded by splendid sea-green toning. (#5581)

Lovely Toned 1880 Quarter, PR66

1250 **1880 PR66 PCGS.** Type One Reverse. This is an extraordinary proof with excellent cameo contrast, although it is not designated as a cameo proof due to the thick sea-green, gold, and iridescent toning on both sides. All design features are boldly detailed. Population: 34 in 66, 15 finer (8/07). (#5581)

1251 **1880 PR64 Cameo PCGS.** Champagne, orange, and blue-green toning graces the shining fields, while the lightly frosted and decisively struck devices show minimal patina. Minor hairlines are present in the fields of this later Seated proof. Population: 18 in 64 Cameo, 21 finer (8/07). (#85581)

Gem Cameo Proof 1880 Quarter

1252 **1880·PR65 Cameo NGC.** Type Two Reverse. Beautiful ocean-blue, honey-gold, and cherry-red shades endow this exactingly struck and unblemished Gem. Cameo contrast is particularly evident on the reverse. Business strikes and proofs combined for fewer than 15,000 pieces. Census: 9 in 65 Cameo, 33 finer (7/07). (#85581)

1253 **1881 PR64 NGC.** Though not noted on the holder, both sides of this Choice Proof display appreciable contrast. Patches of blue and orange peripheral toning surround the minimally patinated inner fields. One of just 975 specimens struck. (#5582)

1254 **1882 PR64 PCGS.** A thin layer of cloud-gray patina appears over the obverse, though that side retains strong reflectivity and the reverse devices show rich frost. A boldly impressed proof with only a handful of faint hairlines in the fields. (#5583)

1255 **1882 PR64 Cameo PCGS.** A veneer of soft champagne color bathes this near-Gem Cameo that is sharply impressed throughout. Nice field-motif contrast on both sides.
From The Beau Clerc Collection. (#85583)

1256 **1883 PR65 PCGS.** Medium intensity cobalt-blue and mauve-gray patina occupy the nicely preserved surfaces of this Gem proof. The design elements are sharply and evenly struck. Population: 36 in 65, 26 finer (8/07).
From The Beau Clerc Collection. (#5584)

Delightful 1884 PR66 Quarter

1257 **1884 PR66 NGC.** Sharp design details and deeply mirrored fields are evident beneath wonderful lilac-gold, sea-green, and iridescent toning on both sides. The designs are lustrous with hidden cameo contrast. Census: 35 in 66, 18 finer (8/07).
From The Beau Clerc Collection. (#5585)

1258 **1884 PR65 Cameo PCGS.** A remarkable cameo proof with hints of champagne toning over deeply mirrored fields. This is a low mintage date, with both proofs and business strikes highly desired by collectors. Population: 8 in 65, 14 finer (8/07). (#85585)

Splendid 1884 Seated Quarter PR66 Cameo

1259 **1884 PR66 Cameo PCGS.** Ex: Gil Clark. This lovely Premium Gem proof is well preserved and nearly pristine. The glassy fields form a splendid backdrop to the sharply defined and thickly frosted central devices. Golden-orange, rose, and blue peripheral toning attractively frames each side. Population: 10 in 66 Cameo, 4 finer (8/07). (#85585)

Enticing Gem Cameo Proof 1885 Quarter

1260 **1885 PR65 Cameo PCGS.** Both sides of this lovely later Seated quarter show unmistakable contrast and clear central detail, though the stars to the right show a hint of softness. The strongly reflective obverse is predominantly silver-gray with a hint of ice-blue, while a touch of spring-green patina visits the reverse rims. Population: 7 in 65 Cameo, 14 finer (7/07). (#85586)

1261 1887 PR65 PCGS. Electric-blue and deep purple toning runs over both faces of this attractive Gem proof quarter, neither of which reveals mentionable blemishes. The motifs are in receipt of a well directed strike. Population: 37 in 65, 22 finer (8/07).
From The Beau Clerc Collection. (#5588)

1262 1890 PR64 PCGS. This near-Gem proof displays considerable field-motif contrast when the coin is rotated beneath a light source. Sharply struck, with well preserved surfaces.
From The Beau Clerc Collection. (#5591)

Ultra Cameo PR66 1890 Quarter

1263 1890 PR66 Ultra Cameo NGC. A white-on-black beauty with boldly struck devices. No hairlines are noticeable, and the fields have minimal detractions. A mere 590 proofs were struck. The final year of low business strike production, although 1890's mintage of 80,000 pieces was multiples of prior years' Philadelphia production. Census: 6 in 66 Ultra Cameo, 16 finer (8/07). (#95591)

1264 1891 PR64 PCGS. Fully struck with pinpoint definition on all of the major and minor design elements, denticles included. Light golden toning occurs on the obverse, and near the upper reverse border. The fields are highly reflective, and a mild cameo effect is noted on both sides of this attractive near-Gem specimen. (#5592)

BARBER QUARTERS

1265 1892 MS66 NGC. Type One Reverse. Swirls of sea-green, cobalt-blue, yellow-gold and bright rose toning dominate each side. Fully struck and nearly unabraded, this lustrous and impressive premium Gem would be a wonderful addition to a high quality first year of issue type set. (#5601)

1266 1894-S MS64 PCGS. The luminous obverse of this near-Gem has lavender and orange toning, while the reverse shows more vibrant luster and bolder amber and ocean-blue hues. An attractive example of this earlier S-mint Barber issue. Population: 40 in 64, 27 finer (8/07). (#5609)

1267 1895 MS65 PCGS. Like other, later Barber issues, the 1895 quarter was not saved in quantity, and Gems are condition rarities today. This shining, well struck example shows lovely amber and sapphire toning in the fields. A faint flaw on Liberty's cheek is of little concern. Population: 11 in 65, 11 finer (8/07). (#5610)

1268 1899-S MS64 NGC. This shining silver-white S-mint quarter, which comes from a mintage of just 708,000 coins, has slightly frosty luster and pleasing detail. Minimally marked with excellent visual appeal. Census: 6 in 64, 16 finer (7/07). (#5624)

1269 1900 MS65 PCGS. A terrific Gem type coin from this popular turn-of-the-century year. Fully struck, much of each side is brilliant still, but almost as much of each side shows an accent of deep reddish-russet toning. Remarkably smooth over the cheek of Liberty and problem-free elsewhere. A lustrous example. (#5625)

Lovely Gem 1900-O Quarter

1270 1900-O MS65 PCGS. Type One Obverse, Type Two Reverse. A faintly toned and thoroughly lustrous Gem with exceptionally smooth fields and devices. The right-side stars, the fletchings, and the right wingtip are typically struck, but the remainder of the design is bold. Rare as a Gem despite a plentiful mintage. Population: 8 in 65, 11 finer (7/07). (#5626)

1271 1900-S MS63 NGC. Type One Obverse, Type Two Reverse. Light tan and ice-blue toning. A razor-sharp strike and refreshingly smooth surfaces ensure the quality of this conditionally rare Barber quarter. Census: 5 in 63, 17 finer (7/07). (#5627)

Key-Date 1901-S Barber Quarter

1272 1901-S Fair 2 ANACS. Original light grayish-brown surfaces are consistent with well worn Barber quarters of all different dates. The obverse has the rim merged into a few stars and letters, but all design elements fully outlined. The reverse has little remaining detail, with all letters essentially worn away, but fortunately with a complete and bold mintmark. (#5630)

Collectible 1901-S Barber Quarter

1273 1901-S Fair 2 NGC. The 1901-S quarter has an impressively low mintage of only 72,664 pieces. This issue was struck before collectors and the general public were aware that a mintage this low was worth setting aside. As a result, almost the entire mintage slipped into circulation and today the vast majority of survivors grade no better than VG. This piece is heavily worn, as one would expect from the grade, but the surfaces are uncleaned and original. Most of each side displays hints of rose coloration with charcoal-gray surrounding the devices. (#5630)

1274 1908 MS65 NGC. Gem and better examples of circulation-strike Barber silver pose a challenge for collectors today, since few examples were saved near the time of striking. This well-defined and shining representative offers elegant veils of gold and sky-blue toning with faint dots of orange at the margins. Census: 12 in 65, 4 finer (8/07). (#5649)

Choice 1909-O Barber Quarter, MS64

1275 **1909-O MS64 PCGS.** This quarter was struck during the final year of coinage operations before the New Orleans Mint permanently ceased production. All three denominations of Barber silver coins were struck during the year, along with a brief coinage of Indian half eagles. Natural gray-brown surfaces are accompanied by splashes of cobalt-blue and iridescent toning. Population: 15 in 64, 7 finer (8/07). (#5655)

Premium Gem 1911-S Barber Quarter

1276 **1911-S MS66 PCGS.** Just 988,000 of these coins were produced, placing the date in 14th position among all Barber quarters. Pristine silver surfaces are fully brilliant, and all design elements are boldly rendered. This delightful Barber quarter ranks close to the finest certified. Population: 30 in 66, 4 finer (8/07). (#5661)

1277 **1913-D MS65 PCGS.** A highly lustrous and largely untoned Gem. The obverse has suitable definition, though the eagle's right (facing) talon is soft. Population: 25 in 65, 10 finer (8/07). (#5665)

1278 **1913-S AG3 ANACS.** Well worn into the rims on each side, this key date example displays nearly full remaining details on GOD WE TRUST, the date, and most of the reverse legends. The tiny mintage of 40,000 pieces was easily the lowest in the entire series. (#5666)

1279 **1913-S Good 6 PCGS.** A heavily circulated, yet pleasing example of this noted Barber quarter key, which has a mintage of only 40,000 pieces. The devices and rims are silver-gray, while the fields are predominantly seal-gray instead. The L and Y of LIBERTY are visible on the headband. (#5666)

1280 **1914-D MS65 PCGS.** With a mintage of just over 3 million pieces, the 1914-D quarter is far from the most common issue, though it does not rank as a key. This strongly lustrous Gem, well-defined save for the eagle's talons, has delicate gold and peach patina over each side. Population: 40 in 65, 9 finer (7/07). (#5668)

PROOF BARBER QUARTERS

1281 **1892 PR65 Cameo NGC.** Type Two Reverse. A gleaming Gem representative from the first year of issue, boldly impressed with essentially untoned fields and richly frosted devices. A touch of tan-orange patina graces the left reverse rim. (#85678)

1282 **1893 PR65 NGC.** Interest in Barber proofs waned after the first year, and in 1893, the Mint struck only 792 pieces for each denomination. This gleaming Gem displays a modicum of contrast and crescents of rich amber-brown patina at the margins. (#5679)

Superb 1893 Quarter, PR67 Cameo

1283 **1893 PR67 Cameo PCGS.** Untoned overall, the heavily frosted devices contrast nicely with the fully mirrored surfaces. For pedigree purposes, a small lintmark is seen on close examination in the wreath on Liberty's head. A carefully preserved first strike. Population: 11 in 67 Cameo, 3 finer (8/07). (#85679)

1284 **1894 PR65 NGC.** This deeply reflective, decisively struck early Barber Gem exhibits regions of toning and brilliance. A splash of ocean-blue toning appears above the portrait, and amber patina covers the lower left reverse. Housed in a prior generation NGC holder. (#5680)

Exemplary PR67 1894 Quarter

1285 **1894 PR67 NGC.** The obverse is brilliant except for a hint of golden-tan color along the border. The reverse, however, is bathed in deep olive and sea-green patina. An intricately struck and essentially pristine Superb Gem, suitable for an advanced collection of Barber proofs. Both sides exhibit a partial wire rim. A scant 972 pieces were struck. Census: 24 in 67, 5 finer (8/07). (#5680)

Outstanding PR68 1894 Quarter

1286 **1894 PR68 NGC.** Dramatic orange and ocean-blue borders surround the brilliant fields and devices. Although the older generation holder lacks a cameo designation, the contrast between the icy devices and flashy fields is undeniable. A scant 972 proofs were struck, and NGC (as of 8/07) has only certified five as PR68 with none finer. (#5680)

Glorious PR68 1895 Quarter

1287 1895 PR68 PCGS. The cherry-red centers cede to ocean-blue and forest-green margins. A powerfully struck specimen that shows cameo contrast on the lightly toned central reverse. A raised lintmark near the eye is as made and diagnostic for the issue. A stingy 880 proofs were struck. Population: 2 in 68, 0 finer (8/07). (#5681)

1288 1896 PR64 PCGS. Iridescent cobalt-blue, olive-green, lavender, and golden-tan patination bathe the proof surfaces of this near-Gem. Sharply struck, with no significant marks. Housed in a green-label holder. (#5682)

Impressive 1896 Quarter, PR65 Cameo

1289 1896 PR65 Cameo PCGS. Brilliant save for a hint of tan patina on Liberty's neck and three or four tiny obverse toning flecks. Obvious icy frost on the devices and deep mirror fields approach a Deep Cameo designation, and the pinpoint-sharp strike is also worthy of mention. Only a few wispy slide marks on the cheek deny assessment at a higher grade. A scant 762 proofs were issued. Population: 6 in 65 Cameo, 13 finer (8/07). (#85682)

Wildly Toned PR67 1899 Quarter

1290 1899 PR67 NGC. Gorgeous pumpkin-orange, lilac, and sky-blue invigorate the obverse. Deep olive and ocean-blue dominate the reverse. This exquisitely struck Superb Gem is splendidly free from hairlines or planchet imperfections. The proof mintage of 846 pieces ensures a paucity of high quality survivors. Census: 20 in 67, 6 finer (8/07). (#5685)

1291 1901 PR64 PCGS. Vivid amber-gold patina with cobalt-blue peripheral toning envelops both sides of this early 20th century Barber quarter. Decisively struck with strongly reflective, faintly hairlined fields. Population: 48 in 64, 51 finer (8/07). (#5687)

Toned 1901 Barber Quarter PR66 Cameo

1292 1901 PR66 Cameo PCGS. Khaki-green, gold, and electric-blue toning adorns the surfaces of this crisply struck Premium Gem. Glassy reflectivity is obvious in the fields, and mild cameo contrast occurs on each side. The 1901 proof Barber quarter issue was limited to 813 pieces, and fewer than half that number are known to survive today. Coins with noteworthy Cameo quality are especially scarce. Population: 12 in 66 Cameo, 3 finer (8/07). (#85687)

Elusive 1901 Quarter, PR67 Cameo

1293 1901 PR67 Cameo NGC. This is an extraordinary opportunity, not only for the Superb technical quality, but also for its cameo contrast. Only a small portion of the 912 proof quarters struck in 1901 have any degree of cameo contrast. The surfaces are fully brilliant with wispy champagne toning at the borders. Deeply mirrored fields bring out the attractive design on this coin. Census: 8 in 67, 4 finer (8/07). (#85687)

Visually Alluring 1903 Quarter PR64 ★ Cameo

1294 1903 PR64 ★ Cameo NGC. This is a flashy, utterly brilliant proof quarter that exhibits stark white-on-black contrast between frosted devices and deeply mirrored fields. The design elements are sharply struck, and surface distractions are minimal. NGC does not include the "Star" as a part of its assigned grade designation very often, but this coin definitely qualifies on the basis of outstanding eye appeal. (#85689)

Impressive 1903 Barber Quarter PR65 Cameo

1295 1903 PR65 Cameo NGC. This is a sparkling Gem proof quarter with razor-sharp striking details and intense field-to-device contrast on both sides. An area of excess die polish is noted along the lower edge of Liberty's jawline and below the ear, but this does not affect the technical grade of the piece. A few small milky spots in the obverse fields prevent an even loftier grade assessment. (#85689)

Pleasing 1904 Quarter, PR66

1296 1904 PR66 NGC. A total of 670 proof quarters were struck in 1904. This Premium Gem displays essentially untoned surfaces that yield a degree of field-motif contrast. The strike is exceptional, imparting exquisite definition to the design elements, and both faces are impeccably preserved. A most pleasing proof Barber quarter. Census: 28 in 66, 35 finer (8/07). (#5690)

1297 1906 PR66 PCGS. The Barber design generated less enthusiasm than its Seated predecessor, and no 20th century proof of the former design reached a four-figure mintage. The gleaming, modestly contrasting silver-white specimen offered here is one of just 675 pieces coined. Population: 31 in 66, 19 finer (8/07). (#5692)

Incredible 1906 Quarter, PR68 ★

1298 1906 PR68 ★ NGC. Fully brilliant silver-white surfaces are entirely void of toning on either side. Light cameo contrast is visible on the obverse, with deeper contrast on the reverse. Considered separately, the reverse seems to have strong enough contrast for a Cameo designation. This example is the single finest 1906 proof quarter that NGC has ever graded. (#5692)

1299 1909 PR64 NGC. An untoned and strongly reflective representative of this later proof Barber quarter issue. Boldly impressed with faint, grade-defining hairlines in the fields. One of just 650 specimens struck. (#5695)

Colorful Superb Gem Proof 1909 Quarter

1300 1909 PR67 NGC. Splashes of jade-green, lilac-red, and ocean-blue enrich this gorgeously toned and flashy Superb Gem. Only the eagle's right shield corner has a hint of softness, and the preservation is exemplary. Just 650 proofs were produced. Census: 24 in 67, 9 finer (7/07). (#5695)

1301 1911 PR65 PCGS. A boldly struck Gem with plenty of eye appeal. Thin rose and gold patina scarcely impedes the deep reflectivity in the fields. Population: 29 in 65, 53 finer (8/07). (#5697)

1302 1912 PR64 NGC. The obverse of this gleaming Choice proof has a touch of champagne patina, while the reverse offers a richer coat of green-gold toning. Decisively struck with faint hairlines and a single contact mark in the right obverse field. A pleasing example of this later Barber issue. (#5698)

1303 1912 PR64 NGC. Fully struck throughout with watery reflectivity in the fields and a slight degree of frost on the devices. Free of contact marks with a few wispy hairlines on the obverse that limit the grade. A low mintage issue of just 700 pieces. (#5698)

1304 1913 PR63 NGC. This Select example is from a scant mintage of 613 pieces, and belongs to one of the key issues in the proof Barber quarter series. It is crisply struck, with deeply reflective fields and mildly frosted devices. A few wispy hairlines on the obverse limit the grade. (#5699)

Low Mintage PR66 1914 Quarter

1305 1914 PR66 NGC. Well struck and unabraded with glassy fields and delicate gold and apple-green toning. A faint lintmark passes through star 4, as made. Only 380 proofs were struck, the lowest proof mintage of the series, and the smallest emission for the denomination after 1858. Census: 26 in 66, 24 finer (8/07). (#5700)

STANDING LIBERTY QUARTERS

Good Key Date 1916 Standing Liberty

1306 1916 Good 4 PCGS. Although graded Good 4, all legends are clear except for the top of the date. The eagle's wings display noticeable plumage detail. A bright example of this famous key date quarter. Light khaki-gold toning deepens slightly near the rims. No marks are worthy of comment. (#5704)

Choice Fine 1916 Standing Liberty Quarter

1307 1916 Fine 15 NGC. Although it shows considerable signs of circulation, the date is complete and bold, arguably the most important consideration when choosing a lower or middle grade circulated example of this low mintage key-date issue. Both sides have natural light silver-gray surfaces with darker charcoal toning along the borders and around the devices.
From The Beau Clerc Collection. (#5704)

VF 1916 Standing Liberty Quarter

1308 1916 VF20 PCGS. The date is generally clear, with only the top of the 6 indistinct. The eagle's plumage is also well defined. This key date quarter has slate-gray devices and subtle ice-blue and almond-gold fields. Faint marks are present beneath the motto. Among 20th century quarters, only the 1913-S has a lower mintage. (#5704)

Select Full Head 1916 Quarter

1309 1916 MS63 Full Head PCGS. The borders exhibit a hint of tan toning, but most collectors would regard this satiny to lustrous key date representative as fully brilliant. Alertly struck, even on the date and the eagle's breast feathers. Evaluation with a lens confirms the unblemished quality of the fields and devices. The coveted 1916 is famous for its tiny emission of 52,000 pieces, released sufficiently late in the year that most folks saw their first Standing Liberty quarter in 1917. By that time, the high mintage 1917 was the predominate new issue, and those pieces were set aside by the curious in greater numbers than the elusive 1916. (#5705)

1310 1917 Type One MS63 Full Head PCGS. Silver-gray surfaces display sharply struck design elements, culminating in a full head and at least partial delineation in the inner shield. A handful of minute marks help define the grade.
From The Beau Clerc Collection. (#5707)

1311 **1917 Type One MS65 Full Head NGC.** Dramatically toned in speckled jade-green, golden-brown, and slate. Luster nonetheless dominates the nearly unabraded surfaces. An exactingly struck Gem of this briefly produced 20th century type. (#5707)

1312 **1917 Type One MS65 Full Head PCGS.** Sharply struck and eminently appealing, jewel-toned sapphire and amethyst at the margins with strongly lustrous silver-gray centers. An enticing Full Head Gem representative of this popular type issue. (#5707)

1313 **1917 Type One MS65 Full Head PCGS.** A luminous and sublimely toned Gem exemplar of this popular type issue, boldly detailed with excellent visual appeal. The lavender patina displays lovely sky-blue and green-gold tints. (#5707)

1314 **1917 Type One MS66 Full Head PCGS.** A satiny and exquisitely preserved representative of this popular type issue, sharply struck with dappled silver-gray and tan-gold toning over both sides. Immensely appealing. (#5707)

1315 **1917 Type One MS66 Full Head NGC.** This coin demonstrates just how attractive a Type One Standing Liberty quarter can be. Fully struck with lovely, pale silver-gold toning that is illuminated by gleaming luster. The matte-like surfaces are virtually pristine. (#5707)

1316 **1917-D Type One MS65 PCGS.** This crisply detailed Type One Gem, which comes from an issue of just over 1.5 million pieces, offers unusually beautiful patina over the shining and well-preserved surfaces. Rich rose and orange peripheral toning yields to subtle green-gold and sky-blue shadings in the centers. Population: 70 in 65 Full Head, 15 finer (8/07). (#5708)

1317 **1917-D Type One MS64 Full Head NGC.** This crisply struck Choice beauty offers delightful luster and delectable dots of plum patina at the margins. The centers are untoned on this carefully preserved quarter, from the only Type One issue struck at Denver. *From The Laguna Niguel Collection, Part Two.* (#5709)

1318 **1917-D Type One MS65 Full Head PCGS.** A shining and solidly struck Gem representative of this popular Type One issue, minimally toned with great eye appeal. Denver struck just over 1.5 million quarters before the change to the less revealing Type Two design. (#5709)

1319 **1917-D Type One MS65 Full Head NGC.** The 1917-D Type One has the second-lowest mintage of four pre-modification issues, behind only the famed 1916. This frosty and solidly struck Gem shows little patina on the obverse, though faint dots of olive-tan toning appear on the reverse. (#5709)

1917-D Type One Quarter, MS66 Full Head

1320 **1917-D Type One MS66 Full Head PCGS.** A frosty Premium Gem with brilliant silver luster and splashes of iridescent toning along the borders and near the devices on each side. All three of the 1917 Type One issues are easily located in any desired grade, including sharply struck Gems like this coin. Needless to say, higher grades translate to lower populations, thus higher desirability. Population: 99 in 66, 17 finer (8/07). (#5709)

Lustrous 1917-D Type One Quarter, MS66 Full Head

1321 **1917-D Type One MS66 Full Head PCGS.** Sharp design elements and brilliant, frosty silver luster are the hallmarks of this lightly toned example. Type One quarters were coined at all three Mints, and examples are typically available in most any grade, although just 17 finer full head examples of the Denver Mint issue have been certified by PCGS (8/07). (#5709)

1322 **1917-S Type One MS64 Full Head NGC.** The fine-grain surfaces display intense mint luster and silver-white color that yields to a bit of pale gold border toning on each side. Sharply struck and impressively preserved, this Type One quarter shows just a few wispy field marks on the reverse. (#5711)

Impressive 1917-S Type One Quarter MS65 Full Head

1323 **1917-S Type One MS65 Full Head PCGS.** This impressive Gem has flashy, intensely lustrous surfaces that reveal fine grain textures under low magnification. It is essentially untoned, except for a streak of red-brown color that occurs on the right center of the obverse. Carefully preserved and free of distractions, this piece is also boldly struck, with full detail on Liberty's head and shield rivets. (#5711)

1324 **1917 Type Two MS66 PCGS.** Though Liberty's head falls shy of full details, the rivets of the shield and other design elements are strong. A shining, minimally toned representative from the first year of the revised Standing Liberty design. Population: 20 in 66, 1 finer (8/07). (#5714)

1325 **1917 Type Two MS66 Full Head PCGS.** A luminous, eminently appealing Premium Gem, boldly impressed with lovely blue-gray patina over both sides. A few tiny flecks of deeper patina are visible on the obverse of this delightful Type One quarter. PCGS has graded only six finer examples (8/07). (#5715)

Premium Gem 1917-S Type Two Quarter

1326 **1917-S Type Two MS66 NGC.** Only one finer non-full head example of this issue has been certified by NGC. This grading company has also graded 12 Full Head pieces in MS66 or finer quality. Despite noticeable design weakness, this piece has exceptional frosty silver luster with wispy gold toning. Population: 15 in 66, 0 finer (8/07).
From The Beau Clerc Collection. (#5718)

1327 **1918 MS65 PCGS.** This Gem example of the early 1918 Standing Liberty quarter reveals a remarkable level of preservation which is not often seen on other survivors. Neither side of the piece displays any mark that is evident to the unaided eye. All of the shield rivets are crisply struck, and Liberty's head detail is nearly full. Population: 61 in 65, 20 finer (8/07). (#5720)

1328 **1918 MS65 Full Head PCGS.** Splashes of gold toning enhance the lustrous ivory surfaces of this frosty Gem. Both sides are sharply detailed, include complete head details and sharp shield elements. The latter is a particularly troublesome area of the design, usually lacking full rivets (#5721)

Elusive 1918-S Quarter, MS64 Full Head

1329 **1918-S MS64 Full Head PCGS.** A scarce San Francisco date in the series exhibiting satiny luster and some very light, natural throughout. The head detail is full and sharp, but some of the rivets are missing from the shield. A few minor contact marks limit the grade. Population: 82 in 64, 34 finer (8/07). (#5725)

VF25 Overdate Standing Liberty Quarter

1330 **1918/7-S VF25 PCGS.** Because of the nature of the raised numerals on Type Two quarters, circulated examples show dates that are more heavily worn than other design elements. This, of course, was corrected in 1925 by recessing the date, but on overdate quarters it is a challenge. This particular coin shows the expected faint definition on the digits in the date. And the all-important 7 underdigit is clearly present as bisects the lower loop of the 8 and eliminates two-thirds of it. The surfaces are moderately bright with a mild overlay of rose and lilac toning. Evenly worn over the remainder of the devices. (#5726)

Pleasing 1918/7-S Quarter, VF30

1331 **1918/7-S VF30 NGC.** This Choice VF piece has splendid medium gray surfaces with darker outlines around the border and the devices. The date is slightly worn, but fully visible and the overdate element is sharp, even without magnification. A nice addition to a higher level circulated collection of Standing Liberty quarters. (#5726)

XF Sharpness 1918/7-S Quarter

1332 **1918/7-S—Improperly Cleaned—NCS. XF Details.** The downstroke of the underdigit 7 is partly separated from the lower loop of the 8. The head is typically struck, but the devices show only minor wear. The gunmetal-gray surfaces are cloudy from moderate hairlines, and a few faint marks are noted above the eagle's tail. (#5726)

Desirable 1918/7-S Quarter, AU58

1333 1918/7-S AU58 NGC. The 1918/7-S quarter is one of the most sought-after overdates in the American coinage series, and after the key-date 1916 issue, is the most expensive coin in the Standing Liberty quarter series in circulated condition. Since comparatively few are thought to have been struck, and the exposed date was especially vulnerable to wear, nice examples of this coin are difficult to acquire.

The high-end AU piece being offered in this lot displays considerable luster, as well as occasional splashes of electric-blue, purple, and olive-tan patination, that are slightly more extensive and deeper in hue on the obverse. Strong definition is noted on the design features, including virtually all of the vertical stripes on the inner shield, and about half of the horizontal ones. Two-thirds or so of the head detail is clear, as well as most of the chain mail. The overdate feature is particularly sharp. Both sides are quite clean. Census: 32 in 58, 44 finer (7/07). (#5726)

Near-Mint 1918/7-S Quarter

1334 1918/7-S AU58 NGC. Many collectors seek coins that fall in the higher numerical level of the AU grade, providing an attractive collection that is still rather affordable. Locating a properly graded AU55 or AU58 example of this overdate is quite a challenge.

This specimen is boldly detailed, save for Liberty's head, with the overdate feature especially prominent. Both sides have nearly full mint luster with satiny silver surfaces. Slight traces of wear on the highpoints of the obverse and reverse designs are consistent with the grade assigned by NGC. An important opportunity for the advanced collector. (#5726)

Near Full Head Gem 1919-S Quarter

1335 1919-S MS65 PCGS. Standing Liberty quarters exist with varying degrees of strike. This example, for instance, has about 75% of the head details visible, being a much better choice than another similar quality Gem with 50% or less of the head details remaining. Brilliant and frosty luster is accompanied by hints of gold and iridescent toning. Population: 41 in 65, 10 finer (8/07). *From The Beau Clerc Collection.* (#5732)

1336 **1920 MS66 PCGS.** A lovely Premium Gem with nearly full head details. Both sides are frosty with brilliant silver luster and wispy gold toning. The shield is fully defined, and only the three leaves on Liberty's head are flat. All other head details are sharp and bold. Clearly far above average for the date. (#5734)

1337 **1920 MS65 Full Head NGC.** This is a beautiful, untoned Gem example of the 1920 Standing Liberty quarter. This type is not often seen with such clear striking definition along with such clean surfaces. Lustrous and bright, the piece exhibits crisp detailing of Liberty's head and shield rivets. On the reverse, a wispy die crack extends across the eagle's breast, slightly blunting the feather definition. The obverse is virtually pristine, while the reverse only shows a couple of minor blemishes.
From The Arnold & Harriet Collection, Part Two. (#5735)

Important 1920 Quarter, MS66 Full Head

1338 **1920 MS66 Full Head PCGS.** The head and shield of this elusive coin are both sharply detailed. Frosty silver surfaces shine through medium ivory, gold, and iridescent toning on both sides. Hints of blue are also evident on the reverse. Full Head examples of this date, especially in Premium Gem or finer condition, are highly elusive. Population: 16 in 66, 3 finer (8/07). (#5735)

1339 **1921 AU58 NGC.** This still-lustrous, attractively toned piece hails from a mintage of under 2 million pieces. The obverse is predominantly silver-gray with orange toning at the margins, while the reverse has richer peach patina. A modicum of highpoint friction precludes a Mint State designation. (#5740)

1340 **1921 AU58 NGC.** A key-date in the series, the 1921 is often lacking from collections of these coins. This piece, with its light gold toning, is attractive and highly desirable. Slight friction on Liberty's knee keeps it away from a Mint State grade. (#5740)

1341 **1923 MS66 PCGS.** The delicate gold and blue patina that graces this Premium Gem yields to deeper orange at the right obverse and reverse rims. Pleasingly lustrous with excellent definition on the shield, though Liberty's head falls just shy of the Full Head mark. PCGS has graded 15 coins finer (8/07). (#5742)

Lustrous Near-Gem 1923-S Quarter

1342 **1923-S MS64 NGC.** An amazing Choice Mint State example of the elusive key-date '23-S quarter, with brilliant silver luster, satiny surfaces, and mostly sharp design features. Faint champagne toning is detected on each side of this near-Gem. Census: 43 in 64, 65 finer (8/07). (#5744)

Impressive MS68 1924 Standing Liberty Quarter

1343 **1924 MS68 NGC.** This is a remarkably attractive coin that exhibits gleaming, frosty luster over silver surfaces that reveal light golden iridescence near the peripheries. The striking details are bold, and a mere whisper away from the Full Head category. The date and the shield rivets are crisply impressed, and both sides of the piece are essentially pristine. One of just six examples to receive the MS68 grade designation at NGC and PCGS combined, with none certified any finer by either service. (#5746)

Full Head Gem 1924-D Quarter

1344 **1924-D MS65 Full Head PCGS.** A shimmering and lightly toned Gem that benefits from impeccably preserved fields and devices. Liberty's waist is sharply struck, and the three helmet sprigs are clearly outlined. The usual two shield rivets are soft, while the remainder of the shield is intricately brought up. Population: 43 in 65 Full Head, 14 finer (8/07). (#5749)

Rare 1924-D Quarter, MS66 Full Head

1345 1924-D MS66 Full Head PCGS. An incredible example, the 1924-D is one of the most difficult Standing Liberty quarters to find with full head details. The typical example has the head almost entirely flat. Noted Standing Liberty quarter authority Jay Cline writes that "there are some screamers out there in MS65 FH and MS66 FH with strong dates, but it takes a lot of shoe leather to find them." According to Cline, examples must have a full, strong date to qualify as MS65 or finer. This example qualifies! The only weakness evident is three of the shield rivets, and even those are still faintly visible. Population: 14 in 66, 1 finer (8/07). (#5749)

1346 1924-S MS63 PCGS. A surprisingly bright, minimally toned Select representative of this mid-date S-mint Standing Liberty quarter. Well struck with a number of light abrasions that preclude a finer grade. (#5750)

1347 1924-S MS65 NGC. Though available in lower grades, true Gems of this issue are scarce and elusive. This is one such coin, solidly struck and largely untoned with soft, pleasing luster and carefully preserved surfaces. A pleasing Type Two piece. Census: 56 in 65, 23 finer (8/07). (#5750)

Choice Full Head 1924-S Quarter

1348 1924-S MS64 Full Head PCGS. Liberty's head is needle-sharp, and the date is also exactingly defined. Only the two shield rivets near the waist lack absolute detail. This brilliant and highly lustrous near-Gem has an outstanding obverse, and is limited in grade only by minor grazes beneath the left (facing) wing. Population: 52 in 64 Full Head, 37 finer (8/07). (#5751)

1349 1925 MS65 Full Head PCGS. Though much more available in lower grades than its 1924 counterpart, the 1925 has a similar survival rate in Gem. This boldly struck and essentially untoned piece offers powerful luster and elegant visual appeal. (#5753)

Beautiful 1925 Quarter, MS66 Full Head

1350 1925 MS66 Full Head NGC. This is an extremely attractive Premium Gem with a sharp strike, intense satiny luster, and light reddish-gold and green peripheral toning. This is a common date in circulated grades, but Mint State examples are surprisingly scarce, especially at the Gem Full Head level or higher. (#5753)

Desirable 1925 Quarter, MS66 Full Head

1351 1925 MS66 Full Head NGC. A boldly defined piece that has pale lavender patina around a champagne center on the reverse. Lustrous and pleasing. Despite a mintage exceeding 12 million coins, true full head pieces are seldom encountered in the marketplace. Census: 23 in 66, 10 finer (8/07). (#5753)

1352 **1926 MS66 PCGS.** A satiny Premium Gem, light silver color is intermingled with gold and iridescent toning. Not fully struck, but sharply detailed in most areas. (#5754)

1353 **1926 MS65 Full Head PCGS.** An attentively struck and attractive Gem exemplar of the first Recessed Date Philadelphia issue. Delicate green-gold, orange, and lavender tints grace the otherwise silver-gray surfaces. Population: 73 in 65 Full Head, 24 finer (8/07). (#5755)

Full Head Near-Mint 1926-S Quarter

1354 **1926-S AU58 Full Head NGC.** The lustrous surfaces appear Mint State to the unaided eye, although a strong loupe locates a trace of friction on the knee and ear hole. Nonetheless, this unmarked quarter has exemplary eye appeal for the grade, since marks are inconsequential. A better date that rarely comes with complete detail on Liberty's head. Census: 3 in 58 Full Head, 37 finer (7/07). (#5759)

1355 **1927 MS66 NGC.** Mottled mint-green, burnt-orange, violet, and crimson toning drapes the shining surfaces. While nicely detailed for the most part, some softness is seen in the central obverse, on the two bottom stars, on the eagle's breast, and on some of the feathers of the left wing. A wonderful Premium Gem example of this Type Three issue. Census: 14 in 66, 2 finer (8/07). (#5760)

1356 **1927 MS64 Full Head PCGS.** Delicate, swirling luster and enticing patina are the hallmarks of this striking, boldly impressed near-Gem. Lilac and champagne tints grace the well-preserved surfaces. (#5761)

1357 **1927 MS66 Full Head PCGS.** A remarkable piece with few peers, the surfaces have frosty luster and splashes of iridescence. All of the design motifs are sharply detailed. Population: 45 in 66, 5 finer (8/07). (#5761)

1358 **1927-D MS64 Full Head NGC.** Delicate golden-tan and silver-gray patina with a touch of crimson graces both sides of this Full Head near-Gem. Well-defined overall, though the lower left shield shows a measure of softness. The 1927-D quarter has a mintage of under a million pieces. (#5763)

1359 **1927-S XF40 ANACS.** This key date example displays moderate wear over Liberty's highpoints, and on the eagle. Light-gray and charcoal-gray coloration yields to sky-blue, amber, and purple-red iridescence along the reverse periphery. (#5764)

1360 **1928 MS65 Full Head NGC.** In addition to the three olive leaves, ear hole, and distinct hairline, Liberty's head displays a faint die crack. This strongly lustrous Gem has faint golden toning at the obverse peripheries and reddish-orange patina in the regions below the eagle's outstretched wings. Census: 44 in 65 Full Head, 23 finer (8/07). (#5767)

1361 **1928-D MS66 PCGS.** The surfaces of this later D-mint Standing Liberty quarter are luminous beneath luminous, ethereal turquoise patina. A well struck and carefully preserved example. PCGS has graded only two finer examples (8/07). (#5768)

1362 **1929 MS66 PCGS.** Intense satiny mint luster radiates from each side of this flashy Premium Gem. The unmarked surfaces are untoned in the centers, with small amounts of brown and russet patina near the peripheries. Boldly struck, but not quite sharply enough to merit a Full Head designation. Population: 23 in 66, 2 finer (7/07). (#5772)

Lavishly Toned Superb 1929 Quarter

1363 **1929 MS67 NGC.** Splashes of apple-green and orange overlie the lustrous pearl-gray surfaces. Remarkably void of contact, and the eye appeal is also exemplary. The strike is good, with the expected slight softness on the center of Liberty's head and on the two shield rivets near Liberty's waist. Housed in an earlier generation NGC holder. Census: 2 in 67, 0 finer (8/07). (#5772)

1364 **1929 MS65 Full Head PCGS.** An important issue among Gem quality type collectors, this lovely example is certainly high-end for the grade. The prime focal areas are free of even the most trivial abrasion and both sides show pleasing cartwheel effects. Housed in an early-generation PCGS holder with a pale green label. (#5773)

1365 **1929 MS65 Full Head PCGS.** Sharply struck with shining luster and essentially brilliant surfaces, though the right reverse shows a touch of milky toning. Close inspection reveals a handful of tiny flaws, though this is mere nitpicking of a fundamentally appealing Gem. (#5773)

1366 **1929-D MS65 NGC,** lightly toned and lustrous with clean surfaces and occasional incompleteness of strike at the borders; and a **1905 Liberty Nickel MS64 PCGS,** booming luster, a suitable strike, a small reverse spot at 9:30. (Total: 2 coins) (#5774)

1367 **1929-S MS66 PCGS.** While not completely struck in other areas, the all-important head detail on Liberty is just an ear hole away from Full Head status. Lustrous with some attractive speckled toning on each side. Population: 89 in 66, 7 finer (7/07). (#5776)

1368 **1930 MS66 Full Head NGC.** Solidly struck and practically untoned with exemplary luster. Though a touch of weakness visits the shield, Liberty's head is bold. A lovely example of this popular Type Three issue. (#5779)

1369 **1930-S MS66 Full Head NGC.** Magenta, gray, and yellow-gold patina embraces the highly lustrous surfaces. This final-year piece offers exquisite detail on Liberty's head, and the fields are carefully preserved. NGC has graded just 20 finer Full Head pieces (7/07). (#5781)

WASHINGTON QUARTERS

1370 1932 MS66 PCGS. Faint speckled russet patina occurs on both sides, while the reverse also displays a significant degree of champagne-tan and lilac toning. Lustrous and well struck, with blemish-free surfaces. An attractive and conditionally scarce Premium Gem from the first year of the Washington quarter series. PCGS has only graded a single coin finer (8/07). (#5790)

1371 1932-D AU58 NGC. Well detailed with lovely satin luster and attractive reddish-russet peripheral patina. The smooth, unmarked surfaces show traces of wear on the design's highpoints, preventing a Mint State grade assessment. A pleasing near-Mint representative of this key issue from the first year of the Washington quarter. (#5791)

1372 1932-D AU58 NGC. Delicate silver-gray patina graces both sides of this near-Mint key, and the upper obverse shows a blush of vivid peach. Minor friction affects the well-defined portrait, and wispy abrasions are present in the fields. Pleasing nonetheless. (#5791)

1373 1932-D MS61 NGC. The 1932-D has a slightly higher mintage than the 1932-S, at 436,800 pieces versus 408,000 pieces, respectively. The '32-D has proven slightly scarcer than its San Francisco Mint counterpart, however. This example displays satin luster and light champagne-gold toning. Three or four tiny milling marks are noted on the upper half of the obverse. (#5791)

1374 1932-D MS62 NGC. Everyone desires Mint State examples of the '32-D and '32-S quarters, long known for their status as key-date coins. Attractive steel, lilac, and golden-brown on both sides masks the satiny luster. (#5791)

1375 1932-D MS62 PCGS. Neither the Denver nor the San Francisco Washington quarter issue had a mintage of over half a million pieces. This D-mint example offers excellent luster and minimal patina. Light abrasions are noted in the fields and on the well struck devices. (#5791)

Lustrous MS64 1932-D Quarter

1376 1932-D MS64 PCGS. The Denver mint 1932 quarters are significantly scarcer to locate than their San Francisco counterparts, in spite of similar mintages. According to Breen, this is because fewer rolls were set aside of the D-mint quarters. This is an exceptionally attractive example that shows luxuriant, satin-like mint luster. Nearly brilliant over most of each side with deeper flecks of russet toning around the margin on the obverse. (#5791)

Originally Toned MS65 1932-D Quarter

1377 1932-D MS65 PCGS. Study of the evolution of the Washington quarter demonstrates how coin designs are seldom (ever?) a straight line from concept to finished product. The Washington design was originally intended for the half dollar. Congress intervened and changed it to a quarter. The winning design was to be chosen from entrants submitted to the Commission of Fine Arts. Instead, Treasury Secretary Andrew W. Mellon chose the design he wanted. At least the coin was issued on the bicentennial of Washington's birth, and the design is based on the Houdon bust of the first president.

The low-mintage 1932-D is rarely offered in Gem condition. This is a lovely, lustrous example that has speckled iridescent toning over the obverse. The reverse is mostly brilliant in the center with the same iridescence around the margin. An outstanding '32-D quarter. Population: 63 in 65, 1 finer (8/07). (#5791)

1378 1932-S MS62 NGC. Not easy to obtain at any grade level, the first-year 1932-S Washington quarter had a relatively tiny mintage of just 408,000 pieces, ensuring its status as a key date. This example is untoned on the obverse and displays a rich coating of mint-green, amber, and red-brown patina over the reverse. Small contact marks limit the grade. (#5792)

1379 **1932-S MS63 NGC.** Lustrous and untoned on the obverse, with golden-bronze and speckled forest-green patina over the reverse. This is a well struck key date from the first year of the Washington quarter series. A few trivial contact marks and luster breaks define the grade. (#5792)

1380 **1932-S MS63 NGC.** Boldly struck, lustrous, and mostly untoned, save for occasional light splashes of olive patina. A handful of trivial marks are noted on each side. One of the two most important key dates in the Washington quarter series. (#5792)

1381 **1932-S MS63 NGC.** Delicate khaki-gold and jade-green freckles are noted along the borders of this alertly struck and attractively preserved rare date quarter. Blazing luster confirms the originality. (#5792)

1382 **1932-S MS63 NGC.** Boldly struck with creamy luster and milky-silver surfaces that show a touch of russet patina near the borders. A few wispy milling marks are not unexpected for the Select Mint State grade level. An important first-year key date in the series. (#5792)

1383 **1932-S MS64 PCGS.** An attractive Choice example of this West Coast Washington quarter key, highly lustrous beneath dappled blue and gold patina over the upper obverse and champagne toning on the reverse. Well-defined with excellent visual appeal for the grade. (#5792)

1384 **1932-S MS64 NGC.** Potent luster sweeps this sharply impressed key date near-Gem. Light to medium golden toning congregates near the rims. A few faint marks on the left obverse determine the grade. (#5792)

1385 **1932-S MS64 NGC.** Near-Gem examples of this key date are extremely scarce, compared to the number of Washington quarter collectors. This piece is lustrous with smooth, only slightly marked surfaces. Faint toning streaks are noted on each side. (#5792)

1386 **1932-S MS64 PCGS.** The obverse of this first-year Washington key is predominantly toned silver-gray, while areas at the margins show lemon-gold patina. The luminous reverse shows only small dots of blood-red at the margins. A pleasingly detailed and well-preserved piece from an issue originally meant as a circulating commemorative. PCGS has graded only 91 finer pieces (8/07). (#5792)

Key Date Gem 1932-S Washington Quarter

1387 **1932-S MS65 NGC.** 1932 was the first year of the Washington quarter series. The Denver and San Francisco Mints only produced 436,800 and 408,000 pieces, respectively, making those the two key dates in the popular, long-lived series. A slight degree of gray-brown color rests near the peripheries of this lustrous example. A grade-defining mark is barely visible in the right obverse field. Census: 54 in 65, 5 finer (8/07). (#5792)

1388 **1934 Light Motto MS66 PCGS.** Impressively preserved, this Premium Gem example of the scarce Light Motto variety displays satiny surfaces that are lightly toned and mark-free. A touch of charcoal-gray color occurs near the lower obverse and reverse peripheries. Conditionally scarce and rare any finer. Population: 62 in 66, 5 finer (8/07). (#5794)

1389 **1934-D Medium Motto MS65 PCGS.** The centers of this strongly lustrous Gem are silver-white, while the margins have varying degrees of lemon-yellow, tan, and bronze toning. An attractive example of this early issue. (#5796)

1390 **1934-D Heavy Motto MS65 NGC.** Lightly toned in honey, ice-blue, and autumn-brown. A beautiful and lustrous Gem of this popular low mintage issue. The mintmark is filled, but the strike is good and only unimportant marks are present. (#85796)

1391 **1934-D Heavy Motto MS65 PCGS.** The Heavy Motto variety of this issue is very scarce at the Gem level of preservation. This piece is well struck and nicely preserved, with bright satiny luster and extensive mottled patina on both sides, in several different hues. Turquoise, russet, and golden-brown are the most prominent. Population: 27 in 65, 13 finer (8/07). (#85796)

1392 **1934-D Heavy Motto MS65 NGC.** Small D. This is the sole example of the Small D, Heavy Motto variety that is certified as such by NGC (on the holder). It is also a frosty, highly lustrous, brilliant Gem example of this Washington quarter semi-key date issue. Boldly struck and well preserved, there are no objectionable marks on either side. (#85796)

1393 **1935-D MS66 PCGS.** Whispers of attractive olive-green toning exhibit gold-orange and crimson accents. Boldly impressed with bright luster and the great luster often found on high-end examples of this early issue. PCGS has graded 12 finer pieces (8/07). (#5798)

1394 **1935-S MS66 PCGS.** A well struck and satiny S-mint Premium Gem, predominantly cloud-gray with dashes of brick-red toning at the margins. This earlier Washington quarter has a low survival rate any finer; PCGS has graded just 20 such pieces (8/07). (#5799)

1395 **1935-S MS66 PCGS.** Beautifully patinated with copper-gold, yellow, russet, olive, and lilac shades over radiant surfaces. These attributes complement the strike, which displays uncommonly strong detail for this earlier S-mint issue. (#5799)

1396 **1936-D MS64 NGC.** Boldly struck with an attractive layer of opaque silver-gray patina over both sides. Faint die polish lines are noted in the fields, and a faint reddish-brown toning streak extends across the eagle's lower left (facing) leg. Third in Mint State rarity for the series, the 1936-D is a highly desirable date. (#5801)

1397 **1936-D MS64 PCGS.** A frosty and attractive near-Gem example of this desirable earlier D-mint issue, solidly struck with clean surfaces for the grade. Examples in finer condition are elusive. (#5801)

1398 **1936-D MS65 PCGS.** Well struck with pleasing silver-gray coloration on both sides. This satiny, appealing Gem shows no flaws of note, an unusual state for this often-elusive Denver issue. (#5801)

1399 **1937-S MS66 NGC.** Exquisitely preserved and solidly struck with soft luster beneath vibrant rose-orange, plum, and green-gold patina. A lovely Premium Gem example of this lower-mintage S-mint issue. NGC has graded 24 numerically finer pieces (8/07). (#5805)

1400 **1939-S MS67 NGC.** Bright and satiny, with exquisitely struck devices and mere traces of speckled patina on each side. Surface marks are minimal. This is a low mintage issue that is rare at the Superb Gem level of preservation. Census: 30 in 67, 0 finer (7/07). (#5810)

1401 **1939-S MS67 NGC.** A hint of golden toning decorates this highly lustrous and splendidly preserved Superb Gem. Well struck save for minor softness on the obverse border. A great example of this popular low-mintage issue. Neither NGC nor PCGS has graded a numerically finer piece (8/07). (#5810)

1402 **1940-D MS67 NGC.** This remarkably preserved Superb Gem is draped in medium lilac, gold, and sky-blue. The lustrous surfaces approach perfection, except for the usual slight incompleteness of strike on the legends close to the rims. IN GOD WE TRUST is minutely die doubled. Census: 36 in 67, 1 finer (8/07). (#5812)

1403 **1940-S MS67 NGC.** A fully struck and highly lustrous Superb Gem, almost completely brilliant and exhibiting only a few tiny blemishes. Certified in a former generation holder.
Ex: Colonel Carmine Penta Collection (Heritage, 3/03), lot 743. (#5813)

1404 **1949 MS64 PCGS.** Rich rust patina covers much of this silver quarter, though areas of gray are present at the left obverse and the reverse margins. Choice and solidly struck with strong luster beneath the toning. (#5839)

1405 **1949 MS65 PCGS.** A delicately toned Gem representative of this early Cold War issue, solidly struck with soft, pleasing luster beneath the patina. Both sides offer a pleasing blend of blue, green, and violet-rose. (#5839)

1406 **1949-D MS65 PCGS.** Well struck and lustrous with immaculately preserved surfaces and luscious amber-red toning across the obverse, as well as along the reverse border. An obverse fingerprint fails to lessen the appeal of this impressive Gem quarter. (#5840)

1407 **1949-D MS66 PCGS.** A rich layer of speckled amber-red and olive patina covers the obverse and the same colors adorn the reverse periphery. The reverse center is essentially untoned, and both sides are free of distracting marks. (#5840)

Impressively Toned MS67 1950-S/D Quarter

1408 **1950-S/D MS67 NGC.** FS-601, formerly FS-022. This *Guide Book* variety clearly shows both mintmarks. A serif of the D is noted near the upper left of the S, and the curve of the D dominates the right border of the overmintmark. As one might expect, the variety is scarce in Mint State, and very rare as a Superb Gem. Well struck and immaculate with dramatic sea-green, tan, and rose-gold obverse toning. Census: 7 in 67, 0 finer (8/07). (#5845)

PROOF WASHINGTON QUARTERS

Popular 1936 Quarter, PR66

1409 **1936 PR66 PCGS.** The reverse of this Premium Gem proof is fully brilliant, while the obverse exhibits some light smoky-opaque patina, which is joined by speckled russet at the lower border. Excellent definition results from a well directed strike, and the surfaces on each side are nicely preserved. Popular first year of proof issue. PCGS has seen only eight pieces finer. (#5975)

1410 **1937 PR67 NGC.** This is a lovely Superb Gem example of the second-year proof Washington quarter issue of 1937. Although brilliant and lacking contrast between the fields and devices, the piece is sharply struck and immaculately preserved, with nary a contact mark or a hairline to be seen on either side. Census: 78 in 67, 11 finer (8/07). (#5976)

1411 **1937 PR67 NGC.** Full brilliance with exceptional surfaces, this Superb Gem has mirrored fields with a hint of frost on the devices. Few finer examples have been certified, 11 by NGC and two by PCGS. (#5976)

1412 **1938 PR67 NGC.** Only the faintest trace of haze visits the gleaming silver-white surfaces of this exquisite Superb Gem. Decisively struck with strongly mirrored fields and excellent visual appeal for this early proof Washington quarter issue. NGC has graded only 11 pieces finer (8/07). (#5977)

1413 **1940 PR68 NGC.** Deeply mirrored with great detail. Arcs of golden patina appear at the periphery, while the rest of the piece has hazy toning. NGC has certified no example in a higher grade, as of (8/07). (#5979)

1414 **1941 PR68 NGC.** Gorgeous lemon-gold, rose, apple-green, and cream-gray iridescence endows this crisply struck Superb Gem. A couple of powder-blue streaks visit the left obverse field. Census: 27 in 68, 0 finer (8/07). (#5980)

1415 **1941 PR68 ★ NGC.** This early proof Washington quarter offers exceptional visual appeal. The obverse is fully toned in shades ranging from light champagne to blue-green and deep russet. The reverse is mostly brilliant at the center, with pleasing peripheral iridescence. Census: 4 in 68 ★, none finer (8/07). (#5980)

1416 **1942 PR67 NGC.** Cloud-gray patina settles over much of the surfaces of this decisively struck Superb Gem, while the obverse and reverse margins are amber-orange. A lovely example of this earlier Washington quarter proof. NGC has graded only 17 numerically finer representatives (8/07). (#5981)

1417 **1950 PR67 Cameo NGC.** 1950 was the year when the Mint began to regularly produce proofs with Cameo and Deep Cameo contrast. This impressive piece displays attractive contrast between the fields and devices. It is sharply struck and well preserved throughout. Census: 44 in 67 Cameo, 12 finer (8/07). (#85982)

1418 **1951 PR67 Cameo PCGS.** This piece has well-balanced mint frost over the devices on each side. Brilliant throughout and nearly defect-free. The 1951 quarter, like the other proof denominations of that year, infrequently appears with contrast. Population: 34 in 67 Cameo, 4 finer (8/07). (#85983)

1419 **1951 PR68 Cameo NGC.** A captivating, nearly as struck specimen with stark contrast between fields and devices. In fact, it seems unlikely that a much finer representative of this early proof Washington quarter could exist. Census: 20 in 68 Cameo, 0 finer (8/07). (#85983)

1420 **1952 Superbird PR67 ★ Cameo NGC.** This variety appears in the Fourth Edition of the *Cherrypickers' Guide*, that indicates an S-shaped mark on the eagle's breast is from an "unknown cause." The name "Superbird," (a take-off on the comics character Superman) was given to the variety. As reported in a June 30, 2004 Heritage press release on a pair of Superbird quarters offered at the 2004 ANA, Ken Potter speculates that the "S" on the breast "... may have been the deliberate work of an engraver. This Superb Gem with the Star designation example is immaculately preserved, with untoned, cameoed surfaces. (#144443)

1421 **1952 PR67 Cameo PCGS.** The devices show pleasing frost on this silver proof Washington quarter, and the fields offer immense reflectivity. Splashes of reddish-tan toning at the obverse margins have minimal impact on the piece's contrast. PCGS has graded just five finer Cameo specimens (8/07). (#85984)

1422 **1953 PR68 Deep Cameo NGC.** This date is rarely seen with the strong contrast found here combined with the nearly flawless surfaces on this piece. Brilliant throughout, the cameo effect would be impressive even if this were a quarter from the 1980s or 1990s, when the Mint made a conscious effort to produce such coins. Census: 10 in 68 Deep Cameo, 1 finer (8/07). (#95985)

1423 **1954 PR68 Deep Cameo NGC.** The jet-black fields are deeply mirrored, and the silver-gray devices are impressively frosted. Close inspection of the obverse and reverse surfaces, with the aid of low magnification, fails to reveal any troublesome hairlines or contact marks. Census: 14 in 68 Deep Cameo, 6 finer (8/07). (#95986)

1424 **1955 PR68 Deep Cameo PCGS.** Pinpoint-sharp, brilliant, and beautiful. High grade proofs from this year are available, but few among them exhibit dramatic frost throughout the devices. Population: 18 in 68 Deep Cameo, 0 finer (8/07). (#95987)

1425 **1956 PR69 Deep Cameo PCGS.** Fully struck with pristine, heavily frosted devices and inky-black deep mirror fields. A conditionally scarce specimen that is close to perfection. Population: 40 in 69 Deep Cameo, 0 finer (8/07). (#95988)

1426 **1956 PR69 Ultra Cameo NGC.** This blast-white piece from the early era of modern cameo coinage offers fathomless fields and richly frosted devices. Amazing quality with only the tiniest of flaws visible under magnification. Census: 37 in 69 Ultra Cameo, 0 finer (8/07). (#95988)

1427 **1957 PR68 Deep Cameo PCGS.** An exceptional proof representative with crisply struck devices and deeply reflective fields. Both sides are distraction-free and essentially pristine. Population: 20 in 68 Deep Cameo, 5 finer (8/07). (#95989)

Bold 1958 PR68 Deep Cameo Quarter

1428 **1958 PR68 Deep Cameo PCGS.** Speckles of faint gold color make infrequent visits to each side of this lovely proof. Sharply struck design elements stand out boldly against deeply mirrored fields. Immaculately preserved throughout. Population: 17 in 68 Deep Cameo, 5 finer (8/07). (#95990)

1429 **1959 PR68 Deep Cameo PCGS.** The fields are jet-black pools of illimitable reflectivity; the devices are crisply struck and fully frosted. Not even the most trivial blemish or hairline can be found on either side of this Superb proof quarter. Population: 34 in 68 Deep Cameo, 0 finer (8/07). (#95991)

1430 **1960 PR69 Deep Cameo PCGS.** Ex: Daniel D. Biddle Collection. With spectacular jet-black fields and heavily frosted devices, the Deep Cameo effect is truly remarkable. A virtually flawless proof Washington quarter. Population: 32 in 69 Deep Cameo, 0 finer (8/07). (#95992)

1431 **1961 PR69 Deep Cameo PCGS.** Ex: Daniel D. Biddle Collection. The fully brilliant surfaces are virtually flawless, and display a pronounced cameo appearance. A couple of faint, milky orange-tan spots are noted on each side. Population: 41 in 69 Deep Cameo, 0 finer (8/07). (#95993)

1432 **1964 PR69 Deep Cameo PCGS.** The richly frosted devices shine and seemingly float above fathomless jet-black fields, on each side of this near-perfect specimen. Fully struck and exquisitely preserved. Population: 79 in 69 Deep Cameo, 0 finer (8/07). (#95996)

EARLY HALF DOLLARS

O-105 1794 Flowing Hair Half Good 6, R.5

1433 **1794 Good 6 PCGS.** O-105, R.5. A better variety from different dies than the usual O-101. The central reverse is well worn, but all legends and stars are bold. The lower reverse has a few tiny pits, but there are no mentionable marks. Toned medium gray with charcoal areas near Liberty's chin and the RI in AMERICA. (#6051)

Possibly the Finest 1794 O-102 Half Dollar, VF35

1434 **1794 VF35 NGC.** O-102, High R.6. In the fourth edition of the Overton half dollar reference, Don Parsley lists the Census of O-102 as 40, 12, 12, 8, 4. The die combination is very rare, with only 13 or 14 examples known in all grades. Stephen Herrman lists just nine auction appearances of this variety since 1995, including repeat appearances of just six coins. This is an impressive example with lovely original toning and traces of underlying luster. A few tiny marks on the obverse are barely worth description.

The following is a record of those pieces known to us:

1. XF40. Recorded by Don Parsley in the third and fourth editions of the Overton reference. Possibly the same piece that is illustrated (reverse only) in Beistle.

2. VF35. The present specimen, not previously known. This example has been graded VF35 on two different occasions by NGC, accounting for two of the three VF coins on the firm's Census report.

3. VF. Another example graded by NGC.

4. Fine 15 PCGS. Eliasberg Collection (Bowers and Merena, 4/1997), lot 1661; Goldberg Coins (2/2001), lot 1720; Westmoreland Collection. This coin will be offered by us early next year.

5. Fine 12 NGC. David Hirt (Pine Tree, 11/1975), lot 554; David Davis (8/1980); Jules Reiver (Heritage, 1/2006), lot 22473. Possibly one of the "12" coins recorded by Overton.

6. VG10. Heritage (9/1988), lot 649. The attribution is assumed accurate, although only the obverse was plated in the catalog. Possibly one of the "12" coins recorded by Overton.

7. Good 6/VG8. Coin Galleries (8/1989), lot 1515. The plate coin in the third and fourth editions of Overton, and probably the piece graded "8" in the Overton/Parsley Census.

8. Good 6 PCGS. Sheridan Downey (5/2001), lot 197. This coin, or one of the following, may be the coin graded "4" by Parsley.

9. Net Good 4 ANACS. Bowers and Merena (6/2003), lot 543; Heritage (2/2004), lot 649; Heritage (10/2006), lot 1106.

10. AG3/Good 4. Brilliant Collection (Bowers and Merena, 1/1992), lot 2; Sheridan Downey (1/1995), lot 1.

In addition to these 10 pieces, the Overton Census suggests that three or four others might exist. (#6051)

1435 **1795 2 Leaves—Cleaned—ANACS. Good 4 Details.** O-105a, R.4. Bright from cleaning, and a pinscratch is noted right of the eagle's neck. The obverse has the sharpness of a higher grade, although STATES and AMERICA each have three faint letters. (#6052)

1436 **1795 2 Leaves Good 6 ANACS.** O-116, R.4. All legends are clear, the portrait has eye, hair, and mouth detail. The slate-gray devices are framed by subtle bands of orange and sea-green toning. A few thin marks are noted near the eagle's beak. (#6052)

1437 **1795 2 Leaves VG8 PCGS.** O-116, R.4. Silver-white motifs contrast with the charcoal-gray fields. Moderately abraded with mildly granular borders and a small circular impression on the reverse at 4:30. (#6052)

1438 **1795 2 Leaves—Tooled, Graffiti—ANACS. Fine 12 Details.** O-105a, R.4. The right obverse field has an illegible cursive name, and the left obverse field is smoothed. Liberty's neck has a curly scratch, and a few rim nicks are distributed, mostly between 2 and 5 o'clock on the obverse. A nicely detailed lavender and slate-gray example of this briefly produced early silver type. (#6052)

1439 **1795 2 Leaves Fine 12 NGC.** O-113a, R.4. Olive and aqua shades bathe this elusive Flowing Hair type coin. The central reverse has a few faint adjustment marks, as made, and reverse protected areas display minor dark buildup. Certified in an early generation, pre-hologram NGC holder. (#6052)

1440 **1795 2 Leaves—Cleaned—ANACS. Fine 12 Details.** O-107a, R.5. The heavy bisecting reverse crack aids attribution. A bit bright from a cleaning, and the powder-blue margins suggest more luster than is possible for the grade. Nonetheless, an unblemished and nicely detailed without distracting adjustment marks. (#6052)

1441 **1795 2 Leaves—Corroded, Cleaned—ANACS. VF Details. Net Fine 12.** O-129, R.4. The popular variety with the second S in STATES cut over a D. The absent-minded engraver thought he was cutting UNITED before realizing the mistake. (The same blunder is also found on the BD-6 1795 half eagle). This cream-gray example is surprisingly free from marks, but is slightly cloudy and has a smattering of small dark spots on each side. (#6052)

1442 **1795 2 Leaves—Scratched, Cleaned—ANACS. Fine 15 Details.** O-104, R.4. The wings and hair display significant remaining detail, and the cleaning is relatively mild. The right obverse field has a few faded marks, and the reverse rim is nicked at 4:30. Overall, an attractive Flowing Hair type coin with medium sea-green and gunmetal-gray toning.
From The Laguna Niguel Collection, Part Two. (#6052)

Choice Fine 1795 Flowing Hair Half, O-113

1443 **1795 2 Leaves Fine 15 PCGS.** O-113, R.3. The popular variety with the A in STATES punched over an errant E. A charming example of this coveted and briefly produced early silver type. Delicate caramel-gold and ice-blue toning visits the smooth and slightly cloudy surfaces. A few adjustment marks of mint origin are noted on the reverse border at 10 o'clock. (#6052)

Worthy O-119 1795 Flowing Hair Half VF25

1444 **1795 2 Leaves VF25 NGC.** O-119, R.4. Identified by repunching on the I in UNITED and a die lump above the final star. The obverse is mostly slate-gray despite an arc of deep russet along the lower border. The reverse is cream-gray with a generous blush of lilac and an upper glimpse of cobalt-blue. (#6052)

Lightly Toned 1801 Half Dollar, XF40, O-101

1445 **1801 XF40 ICG.** O-101, R.3. One of two varieties, this one is identified by the presence of die lumps (as struck) near the arrowheads, as well as by the last A in AMERICA not being embedded in the wing feathers. Whispers of red-tan and aqua-blue patina occur on both sides of this XF40 specimen. Generally well defined, and revealing just a few light circulation marks. (#6064)

1802 Half Dollar VF30, O-101

1446 **1802 VF30 PCGS.** O-101, the only known dies, R.3. This early Draped Bust, Heraldic Eagle half dollar is popular due to its low mintage of 29,890 pieces. Moderately worn with several scattered marks and numerous wispy hairlines on each side. (#6065)

Well Defined 1802 Choice XF Fifty Cent, O-101

1447 1802 XF45 ICG. O-101, R.3. Production in 1802 of 29,890 half dollars was completed using a single obverse die and a single reverse die which was first placed into use in 1801 (Reverse B). This Choice XF example displays traces of luster residing in the recesses of the light silver-gray surfaces. The design elements retain relatively strong definition. A few contact marks are noted, including a small, shallow scrape at the A in STATES and the cloud beneath. (#6065)

1448 1803 Large 3—Corroded, Cleaned—ANACS. XF40 Details. O-101, R.3. Incorrectly designated as O-103 by ANACS. Ample luster glimmers from the margins and devices, but a mild cleaning has subdued the pale gold and ocean-blue surfaces, and granular streaks are noted near the third and first obverse stars. (#6066)

1449 1803 Large 3 XF40 PCGS. O-103, R.3. An impressive piece with bold definition and occasional glimpses of luster. Liberty's cheek and shoulder exhibit moderate wear. Toned gunmetal-gray with infrequent recessed areas of deeper charcoal patina. (#6066)

1450 1803 Large 3 XF40 PCGS. O-103, R.3. This is a pleasing example that is lightly toned on the obverse, while showing moderate olive and some light-gray color on the reverse. The devices are suitably worn for the grade. Clash marks are noted on Liberty's ear, from the eagle's shield. (#6066)

1451 1803 Large 3 XF45 PCGS. O-102a, R.3. The reverse shows a die crack through AMERICA. This lightly worn, richly toned representative exhibits pleasing detail. Plum and golden-tan patina graces the margins, while the centers are predominantly cloud-gray. Population: 27 in 45, 39 finer (8/07). (#6066)

1452 1805—Scratched, Cleaned—ANACS. XF45 Details. O-107, R.5. A faintly hairlined, partly retoned representative of this rare die marriage, well struck overall with a touch of softness present at the upper right stars and clouds on the reverse. The golden-brown and cloud-gray surfaces show a number of fine scratches, including a thin one on Liberty's cheek. (#6069)

1453 1805—Improperly Cleaned—NCS. AU Details. O-112, R.2. Star 9 is recut. Attentively detailed for this earlier issue with only minor wear on each side. The unnaturally luminous surfaces have partly retoned violet-gray and rose. (#6069)

1806 Pointed 6 O-119 Half, MS62

1454 1806 Pointed 6, Stem MS62 PCGS. O-119, R.3. Rich aquamarine toning dominates the obverse periphery and visits the reverse border, but the majority of this satiny representative is only light golden-gray. Smooth aside from a brief thin mark above the shoulder. Multiple sets of clash marks approach Liberty's profile and cleavage. (#6071)

1455 1806 Pointed 6, No Stem VF35 NGC. O-109, R.1. The date shows a pointed 6, and there is not a stem through the eagle's right (facing) claw. This unabraded example displays appropriate wear for the grade and surprising glints of luster, along with amber-gold color; both of which are more noticeable on the obverse. (#6073)

Near-Mint 1806 No Stem Half, O-109

1456 1806 Pointed 6, No Stem AU58 PCGS. O-109, R.1. While the Knob 6, No Stem (Overton-108) is a great rarity, its Pointed 6 counterpart is a readily collectible Guide Book variety. This partly lustrous example is well struck and offers attractive ocean-blue, gold, and lilac-gray toning. Population: 17 in 58, 19 finer (8/07). (#6073)

1457 1806 6 Over Inverted 6 VF25 NGC. O-111, R.3. The distinctive 6 Over Inverted 6 obverse, paired with a reverse that shows arrowheads at the left side of the N. A moderately worn piece that displays rich rose, golden-tan, and violet patina over each side. For all 6 Over Inverted 6 varieties, Census: 4 in 25, 27 finer (8/07). (#6078)

1458 1807 Draped Bust VF35 NGC. O-106, R.3. A rich layer of obviously original patina adorns the obverse of this Choice VF example, with amber, lime-green, and gold toning on display. The same colors also decorate the reverse periphery. An evenly worn example with a few shallow adjustment marks noted on the obverse but no serious abrasions apparent on either side. *From The Arnold & Harriet Collection, Part Two.* (#6079)

1459 1807 Draped Bust—Scratched—ANACS. AU53 Details. O-105, R.1. Orange-gold and aquamarine fill the margins of this partly lustrous and lightly circulated Draped Bust half. The reverse is smooth save for a minor edge nick at 1:30, while the obverse has an interrupted thin vertical mark on the portrait and a couple of faint, brief marks near the mouth and ribbon. *From The Laguna Niguel Collection, Part Two.* (#6079)

Choice AU O-105 1807 Draped Bust Half

1460 1807 Draped Bust AU55 PCGS. O-105, R.2. A die lump between the final S of STATES and the O of OF aids attribution of this final year Draped Bust half. Bright silver surfaces display occasional traces of light tan, and luster in the recessed areas. The design elements exhibit nice delineation, and the obverse field has only faint abrasions. In a green label holder. (#6079)

Patinated O-110a 1807 Draped Bust Half, MS62

1461 1807 Draped Bust MS62 PCGS. O-110a, R.3. The Draped Bust type is much scarcer in Mint State than the Capped Bust type. Both designs were struck in the transitional year of 1807. One wonders how Chief Engraver viewed the passing of his Draped Bust type, and its replacement on denomination after denomination by John Reich's motifs. Mottled forest-green and fire-red envelops this smooth example. Sharply struck save for the stars near the beak. Each side has a network of fine die cracks throughout the borders, as described in the Overton standard reference. The lower loop of the 8 has a small letter H. Population: 22 in 62, 32 finer (8/07). (#6079)

1462 1807 Large Stars, 50 Over 20 VF35 NGC. O-112, R.1. The distinctive "overdenomination" variety, a striking curiosity from the Mint's early years. Though Choice VF by its luminous, gold-toned surfaces, the portrait shows little detail and the reverse displays a pair of significant marks near the denomination. (#6086)

1463 1807 Large Stars, 50 Over 20 XF40 PCGS. O-112, R.1. This variety shares a common reverse with O-111. Per Overton (Third Edition): "The 5 in 50 C was first punched using a 2. This punching error was corrected by punching a 5 over the 2. The 2 shows clearly underneath." This richly toned specimen is evenly worn, with few marks on either side. (#6086)

Choice AU 1807 Capped Bust Half, O-112
Famous 50 Over 20 Mint Error

1464 1807 Large Stars, 50 Over 20 AU55 PCGS. O-112, R.1. A charming first-year Capped Bust half with the engraving blunder 50 Over 20. The diemaker began to enter the denomination as 20 before realizing the mistake. A similar 25 Over error occurs on 1822 and 1828 quarters. This example is tan-gray with gunmetal toning on the device highpoints. Satin luster shimmers from protected areas. Impressively unabraded despite its light circulation. (#6086)

1465 1808/7 AU55 NGC. O-101, R.1. The overdated variety is distinctive for the year. This modestly worn, still-lustrous piece offers predominantly silver-gray surfaces with a touch of apricot near the rims. Excellent peripheral detail, though the portrait and eagle show a degree of softness. (#6091)

1466 1809 VF20 PCGS. O-112, R.5. Dots between the ES of STATES and below the M of AMERICA identify this rare Overton variety. This moderately worn piece, toned in various grays, shows few marks or other distractions. (#6092)

Select O-107 1809 Half Dollar
Experimental III Edge

1467 1809 III Edge MS63 PCGS. O-107, R.3. Parallel die lines above the left (facing) wing help confirm the variety. This satiny and carefully preserved early Capped Bust half is boldly struck save for the area near the right claw. Light golden-brown toning deepens slightly toward the obverse periphery. (#6094)

Dazzling MS64 1810 Half, O-102

1468 1810 MS64 NGC. O-102, R.1. An interesting, common variety from 1810 that shows an extra point on star 12, a defect on the lip that makes Liberty appear to be hairlipped, and the T in UNITED cut over a much lower T. Exceptionally well defined in all areas except the top of the eagle's left (facing) wing—an area that may be weak on all since the Overton plate coin also shows weakness in this area. Brilliant with dazzling mint luster. While it is always tricky trying to establish Condition Census ranking on Bust halves without a list of specific coins, we can at least say that this is one of the finest O-102s sold in recent years. An MS65 was in the Byers' sale and sold for $12,650 in October of last year. (#6095)

Scarce 1811 O-107 Half Dollar, MS63

1469 1811 Small 8 MS63 PCGS. O-107, R.4. This is a scarce 1811 half dollar variety, seldom found in higher Mint State grades. Possibly a Condition Census example, this piece is fully lustrous with satiny silver surfaces and faint traces of gold color. The upper obverse and lower reverse a weakly defined, suggesting either problems with die alignment in the press or perhaps a slightly tapered planchet. (#6097)

Charming Choice 1811 Small 8 Half, O-109

1470 1811 Small 8 MS64 NGC. O-109, R.2. An easy marriage to attribute, thanks to a heavy radial die crack on the reverse at 10 o'clock. All known O-109 halves share this diagnostic, and the reverse die is unique to the variety. The obverse die later struck O-106. This lustrous and boldly struck near-Gem has delicate chestnut and sky-gray toning. (#6097)

1471 1812 AU58 NGC. O-105a, R.2. Orange-red and apple-green toning clings to the margins of this lustrous near-Mint Capped Bust half. Surprisingly unabraded save for a tiny reverse rim nick at 8 o'clock. Liberty's curls display slight friction.
From The Diemer L. Fife Collection. (#6100)

Select Mint State 1812 Half, O-104a

1472 1812 MS63 PCGS. O-104a, R.1. Medium russet-brown dominates the borders, while the centers offer dove-gray toning and the rims are ocean-blue. A charming representative that boasts shimmering luster and impressively unabraded surfaces. Well struck aside from a few star centers. (#6100)

Patinated Gem O-103 1813 Half Dollar

1473 1813 MS65 PCGS. O-103, R.2. Cream-gray, jade-green, and dusky rose toning blend throughout this shimmering and unblemished Gem. A few of the upper stars are soft, but the strike is generally crisp. Multiple sets of clash marks are visible beneath the scroll and above the date. (#6103)

O-101 1813 50C Over UNI Half MS62

1474 1813 Over UNI MS62 NGC. O-101, R.2. The popular Guide Book variety with a blundered reverse. The UNI in UNITED was engraved in place of the denomination, before the error was discovered and partially effaced. This is a lustrous example with light and attractive caramel-gold, rose-gray, and forest-green toning, particularly evident near the borders. The strike is crisp save for star 1 and the PLUR in PLURIBUS. Census: 3 in 62, 8 finer (8/07). (#6104)

Sharp 1814 Half Dollar, MS62, O-104a

1475 1814 MS62 PCGS. O-104a, R.2. The low second 1 in the date, the center dot on crossbar 5, and the low 50 C. confirm the variety, while the obverse and reverse cracks affirm the later die state. Soft luster emanates from silver-gray surfaces that yield cobalt-blue, lavender, and gold-tan peripheral patination. A solid strike brings out nice detail on the motifs. A few minute marks occur on Liberty's portrait. A sharp Capped Bust half dollar. (#6105)

Lushly Toned 1814 Half Dollar MS64, O-105

1476 1814 MS64 PCGS. O-105, R.2. Deep ocean-blue and plum-red toning envelops this satiny Capped Bust half. The strike is precise aside from the right-side star centers and minor incompleteness on the eagle's right (facing) claw. The dies are boldly clashed, as usual for this Overton marriage. Population: 25 in 64, 10 finer (8/07). (#6105)

1477 1817 AU50 NGC. O-110a, R.2. The obverse shows a triple dentil at star 13, and the prominently clashed reverse exhibits a die crack from ERICA through the arrowheads and denomination. This lightly circulated, still-lustrous piece is well struck with faintly toned silver-gray surfaces. (#6109)

Eye-Appealing Choice 1817 Half "Comet" Variety O-106

1478 1817 MS64 NGC. O-106, R.2. The so-called "Comet" variety with a heavy die line from the cap to 1 o'clock. Lovely orange, aqua-blue, and fire-red patina adorns this lustrous and splendidly preserved near-Gem. Certified in a former generation holder. Expect fierce bidding competition for this eye-appealing lot. (#6109)

Probable Finest Known O-101a 1818/7 Half MS65, Ex: Eliasberg

1479 1818/7 Large 8 MS65 NGC. O-101a, R.1. Ex: Eliasberg. One of two overdates from this year, each of which is distinct and collectible, one with a large first 8 in the date and the other (O-102) with a small first 8. As expected from this die state, extended die cracks are seen on each side. This piece is listed in Stephen Herrman's *Prices Realized for Bust Half Dollars* as the finest known. The surfaces are lustrous and the blue-gray patina is accented with deep golden around the devices. Sharply struck in all areas except on the upper left (facing) wing, as indicated in the Eliasberg catalog.
Ex: George H. Earle Collection (Henry Chapman, June 25-29, 1912); John H. Clapp; Clapp Estate, 1942 to Louis E. Eliasberg, Sr.; Eliasberg Collection (Bowers and Merena, 4/97), lot 1746; Phillip Flannagan Collection (Bowers and Merena), lot 4059. (#6115)

Magnificent Gem O-113 1819 Bust Half

1480 1819 MS65 NGC. O-113, R.1. Peach and sky-blue toning adorns the peripheries of this lustrous and magnificent Gem. The fields are remarkably undisturbed by contact, and the strike is needle-sharp with the sole exception of the eagle's claws. Specialists identify O-113 by the center line of the second vertical stripe, which ascends to the third horizontal line. (#6117)

1481 1819/8 Large 9 AU55 NGC. O-104, R.1. The widely recut star 2 confirms the Overton variety. A lightly toned and briefly circulated example with substantial shimmering luster throughout the borders, eagle, hair, cap, and drapery. A hair-thin mark above the jaw is barely worthy of mention. (#6119)

Lovely MS64 1823 Half Dollar O-103

1482 1823 MS64 NGC. O-103, R.2. Impressive cartwheel sheen dominates this pleasing Choice Bust half. The major devices are sharply struck, although several star centers are incompletely brought up. The fields are splendidly smooth, and the cheek has only a pair of unimportant hair-thin marks. (#6131)

1483 1823 Ugly 3 AU50 ICG. O-110a, R.3. A popular Guide Book variety often confused with the similar Patched 3 (O-101a and O-102). This gunmetal-gray piece retains significant luminous pale gold luster. Marks are noted on each side of star 9. (#6134)

Popular Overdate 1824 Half MS62, O-103

1484 1824 Overdate MS62 NGC. O-103, R.1. Potent luster sweeps this beautifully smooth and lightly toned example. The major devices are intricately struck, and only the upper left stars show centril incompleteness. Overton called this dramatic overdate variety "a jumble of recuttings," while the *Guide Book* simply lists it as "4/ Various Dates." Census: 8 in 62, 18 finer (8/07). (#6138)

1485 1825 AU58 NGC. O-112, R.3. The 2 in the date shows prominent recutting, and the letters AME of AMERICA are joined at their bases. This softly struck but shining piece exhibits delicate layers of pink and violet patina at the margins. Minimally marked with excellent eye appeal. (#6142)

1486 1825 MS62 NGC. O-113, R.1. The reverse is distinctive with a tine pointing to the left from the bottom of the shield. Peach, rose, and violet toning drapes the lustrous, lightly abraded surfaces. (#6142)

Patinated O-111 1826 Bust Half MS64

1487 1826 MS64 NGC. O-111, R.2. The obverse has the die crack specified in O-111a, but the reverse lacks the Overton-mentioned die crack near AMERICA. An evenly struck and satiny example with impressively smooth surfaces. The obverse is rose-gray, ocean-blue, and caramel-gold. The reverse has an aquamarine center and light gold and cherry-red margins. (#6143)

Delightful Choice 1826 Half O-112a

1488 1826 MS64 NGC. O-112a, R.2. Die chips inside the N in UNITED, along with a filled top loop of the first S in STATES, determine the Overton marriage. Light golden toning is limited to the margins. Lustrous, well preserved, and crisply struck despite minor blending of detail on the left (facing) claw. (#6143)

Splendidly Toned 1826 O-102 Half MS65

1489 1826 MS65 NGC. O-102, R.1. Eye-catching ocean-blue, gold, and ivory-gray embrace this unabraded and crisply struck representative. The reverse is particularly lustrous. Overton-102 is noteworthy for the location of star 7, which nearly touches Liberty's cap. A flaw on the upper serif of the E within the scroll confirms the attribution. Census: 51 in 65, 24 finer (8/07). (#6143)

Lustrous MS63 1827/6 Half Dollar, O-101

1490 **1827/6 MS63 NGC.** O-101, R.2. Noticeable portions of the 6 are seen on both sides of the 7. Heavily die cracked, as always, around the reverse periphery. The striking details are remarkably strong, especially considering the piece was produced with a screw press, with no localized areas of weakness. Much brilliance remains with a light accent of color around the devices. Only a couple of small marks can be seen, both located in the left obverse field. Several examples are known in mint condition of this variety. (#6147)

1491 **1827 Square Base 2 MS62 PCGS.** O-105, R.3. Attractive gray color with peripheral gold and iridescent toning, reminiscent of coins from old time collections. Both sides have frosty luster beneath the toning. (#6144)

Census Level 1827 O-112a Half, MS64

1492 **1827 Square Base 2 MS64 NGC.** O-112a, R.4. From a Superior sale where it was offered unattributed, it appears that this piece may be the finest known example of the late die state, and probably one of the three or four finest of the variety. Most of the design details of this near-Gem are sharply defined. Satiny luster is hidden beneath attractive gray color with subtle gold and iridescent toning.

The obverse has two prominent die cracks. The first stars at the lower border, passes between the 8 and 2, grazes the left edge of the drapery clasp, and terminates at the hair lock above. The other crack passes between the digit 7 and star 13, continuing faintly through the hair curls to the ear.
Ex: Superior (5/2004), lot 1461. (#6144)

O-120a 1827 Half, MS64

1493 **1827 Square Base 2 MS64 NGC.** O-120a, R.3. This advanced die state is more frequently seen than the earlier (O-120) variant as the a die state is rated R.3 in Overton while the O-120 is R.5. Seven Mint State pieces are listed on Herrman's Prices Realized for the O-120a, but this particular piece does not appear to be included. Sharply struck throughout, the satiny surfaces are mostly brilliant with a slight accent of gold around the margins. There are no obvious abrasions on either side of this attractive coin. (#6144)

Gracefully Toned Choice 1828 O-102 Half

1494 **1828 Curl Base 2, No Knob MS64 NGC.** O-102, R.2. Beautiful powder-blue, plum-red, and orange shades emerge when this high grade silver type coin is rotated beneath a light. Liberty's curls and cap are impressively free from friction, and the semi-prooflike fields lack visible abrasions. An exceptional near-Gem worthy of the ultimate variety collection. (#6148)

1495 **1829 AU58 NGC.** O-105, R.1. A lustrous and attentively struck Borderline Uncirculated Bust half with clean surfaces and faint peripheral peach toning. The obverse die is slightly misaligned toward 11 o'clock. (#6154)

Sharply Struck MS65 1829 Half, O-119 Possible Finest Known

1496 **1829 MS65 NGC.** O-119, R.2. An easily attributable variety that shows several crossbars that extend into the right wing and recutting on the upper left part of A1. Sharply defined in all areas, the satiny surfaces are brilliant in the centers with golden-brown toning around the peripheries. While relatively available in AU and Uncirculated grades, this Gem is certainly one of the finest, if not *the* finest example known. (#6154)

1497 **1830 Small 0 AU58 PCGS.** O-103, R.1. Recutting on the 5 in the denomination and the first A of AMERICA confirms the variety. This well-defined and pleasing piece shows only faint wear on the highpoints and few marks. Amber, amethyst, and turquoise are the major colors of the sumptuously toned surfaces. (#6156)

Near-Gem 1830 Capped Bust Half O-103

1498 **1830 Small 0 MS64 PCGS.** O-103, R.1. Recutting on the first A in AMERICA and the stand of the 5 confirms the variety. Faint golden-brown toning graces the peripheries of this lustrous half dollar. Well struck except for the right side stars. Beautifully preserved, since a pair of pinpoint spots in front of the eye are barely worthy of mention. (#6156)

Satiny MS64 O-110 1830 Half Dollar

1499 **1830 Small 0 MS64 NGC.** O-110, R.3. This obverse/reverse die pairing is a later usage of each, and each side shows patches of die rust. Several Uncirculated examples are known of this slightly scarcer variety, the finest apparently being an NGC MS66. This is a sharply defined example that has satiny luster and even gray-lilac toning over each side. (#6156)

Select 1830 Large 0 Half O-121

1500 **1830 Large 0 MS63 PCGS.** O-121, R.3. O-120 and O-121 are fiendishly difficult to distinguish, but the high 3 in the date and the soft left-side stars are characteristic of the scarcer O-121. Attractively toned in caramel-gold and ice-blue. Lustrous and crisply struck with a few wispy thin marks on the left obverse field. Population: 12 in 63, 28 finer (8/07). (#6157)

Delightful Near-Gem 1830 Large 0 Half, O-123

1501 **1830 Large 0 MS64 PCGS.** O-123, R.1. The distinctive Large 0 distinguishes the obverse, while the reverse has overly long pales protruding from the bottom of the shield. This strongly lustrous example shows pleasing detail overall, with just a touch of softness at Liberty's clasp and the stars. The surfaces are minimally toned with only faint marks. For all Large 0 varieties, Population: 22 in 64, 6 finer (8/07).
From The Mario Eller Collection, Part One. (#6157)

1502 **1831 MS61 NGC.** O-104, R.1. An early die state with parallel die lines beneath the bust truncation. Golden-brown and sky-blue visit the borders, while the fields and devices remain brilliant. Careful study locates a few hairlines, and the RIB in PLURIBUS is soft.
From The Mario Eller Collection, Part One. (#6159)

1503 **1831 MS61 NGC.** O-102, R.1. The filled N of UNITED is diagnostic. Delightful luster swirls beneath vivid blue-green, gold-green, and yellow-orange patina. This piece is well struck overall, though the center of the scroll on the reverse shows weakness; the I in PLURIBUS is not visible. (#6159)

1504 **1831 MS62 NGC.** O-110, R.2. Forest-green and golden-orange grace recessed areas of this lustrous and minimally abraded half dollar. Nicely struck apart from the UR in PLURIBUS and a few star centers. (#6159)

1505 **1831 MS63 PCGS.** O-107, R.3. The obverse has LIBERTY recut and die lines before the bust, while the reverse shows an interrupted arrow shaft. This Select and shining piece offers pleasing overall detail and subtle ice-blue hints in the fields. Minimally marked overall with great eye appeal. (#6159)

Choice Mint State 1831 Bust Half O-103

1506 **1831 MS64 PCGS.** O-103, R.1. The recut upright of the 5 in the denomination is diagnostic for the Overton variety. Blended gold and cream-gray toning embraces this lustrous and unabraded near-Gem. It would be a difficult task to find a higher quality or more attractive example. (#6159)

1507 **1832 Small Letters AU58 NGC.** O-118, R.1. Faint friction is present on the cheek, but the mint luster is close to complete. The almond-gray fields and devices are nearly unabraded, and the strike is good save for a few feathers left of the shield. (#6160)

1508 **1832 Small Letters AU58 NGC.** O-122, R.1. Emerald-green, golden-brown, and slate-gray endow this lightly abraded representative. Liberty's curls and forehead have some wear, but luster dominates the borders and devices. (#6160)

1509 **1832 Small Letters MS63 PCGS.** O-107, R.2. Liberty's hair rises above the band between the R and T on the obverse, and the reverse has a crooked line that protrudes vertically from the right corner of the shield. This luminous and well-defined Select example has pleasing olive patina over much of the surfaces and areas of deeper plum toning at the margins. (#6160)

Near-Gem 1832 Small Letters Half, O-107

1510 **1832 Small Letters MS64 PCGS.** O-107, R.2. Lovely golden-brown and sea-green toning accompanies the borders of this lustrous and attractively preserved near-Gem. The star centers are generally soft, but the legends and devices are sharp, including PLURIBUS and the right claw. A small spot on the U in UNITED is of little import. (#6160)

Elegant O-103 1832 Bust Half MS65

1511 **1832 Small Letters MS65 NGC.** O-103, R.1. The recut stand on the 5 in the denomination narrows the attribution. This evenly struck and nearly mark-free example is attractively toned in steel-gray, peach-gold, and forest-green shades. Desirable in such exemplary quality. Census: 28 in 65, 11 finer (8/07). (#6160)

1512 **1832 Large Letters MS61 NGC.** O-101a, R.1. The sole Large Letters variety for the date, but the prominent die break from the left (facing) wing to the branch is also diagnostic. Smooth blue-green and rose-gold fields encompass the gunmetal-gray devices. Struck from a lightly rusted reverse die. (#6161)

1513 **1833 MS62 PCGS.** O-107, R.3. Medium caramel-gold and ivory-gray toning drapes this satiny and unmarked representative. The star centers and the RI in PLURIBUS are typically defined, but the eye appeal is exceptional for the assigned grade. (#6163)

Eliasberg's Gem O-101 1834 Half Dollar

1514 **1834 Large Date, Large Letters MS65 NGC. Ex: Eliasberg.** O-101, R.1. This lustrous piece is luxuriously toned in lavender, fire-red, and aquamarine shades. The strike is bold aside from the centers of the first four stars. A hair-thin mark crosses the nose, but marks are otherwise absent. Within the (8/07) NGC Census for O-101, the present is the single finest graded, and its closest competitors are four grades back at MS61.
Ex: Louis E. Eliasberg, Sr. Collection (Bowers and Merena, 4/07), lot 1888. (#6164)

1515 **1834 Small Date, Small Letters MS62 NGC.** O-116, R.1. A wavy die line resembling a small worm is seen in the field to the left of Liberty's bust, there are two pair of twin segments opposite star 8, and crossbars 4 and 5 extend into the left (right facing) wing, all of which confirm the variety. Whispers of reddish-tan patina visit the margins. Generally well defined, with a few light obverse handling marks. Some grease marks appear to be struck into the area around AT of STATES. (#6166)

Choice 1834 Bust Half O-116

1516 **1834 Small Date, Small Letters MS64 NGC.** O-116, R.1. Golden-brown, ocean-blue, and plum-red enrich this moderately toned and lustrous near-Gem. The major devices are well struck, while the right-side stars and the A in STATES are indistinctly brought up. Refreshingly mark-free, and a splendid representative of the type. (#6166)

Challenging Choice 1835 Half Dollar O-107

1517 **1835 MS64 NGC.** O-107, R.1. Rich gunmetal-blue, jade-green, and magenta envelop this glimmering and unblemished representative. Boldly struck for the most part, with a couple of soft stars and minor weakness on the RI in PLURIBUS. Scarcer than other Lettered Edge dates from its decade. Census: 35 in 64, 19 finer (8/07). (#6168)

1518 **1836 Lettered Edge AU58 PCGS.** O-117, R.3. The 1 in the date is low compared to the 8 and tilts to the right. This late-state Lettered Edge half shows pleasing gold and gray-blue patina over each side. Pleasingly detailed with minor friction on the highpoints and a degree of spotting above Liberty's cap. (#6169)

PROOF BUST HALF DOLLAR

Rare 1836/1336 Lettered Edge Half, PR63, O-108

1519 **1836 / 1336 Lettered Edge PR63 PCGS.** O-108. While Lettered Edge proofs are known from several different dies of this year, this is certainly the most interesting variant. The 8 in the date was erroneously first punched over a 3, creating this unusual overdate. Several proofs are known from the O-108 dies, but this is the first we have handled since we offered this piece in 1994. It seems obvious to even the most casual observer, that this coin was not struck on a steam press. The screw press used to produce these proofs gave the coin less of a determinant edge, so it is not possible to use the test of "squared off rims" that one expects on later, more "commercial" strikings. The fields are moderately reflective, perhaps being a bit subdued by the medium density gray and blue toning seen over both sides. A splash of blue toning is seen over the eagle's left (facing) wing, and serves as a useful pedigree identifier. The striking details are exceptionally crisp, and judging from that aspect alone, it is difficult to believe the coin was struck using the power generated by the muscles of a horse or man. Extremely rare and highly desirable. *Ex: 1994 ANA (Heritage, 7/94), lot 6573, where it was bought back by the consignor.* (#6221)

REEDED EDGE HALF DOLLARS

Choice XF 1836 Reeded Edge Half

1520 **1836 Reeded Edge XF45 NGC.** The 1836 Reeded Edge half dollar is historic, since it departs from the Mint's former tradition of open collar production. But the real reason it is hoarded has more to do with its minuscule reported mintage of 1,200 pieces. This bright example has a peripheral blush of golden-brown toning. Some luster remains, and the surfaces are only moderately marked. A minor obverse rim ding is detected at 4:30. (#6175)

1521 **1838 MS60 NGC.** Although dipped, this piece is sharply struck with full silver luster and satiny surfaces. A few faint hairlines and tiny abrasions are the only imperfections. (#6177)

1522 **1838 MS63 PCGS.** Rich sea-green and tan toning envelop this satiny and lightly abraded type coin. The centers are precisely struck, while the borders show minor incompleteness. The HALF DOL. reverse and the Capped Bust obverse were combined only for 1838 and 1839. Population: 54 in 63, 42 finer (7/07). (#6177)

1523 **1838 MS63 NGC.** An enticing Reeded Edge, HALF DOL piece that has delicate rose-gold patina over the fields. Warm luster and an absence of distracting marks contribute to the coin's visual appeal. A great example for the type or date collector. (#6177)

1524 **1838 MS63 NGC.** An outstanding Select example of this Reeded Edge issue, part of a two-year type with the Bust obverse and the denomination given as HALF DOL. This well struck and luminous piece exhibits warm rose and orange patina over much of each side. (#6177)

1525 **1839 AU55 NGC.** With a mintage of just under 1.4 million pieces, the 1839 has the lower mintage of the two Reeded Edge, HALF DOL. Philadelphia issues. This well struck, briefly circulated representative has dappled blue-green and tan toning over much of the obverse with a greater degree of silver-gray on the reverse. (#6179)

Choice Mint State 1839 Bust Half

1526 **1839 MS64 PCGS.** While a few of the stars along the lower obverse border are flat, and some letters in the legend on the reverse are also flat, all other details on both sides are remarkably sharp. The surfaces are brilliant and highly lustrous with soft frosty texture. Wavy die cracks are faintly visible on the reverse. Population: 36 in 64, 5 finer (8/07). (#6179)

Rare 1836 Reeded Edge Half, PR63

1527 **1836 Reeded Edge PR63 PCGS.** 1836 Reeded Edge halves are famous as business strikes as only 1,200 pieces were minted. These pieces are widely sought out by collectors in all grades as the first examples of the new half dollar type and the first mass-produced denomination on steam presses. These halves are occasionally available in a wide range of grades, and are always of interest to collectors.

However, little thought is given to the proofs known of this date and type as they are so rare that most collectors have overlooked them. In fact, many do not even know of their existence. Estimates vary from 10 to 12 proofs struck of the 1836. This piece is among the finest known. The fields have a confirmed reflectivity that is plentifully evident through the multiple layers of purple, golden, and blue toning that are splashed over each side. The striking details are strong, but lack absolute fullness, apparently a common trait among several of the known proof 1836 halves. Mint officials were obviously unfamiliar with the striking pressure necessary with the new steam press to completely bring up all the details on these pieces. However, this piece is much stronger defined than the Garrett-Auction '80 coin. Diagnostically correct also, there is a short die crack to the right of the final S in STATES that is present on all genuine proofs of this issue, a trait that is also present on business strikes but is significantly longer on those later strikings. (#6223)

SEATED HALF DOLLARS

1528 **1839 No Drapery AU50 ANACS.** Randy Wiley and Bill Bugert (1993) write that the No Drapery is slightly less available than the With Drapery. Cobalt-blue patina hugs the rims, while splashes of brown glom onto the edges of some of the design elements. Well struck on the obverse, but portions of the eagle are soft. Light roller marks are visible on Liberty's torso.
From The Beau Clerc Collection. (#6230)

1529 **1839 Drapery AU53 PCGS.** Light speckled coloration improves the eye appeal of this AU example. Boldly struck except for the eagle's left (facing) leg and talons, and the arrow fletchings. Surface marks and highpoint wear are minimal, making this piece seem conservatively graded. (#6232)

Colorful Choice 1840 Reverse of 1839 Half Dollar

1530 **1840 Reverse of 1839, Small Letters MS64 NGC.** Lavishly toned in fire-red and mauve with a blush of straw-gold on each side. Crisply struck and lustrous. A moderately abraded representative of the briefly-issued Small Letters subtype, which is more available than its rare Medium Letters counterpart. Census: 12 in 64, 16 finer (8/07). (#6234)

1531 **1841-O MS62 PCGS.** The surfaces of this early O-mint half are luminous beneath dusky seal-gray patina that exhibits orange and violet accents. The central detail is pleasing, and the faint abrasions present on each side are not distracting. The 1841-O half, like other New Orleans minor silver issues, is challenging in Mint State. Population: 11 in 62, 13 finer (8/07). (#6237)

1532 **1845-O—Cleaned—ANACS. VF20 Details.** FS-301, formerly FS-001.5. WB-104. The date is widely repunched east, with the outer right curve of an errant 5 plainly visible. Autumn-brown and sea-green embrace the obverse, while the reverse has deep powder-blue fields. A few minor rim nicks are present, and a faint scratch on the right obverse field is subdued by a cleaning. (#6249)

Well Struck 1846 6 Over Horizontal 6 Half Dollar
AU58, WB-104, VP-001

1533 **1846 6 Over Horizontal 6 AU58 NGC.** WB-104, VP-001. The 6 in the date is repunched over an earlier punched horizontal 6. This AU58 example has a double rim cud below 846, and there is a retained cud above UNI in UNITED, indicating an intermediate die state (Randy Wiley and Bill Bugert, 1993, p.79). Medium intensity multicolored toning covers both sides, and luster resides in the recesses. Well struck throughout. Census: 4 in 58, 8 finer (8/07). (#6254)

Gem Mint State 1852 Half Dollar

1534 **1852 MS65 NGC.** Perhaps the most important observation about this piece is its virtually full strike, with only slight weakness evident on a few of the obverse stars. The surfaces are fully lustrous and brilliant with subliminal champagne toning. Census: 3 in 65, 4 finer (8/07).
From The Beau Clerc Collection. (#6268)

1853 Arrows and Rays Half, MS63

1535 **1853 Arrows and Rays MS63 PCGS.** A hint of pale gold toning can be seen on each side, over lustrous ivory surfaces. Only a few scattered marks interrupt the satiny luster. A one-year type issue with arrows on the obverse and rays on the reverse. Examples are constantly in demand by Seated half dollar specialists and type collectors. (#6275)

1536 **1853-O Arrows and Rays—Cleaned—ANACS. AU55 Details.** The 1853-O is requisite for New Orleans type collectors, since the rays were removed from the design in 1854. This example is noteworthy not only for its ample remaining luster, but for its prominent obverse die cracks at 3 and 7 o'clock. The reverse is multiply clashed. (#6276)

1537 **1854-O Arrows MS64 PCGS.** This shining near-Gem hails from the highest-mintage of the No Motto, Arrows halves, though this antebellum issue remains challenging in Choice and better grades. Minimally marked with vibrant luster, pleasing central detail, and a pair of gold-orange streaks across the reverse. (#6280)

1538 **1855-O Arrows Shipwreck Effect NGC.** Ex: S.S. Republic. We believe this coin has XF details. The stone-white surfaces are granular from 140 years of exposure to saltwater. Some luster remains in design recesses. This lot is accompanied by a presentation box, booklet, DVD, and certificate of authenticity from Odyssey Marine Exploration, Inc.
From The Vanek Collection. (#6283)

Lustrous 1855-O Arrows Half Dollar, MS64

1539 1855-O Arrows MS64 PCGS. The lustrous surfaces of this near-Gem O-mint half display a mix of low to medium intensity multicolored toning resting over both sides. A well executed strike brings out sharp definition on the design features, and just a few minute obverse ticks define the grade. "Halos," often found on this issue, are visible around the stars of this specimen. The halos around these devices were explained by Wiley and Bugert (1993) as the result of coinage dies being used as temporary master dies to create additional dies. The outlines around the various design elements represent the base of the punch being transferred to a new working coinage die. (#6283)

Condition Rarity 1855-O Arrows Half Dollar, MS66

1540 1855-O Arrows MS66 NGC. This stone-white and satiny Premium Gem is essentially free from marks. The strike is crisp overall, and particularly impressive on Liberty's hair and the nearby stars. Stars 12 and 13 show a hint of softness, as does the eagle's left (facing) ankle. The second 5 in the date appears to show slight recutting on the lower right, but this is probably a 'halo' from the die production process, similar to that seen near portions of the stars. As a two-year type, the 1855-O is sought for New Orleans Mint type sets, and although nice Mint State pieces are obtainable, there are not enough to meet demand. At the MS66 level, Seated halves are rare regardless of date or subtype, and the 1855-O is no exception. Census: 5 in 66, 0 finer (7/07). (#6283)

1541 1857-S AU53 PCGS. Golden-gray toning is slightly deeper on the reverse of this AU53 half, and sharp definition characterizes the design elements. A few minute marks are not disturbing. Randy Wiley and Bill Bugert (1993) assign a low R.5 rating to XF/AU examples, though AU53 coins are probably close to R.7. (#6292)

1542 1858 MS64 PCGS. An impressive Choice Mint State piece with frosty silver luster and sharp design details. The head, stars, and claws are all nicely defined. Over 4 million of these were coined, yet this is an elusive date in higher quality. Population: 52 in 64, 14 finer (8/07). (#6293)

1543 1859-S AU58 NGC. Light silver-gray surfaces are quite clean and display traces of luster in the recessed areas. A well executed strike leaves nice definition on the design features. *From The Beau Clerc Collection.* (#6298)

1544 1860-O—Shipwreck Effect—NGC. Ex: *S.S. Republic.* This untoned New Orleans half has Mint State sharpness, but is mildly granular from long-term exposure to seawater. The luster is subdued, but nonetheless present within the devices. Accompanied by a presentation box, a certificate of authenticity, a brochure, a mini-book, and a DVD. (#6300)

1545 1860-O MS64 NGC. Pleasing central detail and attractive luster are among the prime draws of this lovely antebellum half. The obverse shows scattered hints of canary-gold and sky-blue toning, while the reverse has richer orange patina. A few wispy marks in the fields account for the grade. Population: 27 in 64, 18 finer (8/07). (#6300)

1546 1861-O—Shipwreck Effect—NGC. Ex: *S.S. Republic.* Wiley-03, a State of Louisiana marriage. No wear is apparent on Liberty's chest or thighs, although the stone-white surfaces are somewhat porous from more than a century's exposure to saltwater. A cherry-wood presentation case, brochure, DVD, and certificate of authenticity accompany the lot. (#6303)

1547 1861-O—Shipwreck Effect—NGC. Ex: *S.S. Republic.* Wiley-08, a State of Louisiana. The highpoints lack any indication of wear, although the cream-gray fields and devices are mildly to moderately granular from more than a century of sleeping with the fishes. A cherry-wood presentation case, brochure, DVD, and certificate of authenticity are all included. (#6303)

1548 1861-O—Shipwreck Effect—NGC. Ex: *S.S. Republic.* Wiley-02, a Union die marriage. No wear is apparent on the devices, but each side is lackluster and granular from its long sleep at the bottom of the sea. A wooden presentation box, DVD, brochure, and certificate of authenticity accompany the lot. (#6303)

1549 1861-O—Shipwreck Effect—NGC. Ex: *S.S. Republic.* Wiley-04a, a State of Louisiana marriage. This shipwreck recovery piece has little if any circulation wear, but the slate-gray surfaces are granular from its 140-year stint at the bottom of the Atlantic ocean. A wooden presentation box, DVD, brochure, and certificate of authenticity are included. (#6303)

1550 1861-O MS63 NGC. Speckles of purple and cobalt-blue visit the obverse, while the reverse is mostly golden-tan. Sharply struck, and displaying nice luster on generally well preserved surfaces. *From The Beau Clerc Collection.* (#6303)

1551 1861-O MS64 NGC. Wiley-08 with partial drapery near the elbow and clash marks within the eagle's shield. Wiley's research suggests this die pairing was struck by the State of Louisiana, shortly before it joined the Confederacy. Lustrous and virtually brilliant with a unimportant marks on the upper left obverse field. Census: 38 in 64, 13 finer (7/07). (#6303)

Important 1861-S Half Dollar, MS64

1552 1861-S MS64 PCGS. Nearly 1 million examples of this issue were coined during the year, yet Choice and Gem Mint State survivors are rarely seen. This lustrous near-Gem has frosty luster beneath medium gold color with specks of darker toning on both sides. Population: 12 in 64, 4 finer (8/07). *From The Beau Clerc Collection.* (#6306)

1553 **1864 AU55 NGC.** A scarce civil War issue, traces of luster reside in the recesses of this light golden-gray representative. Clean surfaces exhibit sharply struck design elements. A light crack connects the outer edges of the first four stars.
From The Beau Clerc Collection. (#6311)

1554 **1866-S No Motto—Cleaned—ANACS. VF20 Details.** This stone-gray rare date quarter is subdued and mildly granular from a chemical cleaning. The reverse rim has a moderate mark near 10 o'clock. Only 60,000 pieces were struck. (#6315)

Colorful Choice 1867 Half

1555 **1867 MS64 PCGS.** Golden-brown and electric-blue adorn this intricately struck and shimmering near-Gem. Nearly a "No Drapery" variety, but Liberty has a fragment of drapery beneath her raised elbow. The reverse die is interesting for a series of faint vertical die scratches (as made) within the left horizontal shield lines. Desirable in such quality. Population: 10 in 64, 7 finer (7/07). (#6321)

Desirable 1870-CC Seated Half, VF25

1556 **1870-CC VF25 PCGS.** "If I were seeking an attractive middle grade circulated example of the 1870-CC half dollar, I would choose this one." That is the comment made by the cataloger to an associate when this coin was first examined.

While the half dollar and the silver dollar are both reasonably plentiful in comparison to the other denominations struck in Carson City during the opening session of production, examples with fully natural, unimpaired surfaces like this coin are not easy to locate. Both sides have delightful silver-gray surfaces with subdued golden-brown toning. While there are some collectors who expect catalogers to find fault with every coin, the only blemish on this piece is a minute rim bump near star 3.
From The Beau Clerc Collection. (#6328)

Historic 1870-CC Seated Half AU50 Details

1557 **1870-CC—Corroded—ANACS. AU50 Details.** In its first year of operation, the Carson City Mint struck three silver denominations: the quarter, half dollar, and dollar. The 1870-CC has a mintage more than double that of the quarter and dollar combined, but the survival rate was remarkably low, particularly when compared with the 1870-CC silver dollar. Apparently, no one, not even local Mint officials or workers, appreciated the significance of the issue sufficiently to set examples aside. As of (5/07), NGC and PCGS have each certified only one piece as Mint State, both as MS62. In terms of sharpness, the present lot is close to Mint State, but the slate-gray surfaces are subdued and granular. The fields have only a few minor marks. (#6328)

Rare Mint State 1872-S Half Dollar, MS62

1558 **1872-S MS62 PCGS.** The '72-S ranks among the most elusive dates among all San Francisco Mint Seated half dollars, as indicated by the PCGS population data. This piece is fully brilliant with frosty silver luster and a trace of light gold toning near the borders. Most design elements are sharply detailed, although a few stars are flat, and weakness is evident on Liberty's leg. Population: 4 in 62, 10 finer (8/07).
From The Beau Clerc Collection. (#6335)

1559 1873 Arrows MS61 NGC. In 1873, the Mint reprised the arrows of 1853 to denote a weight change, though this shift was much more minor than that of 20 years ago. This luminous and well struck piece has splashes of faint canary-yellow patina and numerous tiny abrasions that account for the grade. (#6343)

Toned MS64 1873 Arrows Half

1560 1873 Arrows MS64 PCGS. WB-107, Small Arrows. Dusky apricot and aqua-blue colors do not deny the unbroken satin luster. Well struck save for the hair on Liberty's forehead. A carefully preserved representative of this important short-lived type, which is surprisingly scarce in better Mint State grades. (#6343)

Desirable 1873-CC Arrows Half, AU50

1561 1873-CC Arrows AU50 ANACS. Light silver surfaces exhibit considerable luster with faint lilac and gold toning near the borders. Although the 1873-CC With Arrows half is not particularly rare, demand far exceeds the available supply, supported prices at generally increasing levels.
From The Beau Clerc Collection. (#6344)

Scarce 1873-CC Arrows Half, AU58

1562 1873-CC Arrows AU58 NGC. WB-103. Large Mintmark. A scarce Arrows issue with only 122,500 pieces produced. High grade pieces are especially difficult to locate. Unlike the majority of CC halves from 1870-1874, this piece is sharply struck on the obverse. The reverse is equally well defined. The subdued surfaces show even gray toning with a light undertone of rose. (#6344)

1563 1873-S Arrows AU58 NGC. Randy Wiley and Bill Bugert in their Seated Liberty half dollar reference indicate the 1873-S with Arrows half is "A scarce date, especially in higher grades. Extremely rare in Mint State." Sharply struck, with ample luster residing on surfaces lightly toned golden-gray. A few minor circulation marks are noted.
From The Beau Clerc Collection. (#6345)

Challenging 1874-CC Arrows Half AU53

1564 1874-CC Arrows AU53 ANACS. The 1874-CC has a mintage of just 59,000 pieces, and is one of only two Carson City Arrows issues. The '74-CC is very scarce in all grades, and is desirable with ample remaining mint luster. This example has medium golden-brown and olive toning. The right obverse field has a few faint hairlines. (#6347)

1565 1874-S Arrows AU58 NGC. Generous amounts of luster remain on the silver surfaces visited by traces of light olive-green. Quite clean throughout, and sharply struck on the design elements. A scarce date, especially in higher circulated grades. Rare in Mint State.
From The Beau Clerc Collection. (#6348)

1566 1875-CC MS62 NGC. Lustrous surfaces exhibit traces of light olive-green and sharply struck devices. A few minute contact marks are scattered about, and what appears to be a light fingerprint is visible in the upper left obverse quadrant.
From The Beau Clerc Collection. (#6350)

1567 1875-S MS63 PCGS. Surprisingly well-detailed for this San Francisco issue with smooth luster below olive-green and plum patina. A number of wispy, isolated marks on each side account for the grade. (#6351)

1568 1875-S MS64 NGC. Dappled gray, light green, mauve, and aqua-blue race over highly lustrous surfaces. Nicely struck, with minimal marks. Census: 52 in 64, 42 finer (7/07). (#6351)

1569 1875-S MS64 NGC. An ivory near-Gem with excellent design definition. Satiny silver luster is only slightly subdued by light gold and pale rose toning. Census: 52 in 64, 42 finer (8/07). (#6351)

1570 1875-S MS64 PCGS. The arrows flanking the date for the previous two years were removed for the 1875 issues, marking the last design change within the Seated series. This frosty near-Gem offers lovely lavender and gold toning over silver-white surfaces and pleasing central sharpness, though a few stars show softness. (#6351)

Sharp 1875-S Gem Half Dollar

1571 1875-S MS65 PCGS. A delicate mix of golden-tan and soft violet patination rests on lustrous surfaces that are devoid of significant contact marks. Sharp definition is apparent on the design elements, save for minor softness in a couple of the star centers and in the right (left facing) claw. Four or five minute toning flecks are noted on the obverse. With a mintage of 3.2 million pieces, the 1875-S is an excellent type coin. This example will fit comfortably in a high-grade Mint State collection. Population: 47 in 65, 11 finer (8/07). (#6351)

1572 **1876 MS64 PCGS.** An enticing, softly lustrous Choice piece from the ever-popular centennial issue. Dusky plum and antique-gold shades drape the faintly marked silver-gray surfaces. Population: 46 in 64, 18 finer (8/07). (#6352)

1573 **1877-CC AU55 PCGS.** This Choice AU Carson City Mint specimen displays bright golden-tan centers framed by cobalt-blue and gold-orange on the obverse margins, and deep olive-green, blue, and golden-brown on the reverse peripheries. Sharply struck, and devoid serious contact marks.
From The Beau Clerc Collection. (#6356)

Exceptional 1877-S Half Dollar, MS66

1574 **1877-S MS66 NGC.** Type One Reverse. A generous number of half dollars from the San Francisco Mint were produced in 1877 (5.356 million pieces), and as might be expected, a goodly number can be located in most grades. Premium Gems, however, such as that in the present lot, are less available. Much prooflikeness is visible underneath the lush toning that features shades of jade-green and ice-blue on each side. The strike is complete, a feature that is seldom seen on these large silver coins, and close scrutiny reveals little evidence of contact. A top-of-the-line example. Census: 18 in 66, 3 finer (8/07). (#6357)

Uncirculated Details 1878-CC Half

1575 **1878-CC—Scratched—NCS. Unc. Details.** At first glance, this is a lovely Mint State example with full cartwheel luster, a penetrating strike, and attractive peripheral golden-brown toning. A few clusters of pinscratches are noted on the field near the eagle, from an attempt to remove a few green flecks. The obverse displays faint hairlines on the right obverse field. A rare Carson City issue, since its production was interrupted to resume silver dollar coinage.
From The Beau Clerc Collection. (#6359)

Breathtaking 1882 Half, MS68

1576 **1882 MS68 NGC.** While the Bland-Allison act spurred the purchase and coinage of vast quantities of silver, practically all of the metal went to dollars, and minor coinage suffered comparative neglect. In 1882, for example, the year's production of half dollars amounted to just 4,400 pieces, a trifling quantity compared to the 11.1 million dollars struck at Philadelphia for that year.

A delicate melange of gold, rose, sea-green, and amber patina graces both sides of this amazing coin, which has boldly impressed devices and vibrant, partly reflective luster. Even under strong magnification, the surfaces betray only the most insignificant of flaws. In addition to its status as one of the two finest known halves from 1882 (one at NGC and one at PCGS), this stupendous representative is one of just seven total With Motto Seated halves awarded the MS68 grade by NGC, with none finer for the series (8/07). (#6364)

1577 **1886 MS64 NGC.** Sharply struck with reflective fields and frosty devices, the surfaces are mostly brilliant with splashes of lilac and steel-blue toning on both sides. Just 5,000 circulation strikes were minted, and high quality survivors are elusive. Census: 26 in 64, 13 finer (8/07). (#6368)

1578 **1886 MS64 NGC.** Strikingly prooflike even by the standards of this low-mintage late-date Seated issue, though the reflectivity falls just shy of the proof standard and the rim is not completely squared. Rich rose patina graces the margins of this near-Gem, while the centers are silver-gray. Census: 26 in 64, 13 finer (8/07). (#6368)

Ebullient Gem 1888 Half Dollar

1579 **1888 MS65 PCGS.** This carefully preserved and low mintage Seated half provides potent luster, and has just a hint of light tan toning. Only 12,000 pieces were struck. A good strike despite slight blending of detail on Liberty's forehead curls. Certified in a green label holder. Population: 20 in 65, 20 finer (8/07). (#6370)

Splendid 1888 Half Dollar, MS67

1580 **1888 MS67 NGC.** This low-mintage half (12,001 business strikes) looks nearly as it did when it came off the presses. Glowing, unbroken luster exudes from essentially white surfaces that exhibit sharply struck design elements, save for minor softness in the centrils of the stars at each side of Liberty's head. A few luster grazes are visible on Liberty's portrait, but they do nothing to take away from the splendid overall eye appeal. Census: 9 in 67, 0 finer (8/07). (#6370)

Flashy Gem 1890 Seated Half

1581 **1890 MS65 NGC.** Although uniformly frosted, the fields are slightly brighter than the devices on both sides. Pale tan-gray iridescence is noted throughout, but the overall appearance is one of full brilliance. The last year of depressed half dollar production, the 1890 is quite scarce in the preferred Mint State grades. Census: 15 in 65, 14 finer (7/07). (#6372)

1582 **1891 MS64 PCGS.** Unlike the nominal mintages of the decade before, the 1891 issue, the last of the Seated halves, has a mintage of 200,000 pieces. This near-Gem exhibits swirling, slightly frosty luster with delicate sky-blue and gold tints. Population: 40 in 64, 27 finer (8/07). (#6373)

PROOF SEATED HALF DOLLARS

1854 Arrows Half, PR65
Rarely Seen and Highly Collectible

1583 **1854 PR65 NGC.** The 1854 Arrows half is a significant 19th century rarity. So few have been seen by any one person, however, that in the past its rarity has been overstated. Breen (1977) said just three pieces were known. Wiley-Bugert estimated that "less than 6 known." The advent of third-part grading has made it possible for two entities (PCGS and NGC) to verify rare proofs and certify them. So, over the course of 20 years, it is probable that most of the proofs of this issue have been seen. Both of the major services combined have certified 26 pieces in all grades, and we estimate that translates into around 20 separate coins.

When he cataloged the Kaufman PR66 1854 half, Mark Borckardt noted: "While separated from Liberty's base and the border, the date and arrows are slightly above center in the exergue. The shield point is over the outer left curve of the 8, and 54 are extremely close but do not touch. Similar to Breen's description, but the stars do not have any extra outlines. No unusual reverse characteristics are noted, other than faint clash marks visible just inside the right shield border. Seated coins of various dates and denominations often show similar clash marks." These diagnostics are present on this piece also.

The fields show the depth of reflectivity one would expect from a proof striking. The surfaces on each side display deep blue, purple, and rose toning. There are no noticeable flaws, but the peripheral obverse stars lack complete striking definition. (#6407)

1584 **1862 PR63 PCGS.** An attractive Select proof with splashes of cobalt-blue, purple, and gold-tan around the borders, leaving the centers brilliant. Exquisitely struck throughout. Some faint hairlines in the fields define the grade.
From The Beau Clerc Collection. (#6416)

Patinated Gem Proof 1862 Seated Half

1585 1862 PR65 PCGS. Type Two Reverse. Attractive orange and aquamarine embraces this razor-sharp specimen. Among the finest survivors of this Civil War issue. A mere 550 proofs were struck, some of which may have been melted by the Mint as unsold. Population: 15 in 65, 3 finer (8/07). (#6416)

Gorgeous Proof 1862 Half, PR66

1586 1862 PR66 NGC. A gorgeous proof with glittering, deeply mirrored fields on both sides, accented by lighter iridescent toning. The obverse has a small circle of ivory-gray, surrounded by lilac, amber, and blue-green toning. The reverse is similarly toned, but lacks the lighter color found on the obverse.

Proof No Motto half dollars are much scarcer than those of the modified With Motto design. Factor in the nature of Civil War issues, with the rarity of business strikes, and this issue qualifies as an important and highly desirable numismatic prize. Census: 6 in 66, 2 finer (8/07). (#6416)

Stunning 1862 Half Dollar, PR65 Cameo

1587 1862 PR65 Cameo PCGS. A stunning half dollar, this Gem Cameo proof example is tied for the finest certified by PCGS. A borderline deep cameo piece, the obverse has full silver brilliance and the reverse has a trace of golden iridescence. Population: 3 in 65, 0 finer (8/07). (#86416)

1588 1863 PR63 Cameo NGC. The frosty devices favorably compare with the glittering mirrored fields. This brilliant proof has a few wispy hairlines, but the strike is intricate save for minor completeness on the left (facing) ankle.

Gem Proof 1864 Seated Half

1589 1864 PR65 NGC. A lovely Gem proof with lilac, sea-green, and gold toning intermingled across both sides. An important low-mintage piece from the Civil War era. Coin collectors preferred proof examples, and there is little doubt that this piece was originally acquired at that time by an active collector. It is unfortunate that no provenance has been preserved. (#6418)

1590 1866 Motto PR63 NGC. A gorgeous Select proof representative of this scarcer issue, from a low mintage of just 725 pieces. Obvious cameo contrast is noted on the obverse, and a milder cameo effect is also observed on the reverse. Census: 20 in 63, 44 finer (7/07). (#6424)

1591 1867 PR63 Cameo PCGS. A goodly number of the 625-piece mintage of 1867 proof halves have apparently survived, judging from the fairly large number certified by PCGS and NGC. Cameos, such as this select specimen, are more challenging. Sharply impressed, with excellent contrast, and a thin coat of champagne-gold color. Some wispy handling marks in the obverse fields limit the grade. *From The Beau Clerc Collection.* (#86425)

1592 1868 PR63 PCGS. Light to medium intensity golden-gray toning occupies the central areas of this Select proof, flanked by iridescent aqua-green, electric-blue, and lavender clinging to the margins. We note an impressive strike on all of the design elements, and well preserved surfaces with just a few minute handling marks. Population: 47 in 63, 45 finer (8/07). *From The Beau Clerc Collection.* (#6426)

Cameo PR64 1868 Half Dollar

1593 1868 PR64 Cameo NGC. A better date in the early With Motto series, in spite of a substantial mintage of more than 400,000 business strikes. However, only 600 proofs were struck. This is a deeply mirrored example that has strongly contrasting mint frost over the devices. Mostly brilliant, there is just a hint of golden toning around the rims. Census: 11 in 64, 7 finer (8/07). (#86426)

1594 1869 PR63 PCGS. An attractive example of this post-war proof issue. The iridescent amber, blue, and green patina creates a two-tone effect next to the essentially brilliant, boldly impressed devices. One of only 600 pieces struck. (#6427)

Untoned 1869 Half Dollar, PR64

1595 1869 PR64 NGC. A crisply struck and untoned specimen with noticeable cameo contrast, particularly on the obverse, although not designated as such on the NGC insert. The reverse field has a few wispy hairlines. Just 600 pieces were struck. Census: 46 in 64, 29 finer (8/07).
From The Mario Eller Collection, Part One. (#6427)

Sharp 1871 Half Dollar, PR66

1596 1871 PR66 NGC. A Premium Gem proof, this impressive half dollar is deeply mirrored with lightly frosted devices. The brilliant surfaces exhibit light heather, gold, and blue toning on both sides, concentrated more heavily near the borders. Census: 5 in 66, 2 finer (8/07).
From The Beau Clerc Collection. (#6429)

1597 1872 PR63 PCGS. Essentially untoned surfaces exhibit sharply impressed design elements. Some faint hairlines in the fields become visible under magnification, nevertheless, a sharp proof with mild field-motif contrast. Housed in a green label holder.
From The Beau Clerc Collection. (#6430)

Scarce 1874 Seated Half Dollar, Small Arrows, PR64

1598 1874 Arrows PR64 PCGS. WB-101. Small Arrows. According to Wiley & Bugert (1993), the Small Arrows variety is: "Usually found as a proof and by far scarcer than WB-102". This example is crisply struck throughout, with mildly reflective fields that only reveal a trace of milkiness and a few stray hairlines. Carefully preserved and free of contact marks. (#6435)

Lovely Gem Proof 1874 Arrows Half

1599 1874 Arrows PR65 NGC. Philadelphia struck just 1,250 With Motto, Arrows proof halves across two years, and the type is popular with collectors. This 1874 representative comes from the second issue, which amounted to 700 specimens. The boldly impressed devices show a measure of frost on each side, and the lightly gold-toned fields offer a modicum of contrast. The margins have deeper amber patina that approaches orange on the obverse. Census: 13 in 65, 7 finer (8/07). (#6435)

1600 1876 PR64 Cameo NGC. Type One Reverse. This amazing PR64 Cameo displays white surfaces and crisp design features. Some light hairlines visible under magnification define the grade. Census: 7 in 64 Cameo, 12 finer (7/07). (#86437)

1601 1876 PR64 Cameo NGC. Type One Reverse. A gleaming specimen with strong contrast on both sides, this near-Gem exhibits solid frost on the sharply struck devices. Aside from a measure of haze at the faintly hairlined lower right obverse, the fields are untoned. Census: 8 in 64 Cameo, 12 finer (8/07). (#86437)

1602 1878 PR63 NGC. Type Two Reverse. A glittering proof that nearly qualifies for a Cameo designation, this brilliant piece has deeply mirrored fields and only faint hairlines to limit the grade. (#6439)

1603 1878 PR63 PCGS. Type Two Reverse. Crisply struck with unmarked surfaces that display milky plum-gray toning over both sides. Only 800 proof half dollars were struck in 1878. Certified in a green label holder. (#6439)

1604 1878 PR63 PCGS. Whispers of gold-tan and olive-green patina make occasional visits to the obverse fields of this Select proof, leaving the remaining surfaces brilliant. The design elements are well impressed, and a few minor handling marks are noted on both sides.
From The Beau Clerc Collection. (#6439)

1605 1878 PR64 Cameo PCGS. Type Two Reverse. The lovely golden-brown patina is especially rich at the borders. A suitably struck near-Gem with good cameo contrast. A few faint obverse hairlines are evident upon intense scrutiny. Only 800 pieces were struck. Population: 8 in 64 as Cameo, with 8 finer (7/07). (#86439)

1606 1879 PR64 PCGS. Type One Reverse. An exquisitely detailed later Seated proof that exhibits delightful, deep patina. Lilac and violet are the predominant shades of the obverse, while the reverse displays yellow-green and ocean-blue hues. A few tiny hairlines are present in the fields. (#6440)

1879 Gem Proof Seated Liberty Half

1607 1879 PR65 PCGS. Type Two Reverse. Mild cameo contrast is present despite light cream and gold toning. The strike is crisp, and the fields are undisturbed. Liberty's drapery near the elbow is partially effaced, as made. A low mintage date, since the Mint was occupied with Morgan dollar production. In a green label holder. Population: 22 in 65, 17 finer (8/07). (#6440)

Colorful Gem Proof 1879 Half Dollar

1608 1879 PR65 ANACS. Type Two Reverse. Beautiful powder-blue, peach, aquamarine, and violet-rose endow this nicely mirrored and unabraded Gem. A good strike despite minor incompleteness on Liberty's hair and the eagle's left (facing) ankle. A low mintage date, since the Philadelphia Mint focused on silver dollar coinage. (#6440)

Dazzling PR66 Cameo 1879 Seated Half

1609 1879 PR66 Cameo NGC. Type One Reverse. An exceptionally reflective and practically untoned Premium Gem. Thick mint frost is consistent throughout the devices and legends. An unobtrusive fingerprint is noted on AMERICA. An appealing example of this low mintage date. Census: 5 in 66 Cameo, 11 finer (8/07).
From The Beau Clerc Collection. (#86440)

1610 1880 PR63 ANACS. Wisps of light golden-tan color gravitate to the obverse margins, while deeper hues of the same palette are joined by lavender and russet on the reverse borders. A sharp strike brings out excellent definition on the design features. Some faint, unobtrusive hairlines preclude a higher grade.
From The Beau Clerc Collection. (#6441)

Beautifully Toned PR65 1880 Half Dollar

1611 1880 PR65 PCGS. Type Two Reverse. A low total issue with only 9,755 halves struck of this date, of which 1,355 were proofs. Both sides are fantastically toned in multiple iridescent colors. The coin is also exceptionally well preserved and the proof mirrors are deeply reflective; but what any viewer will come away with is the memory of the toning on this piece. Population: 28 in 65, 15 finer (8/07). (#6441)

1612 1881 PR64 PCGS. A crisply struck and beautifully toned Choice specimen of this later Seated half issue, blue-green, rose, and orange on the obverse with deeper plum shades on the reverse. One of only 975 pieces coined. PCGS has graded 32 finer examples (8/07). (#6442)

1613 1882 PR61 PCGS. Just the barest hints of tan-gold color at the margins show up under magnification, and all of the design elements are sharply struck. Somewhat subdued reflectivity, particularly on the obverse. Housed in a green label holder.
From The Beau Clerc Collection. (#6443)

Lushly Patinated PR66 1882 Half

1614 1882 PR66 PCGS. Transparent shades of fuchsia and sage evenly cover the surfaces of this delightful Premium Gem proof. Close perusal with a loupe fails to reveal the most trifling evidence of contact. The half dollars of 1879 through 1890 saw proof mintages that were not much smaller than the minuscule business strike emissions. A sharp and pleasing piece. Population: 21 in 66, 2 finer (8/07). (#6443)

Sharp 1882 Half Dollar, PR66

1615 1882 PR66 NGC. This 1882 Premium Gem proof displays mauve-gray patina on the central devices, and a melange of cobalt-blue, lavender, crimson, and yellow-gold in the fields. A well executed strike imparts excellent definition to the design features, and close inspection reveals no significant marks. (#6443)

Cameo Gem Proof 1882 Half

1616 1882 PR65 Cameo NGC. Icy devices and suitably mirrored fields confirm the Cameo designation. A sharply struck, brilliant, and unabraded Gem. Dimes resumed normal production levels in 1882, but half dollars remained on the Mint back burner. Proofs and business strikes combined for only 5,500 pieces. Census: 9 in 65 Cameo, 15 finer (8/07).
From The Mario Eller Collection, Part One. (#86443)

Ultra Cameo PR63 1882 Seated Half

1617 1882 PR63 Ultra Cameo NGC. This brilliant and crisply struck specimen exhibits remarkable contrast between the frosty devices and the darkly mirrored fields. The reverse is exquisitely preserved, and the obverse field is only moderately hairlined. Census: 1 in 63 Ultra Cameo, 7 finer (8/07). (#96443)

1618 1883 PR63 Cameo NGC. Ex: W.J. Skiles Collection. An appealing proof with sea-green toning in the fields and silver-beige patina over the delicately frosted devices. Faint, scattered hairlines in the fields preclude a finer grade, though the eye appeal remains strong. Census: 15 in 63 Cameo, 43 finer (8/07).
From The Mario Eller Collection, Part One. (#86444)

Gem 1883 Half, PR65 Cameo

1619 1883 PR65 Cameo NGC. A wonderful cameo proof with exceptional mint brilliance. The fields are deeply mirrored, the devices lustrous, and the contrast exceptional. We consider this piece to be a borderline Deep Cameo proof, therefore, an outstanding opportunity.
From The Beau Clerc Collection. (#86444)

Sharply Struck 1884 Half Dollar, PR64

1620 1884 PR64 NGC. All of the design elements are crisply impressed, befitting a proof striking on this near-Gem. Just the slightest hint of light tan color is visible at the peripheries under magnification. A few inoffensive contact marks and hairlines on the obverse define the grade.
From The Mario Eller Collection, Part One. (#6445)

Choice Cameo Proof 1886 Half

1621 1886 PR64 Cameo NGC. Ex: W.J. Skiles Collection. Stone-white at first glance, although a faint band of apricot toning adorns UNITED STATES. Razor-sharp aside from trivial merging of detail on the eagle's ankle. A mere 886 proofs were struck, in addition to only 5,000 commercial pieces. Census: 8 in 64 Cameo, 10 finer (8/07). *Ex: FUN Signature (Heritage, 1/05), lot 7418, which realized $1,955.*
From The Mario Eller Collection, Part One. (#86447)

1887 Half Dollar, Choice Proof

1622 1887 PR64 PCGS. This deeply toned proof has thick heather, sea-green, and steel-blue toning over fully mirrored fields. The devices are frosted, presenting a pleasing cameo appearance under the toning. Population: 59 in 64, 30 finer (8/07).
From The Beau Clerc Collection. (#6448)

PR64 Cameo 1887 Seated Half

1623 **1887 PR64 Cameo NGC.** Ex: W.J. Skiles Collection. Light gold patina endows this nicely struck and carefully preserved specimen. The devices offer imposing white-on-black contrast. Proofs and business strikes combined for a mere 5,710 pieces.
Ex: FUN Signature (Heritage, 1/05), lot 7419, which realized $1,955. From The Mario Eller Collection, Part One. (#86448)

Gold Toned 1888 Half, PR65

1624 **1888 PR65 PCGS.** A lightly toned Gem proof, this attractive piece ranks high in the population data. Both sides are deeply and fully mirrored in the fields, with lustrous devices and excellent cameo contrast, despite the lack of such a designation from PCGS.
From The Beau Clerc Collection. (#6449)

1625 **1889 PR62 NGC.** Decisively struck with strong reflectivity beneath layers of cloud-gray patina. The lower obverse rim displays an arc of reddish-orange patina. Light, scattered hairlines and a few pinpoint contact marks limit the grade of this otherwise pleasing late-date proof Seated half. (#6450)

Gorgeous 1890 Half, PR66 Cameo

1626 **1890 PR66 Cameo NGC.** This amazing proof has virtually perfect surfaces with exceptionally deep mirrors and lustrous devices. The obverse is light gold with peripheral russet, lilac, and blue toning. The reverse is mostly brilliant with peripheral iridescence similar to the obverse. Census: 5 in 66 Cameo, 5 finer (8/07). (#86451)

Profoundly Contrasted Deep Cameo PR66 1890 Half

1627 **1890 PR66 Deep Cameo PCGS.** The silver lobby and the Bland-Allison Act of 1878 explain several mysteries in late 19th century numismatics. The Act required the government to purchase between 2 and 4 million ounces of newly coined silver each month. What this translated into is enormous mintages for silver dollars, as a silver dollar was heavier than two halves, four quarters, or 10 dimes. As a result, mintages for lower denomination silver coins from 1878 through 1890 were remarkably low for the most part. The year 1890 was the final year for lower production numbers for half dollars. Still, only 12,000 circulation strikes were produced, plus 590 proofs. This is an outstanding Deep Cameo proof. The fields are deeply reflective and all the devices on each side show thick mint frost. The result is a profound white-on-black cameo effect. Population: 1 in 66, 1 finer (8/07). (#96451)

BARBER HALF DOLLARS

1628 1892 MS63 PCGS. Original dove-gray patina enriches the obverse. The reverse has lighter toning, but the border nonetheless displays gold and aquamarine freckles. Unabraded and attractive with satin luster and minor incompleteness on the right shield corner. (#6461)

1629 1892 MS64 NGC. Fully struck in all areas. The softly frosted mint luster is covered with several layers of gray, olive, and pinkish-rose toning. (#6461)

Fully Lustrous 1892 Gem Half Dollar

1630 1892 MS65 PCGS. A fully lustrous Gem representative of this first year of issue half dollar. Cobalt-blue and purple toning is concentrated at the margins, framing light gray centers, and the design elements are well brought up. There are no significant marks to report. Great eye appeal! (#6461)

Lustrous MS64 1893 Barber Half

1631 1893 MS64 PCGS. Fully struck with satiny mint brilliance and some subtle golden color at the right portions of each side. Sharply defined throughout with thick mint luster. There are no reportable abrasions, and at first glance this piece appears much finer than the stated grade. One of the more popular dates for type purposes, both because of the earliness of the date as well as the numbers set aside as mementoes. Population: 28 in 64, 24 finer (8/07). (#6465)

MS64 1893 Barber Half Dollar

1632 1893 MS64 PCGS. Beautiful rose-pink toning covers both sides fairly evenly on this well-struck piece, which shows good delineation of the hairline from the brow of Liberty and bold reverse detail. Minor marks are noted beneath the date on the obverse and around the left rim, without which this piece would grade considerably finer. (#6465)

Sharp 1893-S Barber Half Dollar, MS63

1633 1893-S MS63 PCGS. This well-struck piece shows pretty amber-gold and steel-blue coloration near the peripheries on each side, with moderate luster visible in the silvery centers. There are a few slide marks on Liberty's cheek, but this coin is nice for the grade. A desirable series key, produced to the extent of only 740,000 coins. Population: 18 in 63, 17 finer (8/07). (#6467)

1634 1898 MS64 PCGS. A crisply impressed 19th century Barber half, subtly lustrous beneath peach, pastel yellow, and amethyst patina at the margins. A faint planchet defect is noted to the left of Liberty's lips. Population: 43 in 64, 20 finer (8/07). (#6480)

1635 1898 MS64 PCGS. Delicate gold toning graces the peripheries of this penetratingly struck and satiny near-Gem. The portrait is well preserved, and the fields are nearly immaculate. Population: 42 in 64, 20 finer (7/07). (#6480)

1636 1902 MS64 PCGS. This mid-date Barber half offers pleasing luster and strong visual appeal for the grade. Rose, blue, and gold toning graces the obverse margins, and the surfaces are silver-gray otherwise. Pleasingly detailed with a few grade-defining ticks on the portrait. (#6492)

Scarce 1903-O Fifty Cent, MS64

1637 1903-O MS64 PCGS. David Lawrence, in his Barber half dollar reference, writes of the 1903-O that: "Like most O-mints, scarcer than mintage (2.1 million pieces) indicates." Splotches of gray, cobalt-blue, lavender, and gold-tan toning rest over the highly lustrous surfaces of this near-Gem specimen. Sharp definition is apparent on the design elements, save for minor softness on some of the star centers and on the upper right shield corner. Population: 33 in 64, 11 finer (8/07). (#6496)

1638 1904 MS64 PCGS. The thin, dusky amber patina that graces the obverse margins appears in a slightly lighter form on the reverse. A well-defined Choice example of this mid-date Barber issue. Population: 45 in 64, 12 finer (8/07). (#6498)

1639 1904-S VF30 PCGS. A degree of luminosity remains at the margins of this moderately worn S-mint semi-key. The lightly marked silver-gray surfaces show gold and tan overtones, particularly at the margins. Population: 3 in 30, 64 finer (7/07). (#6500)

1640 1907-O MS64 PCGS. An important opportunity for the specialist to add this date, with few finer examples certified. Both sides have satiny luster with heather, gold, and steel toning. Population: 39 in 64, 20 finer (8/07). (#6510)

1641 **1909-O MS62 ANACS.** Well struck except near the arrow feathers and the eagle's right (facing) talons. The lustrous, scarcely toned surfaces are blemish-free on the reverse, though wispy, parallel abrasions are evident on the portrait. A noteworthy half from the final year of operation for the New Orleans Mint. (#6517)

1642 **1910 MS64 PCGS.** Boldly struck, highly lustrous, and essentially untoned. This near-Gem Barber half is well preserved, with a moderate abrasion on obverse star 6 that extends onto the back edge of Liberty's cap as its only obvious grade-limiter. A low mintage date that is very scarce at this grade level or finer. Population: 36 in 64, 25 finer (8/07). (#6519)

Lustrous Gem 1910 Barber Half

1643 **1910 MS65 PCGS.** The obverse shows only a hint of gold toning, while the reverse has medium tan patina. Boldly struck with an immaculate reverse and unimportant portrait grazes. A lower mintage than usual for a Philadelphia issue, just 418,000 pieces. Population: 21 in 65, 4 finer (8/07). (#6519)

Near-Gem 1910-S Barber Half

1644 **1910-S MS64 PCGS.** Both sides are fully lustrous with frosty surfaces accented by traces of obverse iridescence and peripheral gold on the reverse. The population is surprisingly low in the higher grades, despite a mintage of nearly 2 million coins. Population: 15 in 64, 24 finer (8/07). (#6520)

Highly Lustrous 1911 Gem Half Dollar

1645 **1911 MS65 PCGS.** Both sides of this 1911 Gem half dollar are awash in gorgeous luster, and whispers of tan-beige and ice-blue patina ride over the obverse, while speckles of olive-green are evenly distributed over the reverse. An impressive strike emboldens the design features. The only mark of any consequence occurs on the cheek, and it is wholly within the parameters of the grade designation. Population: 39 in 65, 9 finer (8/07). (#6521)

Pleasing 1911-S Half Dollar, MS66

1646 **1911-S MS66 NGC.** David Lawrence, in his Barber half dollar reference, calls the 1911-S "Underrated in MS." This Premium Gem exudes glowing luster from satiny surfaces that display hints of light gold-tan color. A solid strike sharpens the design elements, except for minor softness in the upper right corner of the shield and the eagle's left (right facing) claw and adjacent arrow feathers. Impeccably preserved throughout. Census: 1 in 66, 1 finer (8/07). (#6523)

1647 **1912-D MS64 PCGS.** A well-defined and pleasing near-Gem representative of this D-mint Barber issue, shining with delicate golden patina over the obverse and at the reverse rims. One of just over 2.3 million pieces struck. (#6525)

Attractive Gem 1914 Barber Half

1648 **1914 MS65 PCGS.** A precisely struck Gem with pleasing luster and nearly unabraded fields. The light gold toning is consistent throughout. The low mintage 1914 is coveted in all grades by Barber half collectors. Housed in a green label holder. Population: 7 in 65, 2 finer (8/07). (#6530)

PROOF BARBER HALF DOLLARS

Richly Toned 1892 Half, PR65

1649 **1892 PR65 NGC.** Always of interest to type coin collectors, many high grade 1892 halves were set aside both as proofs and business strikes because of the new and distinctly different design. This is a clean Gem example that is richly toned on each side in shades of rose and emerald green. Sharply struck. (#6539)

Attractively Toned PR65 Cameo 1892 Half

1650 **1892 PR65 Cameo NGC.** Strong field-design contrast is apparent on his sharply struck 1892 proof half. Whispers of cobalt-blue, lavender, and golden-tan color gravitate to the peripheries, especially on the obverse, where moderate roller marks reside. Exceptionally well struck on the design elements. Light doubling is seen on some of the reverse lettering, especially HALF DOLLAR. Census: 20 in 65 Cameo, 44 finer (8/07). (#86539)

Splendid, Subtly Toned 1892 Half, PR67 Cameo

1651 **1892 PR67 Cameo NGC.** The 1892 is both a well-produced date as well as one that was widely set aside as a first-year issue. This is a fabulous cameo coin whose thick mint frost is evident over the devices even beneath the toning. Both sides display pale mint-green centers with light rose accents around the margins. A magnificent cameo proof of this first year of the Barber design. Census: 22 in 67, 2 finer (8/07). (#86539)

Well Struck 1895 Gem Proof Half Dollar

1652 **1895 PR65 NGC.** Mint records indicate that 880 proof half dollars were struck in 1895. Walter Breen says in his 1977 proof *Encyclopedia* that "The majority of these have been poorly cleaned." The Gem offered in this lot yields no evidence of cleaning. Some wispy lines on Liberty's cheek and neck are die polish lines, not hairlines. A thin veneer of gold color is noted under magnification, and a well executed strike imparts nice delineation to the design elements. *From The Mario Eller Collection, Part One.* (#6542)

Boldly Struck 1895 Half Dollar, PR67 Cameo

1653 **1895 PR67 Cameo NGC.** Frosty devices compare favorably with the glassy, faintly toned fields. Unlike most proof Barber half dollars, the strike is virtually complete, even on the right shield corner and fletchings. Exceptional preservation ensures the eye appeal. A scant 880 proofs were struck. Census: 9 in 67, 8 finer (8/07). (#86542)

1654 **1896 PR64 Cameo NGC.** Both sides offer distinct contrast through a rich layer of champagne-gray patina. Deeper bronze patina appears in patches at the margins, and faint hairlines are noted in the fields. Census: 6 in 64 Cameo, 27 finer (7/07). (#86543)

Vividly Toned PR67 1899 Half

1655 **1899 PR67 NGC.** Deep powder-blue and plum-red toning adorns this suitably mirrored Superb Gem. The strike is needle-sharp, even on the fletchings and the right shield corner. An exquisite representative of this turn-of-the-century issue. A mere 846 proofs were struck. Census: 11 in 67, 4 finer (8/07). (#6546)

1656 1899 PR64 Cameo NGC. An immensely appealing piece, strongly reflective with distinct contrast beneath elegant champagne patina. Decisively struck with only minor hairlines evident on each side. One of just 846 proofs coined for this Barber issue. Census: 7 in 64 Cameo, 28 finer (7/07). (#86546)

Nearly Perfect 1902 Barber Half, PR67

1657 1902 PR67 NGC. One would be hard pressed to find a more attractive and better preserved proof Barber half. This is just an extraordinary coin. The fields are deeply mirrored on each side, and this intense reflectivity serves to highlight the lovely toning. Both obverse and reverse have the same colors: emerald green and smoky gray-rose, but the configuration is different on each side. Much of the original brilliance still is in evidence in the center of the obverse. There are virtually no flaws on this coin. A check-shaped lint mark is barely visible behind Liberty's mouth, but we do not see any other pre- or post-striking impairments. Census: 14 in 67, 2 finer (8/07). (#6549)

1658 1902 PR63 Cameo PCGS. Fully struck with deeply reflective jet-black fields and icy-white devices. Some wispy slide marks on Liberty's cheek and neck limit the grade of this proof specimen. A scant 777 pieces were produced, and few of the survivors exhibit substantial field-to-device contrast. Population: 5 in 63, 13 finer (7/07). (#86549)

High-End 1903 Barber Half PR64

1659 1903 PR64 NGC. This is a splendid proof striking that seems high-end for the PR64 grade level. The design elements are crisply defined, without any areas of weakness on either side, and the fields display remarkably deep reflectivity. A few microscopic hairlines on the obverse are seemingly all that keeps this attractive piece from a Gem holder. (#6550)

Exquisite 1903 Half Dollar, PR68

1660 1903 PR68 NGC. Though the Barber design proved unpopular with contemporary numismatists, enough collectors purchased proof sets that specimens in typical grades are available and comparably affordable today. An extraordinary survivor such as the present piece, however, is another story. While the obverse shows the lack of contrast that marks most of the early 20th century silver proof issues, the reverse offers a modicum of contrast. Wisps of gold and champagne patina grace the margins, while the centers are essentially untoned. Even under magnification, the minuscule flaws that preclude a perfect grade are difficult to see. Of the 755 specimens struck, this wonderful example ranks among the finest; neither NGC nor PCGS has certified a numerically finer representative, with just seven pieces awarded a grade of MS68 between both services (8/07). (#6550)

1661 1904 PR63 NGC. The grade of this brilliant proof is limited by the presence of a few faint hairlines across Liberty's cheek, probably the result of a plastic slide from a modern coin album. (#6551)

Appealing 1905 Half Dollar, PR67

1662 **1905 PR67 NGC.** The 1905 proof half dollar comes with a mintage of 727 coins. A relatively large number have been certified by NGC and PCGS through PR65, but the numbers drop significantly in higher grades. This Superb example is one of just 18 PR67 pieces, and only five specimens have graded finer. Essentially untoned surfaces display sharply defined design elements. Impeccably preserved, which further enhances the coin's great eye appeal. (#6552)

Bright, Flashy PR64 Cameo 1905 Half

1663 **1905 PR64 Cameo PCGS.** Seldom seen with contrast, only two other proofs have been certified by PCGS as Cameo and a mere seven pieces are finer (8/07). This coin is almost completely brilliant with just the lightest accent of color over the denticles. Deeply reflective fields, there are no obvious or distracting blemishes on either side. (#86552)

Vividly Toned PR67 1908 Half

1664 **1908 PR67 PCGS.** The obverse is dramatically toned in cobalt-blue, cherry-red, and olive shades. The reverse has a pumpkin-gold area framed on each side by ruby-red and blue-green. Precisely struck and undisturbed with exceptional eye appeal. Population: 7 in 67, 3 finer (7/07). (#6555)

1665 **1909 PR62 PCGS.** Fully struck with deep layers of tobacco-brown, rose, and gray coloration on each side. Minimal hairlines are noted in the fields, and bothersome contact marks are nonexistent. A low mintage, late date proof issue of just 650 pieces. (#6556)

Conditionally Scarce Gem Proof 1911 Barber Half

1666 **1911 PR65 PCGS.** Layers of original olive, gold, rose, and sky-blue patina adorn the surfaces of this lovely Gem proof half dollar. Fully struck and nicely preserved, with a couple of faint slide marks noted on Liberty's cheek and a minor handling mark on the lower bust, just above Barber's initial. A conditionally scarce offering from a low mintage of 543 pieces. Population: 27 in 65, 22 finer (8/07). (#6558)

Choice Cameo Proof 1911 Barber Half

1667 **1911 PR64 Cameo NGC.** The eye appeal of this example is fully equal to many Gem proof examples we have seen. Brilliant aside from a touch of gold toning along the rims. The fields are deeply mirrored with trivial hairlines preventing that elusive Gem determination. The devices are radiant with frost and just miss an Ultra Cameo. Census: 8 in 64 Cameo, 20 finer (8/07). *From The Mario Eller Collection, Part One.* (#86558)

WALKING LIBERTY HALF DOLLARS

1668 **1916 MS64 PCGS.** A satiny and crisply struck near-Gem with delightfully original silver-white and russet-brown toning. The reverse is well preserved. A lovely example of this lower-mintage first-year issue. (#6566)

Scintillating 1916 Walker MS66

1669 **1916 MS66 NGC.** A penetratingly struck Premium Gem with vibrant luster and only a hint of peripheral peach patina. A charming example of this introductory issue. The 1916 has the second lowest mintage of any Philadelphia issue of the type, and is seldom encountered above the MS65 level. (#6566)

1670 **1916-D MS64 PCGS.** Total production for this first-year branch mint issue barely exceeded 1 million pieces. This near-Gem shows a measure of detail on the branch hand and delicate golden accents over the subtly lustrous fields.
From The Mario Eller Collection, Part One. (#6567)

1671 **1916-D MS64 NGC.** This shining near-Gem displays a touch of satiny luster. Delicate golden toning graces much of the minimally marked surfaces. In the first year of the design, Denver struck just over a million pieces. (#6567)

1672 **1916-D MS65 PCGS.** The satiny surfaces of this mintmarked first-year Walker exhibit vibrant patina, predominantly rose and silver-gray with crimson and plum accents. Well struck with excellent visual appeal. (#6567)

1673 **1916-S AU55 NGC.** An attractive, briefly circulated representative of this first-year issue, well-defined with ample luster remaining in the fields. The surfaces are largely silver-gray with touches of blue. One of just 508,000 examples coined. (#6568)

1674 **1916-S MS62 NGC.** This well struck and satiny first-year piece displays subtle, pleasing gold-gray patina over each side. Wispy abrasions preclude a finer grade. The 1916-S has a mintage that just exceeds half a million pieces. (#6568)

1675 **1916-S MS63 ANACS.** An attractively toned Select representative of this first-year issue, well struck with a hint of detail on the branch hand. Magenta-accented gold and orange toning graces both sides. (#6568)

Lovely 1916-S Walker, MS64

1676 **1916-S MS64 PCGS.** Bright silver surfaces have soft, frosty luster and splashes of peripheral gold and iridescent toning along the borders. Although this date is not particularly rare, despite a mintage of just 508,000 coins, demand is high and examples are difficult to locate. (#6568)

1677 **1917 MS65 NGC.** Uncommonly strong detail and vibrant luster are the main attractions of this outstanding Gem. The silver-white surfaces are delightfully preserved and appealing. (#6569)

1678 **1917 MS65 NGC.** Light golden-gray patina rests over radiantly lustrous surfaces. A well executed strike brings out nice detail on the design elements, including Liberty's left hand and adjacent branches. A few minor obverse handling marks preclude an even higher grade. (#6569)

1679 **1917 MS66 PCGS.** While the mintmarked Walker issues of 1917 come in two varieties, the Philadelphia pieces have no such distinction. This attentively struck and shining Premium Gem offers delicate patina in shades of silver-gray. PCGS has certified only two finer pieces (8/07). (#6569)

1680 **1917-D Obverse MS64 PCGS.** The obverse mintmark placement on Walker halves lasted for just two issues, and the majority of mintmarked 1917 halves are of the reverse variety. This well-defined Choice piece is largely silver-gray with splashes of brick-red, cobalt, and olive-tan at the margins. (#6570)

1681 **1917-D Reverse AU58 ANACS.** Despite having a higher mintage than its Obverse counterpart, the 1917-D Reverse Walker is more challenging in better circulated grades. This still-lustrous piece shows sky-blue patina with a touch of champagne at the margins. A hint of friction on the softly struck highpoints precludes a Mint State designation. (#6571)

1682 **1917-D Reverse MS62 NGC.** In 1916 and briefly in 1917, branch mint Walker halves had their mintmarks on the obverse, but in February, the location changed to the reverse. This gold-tinged, slightly satiny example has few marks for the grade and pleasing detail on the branch hand. (#6571)

1683 **1917-D Reverse MS63 PCGS.** The position of the mintmark on this type was shifted from the obverse to the reverse, early enough in the year 1917 that considerably more of the Reverse coins were produced. For unknown reasons, however, the Reverse variety is scarcer in Mint State than the Obverse variety. This example is softly struck on Liberty's head and branch hand, with soft satin luster and light, creamy-beige coloration. A few minor marks and a small gray spot, on Liberty's lower skirt area, limit the grade. (#6571)

Scarce and Popular 1917-S Obverse Walker, MS64

1684 **1917-S Obverse MS64 PCGS.** A scarce early Walker, and one that was highly prized in the early years of collecting—so much so that counterfeits were made of the 1917-S by placing an S on a Philadelphia coin. This coin has terrific, thick mint luster. The striking details are strong except on Liberty's skirt lines. Brilliant-gray surfaces. There are only a few tiny abrasions scattered over each side that explain the grade. Population: 95 in 64, 39 finer (8/07). (#6572)

Near-Gem 1917-S Obverse Half

1685 **1917-S Obverse MS64 PCGS.** Boldly struck with slight weakness on Liberty's head and branch hand, as usual. The light-gray surfaces display satin luster and a faint sprinkling of mottled olive patina on the obverse. A couple of trivial milling marks are noted near Liberty's hip area. A challenging early type with the mintmark located on the obverse, below WE TRUST. (#6572)

1686 **1917-S Reverse MS62 ANACS.** Subtle, pleasing luster and faint golden peripheral toning are the most noteworthy characteristics of this S-mint Walker, struck after the mintmark position changed from the obverse to the reverse. While this piece displays few abrasions of note, the centers show distinct softness. (#6573)

Pleasing 1917-S Reverse Half Dollar, MS63

1687 1917-S Reverse MS63 NGC. Speckles of gold-tan toning race over the highly lustrous surfaces of this Select half dollar. The strike is somewhat soft in the centers, as is typical for this issue, but the remaining design elements are boldly impressed. Close inspection reveals that the surfaces are quite clean for the designated grade. All in all, a very pleasing Reverse mintmark Walker. (#6573)

1688 1918 MS64 NGC. Pleasing overall detail and frosty luster are the prime draws for this Choice silver-gray example. An attractive, minimally marked representative of this earlier P-mint Walker. *From The Mario Eller Collection, Part One.* (#6574)

1689 1918-D MS61 ANACS. Luminous and unworn with rich tan and amber patina over all but the centers, which remain silver-gray. This well struck D-mint piece exhibits a degree of contrast on the branch hand. (#6575)

1690 1918-D MS62 ANACS. Speckled brick-red toning is seen near the peripheries of the softly lustrous surfaces. The striking details are weak on Liberty's head and branch hand, as usual. The coin shows relatively few marks for the grade. (#6575)

Sharply Struck 1918-D Half, MS64

1691 1918-D MS64 NGC. Beginning in 1918 and continuing for almost 10 years, the Denver mint had a practice of lengthening die life by setting the dies further apart than optimal. This undoubtedly worked, but the resultant coins almost universally lack highpoint definition. That is the case for the 1918-D half also; however, this particular piece shows uncharacteristically strong central details. The mint luster is strong and frosted, and each side shows just the slightest accent of light golden-rose color. (#6575)

Impressive 1918-D Half Dollar, MS64

1692 1918-D MS64 PCGS. A remarkable piece with frosty silver luster and strong design elements that are weak only on the lower skirt lines, as always for the first several years of the design. Hints of natural champagne toning grace the surfaces on both sides. Just 29 PCGS certified examples of the '18-D half are graded higher. (#6575)

Choice 1918-S Walking Liberty

1693 1918-S MS64 PCGS. Consistent caramel-gold patina graces this pleasing Choice Walking Liberty half. The strike is suitable for an S-mint issue, with the expected merging of detail on the skirt lines, but both sides are impressively free from marks. PCGS has certified only 30 pieces finer (8/07). (#6576)

Bright, Lustrous MS64 1918-S Half

1694 1918-S MS64 NGC. While struck in generous quantities, few 1918-S halves were saved. This is an attractive, highly lustrous example that shows the usual slight softness on the central design elements. The surfaces are mostly brilliant with occasional russet-golden color scattered around the margins. (#6576)

Well Struck 1918-S Gem Half Dollar

1695 1918-S MS65 PCGS. Mint State specimens of the 1918-S half dollar, with a mintage of 10.282 million pieces, are scarce. Moreover, the issue comes weakly struck, as alluded to by Bruce Fox in his Walking Liberty half dollar reference: "Liberty's hand, leg and the branches she holds tend to blend together as one entity."

The Gem in this lot displays an above average strike. The area Fox refers to above, while not quite fully struck on this example, does exhibit sharp delineation. Both faces exude potent luster, and are lightly toned in pastels of sky-blue and gold-tan. A few unobtrusive obverse marks are totally consistent with the grade. Housed in a green-label holder. Population: 28 in 65, 2 finer (7/07). (#6576)

Lovely Gem 1918-S Half Dollar

1696 1918-S MS65 ANACS. Both sides of this lustrous Gem have frosty ivory surfaces with rich peripheral gold toning confined to a portion of the obverse. It is surprisingly well detailed for an early issue that originated with the first design hub. While many of the skirt lines are nearly invisible, the thumb is strong, and the head details are sharp. (#6576)

1697 1919 AU58 ANACS. It takes an experienced eye to note the whisper of friction on the skirt lines, branch hand, and cheek of Liberty. Cartwheel luster sweeps across the lightly marked surfaces. The 1919 has a lower mintage than either of its pricey branch mint counterparts. (#6577)

Strong MS64 1919-D Half

1698 1919-D MS64 NGC. V-101. Doubled D west. The 1919-D is one of the keys to the Walking Liberty half series. It is also a major condition rarity as well as a strike rarity. As one would suspect, it is seldom seen in high grades, and when encountered is a pricey item. While the normal 1919-D has luster that is not as bright as its Philadelphia counterpart, on this example the surfaces have a thick, satiny texture—not particularly bright, that is true, but definitely original and attractive. Only the slightest abrasions are present and account for the less-than-Gem grade. The striking details are strong on Liberty's hand, the skirt lines, and the eagle's plumage; in fact, it is strong in all areas except the head of Liberty, a feature that is expected on virtually all 1919-D halves. Census: 58 in 64, 4 finer (8/07). (#6578)

MS62 Semi-Key 1919-S Walking Liberty

1699 **1919-S MS62 PCGS.** Despite a reasonable mintage of 1,552,000 pieces, the 1919-S ranks among the rarest issues in the series in Mint State. Collectors of the day concentrated on earlier series, and when coin folders arrived some years later, most remaining 1919-S halves were in Fine or lesser grades. This satiny example has light almond-gold toning and only minor blending on Liberty's cheek and branch hand. Marks are unimportant for the grade. (#6579)

Important Gem 1919-S Half Dollar

1700 **1919-S MS65 PCGS.** This amazing Gem is fully brilliant with frosty silver luster and minimal surface marks preventing a higher grade. Subliminal gold toning is present on the obverse. Slight central weakness is evident only on the obverse. Although the Denver Mint half dollar coined this year receives much more attention due to its conditional rarity, the 1919-S is also an elusive issue in top grades, as the population data indicates. A review of the PCGS Set Registry for Walking Liberty half dollars indicates that this coin will improve at least five of the top 10 current sets, with two other sets not viewable on the PCGS website. Population: 38 in 65, 11 finer (8/07). (#6579)

1701 **1920 MS64 PCGS.** Choice with pleasing luster and soft blue and cloud-gray patina overall. The devices are well struck overall with a modicum of definition on the branch hand. A scrape in the right obverse field defines the grade of this P-mint piece. (#6580)

1702 **1920 MS64 PCGS.** Delicate gold and tan accents grace the otherwise silver-gray surfaces of this softly lustrous early Walker. Well struck with faint, scattered marks that preclude a finer grade. (#6580)

1703 **1920 MS64 PCGS.** Sharply struck with crisp details noted on Liberty's head, branch hand, and feet. Satin luster illuminates steel-gray surfaces that show some speckled russet and gold patina near the peripheries. Surface marks are nearly nonexistent. (#6580)

1704 **1920 MS64 NGC.** One of the more frequently encountered P-mints from early in the Walker series. Generally well struck, if slightly weak on Liberty's head and hand, this attractive near-Gem exhibits soft, frosty luster, light toning, and a few minor marks. (#6580)

1705 **1920-D AU58 ANACS.** The vivacious luster appears unbroken at first glance, but the eagle's breast has a hint of wear. An untoned near-Mint example of this popular lower mintage issue. (#6581)

1706 **1920-S MS61 ANACS.** Well-defined for this early San Francisco issue with luminous surfaces beneath violet and amber toning. The fields and devices show surprisingly few marks for the grade. (#6582)

Select Mint State 1920-S Walker

1707 **1920-S MS63 PCGS.** This untoned and lustrous example has the look of a finer grade, since the surfaces are only minimally abraded. The highpoints of the walking Liberty are softly brought up, as usual for this strike-challenging issue. A good value relative to higher grades. (#6582)

1708 **1921-D—Damaged—ANACS. XF40 Details.** A lightly toned and moderately circulated example that has minor reverse rim dings at 11 and 1 o'clock, and a more noticeable reverse rim depression at 8 o'clock. The lowest mintage issue in the series. (#6584)

Bright, Lustrous MS64 1921-D Walker

1709 1921-D MS64 PCGS. The 1921-D is one of the high visibility keys to the Walking Liberty series. One might suspect that from its mintage of 208,000 pieces, the lowest in the series. But additionally it is not an issue that was saved because of its low mintage, as the 1909-S VDB cent or 1916-D dime were, for instance. Part of the reason halves from this year are so scarce is because 1921 was a recession year. Even in good times, a half dollar represented a significant amount of money to set aside, but in a recession year it was just that much more improbable.

The 1921-D is a difficult issue to locate in high grades, and "high grades" is defined as coins in VF and better condition. This piece displays bright, shimmering, satin-like mint luster and there are no mentionable abrasions on either side. The striking details are only slightly soft in the centers, the most notable softness limited to the trailing leg of the eagle. (#6584)

1710 1927-S MS62 ICG. Soft, pleasing luster and a measure of amber and tan patina at the margins are the prime draws of this lightly abraded S-mint Walker. Central striking weakness appears on both sides, consistent with this piece's Roaring Twenties origin. (#6587)

Sharp 1927-S Fifty Cent, MS64

1711 1927-S MS64 PCGS. Bruce Fox (1993) cites the problems of poor striking and numerous abrasions that characterize the 1927-S half dollar. The near-Gem in this lot exhibits sharp definition in most of the gown lines, but is weak in the centers. Highly lustrous surfaces show a few minor, grade-defining contact marks, and some light gold-tan dappled color. All in all, a much better '27-S that typically seen. (#6587)

1712 1929-S MS64 NGC. A few splashes of milky-tan color do not impede the gorgeous luster. A powerful strike brings out excellent definition on the design features, and were it not for a handful of obverse milling marks, this outstanding specimen would have achieved full Gem status. (#6590)

1713 1933-S MS61 NGC. This lower mintage Depression-era half dollar has impressive luster for the MS61 level, and detrimental marks are absent. Nicely struck, and lightly toned in pastel gold and steel-gray shades. (#6591)

1714 1933-S MS62 NGC. The 1933-S Walker, the first such issue of half dollars in four years, offers a convenient demarcation between the more challenging pieces from earlier years and the comparatively easier later coins. This boldly impressed example has a lovely satiny appearance and thin violet and tan patina over both sides. (#6591)

1715 1933-S MS64 PCGS. The brilliant white surfaces display a lovely satiny sheen across both sides. The design elements are boldly rendered, and even Liberty's branch hand shows a fully separated thumb. The reverse is remarkably clean, while the obverse has a few wispy slide marks. (#6591)

Lovely 1933-S Walker, MS65

1716 1933-S MS65 PCGS. Beautifully effulgent mint luster radiates from each side of this lovely, snow-white Gem. Both sides are minimally marked, as expected for the grade, and the striking details are typically bold. A faint splash of gold color occupies the right obverse field. (#6591)

Fully Struck 1933-S Walker, MS66

1717 1933-S MS66 PCGS. An amazing example that is fully detailed and highly lustrous with brilliant silver surfaces. Although the 1933-S is an exception to the usual rule of weakly defined San Francisco Mint issues, this Premium Gem is even sharper than most that are seen. Population: 74 in 66, 7 finer (8/07). (#6591)

Premium Gem 1933-S Walker

1718 1933-S MS66 PCGS. Like most surviving examples of the date, this piece is sharply struck and it exhibits frosty silver luster with hints of gold toning over ivory color. The reverse has a splash of deeper steel toning on the eagle's wing. Population: 75 in 66, 7 finer (8/07). (#6591)

Lightly Toned 1933-S Half Dollar, MS66

1719 1933-S MS66 PCGS. Circulated 1933-S half dollars are plentiful, and even Mint State coins through MS65 can be located with patience and searching. The certified population data show a drop in numbers between MS65 and MS66 pieces. Light golden-champagne color bathes the lustrous surfaces of this Premium Gem, and the design features are well brought up. A few minor obverse marks are consistent with the grade level. Population: 74 in 66, 7 finer (8/07). (#6591)

1720 1934 MS66 NGC. This yellow-gray Premium Gem provides a precise strike and lustrous, nearly mark-free fields. An original and attractive example. (#6592)

1721 1934-D MS65 PCGS. Vibrant luster and excellent detail are among the prime attributes of this attractive Depression-era Gem. The fields offer a touch of sky-blue patina, while the devices are predominantly silver-gray. Carefully preserved and immensely appealing. (#6593)

1722 1934-D MS65 PCGS. Small D mintmark. Essentially brilliant, but the experienced eye will note a few wisps of chestnut toning. Lustrous and lightly abraded with impressive definition on the skirt lines and branch hand. (#6593)

1723 1934-D MS65 PCGS. Delicate golden patina graces the shimmering surfaces of this Depression-era Gem. Well-defined and carefully preserved with small dots of reddish-brown patina just below Liberty's mantle.
From The Mario Eller Collection, Part One. (#6593)

1724 1934-D MS66 NGC. A gleaming and essentially untoned example of this Depression-era issue, crisply detailed with carefully preserved devices. Only a few faint grazes in the right obverse field preclude a finer grade. NGC has graded only one finer example (8/07). (#6593)

1725 1934-D MS66 PCGS. Striking quality and surface preservation vary widely on survivors of this 2.3 million-coin Denver Mint delivery, but this amazing Premium Gem ranks near the apex on both scales. Delicate russet-brown iridescence circles the obverse rim, while the frosty centers show soft gold-gray tints. PCGS has graded two finer pieces (8/07). (#6593)

1726 1934-D MS66 PCGS. Well struck and highly lustrous, with silver-gray surfaces that display faint rose accents on each side. Satiny and carefully preserved, with few marks. Conditionally scarce at this grade level, and PCGS has only graded two pieces finer (8/07). (#6593)

1727 1934-S MS63 NGC. The design elements of this lustrous specimen benefited from an excellent strike (unusual for this issue), as evidenced from the detail on Liberty's thumb and adjacent branches and the eagle's plumage. Freckles of light gray visit the obverse, while speckles of reddish-gold gravitate to the reverse border. Both sides possess great luster. (#6594)

Ebullient Gem 1934-S Walking Liberty

1728 1934-S MS65 PCGS. This essentially brilliant Gem features an impressive strike for an S-mint Walker. Better yet, even thorough examination locates only trivial imperfections. Scintillating luster confirms the originality. An exemplary example of this Great Depression issue. (#6594)

Lustrous Gem 1934-S Half, MS65

1729 1934-S MS65 NGC. Both sides of this Gem have pale heather and champagne toning over frosty luster. Splashes of iridescence add to the overall eye appeal and desirability. All of the designs are boldly defined, and nearly full. Liberty's head is slightly weak, but still shows good detail. Census: 96 in 65, 28 finer (8/07). (#6594)

1730 1935-D MS65 PCGS. A frosty and attractive Gem, untoned on the reverse with delicate peach patina over the obverse. Both sides show pleasing peripheral detail, though the highpoints of this Denver half show softness. (#6596)

1731 1935-D MS65 PCGS. This softly struck and satiny Gem is silver-blue with a hint of tan. The surfaces are carefully preserved with excellent visual appeal for this mid-date Denver issue. (#6596)

Magnificent Brilliant MS65 1935-S Half

1732 **1935-S MS65 PCGS.** A scarcer and often-overlooked issue from the 1930s. Dies were changed frequently and sharply struck coins are available—quite a contrast to the Denver issue from this year. The obverse details are exceptionally well defined, and there is just the slightest softness on the eagle's trailing leg. Brilliant throughout and intensely lustrous. (#6597)

Scarce 1935-S Gem Half Dollar

1733 **1935-S MS65 PCGS.** The 1935-S is relatively scarce in MS64 and higher, with fully struck devices (Bruce Fox, 1993). The Gem we offer in this lot has sharply defined gown lines, but exhibits the usual softness in the centers. Silver-gray surfaces display pleasing luster, and a few minor obverse handling marks are in line with the grade designation.
From The Mario Eller Collection, Part One. (#6597)

Gem 1935-S Walking Liberty Half

1734 **1935-S MS65 PCGS.** Delicate golden patina visits the silver-white surfaces of this well struck and attractive S-mint Gem. A few faint marks are present in the reverse fields, but these are consistent with the grade. This Depression-era issue is available in Mint State, but Gems remain scarce. (#6597)

1735 **1936 MS67 NGC.** A touch of silver-gray patina appears in the obverse fields of this otherwise untoned and beautiful Superb Gem. The surfaces are strongly lustrous, and Liberty's branch hand shows a measure of detail. NGC has certified just three finer representatives (8/07). (#6598)

1736 **1936-D MS65 PCGS.** The silver-gray obverse of this Gem shows subtle luster, while the champagne-tinged reverse has stronger luster. A solidly struck and attractive example of this Depression-era D-mint issue. (#6599)

1737 **1936-D MS66 PCGS.** A frosty representative of this Depression-era D-mint issue, largely silver-white with splashes of peach patina in the fields. A modicum of definition is evident on the branch hand. PCGS has certified 19 finer examples (7/07). (#6599)

1738 **1936-D MS66 PCGS.** An exceptionally sharp strike and vibrant cartwheel sheen proclaim the quality of this pleasing Premium Gem. Encapsulated in a green label generation holder. (#6599)

1739 **1936-D MS66 NGC.** This Premium Gem's frosty luster shimmers softly. The well struck devices are predominantly silver-gray, though the eagle's left (facing) wingtips show a touch of ruby toning. NGC has certified just 22 coins finer (8/07).
From The Mario Eller Collection, Part One. (#6599)

1740 **1936-S MS66 PCGS.** Great luster issues from untoned surfaces that have been well cared for. This Premium Gem possesses a better-than-average strike than ordinarily seen on examples of this date. The gown lines are sharp, and there is partial definition in Liberty's thumb and the adjacent branches. (#6600)

1741 **1936-S MS66 PCGS.** Boldly struck with satiny and well-preserved surfaces. Splashes of green-gold patina grace the otherwise silver-gray fields of this delightful coin. PCGS has certified just five finer representatives (7/07). (#6600)

1742 **1936-S MS66 PCGS.** Lustrous surfaces display wisps of pastel olive-gold, lilac, and ice-blue patina. The design elements are generally adequately struck, though Liberty's branch hand is weak. There are no significant contact marks to report. PCGS has only graded five pieces finer (8/07). (#6600)

1743 **1937 MS67 PCGS.** This Superb Gem Walker shows well defined design elements and lovely, creamy luster over each side. A couple of wispy marks, located between L and I on the left side of the obverse, are noted for the sake of accuracy. Housed in a green label PCGS holder. Population: 94 in 67, 2 finer (7/07). (#6601)

1744 **1937-D MS65 NGC.** Pleasing detail and frosty luster are the prime attractions of this elegant Gem. Subtle periwinkle-blue and sky-blue tints grace both sides of this Denver beauty.
From The Mario Eller Collection, Part One. (#6602)

1745 **1937-D MS66 PCGS.** Sharply struck, including near-full definition on Liberty's left hand and adjacent branches. Lovely mint frost adorns untoned surfaces. A premium example of this scarcer issue from the 1930s. (#6602)

1746 **1937-D MS66 PCGS.** The surfaces of this Premium Gem '37-D are stone-white and brilliant, the strike is bold with a split thumb and sharp gown lines, and elsewhere the appeal is equally high. A few light marks on Liberty's lower torso might preclude an even higher grade. PCGS has certified only 35 coins finer (7/07). (#6602)

1747 **1937-D MS66 NGC.** This is a wondrous example that should be considered by many high grade specialists. The striking details are close to complete on each side. The surfaces are bright and untoned with a semi-reflective sheen in the fields (most evident on the obverse). (#6602)

1748 **1937-D MS66 PCGS.** This precisely struck high grade Walker has dazzling luster and pastel sky-blue and almond-gold toning. Encased in an old green label holder. (#6602)

1749 **1937-D MS66 PCGS.** Pastel blue and canary-gold patina with a touch of tan graces the shining surfaces of this enticing Premium Gem. Solidly struck for this Denver issue with carefully preserved central devices. PCGS has graded 35 finer pieces (8/07). (#6602)

1750 **1937-S MS65 PCGS.** Glowing luster exudes from beige-gold surfaces laced with tinges of powder-blue. Generally well struck, with no marks worthy of individual mention. (#6603)

1751 **1937-S MS65 NGC.** This is a lovely, supremely lustrous, brilliant Premium Gem. Liberty's branch hand is the only design element that seems a bit softly defined. A couple of milky spots are noted in the lower left obverse field area, but they are very faint. Surface marks are minimal for the grade. (#6603)

1752 **1938 MS65 PCGS.** Olive-gold tints adorn this lustrous and crisply impressed Gem. Though this issue was saved in quantity, well-preserved examples remain popular with date and type collectors alike. Housed in a first-generation PCGS holder. (#6604)

1753 **1938 MS66 PCGS.** A crisply struck piece that appears essentially untoned at first glance, though faint elements of ice-blue and champagne patina are present in the strongly lustrous fields. Carefully preserved with incredible visual appeal. (#6604)

1754 **1938-D MS63 PCGS.** Light caramel-gold visits this satiny example. The reverse is well preserved, while the obverse has an inconspicuous graze on Liberty's neck. This low mintage Walking Liberty half is housed in a scarce doily label holder. (#6605)

1755 **1938-D MS65 PCGS.** One of several lower-mintage Walker issues, the 1938-D has a mintage of under half a million pieces, though the issue was saved in quantity and available in Gem. This well-defined piece has amber and gold toning at the margins with delicate blue and lilac shades over the centers. (#6605)

1756 **1938-D MS66 PCGS.** The key date of the short set Walkers with a mintage of only 491,600 coins. Although it is not particularly rare at this grade level, only 22 pieces have been graded finer by PCGS. A highly lustrous example with frosty silver surfaces and sharp design elements. (#6605)

1757 **1938-D MS66 NGC.** An elegant silver-white Denver piece that displays strong overall detail, though the branch hand displays a measure of softness. Carefully preserved with magnificent visual appeal. (#6605)

Low Mintage 1938-D Half, MS67

1758 **1938-D MS67 NGC.** A brilliant Superb Gem with no evidence of toning on either side. This is an exceptional example with satiny white luster created by extensive die polish in the fields on each side. Although not a full strike, the design definition is far finer than usual. This piece is tied for the finest examples certified by either NGC or PCGS. Census: 18 in 67, 0 finer (8/07). (#6605)

1759 **1939-D MS67 NGC.** 1939-D half dollars can be located through MS65, and even Premium Gems are obtainable with a little patience. MS67 examples are more elusive, and finer-graded coins are rare. An arc of deep green, gold, and purple toning rests along the left obverse border of this Superb Gem. Lustrous surfaces exhibit sharply struck motifs, including good definition on Liberty's left hand and adjacent branches. Well preserved on both sides. Census: 57 in 67, 2 finer (7/07). (#6607)

1760 **1940-S MS66 PCGS.** A brilliant and well-defined Premium Gem that would make an excellent addition to a high-end date set, carefully preserved and immensely appealing. PCGS has graded only three finer pieces (7/07). (#6610)

1761 **1940-S MS66 PCGS.** This well struck S-mint Premium Gem offers an intriguing blend of frost and satin. Sky-blue, green-gold, and lavender tints grace the shimmering surfaces. PCGS has graded only three finer pieces (8/07). (#6610)

1762 **1941 MS68 NGC.** Splashes of peach, lime, and sky-blue grace this thoroughly lustrous and penetratingly struck silver type coin. Immaculate aside from reflective grazes on the left (facing) leg. Census: 16 in 68, 0 finer (8/07). (#6611)

1763 **1941-D MS66 NGC.** An alluring Premium Gem example of this late date in the Walking Liberty half dollar series. The satiny alabaster-white surfaces reveal pale antique-gold peripheral accents on the obverse. Boldly struck and free of distracting abrasions. (#6612)

1764 **1941-S MS65 PCGS.** A lovely Gem example of this short-set S-mint issue, frosty with a pillowy strike. The carefully preserved surfaces display a delicate veil of lemon-gold patina over both sides. *From The Mario Eller Collection, Part One.* (#6613)

1765 **1941-S MS65 PCGS.** This San Francisco Gem displays above-average detail for the issue with partial definition on the branch hand. The essentially untoned surfaces are blast-white. One of under 8.1 million pieces struck. (#6613)

1766 **1941-S MS65 PCGS.** This satiny Gem displays lovely beige coloration and smooth, carefully preserved surfaces. Liberty's head and branch hand, and the eagle's right (facing) leg feathers are softly struck, but the remaining design elements are well defined. (#6613)

1767 **1941-S MS66 PCGS.** A carefully preserved short-set Premium Gem, generally well struck with partial definition on the branch hand. Conditionally rare any finer, with only six such pieces certified by PCGS (8/07). (#6613)

Brilliant Superb Gem 1941-S Half

1768 **1941-S MS67 NGC.** This brilliant Superb Gem has potent luster, and retains a freshly minted appearance despite the passage of two-thirds of a century. The strike is decidedly above average, particularly on Liberty's cheek and the skirt lines. The 1941-S is the key to the popular 1941-1947 short set. (#6613)

MS67 1941-S Half Dollar Rarity

1769 **1941-S MS67 NGC.** A sensational example, this Superb Gem specimen is fully brilliant with radiant silver luster. The strike is sharp and just misses the full strike label due to slight central weakness on the obverse. Tied for finest certified by either NGC or PCGS, this is a treat for the connoisseur. Census: 16 in 67, 0 finer (8/07). (#6613)

Frosty Superb Gem 1941-S Walker

1770 **1941-S MS67 NGC.** A Superb Gem example of this important key-date issue with frosty silver luster and excellent design details. Both sides are brilliant. This is an impressive example of this scarce issue and would fit nicely in a high-grade set of Walkers. Neither NGC or PCGS have graded a finer example of this date. Census: 16 in 67, 0 finer (8/07). (#6613)

1771 **1942 MS67 PCGS.** Fully struck with bright satiny luster and nearly pristine surfaces. A swath of red-brown toning across the lower edge of the obverse is the only significant departure from a generally untoned appearance. (#6614)

1772 **1943 MS67 PCGS.** This magnificent Superb Gem is bathed in original olive and golden toning. Sharply struck and lustrous with exceptional preservation. Certified in a first generation holder. As of (7/07), only five finer pieces have been graded by PCGS. (#6618)

1773 **1943-S MS66 PCGS.** Large S. Potent luster bathes this beautifully preserved and essentially brilliant Premium Gem. The strike is impressive for this S-mint issue, although the cheek and branch hand lack absolute detail. (#6620)

1774 **1943-S MS66 PCGS.** Trumpet Tail S. FS-101. IN GOD WE TRUST shows hub doubling. A lustrous and beautiful Premium Gem that has remarkably pristine surfaces. The peripheral gold toning only adds to this coin's strong visual appeal. (#6620)

1775 **1944-D MS67 PCGS.** This frosty and immensely appealing Superb Gem exhibits elegant champagne patina over parts of each side. The branch hand is soft as always, though it does exhibit faint definition. Tied for the finest certified by either NGC or PCGS (8/07). (#6622)

1776 **1944-S MS65 PCGS.** Large S. This impressive Gem is brilliant with dazzling luster. The obverse field is striated, as made, and abrasions are essentially absent. Liberty's head has a bold strike, while the upper skirt lines and branch hand show expected merging of detail. (#6623)

1777 **1944-S MS66 PCGS.** Large S. Delicate ice-blue and tawny-gold hues visit this beautiful Premium Gem. Luster rolls across the unmarked fields and devices. The upper skirt lines are indistinct, but the remainder of the design is well brought up. (#6623)

Exemplary 1945-D Walking Liberty MS68

1778 **1945-D MS68 NGC.** The finest example of this issue certified at either service, and as such destined to keenly interest Registry collectors. Even, light golden toning covers each side with strong underlying mint luster. Sharply struck with immaculate fields and only inconsequential contact on the devices. (#6625)

1779 **1947 MS66 NGC.** Medium intensity golden-orange toning with crimson and aqua-blue accents bathes the obverse, while the reverse displays an array of multicolored patina. Sharply struck, including good definition on Liberty's thumb. Both sides are impeccably preserved. (#6630)

PROOF WALKING LIBERTY HALF DOLLARS

Brilliant PR65 1936 Walking Liberty Half

1780 **1936 PR65 PCGS.** The premier proof issue in the Walking Liberty half dollar series, the 1936 is also the key to the specimen strikes of this type with just 3,901 pieces produced. Razor sharp throughout, both sides are smooth with a glowing, reflective finish. A completely snow-white appearance overall side greets the viewer. (#6636)

Brilliant, Moderately Contrasted PR66 1936 Half

1781 **1936 PR66 PCGS.** There are few 1936 proof halves that have the combination of features seen on this piece. The fields are deeply reflective mirrors, which is not always the case on this date. The devices are moderately frosted and present a mild cameo effect against the deep fields. Additionally, the surfaces are remarkably clean, which explains the grade. Brilliant throughout.
From The Dennis Nelson Collection. (#6636)

1782 **1937 PR64 NGC.** Splashes of light gold visit bright surfaces that have received an attentive strike. A few wispy handling marks visible under magnification limit the grade. Nevertheless, a simply outstanding example of this low-mintage proof issue. (#6637)

1783 **1937 PR65 PCGS.** A thin veil of cloud-gray patina drapes the carefully preserved surfaces of this Gem. A boldly impressed specimen of this earlier proof Walker half, one of just 5,728 such pieces coined. (#6637)

1784 **1937 PR65 NGC.** The glassy fields display a typical, thin layer of milky patina on both sides, with a slight degree of russet color noted near the obverse border. An appealing and well preserved Gem proof, with fully struck design elements. (#6637)

1785 **1937 PR66 PCGS.** A boldly impressed earlier Walker specimen of obvious quality, gleaming with areas of green-gray patina that are thicker at the margins. Housed in a first-generation PCGS holder (8/07).
From The Dennis Nelson Collection. (#6637)

1786 **1937 PR67 NGC.** An enticing Superb Gem specimen from the second of just seven proof Walker issues. This boldly impressed piece gleams beneath hazy khaki-olive patina that deepens near the margins. NGC has graded 17 finer examples. (#6637)

1787 **1937 PR67 PCGS.** Brilliant surfaces have deeply mirrored fields and just a trace of cameo contrast, so seldom seen on this design. This Superb Gem proof may have received a higher grade, except for a short, faint hairline in the right obverse field. Otherwise, both sides are immaculate. PCGS has only certified nine finer examples (8/07). (#6637)

1788 **1938 PR64 ★ NGC.** Full brilliance exudes from both sides of this outstanding near-Gem proof with the coveted Star designation. Exquisite motif detail befits a proof striking. A few wispy field marks define the numerical grade. (#6638)

1789 **1938 PR66 NGC.** Fully struck with immense reflectivity in the jet-black fields, and mild frost on the snow-white central devices. Both sides of the coin seem impeccably preserved and free of even the smallest distraction. (#6638)

1790 **1938 PR66 NGC.** A brilliant Premium Gem proof with bright silver mirrors and a trace of gold toning. Slight cameo contrast is evident on each side. (#6638)

1791 **1938 PR66 PCGS.** Though the revival of the Mint's proof program proved popular, in 1938, two years after its reintroduction, the half dollar mintage amounted to just 8,152 pieces. Both sides of this shining Premium Gem show bold detail and strong reflectivity beneath layers of gold-gray haze.
From The Dennis Nelson Collection. (#6638)

1792 **1938 PR67 NGC.** A Superb Gem, this piece deserves a Cameo designation, in our opinion, as both sides have excellent contrast. The surfaces are fully brilliant with deep mirrors and lustrous devices. (#6638)

1793 **1939 PR66 NGC.** A deeply reflective specimen of this mid-date proof Walker half, impeccably detailed beneath a thin veil of violet and tan patina. Exquisitely preserved with undeniable visual appeal. (#6639)

1794 **1939 PR67 PCGS.** The proof Walker issue of 1939 was the last half dollar with a four-figure mintage. This decisively struck representative exhibits strong luster beneath rich gold-gray toning. PCGS has graded only 24 finer pieces (8/07).
From The Dennis Nelson Collection. (#6639)

1795 **1940 PR66 PCGS.** Crisply detailed with a moderate layer of silver-gray and olive patina over each side. The carefully preserved surfaces of this Premium Gem shine beneath the toning. A lovely example from the fifth of only seven proof Walking Liberty half issues. (#6640)

1796 **1940 PR66 NGC.** Crisply struck and expertly preserved, with nicely reflective fields and a slight degree of mottled tan-beige patina on the silver-gray surfaces. Free of marks or hairlines. (#6640)

1797 **1940 PR66 PCGS.** A gleaming and eminently appealing Premium Gem specimen, boldly impressed with carefully preserved surfaces. Delicate layers of gauzy silver-gray patina grace parts of the fields. Housed in a first-generation PCGS holder.
From The Dennis Nelson Collection. (#6640)

1798 **1940 PR67 NGC.** This is a beautiful, brilliant Superb Gem proof half dollar from the later era of the Walking Liberty series. Fully struck and seemingly pristine, with gorgeous reflectivity noted in the dark fields, and a slight degree of silvery frost on the central devices. (#6640)

1799 **1941 PR66 NGC.** No AW. Orange-red and apple-green shades grace the obverse border and fully occupy the reverse. The obverse center is cream-gray. Sharply struck and unquestionably original. (#6641)

1800 **1941 PR66 NGC.** No AW. This needle-sharp Premium Gem is devoid of hairlines, and the mirrored fields are flashy. Brilliant aside from traces of milk-gray on the upper right obverse field, and a few tiny areas of dark toning on the obverse rim at 12, 1, and 3 o'clock. (#6641)

1801 **1941 PR66 NGC.** No AW. This assertively struck Premium Gem displays peripheral freckles of russet and ocean-blue patina. Well preserved with some frost on the walking Liberty. Certified in a former generation holder. (#6641)

1802 **1941 PR66 NGC.** No AW. Glimpses of apricot toning enrich this otherwise ivory-gray Premium Gem. A loupe confirms the absence of hairlines. The design highpoints are penetratingly struck. (#6641)

1803 **1941 PR66 NGC.** No AW. The low relief designer's monogram was raised on the dies for the Walking Liberty half, and on several occasions the monogram was inadvertently removed by a mint employee during the die preparation. The 1941 proof is the best known example. An immaculate Premium Gem with original cream-gray, ice-blue, and russet toning. (#6641)

1804 **1941 PR66 PCGS.** This proof Walker from the penultimate issue of such coinage exhibits gold-gray patina with dots of deeper amber-brown toning at the reverse. Exquisitely detailed with vibrant reflectivity and excellent visual appeal.
From The Dennis Nelson Collection. (#6641)

1805 **1941 PR67 PCGS.** No AW. Highly reflective with an iridescent crescent of lime-gold and steel-gray toning on each side that deepens to sunset-orange at the lower right side of the reverse. Exquisitely struck and an immensely appealing representative of this penultimate proof Walker half issue. (#6641)

1806 **1941 No "AW" PR67 ★ NGC.** Gorgeous gold, lime-green, and rose hues enliven this well struck and lovingly preserved Premium Gem. The designer's monogram is absent, as made from a lapped die. (#6641)

1807 **1941 PR67 NGC.** No AW. The designer's monogram was lapped off the reverse die during its preparation. Medium apricot toning adorns the borders of this needle-sharp and flawless Superb Gem. (#6641)

Stunning 1941 Half Dollar, PR68

1808 **1941 PR68 NGC.** This piece is tied for the finest that has been certified, with 13 similar pieces graded by PCGS and 59 by NGC (8/07). Both sides of this beauty are fully mirrored, and the devices show a hint of cameo contrast. The opportunity to acquire this amazing proof should not be missed. It is a great coin to match a complete set, either of proof Walkers, or a 1941 proof set. (#6641)

1809 **1942 PR65 PCGS.** Sharply defined with none of the central striking weakness common to business strikes. This Gem proof has flashy, highly reflective fields that only show a modest degree of cloudiness. Expertly preserved and nearly pristine.
From The Arnold & Harriet Collection, Part Two. (#6642)

1810 **1942 PR65 NGC.** Radiant surfaces display dapples of barely discernible orange-gold color, and have been well cared for. The design features exhibit bold definition, as expected for a proof Walker. (#6642)

1811 **1942 PR66 NGC.** Fully struck with deeply reflective fields that show a light layer of cloudy color on both sides. Immaculately preserved and seemingly pristine; a great Premium Gem proof. (#6642)

1812 **1942 PR66 PCGS.** Fully struck and free of contact marks, this Premium Gem reveals slight milkiness in the fields and a couple of reddish-brown areas on each side. An excellent date for proof type purposes, 1942 was the final year of proof Walking Liberty production, and also had the highest mintage of the series at 21,120 pieces. (#6642)

1813 **1942 PR66 NGC.** The silver-gray patina that graces the obverse shows splashes of rose-gold on Liberty's mantle, while the reverse displays distinct champagne and powder-blue elements. Decisively struck with strong reflectivity and excellent visual appeal, a lovely specimen from the final proof Walker issue. (#6642)

1814 **1942 PR66 PCGS.** The popularity of proofs continued to expand through 1942, though wartime exigencies stalled the Mint's program. This immensely reflective Premium Gem shows excellent detail and exquisite reflectivity with just a touch of silver-gray patina in the fields. Housed in a first-generation PCGS holder. *From The Dennis Nelson Collection.* (#6642)

1815 **1942 PR67 PCGS.** An intensely reflective Superb Gem exemplar of the final proof Walker half issue, practically untoned with wonderful visual appeal. PCGS has graded just 35 finer specimens (8/07). (#6642)

1816 **1942 PR67 PCGS.** Cream-gray color in the centers yields to whispers of rainbow iridescence at the peripheries. Boldly struck, as befits a proof, and well preserved throughout. (#6642)

1817 **1942 PR67 PCGS.** This was the last year of proof production (21,120 pieces), and many have suffered from improper handling and imperfect strikes. This Superb specimen is impeccably preserved and exquisitely struck throughout. A few barely discernible wisps of gold tan color are visible under magnification. (#6642)

1818 **1942 PR67 PCGS.** A splendid example, this Superb Gem proof has brilliant silver surfaces with fully mirrored fields and a hint of contrast. PCGS has only certified 35 finer pieces. (#6642)

FRANKLIN HALF DOLLARS

1819 **1949 MS64 Full Bell Lines PCGS.** Not only are the lines on the bell full, but Franklin's hair shows above-average definition as well. Dappled blue-green and cloud-gray patina graces both sides of this lightly marked example, which comes from an issue infrequently offered with the strength of strike shown here. (#86653)

1820 **1949 MS65 Full Bell Lines PCGS.** Swirls of deep, mottled patina blanket the obverse, and lighter speckled toning decorates the reverse border. Satiny and well struck with just two or three small marks on each side. (#86653)

1821 **1949-D MS64 PCGS.** Lustrous and well struck, with lavish, speckled reddish-amber toning over the obverse and bluish-gray color with rose accents on the reverse. A few small abrasions are noticeable on the reverse. An attractive near-Gem example of this second-year issue in the Franklin half dollar series. (#6654)

1822 **1949-D MS65 PCGS.** This is an amazingly well struck Franklin half, with the minute details of the Liberty Bell completely brought up. A rich coating of speckled amber-red patina covers the obverse; the pearl-gray reverse is untoned save for wispy peripheral toning. Surface marks are minimal. Population: 38 in 65, 1 finer (7/07). (#6654)

1823 **1949-S MS66 PCGS.** Beautiful sunset-orange toning adorns the obverse, while lighter speckled patina decorates the reverse. Highly lustrous with fully struck design elements and unblemished surfaces. This first year issue is one of the key dates in the Franklin half dollar series. (#6655)

1824 **1949-S MS66 PCGS.** An attractive example of this early Franklin half, well-defined overall with pleasing luster beneath olive-tan and blue-green patina on the obverse. The reverse offers faint specks of similar color at the margins. PCGS has graded just three finer non-Full Bell Lines examples (7/07). (#6655)

1825 **1951-S MS66 Full Bell Lines PCGS.** A boldly impressed S-mint Franklin that offers effusive luster and dappled bronze and blue-green patina over each side. Tied for the finest Full Bell Lines example certified by PCGS (7/07). (#86660)

Lustrous, Lightly Toned MS66 1952-D Half

1826 **1952-D MS66 NGC.** A scarcer D-mint Franklin half in MS66, from a mintage of only 25.3 million pieces. Only 11 such pieces have been so graded by NGC with two finer (8/07). This is a lovely, frosted example that shows a light overlay of golden-reddish toning on each side and a faint undertone of lilac. (#6662)

1827 **1952-S MS64 Full Bell Lines PCGS.** A frosty, minimally toned representative of this S-mint Franklin half, appealing with solid definition at the lower parts of the bell. Small, isolated abrasions on the devices preclude a finer grade. (#86663)

1828 **1952-S MS65 Full Bell Lines PCGS.** Olive and sky-blue shadings enrich this lustrous and beautifully preserved Gem. A crisply struck prize for the connoisseur of toned silver, challenging any finer. PCGS has graded only 26 such Full Bell Lines pieces (8/07). (#86663)

1829 **1952-S MS65 Full Bell Lines PCGS.** Solidly struck for this issue and quite lustrous with mottled bronze and lavender patina on the obverse. The toning is restricted to the periphery on the reverse, and some abrasions are noted on the bell. (#86663)

1830 **1952-S MS65 Full Bell Lines PCGS.** Essentially untoned and rather frosty, this Gem has only a handful of minor marks on its surfaces. The lines are full, and the eye appeal is strong. (#86663)

Key 1952-S Full Bell Lines Half, MS66

1831 **1952-S MS66 Full Bell Lines PCGS.** A magnificent example of this key to the Full Bell Line series. Obviously popped from a mint set, the obverse has milky gray patina, while the reverse displays rich, speckled rose, olive, and golden toning. The bell lines are strong all the way across the bell, and the overall preservation of the surfaces is exceptional. Population: 26 in 66, 0 finer (8/07). (#86663)

1832 **1954-S MS66 Full Bell Lines PCGS.** Speckles of russet-brown and apple-green patina endow this lustrous and exquisitely preserved Premium Gem. While the 1954-S is readily available in abraded Mint State grades, it becomes decidedly rare in such near-pristine state. Crisply struck and original. PCGS has graded only one coin finer (3/06). (#86669)

1833 1955 MS66 Full Bell Lines PCGS. A richly toned Gem featuring Full Bell Lines. Each side shows deep blue-green and gold mottled toning over lustrous surfaces. PCGS has only certified one example finer than this one, and NGC has graded a mere two pieces higher (7/07). An exceptional coin for the Franklin half dollar devotee. (#86670)

1834 1956 MS66 Full Bell Lines PCGS. Dappled nutmeg-brown, peach, and sky-gray toning graces this shimmering and sharply struck Premium Gem. An outstanding example of this lower-mintage issue, certified in a green label holder. PCGS has graded just nine finer Full Bell Lines pieces (8/07). (#86671)

1961-D Half, MS66 Full Bell Lines
A Late-Date Strike Rarity

1835 1961-D MS66 Full Bell Lines PCGS. A scarce, late-date Franklin half that was recognized about 20 years ago as a strike rarity. This recognition of its rarity seemed to roughly coincide with the advent of third-party grading and the publication of population data. This piece has a hard, metallic sheen over each side. Most of the surfaces are brilliant except for a thin crescent of deeper color around the reverse. Population: 11 in 66, 0 finer (8/07). (#86681)

PROOF FRANKLIN HALF DOLLARS

1836 Complete Set of Proof Franklin Halves PR67 to PR68 PCGS. The set includes: **1950 PR67**, strongly reflective with a touch of russet haze at the obverse margins, tied for the finest graded by PCGS (8/07); **1951 PR67**, gleaming with tiny milk spots on the obverse; **1952 PR67**, minimal patina and a measure of contrast on the obverse; **1953 PR67**, shining with a touch of silver-gray toning at the peripheries; **1954 PR67**, excellent reflectivity and a small milk spot over the date; **1955 PR67**, silver-gray toning over the obverse with a subtle golden aura on the reverse; **1956 PR67**, minor milk spots and elements of contrast on each side; **1957 PR68**, exquisitely preserved with powerful reflectivity; **1958 PR67**, strongly mirrored with delicate silver-gray patina and subtle violet accents; **1959 PR67**, flashy with a pair of milk spots on the bell and contrast on the obverse; **1960 PR67 Cameo**, considerable mirrors and contrast, slightly stronger on the faintly gold-tinged reverse; **1961 PR67**, excellent reflectivity with a measure of peripheral spotting; **1962 PR67**, fathomless, carefully preserved mirrors; and a **1963 PR67**, strongly reflective and essentially untoned. Aside from the 1950, 1952, 1957, and 1960 pieces, all are housed in first-generation holders.
From The Dennis Nelson Collection. (Total: 14 coins) (#6691)

1837 1950 PR65 Cameo NGC. Moderate contrast and minimally toned fields contribute to the outstanding eye appeal of this gleaming Gem. A wonderful representative of the first proof Franklin half issue. (#86691)

1838 1954 PR67 Ultra Cameo NGC. Both sides of this Superb Gem offer excellent contrast, though the reverse shows a touch more frost on the devices. A decisively struck, immensely reflective beauty from the fifth proof Franklin issue. Census: 17 in 67 Ultra Cameo, 7 finer (8/07). (#96695)

1839 1958 PR67 Deep Cameo PCGS. This intensely reflective Superb Gem offers rich frost on the devices and excellent contrast. Only a few pinpoint areas of milky toning affect the surfaces of this mid-date Franklin proof. Population: 32 in 67 Deep Cameo, 14 finer (8/07). (#96699)

1840 1959 PR68 Cameo NGC. Virtual perfection with bright silver mirrors and excellent contrast. NGC has only certified one finer piece, and no better ones have been graded by PCGS. Census: 80 in 68, 1 finer (8/07). (#86700)

1841 1961 PR68 Ultra Cameo NGC. Exquisitely preserved with gleaming silver-white fields and richly frosted, decisively struck devices. An eminently appealing exemplar of this later Franklin proof issue. Census: 61 in 68 Ultra Cameo, 4 finer (8/07). (#96702)

Desirable FS-801 DDR 1961 Half Dollar, PR65

1842 1961 Doubled Die Reverse PR65 PCGS. FS-801, formerly FS-013. E PLURIBUS UNUM and UNITED are dramatically die doubled. The remainder of the legends also show significant doubling. A deeply mirrored and brilliant Gem of this scarce variety, photographed on page 198 of the 2008 *Guide Book*. Population: 8 in 65, 27 finer (7/07). (#6689)

PROOF KENNEDY HALF DOLLARS

1843 1964 Accented Hair PR66 Ultra Cameo NGC. An essentially untoned, strongly contrasted exemplar of the elusive Accented Hair die variant, decisively struck and carefully preserved. A lovely representative from the only 90% silver proof Kennedy issue. Census: 8 in 66 Ultra Cameo, 22 finer (8/07). (#96801)

1844 1979-S Type Two PR70 Deep Cameo PCGS. Fully frosted devices seem to float above highly reflective, inky-black fields. A virtually unimprovable specimen. Population: 40 in 70 Deep Cameo (8/07). (#96819)

1845 1981-S Type Two PR70 Deep Cameo PCGS. Fully struck with attractive copper-gold toning and intense Deep Cameo contrast on both sides. Virtually pristine, with mere traces of cloudiness noted in the fields. The bulbous upper serif helps to distinguish the Type Two mintmark from its Type One counterpart. Population: 24 in 70 Deep Cameo (8/07). (#96822)

1846 2001-S Clad PR70 Deep Cameo PCGS. Stunning white-on-black contrast shows up on both sides of this Deep Cameo. Some faint marks are noted to the left of the olive branch. Population: 12 in 70 Deep Cameo (8/07). (#96914)

Desirable XF Sharpness 1794 Dollar

1847 1794—Obverse Repaired—NCS. XF Details. B-1, BB-1, R.4. Bowers-Borckardt Die State III with shortened curls from a Mint attempt to efface clash marks, which are still evident on the field near the mouth and beneath the jaw. As a rule, silver dollars from this year are rarely offered at public auction, and the demand for these coins far outdistances the supply. This particular coin is whizzed, and stars 13 and 14 are affected by a repair. A planchet flaw near star 8 has been wiped, and a second (and lesser) planchet flaw is concealed within the lower hair curls. Numismatists for many generations have been willing to accept or overlook these defects, as this piece has been in major collections since the 1870s. The surfaces are medium gray with much lighter accents over the highpoints on the reverse. Weakly struck on the stars on the obverse stars, as always, with the left side of the reverse also weak from having been struck from misaligned dies. The only mentionable abrasion is a diagonal scratch across the eagle's neck that continues into the field below. A well detailed and historic 1794 dollar, listed on page 102 of the 2004 Martin Logies reference, *The Flowing Hair Silver Dollars of 1794*.

Ex: Michael Moore Collection (Edward Cogan, May 1-2, 1879), lot 611; John C. Lighthouse Collection (J. C. Morgenthau & Co., February 18-19, 1936), lot 208; F. S. Guggenheimer Collection (Stack's, January 22-24, 1953), lot 945; June Long Beach Signature (Heritage, 6/04), lot 6106.

From The Beau Clerc Collection. (#6851)

1848 **1795 Flowing Hair, Three Leaves VG10 PCGS.** B-7, BB-18, R.3. A Head of 1794 variant with star 1 touching the curl. This significantly worn blue-gray example shows attractive sea-green accents. Appealing despite a number of extended abrasions on and around the portrait. (#6852)

Enticing 1795 Flowing Hair Dollar VF25, B-5

1849 **1795 Flowing Hair, Three Leaves VF25 PCGS.** B-5, BB-27, R.1. The pearl-gray devices are encompassed by light autumn-brown fields. No adjustment marks are visible, and abrasions are generally minor for the grade. The eagle's left wing displays considerable plumage detail. A worthy Flowing Hair type coin. (#6852)

B-6 1795 Flowing Hair Dollar VF30 Details

1850 **1795 Flowing Hair, Three Leaves—Scratched, Cleaned—ANACS. VF30 Details.** B-6, BB-25, R.3. The fields are hairlined, most noticeably on the field near the eagle's head. Moderately abraded, but perhaps unworthy of the "Scratched" designation. Relatively minor rim dings are present at 4 o'clock on the obverse and 1 o'clock on the reverse. The obverse periphery has a few unimportant adjustment marks, as made. (#6852)

VF30 Details, B-6 1795 Flowing Hair Dollar

1851 **1795 Flowing Hair, Three Leaves—Scratched, Cleaned—ANACS. VF30 Details.** B-6, BB-25, R.3. This nicely detailed ivory-gray type coin may have had an encounter with baking soda, and a cluster of unimportant, faint, hair-thin marks crosses the field beneath the chin. The portrait also has a few minor hairlines.
From The Diemer L. Fife Collection. (#6852)

Choice XF B-6 1795 Flowing Hair Dollar

1852 **1795 Flowing Hair, Three Leaves XF45 PCGS.** B-6, BB-25, R.3. Dusky olive and golden-brown blend throughout this nicely detailed Choice XF Flowing Hair dollar. Adjustment marks are nearly absent, limited to a few inconspicuous lines on the obverse border between 3 and 5 o'clock. The subdued surfaces are generally smooth, since a vertical mark on the neck and a pair of faint marks near the right wreath stem are barely worthy of individual mention. The usual Three Leaves variety is Bolender-5, and although B-6 is several times scarcer, it currently carries little if any premium. Those in search of a better value type coin need look no further. (#6852)

1853 **1795 Flowing Hair, Two Leaves Good 4 PCGS.** B-1, BB-21, R.2. A deep cream-gray example of this coveted introductory silver type. The upper reverse legend is worn into the rim, and the lower right stars and the base of the date are partly present. (#6853)

1854 **1795 Flowing Hair, Two Leaves—Cleaned—ANACS. Fine 12 Details.** B-1, BB-21, R.2. Dusky golden-brown, dove-gray, and olive-green shades blend throughout this slightly glossy example. A minor reverse rim ding at 2:30 detracts little from the eye appeal of this formidable silver type coin.
From The Laguna Niguel Collection, Part Two. (#6853)

1855 **1795 Flowing Hair, Two Leaves—Plugged, Whizzed—ANACS. Fine 12 Details.** B-1, BB-21, R.2. Russet-brown borders encompass slate-gray centers. Tooling near the ER in LIBERTY and opposite near the right ribbon end suggests a plug. The centers are hairlined, and both sides are micro-granular from whizzing. (#6853)

Choice VF 1795 Flowing Hair Dollar, B-2

1856 **1795 Flowing Hair, Two Leaves VF35 NGC.** B-2, BB-20, R.3. It is fortunate for the collectors of die varieties that the B-5 and B-1 1795 Flowing Hair dollars are as plentiful as they are, since they reduce type demand on the scarcer B-2 marriage. This is a silver-gray piece with slightly deeper dove-gray toning on the devices. Glowing luster accompanies the legends and stars. The eagle's tail feathers and belly have a few faded thin marks. (#6853)

VF35 1795 Flowing Hair Dollar, B-1

1857 **1795 Flowing Hair, Two Leaves VF35 NGC.** B-1, BB-21, R.2. Gunmetal-blue and caramel-gold embrace this nicely detailed Choice VF Flowing Hair dollar. Both sides are surprisingly unblemished except for a thin mark that crosses Liberty's jaw and exits beneath the chin. The upper reverse has a few minor mint-made adjustment marks. (#6853)

Noble XF B-1 1795 Flowing Hair Dollar

1858 **1795 Flowing Hair, Two Leaves XF40 NGC.** B-1, BB-21, R.2. A cream-gray Flowing Hair dollar that retains traces of luster near design crevices. Evenly struck, and without any adjustment marks or other planchet issues. A trio of toned-over abrasions are noted near star 6, and another subdued mark passes through the first A in AMERICA. (#6853)

1795 Flowing Hair Dollar With Silver Plug Fine 15, Better B-7, BB-18 Variety

1859 **1795 Flowing Hair, Silver Plug Fine 15 NGC.** B-7, BB-18, R.3. The outline of the slightly oval-shaped plug is faintly visible at the center of the obverse. This mint-made plug was inserted to bring the piece up to weight specifications, and was briefly mint procedure instead of simply melting the flan and starting again. The dove-gray surfaces are refreshingly unabraded, and protected areas display glimpses of orange toning. A few inconsequential adjustment marks (as produced) are confined to the reverse margin. Our auction records over the past few years confirm that B-1 and B-7 are the usual silver plug varieties, although B-3, B-4, and B-5 have also appeared with mint-issued silver plugs. (#6854)

Toned, B-15 XF 1795 Draped Bust Dollar

1860 **1795 Draped Bust, Centered XF40 NGC.** B-15, BB-52, R.2. Bowers-Borckardt Die State IV. This charming first-year Draped Bust dollar has dove-gray toning that deepens near the borders. Minor to moderate marks include a curved line on the reverse exergue. The portrait has a few faint adjustment marks, as made. *From The Beau Clerc Collection.* (#6858)

1795 Draped Bust Dollar
AU Details, B-14, BB-51

1861 1795 Draped Bust, Off Center—Whizzed—NCS. AU Details.
B-14, BB-51, R.2. The central reverse has a marbled, glossy texture
characteristic of whizzing, and the remainder of the surfaces are
subdued from a cleaning. Luster nonetheless dominates Liberty's
hair, the eagle's wings, and the wreath. Light wear on the cheek and
shoulder is consistent with the AU level. (#96858)

Scarce 1796 Dollar XF45 Details, B-5

1862 1796 Large Date, Small Letters—Edge Damaged—ANACS. XF45
Details. B-5, BB-65, R.2. The rims of this partly lustrous Small Eagle
dollar are problem-free, and the extent of any edge damage will be
unknown until the piece is freed from its ANACS encapsulation.
The lightly toned surfaces are minimally abraded. The diagnostic
die lump from the I in AMERICA has yet to reach the nearby C.
From The Diemer L. Fife Collection. (#6861)

Appealing 1797 Dollar 9x7 Stars, Large Letters VF25, B-1

1863 1797 9x7 Stars, Large Letters VF25 ANACS. B-1, BB-73, R.3.
This is a gorgeous example for the grade, with well struck design
elements and pleasingly original sea-green and rose toning. A
normal degree of wear has occurred across the central highpoints,
leaving the other devices essentially complete. A couple of minor
rim disturbances are apparent on the obverse: below the date and
just above the B in LIBERTY.
From The Laguna Niguel Collection, Part Two. (#6863)

VF B-1 1798 Small Eagle Dollar

1864 1798 Small Eagle, 13 Stars VF20 PCGS. B-1, BB-82, R.3.
Bolender-1 was likely the final Small Eagle variety struck, since the
obverse die was made after the Mint decision to use only 13 stars
instead of one for every state. This slightly bright example is mostly
pearl-gray with hints of tan, but the obverse border offers sea-green
and gold shades. Certified in a green label holder. (#6867)

Choice XF 1798 Small Eagle Dollar
15 Stars Obverse, B-2, BB-81

1865 1798 Small Eagle, 15 Stars XF45 NGC. B-2, BB-81, R.3. Bowers-
Borckardt Die State II. There are 33 die varieties of 1798 dollars,
and among those, only two bear the Small Eagle reverse first
introduced in 1795. B-2 is the sole 1798 variety with 15 obverse
stars, which implies the obverse die was made prior to June 1796,
when Tennessee became the 16th state. The die was presumably
complete save for the date, which was entered in 1798 when the die
was removed from storage and prepared for coinage. This attractive
example has a pleasing quota of shimmering luster within design
recesses, particularly the hair. The eagle's body and Liberty's cheek
and shoulder show the expected moderate wear, but the cream-gray
and pale autumn-brown surfaces are generally smooth except for a
thin reverse mark near 10 o'clock. (#6868)

1866 **1798 Small Eagle, 15 Stars AU58 NGC.** B-2, BB-81, R.3. Die State II. A transitional year for silver dollars, with two distinct design types produced. Only two die varieties of the Small Eagle dollars have been identified, and each of these is a major variety, distinguished by either 13 stars or 15 stars on the obverse.

The 15 Star obverse has eight stars along the left border and seven stars at the right border, and is considered the first 1798 silver dollar variety produced. The reasoning is sound: the Small Eagle design was discontinued with the new Heraldic Eagle reverse taking its place. This means that the Small Eagle coins were produced at the beginning of the year. Since the obverse of the Small Eagle type with just 13 stars was also used with a Heraldic Eagle reverse, it must have been coined after those with 15 stars.

Just as interesting is the knowledge that this 1798-dated obverse die was actually created a couple years earlier. Since Kentucky became the 15th state in 1792 and Tennessee became the 16th state in June 1796, the die must have been created before that date. In fact, all 1795 and 1796 silver dollars have 15 stars on the obverse, and all 1797 dollars have 16 stars. Finally, in 1798 the decision was made to reduce the star count to 13 stars for the original 13 states. Stylistically, the obverse is similar to some 1796 obverse dies, and was probably made at about the same time, with only the 179 of the date punched in the die.

This near-Mint example has satiny luster beneath deep steel toning, with lighter ivory color through Liberty's hair. Minor criss-crossing adjustment marks on the obverse were not completely eliminated when this piece was coined. (#6868)

1867 **1798 Large Eagle—Obverse Damage—NCS. VF Details.** Ex: Reiver. B-28, BB-118, R.3. Digit 8 out of position, high and leaning slightly right; point of leaf below right half of C. The obverse damage consists of some light vertical and horizontal scratches in the right obverse field, and a couple of minor edge file marks, one on the obverse, another on the reverse. Olive-gray patina graces the moderately worn surfaces. (#6873)

Slate-Gray 1798 Large Eagle Dollar VF30, B-27

1868 **1798 Large Eagle VF30 NGC.** B-27, BB-113, R.2. Bowers-Borckardt Die State II. A slate-gray and chestnut-tan Heraldic Eagle dollar with cloudy and unmarked surfaces. Most letters in E PLURIBUS UNUM are partly to fully legible. This Bolender variety pairs two long-lasting dies, the reverse from BB-110 to BB-113, and the obverse from BB-113 to BB-119. (#6873)

Scarce 1798 Large Eagle Dollar XF45 Details, B-25

1869 **1798 Large Eagle—Corroded, Cleaned—ANACS. XF45 Details.** B-25, BB-123, R.4. Bowers-Borckardt Die State III. Obverse die cracks. Blundered stars reverse. Well centered and well struck, except for noticeable weakness on the eagle's head and breast feathers. Evenly worn across each side. Rim damage is noted between 6 and 7 o'clock on the obverse. A few minor blemishes are observed, as expected for a lightly circulated example. (#6873)

1798 Five Stripes Dollar, XF Details, B-6, BB-96

1870 **1798 Five Stripes—Obverse Scratched, Improperly Cleaned—NCS. XF Details.** Ex: Jules Reiver Collection. B-6, BB-96, R.2. Reiver die state c. Bowers-Borckardt die state V. This is the Reiver plate coin for the obverse of this variety. Both the obverse and reverse show numerous tiny pin scratches when examined with a strong loupe, and there is minor verdigris near the center of the reverse. We note a few nicks on Liberty's face and some surface pits in the field above Liberty's bust. Starting to retone a bit toward a more natural silver gray color. Ever popular for the Knobbed 9 in the date, and the general scarcity of the variety.
Ex: Stack's W. Earl Spies Sale (December, 1974), lot 110. (#6874)

1871 **1798 Large Eagle, 10 Arrows—Scratched—ANACS. Fine 12 Details.** B-21, BB-107, R.5. A better die variety that pairs a 10 arrows reverse die and the obverse with a memorable die lump above the 9 in the date. Designated as "Scratched" by ANACS, but we believe the relatively heavy criss-cross reverse lines are adjustment marks, similar to those seen on Bowers' BB-107 plate coin. A minor scratch is present near obverse star 6, and the devices exhibit some charcoal verdigris. (#6876)

1872 **1798 Wide Date VG10 ANACS.** B-23, BB-105, R.3. On this variety, the 8 in the date firmly touches the bust, the 7th star points directly at the lower left serif end of L in LIBERTY, there are five small berries on the branch, the two above closest together, and the leaf point is under the left foot of I in AMERICA. Just a few light circulation marks are visible on the light gray surfaces, with some semi-circular toning streaks on the upper reverse.
From The Beau Clerc Collection. (#6877)

1873 **1799 7x6 Stars—Damaged, Altered Surface—NCS. Fine Details.** B-9, BB-166, R.1. The obverse is glossy from polishing, and the reverse is hairlined. Unevenly worn, with details indistinct near the eagle's head. The reverse periphery is moderately granular. The reverse rim at 6 o'clock has minor damage. (#6878)

1874 **1799 7x6 Stars—Cleaned—ANACS. VF20 Details.** B-8, BB-165, R.3. Bowers-Borckardt Die State III. Lightly toned in cream-gray and almond-gold. Nicely defined aside from the stars above the eagle's head, which are typically struck. A hairlined representative of this scarce late die state.
From The Laguna Niguel Collection, Part Two. (#6878)

1875 **1799 7x6 Stars—Repaired, Polished—NCS. VF Details.** B-14, BB-167, R.3. A moderately worn and glossy representative of this scarce die marriage, charcoal-gray around the peripheral devices with cloud-gray centers. The upper regions of the portrait and the nearby fields show evidence of repair. (#6878)

VF30 1799 Bust Dollar, B-5, BB-157

1876 **1799 7x6 Stars VF30 NGC.** B-5, BB-157, R.2. Bowers-Borckardt Die State III. Aqua-blue and olive-gray tones envelop this well-defined early dollar, which retains glimpses of luster within the wings and other protected areas. No marks are consequential, and the only hint of a rim ding is on the obverse at 2 o'clock. (#6878)

1877 **1799 7x6 Stars—Cleaned, Scratched—ANACS. VF30 Details.** B-21, BB-169, R.3. This slate-gray early dollar is finely hairlined and a relatively light diagonal scratch on the shield. The eagle's head has moderate parallel scuffs, and the obverse rim has a nick at 1 o'clock. Still a nicely detailed and collectible example of this enormously popular silver type. (#6878)

XF Details 1799 Dollar, B-8A, BB-165

1878 **1799 7x6 Stars—Tooled, Cleaned—ANACS. XF40 Details.** B-8A, BB-165, R.3. No tooling is obvious, although the pearl-gray fields are slightly bright and a cluster of faded marks is present near obverse star 11. Some luster remains within the hair, shield, and plumage. A bold example of this impressive early silver type. *From The Diemer L. Fife Collection.* (#6878)

XF Sharpness 1799 Dollar B-14

1879 **1799 7x6 Stars—Obverse Scratched—NCS. XF Details.** B-14, BB-167, R.3. Bowers-Borckardt Die State IV. A bold representative of this popular early large silver type. The right obverse field is pinscratched, and the left obverse field is slightly bright. Faintly granular gray streaks cross the upper left reverse. Still desirable, since luster beckons from the devices and margins. (#6878)

Near-Mint 1799 Dollar 7x6 Stars, B-9

1880 **1799 7x6 Stars AU58 NGC.** B-9, BB-166, R.1. Bowers-Borckardt Die State IV. Obverse die crack through Liberty's bust extends to star 10 and also downward to first 9 in the date. Deep cobalt-blue and olive-drab toning covers both sides. Well struck with very little highpoint wear and few blemishes evident on either side. Some faint adjustment marks (as struck) are noted just above the eagle's head. (#6878)

Popular XF 1799 Irregular Date Dollar, B-15

1881 **1799 Irregular Date, 13 Stars Reverse XF40 PCGS.** Ex: Highlander. B-15, BB-152, R.3. Bowers-Borckardt Die State II. The fields are lilac, and the remaining luster and highpoints are both silver-gray. Dashes of darker russet visit the upper portions of each side. The obverse has a small edge nick at 3 o'clock, but the surfaces are generally pleasing. (#6880)

Choice AU 1799/8 15 Stars Reverse Dollar, B-3

1882 **1799/8 15 Stars Reverse AU55 NGC.** B-3, BB-141, R.3. Bowers-Borckardt Die State III. The well known blundered die variety with 15 reverse stars. The engraver tried to hide his mistake by greatly enlarging the first and final clouds, yet two telltale points of an errant star emerge from each base of the oversized clouds. Pale aqua-blue luster dominates all but the open fields of this lightly toned overdate dollar. A hint of wear is present on Liberty's cheek and shoulder, and on the eagle's head and breast. Refreshingly unabraded, and a desirable example of this distinctive variety. (#6883)

1883 **1800—Graffiti—ANACS. VF Details. Net Fine 12.** B-16, BB-187, R.2. The obverse has seven faint pinscratches, five of which form a square divided into two triangles. Nonetheless, a nice collector grade early silver dollar with original medium caramel-gold, lilac, and gunmetal-gray toning. (#6887)

1884 **1800—Improperly Cleaned—NCS. VF Details.** B-16, BB-187, R.2. Die dot below left serif of E of LIBERTY, others join tops of RT; reverse die flaws over ES and right; right base of F touches cloud. Lightly cleaned surfaces have retoned light to medium gray, blue, and lavender. Nicely detailed, save for light to moderate wear on the highpoints. Both sides are devoid of significant abrasions. (#6887)

1800 Dollar, AU55, B-16, A Scarce High Grade Example

1885 **1800 AU55 NGC.** B-16, BB-187, R.2. Die State V. This final die state is characterized by new flaws between the ES in STATES, and a new obverse die crack below the 800 in the date. While the B-16 is tied with the B-13 as the most plentiful variety of the year, it is seldom encountered in high grades. This is a bright, untoned coin that is well struck throughout and well centered with even denticles around the peripheries. A thin layer of mint luster can be seen over each side. Behind Liberty's head are a few short grease stains that were struck into the coin at the time of manufacture. (#6887)

1886 **1800 12 Arrows—Cleaned—ANACS. Fine 15 Details.** B-17, BB-196, R.1. A cream-gray early dollar with a glimpse apple-green along the obverse margin. Generally smooth, although the obverse has a pair of unimportant rim nicks near 10:30. (#6890)

1887 **1801—Repaired, Improperly Cleaned—NCS. VF Details.** B-2, BB-212, R.3. Bowers-Borckardt Die State II with double "collar" clashmark above the cleavage. The obverse field is extensively smoothed, and the surfaces are whizzed, hairlined, and glossy. Nonetheless, this pale green-gold piece is sharply defined, particularly on the heraldic eagle. (#6893)

1801 Dollar, VF30, B-2, BB-212

1888 **1801 VF30 PCGS.** B-2, BB-212, R.3. This variety shows the distance from the 1 in the date to the curl being about the same as the distance from star 8 to the upper right serif of Y in LIBERTY, and the 01 in the date closer than the 180. On the reverse, the point of the leftmost arrowhead is under the left edge of the left serif of N in UNITED. Golden-gray patina is accented by deep bluish-gray, and traces of luster reside in the protected areas of the obverse. Nicely defined. A light horizontal grease streak is visible on the obverse. (#6893)

Attractive 1801 Dollar XF40, B-2

1889 **1801 XF40 NGC.** B-2, BB-212, R.3. Die State III. The most common die state for this variety. Well centered and well struck, this example displays an attractive coating of mauve toning over both sides, imbued with bluish-green undertones in the fields. Modest even wear and a few small abrasions are noted on the generally smooth surfaces. (#6893)

Choice AU 1801 Dollar, B-3, BB-213

1890 **1801 AU55 NGC.** B-3, BB-213. R.3. Die State II. All four digits of the date on this coin can be seen incused and reversed under ES and O of STATES OF on the reverse. Sometime in the middle of its life, the reverse die, which was used only to strike this die marriage, clashed with the obverse die, producing the strong effects seen on this piece. The surfaces are bright and silvery with no overly distracting abrasions noted. A highly unusual example worthy of a specialist's collection. (#6893)

Scarce AU55 B-2 1801 Dollar

1891 **1801 AU55 NGC.** B-2, BB-212, R.3. Die State III. Most easily attributed by the double center dot on the obverse, with the one to the left considerably smaller than the prominent dot. This is a well defined coin that is richly toned in shades of deep blue, rose, and yellow-green. Much of the original mint luster remains and is abundantly evident beneath the toning. The only mark that can be used as a pedigree identifier is a planchet flake on the cheek of Liberty. (#6893)

1892 **1802 Narrow Date—Cleaned—ANACS. VF30 Details.** B-6, BB-241, R.1. Bowers-Borckardt Die State III. Steel-blue and almond-gold toning alternates across this subdued middle-grade Bust dollar. The right obverse field has a thin granular area, and a couple of stray adjustment marks are present near obverse star 13. (#6895)

1893 **1802 Narrow Date—Altered Surfaces—ANACS. VF30 Details.** B-6, BB-241, R.1. Medium lilac-brown toning is consistent across this finely granular early dollar. Light adjustment marks are limited to OF and nearby clouds. Sharp for the VF level. (#6895)

1894 **1802 Narrow Date—Damaged, Cleaned—ANACS. VF30 Details.** B-6, BB-241, R.1. Rotation beneath a light reveals glimpses of luster within protected areas. The cream-gray and chestnut-tan fields are hairlined, and the portrait has three small gouges. The reverse rim has several dings, particularly at 2, 7, and 9 o'clock. (#6895)

Partly Lustrous B-6 AU 1802 Dollar

1895 **1802 Narrow Date AU50 NGC.** B-6, BB-241, R.1. B-6 receives a separate *Guide Book* listing as the sole "Narrow Normal Date" variety. Almond-gold and sky-gray tones emerge from this lightly toned and subdued early dollar. Plentiful pockets of luster fill design crevices, and no abrasions are worthy of individual mention. Adjustment marks are faint and localized to 4:30 on the obverse. *From The Beau Clerc Collection.* (#6895)

1802 Narrow Date Dollar AU53, B-6

1896 **1802 Narrow Date AU53 PCGS.** B-6, BB-241, R.1. A still-lustrous example that is solidly struck with predominately light steel-gray color and delicate yellow-gold accents. Scarcely visible is an ancient pinscratch that connects star 7 to the E in LIBERTY. On the reverse, a curious, triangular-shaped stain stays within the boundaries of the eagle's scroll and shield. (#6895)

1897 **1802/1 Wide Date—Improperly Cleaned—NCS. Fine Details.** B-2, BB-233, R.4. This slate-gray early dollar is richly detailed for the Fine details grade, although a bit bright from a cleaning. Scarcer than the usually encountered 1802/1 varieties, B-3 and B-4. (#6899)

VF35 1802/1 Dollar B-3, BB-234

1898 **1802/1 Wide Date VF35 NGC.** B-3, BB-234, R.3. Bowers-Borckardt Die State III. The large die lump near obverse star 8 is diagnostic for this 1802/1 variety. Considerable luster clings to design recesses, although Liberty's cheek and shoulder exhibit wear. Uncommonly free from marks. Areas of charcoal toning is noted near 7 o'clock and beneath the RT in LIBERTY. (#6899)

VF30 Sharpness B-5 1803 Small 3 Dollar

1899 **1803 Small 3—Cleaned—ANACS. VF30 Details.** B-5, BB-252, R.3. This pearl-tan and lilac-gray example is thickly hairlined, and has a couple of unimportant rim nicks at 12 o'clock on the obverse and 7 o'clock on the reverse. A few bright but wispy marks are present on the right-side clouds. Most letters in E PLURIBUS UNUM are bold. (#6900)

Sharp 1803 Large 3 Dollar, VF35, B-6, BB-255

1900 **1803 Large 3 VF35 ICG.** B-6, BB-255, R.2. The 3 in the date has a thick top, and the E in STATES is left of the cloud break on this variety. Light to medium gray patination covers both sides of this VF35 example, and aside from highpoint wear, the design elements are nicely detailed. We note a rough area in the lower left reverse quadrant. (#6901)

Choice XF Large 3 B-6 1803 Dollar

1901 **1803 Large 3 XF45 NGC.** B-6, BB-255, R.2. Luster fills the borders, curls, and plumage of this attractive Draped Bust dollar. Light, even wear is found on Liberty's cheek and shoulder. From the final year of circulation production, although novodel proofs of various dates were issued decades later. (#6901)

Choice XF B-6 1803 Large 3 Dollar

1902 **1803 Large 3 XF45 ANACS.** B-6, BB-255, R.2. This splendidly detailed Draped Bust dollar provides nearly full wing plumage, and E PLURIBUS UNUM is bold. The cream-gray surfaces are only lightly hairlined, and marks are surprisingly few aside from minor contact on the field near the chin and on the obverse rim near 7:30. (#6901)

Rare 1836 Name Below Base Gobrecht Dollar, Proof

1903 **1836 Name Below Base, Judd-58 Restrike, Pollock-61, R.6(?)—Improperly Cleaned—NCS. Proof.** Silver. Die Alignment III: Center of Liberty's head opposite N in ONE. While not numerically graded, we grade the coin PR60. As with all Gobrecht dollars, the Judd-58 is an issue that is not without controversy. There are competing theories but they generally resolve into one question: Were there any Original Name Below Base coins struck, or all they all Restrikes?

It is our belief, based on the recent research by Mike Carboneau, Jim Gray, Saul Teichman, and John Dannreuther, that no Originals are known. This conclusion is based on the fact that no examples have been seen to date that do not have extensive die cracks around the reverse periphery. One coin has been certified by PCGS as an Original in the VG-VF grade range, but it is widely believed this is a mistaken attribution.

The Die Alignment III coins all have well-developed reverse die cracks. More so than those seen on the Die Alignment IV, which are fainter and not as well developed. Which leads one to the conclusion that DA IV coins were struck before the DA III pieces. The development of these die cracks on Judd-58s compared to other DA III Gobrecht dollars has led the above-mentioned researchers to conclude that the Name Below Base dollars were struck in the 1860s.

The story about "the conceited German" (C. GOBRECHT F.) placing his name on the coin is traceable to Edward Cogan in 1867. Since the Name Below Base coins were not struck until the 1860s, this has been recently regarded as a coin dealer fiction. However, there may actually be some truth to the story. But the story may actually refer to the 1836-dated dollars with Gobrecht's name on the base. Subsequent issues from 1838 and 1839 show that C. GOBRECT F. was effaced from the die, with faint "ghosts" of several letters remaining on the 1839 coins. This effacement was just recently discovered (at the ANA) by John Dannreuther.

The fields are deeply mirrored with evidence of crisscrossing hairlines on each side. Mostly brilliant, there is just a hint of light golden toning around the margins. Fully struck in all areas, including Liberty's foot. (#11217)

1836 Gobrecht Dollar, PR35
Die Alignment I

1904 **1836 Name on Base, Judd-60 Original, Pollock-65, R.1, PR35 PCGS.** Silver. Plain Edge. Die Alignment I (Liberty's head opposite DO). This early December striking shows the eagle flying upward with a coin turn. Only 400 pieces are believed to have been produced in this first striking period. While it is generally accepted that the 1836 dollars were struck as circulating proofs, there is no evidence remaining of such a finish on this coin. The fields show a uniform, light gray color, the same as the highpoints of the design. The recesses are a deeper charcoal gray. Several contact marks are scattered over each side, the most obvious ones in the right obverse field and in the fields above and below the eagle. Even wear over the design motifs on each side. (#11225)

Die Alignment IV 1836 Gobrecht Dollar, PR40

1905 **1836 Judd-60 Original, Medal Alignment PR40 PCGS.** Silver. Plain Edge. Die Alignment IV (medallic alignment with the head of Liberty opposite OF). The die scratch above the eagle's right wing is faint, but just barely discernible with magnification. The most recent research into the striking sequence of Gobrecht dollars indicates that between December 1836 and March 1837 the order was: DA I, DA II, DA III, Judd-61, DA IV. Considerable research is being conducted into the die emission sequence of these coins and more an-depth article is expected soon from John Dannreuther, in addition to the long-awaited book Heritage is publishing.

The surfaces of this piece are bright and there is a slight trace of reflectivity still in the fields, in spite of 20 points of wear. Generally untoned, there is a trace of golden color present around the rims. Light, even wear is seen over the design elements, and there are no mentionable or detracting contact marks on either side. (#11226)

Elusive Judd-84 Restrike 1838 Gobrecht Dollar

Toned 1839 Gobrecht Dollar, PR40

1906 **1838 Name Omitted, Judd-84 Restrike, Pollock-93, R.5—Polished, Artificially Toned—NCS. Impaired Proof.** Silver. Reeded Edge. Die Alignment III (head of Liberty opposite the NE of ONE; or equivalently, coin-turn with the eagle flying level). Both sides are unnaturally bright, even for a proof striking, with tinges of orange-gold and violet toning in the recesses. Classified as a "restrike," this term seems superfluous as it appears that all 1838 Dollars that exist today are restrikes. No "original" 1838 Dollar has been authenticated to our knowledge, and it is believed by some numismatists that no 1838 Dollars were actually struck in 1838. If this is correct, then all 1838 Dollars are restrikes.

Of the three die cracks normally found on the reverse, only the short crack connecting the bases of the letters LAR (of DOLLAR) can be detected here with any certainty. The presence and size of these die cracks, when compared with other Gobrecht Dollars struck with the same reverse die, indicate that this piece was probably made during one of Linderman's two terms of office. Most Gobrecht Dollar restrikes are known to have been made between 1857 and 1860 (during Snowden's term of office), or from 1867 to 1869 (during Linderman's first term), or from 1873 to 1878 (during Linderman's second term as U.S. Mint Director). Even though their origin is a bit hazy, the scarcity of these 1838 Restrikes when combined with the popularity of the Gobrecht design make them sought-after numismatic commodities. (#11352)

1907 **1839 Name Omitted, Judd-104 Original, Pollock-116, R.3, PR40 ANACS.** Die Alignment IV. Original. Head of Liberty opposite the O in OF with the eagle flying level following a medal turn. Struck in December 1839, originals of this date do not show die cracks through MERI and other reverse lettering, as seen on later date restrikes.

An interesting feature on 1839 dollars was just discovered at the Milwaukee ANA by John Dannreuther. He observed that C. GOBRECHT F. was effaced from the master die. A definite, oval-shaped depression can be seen on the rock beneath Liberty with graver lines present, and faint "ghosts" of several letters can be seen with strong magnification. The remarkable part of this find is that it took 170 years for someone to discover this! It also gives some credence to what has recently been considered the equivalent of a "numismatic old wives' tale" that Gobrecht's name was positioned too prominently on the coin.

The surfaces are medium russet-brown with underlying lilac color. A couple of shallow pinscratches are located (but barely visible) in the lower right obverse field, and otherwise there are only the small contact marks one would expect from a PR40 coin. Even friction over the highpoints of the design. (#11444)

SEATED DOLLARS

Borderline Uncirculated 1840 Dollar

1908 **1840 AU58 NGC.** The Liberty Seated dollar was introduced in 1840. The Gobrecht dollar obverse was retained, while the reverse discarded the flying eagle in favor of the "sandwich board" eagle in use on silver coins since 1807. A dusky example with blended silver-gray and almond-gold toning. Sharply struck with moderately abraded fields and a thin vertical mark through the cheek. Census: 38 in 58, 31 finer (7/07). (#6926)

1909 **1841 AU58 ANACS.** Most 1841 dollars were apparently placed into circulation. High-end AU examples, such as the AU58 in this lot, are thus what most collectors can aspire to own. Light to medium gray toning displays gold undertones, and remarkably clean surfaces exhibit sharply defined design elements.
From The Beau Clerc Collection. (#6927)

1910 **1843 AU53 PCGS.** An attractive example for the grade, this piece displays generally well struck design elements that show just a bit of weakness on the eagle's neck and the top of Liberty's head. Essentially untoned, with traces of mint luster near the devices. The highpoints are modestly worn, and there are scattered small abrasions over each side.
From The Arnold & Harriet Collection, Part Two. (#6929)

1911 **1844 AU58 Prooflike ANACS.** Light orange-gold and ocean-blue toning visits the borders. A flashy and nicely struck example. The usual 1844 business strike dies with strong die doubling on Liberty's shield and heavy die polish lines beneath the eagle's wings. Only 20,000 circulation strike pieces were struck. (#6930)

1912 **1846 XF45 NGC.** Electric-blue, lavender, and golden-tan toning concentrates at the obverse margin, while golden tan color rims the reverse. Traces of luster rest in the protected areas of this well defined and relatively clean Choice XF specimen.
From The Beau Clerc Collection. (#6932)

Reflective 1846 Seated Dollar, MS63

1913 **1846 MS63 NGC.** The combined population of NGC and PCGS indicate that just 65 examples of this date are certified MS63 or finer, the figure include an unspecified but likely numerous number of resubmissions. Light golden surfaces are fully lustrous with reflective fields. The usual scattered surface marks and faint hairlines prevent a higher grade. (#6932)

Bold 1848 Silver Dollar AU58

1914 **1848 AU58 NGC.** Powder-blue and pale golden-gray toning frequents this richly detailed example, which has its share of subtle satin luster. The right obverse and the field near UNITED display some wispy marks. Only 15,000 pieces were struck. Census: 18 in 58, 11 finer (7/07). (#6935)

1915 **1850-O—Plugged, Repaired, Whizzed—ANACS. XF45 Details.** Perhaps holed at one time between the E and D in ONE DOL. The upper reverse field and the upper left obverse field are repaired, and the entire coin has been whizzed. Toned cream-gray and apricot. The rarest New Orleans silver dollar issue. (#6938)

Pleasing 1850-O Dollar, AU55

1916 **1850-O AU55 PCGS.** While usually available in lower grades, the 1850-O is an important (and pricey) condition rarity in AU, and only a couple of dozen Uncirculated coins are believed known today. This pleasing AU is generally quite well struck. There are a few small abrasions scattered about, but these are largely obscured by the deep gray-blue patina that covers each side. (#6938)

1917 1851 MS62 PCGS. The 1851 is a famous rarity within the Seated Liberty series. It is more rare than the 1852, whose mintage of 1,100 pieces is slightly less than the 1851, for which 1,300 coins were struck. The latter production does not count Restrike proofs, which are readily distinguished by the lower placement of the date. Although Original 1851 dollars have been cataloged as proofs in the past, these are now believed to have been prooflike business strikes. Given the extremely small production, it is not surprising that there are prooflike pieces among the handful of Mint State survivors. Bowers (1993) surmises these prooflike pieces may also have been the outcome of die polishing to remove clash marks.

Only 30 coins have been certified in Mint State by PCGS and NGC combined, some of which are undoubtedly resubmissions. According to our records, only 19 Uncirculated 1851 specimens have made auction appearances through the major houses over the past 15 or so years.

The present MS62 piece displays bright surfaces that are visited by mottled cobalt-blue and light gray patination. The design elements are exquisitely struck, with nice definition on the Liberty and eagle motifs as well as on the peripheral elements. A few minute ticks are scattered here and there, but none are significant. A couple of roller marks at the top of Liberty's head may serve to identify the piece. Population: 7 in 62, 7 finer (8/07).

From The Beau Clerc Collection. (#6939)

Lustrous 1854 Select Dollar

1918 1854 MS63 ANACS. The 1854 dollar, with a circulation strike mintage of 33,140 coins, is a prime rarity in all grades, as most were apparently exported (David Bowers, 2006). Golden-tan patination on this Select example is accented with hints of blue and lavender, and covers lustrous surfaces. Sharply struck, with just a few trivial marks. (#6942)

Rare 1856 Dollar, AU55

1919 1856 AU55 PCGS. The 1856 dollar, from a mintage of 63,500 business strikes, is rare in all grades, as most were exported to China or Europe (David Bowers, 1993). Light champagne-gold patina resides on this Choice AU example. The design elements display better definition than usually seen on this typically weak issue, except for softness in the hair at Liberty's head and the feathers on the right (left facing) leg. A few light marks are inconsequential.
From The Beau Clerc Collection. (#6944)

Prooflike 1857 Seated Dollar, MS62

1920 1857 MS62 PCGS. An elusive date in Mint State grades, from a mintage of just 94,000 coins, with the typical appearance of this issue. The head and several of the top stars are flat, and all remaining details on both sides are bold. The surfaces of this light ivory colored example are fully reflective, revealing minor hairlines and other slight imperfections consistent with the grade. Population: 20 in 62, 21 finer (8/07).
From The Beau Clerc Collection. (#6945)

1921 1859-S—Cleaned—ANACS. AU Details, Net XF45. David Bowers (2006) writes of the 1859-S dollar that: "Most of the mintage was exported to China, where they were melted." Magnification reveals fine hairlines on the golden-gray surfaces, where traces of luster still reside in the recesses. Good definition is apparent on the motifs.
From The Beau Clerc Collection. (#6948)

Scarce 1859-S Seated Dollar AU50

1922 1859-S AU50 PCGS. Only 20,000 examples of this San Francisco Mint issue were coined, making it a scarce date at all grade levels. This lightly circulated piece displays even wear over the dove-gray surfaces that show a small amount of mottled peripheral toning. A few small marks exist on each side, but none of them are individually distracting. (#6948)

1923 1860-O AU58 ANACS. Luster dominates all but the open fields, and the strike is precise aside from the centers of the final stars. The fields show the effects of brief circulation, but the eye appeal is strong for this usually bagmarked issue. (#6950)

1924 1860-O MS62 NGC. A well struck, frosty, and unworn example of this late antebellum issue, the last Seated dollars struck at New Orleans. Though the lower obverse shows areas of vivid orange patina, the remainder of the piece is silver-gray. Numerous tiny abrasions on both sides account for the grade. (#6950)

1925 1864 XF45 NGC. Though years of evidence showed that the pieces were often simply remelted and sold as bullion, Philadelphia persisted in striking silver dollars, including 30,700 of the coins in 1864. This modestly abraded example displays light, even wear across the well struck devices and pale silver-gray fields. Census: 9 in 45, 40 finer (8/07). (#6954)

Near-Gem 1867 Seated Dollar Rarity

1926 1867 MS64 PCGS. An amazing coin, nearly the finest known for the date. The low mintage of just 46,900 coins provides an indication of its rarity. The 1867 has the lowest mintage of any With Motto Seated Liberty dollar coined at the Philadelphia Mint.

The fields are satiny and reflective, nearly prooflike in appearance. The obverse has ivory and pale gray color at the center, framed by deep sea-green and steel toning. The reverse is similar with ivory color surrounded by rich reddish-gold toning. Population: 12 in 64, 3 finer (8/07).
From The Beau Clerc Collection. (#6960)

1927 1869 AU58 NGC. Despite a generous mintage of 423,700 pieces, the 1869 silver dollar was melted in quantity, and only a fraction of the original production survives today. This luminous near-Mint piece has silver-gray centers with areas of orange toning at the rims. Well struck with a number of abrasions in the fields, though actual friction is minimal. Census: 13 in 58, 31 finer (7/07). (#6962)

Untoned 1870 Seated Dollar MS62

1928 1870 MS62 ANACS. Breen-5483. The 1870 is scarce in Mint State, since it was principally struck for export to the Orient. An untoned and satiny example with a good strike and a smooth reverse. The obverse is moderately abraded. IN GOD WE TRUST and the left wing feathers are lightly die doubled. (#6963)

Difficult Very Good 1872-CC Dollar

1929 1872-CC VG8 ANACS. A collectible cream-gray example of this rare Carson City Seated dollar. The center letters of the shield are gone, but the L and Y are plain, and the T is faint but readable. The eagle displays substantial plumage detail. One of just 3,150 examples coined.
From The Beau Clerc Collection. (#6969)

Conditionally Rare 1873 Seated Dollar MS62 Prooflike

1930 1873 MS62 Prooflike NGC. A reflective example of this conditionally rare final year issue; production was interrupted by authorization of the Trade dollar. The strike is good, if not quite full on Liberty's hair and the nearby stars. A few wispy slide marks in the fields and a faint fingerprint fragment near 8 o'clock on the obverse are not troubling for the grade. NGC has certified 127 examples of the business strike 1873 (as of 8/07), but only this piece has received a Prooflike designation. (#6971)

XF Details 1873-CC Dollar

1931 **1873-CC—Fields Tooled, Cleaned—ANACS. XF40 Details.** Darkly toned olive-brown. The obverse field has been skillfully smoothed on each side of the seated Liberty, although it takes patience, a strong light, and an experienced eye to detect the telltale swirls of carefully-moved metal. The 1873-CC is the rarest Carson City silver dollar. Much of the tiny mintage of 2,300 pieces was likely melted when the Trade dollar was abolished and Morgan dollar production began. (#6972)

PROOF SEATED DOLLARS

1932 **1860 PR60 NGC.** A decisively struck, deeply reflective specimen of this pre-war proof Seated dollar issue, one of 1,330 such pieces coined. The significantly hairlined obverse has a measure of cloudy champagne toning, while the reverse is predominantly silver-gray. (#7003)

Choice Proof 1861 Seated Liberty Dollar

1933 **1861 PR64 PCGS.** Business strikes coined during the Civil War are elusive, and in some cases major rarities, placing additional demand on the proofs that have survived through the years. This example is a pleasing example with light gold toning over silver surfaces. Population: 23 in 64, 7 finer (8/07).
From The Beau Clerc Collection. (#7004)

Splendid 1861 Dollar, PR63 Cameo

1934 **1861 PR63 Cameo PCGS.** Although a few light hairlines limit the grade, this lovely proof dollar has brilliant silver surfaces with exceptional contrast that is created by the combination of deeply mirrored fields and fully lustrous devices. True cameo proofs are hard to locate, and this is a delightful example. Population: 4 in 63 Cameo, 10 finer (8/07). (#87004)

Outstanding 1861 Dollar, PR66 Cameo
One of the Two Finest Certified

1935 **1861 PR66 Cameo NGC.** According to mint records, 1,000 proof silver dollars were minted in 1861, and all delivered on April 15 of that year. In his book *Silver Dollars and Trade Dollars of the United States*, David Bowers says that only about 350 were ever sold as part of copper-nickel and silver proof sets, and "... early in 1862 over 600 sets were consigned to the melting pot." Bowers goes on to say: "Today, 1861 Proof dollars are very elusive. Not only was the distribution low ... but those sold seem to have had an unusually high attrition rate." NGC/PCGS population figures show that about 180 coins have been certified, some of which, of course, are likely to be resubmissions. Fewer than 30 Cameo have been seen.

The Premium Gem Cameo in this lot is essentially untoned, and its frosty motifs sit amidst deeply mirrored fields. The strike is outstanding, leaving none of the design elements with even a hint of weakness. A few wispy hairlines in the fields show up under high magnification, and prevent a possibly even higher grade! No pieces have been graded higher by either NGC or PCGS. Census: 2 in 66 Cameo, 0 finer (8/07). (#87004)

1936 **1863 PR61 NGC.** Delicate gold toning is even save for glimpses of a russet streak on the lower reverse. Well struck and typically hairlined. A popular proof Motto issue, due to its Civil War origin and its tiny mintage of 460 pieces.

Select Proof 1864 Silver Dollar

1937 1864 PR63 NGC. Although only 470 proofs were struck in 1864, at least two obverse dies were used. This is the level date variant, easily distinguished from the low 4 variety, an example of which is also in the present auction. The present piece has dusky orange toning with selected cherry-red and ocean-blue highlights. Slightly soft on the top of Liberty's head, although the remainder of the design is well brought up. (#7007)

Delightful 1864 Silver Dollar, PR64

1938 1864 PR64 NGC. This exceptional Choice specimen shows strongly reflective fields through delicate layers of patina, rose-gray in the centers and sea-green at the margins. The 1864 silver dollar had a proof mintage of just 470 pieces, and near-Gem and better examples remain elusive today. NGC has graded 29 finer representatives (8/07). (#7007)

Attractively Toned 1864 Near-Gem Proof Dollar

1939 1864 PR64 NGC. A coating of light gold-tan patina rests on the central devices, highlighted by a melange of light to medium intensity cobalt-blue, purple, lavender, and olive-green in the fields. Exquisite definition on the design elements is befitting of a proof strike. Some inoffensive handling marks preclude full Gem status. Census: 60 in 64, 29 finer (8/07). (#7007)

Colorful Superb Gem Proof 1864 Silver Dollar

1940 1864 PR67 NGC. A window of brilliance at the obverse center is bounded by ruby-lilac and jade-green shades. The reverse alternates between deep aquamarine and cherry-red toning. The strike is unimprovably precise, even on Liberty's hair and the nearby star centers. Careful rotation beneath a strong light fails to locate any surface imperfections. The Civil War date has a proof mintage of just 470 pieces, and the associated business strike emission of 30,700 pieces is also minimal. Unlike the circulation issue, proofs show no trace of repunching on the date. Census: 2 in 67, 3 finer (8/07). (#7007)

PR61 Cameo 1864 Silver Dollar

1941 1864 PR61 Cameo NGC. This proof Civil War Seated dollar has a tiny production of just 470 pieces. The strike is precise, particularly on Liberty's hair and the eagle's left ankle, which are sometimes indistinct on this type. Only a hint of golden toning is present. The devices and legends are nicely frosted. The minor field hairlines are fainter than expected of the grade. (#87007)

Select Proof 1866 Motto Seated Dollar

1942 **1866 Motto PR63 PCGS.** Pale honey and silver-blue toning graces this pleasing and exquisitely struck proof silver dollar. The lower obverse rim shows light sea-green and orange patina. Only 725 proofs were struck, and unimpaired survivors are in demand as the first examples of the Motto type. Population: 64 in 63, 78 finer (7/07). (#7014)

Impressive 1866 Motto Dollar, PR64 Cameo

1943 **1866 Motto PR64 Cameo PCGS.** This wonderful proof is an excellent representative of the first year of issue for the With Motto design, with full cameo contrast. Lustrous silver devices are framed by fully mirrored fields, and the whole is graced by pale lilac and gold toning. Population: 10 in 64 Cameo, 12 finer (8/07).
From The Beau Clerc Collection. (#87014)

Attractively Toned 1867 Select Proof Dollar

1944 **1867 PR63 PCGS.** 625 proof dollars were struck in 1867. This Select example is toned in mauve-gray, violet, and orange-gold. A well directed strike translated into sharp definition on all of the design elements, further enhancing the coin's overall eye appeal. Some wispy marks in the fields, visible only under high magnification, define the grade. (#7015)

Lovely 1867 Seated Dollar, PR63 Cameo

1945 **1867 PR63 Cameo PCGS.** Peripheral gold toning creates excellent aesthetic appeal, enhancing the overall appearance of this splendid cameo proof. Close inspection reveals a few faint hairlines in the fields, consistent with the grade. Population: 8 in 63 Cameo, 17 finer (8/07).
From The Beau Clerc Collection. (#87015)

Fabulous 1867 Seated Dollar PR67 ★ Cameo

1946 **1867 PR67 ★ Cameo NGC.** Only 46,900 business strikes were minted of the 1867 Seated dollar. It is rarely encountered at any grade level, and, in the opinion of John McCloskey, it may well be the rarest P-mint in the With Motto series (in circulated condition). As a date, however, the 1867 does not have the *appearance* of being a scarce issue because proofs are available often enough to satisfy date collectors. Five examples of this issue have been certified at PR67 Cameo, by NGC (8/07), but only two of those have a "Star" designation, and none are finer. When viewing this coin it is easy to take the technical merits of the piece for granted, as one is so enthralled with the color scheme on each side. The mirrored fields are brightly reflective and free from any mentionable defects, as one would surmise from the grade. The devices are nicely frosted against the fields, and each side is spectacularly toned. The centers are brilliant, but soon give way to rich concentric rings of iridescence around the margins. A must-see piece for the serious Seated dollar collector. (#87015)

1947 **1869 PR61 ANACS.** Occasional splashes of faint gray or light tan color visit this sharply struck proof dollar. The surfaces are abrasion free, but show subdued reflectivity.
From The Beau Clerc Collection. (#7017)

Gem Proof 1869 Seated Dollar

1948 **1869 PR65 PCGS.** Splashes of intermingled iridescence take the aesthetic appeal of this piece to a new level. A sharply defined Gem with moderate cameo contrast, the mirrored fields surround lustrous devices. The toning on this piece prevents a Cameo designation. Population: 19 in 65, 6 finer (8/07). (#7017)

Choice Cameo Proof 1869 Seated Dollar

1949 **1869 PR64 Cameo PCGS.** An amazing Cameo proof, this Choice quality piece has few peers certified by PCGS. Both sides are brilliant with glittering silver surfaces splashed by traces of gold and darker speckles. The surfaces are nicely preserved with only a few blemishes that are consistent with the grade. Population: 10 in 64 Cameo, 4 finer (8/07). (#87017)

Elusive PR64 Cameo 1871 Seated Dollar

1950 **1871 PR64 Cameo NGC.** An impressive Cameo proof, this dollar has brilliant silver surfaces with splashes of gold and cobalt-blue toning along parts of the border on each side. The fields are exceptional with deep mirrors, and the devices are frosty and sharply detailed. Census: 5 in 64 Cameo, 5 finer (8/07). (#87019)

1951 **1872 PR61 PCGS.** A richly toned dolphin-gray representative of this penultimate proof Seated dollar issue, which has a mintage of only 950 specimens. The strike is crisp, and the areas with thin patina permit strong reflectivity. Numerous scattered hairlines and a few pinpoint contact marks contribute to the grade. (#7020)

Scarce Select Proof 1872 Seated Dollar

1952 **1872 PR63 PCGS.** Bright, essentially untoned proof surfaces display cameo tendencies, and no marks that are worthy of individual mention. A bold strike manifests itself in exceptional detail on the design elements. According to David Bowers (1993), some of the 950 proofs of this year probably remained unsold, and were melted in 1873. (#7020)

Desirable Proof 1873 Seated Dollar

1953 **1873 PR61 PCGS.** This is the final year of issue for the Seated dollar series, coined continuously since 1840, after the 1836 Gobrecht design. Both sides have moderate hairlines, explaining the lower numerical grade assigned by PCGS. Population reports suggest that nearly half of the 600 coin mintage have been certified, but the figures included a substantial number of resubmissions.
From The Beau Clerc Collection. (#7021)

TRADE DOLLARS

1954 **1873-CC XF45 PCGS.** The 1873-CC Trade dollar is quite scarce in circulated grades, and is rare in Mint State (David Bowers, 1993). Wisps of gold patina rest on the light gray surfaces of this Choice XF specimen that displays sharp definition on the design elements. Some light circulation marks in the fields are only visible under magnification. Housed in a green label holder. *From The Beau Clerc Collection.* (#7032)

1955 **1874-CC—Chopmarked—ANACS. MS60 Details.** Many Trade dollars, such as this one, were exported to China. This example displays bold chopmarks on both obverse and reverse. Lustrous with numerous small abrasions and pale golden toning near the borders. The '74-CC is a scarcer issue, especially in finer Mint State grades. (#7035)

Lustrous MS64 Chop Marked 1874-S Trade Dollar

1956 **1874-S Chop Mark MS64 PCGS.** By definition, one would think that a chop marked dollar would have been handled and thus show signs of circulation, and this is usually the case. But apparently this coin was set aside shortly after the two chops were placed on the obverse. One chop is easily seen in the left obverse field, but the other blends into the folds of the gown around Liberty's knees. Highly lustrous, the surfaces are gray-brilliant and evenly matched over each side. Well struck.

1957 **1875-CC—Reverse Tooled—ANACS. MS60 Details.** Type One Reverse. Wide CC. Judging from the obverse alone, this lightly toned Carson City Trade dollar has an MS62 appearance, but the reverse field has numerous wispy marks near the eagle's wings and neck. *From The Laguna Niguel Collection, Part Two.* (#7038)

1958 **1875-S MS62 PCGS.** Type One Obverse, Type Two Reverse. This silver-white example has flashy luster and pleasing detail overall, though Liberty's head and the eagle's right (facing) talon show softness. Light to moderate abrasions pepper each side. *From The Mario Eller Collection, Part One.* (#7039)

Impressive MS63 1875-S Trade Dollar

1959 **1875-S MS63 NGC.** Type One Reverse. Large S. A lustrous and lightly toned Select Trade dollar. Nicely struck despite slight merging of detail near Liberty's ear and the eagle's right (facing) claw. A few tiny marks on the field near the knees, but abrasions are minimal overall for the designated grade. *From The Beau Clerc Collection.* (#7039)

Attractive 1875-S Near-Gem Trade Dollar

1960 **1875-S MS64 PCGS.** Type One Obverse and Reverse. Large S. The San Francisco Mint made the lion's share of Trade dollars during their heyday from 1874 through 1878, due to its closer location to the Orient, the ultimate destination for much of the coinage. Dappled golden-brown and gunmetal-gray patina embraces this satiny and suitably struck near-Gem. Thorough inspection of the fields beneath a loupe locate no significant marks. A worthy contribution to an originally toned silver type set. (#7039)

Lustrous 1875-S Gem Trade Dollar

1961 **1875-S MS65 ANACS.** Type Two Reverse. Large S. Dusky golden-brown and orange patination at the margins mingles with bluish-gray and lavender, framing champagne-gold and ice-blue centers. Excellent definition shows on the design elements, save for the usual softness in Liberty's hair. Well preserved, highly lustrous surfaces are devoid of any mentionable marks. (#7039)

1962 **1875-S/CC Chop Mark ANACS. MS60 Details.** FS-501, formerly FS-012.5. Type One Reverse. A fully lustrous, lightly toned, and well struck example of this famous overmintmark variety. Two chopmarks are present, one near 9:30 on the obverse and the other above the eagle's right (facing) leg. These chopmarks are deeply entered and make the piece somewhat wavy. (#87040)

Interesting 1875-S/CC Select Trade Dollar

1963 1875-S/CC MS63 NGC. VP-001. FS-501, formerly FS-012.5. Type One Reverse. The more obvious of the two 1875-S/CC varieties, the presence of the C mintmark to the right of the S is irrefutable. David Bowers (1993) writes: "This issue was generally unknown to numismatists until the early 1960s. One of the earliest market appearances of the variety was in New Netherlands Coin Company's sale of December 10-11, 1963." Bowers go on to say: "In 1962-3, the 1875-S/CC overmintmark was considered to be a great rarity, but over a period of time additional specimens came to light. Today it is considered to be moderately scarce in lower grades and quite rare in Mint State."

The lustrous surfaces of this select specimen display electric-blue, lavender, and gray-tan toning, and just a few minor ticks that limit the grade. An impressive strike brings out sharp definition on the design features. Census: 3 in 63, 4 finer (8/07). (#7040)

1964 1876 MS62 PCGS. Type One Obverse (ribbon points left) and reverse (a berry under the claw). Sharply struck, with gold patina, deeper in hue on the reverse, resting on lustrous surfaces. A few light scuffs and luster grazes are noted.
From The Beau Clerc Collection. (#7041)

Scarce MS61 1876-CC Trade Dollar

1965 1876-CC MS61 NGC. Type One Obverse, Type Two Reverse. The lustrous obverse has only a hint of gold toning, while the satiny reverse is a deeper chestnut-gray. Sharply struck, and attractive despite the occasional moderate field mark. Interesting rim die breaks are present on the obverse between 9 and 11 o'clock. Census: 16 in 61, 21 finer (8/07).
From The Beau Clerc Collection. (#7042)

White MS64 1876-S Trade Dollar

1966 1876-S MS64 PCGS. Ex: Daniel D. Biddle. Type One obverse, Type Two reverse. Small S mintmark. This is a transitional issue with the obverse from the 1873 to 1876 hub and the reverse from the 1876 to 1883 (1885) hub. The upper obverse and lower reverse show a little characteristic weakness that is often seen on similar coins. Lustrous surfaces are visible beneath splashes of steel and heather toning. (#7043)

Choice Mint State 1877 Trade Dollar

1967 1877 MS64 PCGS. Typical of the date, Liberty's head and most of the stars are flat. Perhaps less than 1% of all circulation strikes have sharp head details. Aside from the peripheral obverse weakness, the balance of design elements are bold. Frosty surfaces exhibit brilliant silver luster and light champagne toning. Population: 60 in 64, 4 finer (8/07). (#7044)

1968 **1877-S MS62 PCGS.** Traces of deep amber-orange, magenta, and electric-blue toning are noted near the peripheries, mainly on the reverse. The fields are highly reflective and nearly prooflike. Well struck with noticeable hairlines and a few tiny abrasions on each side. (#7046)

Choice 1877-S Trade Dollar

1969 **1877-S MS64 PCGS.** Light autumn-gold toning embraces this highly lustrous and minimally abraded near-Gem. The reverse die is interesting for its cluster of fine die lines near the eagle's right (facing) leg. A crisply struck example from the penultimate year of circulation issue. As of (7/07), PCGS has certified a mere 30 pieces finer. (#7046)

White MS64 1877-S Trade Dollar

1970 **1877-S MS64 PCGS.** A stone-white Trade dollar with dazzling luster and a meticulous strike. Even Liberty's hair and the eagle's ankle have exacting definition. Marks are inconsequential, and the grade appears conservative despite a small obverse spot equidistant from stars 9 and 10. (#7046)

Patinated Choice 1877-S Trade Dollar

1971 **1877-S MS64 ANACS.** Honey-gold, radish-red, lime-green, and ice-blue compete for territory across this lovely semi-prooflike near-Gem. The strike is exemplary, and a search for abrasions fails to find any remotely worthy of mention. Although a high mintage issue, the '77-S was struck for export to the Orient, and quality Mint State examples are scarce. (#7046)

Near-Gem 1877-S Trade Dollar

1972 **1877-S MS64 PCGS.** Splashes of peripheral iridescence enhance the natural golden-ivory surfaces of this frosty silver trade dollar. All of the design elements are bold and the surfaces are pristine. The date is not difficult to locate in Choice Mint State grade, but is nearly impossible to find any finer. We consider an MS64 example of the 1877-S trade dollar to be an excellent value. (#7046)

Impressive Near-Mint 1878-CC Trade Dollar

1973 **1878-CC AU58 PCGS.** The 1878-CC trade dollar is the key-date among all business strike issues of the series. Although official records show a mintage of 97,000 coins during the first part of 1878, records also indicate that 44,148 trade dollars were melted in July of that year. While it is not known what dates were included in the melt, a reasonable assumption is that many or most were 1878-CC coins. Survivors are rare in all grades as the PCGS population data indicates. This example has satiny light gray surfaces with considerable remaining luster beneath iridescent toning. Only a trace of wear is evident on the highpoints of the design. Population: 10 in 58, 24 finer (8/07). (#7047)

1974 **1878-S MS62 NGC.** The Trade dollar issues of 1878 would prove to be the last for all Mints save Philadelphia, which continued the design in proof for several more years. This 1878-S example shows pleasing detail and vibrant luster on the reverse, though the silver-gray obverse is slightly subdued. Pleasing despite a number of wispy abrasions.
From The Mario Eller Collection, Part One. (#7048)

Patinated Choice 1878-S Trade Dollar

1975 **1878-S MS64 NGC.** A prooflike piece with exquisite golden-brown and aquamarine patina. Precisely struck and nearly mark-free save for a thin mark beneath the left scroll end. Lightly die doubled on the lower reverse legends, but not either of the Cherrypickers' varieties (FS-801 and FS-802). Certified in a prior generation holder. (#7048)

PROOF TRADE DOLLARS

Near-Gem Proof 1873 Trade Dollar

1976 1873 PR64 NGC. At the end of the Seated dollar series, a replacement appeared in the form of the trade dollar, although this design was not intended for actual circulation. Of course, contemporary collectors still desired proof examples for their cabinets. Although just shy of Gem quality, this is a delightful proof with lovely heather, lilac, and blue toning, deeper near the borders.
From The Beau Clerc Collection. (#7053)

Elusive 1874 Trade Dollar, PR64 Cameo

1977 1874 PR64 Cameo PCGS. Despite a substantial proof population, Cameo examples are seldom encountered. This Choice proof has brilliant silver surfaces with fully mirrored fields and highly lustrous devices. A few insignificant hairlines and additional contact marks prevent a Gem grade. Population: 9 in 64, 4 finer (8/07).
From The Beau Clerc Collection. (#87054)

Crisply Defined 1879 Trade Dollar, PR62

1978 1879 PR62 NGC. The 1879 Trade dollar is a proof-only issue with a mintage of 1,541 pieces. In his Silver and Trade dollar reference (1993), David Bowers indicates that "Most specimens were saved, but with varying degrees of care." The NGC/PCGS population data bear this out, as relatively few certified coins fall into the Gem- quality classification. Whispers of golden-tan color gravitate to the peripheries of this PR62 specimen, being deeper in hue and more extensive on the reverse, and a powerful strike brings out crisp delineation on the design elements. A faint, short obverse staple scratch, and some wispy hairlines in the fields, preclude a higher grade. (#7059)

Toned 1879 Trade Dollar, PR64

1979 1879 PR64 PCGS. The second proof-only issue in the series, the 1879 had the second highest mintage of any proof trade dollar with a production of 1,541 coins. This near-Gem proof has deep blue and iridescent toning on both sides, with fully mirrored fields beneath. Apparent cameo contrast is also evident, although the toning prevents such a designation by the grading service.
From The Beau Clerc Collection. (#7059)

Cameo PR64 1879 Trade Dollar

1980 1879 PR64 Cameo PCGS. A popular, proof-only date with a mintage of 1,541 pieces. This is an attractive, upper-end PR64 that shows a significant amount of contrast between the frosted devices and deeply reflective proof fields. A few light hairlines account for the less-than-Gem grade. Mostly brilliant, there is just a hint of light golden-rose color on each side. (#87059)

Richly Frosted 1881 Trade Dollar, PR64

1981 1881 PR64 NGC. Great depths of mirrored reflectivity are observed in the obverse and reverse fields. The central devices are richly frosted, allowing for noteworthy cameo contrast. Freckles of russet patina are noted on each side, primarily near the peripheries. A late proof-only issue in the Trade dollar series. (#7061)

Gem Proof 1881 Trade Dollar

1982 1881 PR65 PCGS. Pale heather and iridescent toning grace both sides of this delightful Gem proof. Mintages of the proof-only trade dollars from 1881 to 1883 were each slightly lower than the similarly dated Morgan dollars in proof. Pieces were sold individually, as well as part of complete proof sets, although some collectors preferred proof sets that only included the Morgan dollar. *From The Beau Clerc Collection.* (#7061)

Stunning PR65 Cameo 1881 Trade Dollar

1983 1881 PR65 Cameo NGC. This is a brilliant Gem proof with excellent cameo contrast and bright silver surfaces. All of the design detail on both sides is fully defined, just as William Barber intended when he first created the design nearly a decade earlier. The proof-only Trade dollars are highly popular among type collectors today. Census: 13 in 65 Cameo, 25 finer (8/07). (#87061)

Exceptional 1881 Trade Dollar, PR65 Cameo

1984 1881 PR65 Cameo PCGS. Lavender, electric-blue, and golden-tan patination concentrates at the peripheries of this Gem proof Cameo, leaving the centers coated with a thin veneer of champagne-gold. Spectacular mirrored fields highlight frosted design elements that have benefited from a powerful strike. No significant blemishes can be discerned under high magnification. Indeed, some might argue that this piece was assigned a conservative numerical grade. Population: 18 in 65 Cameo, 9 finer (8/07). (#87061)

1985 1882 PR62 PCGS. This proof-only representative exhibits irregular pastel golden-gray patina on the obverse, and deep smoky gray color on the reverse. Sharply struck, with no significant marks. *From The Beau Clerc Collection.* (#7062)

Desirable 1882 Trade Dollar, PR63

1986 1882 PR63 PCGS. This is a lovely proof trade dollar with sharp design details and hints of cameo contrast. The obverse has light gray color and the reverse is toned deeper grayish-brown. A few grade-consistent hairlines are visible but insignificant. The auction should provide an opportunity to balance quality and price. (#7062)

1987 1882 PR61 Cameo PCGS. Peripheral steel and gold color follow the obverse and reverse borders with light gray mirrors and lustrous white devices. Excellent contrast with minor hairlines and contact marks. (#87062)

Choice Cameo Proof 1882 Trade Dollar

1988 1882 PR64 Cameo PCGS. Lovely golden-brown toning deepens near the rims, which also display ruby-red and forest-green patina. The smooth fields are flashy, and the devices are expertly impressed. An exquisite example of this eagerly pursued proof-only date. Population: 24 in 64 Cameo, 8 finer (8/07). (#87062)

Flashy PR64 Cameo 1882 Trade Dollar

1989 1882 PR64 Cameo NGC. This beautiful proof-only Trade dollar threatens an Ultra Cameo designation, since the frost is seamless throughout the exactingly struck devices. The flashy fields possess a few faint hairlines upon examination beneath a loupe. Census: 30 in 64 Cameo, 35 finer (7/07). (#87062)

Cameo Gem Proof 1882 Trade Dollar

1990 1882 PR65 Cameo PCGS. Ex: Hesselgesser. Lush orange, rose-red, and ocean-blue toning invigorates this exactly struck and unabraded Gem. The devices and legends exhibit consistent frost. The proof-only 1882 is typically seen in PR62 to PR64 grades. Gems are scarce, particularly with significant cameo contrast. Population: 4 in 65 Cameo, 4 finer (8/07). (#87062)

Choice Proof-Only 1883 Trade Dollar

1991 1883 PR64 NGC. Close to a Cameo designation, since the motifs exhibit even and moderate frost. Delicate gold toning prevents full brilliance. This is an intricately struck and attractive near-Gem with only a few stray field hairlines to preclude an even finer grade. By 1883, the Trade dollar had finally found popularity, at least among collectors as a proof-only issue. (#7063)

Impressive 1883 Trade Dollar, PR67 Cameo

1992 1883 PR67 Cameo NGC. This delightful Superb Gem 1883 Trade dollar concludes this notable run of high-grade proof Trade dollars from late in the series. The 1883 is, of course, the final collectible issue of the series, although a few examples are known dated 1884 and 1885. By 1883 the proof emission had once again dropped beneath 1,000 pieces, specifically to 979 recorded coins. This exquisite Superb Gem displays impressive cameo contrast. The obverse has faint lavender toning, while the reverse is fully brilliant, with deeper contrast. A well executed strike brings out sharp detail, and both sides are impeccably preserved. Census: 12 in 67 Cameo, 0 finer (7/07). (#87063)

End of Session Two

SESSION THREE

Live, Internet, and Mail Bid Signature Auction #446
Friday, September 28, 2007, 9:30 AM PT, Lots 1993-2297
Long Beach, California

A 15% Buyer's Premium ($9 minimum) Will Be Added To All Lots

Visit HA.com to view full-color images and bid.

ERRORS

1993 1863 Indian Cent—Struck 70% Off Center—MS64 NGC. Off center toward 12 o'clock with the date intact and most of the shield present. This light brown Civil War cent displays the expected minor planchet abrasions on its unstruck portion.

15% Off Center 1864 Cent MS63
Scarce Bronze L on Ribbon Variety

1994 1864 L On Ribbon Indian Cent—Struck 15% Off Center—MS63 Brown NGC. Off center toward 6 o'clock, but most of the date is intact. A broad area of unstruck surface dominates the upper obverse and lower reverse. A mark-free and satiny golden-brown Civil War cent with minor buildup near ONE CENT. The L on Ribbon variety is much scarcer than its No L counterpart.

1995 1865 Fancy 5 Indian Cent—Struck 5% Off Center on a Type One Planchet—MS63 Brown PCGS. Off center toward 12 o'clock, with the design intact aside from several denticles. A wide band of unstruck surface near 6 o'clock gives the piece a broadstruck appearance. Deep lavender, gold, and forest-green toning embraces the smooth and shimmering surfaces.

1996 1901 Indian Cent—Struck 10% Off Center—AU58 PCGS. Off center toward 1 o'clock with a broad unstruck area centered at 7 o'clock. Ruby-red and apple-green toning embraces this briefly circulated mint error. Unabraded save for a hair-thin mark beneath ONE.

1997 1902 Indian Cent—Off Center—MS61 NGC. Struck approximately 20% off center toward 2 o'clock. A chocolate-brown mint error with hints of steel-blue on the device highpoints. The fields are unabraded, while the jaw and neck each display a thin, faint mark.

1998 1902 Indian Cent—Off Center—MS62 Brown ANACS. Struck about 15% off center toward 3 o'clock. Portions of UNITED STATES are off the flan. Toned in iridescent lime-green and tan hues. Crisply struck and essentially unabraded.

1999 1904 Indian Cent—Struck 10% Off Center—MS63 Brown PCGS. Off center toward 7:30 with only a few dentils off the flan, although UNITED and the upper left shield tip are nearly against the edge. A sharply defined chocolate-brown cent with smooth surfaces save for faint marks within the O in ONE and the C in CENT.

2000 1908-? Indian Cent—Struck 20% Off Center—MS61 Brown NGC. Off center toward 1 o'clock, with the mintmark area off the flan. Most of STATES OF is also absent. The chocolate-brown surfaces are smooth and satiny, and carbon is insignificant.

Double Struck 1918 Cent AU58
Second Strike 85% Off Center

2001 1918 Lincoln Cent—Double Struck, 2nd Strike 85% Off Center—AU58 NGC. The first strike is normal, and the second strike is 85% off center toward 10 o'clock, at 8 o'clock relative to the first strike. No additional planchet was fed between the dies for the second strike. A lustrous and bold example with pleasing blended golden-brown and apple-green toning.

Undated Struck Cent Fragment
With Lincoln Memorial Design, MS62

2002 Undated Lincoln Memorial Cent—Struck Fragment—MS62 Red and Brown NGC. Bronze or brass. 0.52 gm. This undated copper-orange and mahogany error displays much of LIBERTY and Lincoln's profile on the obverse, though the date is missing. A number of abrasions appear at the left obverse, though the surfaces display no trace of wear. An enticing and undeniably interesting piece.

2003 Undated Lincoln Memorial Cent—16% Ragged End Clip—MS63 Red and Brown PCGS. This bronze or brass cent, mahogany with distinct brick-red, pink, and orange overtones, has a void that affects much of the right obverse rim. The planchet was punched overlapping the ragged end of the planchet strip. The void affects the area where the last two digits of the date and the mintmark would be.

1980 Cent on a 1980-P Dime MS66

2004 **1980 Lincoln Cent—Struck on a 1980-P Dime—MS66 NGC.** The dime date and mintmark are legible at 10 o'clock relative to the cent strike. The cent date is bold. Roosevelt's inverted bust outlines the portrait of Lincoln. The flame of the torch reaches the E in ONE. Lustrous and lightly toned with an unabraded appearance.

2005 **1986 Lincoln Cent—Struck on a Struck 1986 Dime—MS65 NGC.** Areas of peach and silver-white converge on this double-denomination piece. While the dates of the Lincoln impression and the Roosevelt undertype are interrupted, all four digits of each are legible. A carefully preserved, dramatic error.

2006 **Undated Lincoln Cent—Struck on a 1990 Struck Dime—MS62 ANACS.** Though only the first two digits are visible on the Lincoln overtype, the visible date on the Roosevelt undertype gives a strong sense of where and when this error was minted. Delicate apricot patina drapes the lustrous surfaces.

1991 Cent Struck on a 1991-P Dime MS67

2007 **1991 Lincoln Cent—Struck on a 1991-P Dime—MS67 NGC.** Potent luster sweeps this exciting double denomination error. About 80% of the cent date and dime mintmark are bold, and about 75% of the dime date is discernible. Roosevelt faces south-southwest relative to the portrait of Lincoln. The obverse edge is nicked at 3:30, as made.

Gem 1996 Cent on a 1996-P Dime

2008 **1996 Lincoln Cent—Struck on a 1996-P Dime—MS65 ANACS.** The final two digits of the cent date are clear, as is the dime mintmark. The dime date is faint but readable near the U in UNITED. Roosevelt gazes northeast relative to the Lincoln Memorial. The flame of the torch flickers behind Lincoln's shoulder. Lustrous and lightly toned.

2009 **Undated (?) Lincoln Memorial Cent—Struck on a Struck Dime, Corroded—ANACS. MS60 Details.** Though ANACS has certified this piece as undated, fragments of a final 9 are visible on the Lincoln obverse overtype, and on the other side, the Roosevelt obverse undertype shows a distinct P mintmark and fragments of digits that appear to form '199,' which would suggest a 1999-P origin, a date for which a number of double-denomination cents are known. Areas of corrosion at the upper obverse and left reverse account for the details grade.

Multiple Error 1999 Cent MS66 Red Double Struck, 95% Obverse Indent

2010 **1999 Lincoln Cent—Double Struck, Second Strike 95% Obverse Indent—MS66 Red NGC.** The first strike was normal, but the piece clung to the reverse die instead of being rejected. The second strike is a broadstrike, with a newly fed planchet (not included) between the obverse die and the present piece. This planchet caused a 95% obverse indent, expanding and distorting the portrait of Lincoln from the first strike. The reverse is cup-shaped from a partial wrapping about the reverse die.

XF45 Liberty Nickel With Full Obverse Brockage

2011 **Undated With Cents Liberty Nickel—Full Late Stage Brockage—XF45 PCGS.** This partly lustrous slate-gray Liberty nickel has a normal reverse. The obverse shows an incused, reversed, and distorted impression of the reverse, as made. A previously struck nickel (not included) clung to the obverse die (as an obverse die cap), and its reverse served as a die to a series of newly fed planchets, one of which became the present coin. The reverse of the die cap became blurry and distorted as the strikes progressed.

1905 Liberty Nickel With 10% Curved Clip AU55

2012 **1905 Liberty Nickel—10% Curved Clip—AU55 NGC.** The obverse has a curved clip from 12:30 to 2 o'clock. The Blakesley effect is apparent, with considerable weakness on the obverse rim near 7:30, but only minor incompleteness on the rim above the ST in STATES. This satiny nickel has chestnut and dove-gray toning. A small but interesting spoon-shaped flaw is present on Liberty's cheek.

Gem Off Center 1919 Buffalo Nickel

2013 **1919 Buffalo Nickel—Struck 5% Off Center—MS65 PCGS.** Moderately off center toward 11:30. All design elements are intact, but each side has a broad area of unstruck surface, widest near 5 o'clock on the obverse. Beautifully toned in dusky golden-tan and luminous powder-blue, gold, lime, and violet-red.

2014 **1935-? Buffalo Nickel—20% Straight Clip—MS64 NGC.** A straight clip from 10 o'clock to 12:30 prevents the mintmark (if any) from appearing on the lower reverse. A satiny cream-gray and chestnut-tan nickel with the expected softness of strike on the eagle's front leg.

2015 **Mated Pair of 1944-P Jefferson Nickel Split Halves, AU55 ANACS.** Consecutively numbered holders. This dramatic error occurred when the planchet split after striking. The obverse half shows a ghostly negative image of Jefferson, while the reverse half exhibits a positive image. Dusky patina overall with excellent views of the interiors. (Total: 2 coins)

2016 **1957 Jefferson Nickel—On a Cent Planchet—MS63 Red and Brown ANACS.** Slightly uncentered toward 3 o'clock, with about 50% of the date visible. The devices are toned steel-blue and violet, and the fields are pumpkin-orange. Lustrous and mark-free.

2017 **1978 Jefferson Nickel—Struck on a Cent Planchet—MS64 PCGS**, softly detailed with warm violet and olive patina; and a **1962 Franklin Half—Obverse Planchet Lamination—AU50 PCGS**, a lightly worn piece, silver-gray with splashes of brick-red and plum, that shows a wide diagonal lamination that encompasses the truncation of the bust. (Total: 2 coins)

12% Off Center 1873 Arrows Dime AU55

2018 **1873 Arrows Dime—Struck 12% Off Center—AU55 PCGS.** Struck off-center toward 2:00. As rare as Seated Liberty errors are (in all denominations), they are obviously rarer still within the short-lived Arrows design type. This is a partly lustrous piece with attractive peripheral toning and just a trace of wear on the highest design points. Sharply struck including prominent clash marks on both sides.

Broadstruck Choice AU 1904-S Dime

2019 **1904-S Barber Dime—Broadstruck—AU55 NGC.** An uncentered broadstrike with a large lip of unstruck surface widest at 6 o'clock. Untoned and partly lustrous with a pair of minor marks on the cheekbone. The 1904-S is scarce in AU, broadstruck or not, due to its low mintage of 800,000 pieces.

Mercury Dime Adjustment Strike AU55

2020 **Undated Mercury Dime—Die Adjustment Strike—AU55 PCGS.** Only ghostly outlines of the central devices are visible on this fascinating adjustment strike. Smooth aside from a hair-thin mark near Liberty's chin. Silver-gray, orange, rose, and violet-charcoal patina adds to the eye appeal.

Undated Mercury Dime—Struck Off-Center
With Blank Obverse—AU58 PCGS

2021 Undated Mercury Dime—Struck Off-Center With Blank Obverse—AU58 PCGS. A surprising error that likely resulted when two planchets were fed into the dies at the same time, slightly off-center. The other planchet shielded this piece from the obverse die, though the other side received an impression from the reverse die. While this lightly rubbed example would not qualify as Full Bands, the strike is sharp, and only a touch of patina is present in the lightly marked fields.

MS63 Roosevelt Dime Error
Flipover Double Struck on a Silver Planchet

2022 Undated Roosevelt Dime—Flipover Double Strike on a Silver Fragment—MS63 PCGS. 11 grains. A small fragment of a silver planchet found its way into the coining dies. Upon striking, the fragment momentarily adhered to one of the dies and subsequently flipped over and did not eject, thus receiving another blow of the press. This resulted in both obverse and reverse details being visible on each side. Fully brilliant and highly lustrous, a highly unusual error coin.

Undated Silver S-Mint Roosevelt Dime
Struck Fragment, MS62

2023 Undated San Francisco Silver Dime—Struck Fragment—MS62 NGC. Whispers of pink, orange, and silver-gray patina visit the unworn surfaces of this roughly wedge-shaped struck fragment. While no part of the date is visible, an 'S' mintmark is present just to the left of the torch. An intriguing error piece that hails from somewhere in the decade from 1946 to 1955.

FS-801 DDR 1970 Dime MS62
Struck on a Philippines Sentimo Planchet

2024 1970 Roosevelt Dime—On an Aluminum Philippines Sentimo Planchet—MS62 PCGS. FS-801, formerly FS-020.6. UNITED STATES OF is nicely die doubled. *Cherrypickers'* calls this variety "extremely rare." Perhaps the only example from these dies struck on an aluminum Philippines sentimo planchet. (The U.S. Mint struck Philippines sentimos, KM-196, in 1970.) The fields are prooflike, and the obverse rim is prominently raised (and abraded) between 5 and 9 o'clock.

2025 Undated Washington Quarter—Struck on a Silver Dime Planchet—MS64 PCGS. Surprisingly well-centered with most of the central devices visible, though the planchet was too small to reach the date. The void below the bow of the wreath establishes this silver-planchet piece as a Philadelphia product. Shining with minimal patina.

2026 1967 Washington Quarter—Struck on a Cent Planchet—MS63 Brown NGC. 3.1 grams. Deep reddish-turquoise toning covers the surfaces of this wrong planchet error. Uncentered toward 10 o'clock with the right side of the obverse and reverse complete. Most of the date is also present.

2027 1967 Washington Quarter—On a Dime Planchet—MS63 ANACS. A lustrous and lightly toned sky-blue and gold example. Uncentered toward 12 o'clock with LIBERTY and the denomination off the flan. Struck from worn dies, a secondary mint error.

Obverse Cud on SMS Quarter MS64

2028 Undated (1965 to 1967) Washington Quarter—Obverse Cud Die Break—SMS MS64 PCGS. Type Three Reverse with leaf tip very close to the A in DOLLAR. This Special Mint Set quarter has satin luster and unabraded pearl-gray surfaces, but is noteworthy for its dramatic die break or "cud" on the lower obverse. The die break consumes all but a sliver of the date, and metal flow into the break weakens TES OF AM on the reverse, directly opposite the cud.

2000-P Maryland Quarter MS64
Struck on a Clad Dime Planchet

2029 **2000-P Maryland Statehood Quarter—Struck on Clad Dime Planchet—MS64 PCGS.** THE OLD LINE STATE is complete, as is virtually all of MARYLAND and LIBERTY. The mintmark is near the rim, but identifiable. State quarters struck on dimes are rarely encountered due to improved riddlers, and this lustrous and problem-free example will impress even the jaded error collector.

Amazing Superb Gem 1962-D Franklin Half
Struck on a Nickel Planchet

2030 **1962-D Franklin Half—Struck on a Five Cent Planchet—MS67 NGC.** 5.0 grams. LIBERTY and HALF DOLLAR are off the undersized flan, which is uncentered toward 10 o'clock. Satiny and essentially brilliant with immaculate surfaces. Surprisingly, neither NGC nor PCGS has certified any 1962-D half dollars above the MS66 level, the present mint error excepted (8/07). A desirable wrong planchet combination, especially with such spectacular preservation. (#6683)

1963 Franklin on a Cent Planchet MS64

2031 **1963 Franklin Half—Struck on a Cent Planchet—MS64 Brown PCGS.** Uncentered toward 12 o'clock with LIBERTY and HALF DOLLAR absent. The date is intact, as is the field above the Liberty Bell. The lustrous surfaces are richly patinated olive-green, rose-red, and gold. The bell has a hair-thin diagonal mark, but otherwise a beautifully preserved example of this desirable off-metal combination.

1964 Half on a Quarter Planchet MS65

2032 **1964 Kennedy Half—Struck on a Planchet—MS65 PCGS.** Type Two Reverse. The centering favors the Great Seal, which is intact from the rays to the fletchings. Only the top of Kennedy's head is off the flan. The legends range from partly to fully absent, but 50% of the date is present. Lustrous and lightly toned with clean fields and minor marks above the jaw. A one-year subtype, since the silver alloy was reduced to 40% in 1965.

1964 Half Dollar Capped Die Pair, MS65

2033 **1964 Kennedy Half—Capped Die Set—MS65 PCGS.** Coin one is a uniface die cap with the obverse impression and coin two is a uniface reverse impression. Two planchets entered the coining chamber simultaneously, each planchet receiving an impression from a single die. The obverse half capped the die and continued to strike a few more uniface reverse pieces. Finally, it fell away, and remained with the last reverse piece that it struck. A delightful pair, showing the Mint at its worst. (Total: 2 coins) (#6706)

2034 **Undated 40% Silver Kennedy Half—Struck 55% Off-Center—MS63 NGC.** More than half of the design is missing on this sizable error, with the imprint oriented just south of 9 o'clock on the obverse. The uppermost part of a curved final digit is visible, though the rest of the date and the possible mintmark are not. The surfaces are strongly lustrous with elements of peach and rose. Numerous tiny abrasions appear on the unstruck areas.

Gem Multiple Struck on Scrap Kennedy Half

2035 **19??-? Kennedy Half Dollar—Multiple Struck on Scrap—MS65 PCGS.** 68 gn. The scrap resembles a half dollar planchet irregularly cut in half. It has a copper core thinly plated on both sides with a nickel alloy. This scrap covered the left half of a die pair, and was struck at least twice. For the first strike, only the scrap was present between dies. For the final strike, a newly fed planchet obstructed the obverse die, causing the obverse design of the present piece to expand and distort.

Double Struck, 90% Off Center
1921-S Morgan AU58

2036 **1921-S Morgan Dollar—Double Struck, Second Strike 90% Off Center—AU58 PCGS.** The first strike was normal, but the piece failed to fully eject from the dies, and was struck a second time 90% off center toward 6 o'clock. The second strike is at 6 o'clock relative to the first strike, but the top of the date is apparent, and its status as a 1921-S is confirmed by the minute mintmark and spade-shaped eagle's breast. No additional planchet was fed in between the two strikes. A satiny cream-gray silver dollar with a typical strike and a mere whisper of highpoint friction.

MS64 1999-P Susan B. Anthony Dollar
Struck on a Sacagawea Dollar Planchet

2037 **1999-P Anthony Dollar—Struck on a Sacagawea Dollar Planchet—MS64 PCGS.** A lustrous pale honey-gold off metal error. The silver-colored 1999-D Anthony dollar was struck to fulfill post office demand, since the gold-colored Sacagawea dollar was withheld until 2000. Anthony and Sacagawea production likely overlapped in the second half of 1999.

MS63 2000-P Sacagawea, Struck 15 Times

2038 **2000-P Sacagawea Dollar—Struck 15 Times—MS63 ANACS.** The dies kept coming together, but this stubborn Sacagawea dollar remained in the coinage chamber without the addition of any newly fed planchets. There is a fairly wide spread between the first two strikes, but the remaining strikes are closely spaced. Evidence of each strike, similar in appearance to a tree ring, is present above LIBERTY. The final strike shows mint-caused scraping on the reverse rim between 9 and 12 o'clock.

1901/0-S Five Dollar, MS64
Rare Uncentered Broadstrike

2039 1901/0-S Half Eagle—Uncentered Broadstrike—MS64 Prooflike NGC. The scarcity of gold errors is well known to anyone who has a passing acquaintance with error coinage. The reason is perhaps not as well known. Until 1910, the mint employed "lady adjustors" who weighed every blank and every gold coin. Which means if a gold planchet was underweight it was sent back to be melted and recast into another planchet. If it was overweight, the planchet was filed until it was within the weight tolerance for that denomination. Since theoretically each gold planchet and each gold coin was inspected, it is no wonder so few gold errors exist.

This particular coin is a double error. The date shows a pronounced underdigit beneath the final 1 in the date. These overdates are rare in all grades, and especially so in mint condition. This piece was produced as an uncentered broadstrike—that is, struck with no collar and off center. In this case, there is significant (perhaps 10%) blank flan at the bottom of the obverse and top of the reverse. The fields are bright and prooflike, a feature we have observed on many off-centered coins. Fully struck (another feature seen on many off-center coins), the surfaces show just a hint of reddish patina on each side.

A premium coin for an advanced error set. (#78403)

COMMEMORATIVE SILVER

2040 1893 Isabella Quarter MS63 PCGS. A strongly lustrous Select example that has better-than-average detail, evidenced by the unbroken line of the thread on the reverse. Hints of sky-blue and lemon-gold patina grace the fields. (#9220)

2041 1893 Isabella Quarter MS64 PCGS. A brilliant and boldly struck Choice Isabella with clean fields and potent luster. The mintage of 24,214 pieces is only a fraction of the 1.55 million pieces coined for the 1893 Columbian half. (#9220)

2042 1893 Isabella Quarter MS64 PCGS. Pleasing preservation and uncommonly strong detail are the prime draws of this attractive Isabella quarter. Subtle luster shines beneath warm rose, amber, and violet patina. A great representative of this early classic commemorative. (#9220)

2043 1893 Isabella Quarter MS64 PCGS. The thick mint luster shines forcefully through the layers of gray, blue, and rose toning seen on each side. Kept from an even higher grade by the presence of a shallow (but long) mark in the left reverse field. (#9220)

2044 1893 Isabella Quarter MS64 NGC. The level of detail on this Choice commemorative quarter is significantly above-average, and both sides display excellent luster. Whispers of apricot patina visit the margins. Minimally marked with great eye appeal, though a luster graze in the left obverse field precludes a finer grade. (#9220)

2045 1893 Isabella Quarter MS64 PCGS. Sharply struck and intensely lustrous, with lovely rose peripheral toning on both sides. The surfaces are impressively preserved and only show a few trivial field marks. A high-end example from the first date of American commemorative coinage.
From The Beau Clerc Collection. (#9220)

Beautiful Gem 1893 Isabella Quarter

2046 1893 Isabella Quarter MS65 NGC. This splendid Gem provides potent luster and a penetrating strike. A whisper of marigold toning denies full brilliance. The preservation is exemplary. The Isabella quarter is rare in comparison with the other Columbian Exposition type, the Columbus half. (#9220)

Pretty 1893 Isabella Quarter MS67

2047 1893 Isabella Quarter MS67 NGC. A lovely example of this popular early issue. This piece has layers of olive-green, rose, and golden patina over the bright mint frost that glows over each side. The toning is not overpowering and adds a delicate look to the coin. Dazzling cartwheel sheen illuminates the carefully preserved fields. The strike is sufficiently sharp that both sides exhibit a wire rim. Census: 40 in 67, 9 finer (7/07). (#9220)

2048 1900 Lafayette Dollar MS62 NGC. DuVall 1-B. Delicate almond-gold toning graces this satiny and nicely struck commemorative dollar. Few marks are present, given the third party grade. *From The Diemer L. Fife Collection.* (#9222)

2049 1900 Lafayette Dollar MS63 PCGS. DuVall 1-B. Lustrous and lightly toned with a pleasing strike and a smooth obverse. Light abrasions appear on the field near the statue. (#9222)

2050 1900 Lafayette Dollar MS63 ANACS. Variety 2-C. This issue honors General Lafayette, who voluntarily traveled from France at age 19 to join the American Revolution, and served ably on the staff of George Washington. This Select example is well struck and lightly toned, showing gold-gray color with attractive russet and forest-green peripheral accents. Surface marks are minimal for the grade. (#9222)

2051 1900 Lafayette Dollar MS63 PCGS. Variety 1-B. Boldly detailed with lovely red-orange peripheral toning on each side. Faint die polish lines are noticeable in the reverse fields. On the obverse, several small dark-green spots are noted, along with some wispy contact marks on George Washington's cheek. A Select Mint State example of the first American commemorative silver dollar issue. (#9222)

Clean, Upper-End MS64 1900 Lafayette Dollar

2052 1900 Lafayette Dollar MS64 PCGS. DuVall 1-B. On this variety, the leaf on the reverse points between the 1 and 9 in the date, and on the obverse the A in DOLLAR is low and leans left. For an early commemorative, the surfaces are uncommonly clean. Close examination with a magnifier shows a few minor imperfections, but these are subdued almost into invisibility by the even, deep gray toning that covers each side. Strong mint luster also underlies the toning. (#9222)

Satiny MS64 1900 Lafayette Dollar

2053 1900 Lafayette Dollar MS64 PCGS. DuVall 1-B. Just the slightest hint of toning is seen on the obverse and there is none on the reverse. This brightness allows the satiny mint luster to shine on each side. A remarkably clean coin with just a few minor abrasions present, the only one that is visible without a magnifier is on the highpoint of Washington's cheek. (#9222)

Choice Mint State 1900 Lafayette Dollar

2054 1900 Lafayette Dollar MS64 PCGS. DuVall 1-B. A pleasing Mint State example, this Choice representative has delicate olive and steel toning on both sides. Most of the obverse design is sharply defined, and the reverse has slight weakness on the seated figure. The Lafayette design is the only silver dollar commemorative produced prior to the modern era. (#9222)

MS64 1900 Lafayette Dollar, Variety 2-C

2055 1900 Lafayette Dollar MS64 NGC. DuVall 2-C. Varieties 1-B and 2-C are the common varieties of the Lafayette dollar as described by Frank DuVall. This piece is a lovely Choice Mint State example with sharp details and satiny brilliance, accented by pale gold toning on both sides. (#9222)

2056 1921 Alabama MS64 PCGS. An exceptionally bright and highly lustrous Alabama half. There are minor abrasions present which account for the less-than-Gem grade. A lovely example with eye appeal far in excess of the stated grade. (#9224)

2057 1921 Alabama MS65 PCGS. Wisps of silver-gray patina grace the margins of this otherwise untoned Alabama half, design by Laura Gardin Fraser. Well struck with soft luster and only a handful of isolated marks that are consistent with the grade. (#9224)

2058 1921 Alabama MS65 NGC. An amazing example of this popular early commemorative with frosty silver luster that is accented by pale gold toning. (#9224)

2059 1921 Alabama 2x2 MS64 PCGS. The obverse of this well struck piece is luminous and silver-gray, while the reverse has slightly lighter color and stronger luster. A well-preserved and pleasing representative of this low-mintage Alabama variant, distinguished by a small, incuse 2x2 in the right obverse field. (#9225)

2060 1921 Alabama 2x2 MS64 NGC. Rich, attractive golden-russet toning is seen over each side, but is considerably deeper in hue around the devices. Strong underlying mint luster, a common trait on most MS64 and finer Alabama halves. *From The Diemer L. Fife Collection.* (#9225)

2061 1921 Alabama 2x2 MS65 NGC. Ex: Foxfire. Khaki-gold and sky-blue adorn this shimmering and sharply struck Gem. Only 6,000 pieces were struck of the 2x2 variety, discounting the six pieces destined for assay. (#9225)

Lovely Toned 1921 Alabama 2x2 Half, MS66

2062 1921 Alabama 2x2 MS66 PCGS. Frosty surfaces, sharp details, and lovely gold toning with peripheral iridescence are the characteristics that make this Premium Gem so desirable. Only a few finer examples have been graded by PCGS to date. This is an important opportunity for the Set Registry collector or the connoisseur. Population: 65 in 66, 5 finer (8/07). (#9225)

Pleasing MS66 1921 Alabama 2x2 Half

2063 1921 Alabama 2x2 MS66 PCGS. Although dated 1921, the Alabama half commemorated a centennial that occurred in 1919. Only 6,006 coins were struck with the special 2x2 notation in the right obverse field with another 64,000 coins struck with a "plain" field. This is an attractive, highly lustrous example that has golden-rose toning over each side, more evenly spread over the reverse and more concentrated around the margin on the obverse. Population: 65 in 66, 5 finer (8/07).
From The Beau Clerc Collection. (#9225)

2064 1936 Albany MS67 NGC. A tab-toned beauty with original orange-red and sea-green patina. Scintillating luster rolls across the unperturbed fields and devices. As of (7/07), NGC has certified just seven pieces finer. (#9227)

2065 1936 Albany MS67 NGC. The reverse exhibits gold, russet, and pearl-gray tab toning, and the obverse displays variegated honey, russet, and battleship-gray patina. A wonderful Superb Gem exemplar of this local-interest silver commemorative. NGC has graded just seven finer pieces (8/07). (#9227)

2066 1937 Antietam MS65 NGC. The obverse of this luminous Gem is gray-gold, while the reverse's patina is closer to tan. A solidly struck representative of this Civil War issue, carefully preserved with a solitary mark at McClellan's brow. (#9229)

2067 1937 Antietam MS66 PCGS. Beautifully radiant luster glistens over each side of this Premium Gem Antietam half dollar. Well struck with bright surfaces that only show a trace amount of terra cotta toning on the lower half of the obverse. The Battle of Antietam was one of the bloodiest battles of the Civil War. (#9229)

2068 1937 Antietam MS67 PCGS. Dappled khaki-gold, rose, and aqua shades enrich the peripheries of this lustrous Superb Gem. Exceptional aside from a nearly imperceptible hairline to the left of Grant's ear. Housed in a green label holder. (#9229)

2069 1935-D Arkansas MS66 PCGS. This satiny Premium Gem offers better detail than the typical representative of this D-mint issue. Soft blue-gray patina graces much of the surfaces, while the margins have splashes of orange and gold. (#9234)

Tied for Finest at PCGS 1936-D Arkansas, MS67

2070 1936-D Arkansas MS67 PCGS. A Superb Gem specimen with highly lustrous surfaces beneath pale heather and iridescent toning. This piece is tied for the finest certified by PCGS, and it survives from a mintage of less than 10,000 coins. Population: 18 in 67, 0 finer (8/07). (#9238)

2071 1936-S Arkansas MS66 NGC. Delicate ice-blue and lavender patina graces both sides of this S-mint Arkansas half, and the upper reverse periphery shows elements of gold-orange as well. Solidly struck and carefully preserved. Census: 55 in 66, 4 finer (7/07). (#9239)

2072 1937-S Arkansas MS66 PCGS. The Arkansas is one of the most challenging type coins in the commemorative series. However, the 1937-S is one of the more available issues in this difficult type. The bright, satiny mint luster shines forcefully through the rose and lilac toning seen over each side. Sharply struck also. Population: 53 in 66, 3 finer (8/07). (#9243)

2073 1937 Arkansas PDS Set MS66 PCGS. The set includes: **1937**, a satiny silver-gray piece with hints of olive and cobalt-blue at the rims; **1937-D**, lilac-inflected, softly lustrous surfaces that exhibit deep dots of violet at the margins; and a **1937-S**, delicate gold-gray tints overall with zones of seal-gray and charcoal, primarily at the peripheries. (Total: 3 coins) (#9244)

2074 1938 Arkansas MS66 PCGS. By 1938, the distributors of the Arkansas halves were pandering to a collapsed market, and the net mintage for the Philadelphia issue amounted to just 3,156 pieces. This silver-gray Premium Gem has soft luster, pleasing detail, and a thin band of orange patina at the obverse and reverse rims. PCGS has certified just seven finer examples (7/07). (#9245)

2075 1938 Arkansas MS66 PCGS. The predominantly silver-gray surfaces of this Premium Gem have an undercurrent of orange that is readily apparent at the reverse periphery. A well-defined example of this Arkansas issue, which has a low mintage worthy of note. Population: 69 in 66, 7 finer (7/07). (#9245)

2076 1939-D Arkansas MS66 NGC. The surfaces are predominantly silver-gray with a measure of orange patina near the rims. An intricately struck and beautifully preserved Premium Gem. Certified in a prior generation holder. Census: 29 in 66, 7 finer (7/07). (#9250)

2077 1935/34 Boone MS67 NGC. Unlike its mintmarked counterparts, the 1935/34 is one of the more available Boone pieces, as it has a five-figure mintage. This well struck, shining piece has areas of tan and sage at the periphery, while the centers are silver-gray. NGC has certified no numerically finer examples, while PCGS has graded just two (8/07). (#9262)

2078 1935/34-D Boone MS66 PCGS. Pristine save for a single mark on Boone's jaw and a few tiny ticks and the frontiersman's lower legs. The luminous surfaces have soft powder-blue toning overall with elements of rose and gold. An attractive example of the lowest-mintage silver classic commemorative issue, one of only 2,003 pieces struck. (#9263)

2079 1935/34-D Boone MS67 NGC. A boldly struck silver-white Superb Gem representative of this issue, famous or possibly notorious as the lowest-mintage classic silver commemorative. The surfaces are carefully preserved, as demanded of the grade. NGC has certified just five finer examples (8/07). (#9263)

Superb Gem 1936 Bridgeport Half Dollar

2080 1936 Bridgeport MS67 PCGS. The obverse of this Superb Gem has satiny luster with subtle reflectivity in the fields and the reverse has frosty luster. Faint champagne and gold toning appears on each side. This example, in a green-label PCGS holder, is tied for the finest certified. Population: 59 in 67, 0 finer (8/07). (#9279)

Iridescent MS67 1936 Bridgeport Half

2081 1936 Bridgeport MS67 PCGS. Deep iridescent toning is splashed on both sides of this Superb Gem Bridgeport half dollar. For the connoisseur who appreciates the finest, this piece is unimprovable, being tied for the best PCGS has certified Population: 59 in 67, 0 finer (8/07). (#9279)

2082 1925-S California MS65 PCGS. Champagne and antique-gold patina graces the margins of this California Diamond Jubilee commemorative, while the centers are largely untoned. A boldly struck and shining Gem. (#9281)

2083 1925-S California MS65 NGC. A well-defined Gem that shines beneath silver-gray patina with charcoal peripheral accents. Though the California commemorative was the only coin design credit for sculptor Jo Mora, it remains one of his most popular and widely admired works. (#9281)

2084 1925-S California MS65 PCGS. A flashy and nearly brilliant Gem with a remarkably clean appearance. UNUM is softly brought up, but the remainder of the design is sharply struck. Certified in a green label holder. (#9281)

2085 1925-S California MS66 PCGS. A thoroughly lustrous and virtually unabraded Premium Gem. Plum-red and golden-brown freckles grace the lower obverse. Encased in a green label holder. (#9281)

Spectacular Superb Gem 1925-S California Half

2086 1925-S California MS67 NGC. Swirls of lime-green, violet-blue, and gold patina graces the strongly lustrous surfaces of this California commemorative. The strike is solid, and the visual appeal is strong. This was one of the first issues to recruit local talent for this time, in this case the noted sculptor Jo Mora. NGC has graded only 12 numerically finer pieces (7/07). (#9281)

2087 1936-D Cincinnati MS66 PCGS. The satiny surfaces are attractively toned in subtle pastel shadings on the obverse, while the reverse shows irregular patches of russet color. A clean and appealing high-grade type coin. (#9284)

2088 1936 Cincinnati PDS Set MS64 to MS65 PCGS. A consecutively numbered set that includes: **1936 MS64**, lightly toned and kept from Gem status by a cluster of marks in the upper left reverse field; **1936-D MS65**, colorful reddish-orange toning lines much of the reverse border; and **1936-S MS65**, relatively smooth beneath delicate golden patina. (Total: 3 coins) (#9286)

MS67 1936 Cleveland Half Dollar

2089 1936 Cleveland MS67 PCGS. The issue depicts Moses Cleaveland, of the Connecticut Land Company, which bought more than 3 million acres of land in northeastern Ohio. Creamy-smooth surfaces are softly patinated with dove-gray and deeper splashes of lime-gold and deep crimson toning about the obverse margin. (#9288)

2090 1936-S Columbia MS67 NGC. A splendid example that displays speckled charcoal-brown and forest-green patina near the peripheries. Satiny with a sharp strike and beautifully preserved surfaces. A notable example of this city-celebration design; NGC has graded just six finer representatives (7/07). (#9293)

2091 1892 Columbian MS65 PCGS. FS-301. The peak of the 2 is repunched. The nicest of the three repunched date varieties listed in the fourth edition, Volume 2 of the *Cherrypickers' Guide.* Rich golden-brown, powder-blue, and plum-red toning adorns this satiny and suitably struck Gem. (#9296)

2092 1892 Columbian MS66 PCGS. Cobalt-blue and lavender patination hugs the peripheries of this highly lustrous Columbian, the nation's first silver commemorative. Decisively impressed motifs enhance the coin's eye appeal, and the surfaces are impeccably preserved. PCGS has certified just nine coins finer (8/07). (#9296)

2093 1893 Columbian MS65 NGC. Exquisitely toned in bands of aquamarine, butter-gold, ruby-red, and powder-blue. Nicely struck and moderately abraded. The reverse has prominent cartwheel sheen. (#9297)

2094 **1893 Columbian MS65 PCGS.** Along with the Isabella quarter, the Columbian half dollar was one of the first American commemorative coins, struck in conjunction with the enormous Columbian Exposition held in Chicago. Boldly struck and highly lustrous, with light golden-gray toning and few surface marks. (#9297)

2095 **1893 Columbian MS66 PCGS.** Pieces from this second year of issue are seldom located in MS66 condition. The obverse has the typical reddish-brown patina and is surrounded by blue at the margin. The reverse is mostly brilliant with a slight accent of golden at the perimeter. Highly lustrous. PCGS has graded just seven coins finer (7/07). (#9297)

2096 **1893 Columbian MS66 NGC.** Golden-brown and sea-green colors consume the borders, while the radiant centers have pearl-gray color. A splendidly preserved and gorgeous Premium Gem example of the second American silver commemorative issue. (#9297)

2097 **1893 Columbian MS66 PCGS.** Swirling blue-green and violet patina graces the softly lustrous obverse, while the mostly untoned reverse has similar colors in a crescent at the top. Well struck with surprisingly clean surfaces. The 1893 Columbian was the first classic commemorative with a mintage of over a million pieces. (#9297)

2098 **1893 Columbian MS66 PCGS.** Columbian halves have a distinctive palette of colors. They are usually seen with gray-blue centers and iridescently toned peripheries, as seen on this piece. This large-production second year of issue has strong mint luster and there are no noticeable marks on either side. (#9297)

Gorgeous 1893 Columbian, MS66

2099 **1893 Columbian MS66 PCGS.** Both sides of this Premium Gem have light silver color at the centers, ringed by outstanding gold, lilac, and blue toning, resulting in excellent eye appeal. While quite a number of these have been certified at this grade level, PCGS has only graded seven finer pieces (8/07). (#9297)

Impeccable 1893 Columbian Half, MS67 ★

2100 **1893 Columbian MS67 ★ NGC.** A Superb Gem with frosty luster and impeccable rainbow iridescence on both sides. This gorgeous Columbian half dollar will easily impress the connoisseur with its high degree of aesthetic appeal. Two finer NGC examples are the only better ones certified, as PCGS has never certified a higher grade piece. Census: 25 in 67, 2 finer (8/07). (#9297)

2101 **1935 Connecticut MS66 NGC.** A wonderful example that showcases the daring, acclaimed composition of Henry Kreis. Well struck with softly lustrous silver-gray surfaces that show narrow bands of orange and magenta patina at the upper and lower obverse. *From The Laguna Niguel Collection, Part Two.* (#9299)

2102 **1935 Connecticut MS66 NGC.** Dappled russet, gold, and purple patination races over the lustrous surfaces of this Premium Gem commemorative. A well executed strike brings out excellent definition on the design elements, and both sides are impeccably preserved. (#9299)

2103 **1935 Connecticut MS66 NGC.** Vivid reddish-orange peripheral toning complements the silver-white centers of this classic commemorative. The well-defined obverse, which features an Art Deco interpretation of the Charter Oak framed by the patina, offers exceptional aesthetic appeal. *From The Diemer L. Fife Collection.* (#9299)

2104 **1935 Connecticut MS66 PCGS.** Apricot toning confirms the originality of this lustrous and evenly struck silver commemorative. The obverse is particularly well preserved. (#9299)

2105 **1936 Delaware MS66 PCGS.** A luminous and well-defined representative of this colonial-history commemorative, olive-gold in the centers with soft sky-blue toning at the margins. A pair of small, shallow marks are noted at the right side of the church. (#9301)

2106 **1936 Delaware MS66 PCGS.** Pale lavender-gray patina covers the lustrous centers, while the periphery has lemon-yellow accents on each side and russet patina on the reverse that suggests tab toning. Minimally marked and pleasing, a lovely example of this commemorative with a Swedish connection. (#9301)

2107 **1936 Gettysburg MS65 NGC.** Clean surfaces, as usual, the satiny mint luster shows just the slightest overlay of golden-lilac toning. A perennial favorite for Civil War-theme collections. *From The Diemer L. Fife Collection.* (#9305)

2108 **1922 Grant no Star MS64 PCGS.** A luminous near-Gem example of this presidential birth centennial issue, silver-gray with reddish-orange patina over large swaths of the obverse and the reverse margins. Minimally marked and attractive. (#9306)

2109 **1922 Grant no Star MS66 PCGS.** Peripheral iridescence enhances the ivory luster of this satiny Premium Gem. The strike is sharper than usual for this issue with virtually full details on both sides. By comparison with other commemorative issues from the early 20th century, the mintage of 67,405 Grant half dollars is rather low, with most survivors in lower Mint State grades, or even lightly circulated. PCGS has only graded 33 finer pieces (8/07). (#9306)

2110 **1922 Grant with Star MS62 NGC.** Boldly struck save for typical softness on Grant's hair, and on the second tree trunk from the left on the reverse. Wispy die polish lines and a few minor slide marks are noted on the obverse. An essentially untoned, Mint State example of this popular commemorative issue. (#9307)

2111 **1922 Grant with Star MS63 PCGS.** This low-mintage Grant variant was actually an accident, as the beneficiaries of the Grant pieces had asked for stars on part of the gold dollar mintage, but not the halves. The Select example offered here is lightly marked overall and luminous beneath green-gold and blue toning on the obverse. The reverse has thinner, paler patina. (#9307)

Dazzling MS64 1922 Grant With Star Half

2112 **1922 Grant with Star MS64 PCGS.** The Grant with Star is one of the undisputed keys to the commemorative half series. Only 4,256 pieces were struck, and an instant rarity was produced in 1922 with the addition of the star. This is a bright, untoned example that has no obvious abrasions, although a few minor field marks can be found with a magnifier. (#9307)

Choice 1922 Grant With Star Half

2113 **1922 Grant with Star MS64 PCGS.** Light golden-tan and red-russet toning confirms the originality of this semi-prooflike and sharply struck near-Gem. The 1922 Grant continued the pattern of the 1921 Missouri and Alabama. Those programs had a low mintage issue with a special symbol, as did the Grant. Only 4,256 pieces were struck with a star above the N in GRANT. Survivors are elusive compared to the No Star variety, of which 67,405 pieces were produced. (#9307)

Original Choice 1928 Hawaiian Half

2114 **1928 Hawaiian MS64 NGC.** Autumn-gold and gunmetal-gray alternate across this satiny and carefully preserved near-Gem. The strike is crisp throughout the design elements. The Hawaiian type is the scarcest in the silver commemorative series, and originally toned pieces are under formidable demand. (#9309)

Lovely 1928 Hawaiian Half MS64

2115 **1928 Hawaiian MS64 PCGS.** Silky luster traverses this minimally abraded near-Gem. The obverse is particularly void of contact. Delicate chestnut-gold and ice-blue toning denies full brilliance. Precisely struck and undeniably desirable, since the Hawaiian is the key to the 50-piece classic silver commemorative type set. (#9309)

Lustrous MS64 1928 Hawaiian Half

2116 **1928 Hawaiian MS64 NGC.** Satiny mint luster races around each side of this impressive near-Gem. Both sides show scattered gray-rose toning, and abrasions are held to a minimum. Long considered a key issue in the commemorative series, Hawaiian halves are difficult to locate in all grades.
From The Diemer L. Fife Collection. (#9309)

Satiny MS64 1928 Hawaiian Half

2117 **1928 Hawaiian MS64 PCGS.** Rather than the greenish patina usually seen on Hawaiian halves, this piece has taken on the more traditional coin colors of rose and lilac on the obverse with a nearly brilliant reverse. Matte-like and sharply defined with no singularly mentionable abrasions.
From The Beau Clerc Collection. (#9309)

Attractively Toned MS65 1928 Hawaiian Half

2118 **1928 Hawaiian MS65 NGC.** Rose, orange, and lime tints enrich this lustrous and crisply struck Gem. The obverse is splendidly preserved, as is the reverse, but close examination will show a couple of minor marks on that side. The Hawaiian is a formidable rarity for any collector who attempts to assemble a type set of silver commemoratives. (#9309)

2119 **1935 Hudson—Cleaned—ANACS. MS60 Details.** An unworn representative of this challenging local-interest issue, well struck with delicate blue, violet, and gold retoning over suspiciously subdued surfaces. Faintly hairlined but appealing nonetheless. (#9312)

2120 **1935 Hudson MS63 NGC.** Powder-blue and sun-gold patina endows this satiny and unmarked low mintage commemorative. A small spot near the left-side flag is the sole detraction. In an older generation holder. (#9312)

2121 1935 Hudson MS64 PCGS. The Hudson half celebrates the sesquicentennial of the founding of Hudson, New York, in 1785. This piece offers dusky amber-gold rims with silvery centers. A few tiny ticks on the devices preclude a Gem grade. (#9312)

2122 1935 Hudson MS64 NGC. The satiny surfaces are bright and essentially untoned. What is most unusual is how clean the figures of Neptune and the narwhale are. A couple of light abrasions are seen on the sails on the reverse, but this coin is actually quite close to a Gem grade.
From The Diemer L. Fife Collection. (#9312)

2123 1935 Hudson MS65 PCGS. Pale caramel-gold and lime toning endows this crisply struck and splendidly smooth Gem. The low-mintage Hudson type is a popular issue that becomes challenging any finer. (#9312)

2124 1935 Hudson MS65 NGC. Creamy luster and pale ivory-gold toning are highlights of this Gem Hudson commemorative half. The surface preservation of the piece is excellent, as expected for the grade. (#9312)

2125 1935 Hudson MS65 PCGS. A touch of softness on the central devices is typical for this low-mintage classic commemorative. Both sides of this luminous Gem exhibit rose, gold, and violet patina of varying thickness. (#9312)

Lightly Toned 1935 Hudson Half Dollar, MS66

2126 1935 Hudson MS66 PCGS. A thin veneer of violet, ice-blue, and golden-tan toning rests upon the radiantly lustrous surfaces of this Premium Gem commemorative half dollar, joined on both sides by occasional freckles of russet. Sharply struck throughout, and possessing just a few obverse milling marks that are consistent with the grade. Housed in a green label holder. (#9312)

Splendid 1935 Hudson Half, MS66

2127 1935 Hudson MS66 PCGS. A satiny and sharply struck example. Splendidly preserved and desirable. The low mintage Hudson is a stopper to a silver commemorative type set. One of the more curious types within the commemorative series, the obverse depicts Neptune riding a whale while facing backward; his emergence from the depths proclaimed by a mermaid blowing a seashell. PCGS has only graded six finer pieces. (#9312)

2128 1918 Lincoln MS66 PCGS. Both sides of this pleasing Premium Gem show strong luster beneath a thin veil of gold-gray patina. This example's bold strike highlights the sculptural qualities of this early commemorative design. (#9320)

2129 1934 Maryland MS67 PCGS. Tied for the finest certified by PCGS (8/07), this frosty, richly toned Superb Gem offers excellent visual appeal. Lavender-gray and olive-gold patina covers most of both sides, while the area below the coat of arms displays a dash of magenta. (#9328)

2130 1921 Missouri MS63 ANACS. The surfaces of this well struck Select example are luminous beneath rich lavender, blue, and green-gold patina. The surfaces show only a few scattered abrasions, though these combine to preclude a finer grade. Still, an appealing representative of this earlier statehood centennial commemorative. (#9330)

2131 1921 Missouri MS64 NGC. Satiny luster and light, speckled bronze patina are present on both sides of this near-Gem, a lovely representative of this often-challenging early commemorative issue. Carefully preserved with minimal marks for the grade. (#9330)

2132 1921 Missouri MS64 PCGS. A blend of bronze and pinkish-gray patina covers both sides of this near-Gem. This attractive statehood centennial commemorative issue was heavily marketed at the state fair in Sedalia, and the town's name appears within the exergue on the reverse. (#9330)

2133 1921 Missouri MS64 PCGS. A beautiful tan-gold and steel-blue piece with a good strike and only moderate contact on the left obverse field. Among the scarcer silver commemorative types. Encapsulated in a green label holder. (#9330)

2134 1921 Missouri MS64 PCGS. Rich layers of lilac, amber-gold, and purple toning adorn the surfaces of this well preserved Missouri commemorative. Boldly struck and free of distracting marks, with pleasing satin luster. (#9330)

2135 1921 Missouri 2★4 MS63 PCGS. A well struck and luminous Select example of this low-mintage Missouri variant, gold-gray with faint tan accents. Light, scattered abrasions on each side account for the grade. (#9331)

2136 1921 Missouri 2★4 MS63 NGC. Select and well struck with a predominantly silver-white obverse and faintly blue-tinged reverse margins. Light, scattered abrasions appear on both sides of this lower-mintage Missouri variant. (#9331)

2137 1921 Missouri 2★4 MS64 PCGS. Deeply toned in shades of charcoal-gray, violet, and forest-green. Pleasing satin luster and boldly defined motifs are evident on each side. The 2★4 variety is a scarce key issue in the silver commemorative series. (#9331)

1921 Missouri 2★4 Half Dollar, MS65

2138 1921 Missouri 2★4 MS65 PCGS. A small incuse 2★4 in the left obverse field tells of Missouri statehood as the 24th of our 50 states, entering the Union in 1821. Varieties were issued with and without this symbol, much to the delight of coin collectors, who now needed two different examples for their collections. This piece has delightful ivory color with soft luster, and accents of peripheral iridescence on the obverse. (#9331)

MS66 Tied for Finest 1921 Missouri 2★4 Half

2139 **1921 Missouri 2★4 MS66 PCGS.** Tied for the finest certified by either NGC or PCGS, this Premium Gem has frosty silver luster with brilliant silver surfaces and traces of pale lilac toning. It has remarkable eye appeal and sharp design features, with strong central obverse and reverse details. Unlike certain other commemoratives of the era, the Missouri Centennial half dollar was actually struck during the centennial year of statehood in 1921. For comparison, the Alabama Centennial half dollar was also struck in 1921, even though Alabama became a state in 1820. Population: 22 in 66, 0 finer (8/07). (#9331)

2140 **1923-S Monroe MS64 PCGS.** Boldly struck with creamy luster and essentially untoned alabaster surfaces. A few superficial luster grazes and pinscratches preclude a finer grade assessment, but this is still an attractive near-Gem example of the popular Monroe commemorative half dollar. (#9333)

Colorful 1923-S Monroe Half, MS65

2141 **1923-S Monroe MS65 PCGS.** Strongly lustrous throughout with streaks of rainbow toning on both the obverse and reverse. The surfaces of this Gem, which comes from a well-known and often-challenging commemorative issue, shows only a handful of tiny flaws. An uncommonly appealing Monroe that would fit well in a similarly graded commemorative type or date set. (#9333)

Enticing Gem 1923-S Monroe Half

2142 **1923-S Monroe MS65 PCGS.** A surprisingly attractive example of the Monroe half dollar, an issue that some have suggested never comes nice. This piece is brilliant in the centers with frosty and highly lustrous silver-white surfaces. The surfaces are surprisingly well-preserved for the grade assigned, and each side exhibits faint peripheral toning. (#9333)

Frosted MS65 1923-S Monroe Half

2143 **1923-S Monroe MS65 PCGS.** The novel reverse design of the Monroe half was based on an 1899 medal by Ralph Beck and used in 1901 for the Pan-American Exposition seal. From a design perspective, this central reverse motif is the most distinctive aspect of these coins. This particular piece shows thick mint luster, and the gray-brilliant centers are surrounded by golden-brown toning. A clean and attractive Gem representative. (#9333)

2144 **1938 New Rochelle MS66 PCGS.** Light almond-gold toning endows this nicely struck and well preserved Premium Gem. A lower mintage type, housed in an old green label holder. (#9335)

2145 **1938 New Rochelle MS66 PCGS.** This pleasingly defined local-interest half has silver-gray centers with thin rose patina and dots of crimson at the margins. Strongly lustrous with excellent visual appeal. (#9335)

2146 **1925 Norse Thin Planchet MS65 NGC.** An honorary commemorative of sorts, the 1925 Norse medal was one of several such non-coin substitutes for the half dollars sought by various petitioners. This carefully preserved Thin Planchet piece is essentially untoned and has excellent detail. (#9451)

2147 **1925 Norse Thin Planchet MS65 PCGS.** Attractive apple-green, honey-gold, and ice-blue toning visits this shimmering and evenly struck Norse medal. Faintly abraded above 1000, and a thin vertical mark is noted beneath the U in UNITED. Population: 21 in 65, 3 finer (7/07). (#9451)

2148 **1926-S Oregon MS67 NGC.** The fine details of Laura Gardin Fraser's beautiful design are crisply brought up on each side of this impressive Oregon Trail commemorative. Mottled green, russet, and rose patina increase the eye appeal of this lustrous, immaculately preserved example. (#9341)

2149 **1928 Oregon MS67 PCGS.** Outstanding quality and eye appeal, as always seen on high grade examples of this inspired design. The centers are pearl-gray with golden-brown peripheral toning on each side. Population: 61 in 67, 0 finer (8/07). (#9342)

2150 **1933-D Oregon MS67 PCGS.** Satiny luster rolls across the original light golden-brown and pearl-gray surfaces. The trailblazing pioneer and the back of the Conestoga wagon are not fully struck, but the design elements are otherwise crisp. A splendid representative from the middle years of this long-lived commemorative type. Population: 62 in 67, 0 finer (8/07). (#9343)

2151 **1936 Oregon MS67 PCGS.** A fully brilliant and intricately struck Superb Gem, the frosty mint luster and attractive surfaces further confirm the imposing eye appeal. As of (8/07), NGC and PCGS have certified a total of just four pieces finer. (#9345)

2152 **1936-S Oregon MS67 PCGS.** Well struck with satiny, exquisitely preserved silver-gray surfaces. A lovely high grade example of this elegantly designed commemorative type. PCGS has certified only four coins finer (7/07). (#9346)

2153 **1937-D Oregon MS68 NGC.** Both sides are beautifully toned in mottled lime-green, russet and champagne-apricot shades that are partially ringed by golden-green and crimson peripheral toning. The strike is well above average for this often poorly impressed D-mint issue, and surface marks are simply nonexistent. Census: 46 in 68, 1 finer (8/07). (#9347)

2154 **1938 Oregon MS67 NGC.** Crisply struck and minimally toned with just a touch of ice-blue at the margins. This Superb Gem Oregon piece comes from an issue of only 6,006 pieces. NGC has graded just four numerically finer representatives (8/07). (#9348)

2155 **1938-S Oregon MS67 PCGS.** This softly lustrous silver-gray representative of the penultimate S-mint Oregon issue displays hints of gold at the margins. Well-defined and carefully preserved. PCGS has certified only nine finer examples (8/07). (#9350)

2156 **1938 Oregon PDS Set MS66 PCGS.** The set includes: 1938, thin lines of violet and olive at the peripheries; 1938-D, primarily satiny and untoned with a line of violet at the upper obverse rim and small dots of crimson on the reverse; and a 1938-S, silver-gray with elements of rose-violet and charcoal at the margins. (Total: 3 coins) (#9351)

2157 **1939-D Oregon MS65 NGC.** This D-mint piece comes from the final year of the Oregon design, and the issue had a paltry mintage of just 3,004 pieces. The present Gem offers well-preserved surfaces, largely silver-gray on the obverse with a touch of sky-blue and gold on the reverse. (#9353)

2158 **1915-S Panama-Pacific MS64 PCGS.** FS-501. The mintmark is repunched east. Autumn-gold and pearl-gray toning drape this satiny and splendidly unabraded near-Gem. A lovely early commemorative half that is considerably more appealing than the Choice grade might suggest. (#9357)

2159 **1915-S Panama-Pacific MS64 PCGS.** The shining surfaces of this Choice Panama-Pacific half are predominantly silver-white with occasional splashes of cloud-gray patina. Well struck with a handful of scattered abrasions on the higher areas of the devices, such as Columbia's arm. (#9357)

2160 **1915-S Panama-Pacific MS65 PCGS.** Satiny and nicely preserved, with light cream-gray toning and boldly struck design motifs. A few small marks are observed on each side, but they seem minimal for the assigned grade. Conditionally scarce as a Gem. (#9357)

2161 **1915-S Panama-Pacific MS65 PCGS.** A lovely, luminous Gem representative that offers a thin layer of gold patina over each side and a ring of deeper reddish-orange toning at the reverse margins. Well-defined with excellent surface quality for this early commemorative half dollar issue. (#9357)

2162 **1915-S Panama-Pacific MS65 PCGS.** This popular commemorative displays glowing luster through a light coating of delicate golden-gray patination that is imbued with faint whispers of mauve and sky-blue. Both faces have the design features emboldened by a well executed strike. The mintmark is lightly repunched north. (#9357)

Bright, Lustrous MS65 1915-S Panama-Pacific Half

2163 **1915-S Panama-Pacific MS65 PCGS.** While a significant number of Pan-Pac halves were issued (27,134 pieces), many were bought by fair attendees who were not numismatically inclined. Thus, most are not well preserved. This is a bright, lustrous, sharply struck example that is almost brilliant in the centers with rich golden-brown toning around the peripheries. (#9357)

2164 **1920 Pilgrim MS66 PCGS.** Lightly and evenly toned over each side with shimmering, satin-like mint luster. A lovely, high-end example of this popular, early commemorative. (#9359)

Superb Gem 1920 Pilgrim Half

2165 **1920 Pilgrim MS67 PCGS.** Beautiful caramel-gold, campfire-red, and emerald-green enrich the peripheries of this lustrous and boldly struck Pilgrim half. The reverse appears immaculate, and the obverse has only moderate contact. This example has a dramatic J-shaped die break within the ship's rigging, certain to be of interest to commemorative specialists. Housed in a green label holder. (#9359)

2166 **1921 Pilgrim MS65 NGC.** Pleasing mint frost enlivens the surfaces of this well preserved Gem. Essentially untoned except for some faint peripheral traces. Nearly blemish-free on both sides. (#9360)

2167 **1937 Roanoke MS67 NGC.** An attractive blend of olive and plum patina visits the strongly lustrous surfaces of this attentively struck Superb Gem. Carefully preserved and highly appealing. The event celebrated, the founding of Roanoke Colony, ended in one of the most puzzling mysteries of its era of adventure. Housed in an older generation holder. (#9367)

Remarkable 1937 Roanoke, MS68

2168 **1937 Roanoke MS68 NGC.** An amazing, original tab toned specimen, the obverse has a ring and tabs of lighter silver color where it was protected from the actual tabs on the original toning, and deep iridescent toning in the exposed areas, matching the reverse display. An amazing piece that is tied for the best ever certified. Census: 23 in 68, 0 finer (8/07). (#9367)

2169 **1936 Robinson MS66 PCGS.** Mottled russet-brown, lime-green and gold margins confirm the originality of this lustrous and precisely struck Premium Gem. Joseph T. Robinson was (along with Carter Glass) one of two living Senators featured on 1936 commemorative coins. (#9369)

2170 **1936 Robinson MS66 PCGS.** Both sides of this Premium Gem have satiny luster beneath ivory-gray color, with hints of peripheral gold toning on the obverse. This issue is closely related to the Arkansas commemorative half dollar as both varieties share a common reverse design. (#9369)

2171 **1936 Robinson MS66 PCGS.** This attractive Arkansas-variant piece shows strong luster and pleasing detail. The obverse displays dappled gold, orange, and mint-green patina, while the reverse has similar colors above the eagle's wings and is untoned below. PCGS has certified 60 finer representatives. (#9369)

2172 **1935-S San Diego MS67 NGC.** Fully patinated in sea-green, yellow-gold, violet-red, and dove-gray. This satiny Superb Gem is crisply struck and nearly void of marks. A find for the connoisseur of lavishly toned silver commemoratives. (#9371)

2173 **1926 Sesquicentennial MS64 PCGS.** A strongly lustrous, attractively toned Choice representative of this historic issue, one that is elusive any finer. Well struck with gold-tinged cloud-gray patina over each side with gunmetal toning present at the margins. (#9374)

Colorful 1926 Sesquicentennial Half MS65

2174 **1926 Sesquicentennial MS65 PCGS.** Rose-red, gold, and apple-green endow this lightly abraded example. The strike is good aside from the unavoidable incompleteness on Washington's cheek. Although the Sesquicentennial is an available type, it is surprisingly elusive in Gem, and none have been certified above MS66. (#9374)

Gem 1926 Sesquicentennial Half

2175 **1926 Sesquicentennial MS65 NGC.** Golden-tan, lemon, and pink-rose shades endow this shimmering and nearly unabraded Gem. The cheek of Washington retains the surface of the planchet prior to the strike, as always for this conditionally scarce type. Calvin Coolidge is noteworthy as the only President to appear on U.S. coinage during his term of office, the counterpart to Lincoln's depiction on Civil War Federal currency. (#9374)

Originally Toned Gem 1926 Sesquicentennial Half

2176 **1926 Sesquicentennial MS65 PCGS.** The mint occasionally overestimates how popular certain coins will be with the public. That happened to proofs from 1859-1860, modern mint products, and it certainly happened with the Sesquicentennial half dollar. Just over a million pieces were struck in anticipation of brisk sales at per coin, but 859,408 pieces were returned to the mint to be melted. Of those 140,592 sold, few were set aside in pristine condition. This is a lovely example that show excellent mint luster with an irregular overlay of golden-brown and russet toning on the obverse, and golden-lilac color on the reverse. (#9374)

Lustrous MS65 1926 Sesquicentennial Half

2177 **1926 Sesquicentennial MS65 NGC.** The conditional scarcity of the Sesquicentennial half dollar was slowly recognized by collectors and dealers. About 25 years ago, dealers raised their buy prices for "real Gem" coins, and found there were virtually none to be had. Prices rose and rose, then third-party grading came along, and soon published population figures confirmed the difficulty of this coin in Gem condition. The luster on this piece is exceptional and each side is covered with even golden-rose toning. (#9374)

2178 **1935 Spanish Trail MS65 PCGS.** Highly lustrous surfaces reveal traces of light tan-gold and violet color under magnification. Nicely struck, with no marks worthy of individual mention. Housed in a green-label holder. (#9376)

2179 **1935 Spanish Trail MS65 NGC.** Subtle baby-blue, champagne, and iridescent tints visit the shining surfaces of this solidly struck Gem. A well-preserved and noteworthy example of this low-mintage single-issue classic commemorative design. (#9376)

2180 **1935 Spanish Trail MS66 NGC.** A boldly struck, uncommonly bright Premium Gem example of this tougher single-issue commemorative design. The fields are minimally toned, and the simple central devices are clean.
From The Diemer L. Fife Collection. (#9376)

2181 **1935 Spanish Trail MS66 PCGS.** Lovely original toning ensures the eye appeal of this splendidly preserved Spanish Trail commemorative. Well struck and carefully preserved, with a couple of tiny milling marks on the lower left reverse field that are barely noticeable, even under low magnification.
From The Beau Clerc Collection. (#9376)

Immaculate and Beautifully Toned MS68 1935 Spanish Trail Half

2182 **1935 Spanish Trail MS68 NGC.** This satiny Superb Gem is gorgeously preserved and has a bold strike. Each side displays a coating of medium gray-blue patina with a little darker color about the borders, and there are no blemishes or distractions to be seen. Future ANA President L.W. Hoffecker designed the Spanish Trail, and also assisted in its distribution. Tied with one other example at PCGS at the MS68 level, this is the finest certified Spanish Trail we have handled and it should prove to be a prize for the specialist. Census: 5 in 68, 0 finer (8/07). (#9376)

2183 **1938-S Texas MS67 PCGS.** This intricately designed commemorative displays sharp definition, and light gray patina on highly lustrous surfaces. Both faces are devoid of mentionable marks. Population: 44 in 67, 1 finer (8/07).
From The Beau Clerc Collection. (#9396)

2184 **1925 Vancouver MS65 NGC.** The carefully preserved surfaces of this Vancouver Gem retain soft, pleasing luster beneath warm gold, orange, and blue patina. A well struck example of this Laura Gardin Fraser design. (#9399)

2185 **1925 Vancouver MS65 NGC.** FS-102. The date and WE TRUST is lightly die doubled. Booming luster and unblemished fields ensure the eye appeal of this crisply struck Gem. A lower mintage type. (#9399)

2186 **1925 Vancouver MS65 NGC.** This well struck, softly lustrous silver-gray Vancouver half is carefully preserved with a hint of deeper toning near the rims. A pleasing Gem example of this local-interest West Coast issue. (#9399)

2187 **1925 Vancouver MS65 PCGS.** Sparkling luster graces both sides of this Vancouver Gem, and just the faintest whispers of gold color visit the obverse. The design elements are well impressed. Some minute marks on the portrait of McLoughlin preclude an even finer grade. (#9399)

2188 **1927 Vermont MS66 NGC.** Pastel sky-blue, pink, gold, and cream-gray colors enrich this lustrous and well struck Premium Gem. An exemplary piece that will impress even the most seasoned specialist. (#9401)

2189 **1946-S Booker T. Washington MS67 NGC.** Attractive fire-red, gold, and aquamarine patina envelops the carefully preserved fields. This lustrous first-year Superb Gem has a solid strike, although the texture of the planchet is sometimes visible on the portrait. NGC has certified just four numerically finer examples (8/07). (#9406)

2190 **1946-S Booker T. Washington MS67 NGC.** This first-year S-mint issue had a mintage of over half a million pieces, but between melting and circulation, Superb Gem examples are elusive today. This frosty piece is well-defined and untoned save for areas of reddish-orange at the lower left obverse and the upper left reverse. NGC has graded only four coins finer (7/07). (#9406)

2191 **1947-D Booker T. Washington MS66 PCGS.** Intense mint frost shimmers over each side of this impressive Booker T. Washington half dollar. Boldly struck with a few wispy die striations (as made) on the upper obverse field and some faint toning specks on the reverse. Population: 73 in 66, 0 finer (8/07). (#9409)

2192 **1948-S Booker T. Washington MS67 NGC.** Unlike a number of other issues, the 1948-S Booker T. Washington half has a minor mintage of just 8,005 pieces. This well-defined and highly lustrous piece has pale golden patina overall with dots of gunmetal at the peripheries. NGC has graded just one finer representative (7/07). (#9414)

Appealing 1949 Booker T. Washington
Commemorative Half Dollar, MS67

2193 1949 Booker T. Washington MS67 PCGS. This highly lustrous Superb Gem exhibits sharply struck design elements, and is lightly toned gold-gray with a splash of violet-russet patina evident at the lower obverse rim. A few light marks are scattered over the obverse portrait, but these do not detract in the least from the coin's great overall eye appeal. (#9416)

Exceptional 1949-S Booker T. Washington Half MS67

2194 1949-S Booker T. Washington MS67 PCGS. Only 6,004 examples of this San Francisco Mint issue were produced, a number that seems tiny compared to the relatively monstrous mintages of today's commemorative coins. This Superb Gem displays intense mint luster over bright silver surfaces that reveal mere traces of golden color on each side. Expertly preserved and nearly pristine, this is a truly exceptional representative of the Booker T. Washington type. Population: 14 in 67, 0 finer (8/07). (#9418)

2195 1950-S Booker T. Washington MS67 NGC. Though this issue has a stated mintage of over half a million pieces, many of those coins were melted or placed into circulation. Neither fate befell this eminently appealing Superb Gem, satiny beneath pastel gold and ice-blue patina. Neither NGC nor PCGS has graded an MS68 representative (8/07). (#9422)

2196 1951 Booker T. Washington PDS Set MS66 to MS67 PCGS. The set includes: **1951 MS66 PCGS**, vibrant luster, hints of golden patina, and a degree of planchet roughness at Washington's lower jaw; **1951-D MS66 PCGS**, gleaming with tiny dots of rose and violet patina on both sides of Washington's head; and a **1951-S MS67 PCGS**, carefully preserved with delightful luster and arcs of crimson patina at the right obverse and revere margins. (Total: 3 coins)

Superb Toned Gem 1951 Booker T. Washington Half

2197 1951 Booker T. Washington MS67 PCGS. PCGS has only certified four Superb Gem examples with none achieving a grade above MS67 (8/07). Both sides have shimmering steel and lilac toning with a ring of light gold following the borders. The mintage was 210,082 coins, one of a trio with mintages in the six figure range. (#9424)

2198 1951-S Booker T. Washington MS67 PCGS. Brilliant throughout, this lovely coin displays bright, frosted mint luster and nearly abrasion-free surfaces. Very scarce as such. Census: 43 in 67, 0 finer (8/07). (#9426)

2199 1952-S Washington-Carver MS66 PCGS. Green-gold peripheral toning fades to turquoise and blue-green in the centers. This frosty and well struck second-year commemorative has an unusually pleasing appearance. PCGS has graded just two finer examples (8/07). (#9436)

2200 1936 Wisconsin MS67 NGC. Golden-tan and purple toning cling to the rims of this Superb Gem commemorative. An impressive shrike emboldens the design elements, and intense luster radiates from well preserved surfaces. (#9447)

Resplendent MS68 1936 York Half Dollar

2201 1936 York MS68 PCGS. This superlative piece remains in a green label PCGS holder, and it is tied for the finest PCGS has certified since they began grade in 1986. With just 21 pieces graded so fine, that firm grades about one MS68 per year. This ivory example has brilliant silver luster with a few traces of toning. The surfaces are virtually perfect. (#9449)

COMMEMORATIVE GOLD

2202 **1903 Louisiana Purchase/Jefferson MS62 NGC.** The luminous yellow-gold surfaces exhibit warm luster, and the devices display pleasing detail. If not for scattered, wispy abrasions in the fields, this early classic gold commemorative could have reached an even finer grade. (#7443)

2203 **1903 Louisiana Purchase/Jefferson MS63 PCGS.** Greenish-gold patina covers lustrous surfaces that exhibit sharply struck design elements. Well preserved for the numerical grade designation. Housed in a green-label holder. (#7443)

2204 **1903 Louisiana Purchase/Jefferson MS63 PCGS.** Bright luster exudes from peach-gold surfaces splashed with mint-green. A powerful strike leaves excellent delineation over the design elements, adding to the coin's eye appeal, and a minuscule, light copper spot on each side does not detract. (#7443)

2205 **1903 Louisiana Purchase/Jefferson MS64 PCGS.** A pleasing and unmarked near-Gem that displays vibrant luster and light apricot toning. The strike is sharp except for the HA in PURCHASE. Certified in a first generation holder. (#7443)

1903 Jefferson Gold Dollar MS66

2206 **1903 Louisiana Purchase/Jefferson MS66 NGC.** A precisely struck and radiant example with ebullient luster and light straw-gold toning. The reverse appears immaculate, and the left obverse has only a few delicate grazes. The 1903 Louisiana Purchase Exposition commemoratives revived the gold dollar denomination, out of production since 1889. (#7443)

2207 **1903 Louisiana Purchase/McKinley MS63 PCGS.** Unlike the Jefferson issue of this commemorative series, the McKinley depicted a recently departed president, with the timing remotely suggestive of certain 1866 patterns depicting Lincoln. This butter-yellow example offers pleasing detail and warm luster. A thin abrasion parallel to AMERICA on the obverse defines the grade. (#7444)

2208 **1903 Louisiana Purchase/McKinley MS64 PCGS.** Vibrant sun-gold surfaces are the norm for this Louisiana Purchase/McKinley dollar, though areas of lemon-gold appear at the lower obverse and upper reverse. Solidly struck with few marks and excellent visual appeal for the commemorative type. (#7444)

2209 **1903 Louisiana Purchase/McKinley MS64 PCGS.** The butter-yellow obverse has flashy luster, while the orange-gold reverse has a slightly subdued, frosty appearance. A solidly struck representative of this McKinley-portrait commemorative, struck just two years after his assassination. (#7444)

2210 **1903 Louisiana Purchase/McKinley MS63 Prooflike NGC.** An unusually reflective example, with a touch of olive on the reverse of this otherwise yellow-gold piece with crisply defined devices. A set of parallel abrasions behind McKinley's head account for the grade. Prooflike examples are elusive; NGC has granted the Prooflike designation to only seven of the Louisiana Purchase/McKinley commemoratives. Census: 3 in 63 Prooflike, 1 finer (7/07). (#77444)

Vibrant Choice 1904 Lewis and Clark Dollar

2211 **1904 Lewis and Clark MS64 PCGS.** The butter-yellow surfaces of this shining gold commemorative are well-preserved for the issue, and the portraits show uncommonly strong detail. Though Farran Zerbe, the primary promoter of the 1904 Lewis and Clark dollar and its 1905 counterpart, had high hopes for the pieces, neither sold well, and better examples are challenging today. (#7447)

2212 **1905 Lewis and Clark AU58 ANACS.** A reflective light yellow example of this issue, with a trace of wear as indicated by the grade. The budget-minded collector will delight at the opportunity. (#7448)

2213 **1905 Lewis and Clark MS62 PCGS.** A luminous sun-gold representative of this popular "two-faced" commemorative issue, struck during the second year of production. Well-defined with a slightly hazy appearance and small, scattered abrasions that preclude a Select grade. (#7448)

2214 **1905 Lewis and Clark MS62 NGC.** Bright overall with attractive, semi-prooflike fields. An affordable example of this scarce commemorative gold coin. (#7448)

2215 **1915-S Panama-Pacific Gold Dollar AU58 PCGS.** Lovely apricot-gold patina is accented with traces of lavender and mint-green at the peripheries. Both sides are remarkably clean, possess ample residual luster, and exhibit sharply impressed design features. Housed in a first generation holder. (#7449)

2216 **1915-S Panama-Pacific Gold Dollar MS64 PCGS.** This luminous butter-yellow example shows a trace of frost on the highpoints of the devices. Well-defined with few marks for the grade, and an attractive representative of Charles Keck's first commemorative design credit. (#7449)

2217 **1915-S Panama-Pacific Gold Dollar MS65 PCGS.** The shining lemon-gold and butter-yellow surfaces of this attractive Gem are carefully preserved and host solidly struck devices. An attractive representative of this Charles Keck design. (#7449)

2218 **1915-S Panama-Pacific Gold Dollar MS65 PCGS.** A satiny khaki-gold Gem. Well struck with the sole exception of the snout of the lower dolphin, opposite the high relief of the laborer's cap. The mintmark is faintly (but widely) repunched southeast. (#7449)

Splendid 1915-S Panama-Pacific Gold Dollar, MS66

2219 **1915-S Panama-Pacific Gold Dollar MS66 PCGS.** An exceptional Premium Gem with satiny yellow-gold luster that is enhanced by delicate rose toning on both sides. Examples at this grade level are not difficult to locate, but finer Superb pieces are seldom encountered. PCGS has only graded 46 better pieces, less an uncertain number of resubmissions. (#7449)

2220 **1915-S Panama-Pacific Quarter Eagle AU55 ICG.** Bright yellow-gold surfaces abound on both sides of this Choice AU Pan-Pac quarter eagle, and each exhibits sharply defined design elements. A shallow linear mark is visible in the upper right obverse field. (#7450)

Gem 1915-S Panama-Pacific Quarter Eagle

2221 **1915-S Panama-Pacific Quarter Eagle MS65 NGC.** An impressively smooth straw-gold Gem with satin luster and a good strike. Veteran mint engravers Charles Barber and George Morgan are credited with the designs, the eagle on the reverse similar to that on the Judd-1608 1879 Schoolgirl dollar. One of only two quarter eagle commemorative types, unless the 1848 CAL counts. (#7450)

THE DIEMER L. FIFE PANAMA-PACIFIC SET

COMMEMORATIVE SILVER

Colorful 1915-S Panama-Pacific Half, Unc Details

2222 **1915-S Panama-Pacific Half Dollar—Obverse Improperly Cleaned—NCS. Unc Details.** Both sides of this well struck Panama-Pacific half exhibit rich blue, rose, and plum patina. While the reverse displays strong luster, the obverse is somewhat dulled with hairlines from cleaning. Still, a surprisingly attractive example of this earlier commemorative half.
From The Diemer L. Fife Collection. (#9357)

COMMEMORATIVE GOLD

Lovely Choice 1915-S Panama-Pacific Gold Dollar

2223 **1915-S Panama-Pacific Gold Dollar MS64 NGC.** The deep yellow-gold surfaces of this delicately frosted near-Gem show distinct peach overtones in the fields. Crisply detailed with attractive luster and only a handful of wispy marks, an appealing example of the first commemorative design by noted sculptor Charles Keck.
From The Diemer L. Fife Collection. (#7449)

Luminous 1915-S Panama-Pacific Quarter Eagle, Unc Details

2224 **1915-S Panama-Pacific Quarter Eagle—Improperly Cleaned—NCS. Unc Details.** The pink-gold and butter-yellow surfaces of this commemorative are subdued with a number of hairlines, the result of a past cleaning. Otherwise, a well struck piece with no trace of wear, from one of the last coin designs to which Charles Barber contributed. Interestingly, the NCS holder describes this piece as a half eagle.
From The Diemer L. Fife Collection. (#7450)

2225 1915-S Panama-Pacific 50 Dollar Round MS62 NGC.
The fifty dollar denomination has had an interesting history in United States coinage, though it never reached national circulation. In the original Mint Act, the largest denomination authorized was the eagle; the sum of fifty dollars seemed entirely too large for a single coin. Beginning in 1851, Augustus Humbert worked on behalf of the federal government to strike his fifty-dollar "ingots," which the 2008 *Guide Book* notes had numerous nicknames, among them the "slug," "quintuple eagle," and "five-eagle piece." The iconic and singular Judd-1548 half union pattern by William Barber, later the source of much scandal when it appeared in private hands, was a Mint prototype that never reached production.

The next appearance of the denomination came in 1915, when the San Francisco Mint coined the Panama-Pacific fifty dollar commemoratives in round and octagonal formats. Finally, while the denomination was not struck again until 1986, it has been in production every year since, as fifty dollars is the nominal face value of the one-ounce gold American Eagle coins. The half-ounce American Eagle platinum pieces, struck since 1997, have a denomination of fifty dollars as well.

More readily collectible in unimpaired Mint State than the nigh-unobtainable half union patterns or the Augustus Humbert ingots, the Panama-Pacific fifties are much-heralded in the numismatic marketplace. Most collectors put a slight premium on the lower-mintage round variant, which has a net production of just 483 pieces. The example offered here displays pleasing yellow-gold surfaces, luminous with a touch of alloy near the owl's right (facing) wing. Though this well struck piece shows a few wispy abrasions on the portrait and in the surrounding fields, the coin's overall visual appeal remains strong, and it is sure to delight the winning bidder.
From The Diemer L. Fife Collection. (#7451)

Distinctive 1915-S Panama-Pacific Fifty Dollar Octagonal, AU Details

Original Shreve & Co. Panama-Pacific Five-Piece Set Holder

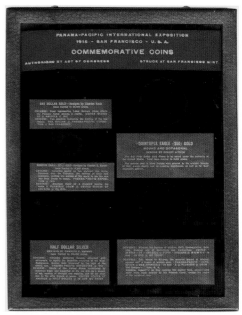

2227 Original Holder for the Five-Piece Panama-Pacific Set. An original hammered copper frame made by Shreve & Co. of San Francisco, designed to hold an original five-coin set of the Panama-Pacific commemorative coins. The plush violet interior and informational tags show only the slightest evidence of fading, and the frame and glass are carefully preserved with lovely olive patina on the former. The only significant flaws appear on the reverse, where the pull-out tab to make the holder a standalone display is missing. A small puncture appears in the center of the void as well. Still, the piece displays beautifully.

Also included is a typed letter signed and dated December 3, 1968, by one Wes Ford, attesting to the authenticity of the coins once housed in the holder. It is an interesting addition to the provenance of this fascinating lot.

From The Diemer L. Fife Collection.

2226 1915-S Panama-Pacific 50 Dollar Octagonal—Improperly Cleaned—NCS. AU Details. The ceremonial strikings that accompany most modern commemoratives have their roots in similar pomp that accompanied classic commemorative issues. Swiatek-Breen (1981) recounts the illustrious dignitaries who participated in early coinings of the octagonal Panama-Pacific fifties: the first was struck by T.W.H. Shanahan, Superintendent of the San Francisco Mint; the second was struck by Charles C. Moore, President of the Panama-Pacific Exhibition; and later participants included Representative Julius Kahn, a Republican from California who sponsored the bill authorizing the commemoratives. Also involved were master numismatic promoter Farran Zerbe and the then-Mayor of San Francisco, James Rolph, Jr.

Though no famous name is attached to the present example, it is a highly desirable piece nonetheless. The luminous yellow-orange surfaces show hairlines from a past cleaning, a measure of friction affects the well struck devices, and minor damage is present at the upper right dolphin on the obverse. Still, as one of only 645 pieces in the issue's net mintage, it remains a coveted exemplar from one of the rarest and most distinctive of America's commemorative issues.
From The Diemer L. Fife Collection. (#7452)

ADDITIONAL COMMEMORATIVE GOLD

2228 **1915-S Panama-Pacific Five-Piece Holder.** An attractive box that is far above average for Pan-Pac boxes. There is no gold imprint on the top or bottom, and the top is not buckled as most are. Even matte black finish on the outside with minor edge wear and a working clasp. The purple velvet and felt interior is pristine and unfaded. The descriptive cardboard insert of issue is also present, but no coins are included in this lot.

2229 **1916 McKinley MS64 PCGS.** The obverse of this first-year McKinley dollar has sun-gold surfaces with elements of orange, while the reverse offers a lighter yellow-gold appearance. An attractive example of this later classic gold commemorative, the second such issue to depict the assassinated president. (#7454)

Richly Patinated 1922 Grant no Star Gold Dollar, MS65

2230 **1922 Grant no Star MS65 PCGS.** This coin really benefits from examination with a loupe. With magnification one is better able to see and appreciate the deep, rich orange-gold color on the coin, but more importantly the occasional patches of deep lilac. Bright and highly lustrous with no noticeable abrasions. (#7458)

2231 **1926 Sesquicentennial MS64 PCGS.** A well struck and shining representative of this final gold classic commemorative issue, yellow-gold with peach accents. Affordable and appealing, though kept from the coveted Gem grade by a few scattered marks in the obverse fields. (#7466)

2232 **1926 Sesquicentennial MS64 PCGS.** This is a pretty near-Gem example of the popular Sesquicentennial quarter eagle. The satiny mint luster is quite intense, and the variegated reddish-apricot and lime-green toning is lovely. An abrasion that removes the lower edge of U in UNUM precludes a Gem grade designation. (#7466)

2233 **1926 Sesquicentennial MS64 PCGS.** The pale straw-gold surfaces of this pretty Choice Sesquicentennial quarter eagle offer pleasing luster and a handful of faint abrasions. A well struck representative of above-average quality for the grade assigned. (#7466)

2234 **1926 Sesquicentennial MS64 PCGS.** A well struck yellow-gold example that offers soft, frosty luster, a distinctive finish for this commemorative issue. The surfaces are surprisingly clean overall, though faint marks are noted at the knee. (#7466)

2235 **1926 Sesquicentennial MS64 PCGS.** This lovely yellow-gold example displays attractive mint-green accents near the margins. A well-defined gold commemorative that shows just a few too many marks to qualify for a finer grade. (#7466)

2236 **1926 Sesquicentennial MS64 PCGS.** A Choice sun-gold representative of the final gold classic commemorative issue, well-defined with uncommonly attractive luster. Faint, scattered abrasions keep this piece from the coveted Gem grade. (#7466)

2237 **1926 Sesquicentennial MS64 ICG.** Both sides of this shining butter-yellow quarter eagle have splashes of orange. A well-defined and minimally marked representative of this final classic commemorative gold issue, notoriously elusive any finer. (#7466)

MS65 1926 Sesquicentennial Quarter Eagle

2238 **1926 Sesquicentennial MS65 NGC.** Blazing luster dominates this evenly struck green-gold Gem. A few small areas near the right border of each side are mildly prooflike. The Sesquicentennial was the final gold commemorative until the Olympic Games returned to Los Angeles in 1984. (#7466)

1926 Sesquicentennial Two and a Half MS65

2239 **1926 Sesquicentennial MS65 PCGS.** Dynamic cartwheel luster invigorates this attractively toned representative. Pastel olive-green margins gradually cede to canary-gold centers. Alertly struck, and both sides exhibit only faint abrasions. The final commemorative type of the denomination. (#7466)

Lustrous 1926 Sesquicentennial Two and a Half MS65

2240 **1926 Sesquicentennial MS65 PCGS.** A peach-gold piece with peripheral tinges of aqua-green. This well struck and moderately abraded commemorative benefits from booming luster. July 4, 1926, was the sesquicentennial of the Declaration of Independence, and also the exact centennial of the deaths of Thomas Jefferson and John Adams. (#7466)

Gem 1926 Sesquicentennial Quarter Eagle

2241 1926 Sesquicentennial MS65 PCGS. The sun-gold interiors are framed by green-gold margins. A well preserved, crisply impressed, and highly lustrous example of this popular type. Independence Hall, featured on the reverse, would later appear on the Bicentennial Kennedy half dollar. (#7466)

Dynamic 1926 Sesquicentennial Quarter Eagle, MS65

2242 1926 Sesquicentennial MS65 PCGS. Vivid butter-yellow surfaces and vibrant luster are the most immediately apparent characteristics of this outstanding Gem. Closer examination reveals exceptional detail and carefully preserved surfaces that are entirely worthy of the grade. A wonderful exemplar of this final gold classic commemorative. (#7466)

Well Struck Gem 1926 Sesquicentennial Quarter Eagle

2243 1926 Sesquicentennial MS65 PCGS. Because of the low-relief design, examples of this issue that are well struck can be elusive. This is one such piece, however, with good articulation on Liberty's face and hands, and the facade of the building on the reverse. Booming luster complements the pleasing orange-gold coloration. An elusive issue at the next grade level. (#7466)

Amazing 1926 Sesquicentennial Quarter Eagle, MS66

2244 1926 Sesquicentennial MS66 PCGS. Seldom do examples of this commemorative gold piece appear in such high quality, tied for the finest certified by PCGS. Approximately 46,000 coins were sold, far fewer than Congress authorized, but far greater than any other gold commemorative issue. The production represents a third of the total mintage of all gold commemoratives from 1903 to 1926. The surfaces of this Premium Gem have frosty yellow-gold luster with traces of pink toning at the centers. It is sharply struck and nearly free of marks. Population: 104 in 66, 0 finer (8/07). (#7466)

MODERN ISSUES

1995-96 Olympic Silver Dollar Reverse Die

2245 1995-1996 Olympic Silver Dollar Reverse Die. A canceled reverse die used for the 1995-1996 Olympic silver dollars, mintmarked P, as used for the proof issues of the series. The 1996 Olympics, held in Atlanta, marked the Centennial of the modern Olympic Games. During the two year commemorative program, the standard reverse silver dollar design was combined with eight different obverse designs, and these pieces were coined in proof at Philadelphia, and Mint State at Denver. (#9716)

2246 1995-W Olympic/Torch Runner Gold Five Dollar MS70 NGC. A technically perfect Mint State representative of this modern Olympic commemorative issue, boldly impressed with pristine yellow-gold surfaces. The Torch Runner design proved to be the most popular half eagle offered for the Atlanta commemorative series. (#9732)

2247 1995-W Olympic/Torch Runner Gold Five Dollar MS70 PCGS. The five dollar gold commemoratives of the 1996 Olympic games all have low mintages, particularly for the Uncirculated finish issues. This is a perfect straw-gold example with seamless satin surfaces. (#9732)

2248 1996-W Smithsonian Gold Five Dollar MS69 PCGS. A wonderful example of this lower-mintage modern half eagle, decisively struck with warm luster and exquisite straw-gold surfaces. Even under magnification, the faint flaw that keeps this piece from perfection is difficult to spot. (#9744)

2249 1997-S Jackie Robinson Silver Dollar MS70 NGC. A technically perfect exemplar of this uncirculated-finish modern commemorative. One of just 63 pieces so graded by NGC, compared to a mintage of just over 30,000 coins (7/07). (#9757)

MS69 1997-W Jackie Robinson Gold Five Dollar

2250 1997-W Jackie Robinson Gold Five Dollar MS69 NGC. A virtually pristine example of this desirable issue. The 50th anniversary of Jackie Robinson breaking the color barrier and winning Rookie of the Year would appear to be a popular sports-related theme, yet the Uncirculated Robinson half eagle has the lowest mintage of any modern commemorative. Only 5,174 pieces were struck. (#9759)

2251 1997-W Franklin D. Roosevelt Gold Five Dollar PR70 Deep Cameo PCGS. This low mintage issue features President Roosevelt in a oversized boating jacket. The 1933 date on the reverse refers to his inauguration, rather than the notorious gold recall of the same year. A pristine piece with rich peach-gold and mauve toning. Population: 20 in 70 (4/07). (#9749)

Perfect MS70 2000-W Library of Congress $10

2252 2000-W Library of Congress Bimetallic Ten Dollars MS70 PCGS. The nation's first and only bimetallic commemorative issue is also the first to incorporate platinum as a coinage metal. Precisely detailed with wonderful contrast between the butter-yellow outer ring of gold and the satiny surfaces of the inner ring of platinum. This is a flawless example. One of the most elusive modern commemoratives, with just 7,261 pieces struck. Population: 88 in 70, 0 finer (8/07). (#9784)

2253 2001-W Capitol Visitor's Center Half Eagle MS70 PCGS. A technically perfect example of this modern gold commemorative. Only 67 pieces have been so graded by PCGS. (#9792)

2254 2001-D Buffalo Silver Dollar MS70 PCGS. A popular reuse of James Earl Fraser's 1913 Buffalo nickel, but seen here in the size of a silver dollar and in silver. Of interest, of course, to Registry Set collectors who will need this issue in the ultimate grade. One of only 120 pieces so graded by PCGS. Brilliant throughout and perfect as far as we can determine. (#9793)

2255 2001-P Buffalo Silver Dollar PR70 Deep Cameo PCGS. An impressive coin with bright, silky mint luster over the devices that contrasts sharply with the deep mirrors seen in the fields. Brilliant throughout. One of only 99 pieces so graded by PCGS (8/07). (#99793)

MODERN BULLION COINS

2256 1986-W One-Ounce Gold Eagle PR70 Deep Cameo PCGS. A gleaming, perfect proof from the premiere issue of American Eagles. Both sides show strong mirrors and rich frost, though the obverse offers a greater degree of contrast. One of 96 specimens so graded by PCGS (8/07). (#9807)

2257 1987 One-Ounce Gold Eagle MS70 PCGS. The centers of this piece are sun-gold, while the margins display slightly paler color. A visually interesting representative from the early years of the successful American Eagle program, perfect in every way. PCGS has awarded the MS70 grade to just 33 examples (8/07). (#9814)

2258 1987-W One-Ounce Gold Eagle PR70 Deep Cameo PCGS. An immaculate and deeply reflective specimen of this second-year proof issue. This vibrant piece showcases the technical perfection made possible by modern minting technology. (#9815)

2259 1988-W One-Ounce Gold Eagle PR70 Deep Cameo PCGS. A vibrant yellow-gold example that shows particularly impressive contrast between the frosted fields and the mirrored devices, this is the perfect choice to represent the third year of issue in one's proof American Eagle set. PCGS has assigned the ultimate grade to only 78 specimens (8/07). (#9825)

2260 **1988-W One-Ounce Gold Eagle PR70 Deep Cameo PCGS.** The obverse has predominantly straw-gold mirrors with a splash of orange at Liberty's feet, while the reverse takes on a distinct butter-yellow tone. Boldly struck with gleaming, impeccable mirrors. One of 78 pieces so graded by PCGS (8/07). (#9825)

2261 **1989-W One-Ounce Gold Eagle PR70 Deep Cameo PCGS.** One of 98 pieces assigned the ultimate grade by PCGS (8/07). Both sides of this impeccable butter-yellow proof show impeccable contrast and impressive visual appeal. (#9835)

2262 **1991 One-Ounce Gold Eagle MS70 PCGS.** An exquisitely detailed yellow-gold American Eagle that offers lovely luster and unimpeachable surfaces. One of 29 pieces assigned a perfect grade by PCGS (8/07). (#9854)

Magnificent Key 1995-W Silver Eagle, PR69 Deep Cameo

2263 **1995-W Silver Eagle PR69 Deep Cameo PCGS.** A white-on-black beauty that boasts a full strike and exemplary preservation. The unchallenged key to the enormously popular silver eagle series, due to its low emission of 30,125 pieces. Originally issued only as part of an American eagle gold proof set. (#9887)

2264 **1995-W Silver Eagle PR69 Deep Cameo PCGS With 10th Anniversary Gold Set.** The first of the proof W-mint silver American Eagle coins, and a piece that was made doubly popular in 2006 with the 2006 release of the three-piece silver American Eagle sets containing the 2006-P reverse proof, the 2006-W regular proof, and the 2006-W burnished issue. The silver 1995-W was, of course, only released in a limited mintage of 30,125 pieces to those who purchased the 10th Anniversary Set, included. The present example, graded PR69 Deep Cameo by PCGS, boasts essentially flawless, deeply cameoed surfaces. Includes the four-piece proof gold American Eagle set, each a deep cameo, flawless coin, in their original U.S. Mint packaging. (Total: 5 coins) (#9887)

2265 **1998-W One-Ounce Gold Eagle PR70 Ultra Cameo NGC.** A perfect proof gold eagle with luminous devices, mirrored fields, and flawless features. What more could be desired? (#9938)

2266 **1999-W Tenth-Ounce Gold Eagle—Struck With Unfinished Proof Dies—MS69 PCGS.** The mintmarked obverse dies for gold American Eagles of this year were intended only for proofs, but for an unknown reason, a number of uncirculated-finish tenth-ounce pieces were struck using mintmarked dies that lacked a mirror finish. This boldly impressed, borderline perfect example has a sun-gold obverse and a butter-yellow reverse. (#99940)

2267 **2001 Four-Piece Gold American Eagle Set MS70 NGC.** The set includes: **2001 MS70 Tenth-Ounce,** technically perfect with luminous wheat-gold surfaces; **2001 MS70 Quarter-Ounce,** boldly impressed with flawless sun-gold fields; **2001 MS70 Half-Ounce,** a delightful, impeccable yellow-gold example of this half-ounce issue; and a **2001 MS70 One-Ounce,** an unbeatable representative of this hefty denomination. (Total: 4 coins)

2268 **2006-W One-Ounce Gold American Eagle MS69 PCGS.** First Strike and 20th Anniversary Set, according to the PCGS insert. Perfect aside from trivial incompleteness of strike on the top of the second T in STATES. (#89993)

2269 **2006-W One-Ounce Gold American Eagle MS70 PCGS.** 20th Anniversary Set and First Strike, per the PCGS insert. An immaculate and satiny example of this popular mintmarked issue. (#89993)

2270 **Certified Three-Piece American Eagle 20th Anniversary Gold Coin Set MS69 to PR69 Ultra Cameo NGC.** The set includes: **2006-W One-Ounce Gold American Eagle 20th Anniversary MS69,** shining with peach inflections on the yellow-gold surfaces; **2006-W One Ounce Gold American Eagle 20th Anniversary PR69 Ultra Cameo,** boldly impressed with richly frosted devices and black-and-gold contrast; and a **2006-W One-Ounce Gold American Eagle Reverse Proof 20th Anniversary PR69,** striking and exquisitely preserved with gleaming devices and frosted fields. The three certified pieces are housed in an attractive maroon hard presentation case with plush royal-blue velvet interior, and the lot includes the original Mint packaging and accompanying literature. (Total: 3 coins) (#89994)

2271 **2006-W One-Ounce Gold American Eagle Reverse Proof PR69 NGC.** An exquisite example of this modern curiosity, boldly struck with gleaming devices and richly frosted microgranular fields. The tiny flaw that bars the way to a perfect grade is difficult to see, even under magnification. (#89994)

2272 **2006-W One-Ounce Gold American Eagle Reverse Proof PR70 PCGS.** The shining, deep black-gold devices project from the satiny fields of this technically perfect exemplar. Part of the three piece 20th Anniversary set, which contains a **2006-W One-Ounce Gold American Eagle** and a **2006-W One Ounce Proof Gold American Eagle,** each of which is also included in this lot, along with the full original Mint packaging. (Total: 3 coins)

2273 **2006-W One-Ounce Gold American Eagle Reverse Proof PR70 PCGS.** An utterly flawless exemplar of the distinctive Reverse Proof American Eagle one-ounce gold, attentively struck with exquisite finishes. This certified piece comes with the original Mint box, holder, literature, and the **2006-W One-Ounce Gold American Eagle** and **2006-W One-Ounce Proof Gold American Eagle** as issued. (Total: 3 coins)

2274 **2006-W One-Ounce Platinum MS70 PCGS.** First Strike. A boldly impressed piece of practically pure platinum with perfect surfaces. The reverse shows a woman with a bound book and quill pen, flanked by two eagles. This modern bullion piece is one of just 24 so graded by PCGS (8/07). (#821119)

COINS OF HAWAII

2275 **1847 Hawaii Cent MS63 Brown PCGS.** Crosslet 4, 15 berries. M. 2CC-2. An impressive Hapa Haneri with satiny chocolate-brown toning and uncommonly blemish-free surfaces. The strike is soft in selected areas, and this may be all that prevents an even higher grade. (#10965)

2276 **1883 Hawaii Ten Cents AU58 NGC.** Both centers are slate-gray, but the obverse border has golden toning, while the reverse features ocean-blue patina across the periphery. Faint, wispy marks are present in the fields. Unlike most monarchs, David Kalakaua, whose portrait appears on this piece, was elected by a legislature rather than inheriting his title. (#10979)

2277 **1883 Hawaii Quarter MS65 PCGS.** An attractively toned Gem representative of this Hawaii quarter, the most available of the kingdom's issues in Mint State. Patches of rose, forest-green, and jade appear within a green-gold matrix. Boldly struck and enticing. *From The Diemer L. Fife Collection.* (#10987)

2278 **1883 Hawaii Half Dollar MS62 NGC.** Despite its status as the highest-mintage Hawaii denomination of 1883, the half dollar is considerably less available than the quarter, particularly in Mint State. This crisply struck silver-white example shines beneath minor, gauzy haze over the reverse fields. Small, scattered abrasions account for the grade. (#10991)

2279 **1883 Hawaii Dollar AU55 NGC.** The Hawaii dollar, owing to its large size and considerable silver content, was heavily redeemed and melted in the islands' post-kingdom years, and today it is the most challenging of the official 1883 issues. Amber, forest-green, and silver-gray toning drapes the still-lustrous, minimally marked surfaces of this lightly circulated piece.
From The Beau Clerc Collection. (#10995)

Key Date 1883 Hawaii Dollar, MS64

2280 **1883 Hawaii Dollar MS64 PCGS.** Walter Breen (1988) writes of the 1883 Hawaii dollar: "... in 1883 Claus Spreckels (banker, sugar tycoon, and power behind the thrown) came to the King (Kalakaua I) with a proposal to have the United States strike silver coins for the Islands. Conveniently, an Act of Jan. 29, 1874 had already authorized the federal mints to strike coins for foreign countries. Under its terms, the royal government formally applied to have 1 million Dala coined in silver." Breen continues to say that the original mintage consisted of 500,000 pieces less 453,622 melted. It is the key to the 1883 Hawaii business strike series.

The lustrous surfaces of this near-Gem example consist of an array of purple, violet, forest and apple-green, and red-orange toning on the obverse, and lavender and sky-blue coloration on the reverse. The strike is impressive, leaving strong definition on all of the design elements. The surfaces on both sides are well preserved. Population: 20 in 64, 12 finer (7/07). (#10995)

MINT SET

2281 **1948 Double Mint Set MS63 to MS66 Uncertified.** The coins have light to medium original toning. The cents are mostly full red. The half dollars grade MS63 to MS64, and the Philadelphia halves have full bell lines. No 1948-S Franklin halves were struck. (Total: 28 coins)

MEDALS AND TOKENS

2282 **1837 Feuchtwanger Cent MS64 NGC.** Low-120, HT-268, Breen 6-I, R.1. One of the most available Feuchtwanger cent die pairings, with a berry to the left of the bow on the wreath and the N and E of one even at their tops. Well struck for this issue with green-gold toning overall and dabs of olive to the right of the eagle. (#20001)

Interesting 1837 Feuchtwanger Three Cents, XF Details

2283 **1837 Feuchtwanger Three Cents—Repaired—NCS. XF Details.** Low-118, HT-263, R.5. A defiant eagle faces left and stands on a rock. The denomination is spelled out on the reverse with no numerals. Struck in German silver. Though he was among the most persistent of the petitioners who stumped for a novel composition for American coinage, Lewis Feuchtwanger never saw his pet composition adopted by the government. His one cent and three cent trial pieces, however, circulated extensively alongside other Hard Times tokens. This lightly worn example of the elusive three cent, eagle obverse design issue shows luminous olive-gray toning. The date area is smoothed over, likely due to past damage, and this repair accounts for the details grade. (#20004)

2284 **1837 Feuchtwanger Cent MS64 PCGS.** Low-120, HT-268, Breen 6-I, R.1. Apricot and rose patina graces the unworn surfaces of this well-defined Feuchtwanger cent. Pleasingly lustrous with few marks for the grade, an attractive example of this well-known German silver token. (#20001)

ADDITIONAL CERTIFIED COINS

2285 **1886-S Morgan Dollar MS65 Paramount International (MS63).** Ex: Redfield Collection. VAM-2. A Top 100 Variety. The mintmark is lightly repunched. A thoroughly lustrous example with light sun-gold toning near the rims. (#7170)

2286 **1888-S Morgan Dollar MS65 Paramount International (MS63).** Ex: Redfield Collection. A highly lustrous silver dollar with attractive peripheral golden-brown toning and a well preserved reverse. The chin and hair above the ear are abraded. (#7186)

2287 **1892-CC Dollar Paramount International MS65 (MS63).** Ex: Redfield Collection. Apple-green and honey-gold freckles endow the margins of this lustrous and nicely struck better date Carson City dollar. The reverse is impressively smooth. (#7214)

Redfield 1893-CC Morgan Dollar MS62

2288 1893-CC Dollar MS65 Paramount International (MS62). Ex: Redfield Collection. One suspects that the key 1893-CC dollar is a rarity in a Redfield holder, although Heritage has handled a few of these in the past few years. This crisply struck piece has lovely golden-brown and forest-green patina at the borders. A reeding mark on the cheek determines the grade. (#7222)

2289 1898-S Dollar MS65 Paramount International (MS64). Ex: Redfield Collection. VAM-6. The mintmark is sharply repunched south. This flashy near-Gem has a good strike and delicate peripheral tobacco-brown toning. A mark on the chin is barely worthy of mention. (#7256)

GSA DOLLARS

Enticing GSA 1879-CC Capped Die Dollar, MS62

2290 1879-CC Capped Die MS62 NGC. VAM-3. A Top 100 Variety. The so-called "Capped Die," with a medium mintmark over a small mintmark. This frosty piece displays a touch of silver-gray toning and pleasing detail, though the surfaces show a number of abrasions. The GSA population of 1879-CC dollars of all varieties was a tiny fraction of the original mintage, which only enhances the distinctiveness of the present piece. Band-certified in the original holder with accompanying outer packaging. (#7086)

2291 1880-CC MS65 NGC. Band-certified in the original holder of issue. Delicate pink and opaque cream patina graces parts of the margins of this frosty Carson City Gem. A crisply struck example that shows only a few scattered luster grazes. Eminently appealing. (#7100)

2292 1881-CC MS65 NGC. A lustrous and largely untoned Gem of this popular low mintage CC-mint date. The fields are unabraded, and the cheek has only trivial contact. Most '81-CC GSA dollars are somewhat scuffy, and the present piece is a happy exception. (#7126)

2293 1884-CC MS64 ★ NGC. Housed in the original case of issue and band-certified. The reverse of this near-Gem is essentially untoned and pleasingly defined, while the obverse displays enticing bands of rainbow patina, from blue-violet on the left to magenta, orange, and forest-green. Minimally abraded, though the cheek shows a patch of roller marks. (#7152)

2294 1885-CC MS64 NGC. A brilliant and crisply struck Carson City dollar with booming luster and a well preserved reverse. The portrait is faintly abraded. The box and certificate of GSA issue accompany the lot. (#7160)

2295 1885-CC MS64 NGC. Only a dollop or two of golden toning visits this boldly struck and flashy near-Gem. The reverse is gorgeously smooth, and the obverse lacks noteworthy marks. Included with the lot is the government-issued box and certificate. (#7160)

Noteworthy 1890-CC GSA Dollar, MS62

2296 1890-CC MS62 NGC. Though the 1890-CC has a high original mintage, most of the pieces were paid out, either near the time of manufacture or in later decades. The GSA inventory of the pieces showed fewer than 4,000 examples. This attentively struck example displays lovely gold and apricot overtones, as well as swirls of milky patina. Decisively struck with strong luster, though the fields and devices show a number of abrasions. Band-certified in the original holder with accompanying box and informational insert. (#7198)

Surprising 1891-CC GSA Dollar, MS63

2297 1891-CC MS63 NGC. Band-certified in the original holder of issue. The 1891-CC was a comparatively under-represented issue in the GSA sales, with only 5,687 pieces in the inventory after 1964, according to statistics cited by Bowers in his *A Guide Book of Morgan Silver Dollars* (2005). This minimally toned and lustrous dollar is well struck with light, scattered abrasions that account for the grade. The original box and documentation accompany the lot. (#7206)

End of Session Three

SESSION FOUR

Live, Internet, and Mail Bid Signature Auction #446
Friday, September 28, 2007, 1:00 PM PT, Lots 2298-3003
Long Beach, California

A 15% Buyer's Premium ($9 minimum) Will Be Added To All Lots

Visit HA.com to view full-color images and bid.

THE 'MILE HIGH' REGISTRY SET OF CARSON CITY MORGAN DOLLARS

Exemplary 1878-CC Morgan Dollar MS66

2298 1878-CC MS66 PCGS. A stone-white Premium Gem of the initial Carson City Morgan dollar issue. The strike is intricate, although a few faint parallel roller marks (as produced) cross the obverse. The fields and portrait are exceptionally preserved. As of (7/07), PCGS has certified only four pieces finer.
From The #3 PCGS 'Mile High' Registry Set of Carson City Morgan Dollars. (#7080)

Carson City Mint – 1879

Key 1879-CC Morgan MS65

2299 1879-CC MS65 PCGS. A whisper of almond-tan and ice-blue toning is present on the portrait, but most would regard the present piece as fully brilliant. Potent cartwheel luster sweeps unencumbered across this alertly struck key date silver dollar. The centers display only a trace of mint-made roller marks, and the reverse is virtually immaculate. The obverse field is also well preserved, and a wispy graze on the jaw is all that stands in the way of an even finer grade. The 1879-CC is the key Morgan dollar within the first period (through 1885) of Carson City production.
From The #3 PCGS 'Mile High' Registry Set of Carson City Morgan Dollars. (#7086)

Superb Gem 1880-CC Silver Dollar

2300 **1880-CC MS67 PCGS.** With just over a half million pieces struck, the 1880-CC is an issue that has always been of interest to collectors who are sensitive to original mintages. Rarely seen in Superb condition, this lovely piece has thick, frosted mint luster and a moderate overlay of pearl-gray and almond-gold patina on each side. Sharply struck throughout, the surfaces are almost free from abrasions. The reverse die is lightly rusted, most noticeable within IN GOD WE TRUST. An outstanding 1880-CC dollar. Population: 23 in 67, 0 finer (7/07).
Ex: Clear Lake Collection (Heritage, 9/04), lot 8351.
From The #3 PCGS 'Mile High' Registry Set of Carson City Morgan Dollars. (#7100)

Beautiful 1881-CC Morgan MS67

2301 **1881-CC MS67 PCGS.** VAM-2, an interesting variety with die fill suggestive of repunching within the upper loops of the 8s. This precisely struck and well preserved representative has vibrant luster and barely a hint of honey toning. Among the CC-mint issues, only the 1885-CC has a lower mintage.
From The #3 PCGS 'Mile High' Registry Set of Carson City Morgan Dollars. (#7126)

Splendid Superb Gem 1882-CC Dollar

2302 **1882-CC MS67 PCGS.** Light golden patina graces this thoroughly lustrous and alertly struck Superb Gem. A dab of slightly deeper obverse toning is noted at 2 o'clock. The 1882-CC is plentiful in typical Mint State, but surprisingly few pieces can aspire to the MS67 level. Population: 47 in 67, 1 finer (7/07).
From The #3 PCGS 'Mile High' Registry Set of Carson City Morgan Dollars. (#7134)

Extraordinary MS68 1883-CC Dollar

2303 **1883-CC MS68 PCGS.** A gleaming, snowy-white Superb Gem with peerless fields and a creamy-smooth portrait. The appearance of an MS68 Morgan is always cause for excitement among enthusiasts of this popular series. Add to the equation the presence of a CC mintmark and widespread interest soon follows. Over the years we have offered dozens of 1883-CC dollars at the MS67 level, but only a single MS68 has previously appeared in a Heritage auction. That piece is the same as the present coin, and it realized $46,000 in our 2006 FUN Signature. Once it has been sold, years may pass before its equal again emerges in the marketplace.

According to Q. David Bowers, the Federal government stopped paying out silver dollars in March 1964, although more than a million pieces remained in Treasury holdings. These were inventoried, and it turned out that many of these were Uncirculated 1883-CC examples. Those pieces were eventually dispersed in a series of GSA auctions, held between October 1972 and February 1980. Today, if a GSA dollar is sighted on the bourse floor, the chances are it will be a Carson City issue struck between 1882 and 1884. Over the past twenty years, most high grade GSA dollars were broken out of their holders and submitted to PCGS and NGC. Examples through the MS65 grade are plentiful, although always in demand as a souvenir of the legendary Western branch mint. In MS66, the issue becomes scarce relative to its formidable demand, and MS67 examples are seldom encountered. The appearance of an MS68 provides a major opportunity to those who will not settle for less than the finest obtainable quality. Population: 3 in 68, 0 finer (7/07).
From The #3 PCGS 'Mile High' Registry Set of Carson City Morgan Dollars. (#7144)

Dazzling 1884-CC Morgan MS67

2304 **1884-CC MS67 PCGS.** Ex: Mike Casper Collection. The fields are essentially immaculate, and Liberty's cheek and the eagle's breast have only inconsequential grazes. A boldly struck example with dazzling luster and imposing eye appeal. A good candidate for a high grade Carson City type collection. Population: 54 in 67, 3 finer (7/07).
From The #3 PCGS 'Mile High' Registry Set of Carson City Morgan Dollars. (#7152)

2305 1885-CC MS67 PCGS. Ex: R. Dier Collection. This virtually brilliant Superb Gem has flashy fields and potent luster. Sharply struck and well preserved with obvious eye appeal. The lowest mintage Carson City Morgan dollar, and in circulated condition, the rarest issue in the series, aside from the 1895. Population: 36 in 67, 1 finer (7/07).
From The #3 PCGS 'Mile High' Registry Set of Carson City Morgan Dollars. (#7160)

Choice Mint State 1889-CC Dollar – The Key to the Carson City Series

2306 1889-CC MS64 PCGS. The 1889-CC is the king of the Carson City Morgan dollars. The 1881-CC and 1885-CC have lower mintages, but are far more plentiful in Mint State, principally due to the GSA hoard. Only a single 1889-CC was present in the GSA holdings. The 1892-CC and 1893-CC also had just one representative in the GSA sales, but are available in Mint State compared to the 1889-CC.

The reason for this is a hoard of Carson City dollars released in 1955. According to the December 1955 Numismatist, The Montana Bank in Great Falls, Montana received a routine shipment of silver dollars from the Minneapolis Federal Reserve Bank, which contained 1,000 1893-CC dollars. The 1955 Treasury dispersal also included 50 bags (per dealer Steve Ruddel) of the 1892-CC.

Some 1889-CC dollars were paid out from the Treasury between the 1920s and 1950s, but most pieces were probably released into circulation in 1889. The Carson City Mint had ceased coinage in 1885, and surplus dollars were likely shipped by rail to San Francisco. Silver dollars may have scarce in Nevada by 1889, when changes in political winds allowed the Mint to resume production.

The typical 1889-CC dollar has XF sharpness but has been cleaned or is otherwise impaired. Examples are found in all circulated grades, and in fact PCGS has certified four pieces as Fair 2. Even low grade examples are coveted by collectors, due to the allure of the Carson City Mint. The 1889-CC becomes very scarce in Mint State, and is essentially uncollectible above the MS64 grade.

PCGS has certified only two such pieces, an MS65 and an MS68.

The present MS64 example is highly attractive for the grade. The cartwheel luster is unbroken, and the light gold toning only affirms the originality. Even the cheek lacks noticeable marks, and the central strike is good, with only minor incompleteness on the hair above the ear. A trace of a fingerprint on the reverse at 6:30 is of no importance. This high end near-Gem is certain to be cherished by its fortunate next owner.
From The #3 PCGS 'Mile High' Registry Set of Carson City Morgan Dollars. (#7190)

Beautiful Gem 1890-CC Dollar

2307 **1890-CC MS65 PCGS.** This remarkable Gem is lightly toned, and has vibrant luster and outstanding preservation. By Carson City standards, the mintage of the 1890-CC is relatively high. More than 2.3 million pieces were struck. This quantity was more than ten times the production of the 1885-CC, yet the 1885-CC is more than ten times as available as the 1890-CC in MS65. The difference is primarily due to the GSA hoard, which had plenty of '85-CC dollars but very few quality '90-CC dollars.
From The #3 PCGS 'Mile High' Registry Set of Carson City Morgan Dollars. (#7198)

MS66 1891-CC Dollar
Ex: Greg Bingham NFL Set

2308 **1891-CC MS66 PCGS.** Ex: NFL Set. VAM-3. A Top 100 Variety. A blush of tan patina graces the portrait, but this lustrous premium Gem is generally only lightly toned. The centers are sharply struck, and only the eagle's claws do not possess meticulous detail. The fields are gorgeously preserved, and even Liberty's cheek and neck have only a whisper of contact. The 1891-CC issue is more elusive in finer grades than the GSA hoard dates from the 1880s. Population: 33 in 66, with only 1 finer (2/04).
Greg Bingham NFL Collection, FUN Signature Sale (Heritage, 1/01), lot 7958; Mike Casper Collection; FUN Signature Sale (Heritage, 1/02), lot 7494.
From The #3 PCGS 'Mile High' Registry Set of Carson City Morgan Dollars. (#7206)

Splendid 1892-CC Dollar MS66

2309 **1892-CC MS66 PCGS.** Although the 1891-CC emerged in quantity from the GSA holdings, the 1892-CC was apparently dispersed from Treasury vaults prior to 1964. Uncirculated examples of the 1892-CC are obtainable, but only for a price, because the GSA auctions increased demand for all Carson City Morgan dollar dates. The 1892-CC becomes an important conditional rarity at the MS66 level, since most survivors have too many facial marks to achieve that lofty grade. The present untoned piece is an exception. The reverse is immaculate, the obverse field is unabraded, and the portrait has only inconsequential grazes. A precise strike further ensures the eye appeal. Population: 20 in 66, 2 finer (7/07).
From The #3 PCGS 'Mile High' Registry Set of Carson City Morgan Dollars. (#7214)

Scarce Near-Gem 1893-CC Dollar

2310 1893-CC MS64 PCGS. A well struck example of this difficult final-year Carson City dollar. Light gold patina visits the lustrous and unblemished fields and devices. Struck from multiply clashed dies. In the early 1960s, the Treasury holdings of silver dollars was nearly depleted by speculators. Most of the remaining million plus pieces were Uncirculated examples from the storied Carson City Mint. These were auctioned by the General Services Administration during the 1970s. While large quantities of 1880 to 1885 CC-mint dollars were sold, three dates did not appear in the GSA sales: the 1889-CC, 1892-CC, and 1893-CC. The indifferent storage and handling of certain hoards, such as Redfield's, has also contributed to the high grade scarcity of the 1893-CC.
From The #3 PCGS 'Mile High' Registry Set of Carson City Morgan Dollars. (#7222)

ADDITIONAL MORGAN DOLLARS

2311 1878 8TF MS65 PCGS. VAM-14.1. The frosty Gem has brilliant silver luster on both sides with a few slight tawny splashes on the reverse. It is fully struck and seldom found any finer. PCGS has only holdered 32 finer ones in over 20 years of coin certification. (#7072)

Impressive 1878 7/5TF Strong MS65 Dollar
Finer Than Any PCGS Has Certified as VAM-40

2312 1878 7/8TF Strong MS65 PCGS. Strong VAM-40 7/5. Five underfeathers show on this VAM-40 variety, attributed by the bold bottom berry on the branch held in the eagle's right (left facing) claw (photo on page 151 of the *Comprehensive Catalog and Encyclopedia of Morgan & Peace Dollars*, Fourth Edition). This Gem "Strong" example displays bright luster radiating from untoned surfaces, and a well executed strike impart sharp definition to the design elements, including the hair over Liberty's ear and the eagle's breast feathers. A few minor luster grazes prevent an even higher grade. The present lot is higher graded than any of the 19 examples certified as VAM-40 by PCGS.
From The Arnold & Harriet Collection, Part Two. (#134037)

2313 1878 7/8TF Weak MS65 NGC. VAM-33. Designated only as a 7TF Reverse of 1878 by NGC. The right reverse border is powder-blue and golden-brown, while the remainder of this lustrous Gem is brilliant. Well struck and thoroughly attractive. (#7070)

2314 1878 7/8TF Weak MS65 NGC. VAM-33. A "doubled legs" VAM with portions of four tailfeathers beneath the prominent seven tailfeathers. Lustrous and nearly brilliant with a well preserved obverse field and a few small strike-throughs (as made) on the chin. Clashed near Liberty's mouth. (#134032)

2315 1878 7TF Reverse of 1878 MS65 ANACS. A fresh, untoned example with swirling mint frost and a prooflike appearance in the reverse field. The features are crisply defined, and the surfaces are unusually clean. (#7074)

2316 1878 7TF Reverse of 1878 MS65 Prooflike PCGS. The 7 Tail Feather Reverse style was used in about a 10:1 ratio over the short-lived 8 Tail Feather Reverse, but Gem 7 Tail Feather Reverse specimens are nonetheless elusive. Brilliant silver-white and fully prooflike on both sides, certified in an old-style PCGS green-label holder. A nice coin for the grade. (#7075)

2317 1878 7TF Reverse of 1879 MS64 PCGS. Orange, dove-gray, fire-red, and apple-green consume the obverse, while the reverse is generally untoned except for slender peripheral bands of golden-brown and ruby-red. A well struck and attractive example of this first-year issue, struck from redesigned reverse dies. (#7076)

Highly Lustrous 1878 7TF Reverse of 1879 Dollar, MS65

2318 1878 7TF Reverse of 1879 MS65 ANACS. The "Slanting Arrow Feather" variety. Light gold color resides on the highly lustrous surfaces of this wonderful Gem. Well struck throughout, and showing just a few minor marks and luster grazes. Some prooflike tendencies are noted in the fields. (#7076)

Sharply Struck 1878 7TF Reverse of 1879 Gem Dollar

2319 **1878 7TF Reverse of 1879 MS65 PCGS.** Leroy Van Allen and A. George Mallis (1991) write that: "This design type uses the seven tail feather C reverse with round eagle's breast and slanted arrow feathers that was used on later years from 1879 to 1904." A hint or two of light gold-tan color visits the obverse of this highly lustrous Gem that reveal just a few minute, grade-consistent marks. All of the design elements are well brought up. PCGS has seen just six examples finer (7/07).
From The Arnold & Harriet Collection, Part Two. (#7076)

Gem 1878 7TF Reverse of '79 Dollar

2320 **1878 7TF Reverse of 1879 MS65 PCGS.** The uppermost feather in the fletching on the arrows appears askew to the rest, a distinguishing feature of the Reverse of 1879. This lovely example displays strong detail at the often-soft hair above the ear and pleasing luster beneath swirling cloud-gray, azure, peach, and rose patina. PCGS has certified just six pieces finer (8/07). (#7076)

2321 **1878-CC MS65 PCGS.** A boldly impressed and delightful Carson City dollar from the first year of the Morgan design. The surfaces shine beneath vibrant gold, peach, and cornflower-blue patina with silver-gray overtones. (#7080)

2322 **1878-CC MS65 NGC.** A frosty and delightful Gem from the first of many issues that would make the Carson City silver dollar a numismatic icon. Though the coin is practically brilliant at first glance, modest haze appears in the fields, which also exhibit subtle ice-blue iridescence. (#7080)

Exquisite 1878-CC Dollar, MS66

2323 **1878-CC MS66 NGC.** This exquisitely struck Carson City Mint specimen displays smooth silver-gray surfaces that exude glowing luster. Nicely preserved, with just one minor mark on the jaw. David Bowers (2006) estimates that a little less than one-half of the 2.212 million-piece mintage was melted under the Pittman Act. (#7080)

Beautiful Premium Gem 1878-CC Morgan Dollar

2324 **1878-CC MS66 PCGS.** All the components of a great type coin are exhibited by this visually alluring Premium Gem. From the first year of issue for the immensely popular Morgan dollar series, this piece is fully struck and displays intense, coruscating mint frost over both sides. Vivid red-gold and cobalt-blue obverse peripheral toning greatly increases the eye appeal of the coin. A few wispy field marks preclude an even loftier grade assessment. (#7080)

Lovely Premium Gem 1878-CC Morgan Dollar

2325 **1878-CC MS66 NGC.** This example has a sharp striking impression, with frosty luster and bright silver-white surfaces with glints of rose at the centers. A faint patch of roller marks is present on the chin. A vibrant representative from the first year of issue, struck at the newest Mint at the time; the Carson City facility opened in 1870. NGC has certified just seven coins finer (7/07). (#7080)

2326 **1878-CC MS64 Prooflike PCGS.** A fully brilliant piece with delightful mirrored fields and excellent cameo contrast. This piece will appeal to Morgan dollar collectors, Carson City Mint collectors, and first-year of issue type collectors. (#7081)

2327 **1878-CC MS64 Prooflike NGC.** The brilliantly mirrored fields show some minor contact on each side, but the devices drip with thick mint frost. A golden-ringed obverse complements blushes of rose-pink on the reverse. (#7081)

2328 **1878-CC MS63 Deep Mirror Prooflike NGC.** A white-on-black Carson City dollar with outstanding contrast and an exemplary strike. Light marks on the left obverse field prevent an even finer assessment. (#97081)

2329 **1878-CC MS63 Deep Mirror Prooflike PCGS.** The fields offer blinding reflectivity even at a distance, and the sharply struck devices offer rich, creamy frost. An impressive first-year Carson City Morgan dollar, appealing despite the light, scattered abrasions that account for the grade. (#97081)

2330 **1878-CC MS64 Deep Mirror Prooflike ANACS.** Richly frosted, boldly impressed devices and blazing, reflective fields combine for stellar contrast on this first-year Carson City Morgan dollar. The margins have a thin band of gold-orange patina with a touch of violet at the upper obverse. (#97081)

2331 **1878-S MS65 PCGS.** The obverse has gorgeous concentric bands of golden-brown, powder-blue, and rose-gold patina. The reverse displays deep rose and sea-green color. A lustrous Gem that has a razor-sharp strike and a well preserved reverse. The cheek has a few minor abrasions, which do not interfere with the coin's eye appeal. (#7082)

Iridescently Toned MS67 1878-S Morgan Dollar

2332 **1878-S MS67 PCGS.** Splendidly patinated in mottled rose, gold, blue-green, and cream-gray hues. Mint luster shines through the multicolored toning. This exactingly struck Superb Gem is remarkably unabraded, and is certain to be a subject of admiration from its fortunate next owner. Housed in a green label holder. Population: 19 in 67, 1 finer (8/07). (#7082)

Stunning 1878-S Superb Gem Dollar

2333 **1878-S MS67 NGC.** A stunning, absolutely Superb example of this popular first-year San Francisco Mint issue. Well struck, including sharp delineation in the hair over Liberty's ear and the eagle's breast feathers. The impeccably preserved surfaces are mostly brilliant except for irregular splotches of gray color on the cheek, and reddish-purple patina on the upper reverse. Census: 29 in 67, 0 finer (8/07). (#7082)

2334 **1879 MS65 PCGS.** This conditionally scarce silver dollar has sweeping luster and a good strike. Nearly brilliant and carefully preserved. Certified in an old green label holder. (#7084)

2335 **1879 MS65 PCGS.** The 1879 Morgan dollar is an underrated and elusive coin in Gem condition, despite its large mintage approaching 15 million coins. Its subsequent scarcity in high grade is almost certainly a function of melting under the 1918 Pittman Act. The present piece is a radiant, frosty silver Gem, certified in an old-style green-label holder, pristine for the grade. (#7084)

Amazing Gem 1879 Morgan, MS66

2336 **1879 MS66 PCGS.** An amazing example with cameo contrast and exceptional eye appeal. The devices are highly lustrous and brilliant with frosty texture, surrounded by reflective fields. Both sides have peripheral lilac, gold, and blue toning serving to frame the central motifs. Population: 75 in 66, 1 finer (8/07). (#7084)

2337 **1879 MS64 Deep Mirror Prooflike ANACS.** Delicate haze settles over the immensely reflective surfaces of this second-year Morgan dollar, and the rims show amber patina. The well-defined, richly frosted devices are largely clean, though a cluster of marks is noted in the right reverse field. (#97085)

2338 **1879-CC AU58 ANACS.** Close to Mint State in terms of wear, but this piece shows light rim filing and signs of cleaning that have left it overly shiny. A couple of abrasions are noted on the cheek, but this coin still has much attraction and would fit well into a Mint State set at an advantageous price. (#7086)

Charming MS60 Details 1879-CC Dollar

2339 **1879-CC—Cleaned—ANACS. Unc. Details. Net MS60.** Freckles of golden-brown and forest-green cling to the peripheries of this lustrous key date Carson City dollar. Although designated as "Cleaned" by ANACS, even the experienced collector will have difficulty detecting any impairment, and we suggest in person examination to confirm the true quality of this attractive example. *From The Mario Eller Collection, Part One.* (#7086)

Popular 1879-CC Morgan Dollar MS62

2340 **1879-CC MS62 NGC.** This lustrous and suitably struck key date Carson City dollar is primarily brilliant, although the margins have blushes of apricot toning. The left obverse is typically abraded, but the remainder of the coin is well preserved. Housed in a prior generation holder. (#7086)

Lovely Near-Gem 1879-CC Morgan Dollar

2341 1879-CC MS64 PCGS. Whispers of tan-gold color gravitate to the margins of this near-Gem Carson City issue. Attractive mint frost adorns both sides, and a powerful strike makes itself known in sharp definition on Liberty's hair, particularly that over the ear. Noticeable motif-field contrast is apparent when the coin is tilted beneath a lamp. The '79-CC becomes more difficult to acquire any finer. (#7086)

2342 1879-CC Capped Die—Cleaned—ANACS. AU50 Details. VAM-3. A Top 100 Variety. Luster outlines the legends and fills design recesses. This pearl-gray example is subdued from a dip, but the devices show only moderate wear. A faded V-shaped mark is noted near the M in UNUM. A popular CC-mint key. (#7088)

2343 1879-CC Capped Die AU55 NGC. VAM-3. A Top 100 Variety. This chestnut-gray semi-key silver dollar has minimal marks, and although the centers show slight wear, satin luster is nonetheless extensive. The reverse has a minor ding at 8 o'clock. (#7088)

MS62 1879-CC Capped Die Dollar

2344 1879-CC Capped Die MS62 PCGS. VAM-3. A Top 100 Variety. A classic example of the Capped Die VAM, with numerous minute die chips near the mintmark. The cream-gray fields and devices are bounded by honey-gold and ice-blue toning. The centers are slightly soft, but the remainder of the piece is sharply defined. (#7088)

Select 1879-CC Capped Die Dollar

2345 1879-CC Capped Die MS63 ANACS. VAM-3. A Top 100 Variety. A satiny pearl-gray representative of this elusive CC-mint issue. Reasonably struck and carefully preserved. The Capped Die variety is now believed to be a repunched Medium over Small CC mintmark, and is more widely collected than before its true nature was revealed. (#7088)

2346 1879-O MS64 PCGS. An astonishing melange of variegated coloration occurs over the obverse of this lovely near-Gem dollar from the New Orleans Mint. Sky-blue, amber, and olive hues are the most prominent. The design features are sharply struck and the highly lustrous surfaces only display a few grade-limiting blemishes. (#7090)

Scarce Gem 1879-O Morgan Dollar

2347 1879-O MS65 ANACS. Well struck and highly lustrous, with intense cartwheel flash in the obverse and reverse fields. A slight degree of pastel color occurs over Liberty's portrait, but the remaining surface areas are brilliant and snowy-white. Surface marks are minor on both sides. The 1879-O is a scarce New Orleans issue at the Gem level of preservation that becomes rare any finer. (#7090)

Pleasing MS65 1879-O Dollar

2348 1879-O MS65 PCGS. This is the first Morgan dollar struck at the New Orleans Mint. Occasional freckles of light tan-gold color are visible on semi-prooflike surfaces that reveal fewer marks than are ordinarily seen on the issue. Generally well struck, and housed in a green label holder. David Bowers (2005) says: MS64 coins are scarce, and in proportion to the demand for them, MS65 pieces are rare." *From The Arnold & Harriet Collection, Part Two.* (#7090)

Conditionally Scarce Gem 1879-O Morgan Dollar

2349 1879-O MS65 PCGS. Long regarded as one of the more important condition rarities among New Orleans Morgan dollars, the typical '79-O is far too bagmarked and poorly struck to merit consideration at such a lofty level as this piece. This is an extraordinary example that should interest even the most advanced collector in this series. The devices are sharply struck and exceedingly frosty while the fields are bright and lustrous, and have avoided virtually all signs of coin-to-coin contact. Brilliant and untoned throughout. (#7090)

2350 **1879-S MS65 ICG.** Lustrous surfaces display an untoned obverse, and a reverse toned in gold-yellow, crimson, sky-blue, and emerald-green. Well struck and nicely preserved. The "third reverse" with a slanting top arrow feather. (#7092)

2351 **1879-S MS67 NGC.** An attractive Superb Gem, this largely untoned S-mint offers occasional hints of silver-gray patina in the fields. Boldly impressed with traces of frost on the devices. A single minuscule luster graze is noted on Liberty's cheek. (#7092)

2352 **1879-S MS67 PCGS.** The design features are boldly impressed, and the lustrous surfaces are virtually free of toning and contact marks. An outstanding '79-S dollar and an excellent type coin. (#7092)

2353 **1879-S MS67★ NGC.** A brilliant Superb Gem that is specially designated by NGC for its exceptional quality, this piece has a prooflike obverse and a satiny reverse. (#7092)

2354 **1879-S MS65 Deep Mirror Prooflike PCGS.** A flashy Gem with good white-on-black contrast. Exactingly struck, and the fields are nearly unabraded. Encased in a green label holder. (#97093)

2355 **1880 8/7 MS64 NGC.** VAM-9. A Top 100 Variety. The "Stem" overdate with suggestive die fill within the loops of the second 8 in the date. The obverse features rich orange, gunmetal-gray, and cobalt-blue patina. The brilliant reverse center is framed by peach iridescence. (#7096)

2356 **1880-CC 8 Over Low 7 MS65 PCGS.** VAM-6. A Top 100 Variety. Well struck with electric blue in the center of the obverse and russet-gold around. The lustrous reverse has peach patina at the rims and light frost on the eagle. Housed in an old green label holder. (#7100)

Beautiful Premium Gem 1880-CC Morgan Dollar, VAM-3

2357 **1880-CC MS66 PCGS.** VAM-3. A tiny dash occurs just below the second 8 in the date. Both Cs in the mintmark are filled by die chips, and an amazing amount of extra metal fills the recesses of IN GOD WE TRUST. This is a singularly lovely Premium Gem, with softly radiant luster and a thick coating of silver mint frost over both sides. An arc of beautiful rainbow toning lies across the top of the obverse. (#7100)

Pleasing MS66 1880-CC Dollar

2358 **1880-CC MS66 NGC.** This 1880-CC is the variety with the Reverse of 1879 with slanted top arrow feather. David Bowers (2005) writes that many of these coins are extensively bagmarked. This Premium Gem, however, displays gorgeous, radiantly lustrous surfaces that are devoid of mentionable marks. Nicely struck despite the usual '80-CC weakness in the hair over Liberty's ear. Both sides are essentially untoned. (#7100)

Lustrous 1880-CC Premium Gem Dollar

2359 **1880-CC MS66 PCGS.** This Premium Gem example is the Reverse of 1879, with slanting top arrow feather and rounded eagle's breast. Wisps of faint tan-gold color adhere to highly lustrous surfaces that exhibit well impressed design elements. A few grade-consistent luster grazes on the cheek and neck are not at all bothersome. (#7100)

Impressive Premium Gem 1880-CC Dollar

2360 **1880-CC MS66 PCGS.** Reverse of 1879. This variety is attributed by its rounded eagle's breast and a slanted top arrow feather. Intense mint frost covers the essentially untoned silver-white surfaces, and the striking details are generally bold, if a trifle weak at the centers. Faint luster grazes are noted on the obverse, and a few small contact marks on the reverse. (#7100)

Popular 1880-CC 8 Over High 7 Dollar, MS66

2361 1880-CC 8 Over High 7 MS66 PCGS. VAM-5. A Top 100 Variety. The overdate feature and VAM are undesignated on the PCGS green label, but there is clear evidence of the crossbar and upright of a high underdigit 7 within the second 8 of the date; just a slight portion of the base of the 7 shows beneath the 8. The radiantly lustrous surfaces of this Premium Gem display just the slightest hint of light tan speckles under high magnification. Partially prooflike fields establish mild contrast with the well struck motifs. A few minor luster grazes are consistent with the grade designation, and there are some light obverse as-made roller marks. Population: 58 in 66 8 Over High 7, 5 finer (7/07).
From The Arnold & Harriet Collection, Part Two. (#7102)

2362 1880/79-CC Reverse of 1878 MS64 PCGS. VAM-4. A Top 100 Variety. Portions of the underdigits 7 and 9 are clearly visible under 80. Light silver-gray surfaces exhibit pleasing luster and well struck devices on this pretty near-Gem. (#7108)

2363 1880/79-CC Reverse of 1878 MS64 PCGS. VAM-4. A Top 100 Variety. Although not a particular rarity, this piece always draws attention from collectors. A frosty and fully brilliant near-Gem. (#7108)

2364 1880/79-CC Reverse of 1878 MS64 NGC. VAM-4. A Top 100 Variety. An essentially brilliant Choice Carson City dollar with unabraded fields and faint facial grazes. One of the more dramatic overdates in the Morgan dollar series. (#7108)

1880/79-CC VAM-4 Dollar MS65

2365 1880/79-CC Reverse of 1878 MS65 PCGS. VAM-4. A Top 100 Variety. Light yellow-gold toning graces the right obverse margin, but this lustrous Carson City dollar is otherwise brilliant. A well struck representative with an impeccably preserved obverse. A concealed mark on the eagle's left leg will be missed by many observers. (#7108)

Sharp 1880-CC 8/7, Reverse of 1878 Dollar MS66 VAM-7

2366 1880-CC 8/7 Reverse of 1878 MS66 PCGS. VAM-7. A less dramatic overdate variety than some of the others from the Carson City Mint this year. VAM-7 is distinguished by the presence of a slight dash under the second 8 in the date. This Reverse of 1878 has seven tail feathers, a concave eagle's breast, parallel arrow feathers, and small CC. David Bowers, in his Silver and Trade dollar reference work (1993), says: "Probably about 10% to 20% of surviving 1880-CC Morgan dollars in Mint State are of this type.
  A well directed strike imparts excellent definition to the design elements of this Premium Gem example, including the hair over Liberty's ear and the eagle's breast feathers. Highly lustrous surfaces are essentially untoned and well cared for, revealing just a few minor luster grazes. (#7110)

2367 1880-O MS64 NGC. Micro O. A beautiful and splendidly lustrous near-Gem with remarkably smooth fields for the MS64 grade. Even the cheek and neck display minimal contact. Virtually untoned and precisely struck. (#7114)

2368 1880-O MS64 ANACS. Sharply struck and highly lustrous, with scattered reddish-gold accents on each side. Minor scuffiness on the cheek and a few scattered field marks limit the grade. A scarce New Orleans issue in the higher Mint State grades, and truly rare in Gem condition. (#7114)

2369 1880-O MS64 PCGS. Oval O. Lustrous and well struck with light autumn-gold toning. Smooth for the grade, and surprisingly scarce at the MS64 level. (#7114)

2370 **1880-O Hangnail MS64 PCGS.** VAM-48. A Top 100 Variety. The popular "Hangnail" variety, not noted on the PCGS insert. This near-Gem is well struck and untoned, with an intense cartwheel sheen across both sides. Mild scuffiness on Liberty's cheek and scattered minor field marks define the grade. A great opportunity for the collector of Top 100 Morgan dollar VAMs. *From The Arnold & Harriet Collection, Part Two.* (#133879)

2371 **1880-O Second 8/7 MS62 Deep Mirror Prooflike ANACS.** VAM-5. A Top 100 Variety. Medium O. This nicely mirrored New Orleans dollar is brilliant save for a hint of peach toning near the rims. Considered scarcer than VAM-4, which has similar die fill within the upper loop of the second 8. (#97115)

2372 **1880/79-O MS63 ANACS.** VAM-4. A Top 100 Variety. Micro O. Booming luster and a bold strike assert the quality of this carefully preserved overdated dollar. (#7116)

2373 **1880/79-O MS64 PCGS.** VAM-4. A Top 100 Variety. Micro O. The overdate feature is undesignated on the PCGS holder. A lustrous chestnut-gold near-Gem that has a sharp strike and smooth fields. (#7116)

2374 **1880-S MS63 ★ NGC.** Medium S. Magnificent gold, violet-red, and steel-blue endow the reverse of this moderately prooflike silver dollar. (#7118)

2375 **1880-S MS64 PCGS,** Medium S, the reverse features dramatic cherry-red, sea-green, and gold patina; **1881-S MS64 PCGS,** the obverse is ocean-blue with peripheral lemon and ruby-red shades, the right reverse has lemon, peach, powder-blue, and apple-green toning; **1882-S MS64 NGC,** the obverse is pink-red and blue-green, the reverse has a brilliant center bounded by golden-brown and forest-green margins. (Total: 3 coins) (#7118)

2376 **1880-S MS65 NGC.** Medium S. Impressive violet-red, apple-green, sky-blue and orange-gold dominate the reverse. The obverse is largely untoned, but offers slender orange, rose, and blue-green bands near the left border. (#7118)

2377 **1880-S MS66 ★ NGC.** Medium S. Gorgeous bands of cherry-red, apple-green, gold, and sky-blue alternate across this crisply struck Morgan dollar. The reverse and the portrait are well preserved, and the obverse field has only minor contact. An opportunity for the connoisseur of original toning. (#7118)

2378 **1880-S MS66 NGC.** Medium S. A satiny Premium Gem fully patinated in orange, rose-red, and apple-green. Encapsulated in a prior generation holder. (#7118)

2379 **1880-S MS66 PCGS.** Boldly impressed with vibrant luster, two hallmarks of this popular type issue. The obverse exhibits rich lime-green patina with mint and jade accents, while the reverse is silver-gray. (#7118)

2380 **1880-S MS67 NGC.** Medium S. A remarkably smooth Superb Gem that has only a whisper of gold toning along the obverse periphery. The strike is good, with minor incompleteness limited to the hair above the ear. (#7118)

2381 **1880-S MS67 PCGS.** Bands of golden-russet, rose, and aqua-blue toning grace the lower left obverse border. This thoroughly lustrous Superb Gem is magnificently preserved. Nearly imperceptible roller marks (as made) cross the forehead. The large S mintmark is repunched on the upper serif. (#7118)

2382 **1880-S MS67 NGC.** Medium S. A precisely struck Superb Gem with booming luster and virtually pristine fields. A trace of gold and ice-blue toning precludes full brilliance. Certified in a green label holder. (#7118)

2383 **1880-S MS67 NGC.** Large S. Deep golden-brown, mauve-red, and navy-blue envelop this well-preserved and sharply struck silver dollar. A noteworthy and immensely lustrous example of this popular type issue. (#7118)

2384 **1880-S MS67 NGC.** The reverse is fairly prooflike, the obverse a bit less so, with good mirrors on the reverse and more frosty fields on the obverse. Neither side shows any mentionable distractions, although some faint toning lines are seen in the left obverse field before the face of Liberty. (#7118)

MS68 ★ 1880-S Silver Dollar

2385 **1880-S MS68 ★ NGC.** Medium S. The obverse is prooflike and features obvious cameo contrast between the frosty portrait and the glassy field. The reverse is merely semi-prooflike. The borders display light gold toning. The fields are immaculate, and the devices possess only the faintest grazes. (#7118)

Lovely 1880-S Dollar, MS68

2386 **1880-S MS68 PCGS.** Ex: Mike Casper Collection. A well executed strike leaves sharp definition on the motifs, including the hair over Liberty's ear and the eagle's breast feathers. The barest hint of occasional light tan color is visible under magnification, but does not obscure the noticeable field-device contrast. Immaculately preserved throughout. (#7118)

Sharp MS68 1880-S Dollar

2387 **1880-S MS68 PCGS.** With a mintage approaching 9 million pieces, the 1880-S is one of the most plentiful of all early Morgan dollars, several tens of thousands having been certified by PCGS and NGC. Sharp definition shows on this MS68 coin, complementing vibrant luster and impeccably preserved surfaces. Both faces are essentially untoned. (#7118)

2388 **1880-S MS66 Prooflike NGC.** Medium S. Lemon, ruby-red, sea-green, and light mauve hues endow this beautiful older holder Morgan dollar. A minimally abraded example with an interesting and small mint-made planchet flaw on the nose. (#7119)

2389 **1880-S MS67 ★ Prooflike NGC.** Medium S. The prominently mirrored fields approach a DPL designation, and the icy devices provide impressive white-on-black contrast. A gorgeously preserved example of this popular 19th century type. (#7119)

2390 **1880-S MS67 Prooflike PCGS.** Medium S. This faintly toned Superb Gem exhibits dazzling luster, and the strike is precise, particularly on the eagle's breast feathers and claws. The obverse is practically pristine. (#7119)

2391 **1880-S MS67 Prooflike PCGS.** Snow-white devices contrast against the deeply reflective fields. Brilliant and sharply struck with good portions of mint frost on the devices. A small graze on Liberty's lower jaw is noteworthy as the only mark on either of the central devices, and field blemishes are nearly as scarce. A beautiful and extraordinary prooflike Superb Gem. (#7119)

2392 **1880-S MS66 Deep Mirror Prooflike PCGS.** Large S. A prominently mirrored and lightly toned Premium Gem that boasts the penetrating strike often seen on this well made issue. Frosty devices provide obvious cameo contrast. (#97119)

Impressive 1880-S Dollar, MS67 Deep Mirror Prooflike

2393 **1880-S MS67 Deep Mirror Prooflike NGC.** The 1880-S dollar, with a mintage of nearly 9 million pieces, is one of the most plentiful of early Morgans. Even Deep Mirror Prooflike specimens through the MS65 level of preservation can be located without too much trouble. Superb Deep Mirror pieces, however, are much more elusive. This essentially untoned MS67 example displays stunning field-motif contrast, and has been well cared for. These attributes are complemented by a powerful strike that emboldens the design elements. Census: 14 in 67 Deep Mirror Prooflike, 3 finer (8/07). (#97119)

Superb Gem 1880/9-S Morgan Dollar

2394 **1880/9-S MS67 PCGS.** VAM-11. A Hot 50 Variety. Parts of the undertype are visible on the 0 in the date. Essentially untoned surfaces exhibit intense cartwheel luster and sharply impressed design elements, including strong definition in the hair over Liberty's ear and on the eagle's breast feathers. A couple of faint obverse luster grazes do not distract. (#7122)

2395 **1881 MS65 PCGS.** Both sides of this boldly impressed P-mint Gem show vibrant luster beneath captivating patina. Impressive gold, rose, blue-green, and lavender-plum toning saturates the obverse, while the reverse shows only slightly less muted patina. (#7124)

2396 **1881 MS65 PCGS.** While the 1881 dollar issue had a mintage nearly three-quarters that of its S-mint counterpart, the P-mint pieces are much more elusive in Mint State grades, particularly Gem and better. This crisply struck and strongly lustrous piece offers a veil of gold-orange patina over each side with deeper toning near the date. (#7124)

2397 **1881-CC MS65 PCGS.** Exquisitely struck, including the hair at Liberty's ear and the eagle's breast feathers. Lustrous light gray surfaces reveal just a few minor obverse marks. (#7126)

2398 **1881-CC MS65 NGC.** Remarkable quality with light silver luster and peripheral gold toning. Both sides are fully detailed, including excellent hair details over Liberty's ear. (#7126)

2399 **1881-CC MS65 PCGS.** A crisply struck Gem representative of this earlier Carson City issue, appealing with soft, frosty luster and a blush of rose toning at the center of the obverse. Minimally marked and pleasing, one of only 296,000 pieces struck. (#7126)

2400 **1881-CC MS66 PCGS.** This Premium Gem displays semi-prooflike fields and mildly frosted motifs, resulting in a cameo-like effect on both sides. Hints of light tan-gray color are more noticeable on the reverse. A well struck beauty from this noteworthy Carson City issue. (#7126)

2401 **1881-CC MS66 NGC.** A frosty and exquisite representative of this popular Carson City issue, one of several heavily popularized by the GSA sales. Wisps of hazy golden patina grace both sides, and strong luster shines beneath the toning. (#7126)

Flashy 1881-CC Superb Gem Dollar

2402 **1881-CC MS67 PCGS.** This flashy 1881-CC Superb Gem exhibits a powerful strike that emboldens the design elements, including excellent delineation in the hair at Liberty's ear and the eagle's breast feathers. A wisp or two of light olive-green patina graces the obverse, and noticeable field-motif contrast is evident on both sides. Impeccably preserved surfaces reveal no more than a few unobtrusive luster grazes. PCGS and NGC each have graded a mere three pieces finer (7/07).
From The Arnold & Harriet Collection, Part Two. (#7126)

2403 **1881-CC MS65 Prooflike PCGS.** The frost on the sharply struck devices is thick, and the reflectivity of the mirrors is deep. A few wisps of haze are noted over the flashy fields of this outstanding Carson City Gem. (#7127)

2404 **1881-CC MS65 Prooflike PCGS.** VAM-2. Die fill within the upper loop of the second 8 in the date somewhat resembles the "8 Over Low 7" 1880-CC variety. The prominently mirrored fields are brilliant, and the centers are penetratingly struck. (#7127)

2405 **1881-CC MS64 Deep Mirror Prooflike ANACS.** VAM-2. An interesting VAM for its die fill in the upper loop of the second 8, suggestive of the crossbar of a 7. This low mintage CC-mint dollar has lemon-gold borders and brilliant mirrored fields. Well struck with a beautifully smooth reverse. (#97127)

2406 **1881-O MS65 NGC.** The 1881-O Morgan dollar commands a price comparable to its more available S-mint counterpart through Select Mint State, but the former is elusive in Gem. Both sides of this flashy example show frosty, boldly impressed devices. Traces of milky patina mingle with faint traces of iridescence. (#7128)

2407 **1881-S MS65 PCGS.** The semi-prooflike fields serve to brighten each side. This has a minimal effect on the light, golden-toned obverse. However, the magnificent, iridescently toned reverse is considerably enhanced by the flashy fields. (#7130)

2408 **1881-S MS65 NGC,** brilliant, good luster, well struck, an immaculate cheek; **1882 MS65 NGC,** lustrous and suitably struck with faint grazes on the portrait; **1898 MS65 Prooflike PCGS,** a flashy Gem with light gold toning and a small strike-through inside the wreath. (Total: 3 coins) (#7130)

2409 **1881-S MS66 ★ NGC.** Medium intensity multicolored toning covers the obverse, while the reverse is essentially brilliant. A light mark on Liberty's cheek is mentioned for accuracy. The eye appeal of this colorful Premium Gem is simply extraordinary, as confirmed by the coveted "Star" designation from NGC. (#7130)

2410 **1881-S MS66 ★ NGC.** Swaths of ruby-red, lemon, and pale electric-blue enrich the obverse of this flashy and razor-sharp Premium Gem. (#7130)

2411 **1881-S MS66 ★ NGC.** This semi-prooflike silver type coin has gorgeous arcs of ice-blue, gold, sea-green, and rose-red across most of the obverse. The reverse is mostly brilliant despite glimpses of russet along the rims. (#7130)

2412 **1881-S MS66 PCGS.** This Premium Gem displays dazzling luster, and the toned reverse takes on an array of variegated lime-green, crimson, yellow-gold, violet, and forest-green coloration, leaving the obverse brilliant. A solid strike leaves sharp definition on the design elements, including the hair at Liberty's ear and the eagle's breast feathers. Well preserved throughout. (#7130)

2413 **1881-S MS67 NGC.** Strongly lustrous and decisively struck, as are most examples of this type issue. A thin veil of milky haze drapes both sides, while the lower left reverse rim has a thin line of honey-orange patina. Carefully preserved and appealing. (#7130)

2414 **1881-S MS67 PCGS.** An enticing representative of this ubiquitous S-mint Morgan dollar. Arcs of dusky olive-green, gold, and cherry-red toning are particularly dramatic on the reverse. This well struck and thoroughly lustrous Superb Gem is housed in a green label holder. (#7130)

2415 **1881-S MS67 PCGS.** The surfaces of this Superb Gem display satiny, reflective silver luster with colorful rainbow toning over much of the obverse and close to the border on the reverse. Collectors of toned Morgan dollars have nearly limitless opportunity to acquire different pieces. (#7130)

2416 **1881-S MS67 PCGS.** The gleaming surfaces of this enticing Superb Gem are untoned save for crescents of blue-green and reddish-orange at the left obverse and a short arc of peach at the upper reverse. Decisively struck and carefully preserved, a delightful type piece. (#7130)

2417 **1881-S MS67 ★ NGC.** The Star designation for superior eye appeal in this case is a product of the pristine fields and the light ring of cerise and mint-green that encircles portions of the obverse. The reverse is untoned. A superb choice for a type collection. (#7130)

2418 **1881-S MS67 ★ NGC.** Sharply struck and wonderfully preserved, with a thin crescent of golden color along the base of the obverse and spectacular multicolored hues on the reverse. (#7130)

2419 **1881-S MS67 NGC.** When impeccable surface quality is combined with multicolored toning, the results can be quite dramatic. Better than half of the obverse on this splendid example is overlaid in the most vivid green, gold, and violet imaginable. (#7130)

2420 **1881-S MS67 ★ NGC.** This flashy Superb Gem is mostly brilliant, but has beautiful arcs of powder-blue, lemon, and fire-red along the lower right obverse border. Sharply struck, as usual for an '81-S, and the cheek is immaculate. (#7130)

Radiant 1881-S MS67 ★ Dollar

2421 **1881-S MS67 ★ NGC.** The 1881-S, with a mintage approaching 13 million coins, is one of the commonest Mint State Morgan dollars. Examples possessing the coveted Star designation, however, especially in the lofty grade of MS67, are quite scarce. The radiantly lustrous surfaces of the Superb Gem with Star coin in this lot display splashes of vivid crimson, forest-green, and gold toning on the obverse, while remaining nearly untoned on the reverse. An impressive strike emboldens the design elements, and close scrutiny reveals no mentionable marks. (#7130)

2422 **1881-S MS67 ★ NGC.** An amazing Superb Gem specimen with pristine, virtually perfect surfaces, this piece has satiny silver luster with a trace of delightful gold and iridescent toning along the borders. (#7130)

2423 **1881-S MS67 PCGS.** Pure white surfaces have a prooflike obverse exhibiting cameo contrast, and a frosty reverse. Both sides have a sharp, nearly full strike. (#7130)

Colorful MS68 ★ 1881-S Dollar

2424 **1881-S MS68 ★ NGC.** Splashes of aquamarine, peach, gold, and rose-red adorn the obverse of this needle-sharp silver dollar. The reverse is only lightly toned, although the upper border has lemon and pink shades. Occasional minor contact cannot deny the eye appeal of this attractive silver type coin. (#7130)

Dynamic 1881-S Silver Dollar, MS68 ★

2425 **1881-S MS68 ★ NGC.** Both sides of this solidly struck representative offer outstanding luster. While the reverse shows just a touch of lemon-yellow toning at the margins, the obverse displays a broad range of colors, including mint-green, canary-yellow, orange, and magenta. An uncommonly appealing, distinctive, and pristine example for the type collector. (#7130)

Outstanding 1881-S MS68 Dollar

2426 1881-S MS68 PCGS. Ex: Jackson Hole. An MS68 1881-S Morgan dollar—among the most attractive and best-produced of the series—never fails to elicit well-deserved gasps of admiration, and this piece is no exception. The swirling cartwheel luster is deep and unimpeachable, and the coin offers stupendous eye appeal throughout. Liberty's face and neck are free of all but a couple of the most insignificant ticks; diligent searching reveals only a single small luster graze in the right (facing) obverse field. The strike is well executed over the ear, although light roller marks are seen there. The surfaces show just a hint of light tan color through the date area. Population: 80 in 68, 2 finer (8/07). (#7130)

Exquisite 1881-S Dollar, MS68

2427 1881-S MS68 PCGS. Bands of cherry-red, forest-green, peach, and powder-blue toning endow the obverse periphery. The reverse shows only a brief blush of golden toning near 1 o'clock. This exquisitely struck Superb Gem is uncommonly void of marks, even for an 1881-S, which often comes nice. Those who wish only the finest quality within their holdings should consider the present piece. Population: 80 in 68, 2 finer (8/07). (#7130)

2428 1881-S MS63 Prooflike PCGS, the obverse has a wide crescent of rainbow iridescence to the right; **1884-O MS63 PCGS,** the entire obverse is toned with golden-olive, lilac, sky-blue, and sea-green, the reverse is brilliant; **1884-O MS63 ★ NGC,** the obverse is brilliant, the reverse has a splendid display of rainbow toning in three distinct sections; **1885-O MS63 PCGS,** the brilliant obverse has a thin crescent of pale gold from 5 o'clock to 9 o'clock, the reverse has vivid gold, lilac, green, and blue toning over an over of brilliance; **1885-O MS63 ★ NGC,** both sides are toned, the obverse with pastel gold, lilac, blue, and green, the reverse with bluish-gray splashed by lighter gold; **1887 MS63 PCGS,** lustrous and brilliant obverse with an unusual pattern of iridescent toning on the reverse. (Total: 6 coins) (#7131)

2429 1882 MS64 Deep Mirror Prooflike PCGS. A flashy and precisely struck silver dollar with delicate rose and gold toning. A spot between the LA in DOLLAR is all that limits the grade. Housed in a first generation holder. Population: 90 in 64 Deep Mirror Prooflike, 18 finer (7/07). (#97133)

2430 1882-CC MS66 PCGS. Sharply struck and untoned, with beautiful mint frost over the silver-white surfaces, and flashy cartwheel luster in the fields. A handful of trivial marks are noted just to the right of Liberty's mouth, and a few more are observed in the upper reverse field. A beautiful Premium Gem dollar from the Carson City Mint. (#7134)

2431 1882-CC MS66 NGC. Dazzling luster radiates from the untoned surfaces of this Carson City Premium Gem. The design elements have benefited from a well directed strike, and both sides are devoid of significant abrasions. (#7134)

2432 1882-CC MS66 NGC. Well struck with vibrant luster and a touch of tan at the rims. The carefully preserved surfaces exhibit a modicum of haze. An appealing, high-grade representative of this earlier CC-mint Morgan dollar issue. (#7134)

2433 1882-CC MS66 NGC. This is a blindingly brilliant Premium Gem with lovely mint frost over both sides. The design elements are well struck and the surfaces are very clean, as expected for the grade. A readily available issue that is ideal for Carson City type collectors. *From The Arnold & Harriet Collection, Part Two.* (#7134)

Lovely 1882-CC Deep Mirror Prooflike Dollar, MS66

2434 1882-CC MS66 Deep Mirror Prooflike PCGS. Deeply mirrored fields highlight the lightly frosted motifs on this lovely Premium Gem. A sharp strike emboldens the design elements, and just a hint of light gold color gravitates to the obverse periphery. A few minor obverse luster grazes do not disturb. Population: 59 in 66 Deep Mirror Prooflike, 1 finer (8/07). (#97135)

2435 1882-O MS65 PCGS. The vibrant luster of this O-mint Gem borders on flashy. A solidly struck representative with delicate layers of milky patina in the fields. PCGS has graded 19 finer examples (8/07). (#7136)

2436 1882-O MS65 PCGS. A crisply struck and strongly lustrous Gem example of this comparatively available O-mint issue, minimally marked with small dots of milky patina over the obverse. Highly appealing with a handful of scattered luster grazes on each side. *From The Mario Eller Collection, Part One.* (#7136)

2437 1882-O MS65 Prooflike NGC. The bright surfaces show bright, reflective fields on each side. A well-balanced coin that is fully struck and mostly brilliant with just a hint of peripheral color. Census: 18 in 65, 0 finer (8/07). (#7137)

2438 1882-O/S MS63 NGC. VAM-4. A Top 100 Variety. Lushly toned in dusky plum-red, sea-green, and canary-gold shades. Lustrous and sharply struck with a well preserved obverse field. (#7138)

2439 1882-O/S MS63 NGC. VAM-3. A Top 100 Variety. The "O/S Flush" VAM. Golden-brown and blue-green margins invigorate this lustrous and attentively struck Select Morgan dollar. Well preserved for the grade. (#7138)

Untoned 1882-O/S Dollar, MS64, VAM-4

2440 1882-O/S MS64 PCGS. Ex: Larry Shapiro Collection. VAM-4. A Top-100 Variety. A diagonal, recessed crossbar within the O mintmark confirms the variety, as do parallel die polishing lines within the confines of Liberty's ear, and two short lines from the edge of Liberty's hair below the upper end of the cap band. Both sides of this near-Gem are awash in luster, and color free. Nicely struck, with just a few grade-defining marks. PCGS has seen a solitary piece finer (7/07).
From The Arnold & Harriet Collection, Part Two. (#7138)

2441 1882-S MS65 PCGS. Both sides of this frosty dollar have brilliant silver luster with gorgeous rainbow toning over the lower obverse. (#7140)

2442 1882-S MS66 NGC, lightly toned and lustrous with a pinpoint-sharp strike and a pristine appearance; **1900-O MS66 NGC,** well struck, booming luster, nearly untoned, an inconspicuous mark on the nose. (Total: 2 coins) (#7140)

2443 1882-S MS67 NGC. A solidly struck example of this early S-mint issue, blast-white with powerful luster. The fields and devices on both sides are marvelously well-preserved. An excellent choice for the type collector. (#7140)

2444 1882-S MS67 ★ NGC. A fully defined Superb Gem with brilliant silver surfaces, this piece should have received a prooflike designation in our opinion. (#7140)

Deep Mirror Prooflike 1882-S Morgan MS66

2445 1882-S MS66 Deep Mirror Prooflike NGC. Because it is a well produced and fairly obtainable issue, the 1882-S is understandably overlooked as a scarcity in DMPL condition. The present example displays prominently reflective fields and pleasantly frosted devices with light peripheral apricot and sea-green toning. Population: 8 in 66, 0 finer (1/05).
Ex: Dr. Hoffnagle Collection of Morgan Dollars (Heritage, 1/05), lot 11217. (#97141)

Beautifully Toned 1883 Morgan Dollar MS65 ★

2446 1883 MS65 ★ NGC. Both sides show exquisite electric-blue and golden-brown patina. A lustrous and nearly immaculate Gem that would surely grade even higher if the strike was a bit sharper in the centers. The eye appeal of this piece is simply outstanding, however, as noted by the NGC "Star" designation. Census: 14 in 65 ★, 5 finer with ★ (7/07). (#7142)

2447 1883 MS66 NGC. The obverse of this well struck Premium Gem has lovely silver-white surfaces with pleasing cartwheel luster, while the reverse shows immense reflectivity and richly frosted devices. An attractive Philadelphia dollar. (#7142)

2448 1883 MS66 NGC. Outrageously toned on both sides with vivid bands of violet, rose, electric-blue, and golden-brown patina. A lustrous Gem with a good strike and well preserved surfaces. (#7142)

2449 1883 MS66 PCGS. Light blue, green, and amber toning accompanies pastel gold color on both sides of this delightful Premium Gem. (#7142)

Lustrous 1883 MS67 Dollar

2450 1883 MS67 PCGS. Radiantly lustrous surfaces yield soft yellow-gold patina on the obverse, that gives way to deep forest-green, crimson, and gold toning on the reverse. Sharp delineation is apparent on all of the design elements, and there are no significant marks to report. Readily available through MS65, but quite challenging in Superb Gem, and very rare any finer. Population: 51 in 67, 3 finer (8/07). (#7142)

2451 1883-CC MS65 NGC, the right reverse has splashes of violet-red, emerald-green, and orange; and an **1884-CC MS64 PCGS,** the obverse is dominated by gold, lilac, sky-blue, and apple-green, the left obverse is typically abraded. (Total: 2 coins) (#7144)

2452 1883-CC MS66 NGC. Intense mint luster shines forth from the brilliant silver surfaces of this impressive Premium Gem. Boldly struck and minimally marked, this piece would make an ideal representative for Carson City type purposes. (#7144)

2453 1883-CC MS66 NGC. The dazzling, snowy-white surfaces of this lovely Premium Gem reveal boldly rendered design elements and a beautiful cartwheel sheen across each side. The obverse is remarkably clean, and a shallow scrape beneath ATE on the upper reverse is the only minor detraction. (#7144)

2454 1883-CC MS66 PCGS. Luxuriant mint frost gives this Carson City dollar a nearly matchless degree of visual appeal. The blazing surfaces are entirely untoned and silver-white on the obverse, while a faint touch of red-gold color enhances the reverse border. A couple of shallow luster grazes are noted on the cheek, but other marks are nearly nonexistent. (#7144)

Outstanding 1883-CC Superb Gem Dollar

2455 1883-CC MS67 NGC. This Carson City representative possesses deep, frosty luster on bright, highly attractive surfaces. Both sides are essentially untoned and impeccably preserved, revealing just a couple of insignificant marks that in no way detract from the coin's outstanding eye appeal. An attentive strike results in sharp definition on the design features. Extremely difficult to acquire this nice! Census: 89 in 67, 0 finer (7/07).
From The Arnold & Harriet Collection, Part Two. (#7144)

2456 1883-CC MS66 Prooflike PCGS. A moderately reflective piece that displays a degree of cartwheel luster in the untoned fields as well. Solidly struck with a touch of peach on the richly frosted devices. A few small scrapes are noted to the right of the eagle. PCGS has certified only seven finer Prooflike representatives (7/07). (#7145)

2457 1883-CC MS65 Deep Mirror Prooflike PCGS. Both sides of this flashy Gem show excellent reflectivity and a measure of frost on the devices, though the reverse has better contrast. A touch of hazy peach-tinged patina graces both sides of this attractive piece, which comes from an issue popularized by the GSA sales.
From The Mario Eller Collection, Part One. (#97145)

2458 1883-O MS63 ★ NGC. More than half of the obverse is consumed by alternating bands of cherry-red, sun-gold, and emerald-green. An opportunity for the toning specialist. (#7146)

2459 1883-O MS64 ★ NGC. Exciting blue-green, gold, and rose-red shades dominate the reverse. The obverse has an almond-gold margin accompanied by a brilliant field and portrait. (#7146)

2460 1883-O MS64 PCGS. Delightful emerald, cobalt, crimson, and gold toning hide the satiny obverse luster with the brilliant reverse framed by a ring of light gold. (#7146)

2461 1883-O MS65 PCGS, honey-gold, ruby-red, and jade-green obverse toning; and **(2) 1884-O MS64 PCGS,** both have dramatic bands of gold, powder-blue, aquamarine, and fire-red across much of the reverse. (Total: 3 coins) (#7146)

2462 1883-O MS66 NGC. A stunning coin with deep orange-pink patina through the centers of each side, complementing a thin peripheral ring of ice-blue. Few signs of contact are noted. (#7146)

2463 1883-O MS65 Deep Mirror Prooflike ANACS. Light gold peripheral toning is joined by wisps of cobalt-blue on the reverse. Both sides reveal excellent field-motif contrast, and have been well cared for. While the 1883-O is relatively common in Mint State, Deep Mirror Prooflike examples are much more difficult to obtain. (#97147)

2464 1883-S MS63 ANACS. A flashy and sharply struck Select example of this earlier S-mint Morgan dollar issue. Hints of silver-gray patina appear on each side, as do a number of tiny abrasions. (#7148)

2465 1883-S MS63 NGC. This solidly struck S-mint example is predominantly silver-white with scattered ice-blue tints. Lightly abraded overall with strong luster on the obverse and a flashy reverse.
From The Mario Eller Collection, Part One. (#7148)

2466 1883-S MS63 PCGS. A stunning beauty in an older green-label PCGS holder, this piece has satiny silver luster with mostly brilliant surfaces framed by a ring of peripheral gold toning. (#7148)

Bright, Lustrous MS64 1883-S Dollar

2467 1883-S MS64 PCGS. More than 6 million pieces were struck of the 1883-S, but this issue does not have an availability in Uncirculated of a coin with that mintage. Numerous lower grade circulated 1883-S dollars can be found for a nominal premium. However, in Uncirculated grades the availability decreases dramatically. This is a lovely coin that has bright, frosted surfaces and a glimmer of semi-reflectivity in the fields. There are no noticeable abrasions, and the coin has an overlay of light gray-rose toning on each side. (#7148)

Bright 1883-S Near-Gem Dollar

2468 1883-S MS64 NGC. The 1883-S dollar is extremely difficult to locate in Gem quality condition, and even near-Gems are not all that available. The MS64 coin we offer in this lot displays pleasing bright luster that exudes from untoned surfaces. All of the design elements exhibit crisp definition, further enhancing the coin's eye appeal. A few inoffensive marks are all that stands in the way of a higher grade.
From The Arnold & Harriet Collection, Part Two. (#7148)

Brilliant MS64 1883-S Dollar

2469 1883-S MS64 PCGS. An extraordinary example of this difficult S-mint issue, seldom seen in near-Gem and quite elusive in Gem grade. This piece has untoned silver surfaces with excellent cartwheel luster. A few abrasions, including some reeding marks and a luster graze on Liberty's cheek, limit a higher grade, but this piece nonetheless offers good eye appeal. PCGS has certified 17 coins finer (8/07). (#7148)

2470 1884 MS66 PCGS. This is a frosty Gem with exceptional eye appeal. The surfaces are brilliant, with only a trace of ivory color on the highest design points. Surface marks are minimal. (#7150)

2471 1884 MS66 PCGS. Steel-gray and peach do not deny the blazing cartwheel luster. This older holder Premium Gem is boldly struck and gorgeously unblemished. A common date in typical Mint State, but elusive in such stellar quality. (#7150)

2472 1884-CC MS66 PCGS. This Carson City dollar exhibits splendid mint frost and a delightful cartwheel sheen across both sides. Razor-sharp striking details are evident on all of the design elements. Surface marks are minimal, and Liberty's cheek and the eagle's breast are exceptionally clean. (#7152)

2473 1884-CC MS66 PCGS. A beautiful semi-prooflike Premium Gem with exquisite preservation and a penetrating strike. Because of the GSA hoard, the 1884-CC remains available in this grade, though it seldom appears any finer. (#7152)

2474 1884-CC MS66 PCGS. An absolutely beautiful coating of silver-white mint frost covers each side of this Carson City dollar. The design elements are crisply rendered, with minimal weakness noted just above Liberty's ear, and surface marks are negligible. (#7152)

2475 1884-CC MS66 NGC. Well-defined with sharp detail on the hair over Liberty's ear and on the eagle's breast feathers. Its highly lustrous surfaces are essentially untoned and possess just a few minuscule obverse marks. A light die crack encircles the margins on each side. An attractive example of this popular Carson City issue. (#7152)

2476 1884-CC MS66 PCGS. A lovely Carson City Premium Gem. The surfaces show thick mint frost with semi-prooflike fields. Fully struck and highly attractive. (#7152)

2477 1884-CC MS66 PCGS. An outstanding and highly colorful example with mottled rainbow toning on the obverse. The reverse is fully brilliant. This sharply struck dollar has underlying frosty mint luster and nearly pristine surfaces. (#7152)

Lovely Superb Gem 1884-CC Morgan

2478 1884-CC MS67 NGC. This semi-prooflike Superb Gem is well struck save for the eagle's claws and belly. Liberty's cheek is remarkably smooth, and the overall quality is exceptional for this popular Carson City issue. Nearly brilliant with just a hint of gold toning. Population: 75 in 67, none finer (7/07). (#7152)

Fantastic 1884-CC Dollar, MS67 Prooflike

2479 1884-CC MS67 Prooflike NGC. While the 1884-CC dollar is relatively common with a Prooflike finish, locating one in this lofty grade is extremely difficult. Both sides of this Superb Gem exhibit fantastic field-motif contrast, and are entirely color free. A well executed strike emboldens the design features, and the surfaces are immaculately preserved. Census: 6 in 67 Prooflike, 0 finer (7/07). *From The Arnold & Harriet Collection, Part Two.* (#7153)

2480 1884-CC MS65 Deep Mirror Prooflike PCGS. A dazzling Gem with frosty surfaces and a hint of die rust on Liberty's portrait. The piece is essentially untoned, except for a tiny bit of speckled peach patina near the center of each side. The fields are intensely prooflike and the flashy surfaces only show scattered, trivial bagmarks. (#97153)

2481 1884-CC MS65 Deep Mirror Prooflike PCGS. Magically deep reflectivity is evident in the jet-black fields, and the snow-white devices are fully frosted. Well struck with a few scattered, light abrasions. The technical and aesthetic quality of this Gem should excite the interest of any specialist in Deep Mirror Prooflike dollars. (#97153)

2482 1884-CC MS65 Deep Mirror Prooflike PCGS. Prooflike 1883-CC and 1884-CC Morgan dollars are among the real glories of the series when found in high grade. This brilliant piece offers blinding mirrors, thick frost on the devices, and a couple of tiny field ticks that limit an even finer grade. (#97153)

Pleasing 1884-CC Deep Mirror Prooflike Dollar, MS66

2483 1884-CC MS66 Deep Mirror Prooflike NGC. The 1884-CC dollar in DMPL is readily available in Mint State grades, but starts to become scarce at the Premium Gem level. As of August 2007, NGC has seen only 39 specimens, and a mere three finer. The MS66 coin we present here displays sharply struck design elements, though the hair above Liberty's ear is soft. The deep mirror fields establish a strong contrast with the motifs. A touch or two of faint tan color visits Liberty's cheek and the lower left obverse quadrant, otherwise the coin can be considered brilliant. A few minor marks on Liberty's cheek and neck are not bothersome. (#97153)

2484 Six-Piece Set of Toned New Orleans Morgan Dollars. The six pieces are housed in three custom NGC holders, each holding two examples of the same issue. The obverse and reverse displayed show spectacular toning, while the other sides show little or no patina. The set includes: **1884-O MS64 (obverse) and MS62 (reverse),** plum, rose, orange, lime-green, and silver-white on the obverse with a muted rainbow effect from left to right across the reverse; **1884-O MS63 (obverse) and MS62 (reverse),** captivating rainbow patterns on both sides with a splash of sage patina at the date on the otherwise untoned lower obverse; and **1885-O MS61 (obverse) and MS64 (reverse),** rich lime-green, magenta, and cerulean on the obverse and olive-green, magenta, and orange on the reverse. (Total: 6 coins) (#7154)

2485 1884-O MS65 ★ NGC. Ruby-red, forest-green, and peach adorn the obverse of this lustrous example. The reverse margin has a hint of gold and sky-blue toning. The left obverse has a few light marks. (#7154)

Toned Premium Gem 1884-O Morgan Dollar

2486 **1884-O MS66 PCGS.** The mintmark is lightly repunched within the loop. The obverse is blanketed by beautifully deep olive, violet, and electric-blue coloration, while the reverse shows a ring of sea-green and tan. Lustrous, well struck, and immaculately preserved. Struck from lightly clashed dies. (#7154)

2487 **1884-O MS66 PCGS.** Both sides of this Premium Gem are entirely covered by original pastel gold, violet, blue, and steel toning. (#7154)

2488 **1884-O MS65 Deep Mirror Prooflike NGC.** Beautiful golden-brown, electric-blue, and rose colors embrace the margins of this nicely struck and prominently mirrored Gem. The cheek and the reverse are relatively undisturbed. (#97155)

2489 **1884-S AU58 NGC.** Nicely struck, except on the eagle's breast feathers, with only mildly reduced luster and essentially untoned surfaces that have a pleasingly smooth appearance. Slight highpoint wear and a few small abrasions are noted on each side, along with some faint hairlines. (#7156)

2490 **1884-S AU58 ANACS.** Dappled gold toning gravitates to the borders of this high-end AU S-mint representative, and the design elements are better struck than is typical for the issue. Both faces are relatively clean, and possess ample luster. (#7156)

2491 **1884-S AU58 ICG.** An attractive example of this earlier S-mint issue, boldly impressed with ample luster and only a touch of highpoint friction. Golden accents and dots of deeper color grace the lightly marked fields. An abrasion is noted on the eagle's neck. (#7156)

Impressive 1884-S Dollar MS61

2492 **1884-S MS61 NGC.** This untoned and suitably struck example has unbroken cartwheel luster, and the centers lack the friction that almost invariably accompanies examples of this conditionally rare issue. Marks are minimal given the grade, with the sweet spot of the cheek surprisingly unabraded. (#7156)

Elusive 1884-S Silver Dollar, MS61

2493 **1884-S MS61 NGC.** Beginning in 1878 the San Francisco Mint made large totals of beautifully produced Morgan dollars, continuing in an unbroken run through 1882 and generally on the order of 9 million to 12 million coins per year. In 1883, however, the S-mint emission dwindled to 6.25 million, dropping even further the following year, to 3.2 million dollars. The 1884-S is the first truly elusive Mint State San Francisco Morgan dollar, although even 1883-S dollars in Mint State can be pricey. This example offers lustrous silvery surfaces with glints of gold on the obverse, while the reverse displays bolder color in amber hues. The strike is typically soft on the hair above the ear and on the eagle's breast, but contact marks are fewer and less severe than might be expected for the grade. (#7156)

Lustrous 1884-S Dollar, MS61

2494 **1884-S MS61 NGC.** While circulated examples of the 1884-S dollar are plentiful, Mint State pieces are elusive at all levels. Barely discernible wisps of light tan and ice-blue rest over the lustrous surfaces of this MS61 specimen, and a well directed strike brings up better-than-average definition on the design features. A few marks are scattered about, including a hair-thin one behind the cap. *From The Arnold & Harriet Collection, Part Two.* (#7156)

2495 1884-S MS61 Deep Mirror Prooflike NGC. As late as 2005, in his *Guide Book of Morgan Silver Dollars*, Q. David Bowers described this issue as "unknown" in Deep Mirror Prooflike, going so far as to describe such a coin as "a Holy Grail in the Morgan series." Yet the facts of numismatics are susceptible to change, and new discoveries can render decades of common wisdom obsolete. Far from being "merely" Prooflike, this coin has powerful, flashy mirrors that unquestionably merit the Deep Mirror Prooflike designation, and the piece stands alone as the **only** Deep Mirror Prooflike representative ever graded by either NGC or PCGS (5/07).

The 1884-S, while an available issue in circulated grades, becomes distinctly elusive in any Mint State grade. Unlike the famous S-mint issues from a few years before, the vast majority of 1884-S dollars saw considerable circulation, leaving only a handful of unworn survivors. With Mint or near-Mint condition as an inflexible prerequisite for Prooflike status, it is little wonder that few such pieces survive today, and that the survival of a Deep Mirror Prooflike coin would seem impossible.

The surfaces of this distinctive coin exhibit powerful mirrors despite minor haze, and while the piece has little contrast (as Wayne Miller described Prooflike representatives of the issue in 1982), the fields offer reflectivity even at arm's length. The devices have crisp detail overall, with just a touch of the usual weakness present at the hair over Liberty's ear. While the dollar displays a number of scattered abrasions that justify the grade, including a number in the fields and on the lower right cheek, these flaws have surprisingly little impact on the overall eye appeal. A noteworthy example that should appeal to even the most discerning collector of the series. (#97157)

2496 **1885 MS64 ★ NGC.** Ex: Battle Creek Collection. Peach, sea-green, ruby-red, and ice-blue patina graces the obverse. The reverse remains brilliant. A fingerprint is noted on the reverse at 3 o'clock. (#7158)

2497 **1885 MS64 Deep Mirror Prooflike PCGS.** An impressive near-Gem with deeply mirrored fields and excellent contrast, hidden beneath colorful rainbow toning on the obverse. The reverse has a brilliant silver surface that closely resembles a proof strike. (#97159)

2498 **1885 MS66 ★ Deep Mirror Prooflike NGC.** Both sides of this exquisite Premium Gem show strong reflectivity and contrast, with only a few points of scattered haze in the fields. A delightful representative of this popular P-mint issue, the present piece is the *only* MS66 Deep Mirror Prooflike example awarded the Star Designation by NGC, with just five numerically finer representatives (8/07). *From The Mario Eller Collection, Part One.* (#97159)

2499 **1885-CC MS65 PCGS.** A frosty Gem representative of the quintessential GSA dollar issue, boldly impressed and untoned save for a spot of reddish-brown patina below the A in STATES and a tiny fleck on the cheek. The fields are clean, and the devices show only a handful of tiny luster grazes. (#7160)

2500 **1885-CC MS65 NGC.** Lustrous and highly attractive, with light golden toning over both sides and a lovely cartwheel sheen in the fields. Minor striking weakness is noted above Liberty's ear and on the two leaves of Liberty's crown below RI in PLURIBUS. A popular Carson City issue that is readily available at most grade levels up to and including MS65. (#7160)

2501 **1885-CC MS65 PCGS.** A colorful Gem that has modest reflectivity on the reverse. The dappled gold and silver-blue of the obverse is confined to the periphery on the other side. (#7160)

Dramatically Toned MS66 ★ 1885-CC Morgan

2502 **1885-CC MS66 ★ NGC.** Waves of peach, navy-blue, emerald-green, and ruby-red dominate this lustrous and low mintage Carson City dollar. The centers show slight inexactness of strike, and the left obverse has a few faint marks. A memorable example certain to find a place of honor within a colorfully toned collection. (#7160)

2503 **1885-CC MS66 PCGS.** A boldly impressed exemplar of this ever-popular Carson City dollar, one that is readily available despite a paltry mintage of 228,000 pieces. Faint veils of cloud-gray patina grace otherwise silver-white surfaces. (#7160)

Radiant 1885-CC Dollar, MS67

2504 **1885-CC MS67 NGC.** The vast majority of 1885-CC dollars still exist in Mint State grades, right through Gem quality. The population diminishes in MS67, the grade of the piece in this sale. Radiantly lustrous, untoned surfaces display sharply struck design elements. Some minor obverse luster grazes do not distract. Census: 47 in 67, 5 finer (8/07). (#7160)

2505 **1885-CC MS64 Prooflike NGC.** Both sides of this boldly impressed Carson City dollar offer distinct reflectivity beneath thin yellow-gold patina, though the fields show a measure of cartwheel luster as well. An attractive near-Gem that show just a few too many marks to reach a finer grade. (#7161)

Attractively Toned 1885-CC Dollar, MS66 Prooflike

2506 **1885-CC MS66 Prooflike NGC.** Splendid cherry-red, apple-green, yellow-gold, sea-green, and apricot patina graces this exceptional Carson City dollar. Though both sides display cartwheel sheen, the fields are also moderately mirrored. Suitably struck and worthy of personal evaluation. Census: 20 in 66, 3 finer (8/07). (#7161)

2507 **1885-CC MS63 Deep Mirror Prooflike PCGS.** The magnificently mirrored fields contrast with the meticulously struck and icy devices. The reverse is impressively void of marks. A low mintage date. (#97161)

2508 **1885-CC MS64 Deep Mirror Prooflike ANACS.** The near-brilliant surfaces display just a whisper of dappled gold patina around the rims. The motifs stand out against deeply mirrored fields, especially when the coin is tilted beneath a light source, adding to its eye appeal. The design features are generally well struck, except for weakness in the hair overlying Liberty's ear. Minor luster grazes on Liberty's cheek and neck and in the left (facing) obverse field limit the grade. (#97161)

2509 **1885-CC MS64 Deep Mirror Prooflike PCGS.** A amazingly frosty near-Gem with deeply prooflike fields and mildly frosted devices. Entirely untoned on both sides. A few minor abrasions on Liberty's cheek and in the adjacent field area preclude a Gem grade assessment. A popular Carson City issue in the Morgan dollar series. (#97161)

2510 **1885-CC MS64 Deep Mirror Prooflike PCGS.** An increasingly popular CC-mint issue, here with deeply contrasting surfaces and a decent strike, despite the light roller marks appearing on the chin. Certified in a green-label holder. (#97161)

Deep Mirror Prooflike Gem 1885-CC Morgan

2511 **1885-CC MS65 Deep Mirror Prooflike PCGS.** A breathtaking dollar with amazing contrast between the mirrored fields and lustrous devices on both sides. There is no evidence of toning on this sharply struck brilliant Gem. A few tiny abrasions on each side prevent a higher grade. (#97161)

2512 **1885-O MS62 PCGS; and an 1885-O MS63 PCGS.** Both coins have multi-color "end of roll" toning on one side, while the other side has only faint gold and gray patina. (Total: 2 coins) (#7162)

2513 **1885-O MS65 PCGS.** Waves of orange, violet, sky-blue, and gold adorn the obverse of this lustrous Gem. The reverse is bathed in aquamarine. The centers are typically defined for an O-mint of the era. (#7162)

2514 **1885-O MS65 ★ NGC.** The obverse is exuberantly toned in splashes of blue-green, radish-red, lemon, and powder-blue. The reverse is nearly untoned, and has a rim mark at 7:30. (#7162)

2515 **1885-O MS67 NGC.** Fully struck and untoned, with a beautifully frosty sheen across both sides. The ivory-white surfaces reveal faint golden accents near the obverse periphery. Surface marks are nearly nonexistent. NGC has only graded nine pieces finer (8/07). (#7162)

2516 **1885-S MS64 PCGS.** A shining representative of this S-mint Morgan issue, generally well-defined with small regions of haze in the fields. This Choice example is untoned otherwise. The 1885-S has a mintage of just under 1.5 million pieces, a steep drop from the production of just a few years before. (#7164)

Conditionally Scarce 1885-S Dollar MS64 Prooflike

2517 **1885-S MS64 Prooflike PCGS.** The 1885-S is an unremarkable date in the Morgan dollar series, being neither scarce nor overly common. In Prooflike condition, however, this issue becomes very scarce. The current offering is a highly attractive near-Gem that displays intense reflectivity in the fields and nicely frosted devices. A slight degree of cloudiness is noted on each side, but surface marks are minimal for the grade. (#7165)

2518 **Six Toned Morgan Dollars MS63 NGC.** The six pieces are housed in three custom NGC holders, each holding two examples of the same issue. The obverse and reverse displayed show spectacular toning, while the other sides show little or no patina. The set includes: **1886 MS63 (obverse) and MS63 ★ (reverse)**, rainbow toning from sky-blue to lemon-gold in a crescent centered at the right rim on the obverse with vivid rainbow toning on the reverse; **1900 MS63 (obverse and reverse)**, pale green at the top fading to gold, orange, and magenta at the bottom of the obverse, with zones of ruby, gold-green, and blue on the reverse; and **1904-O MS63 ★ (obverse and reverse)**, an attractive duo with sea-green at the left obverse that fades through blue-violet and orange and bands of rose and orange patina around a mint-green core that is left-of-center on the reverse. (Total: 6 coins) (#7166)

2519 **1886 MS66 ★ NGC.** Ex: Battle Creek Collection. Iridescent bands of peach, sky-blue, gold, cherry-red, and jade-green take turns consuming the reverse. The obverse is comparatively brilliant. The cheek has a few faint marks. (#7166)

2520 **1886 MS67 NGC.** Well struck, highly lustrous, and nearly pristine, with lovely reddish-brown peripheral toning on the obverse that increases the eye appeal of the piece. A common date which becomes relatively uncommon at the Superb Gem level of preservation. (#7166)

Exceptional MS68 1886 Dollar

2521 **1886 MS68 NGC.** In PCGS's *The Official Guide to Coin Grading and Counterfeit Detection* they state that "Morgan dollars were usually transported in bags; thus most have marks and other surface impairments." Superb Gem Uncirculated Morgan dollars are scarce to rare depending on the date. For instance, of the 1,753,661 Morgan dollars graded by PCGS, only 349 are MS68 and 10 are MS69. Of those graded MS68, only nine come from the Philadelphia Mint. Similar figures are found in the NGC *Census Report*. Most MS68s are from the Carson City Mint and San Francisco Mint. The Philadelphia Mint count shows only six years—all in the 1880s—with examples graded at MS68. This 1886 falls into that category. The popularity of high quality silver dollars seems unabated; therefore, this offering represents a rare opportunity to own a Superb Morgan that is needed to build a winning registry set.

    The surfaces of this piece are virtually perfect, as one would expect. The mint luster is silky-smooth and the only hint of toning is around the margins. Fully struck as well. NGC Census: 8 in 68, 0 finer (8/07). (#7166)

2522 **1886-O MS60 NGC.** An unworn, well struck representative of this O-mint issue, predominantly silver-white with hints of gold. Numerous wispy abrasions and a number of more significant marks affect each side. (#7168)

2523 **1886-O MS61 NGC.** An unworn and decisively struck example of this available O-mint issue, more appealing than the MS61 designation might suggest. A thin veil of rose-gold patina graces the faintly abraded surfaces. (#7168)

2524 **1886-O MS61 ICG.** A well-defined example of this available O-mint issue, luminous beneath dappled silver-blue and tan patina. Scattered marks and a number of wispy abrasions account for the grade. (#7168)

2525 **1886-O MS61 NGC.** Delicate blue and gold tints visit the shining surfaces of this O-mint dollar. Well struck with a surprisingly clean reverse, though the portrait and the surrounding fields show a number of significant abrasions. (#7168)

2526 **1886-O MS61 PCGS.** A key issue, this Mint State piece is fully lustrous with frosty silver surfaces and natural ivory coloration. (#7168)

2527 **1886-O MS62 PCGS.** Lightly toned and lustrous with the usual indifference of strike at the centers. Clean aside from a cluster of wispy grazes on the cheek. Housed in a first generation holder. (#7168)

2528 **1886-O MS62 NGC.** A strongly lustrous representative of this New Orleans issue, pleasingly detailed with only a touch of softness at the highpoints of the portrait. Though the 1886-O is available in this grade, Select and better pieces are comparatively elusive. (#7168)

2529 **1886-O MS62 NGC.** Dots of milky patina visit the right reverse, and pale golden accents grace both sides of this unworn New Orleans Morgan dollar. The strike is solid overall, and the minor weakness at the hair above the ear is typical for the issue. (#7168)

Impressive Select 1886-O Morgan

2530 **1886-O MS63 PCGS.** Despite its heavy production of more than 10.7 million pieces, the 1886-O is scarce in Mint State, and becomes one of the keys to the series at the MS65 level. The centers are softly defined, as usual for a New Orleans dollar from the era, but the luster is comprehensive, and the medium rose-gold toning is attractive. (#7168)

Well Struck 1886-O Select Dollar

2531 **1886-O MS63 PCGS.** Ex: Cajun Collection. Bright luster adorns both sides of this Select O-mint, each of which is essentially devoid of toning. While the issue is usually weakly struck, the present example displays relatively sharp overall detail, including partial definition in the hair at Liberty's ear, and strongly impressed breast feathers. A few light marks account for the grade. David Bowers estimates that 6 to 8 million pieces of the nearly 11 million coins originally produced were probably melted under terms of the 1918 Pittman Act.
From The Arnold & Harriet Collection, Part Two. (#7168)

Satiny MS64 1886-O Dollar

2532 **1886-O MS64 PCGS.** This is an impressive example of the issue, with satiny silver surfaces and fully brilliant luster on both sides. The strike is sharp for the date, and the eye appeal is considerable for an '86-O. With 189 pieces certified at this grade level, the population certainly seems plentiful enough, but only three finer examples have been graded by PCGS (8/07). Therefore, nearly all collectors of otherwise Gem quality collections must necessarily choose a near-Gem specimen of this date. (#7168)

Pleasing 1886-S Gem Dollar

2533 **1886-S MS65 NGC.** Most Uncirculated 1886-S dollars exist in the lower grade ranges of MS60 to MS63 or MS64. A sharp drop occurs in the certified population at the MS65 level. The current Gem received an attentive strike, and possesses attractive luster. Essentially untoned surfaces are generally better preserved than what might be expected for the grade designation.
From The Arnold & Harriet Collection, Part Two. (#7170)

2534 **1886-S MS64 Prooflike NGC.** Both sides are reflective beneath thin veils of hazy amethyst and silver-gray patina. Solidly struck with more luster grazes than actual marks, though a planchet flaw appears above the first 8 in the date.
From The Mario Eller Collection, Part One. (#7171)

2535 **1887 MS67 NGC.** Ex: Jack Lee Collection, Part III. Without a doubt, this is one of the most common dates in the entire Morgan dollar series, *except* in Superb condition. In fact, fewer than 265 examples have been certified by both NGC and PCGS for this date in MS67 or finer quality, and only three of those coins received a higher grade. This is a frosty and Superb Gem with remarkable eye appeal. Both the obverse and the reverse are fully brilliant without any evidence of toning. Careful examination with a magnifier is necessary to find even the smallest ticks on the surface. (#7172)

2536 **1887 MS64 Deep Mirror Prooflike PCGS.** The obverse shows fabulous bag toning in successive arcs of deep iridescent color. Fully struck and deeply mirrored in the fields, the reverse is bright and untoned. (#97173)

2537 **1887 MS65 Deep Mirror Prooflike PCGS.** A flashy, deeply reflective Gem example of this popular P-mint dollar. Well-matched from side to side, the surfaces are brilliant for the most part except for a light accent of peripheral golden color. The devices are noticeably frosted and present excellent contrast against the mirrored fields. (#97173)

2538 1887/6 MS64 PCGS. VAM-2. A Top 100 Variety. The underdigit 6 is discernible without magnification. A nicely struck example with well preserved fields. The obverse is virtually brilliant, while the reverse has faint blushes of olive-gold and steel-gray. (#7174)

2539 1887/6 MS64 PCGS. A gorgeous near-Gem with satiny silver surfaces and full mint brilliance. The fields are mildly reflective, nearly enough to warrant a prooflike designation. A highly desirable representative of the overdate. (#7174)

2540 1887/6 MS64 NGC. Sharply detailed, the overdate is strong and visible without magnification. Both sides are untoned and exhibit frosty, brilliant silver luster. (#7174)

2541 1887/6 MS64 PCGS. VAM-2. A Top 100 Variety. Dazzling cartwheel luster and pleasantly preserved surfaces confirm the exemplary quality of this precisely struck near-Gem. Faint sky-gray toning visits the upper half of the reverse. (#7174)

2542 1887/6 MS64 NGC. Remarkable quality for the grade with highly lustrous silver surfaces. The fields are satiny and the devices are frosty. At current market levels, this overdate seems to be a good value. (#7174)

Attractive 1887/6 Dollar, MS65, VAM-2

2543 1887/6 MS65 NGC. VAM-2. A Top 100 Variety. A portion of the underdigit 6 is easily seen below the lower part of the 7 under low magnification. Nearly untoned surfaces depict partially prooflike fields that yield a degree of contrast with the well struck devices. Well preserved throughout. Census: 93 in 65, 4 finer (8/07). (#7174)

Popular 1887/6 Gem Dollar, VAM-2

2544 1887/6 MS65 PCGS. VAM-2. A Top 100 Variety. The bottom of the lower loop of the underlying 6 is visible as a curved line through the lower stem of the 7. Whispers of golden-tan, lavender, and electric-blue toning gravitate to portions of the borders of this Gem example. Generally well struck, with pleasing luster. A few grade-consistent marks do not disturb. In their 1996 VAM reference book, Michael Fey and Jeff Oxman contend that "this issue's popularity has increased to the point it's now considered an integral part of a complete Morgan dollar set."
From The Arnold & Harriet Collection, Part Two. (#7174)

Highly Lustrous Gem 1887/6 Dollar VAM-2, A Top 100 Variety

2545 1887/6 MS65 NGC. VAM-2. A Top 100 Variety. The lower curved remnants of a 6 are visible below the 7. This overdate was discovered in the mid 1970s. Dazzling luster emanates from each side of this well struck Gem example, and faint hints of light tan are occasionally seen under magnification. A few minor marks are well within the parameters of the grade designation. Census: 93 in 65, 4 finer (8/07). (#7174)

Sharp 1887/6 VAM-2 Gem Prooflike Dollar

2546 1887/6 MS65 Prooflike PCGS. VAM-2. A Top 100 Variety. Under magnification, remnants of a 6 can be discerned at the base of the 7. Sharp field-motif contrast is evident at all angles on this Gem example. Well struck, with just a few light grade-consistent marks. A hint or two of barely discernible light tan color is seen on the central devices. Population: 30 in 65 Prooflike, 2 finer (8/07). (#7175)

2547 1887-O MS64 PCGS. Pleasing luster exudes from color-free surfaces, and the design features are well impressed on this near-Gem Morgan dollar. Some obverse luster grazes limit the grade. (#7176)

2548 1887-O MS65 ANACS. This is a splendid Morgan dollar that exhibits all of the desirable characteristics of a Gem. All of the design elements are sharply struck and the untoned surfaces display beautiful cartwheel luster. Few trivial surface marks are observed on either side of the coin. (#7176)

2549 1887-O MS65 NGC. Well struck with intense mint frost and a beautifully bright sheen over both sides. Essentially untoned but with hints of pale gold color near the centers. A few wispy marks preclude an even finer grade assessment. The 1887-O Morgan dollar is a conditionally scarce issue at the Gem grade level that becomes excessively rare any finer.
From The Arnold & Harriet Collection, Part Two. (#7176)

Deep Mirror 1887-O Dollar MS64

2550 **1887-O MS64 Deep Mirror Prooflike NGC.** An impressive New Orleans dollar that has splendidly mirrored fields and an above average strike. Gentle gold toning visits both sides. Marks are minor for the grade, and the eye appeal is undeniable. Census: 47 in 64 Deep Mirror Prooflike, 3 finer (8/07). (#97177)

2551 **1887/6-O MS63 PCGS.** VAM-3. A Top 100 Variety. A lovely Select example of this branch mint overdate, strongly lustrous with a measure of peach patina at the upper obverse and untoned surfaces elsewhere. Lightly abraded overall with this issue's usual soft definition at the centers.
From The Mario Eller Collection, Part One. (#7178)

Colorful Choice 1887/6-O Dollar

2552 **1887/6-O MS64 PCGS.** VAM-3. A Top 100 Variety. Medium golden-brown, plum-gray, and ocean-blue endow much of the obverse, although the cheek and left obverse field are nearly brilliant. The reverse is untoned aside from an occasional wisp of tan-gold. The eagle's breast and the hair above the ear are typically struck for this scarce *Guide Book* VAM. (#7178)

Lustrous 1887/6-O Dollar, MS64

2553 **1887/6-O MS64 PCGS.** VAM-3. A Top 100 Variety. The right outside curve of the underlying 6 is barely visible to the lower right of the 7. Occasional hints of light tan-gold color adhere to the highly lustrous surfaces of this near-Gem specimen that is generally well struck, except for the usual softness in the centers. A few minute obverse marks define the grade. Rarely available any finer. Population: 79 in 64, 0 finer (7/07).
From The Arnold & Harriet Collection, Part Two. (#7178)

Well Struck 1887-S Dollar, MS65

2554 **1887-S MS65 NGC.** Striking varies on the 1887-S, but many show weakness on the hair over Liberty's ear and on the eagle's breast feathers (David Bowers, 2005). The Gem in this lot was in receipt of a solid strike, as all of the design features exhibit sharp detail, including the aforementioned areas. A few wisps of light tan color appear under magnification, and lustrous surfaces reveal just a few grade-consistent marks.
From The Arnold & Harriet Collection, Part Two. (#7180)

Sparkling 1887-S Gem Dollar

2555 **1887-S MS65 PCGS.** David Bowers (2006) mentions that the 1887-S is relatively available in low Mint State grades, but is elusive in MS65. Sparkling luster adorns this untoned Gem that exhibits well defined design features. A few minute marks are within the parameters of the grade designation. (#7180)

2556 **1888-O MS65 PCGS.** A touch of rainbow toning graces the upper left obverse border. Well struck, save for softness in the hair above Liberty's ear. Lustrous and carefully preserved, with few marks on either side. (#7184)

2557 **1888-O MS66 PCGS.** A gorgeous Premium Gem, tied for the finest that PCGS has graded, with fully brilliant silver surfaces on the obverse and reverse. Delightful gold and iridescent toning near the borders on each side adds to the eye appeal of this piece. (#7184)

2558 **1888-S MS64 NGC.** Wisps of gold and violet patina grace the margins of this immensely lustrous near-Gem. Well struck with faint, scattered abrasions on both sides and a patch of roller marks on Liberty's chin. An attractive example of this lower-mintage S-mint Morgan dollar. (#7186)

2559 **1888-S MS64 NGC.** An essentially untoned, immensely lustrous Choice example of this S-mint issue, struck a decade after the introduction of the Morgan design. Light, scattered marks appear on the well struck devices, while the fields are comparatively clean. (#7186)

2560 **1888-S MS64 PCGS.** This essentially untoned representative hails from a lower-mintage San Francisco issue of only 657,000 coins. A gleaming and well-defined near-Gem that is housed in a green label holder. (#7186)

2561 **1888-S MS64 PCGS.** The skimpy mintage of only 657,000 pieces means that this issue is elusive in the higher Mint State grades, especially when found well struck. This frosty coin is such a piece, and only a couple of tiny luster grazes away from Gem. (#7186)

Radiant 1888-S Gem Dollar

2562 1888-S MS65 PCGS. A thin coat of mauve-gold color bathes both sides of this MS65 Morgan, each of which is awash in cartwheel luster. Sharp definition is apparent on the design elements, though minor softness typical for the issue occurs in the centers. Some minute obverse marks do not detract from the coin's overall eye appeal. Housed in a green-label holder.
From The Arnold & Harriet Collection, Part Two. (#7186)

Colorful 1888-S Gem Dollar

2563 1888-S MS65 PCGS. A medley of aqua-blue, lavender, and golden-tan patination adorns radiantly lustrous surfaces, and a well directed strike brings out sharp impressions on the design elements. A handful of tiny, grade-consistent handling marks are well concealed within the toning. This issue is one of the scarcer Morgan dollars of its era. Anything finer becomes difficult to locate. (#7186)

2564 1888-S MS64 Prooflike PCGS. While the flashy fields have a degree of cartwheel luster, the surfaces' reflectivity is undeniable. Solidly struck with minimal contrast and hints of peach patina at the margins. A patch of roller marks is present on the cheek. PCGS has graded just three finer Prooflike examples (7/07). (#7187)

2565 1889 MS66 NGC. The well struck obverse of this P-mint Premium Gem is luminous beneath rich waves of plum, blue, and forest-green patina. The reverse displays subtle sky-blue toning with gold-green accents at the periphery. NGC has certified only two finer representatives (8/07). (#7188)

2566 1889 MS66 PCGS. A solidly struck and enticingly toned Premium Gem, strongly lustrous with great visual appeal. The obverse has broad areas of dusky peach and lavender toning, while the reverse shows fainter sky-blue and champagne toning. PCGS has graded just five coins finer (8/07). (#7188)

2567 1889 MS66 PCGS. The upper obverse shows lovely rose-orange patina, and fainter sun-gold color graces the reverse. The shining surfaces of this well struck P-mint Morgan are silver-gray otherwise. PCGS has certified only five finer examples (8/07). (#7188)

2568 1889 MS66 PCGS. A radiant and carefully preserved Premium Gem bathed in cobalt-blue, golden-brown, and lavender on each side, with slightly deeper and broader toning on the obverse. Generally well struck, except for the usual softness in the centers. Students of the series note that this issue was heavily melted under the Pittman Act. PCGS has certified only five coins finer (8/07). (#7188)

2569 1889-CC Fine 15 PCGS. Slate-gray with hints of chestnut-tan toning. All legends are bold on this collectible key date Carson City dollar. The obverse is surprisingly unabraded, while the reverse has a few stray but minor marks. Housed in an old green label holder. (#7190)

2570 1889-CC—Scratched—ANACS. Fine 15 Details. A single straight scratch from Liberty's mouth down below star 4 is responsible for the designation, but it is nonetheless not overly bothersome in the context. Dove-gray surfaces show full rims and considerable detail remaining. (#7190)

2571 1889-CC—Cleaned—ANACS. VF Details, Net Fine 15. Light gray surfaces display hints of gold and lilac. Some fine hairlines show up under magnification, but should not intimidate the collector wanting to acquire this key-date for her/his Morgan dollar set. (#7190)

2572 1889-CC—Cleaned—ANACS. VF30 Details. A decent coin despite the ANACS caveat, not overly bright and displaying only a few grade-consistent abrasions. From one of the most frequently seen obverse dies, with a small straight-line die marker between the maple leaf and the wheat stalk to its left. (#7190)

2573 1889-CC—Scratched, Cleaned—ANACS. VF30 Details. Medium chestnut toning helps conceal the straight obverse marks on Liberty's neck, above the ear, and behind the cap. Three reeding marks are also noted on the portrait. The 1889-CC is usually the final Carson City issue added to a Morgan dollar collection. (#7190)

Lightly Toned 1889-CC Dollar, VF35

2574 1889-CC VF35 ANACS. Whispers of cobalt-blue, lavender, and golden-brown patina concentrate at the margins of this high-end Very Fine, key-date Morgan. The design elements retain good definition, and reveal relatively few minute contact marks, despite light to moderate circulation. This is an ideal piece for a mid to high-grade circulated Morgan dollar collection. (#7190)

Desirable 1889-CC Dollar, XF40

2575 1889-CC XF40 ICG. Traces of luster reside in the protected areas of this key date Carson City representative, and a film of champagne-gold color shows over each side. The design elements are well defined, and the few minute marks scattered about are not out of the ordinary for a coin that has seen some circulation. (#7190)

Pleasing Key Date 1889-CC Morgan Dollar XF40

2576 1889-CC XF40 ANACS. This is a pleasingly original example of the most important Carson City Morgan dollar issue. The surfaces are smooth and largely abrasion-free. Even highpoint wear is typical for the assigned grade level. The '89-CC is one of the key dates in the entire series, with an original mintage of only 350,000 pieces. (#7190)

Choice XF Key Date 1889-CC Morgan Dollar

2577 1889-CC XF45 PCGS. The 1889-CC issue has long been touted as one of the key dates in the Morgan dollar series, and rightfully so. Only 350,000 pieces were struck, and survivors are scarce at all grade levels. This Choice XF example has relatively clean, pearl-gray surfaces, with traces of peripheral color and typical highpoint wear for the grade. (#7190)

Desirable 1889-CC Morgan Dollar AU50

2578 1889-CC AU50 PCGS. Among all Morgan dollars, the '89-CC is one of the most prominent key dates, and is instantly recognizable as such by any knowledgeable collector. This AU example will generate intense interest when it crosses the auction block. Evenly toned in mauve-gray, with iridescent amber-golden accents in the reverse fields, this coin is also surprisingly lustrous for the grade. Modest highpoint wear and a few tiny marks are noted on both sides. (#7190)

1889-CC Morgan Dollar, AU53 Details

2579 1889-CC—Cleaned—ANACS. AU53 Details. Lightly cleaned with the obverse retoned, the reverse is mostly brilliant with peripheral gold color. Although this piece has its imperfections, it will still make a nice addition to a set of Morgan dollars, representing the rarest Carson City dollar of the design. (#7190)

AU53 Details 1889-CC Dollar

2580 1889-CC—Cleaned—ANACS. AU53 Details. Light gray surfaces have hints of peripheral gold toning that has been reacquired after the coin was cleaned at some point in the past. A few minor slide marks are visible on Liberty's cheek. Still and all, this is an attractive and desirable example of the key-date Carson City dollar. (#7190)

Key Choice AU 1889-CC Dollar

2581 1889-CC AU55 NGC. Light golden-brown and powder-blue freckles adorn the peripheries of this problem-free key date Carson City dollar. Luster brightens the margins and devices. No marks are remotely worthy of singular mention. Unlike other low mintage CC-mint Morgans, the '89-CC never emerged from Treasury vaults in quantity in Mint State during the 19th century. (#7190)

Attractive Near-Mint 1889-CC Morgan Dollar

2582 1889-CC AU58 NGC. Boldly struck for the issue and lacking noticeable highpoint wear, this pleasing near-Mint example displays light cream-gray toning and attractive pale golden accents on each side. A small abrasion is noted on the eagle's upper right breast, and wispy hairlines occur in the fields. The '89-CC is an important Morgan dollar key date, and one of the few issues rarely seen in bag quantities, by coin dealers, during the 20th century. Coin production was resumed at the Carson City Mint in 1889, after a four-year hiatus, but only 350,000 silver dollars were struck. (#7190)

2583 1889-O MS64 PCGS. A crisply struck example of this desirable O-mint Morgan dollar issue, strongly lustrous with only a trace of color in the fields. Light, scattered marks dot the surfaces of this pleasing Choice piece. (#7192)

2584 1889-S MS64 PCGS. This flashy near-Gem is essentially untoned and exhibits splendid cartwheel effects on both obverse and reverse. All of the design elements are well struck. A few wispy marks on each side prevent the Gem grade designation. (#7194)

2585 1889-S MS64 PCGS. Both sides offer plenty of flash, and the reverse is semi-prooflike at a minimum. An essentially untoned, solidly struck Choice example of this lower-mintage San Francisco issue, which amounted to just 700,000 pieces. (#7194)

2586 1889-S MS65 PCGS. Slightly soft over the centers, but well struck elsewhere, this attractive Gem displays a rich layer of mottled russet patina over the reverse, and variegated russet and olive peripheral toning on the obverse. Lustrous and nicely preserved, with a handful of small abrasions noted on the eagle's breast. (#7194)

2587 1889-S MS65 PCGS. Mottled peach and dove-gray toning blankets this satiny and exquisitely struck Gem. The fields are splendidly preserved, and the cheek shows only minor marks. Housed in a green label holder. (#7194)

2588 1889-S MS65 PCGS. A strongly lustrous Gem example of this lower-mintage S-mint issue, well struck with surfaces that shine beneath layers of blue, champagne, and plum patina. Carefully preserved with excellent visual appeal. (#7194)

2589 1889-S MS65 PCGS. This essentially brilliant Gem has a bright, flashy, semi-prooflike appearance that is only enhanced by the myriad die striations in the fields. The piece is fully struck throughout, with few surface blemishes and some faint roller marks (as struck) on Liberty's chin.
From The Arnold & Harriet Collection, Part Two. (#7194)

2590 1889-S MS64 Prooflike PCGS. Untoned, prooflike surfaces yield a generous amount of field-motif contrast. Adequately struck, save for weakness in the centers. Population: 34 in 64 Prooflike, 6 finer (7/07). (#7195)

2591 1890 MS65 PCGS. Strongly lustrous with above-average detail for this mid-date Philadelphia issue. The obverse offers dusky gold-orange and jade patina, while the reverse shows similar peripheral colors around an untoned center. While available as a Gem, the 1890 is extremely rare any finer; PCGS has certified just one such coin (8/07). (#7196)

Select Tail Bar 1890-CC Dollar

2592 1890-CC Tail Bar MS63 PCGS. VAM-4. A Top 100 Variety. A bold, straight line of relief links the eagle's tailfeathers and the lower wreath on this distinctive die variety. The coin offered here displays strong luster and just a hint of ice-blue patina in the fields. Solidly struck with a comparatively clean reverse, though a number of small abrasions on the obverse restrict the grade. (#87198)

Brilliant MS63 1890-CC 'Tail Bar' Dollar

2593 1890-CC Tail Bar MS63 PCGS. VAM-4. A Top 100 Variety. Fortunately for collectors, the 'Tail Bar' variety is not significantly scarcer than the regular 1890-CC dollar. The 'bar' (actually a die gouge) is strong and easily seen with the unaided eye. A brilliant coin, the surfaces are bright and lustrous. The abrasions that account for the MS63 grade are almost all located on the obverse. (#87198)

Lustrous 1890-CC Tail Bar Dollar, MS64

2594 **1890-CC Tail Bar MS64 PCGS.** VAM-4. A Top 100 Variety. The prominent bar is evident between the feathers and wreath. Essentially untoned surfaces display great luster, and a sharp strike defines the design elements. A few minor marks and luster grazes account for the near-Gem classification. (#87198)

2595 **1890-CC MS62 ANACS.** Crisply struck with flashy luster and an excellent appearance overall. The margins of this Carson City dollar exhibit a pleasing blend of gold, rose, and plum, while the lightly abraded centers are untoned. (#7198)

2596 **1890-CC MS63 NGC.** A solidly struck Select representative of this later Carson City silver dollar issue, lightly toned silver-blue with elements of sea-green. Uncommonly appealing for the grade with few marks, particularly on the devices. (#7198)

2597 **1890-CC MS63 NGC.** Powerful luster and practically untoned surfaces are the prime draws for this Carson City Morgan dollar. A well-defined example that has light, scattered abrasions on the portrait and in the fields. (#7198)

2598 **1890-CC MS63 NGC.** Potent cartwheel luster is the greatest asset of this attractive Select CC-mint dollar. Boldly struck with light, scattered abrasions and a thin ring of gold-orange patina at the rims. (#7198)

2599 **1890-CC MS63 NGC.** A well-defined example of this later Carson City Morgan dollar issue, strongly lustrous with hints of peach patina in the fields. Light, scattered abrasions account for the grade. (#7198)

2600 **1890-CC MS63 PCGS.** VAM-5. The second C in the mintmark is sharply repunched north. This scarce Carson City dollar has potent luster and is virtually brilliant. A few faint roller marks (as produced) are noted on Liberty's jaw. (#7198)

2601 **1890-CC MS63 PCGS.** This solidly struck Select CC-mint example offers pleasing detail and minimal patina. The fields are well-preserved, though three horizontal abrasions at Liberty's lower jaw define the grade.
From The Mario Eller Collection, Part One. (#7198)

2602 **1890-CC MS64 PCGS.** A pleasingly detailed representative of this later Carson City Morgan issue, strongly lustrous with intermittent areas of silver-gray patina. While the surfaces show no individually mentionable abrasions, a number of faint marks combine to preclude a Gem grade. (#7198)

2603 **1890-CC MS64 PCGS.** Ex: Carson City Collection. A sharply struck example with strong luster beneath faint sky-blue and ice-blue patina. A touch of haze visits the moderately abraded surfaces of this later CC-mint silver dollar. (#7198)

2604 **1890-CC MS64 PCGS.** Isolated patches of cloud-gray patina grace the shining surfaces of this pleasingly detailed Carson City dollar. While the obverse shows a number of scattered marks, the reverse is comparatively clean. (#7198)

2605 **1890-CC MS64 PCGS.** Both sides of this piece have natural silver-gray surfaces beneath muted blue-gray toning. An outstanding example for the grade. (#7198)

2606 **1890-CC MS64 PCGS.** Fully struck and brilliant throughout. The surfaces are notably free from abrasions and the coin is clearly suggestive of an even higher grade. (#7198)

Radiant 1890-CC Dollar, MS65

2607 **1890-CC MS65 NGC.** Purple, golden-tan, and cobalt-blue toning concentrates at the margins of this radiantly lustrous Carson City Gem. Well struck throughout, including good detail in the hair over Liberty's ear and on the eagle's breast feathers. Some minor marks in the left obverse filed likely prevent an even higher grade. Census: 56 in 65, 2 finer (7/07).
From The Arnold & Harriet Collection, Part Two. (#7198)

2608 **1890-CC MS64 Prooflike PCGS.** Mint State 1890-CC dollars with prooflike surfaces are relatively scarce, especially in the higher grades. The current near-Gem specimen displays excellent field to device contrast, and is essentially untoned except for a wisp or two of light tan-gold color. Both sides exhibit bright luster. The design features are well brought up, with the hair over Liberty's ear revealing partial definition. The grade is defined by a few minute contact marks and luster grazes on the cheek and in the upper obverse fields. Population: 68 in 64 Prooflike, 10 finer (7/07). (#7199)

2609 **1890-CC MS62 Deep Mirror Prooflike NGC.** Although the surfaces are somewhat abraded, deeply mirrored fields serve as a fine background for the lustrous devices. (#97199)

2610 **1890-O MS65 PCGS.** A vibrant, wholly original example, typically softly struck in the centers and virtually untoned, with very few marks on either side. (#7200)

2611 **1890-O MS65 PCGS.** Highly lustrous with traces of gold toning on mostly untoned, creamy-white surfaces. Boldly struck save for flatness in the hair detail just above Liberty's ear. A few scattered marks are noted, along with some faint roller marks across Liberty's lower cheek, jaw, and ear. (#7200)

2612 **1890-O MS65 PCGS.** Mauve and golden-orange patina covers both sides of this highly lustrous Gem. While not fully struck, the centers are certainly better detailed than the usually seen 1890-O dollar. Smooth and satiny, the rich toning cannot subdue the underlying luster. (#7200)

2613 **1890-O MS64 Deep Mirror Prooflike ANACS.** Orange patina graces the margins, and the well-defined devices offer a surprising amount of contrast. A strongly reflective, immensely appealing near-Gem example of this popular New Orleans issue. (#97201)

2614 **1890-S MS65 PCGS.** A beautiful Gem example that has bright, semi-prooflike fields. The brilliant surfaces are extraordinarily clean and the striking details are strong on each side. (#7202)

2615 **1890-S MS65 PCGS.** Potent luster sweeps this attractively preserved and assertively struck Gem. The portrait and the reverse are surprisingly unabraded. The 1890-S has a high mintage, but is scarce in such exemplary quality. (#7202)

2616 **1890-S MS65 NGC.** Pleasing luster radiates from the lightly toned, well preserved surfaces that show only a couple of trivial blemishes. The strongly impressed design elements further enhance the beauty of this gorgeous S-mint Morgan. (#7202)

2617 **1890-S MS65 PCGS.** Booming luster sweeps this unmarked Gem. Delicate peripheral orange toning confirms the originality. Crisply struck, and certified in an old green label holder. (#7202)

Appealing 1891 Gem Dollar

2618 **1891 MS65 NGC.** A perusal of the NGC/PCGS population figures reveals that Mint State 1891 dollars are abundant throughout the MS64 grade level, but the numbers fall precipitously in MS65 (specifically, from about 2,100 near-Gems to 145 MS65 pieces, and five specimens finer). A medley of soft golden-tan, violet, and powder-blue patina exhibits slightly deeper hues on the obverse, and glowing luster emanates from both sides. The design elements are well defined, and well preserved surfaces have a grainy finish, which is typical for the issue. Great overall eye appeal! Census: 65 in 65, 2 finer (7/07).
From The Arnold & Harriet Collection, Part Two. (#7204)

2619 **1891 MS63 Prooflike PCGS.** Although 1891 is not a rare date, it is elusive in prooflike, with a low population. Highly lustrous and brilliant silver surfaces are void of toning on either side. Population: 27 in 63, 16 finer (8/07). (#7205)

2620 **1891-CC MS63 NGC.** VAM-3. A Top 100 Variety. The best-known VAM for this popular Carson City issue, named the "Spitting Eagle" variety for the small die lump beneath the eagle's beak. Crisply struck and faintly toned with pleasing preservation. (#7206)

2621 **1891-CC MS63 PCGS.** VAM-3. A Top 100 Variety. The reverse is remarkably toned in beautiful ruby-red, forest-green, ice-blue, and yellow-gold shades. The obverse is also originally toned, but in more subtle autumn-brown and aqua tints. (#7206)

2622 **1891-CC MS64 PCGS.** VAM-3. A Top 100 Variety, the "Spitting Eagle." We offer here a bright near-Gem with sparkling mint luster over each side. Sharply struck, except for the centers, and brilliant throughout. (#7206)

2623 **1891-CC MS64 PCGS.** A lovely near-Gem representative of this later Carson City issue, well struck with creamy luster and splashes of milky patina on the obverse. Light, scattered abrasions appear on each side, and a patch of roller marks is present on the cheek. (#7206)

2624 **1891-CC MS64 PCGS.** VAM-3. A Top 100 Variety. Occasional wisps of light tan color reside on highly lustrous surfaces. Light mint-made roller marks are evident near Liberty's ear, but there are no relevant abrasions. (#7206)

2625 **1891-CC MS64 PCGS.** VAM-3. A Top 100 Variety. The well-known "Spitting Eagle," present on perhaps half of all Uncirculated 1891-CC dollars. This lustrous near-Gem is nicely struck and possesses faint golden toning. (#7206)

2626 **1891-CC MS64 PCGS.** VAM-3. A Top 100 Variety. Delicate chestnut toning precludes full brilliance. Booming luster dominates this carefully preserved and nicely struck near-Gem. (#7206)

2627 **1891-CC MS64 PCGS.** Wonderful luster and a generally strong strike are the prime features of this pleasing Carson City dollar. Choice with only a few isolated marks and luster grazes that preclude an even finer grade. (#7206)

2628 **1891-CC MS64 PCGS.** VAM-3. A Top 100 Variety. Plum toning adorns the obverse periphery, and occurs briefly along the upper reverse border. Satin luster gleams across both sides. Boldly struck with a normal number of abrasions for the Select Mint State grade designation. (#7206)

2629 **1891-CC MS64 NGC.** A shining Choice example that exhibits wisps of soft gold-gray patina over well-preserved surfaces. Well struck overall with only a touch of softness noted at the hair over the ear. (#7206)

2630 **1891-CC MS64 NGC.** VAM-3. A Top 100 Variety. An elegantly frosty appearance enhances the visual appeal of this lustrous near-Gem. Only faintly toned on the obverse, with light champagne patina on the reverse. Faint grazes on Liberty's cheek and the left obverse field preclude an even finer grade. (#7206)

2631 **1891-CC MS64 PCGS.** A shining silver-gray Choice example of this later Carson City silver dollar issue, minimally marked for the grade with above-average definition overall. An appealing example from an issue of just over 1.6 million pieces.
From The Mario Eller Collection, Part One. (#7206)

2632 **1891-CC MS64 PCGS.** Though the hair above the ear shows slightly soft detail and a patch of roller marks, the surfaces of this strongly lustrous Carson City near-Gem are minimally flawed for the grade and attractive. Delicate canary patina settles over parts of the otherwise silver-gray surfaces. (#7206)

Remarkable 1891-CC Dollar, MS65 Prooflike

2633 **1891-CC MS65 Prooflike NGC.** David Bowers (2005) writes that 1891-CC Prooflike dollars "usually have low contrast in relation to the design features, and, accordingly, the demand for them is not great." On this Prooflike Gem, the motif-field contrast is pronounced at all angles, but especially when the coin is tilted under a light source. The white surfaces exhibit sharply impressed design elements, and are remarkably well preserved. Census: 5 in 65 Prooflike, 1 finer (7/07).
From The Arnold & Harriet Collection, Part Two. (#7207)

2634 **1891-CC MS61 Deep Mirror Prooflike NGC.** VAM-3. A Top 100 Variety. A boldly impressed, deeply reflective example of this ever-popular Carson City VAM. Scattered haze graces the surfaces. While the obverse shows a number of grade-defining abrasions, the reverse is comparatively clean. (#97207)

2635 **1891-CC MS63 Deep Mirror Prooflike PCGS.** Seldom seen with the Deep Mirror Prooflike designation, and accordingly prized when so encountered. Most example of this issue possess low contrast, and this high-contrast example, with light field marks, will make some new owner quite happy. Silvery and untoned, with excellent eye appeal and a decent strike. A couple of contact marks on the eagle's breast are noted. (#97207)

2636 **1891-O MS64 NGC.** Both sides show pleasing peripheral definition, though the highpoints show softness on this New Orleans near-Gem. The lower obverse and the reverse are largely untoned, while the rest of the coin shows lovely peach-orange patina. A pleasing example of this popular issue. (#7208)

2637 **1891-O MS64 NGC.** Well-defined for this O-mint issue with soft, swirling luster beneath vibrant patina. The carefully preserved surfaces boast a lovely melange of orange, amethyst, peach, and rose. (#7208)

2638 **1891-O MS64 NGC.** A pleasing example of this mid-date O-mint Morgan issue, strongly lustrous with a pillowy strike. Delicate tan accents grace the rims of this minimally marked near-Gem. NGC has graded 76 finer examples (8/07). (#7208)

2639 **1891-O MS64 PCGS.** This O-mint Morgan shows swirling luster and typical detail on both sides. Small splashes of reddish-orange patina appear intermittently along the rims, and a streak of cloud-gray toning crosses the lower portrait. (#7208)

2640 **1891-O MS64 NGC.** Radiant cartwheel luster and a relative absence of contact make this an alluring and distraction-free example of this scarcer New Orleans issue. Despite the generous mintage, few examples are found in Gem condition, currently numbering only a few dozen pieces at both services combined, including resubmissions. A typically struck piece, in the optimal grade for most collectors. (#7208)

Exceptional 1891-O Gem Dollar

2641 **1891-O MS65 NGC.** David Bowers (2006), says: "The 1891-O is the worst struck of all Morgan dollars. Some are flat at the centers." The Gem in this lot displays an above average strike, as at least partial definition is visible in the hair at Liberty's ear and the eagle's breast feathers. Highly lustrous surfaces are essentially untoned, and are well preserved for the grade designation. (#7208)

Beautiful 1891-O Dollar, MS65

2642 **1891-O MS65 PCGS.** The 1891-O dollar carries the reputation of "the worst struck of all Morgan dollars. Nearly all show weakness to one degree or another" (David Bowers, 2006). The Gem we present in this lot exhibits better-than-average definition, though some softness is visible in the hair at Liberty's ear and the eagle's breast feathers. The date, often weak, is bold on this specimen. Pleasing luster issues from well preserved surfaces that bear just a touch of light tan-gold color at some of the margins. *From The Arnold & Harriet Collection, Part Two.* (#7208)

2643 **1891-S MS65 PCGS.** Orange-gold toning dominates both sides, and is slightly deeper on the obverse. Lustrous and crisply struck with a smooth cheek. A pleasing late 19th century S-mint Morgan dollar, encapsulated in an old green label holder. (#7210)

2644 **1891-S MS65 NGC.** This San Francisco Mint product has terrific eye appeal, boasting rich luster and clean, untoned surfaces. Two or three unimportant blemishes and luster grazes on each side. NGC has only graded 20 pieces finer than MS65 (7/07). *From The Arnold & Harriet Collection, Part Two.* (#7210)

2645 **1892 MS64 PCGS.** VAM-3. The reverse legends are lightly die doubled, but of greater collector interest is the low mintage, which barely exceeds 1 million pieces. A lustrous near-Gem with clean fields and delicate tawny-gold toning. Certified in an old green label holder. (#7212)

2646 **1892 MS64 ANACS.** Solidly defined overall with only a hint of softness at the uppermost part of the obverse. This pleasing P-mint near-Gem offers shining luster and a thin veil of peach-gold patina over the obverse and reverse margins. (#7212)

2647 **1892 MS64 ANACS.** This shining Choice P-mint issue has excellent luster and only a hint of highpoint softness. The faintly marked surfaces are minimally toned aside from a touch of haze. A lovely example from an issue of just over 1 million pieces. (#7212)

2648 **1892 MS64 NGC.** Natural silver-gray surfaces with peripheral gold toning and decent definition of the designs accompany fully lustrous mint frost. (#7212)

2649 **1892 MS64 PCGS.** Delicate layers of gold and peach patina add color to this otherwise silver-gray Philadelphia piece. Pleasingly detailed with few marks overall, though a shallow abrasion at the upper left obverse precludes a Gem grade. (#7212)

Condition Scarcity 1892 Gem Dollar

2650 **1892 MS65 PCGS.** The 1892 dollar is generally obtainable through the lower grades of Mint State, but Gem quality examples are scarce. Vibrant luster graces the untoned, well cared for surfaces of this MS65 piece, and the design features are well brought up, including the feather detail on the eagle's breast. PCGS has seen only two coins finer, and NGC a mere one in higher grade (7/07). *From The Arnold & Harriet Collection, Part Two.* (#7212)

2651 **1892-CC—Surface Residue, Cleaned—ANACS. AU55 Details.** This briefly circulated scarcer date Carson City dollar retains most of its initial luster. The cleaning is inoffensive at worst, and the "surface residue" consists of subtle milk-gray patina on the lower left reverse. (#7214)

2652 **1892-CC MS62 NGC.** A charming, untoned example of this late Carson City silver dollar issue. Lustrous and well struck, with a few scuffy marks on Liberty's cheek that reduce the grade. (#7214)

2653 **1892-CC MS63 PCGS.** A die chip rests atop the lower right serif of the 2 in the date. This example is bright and brilliant, with semi-reflective fields. Sharply struck with numerous trivial field marks that limit the grade. A nice Select example of this elusive Carson City issue, which went unrepresented in the great Treasury hoard releases of the 1960s and 1970s. (#7214)

2654 **1892-CC MS63 PCGS.** Partially prooflike fields establish good contrast with the mildly frosted, well struck motifs. Both sides are essentially untoned, and reveal a few grade-limiting marks. (#7214)

2655 **1892-CC MS63 PCGS.** This attractive silver-gray piece shows a touch of frost on the solidly struck devices. Whispers of cloud-gray toning visit the shining obverse fields, and the portrait shows more luster grazes than actual marks. A lovely example of this later Carson City dollar issue. (#7214)

2656 **1892-CC MS63 NGC.** Powerful luster and minimal milk-white patina contribute to the eye appeal of this Morgan dollar, which comes from the penultimate Carson City issue. Aside from softness at the highpoints, the devices are well struck. (#7214)

2657 **1892-CC MS63 PCGS.** The 1892-CC dollar tends to be found heavily bagmarked. This Select specimen, while possessing some obverse luster grazes, displays pleasing lustrous surfaces. Untoned, with well struck design elements, except for the usually-seen softness in the centers. (#7214)

2658 **1892-CC MS63 ANACS.** Golden-rose and ocean-blue invigorate the peripheries of this lustrous and pleasing scarce date Carson City dollar. Housed in an ANA cache holder. (#7214)

2659 **1892-CC MS63 PCGS.** A solidly struck and appealing Select example that shows semi-prooflike silver-gray surfaces on both sides. The fields have few marks for the grade, though the devices show faint abrasions. A lovely representative of the penultimate Carson City silver dollar issue. *From The Mario Eller Collection, Part One.* (#7214)

Splendid 1892-CC Dollar MS64

2660 1892-CC MS64 PCGS. Well struck and lightly toned with booming luster and splendidly smooth fields. The cheek has only minor grazes. The date and mintmark have minor die fill. A better Carson City dollar that failed to appear in the famous GSA auctions, unlike the much lower mintage '81-CC and '85-CC. (#7214)

Lustrous 1892-CC Morgan Dollar, MS64

2661 1892-CC MS64 NGC. The penultimate silver dollar issue from Carson City, here represented by a lustrous silver piece with tinges of gold on the reverse. The surfaces are quite clean, with a moderately prooflike appearance, and only a few tiny luster grazes on the cheek appear to preclude a finer grade. The reverse is slightly rotated clockwise from the obverse, perhaps 10 degrees. (#7214)

Attractive Near-Gem 1892-CC Morgan Dollar

2662 1892-CC MS64 ANACS. Attractive and highly lustrous, with semi-reflective fields and iridescent peripheral toning, in shades of rose, gold, and cobalt-blue, that is heavier on the reverse. The design motifs are boldly struck overall, although softness is noted on the hair detail just above Liberty's ear. A scarcer Carson City date that becomes extremely challenging any finer. (#7214)

MS64 1892-CC Morgan With Interesting Die Break

2663 1892-CC MS64 PCGS. One of the more popular dates in the Carson City series, although not in the front rank of rarities. The meager mintage of only 1.35 million coins was likely further reduced by Pittman Act meltings. This silvery and lustrous piece is well produced, although it does show light roller marks at the center obverse under magnification. Contact marks are at a minimum. This piece also shows a nifty die break/fill on the lower loop of the 2 in the date that joins, on the right, stars 13-11 and 9-8 with the (UNU)M, and on the left with the other date digits, the rim, and stars 2-4. A nice piece for the grade, and one that should see a good premium as a variety. (#7214)

Appealing 1892-CC Dollar, MS65

2664 1892-CC MS65 PCGS. While many Mint State 1892-CC Morgans are flat in the centers and heavily bagmarked (David Bowers, 2006), the Gem we present in this lot displays excellent technical quality and aesthetic appeal. All of the design elements have benefited from a well executed strike, including the hair at Liberty's ear and the eagle's breast feathers. Partially prooflike fields highlight lightly frosted motifs, and essentially untoned surfaces are well preserved. *From The Arnold & Harriet Collection, Part Two.* (#7214)

2665 1892-CC MS63 Prooflike NGC. This satiny, brilliant, and intricately struck Select Prooflike dollar has clean fields and a smooth cheek. A high-end example of this scarcer Carson City emission. (#7215)

Charming Prooflike Near-Gem 1892-CC Morgan Dollar

2666 1892-CC MS64 Prooflike PCGS. Ex: Ray George. A charming Prooflike example from the penultimate CC-mint Morgan dollar issue. A liberal coating of icy mint frost covers the devices, while the brilliantly mirrored fields lack any trace of toning and possess only minor abrasions. Population: 74 in 64 Prooflike, 10 finer (8/07). (#7215)

Deep Mirror Prooflike MS62 1892-CC Dollar

2667 1892-CC MS62 Deep Mirror Prooflike PCGS. This stone-white elusive date CC-mint dollar has nicely mirrored fields that provide desirable contrast with the frosty devices. Well struck, even on the hair above the ear, and no marks merit an individual description for the grade. Population: 60 in 62 Deep Mirror, 70 finer (8/07). (#97215)

Elusive 1892-CC Dollar MS64 Deep Mirror Prooflike

2668 1892-CC MS64 Deep Mirror Prooflike PCGS. Surprisingly absent from the Treasury hoard releases of the early 1960s, the '92-CC has enjoyed increased status ever since. This near-Gem example is boldly struck with deeply prooflike surfaces and exceptionally frosted devices that appear snow-white against the jet-black fields. Superficial luster grazes on Liberty's face, and in the left obverse field, prevent an even higher numerical grade designation, but the Deep Mirror Prooflike label definitely seems warranted. Population: 28 in 64 Deep Mirror Prooflike, 2 finer (8/07). (#97215)

2669 1892-O MS64 PCGS. At first glance, this piece has the appearance of a Gem, partly because of noticeably better-than-average striking definition. Only the area directly above Liberty's ear exhibits typical flatness, and the eagle's breast feathers have partial definition. Highly lustrous with appealing light peripheral toning and nicely preserved surfaces for the grade. (#7216)

2670 1892-O MS64 NGC. A light ring of amber-gold encircles each side of this lustrous near-Gem, a popular issue produced to the extent of only 2.7 million pieces in the year before the Panic of '93. The strike through the center is soft, revealing considerable roller marks on each side, the product of incompletely struck planchets. (#7216)

Exceptional 1892-O Gem Dollar

2671 1892-O MS65 PCGS. Light reddish-gold patination gravitates to the borders of this Gem O-mint dollar, and dazzling luster radiates from both sides. The design elements are well impressed, including relatively strong definition on the eagle's breast, and partial detail in the hair over Liberty's ear. This is a significant attribute for the coin, for as Leroy Van Allen and George Mallis indicate of the 1892-O in their Morgan and Peace dollar reference book: "This is probably the most consistently flat struck date of the entire Morgan series." Well preserved surfaces round out the coin's technical quality and aesthetic appeal. Housed in a green-label holder.
From The Arnold & Harriet Collection, Part Two. (#7216)

Conditionally Elusive Gem 1892-O Morgan Dollar

2672 1892-O MS65 NGC. Intense coruscating mint frost shines over each side of this conditionally scarce Gem dollar from the New Orleans Mint. The design elements are generally bold, but typical softness is noted above the ear and on the eagle's breast feathers. Other than a few small grease specks (as struck) the surfaces of this bright example are snow-white and untoned. Census: 70 in 65, 4 finer (8/07). (#7216)

2673 1892-S AU50 NGC. Dashes of orange and electric-blue frequent the rims. Luster is substantial for the grade. The older generation holder has a small chip absent with no effect on the coin's preservation. (#7218)

2674 1892-S AU53 PCGS. The pale silver-gray surfaces of this lightly circulated S-mint dollar show traces of sky-blue and lemon-gold patina. Well struck with a number of wispy abrasions on each side, though this piece remains appealing and an attractive example of this conditionally elusive issue.
From The Mario Eller Collection, Part One. (#7218)

2675 1892-S—Cleaned—ANACS. AU55 Details. This rare date Morgan dollar has only slight wear in the centers, but the remaining luster is subdued, and the nearly untoned surfaces are glossy. Clusters of wispy marks are noted near the lips, behind the cap, and beneath TRUST. (#7218)

Scarce 1892-S Dollar, AU55

2676 1892-S AU55 NGC. Most of the 1892-S dollars were placed into circulation, resulting in it being common in the circulated grades of VF and XF, scarce in AU, and very rare in Mint State. Luster resides in the protected areas of this Choice AU example, and the surfaces are quite clean for a coin that has seen limited circulation. The design elements are well defined.
From The Arnold & Harriet Collection, Part Two. (#7218)

2677 1892-S—Cleaned—ANACS. AU55 Details. Noticeable traces of mint luster are seen around the devices on each side. Bright from cleaning, the surfaces are generally free from abrasions. (#7218)

2678 1893 MS62 NGC. Unusually well detailed for the issue, the surfaces show just the slightest hint of color on the obverse. (#7220)

2679 1893 MS62 PCGS. VAM-3. The Closed 3 in the date is doubled along the upper edge. Well struck with bright, satiny luster and lovely lilac splashes near the periphery. Surface marks are not excessive for the grade. The 1893 Morgan dollar had one of the lowest mintages from the Philadelphia Mint, at 389,792 pieces. (#7220)

2680 1893 MS63 NGC. Among the lowest-mintage P-mint business strike Morgans, the 1893 issue saw only 389,000 pieces produced. This example offers considerable frosty luster over the untoned surfaces, and appears a bit conservatively graded, as Liberty's cheek and the surfaces elsewhere are relatively free of distractions. (#7220)

2681 1893 MS63 PCGS. In 1893, though Philadelphia, Carson City, New Orleans, and San Francisco all produced Morgan dollars, no one Mint struck more than a million coins. This Select P-mint piece has pleasing detail and strong luster beneath soft silver-gray patina. Splashes of rose appear at the upper and lower obverse. (#7220)

2682 1893 MS63 NGC. Boldly struck and thoroughly lustrous with attractive russet and electric-blue peripheral toning. Conservatively assessed despite a pair of faint slide marks on the chin. Certified in a former generation holder. (#7220)

2683 1893 MS63 NGC. Nice luster emanates from satiny surfaces that possess a silver-gray cast. Generally well defined, with just a few minor obverse luster grazes. (#7220)

2684 1893 MS64 PCGS. The surfaces are mostly silver, with irregular areas of copper-bronze patina before and behind Liberty. A nice piece for the grade with a minimum of marks and an untoned reverse, certified in an old-style green-label holder. (#7220)

2685 1893 MS64 PCGS. VAM-3. The Closed 3 in the date is doubled along the upper edge. Well struck with intense mint luster over flashy, essentially untoned surfaces. The reverse only has a few slight field blemishes, while the obverse shows a small disturbance along the rim near 6 o'clock, and a shallow graze near Liberty's mouth.
From The Arnold & Harriet Collection, Part Two. (#7220)

2686 1893 MS64 PCGS. While its S-mint counterpart attracts more attention, the 1893 presents its own challenges and has a mintage of under 400,000 pieces. This well struck, strongly lustrous representative displays delicate gold, rose, and blue tints. (#7220)

2687 1893-CC VF30 ANACS. A moderately worn representative of this lower-mintage final-year Carson City issue, predominantly cloud-gray with reddish-orange patina at the margins. Well struck with a number of abrasions on the cheek. (#7222)

2688 1893-CC VF35 NGC. An appealing Choice VF representative of this popular final-year Carson City Morgan dollar issue. The moderately worn silver-gray surfaces show faint, scattered abrasions, as expected for the grade. (#7222)

2689 1893-CC VF35 PCGS. This semi-key date dollar is nicely detailed for the grade, with untoned surfaces that are moderately worn across the highpoints. A few small abrasions and numerous wispy hairlines are observed on each side. From the final year of coin production at the Carson City Mint. (#7222)

2690 1893-CC VF35 ANACS. A pleasing light gray example of this popular issue, with typical scattered abrasions on each side, consistent with the grade. (#7222)

2691 1893-CC VF35 PCGS. A moderately circulated example of the popular final issue from Carson City, with minor marks that are expected for the grade. The light gray surfaces have slightly deeper peripheral toning. (#7222)

2692 1893-CC XF45 NGC. The luminous surfaces of this Choice XF piece are predominantly light silver-gray with a hint of gold at the obverse rim and a band of peach and violet at the upper reverse. Well struck with faint, scattered abrasions. Overall, an appealing, lightly circulated example of this noted issue. (#7222)

2693 1893-CC—Cleaned—ANACS. AU50 Details. This nearly untoned silver dollar has been dipped and exhibits fine hairlines on each side. Substantial luster emerges from the crisply defined devices. A difficult Carson City issue. (#7222)

Flashy Mint State 1893-CC Morgan

2694 1893-CC MS60 PCGS. This semi-prooflike semi-key CC-mint dollar has glimpses of butter-gold near the rims, but the fields and devices are essentially brilliant. The centers are typically impressed, and the cheek has several individually light abrasions. Housed in a green label holder. (#7222)

Lustrous 1893-CC Morgan Dollar MS61

2695 **1893-CC MS61 NGC.** The most noteworthy attribute of this Carson City dollar is the intense mint frost over each side, followed by the vivid orange-gold peripheral toning that likewise occurs on both obverse and reverse. Striking weakness on the central design details and extensive bagmarks are both typical for this popular issue. (#7222)

Exceptional 1893-CC Dollar, MS62

2696 **1893-CC MS62 NGC.** This key Carson City issue has an impressively low mintage of only 677,000 pieces. Relatively few Uncirculated coins are extant today, and of the ones that are known many are weakly struck, cleaned, or heavily bagmarked. This is an attractive coin that is sharply struck on each side and accented with light, even lilac-gray patina. Semi-reflective in the fields. There are a few light ticks and luster grazes, but these are not as numerous or severe as is usually the case with this issue. (#7222)

Wonderful 1893-CC Select Dollar

2697 **1893-CC MS63 NGC.** David Bowers (2006) notes of the 667,000-piece 1893-CC dollar that "Probably several hundred thousand (were melted) under the 1918 Pittman Act." Lustrous surfaces abound on this Select example, and reddish-gold patina gravitates to the peripheries, more extensively and deeper on the reverse. Better struck than is typical for the issue, and revealing fewer and less severe bagmarks than typically seen. (#7222)

Impressive 1893-CC Near-Gem Dollar

2698 **1893-CC MS64 PCGS.** We present in this lot an exceptional near-Gem 1893-CC dollar. This piece displays marvelous prooflike surfaces that reveal just a few minute contact marks and luster grazes that barely preclude full Gem classification. In this regard, David Bowers (2005) writes: "Mint State 1893-CC dollars are well known for being extensively bagmarked, some actually appearing quite abused. Accordingly, the majority of Mint State pieces are in lower MS grades. A piece MS63 or finer, with minimum bagmarks, is a numismatic find and is very special." Save for the usual softness in the centers, the design elements are quite well struck. Housed in a green-label holder. This piece exhibits the highest grade that most collectors will encounter, and is also among the best technical quality and aesthetic appeal.
From The Arnold & Harriet Collection, Part Two. (#7222)

Sharply Struck 1893-CC Near-Gem Dollar

2699 **1893-CC MS64 PCGS.** The 1893-CC dollar has always been a collector's favorite due to its scarcity and status as the last Carson City Mint coin of its denomination. In his Silver and Trade dollar reference (1993), David Bowers writes:

> "Mint bags of 1893-CC dollars came on the market as early as 1920 at face value through the Cash Room at the Treasury in Washington and, in particular, from storage at the San Francisco Mint. However, the quantity was small in comparison to certain other Carson City dates, particularly those of the early and mid-1880s. The supply seems to have been exhausted by the late 1950s, and there are no records of any quantities being paid out after that time."

A hint or two of light tan color appears under magnification on the near-Gem being offered in this lot. Lustrous surfaces yield some prooflike tendencies in the fields, with the consequent mild contrast with the motifs. A well executed strike leaves its mark on the design features, being manifested in sharpness in the hair at Liberty's ear and the eagle's breast feathers. A few minute obverse marks and luster grazes preclude the assignment of full Gem classification. (#7222)

Prooflike MS62 1893-CC Dollar

2700 **1893-CC MS62 Prooflike NGC.** This brilliant rare date dollar has flashy fields and a clean reverse. The centers are typically indistinct, while the remainder of the design is sharp. Minor obverse grazes combine to determine the grade. The final year of Carson City production, although the mintmark also appears on certain 1900-O VAMs. (#7223)

2701 **1893-O AU50 ANACS.** Conservatively graded and showing more remaining design detail than expected for the grade. Untoned except for trace amounts of gold peripheral toning. Wispy hairlines and a few small abrasions are noted on both sides. A scarce New Orleans issue with a paltry mintage of just 300,000 pieces. (#7224)

2702 **1893-O AU55 PCGS.** The 1893-O is part of a string of low-mintage issues from 1893 to 1895, with just 300,000 pieces coined. This briefly circulated piece, luminous with typical detail, has a predominantly lavender obverse with bold orange toning over the reverse. (#7224)

2703 **1893-O AU55 NGC.** A hint of wear is present on the softly struck highpoints of this lower-mintage O-mint dollar. A pleasing representative that retains ample luster in the rose-tinged fields. (#7224)

2704 **1893-O AU58 NGC.** Just a touch of friction is noted on the highpoints and in the fields. This otherwise delightful O-mint coin retains ample luster and shows few marks overall, with just one abrasion of note below the E in STATES on the reverse. Minimally toned and eminently appealing, one of just 300,000 representatives of the issue. (#7224)

Low Mintage 1893-O Morgan Dollar MS61

2705 **1893-O MS61 ANACS.** 1893 was a year of low mintages for the Morgan dollar, at all four of the U.S. mints. New Orleans was no exception, as just 300,000 pieces were produced. This Mint State example is untoned and exhibits dazzling cartwheel luster on the reverse, while the obverse shows slightly more subdued, creamy luster. There is a noticeable scrape on Liberty's jaw, and a number of smaller abrasions are scattered around the obverse, limiting the grade. (#7224)

Low Mintage 1893-O Morgan Dollar MS61

2706 **1893-O MS61 PCGS.** Lustrous and essentially untoned, save for a bit of golden-brown color along the upper obverse, this conditionally scarce Mint State example is housed in a first-generation PCGS holder. The design elements are generally bold, except over the centers, as usual. This year's mintage was the lowest among all Morgan dollar issues from the New Orleans Mint. (#7224)

Sharp 1893-O Select Dollar

2707 **1893-O MS63 NGC.** The 1893-O is the lowest mintage New Orleans Morgan dollar (300,000 pieces), and is scarce in circulated grades and scarce to rare in Mint State. The lustrous surfaces of this Select example are toned in cobalt-blue, lavender, and gold-tan at the margins, and the design elements exhibit sharp detail, save for the usually seen softness in the centers. The few minuscule marks scattered about are perhaps fewer than what might be expected for the grade classification.
From The Arnold & Harriet Collection, Part Two. (#7224)

Affordable Key Date 1893-S Morgan Dollar Good 4

2708 **1893-S Good 4 ANACS.** This is a nicely original, well worn example of the primary Morgan dollar key date. The central design elements are worn smooth, but most of the peripheral details are still evident, including the date and the mintmark. What appears to be a large planchet lamination (as struck) resides on the upper reverse, extending from the rim onto the lower half of the first A in AMERICA. (#7226)

2709 **1893-S—Cleaned—ANACS. Good 4 Details.** The date is bold, and although the mintmark is filled, its outline is unmistakable. The cream-gray devices contrast with darker medium brown fields. Only mildly cleaned. An affordable example of the series key. (#7226)

Desirable Key 1893-S Dollar, Good 6

2710 **1893-S Good 6 NGC.** Very Fine seems to be about the "norm" grade for a circulated 1893-S dollar. Indeed, in a September 5, 2005 *Coin World* article, Paul Gilkes writes that "... very few are known in lower grades such as Fair, Good and Very Good." The appearance of a Good 6 example at auction thus provides an excellent opportunity for the collector who desires to acquire a relatively inexpensive specimen of this key date in a collectible grade. This piece displays light to medium gray color on surfaces that are, for the most part, remarkably clean despite extensive circulation. We also note relatively good design definition for the grade. (#7226)

Choice Good 1893-S Dollar

2711 **1893-S Good 6 PCGS.** This key date Morgan dollar provides dove-gray fields and slate-gray devices. The obverse has a tiny rim nick at 4 o'clock and the cheek and jaw have minor contact, but the overall surfaces are superior for the Good 6 grade. More than half of the feathers show on the eagle's wings. (#7226)

Exceptional 1893-S VG8 Dollar

2712 **1893-S VG8 NGC.** Light to medium gray toning takes on a faint pinkish hue, and after accounting for the moderate to heavy highpoint wear, excellent definition is apparent on the design elements. Additionally, close inspection reveals remarkably clean surfaces for a large, heavy coin in the VG level of preservation. This is a most pleasing key-date '93-S, and as such will fit comfortably in any circulated Morgan dollar collection. (#7226)

1893-S Dollar With VG8 Details

2713 **1893-S—Scratched—ANACS. VG8 Details.** This Morgan dollar has a faint vertical mark near Liberty's profile, but most collectors in need of this series key will overlook this abrasion, which is minor for the VG8 level. Every silver dollar enthusiast quickly learns the mintage of the '93-S: just 100,000 pieces. (#7226)

Key 1893-S Dollar VG Details

2714 **1893-S—Improperly Cleaned—NCS. VG Details.** Ocean-blue and golden-brown toning hugs the borders, while the slate-gray fields contrast mildly with the lavender devices. Somewhat bright for the grade, but no abrasions need individual description, and some wing and tail feather detail remains. Coveted as the key to the business strike series. (#7226)

Choice VG 1893-S Morgan Dollar

2715 **1893-S VG10 PCGS.** All of the major design elements are intact, and the mintmark is easily discernible on this well circulated Morgan dollar. The evenly worn surfaces display dove-gray toning and few noticeable marks. The 1893-S had a tiny mintage of 100,000 pieces, ensuring its status as the most famous key date in the Morgan dollar series. (#7226)

Pleasing 1893-S Morgan Dollar, VF25

2716 **1893-S VF25 PCGS.** Medium bluish-gray toning in the fields highlights the silvery-gray design elements on this VF25 key date Morgan dollar. Sharp design definition remains for the grade, and the surfaces are quite clean. A rather pleasing example that will fit well into a mid-grade collection. (#7226)

Desirable VF25 1893-S Dollar

2717 **1893-S VF25 NGC.** Morgan dollar collectors desire the 1893-S in all grades, and the demand-supply equation is such that the issue is valued in four figures even in lower grades. Bright silver-gray surfaces are seen on the VF25 example in this lot, and exhibit ample detail on the design elements. A few minute circulation marks do not detract. (#7226)

Sharp 1893-S Morgan Dollar, VF25

2718 **1893-S VF25 NGC.** Whispers of olive-green color dance about the obverse of this key-date Morgan, and concentrate at the margins of the reverse. The design features reveal good definition, and just a few minute marks consistent with light to moderate circulation are scattered about. An excellent example for a mid to high-grade circulated Morgan dollar collection. (#7226)

Key Date 1893-S Morgan Dollar VF35

2719 1893-S VF35 ANACS. This is the primary key date in the immensely popular Morgan dollar series and, as such, it commands a significant premium at any grade level. This Choice VF example is eminently more affordable than an AU or Mint State piece. Well detailed with a smooth, original appearance, the surfaces display medium-gray color, with occasional glimpses of darker patina near the borders. (#7226)

Key VF35 1893-S Morgan Dollar

2720 1893-S VF35 NGC. This Choice VF example has a pleasing appearance for the grade, and is free of any overtly distracting surface blemishes or abrasions. A couple of minor rim dings are noted on the reverse. The 1893-S Morgan dollar was destined to be an important key date, with its tiny mintage of 100,000 pieces, and many numismatists would gladly pay a premium price in order to own one. (#7226)

Pleasing 1893-S Dollar, XF40

2721 1893-S XF40 NGC. Many numismatists consider the 1893-S to be the most desirable single Morgan dollar issue struck at a branch mint. In addition to its minuscule mintage (100,000 pieces), tens of thousands may have been melted under provisions of the 1918 Pittman Act (David Bowers, 2006). Traces of luster cling to the design elements of this light gray XF40 example, and aside from wear on the highpoints, these display nice detail. There are fewer marks than what might be expected for the grade. All in all, a pleasing, original key-date specimen.
From The Arnold & Harriet Collection, Part Two. (#7226)

Appealing 1893-S Dollar, XF40

2722 1893-S XF40 PCGS. Traces of luster cling to the design elements of this most pleasing XF key date Morgan dollar. Its light gray surfaces are remarkably clean for a large, heavy coin that has seen some circulation. Likewise, nice detail remains on the devices, enhancing its overall eye appeal. (#7226)

Desirable Choice XF 1893-S Morgan Dollar

2723 1893-S XF45 PCGS. In his *A Guide Book of Morgan Silver Dollars*, Q. David Bowers (2005) enthuses about this issue: "The 1893-S is the object of great desire in the Morgan dollar series. No single issue has greater popularity across the board." He further notes that the pieces circulated in the American West, and that the grade distribution is clustered around Very Fine.

For the collector who desires a better example, this well-defined example offers an enticing alternative. The lightly abraded surfaces are predominantly pale silver-gray, though both sides show elements of pale blue and gold. The obverse margins and the reverse exhibit considerable remaining luster, and the overall visual appeal is considerable. A noteworthy choice for the silver dollar enthusiast. (#7226)

Key Issue 1893-S Morgan Dollar XF45 Details

2724 **1893-S—Cleaned—ANACS. XF45 Details.** The sharp design detail still evident on each side of this key date specimen gives it the immediate, arms-length appearance of an AU coin. At close range, however, numerous small hairlines are noted, especially in the reverse fields; indicating that the piece was harshly cleaned at some point in its history. Evenly worn over the central highpoints, with few abrasions and light, cream-gray coloration. (#7226)

2725 **1894—Reverse Rim Damaged—ANACS. VG8 Details.** A rim nick at 10 o'clock on the reverse is less consequential than the ANACS designation suggests. A circulated but collectible example of this difficult low mintage date. (#7228)

2726 **1894 XF40 NGC.** A well struck example from this tiny-mintage issue of 110,000 pieces, luminous at the margins with gold-gray and rose patina over each side. The devices exhibit light, even wear, and the fields show a number of light, scattered abrasions that contribute to the grade. (#7228)

2727 **1894—Cleaned—ANACS. XF40 Details.** A subdued appearance characterizes the surfaces of this improperly cleaned example. The dove-gray coloration is augmented by traces of golden luster along the edges and near the devices. A key issue among Morgan dollars, due to the exceedingly low mintage. (#7228)

2728 **1894 XF40 ANACS.** Hints of luster emerge as this primarily slate-gray, semi-key date dollar is rotated beneath a light. Light golden patination is also encountered near the borders. No marks pose a singular distraction. Far more affordable than the similar mintage 1893-S. (#7228)

2729 **1894 XF45 NGC.** Whispers of olive-green visit both sides of this Choice XF specimen that displays traces of luster in the protected areas. Nicely defined, and devoid of significant marks. The 1894 is elusive in all grades. (#7228)

2730 **1894—Cleaned—ANACS. AU50 Details.** This low mintage Morgan dollar is a bit cloudy from hairlines, but the devices display only moderate wear, and the only mentionable mark is a small obverse rim ding at 5:30. (#7228)

AU 1894 Morgan Dollar

2731 **1894 AU50 PCGS.** The ultra-low mintage 1894 has long been eagerly pursued by the thousands of collectors of this popular series. This silver-gray representative displays slight wear on the centers, but marks are minor and unworthy of further description. Satin luster is evident at the borders and across the devices. (#7228)

2732 **1894—Whizzed—ANACS. AU50 Details.** It is our opinion that this piece may have been cleaned less judiciously than necessary, but the description by ANACS seems quite strong. Take a look for yourself. (#7228)

Choice AU 1894 Dollar

2733 **1894 AU55 NGC.** The Choice About Uncirculated 1894 Morgan being offered in this lot displays traces of luster in the recesses, and is covered by whispers of pastel olive-green, tan, and gray patination. Slight wear on the highpoints does little to diminish the design elements' detail. What few marks that are present are completely inoffensive. A truly "Choice" specimen. (#7228)

Elusive 1894 Morgan Dollar, AU58 Details

2734 **1894—Cleaned, Retoned, Rim Damage—ANACS. AU58 Details.** Light hairlines indicate that it has been cleaned, but the obverse of this piece has delightful silver luster with hints of gold toning. The reverse has slightly reflective fields beneath deep lilac and steel toning. The rims have been noticeably filed on both sides, around nearly the entire circumference. (#7228)

Borderline Uncirculated 1894 Silver Dollar

2735 **1894 AU58 PCGS.** The cartwheel luster appears complete, but a trace of friction is noted on the eagle's breast and on the hair above the ear. The fields are refreshingly unmarked. The cheek has an inconspicuous thin and shallow scrape. The lowest mintage regular issue Philadelphia Morgan dollar. Encapsulated in a green label holder. (#7228)

2736 **1894—Cleaned—ANACS. MS60 Details.** Well struck with satiny luster and light creamy-gold coloration. A shallow scrape is detected on Liberty's cheek, and a couple of minor abrasions reside on her neck. The reverse seems blemish-free. An affordable example of the first Philadelphia Mint key date Morgan dollar, which suffers minimally from the effects of improper cleaning. (#7228)

Desirable 1894 Dollar, MS61

2737 **1894 MS61 NGC.** Satiny silver-gray surfaces take on an occasional wisp of olive-green color around some of the design elements of this 1894 dollar. Adequately struck, with softness noted in the hair over Liberty's ear. Several luster grazes are visible, especially on the obverse. David Bowers writes that "A few bags were released in the 1950s and early 1960s. Quantities are virtually unheard of in the present market." (#7228)

Low Mintage 1894 Dollar, MS62

2738 **1894 MS62 ANACS.** Whispers of electric-blue and brown toning are restricted to the borders of the obverse, but travel throughout the reverse, where they are joined by splashes of muted lavender. Generally well struck, with soft luster, and a few minute obverse marks. The low mintage 1894 is desirable in all grades. (#7228)

Scarce 1894 Morgan Dollar MS62

2739 **1894 MS62 ANACS.** The 1894 Morgan dollar may not be immediately thought of as an important key date in the series, but perhaps it should be. It is certainly a key date among the Philadelphia Mint issues; with the lowest Morgan dollar mintage ever seen at that facility. This example is well struck and lustrous, with attractive light peripheral patina and minor marks for the grade. Perhaps even a candidate for a one-point upgrade. *From The Mario Eller Collection.* (#7228)

Elusive 1894 Near-Gem Dollar

2740 **1894 MS64 NGC.** The 1894 dollar is elusive in all grades. Mint State coins are mostly in the MS60 to MS63 range. The availability falls off in MS64, and Gem quality pieces are rare. This near-Gem example possesses bright luster radiating from silver-gray surfaces that display generally well defined motifs. A handful of obverse marks define the grade. Census: 97 in 64, 4 finer (7/07). *From The Arnold & Harriet Collection, Part Two.* (#7228)

Sharply Defined MS64 1894 Dollar

2741 **1894 MS64 PCGS.** Although popular among today's collectors, the Morgan dollar was a seemingly unnecessary coin that cluttered Treasury Department vaults through the early 1970s. The 1894 was produced to the extent of only 110,000 business strikes, few of which were released into circulation at the time of issue. Although the Treasury Department released several bags of Mint State examples in the 1950s and 1960s, this issue is still a significant rarity above the BU level. Lightly toned in a somewhat mottled fashion on the obverse in golden-tan hues, both sides are dripping with mint frost. The strike is above average for the series and the surfaces are free of unduly bothersome abrasions. (#7228)

2742 **1894 MS66 PCGS.** The model for the Morgan dollar, Ms. Anna Williams, was apparently unaffected by the celebrity status bestowed upon her by the hundreds of millions of silver dollars that showed her profile. The following commentary was included in her obituary in *The Numismatist* in 1926: "The story of how Miss Williams came to be the model has not been told often. She was besieged for the story many times, but in later years she smilingly referred to it as 'an incident of my youth,' and preferred to talk of her work in the kindergarten schools of the city (Philadelphia) which she supervised."

The portrait of Ms. Williams is the critical area for grading Mint State Morgan dollars. It is seldom found unblemished with a smooth, rounded cheek. This is especially true for the 1894, the second scarcest Philadelphia issue in the series. Several bags and numerous rolls were released in the 1950s and 1960s, but most of these coins were lower graded examples in the MS60-64 range. To date, only three other examples of the 1894 have been certified in MS66 condition (all four are PCGS), and predictably none are finer.

As mentioned, the portrait of Liberty is remarkably smooth and free from the abrasions normally encountered. The surfaces are smooth, satiny, and brilliant throughout. Each side is fully struck with fine detailing over the ear of Liberty as well as the breast of the eagle. A rare opportunity for the Morgan specialist. (#7228)

2743 **1894-O AU50 ANACS.** Delicate gold toning visits this attractive AU better date dollar. Highpoint wear is minimal, and there are no significant marks. (#7230)

2744 **1894-O MS61 NGC.** The design elements display weakness in the hair over Liberty's ear and on the eagle's breast feathers. Several minute marks are visible on Liberty's cheek and neck and in the left (facing) obverse field. Nevertheless, a pleasing and unworn example of this popular New Orleans issue. (#7230)

2745 **1894-O MS62 NGC.** The 1894-O is fairly scarce in mint State, and also comes weakly struck (David Bowers, 2006). This lustrous piece is untoned, and shows some definition in the hair at Liberty's ear and on the eagle's breast. Minute obverse marks limit the grade. (#7230)

2746 **1894-O MS62 ICG.** While the central highpoints have the soft detail often associated with this issue, the devices are well-defined otherwise. Strongly lustrous with minimal patina and light, scattered abrasions that account for the grade. (#7230)

Challenging Select 1894-O Morgan Dollar

2747 **1894-O MS63 ICG.** While the 1894-O is the highest-mintage silver dollar issue for the year, many examples experienced significant circulation, and Mint State pieces, particularly those Select and finer, remain elusive. This minimally toned and strongly lustrous example, well-defined save for the hair above the ear, shows faint, scattered abrasions that account for the grade. Appealing despite its flaws. (#7230)

1894-O Dollar, MS64

2748 **1894-O MS64 PCGS.** Potent luster invigorates both sides of this near-Gem O-mint dollar, and the motifs reflect a better strike than usually seen on the issue, except for weakness in the hair at Liberty's ear. The lightly marked surfaces display just the faintest hint of occasional tan color under magnification. PCGS has seen only nine coins finer (7/07).
From The Arnold & Harriet Collection, Part Two. (#7230)

2749 **1894-S MS61 NGC.** A luminous representative of this lower-mintage San Francisco issue, solidly struck with dusky rose and peach patina over each side. Though both sides show a number of faint abrasions, the overall visual appeal is better than the MS61 designation might suggest. (#7232)

2750 **1894-S MS62 ANACS.** Bright, untoned surfaces yield exceptionally well struck motifs. A few small marks on Liberty's cheek and neck define the grade. (#7232)

2751 **1894-S MS63 PCGS.** An impressive Select better date silver dollar with sweeping luster and delicate tan patina. Crisply struck and superior for the grade. Housed in an old green label holder. (#7232)

2752 **1894-S MS63 PCGS.** This well struck Select piece shines beneath thin, intermittent layers of silver-gray haze. A touch of reddish-orange patina is noted in the left obverse field. Pleasing despite scattered, grade-defining abrasions. (#7232)

2753 **1894-S MS63 NGC.** Both sides have bands of gold-orange and bronze patina at the margins, while the highly lustrous obverse has a thin ring of violet as well. A well-defined, lightly abraded example of this interesting S-mint issue, which has a mintage of just 1.26 million pieces. (#7232)

2754 **1894-S MS63 NGC.** A sharply struck example of this popular S-mint dollar. The mint luster is bright and highly frosted. Brilliant throughout. (#7232)

2755 **1894-S MS63 ANACS.** Subtle lilac toning is barely visible on each side of this otherwise brilliant Mint State example. While scattered abrasions keep it from a higher grade, none are of any significance. (#7232)

2756 **1894-S MS64 PCGS.** The frosty reverse is practically untoned, while dappled lemon-yellow, orange, and silver-gray patina graces the obverse. A well-defined and pleasing S-mint dollar. (#7232)

2757 **1894-S MS64 NGC.** Highly lustrous, the mint frost rolls around each side with only minimal impediments from a few light abrasions. Light golden peripheral toning is seen on each side of this better date S-mint. (#7232)

2758 **1894-S MS64 PCGS.** An extremely bright, semi-prooflike sheen encompasses both sides of this brilliant silver-white example. The design elements are boldly detailed, with minimal softness observed over the central regions. A moderate scrape is noted along Liberty's jawline.
From The Arnold & Harriet Collection, Part Two. (#7232)

2759 **1894-S MS64 NGC.** Following the repeal of the silver purchase provisions of the Bland-Allison act, silver dollar production slowed dramatically, and for the period from 1893 to 1895, the 1894-S, with a mintage of just 1.26 million pieces, had the second-highest production for any issue. This crisply struck near-Gem shines beneath rich plum and orange toning over the outer areas and silver-gray over the centers. (#7232)

2760 **1894-S MS64 PCGS.** A shining Choice representative of the issue that bridges the key 1893-S and the challenging 1895-S Morgan dollars. This well-defined piece has regions of scattered haze over the portrait and the obverse and reverse fields. (#7232)

2761 **1894-S MS64 Prooflike ANACS.** The fields of this near-Gem shine through gold-gray haze that turns to peach at the lower margins. Well struck with clean devices for the grade, though marks are present in the fields. (#7233)

2762 **1895-O VF35 NGC.** Evenly worn with substantial design details still clearly outlined. Olive-gray toning adorns both sides. Minor abrasions on Liberty's jaw and neck areas are the only individually noticeable marks. A pleasing Choice VF example of this scarce key date issue from the New Orleans Mint. (#7236)

2763 **1895-O XF45 PCGS.** The blue-gray surfaces of this dollar retain subtle luminosity at the margins. A well struck, lightly worn piece that shows areas of deeper color near the peripheral elements. An attractive example of this popular lower-mintage O-mint issue. (#7236)

2764 **1895-O AU50 ANACS.** Light, even wear affects the well struck devices of this delicately toned, still-lustrous O-mint key. Wispy, scattered abrasions appear below thin veils of champagne patina. (#7236)

2765 **1895-O—Rim Filed—NCS. AU Details.** Pleasing silver-gray surfaces exhibit traces of luster in the recesses and are quite clean for a coin that has seen some circulation. Nicely defined, save for the usual softness in the centers. Any rim filing is extremely minor. In other words, the interested bidder should not be intimidated by the NCS disclaimer. (#7236)

2766 **1895-O AU50 NGC.** Dusky amethyst, cloud-gray, and pumpkin-orange patina graces both sides of this lightly worn and luminous AU dollar. A well struck and pleasing representative of this noted New Orleans issue, famous for its small mintage of only 450,000 pieces.
From The Diemer L. Fife Collection. (#7236)

2767 1895-O—Cleaned—ANACS. AU53 Details. This lightly circulated key date O-mint dollar displays considerable glowing luster. The pearl-gray surfaces are slightly subdued, and faded marks are noted on the cheek and on the field beneath the left (facing) wing. (#7236)

2768 1895-O AU55 NGC. Bowers' *Guide Book of Morgan Silver Dollars* points out that the 1895-O is the single business-strike Morgan not to have been found in any bags of silver dollars from the Treasury releases. AU coins prevail in the marketplace, such as this silvery piece with little evidence of contact. (#7236)

Desirable Near-Mint 1895-O Morgan Dollar

2769 1895-O AU58 NGC. This New Orleans Mint issue had a low mintage of 450,000 coins, assuring its status as a desirable and highly coveted date in the Morgan dollar series. Survivors are scarce enough at the current grade level, but Mint State specimens are especially dear. This example is satiny and essentially untoned, with minimal highpoint wear and a few small abrasions on each side. (#7236)

Lustrous, Iridescently Toned 1895-O Dollar, AU58

2770 1895-O AU58 NGC. The scarcity of the 1895-O dollar is beyond question in the Morgan series, and the AU58 grade level is the breaking point for availability and price for this issue. Several hundred pieces have been certified, but most near-Mint examples are only available in major offerings of dollars in public auctions. Above this, at the MS60 and finer level, the 1895-O is a major condition rarity with only a few dozen pieces known. This piece retains generous amounts of mint luster, especially on the reverse. Both sides are enveloped in rich green, rose, and gray toning. The only mentionable abrasion is located at the bottom of the eagle's breast. (#7236)

Condition Rarity 1895-O Dollar, MS61

2771 1895-O MS61 PCGS. As evidenced by the PCGS/NGC population figures, 1895-O dollars are often seen in lower grades. Even About Uncirculated coins are seen with some frequency. However, in the words of David Bowers (2006): "In Mint State the 1895-O dollar is very rare." Bowers also indicates: "Striking is usually below average to average, not often sharp. Cherrypicking is encouraged, not easy to do with 1895-O as Mint State pieces are quite elusive."

Pleasing satiny luster exudes from both sides of the MS61 coin offered in this lot. Occasional whispers of faint olive-green patina show up under magnification, but the surfaces essentially display a silver-gray cast. The strike is a tad better than usually seen on representatives of this issue, but the centers are soft. Some minute contact marks and luster grazes help to account for the grade (#7236)

Scarce 1895-O Dollar, MS61

2772 1895-O MS61 NGC. The NGC/PCGS population figures indicate that 1895-O dollars are available in circulated grades, but are not easily acquired in Mint State. In a February 15, 2005 *Numismatic News* article entitled "1895-O Morgan Dollar Scarce in High Grades" by Paul Green, the author sates: "There was not likely to be much saving of 1895-O Morgan dollars, since few collectors were assembling sets by date and mintmark—that would take about 20 more years. By then, an 1895 was likely to have circulated heavily."

Wisps of golden-tan and gray patina take up residence over each side of the MS61 coin offered in the present lot, and a better-than-average strike sharpens the design features, save for softness in the hair at Liberty's ear. Only slight interruption in the luster flow is noted on the lightly marked surfaces. All in all, a rather pleasing specimen for the grade. Census: 35 in 61, 43 finer (8/07). (#7236)

2773 1895-S XF45 ANACS. Some luster is still evident on this popular key date. Fortunately, there are no hits or gauges to report on the surfaces of this wholly original specimen. Quite appealing for the grade. (#7238)

2774 1895-S—Altered Surfaces—ANACS. AU50 Details. Close to Mint State in terms of sharpness, but this better date dollar is both granular and unnaturally prooflike. The reverse field is faintly abraded from an attempt to remove a green-gold patina. (#7238)

2775 1895-S—Polished—ANACS. AU50 Details. This low mintage silver dollar is bright from a moderate polishing, but the devices exhibit minimal wear. A minor rim ding is noted at 3:30. The key to a date set of Morgan dollars. (#7238)

2776 1895-S/S AU53 ANACS. VAM-3. A Hot 50 Variety. The mintmark was initially entered with too far northwest with a wild tilt to the left. The mint worker made a partially successful attempt to efface the errant mintmark, then repunched it in proper position. But any 1895-dated dollar is desirable, regardless of mintmark or VAM variety. Lightly toned and partly lustrous. (#7238)

Shining Near-Mint 1895-S Dollar

2777 1895-S AU58 NGC. Just a touch of highpoint friction comes between this attractive semi-key piece and a Mint State grade. The strike is pleasing overall, and hints of cloud-gray and gold patina grace the still-lustrous surfaces. An attractive example of this well-known issue, which has a mintage of only 400,000 coins. (#7238)

Challenging MS61 1895-S Morgan

2778 1895-S MS61 PCGS. VAM-4. A Top 100 Variety. The popular S over Horizontal S VAM of this better date. This semi-prooflike example appears brilliant at first glance, but each side has an infrequent wisp of gold patina. Marks are inconsequential, and the luster is only slightly diminished. Certified in a green label holder. (#7238)

Desirable 1895-S Dollar, MS64

2779 1895-S MS64 PCGS. Mint State 1895-S dollars are usually heavily bagmarked, presumably from rough handling while in treasury storage. The near-Gem specimen for sale in this lot, while displaying a few minor marks that prevent full Gem status, still retains a high level of eye appeal. Pleasing luster exudes from untoned surfaces that exhibit sharply struck design elements.
From The Arnold & Harriet Collection, Part Two. (#7238)

Sparkling MS64 1895-S Dollar

2780 **1895-S MS64 PCGS.** The 1895-S is one of the keys to the S-mint series of Morgans. The mintage was low at only 400,000 pieces. While a few smaller hoards have surfaced over the years, there have never been enough coins available to satisfy collector demand, especially in the better grades of Uncirculated. This is a sparkling coin that has the semi-prooflike glimmer in the fields that is often seen on '95-S dollars. Fully struck, the surfaces are free from any noticeable abrasions, and there is just a bit of golden-brown toning around the peripheries of this otherwise brilliant coin. (#7238)

2781 **1896 MS66 PCGS.** Vibrant luster is the most evident characteristic of this exquisitely preserved and eminently appealing P-mint Premium Gem. The strike is solid, and the surfaces are essentially untoned. PCGS has graded 23 finer representatives (8/07). (#7240)

Splendid 1896 MS67 Dollar

2782 **1896 MS67 NGC.** The 1896 dollar, with a circulation strike mintage approaching 10 million pieces, is readily available through the MS65 grade level. Even Premium Gems can be obtained with patience. MS67 coins, however, are elusive, as evident from less than 70 examples certified by NGC and PCGS combined, and none finer. Potent luster invigorates this suitably struck specimen. Close examination of the untoned surfaces reveals no mentionable marks. Census: 43 in 67, 0 finer (7/07). (#7240)

2783 **1896 MS66 Prooflike NGC.** A stunning Premium Gem with full prooflike surfaces around lustrous white devices. Both sides are exquisite with no toning. Census: 8 in 66 Prooflike, 1 finer (8/07). (#7241)

2784 **1896 MS64 Deep Mirror Prooflike NGC.** Well struck with barely a trace of softness in the hair detail above Liberty's ear. A few minor marks on the cheek and in the left obverse field limit the grade. The fields are decidedly prooflike and show deep, watery reflectivity on both sides of the coin. A common date which becomes considerably scarcer in Deep Mirror Prooflike condition. (#97241)

2785 **1896 MS65 Deep Mirror Prooflike PCGS.** Amazing silver surfaces have deeply mirrored fields with satiny devices and sharp details. PCGS has only graded 11 finer deep mirror examples of the date. (#97241)

2786 **1896-O MS60 ANACS.** Though both sides of the piece show a number of abrasions, the piece's overall eye appeal is better than the MS60 designation would suggest. Well struck with strong luster for this O-mint issue and scattered areas of tawny-gold patina. (#7242)

2787 **1896-O MS61 NGC.** Following a string of lower-mintage issues, New Orleans dollar production rebounded in 1896, with 4.9 million pieces coined. Delicate golden-tan patina graces the obverse of this luminous piece, while the reverse is silver-gray. Wispy abrasions in the fields and on the devices account for the grade. (#7242)

2788 **1896-O MS61 ANACS.** Hints of goldenrod and amethyst patina grace the rims of this lovely, highly lustrous New Orleans Morgan dollar. Both sides show marks, though the obverse abrasions that account for the grade are more wispy than distracting. (#7242)

Attractive 1896-O Dollar, MS62

2789 **1896-O MS62 PCGS.** This attractive example has good luster and generally clean surfaces. A solitary hair-thin vertical mark on the cheek is all that limits the grade. The centers are only slightly soft for this conditionally rare New Orleans issue. Brilliant aside from a dash or two of russet patina at 7:30 on the reverse. (#7242)

Conditionally Scarce 1896-O Morgan Dollar MS62

2790 **1896-O MS62 PCGS.** Well struck save for typical minor softness near the centers. This piece also displays fine satin luster that seems a bit better than average, for the issue. Pale gold toning near the peripheries attractively frames the creamy, untoned centers. This issue is relatively scarce at the current grade level, considering its high mintage of 4.9 million pieces, and becomes rare any finer than MS63. (#7242)

Exceptional 1896-O Select Dollar

2791 **1896-O MS63 PCGS.** Ex: Larry Shapiro Collection. Many numismatists contend that the typical 1896-O dollar comes with considerable problems. Wayne Miller, for example, in his Morgan and Peace dollar reference, says: " No other Morgan dollar is as consistently deficient in luster, strike, and degree of surface abrasions as the 1896-O." The Select coin in this lot digresses significantly from Miller's profile. Its untoned surfaces are fully lustrous, and exhibit sharp definition on most of the design elements. The hair over Liberty's ear is weak, but fairly good detail is apparent on the eagle's breast. The reverse is quite well preserved, while a few marks on Liberty's cheek and neck preclude a higher grade. All in all, a nice example for the issue and the grade.
From The Arnold & Harriet Collection, Part Two. (#7242)

Conditionally Scarce Select Mint State
1896-O Morgan Dollar

2792 1896-O MS63 NGC. Well struck and lacking most of the typical weakness over the centers common to Morgan dollars from the New Orleans Mint, this piece is also frosty and highly lustrous. The gleaming surfaces are snow-white in the centers, and show an attractive ring of golden rim toning on both sides. Minor scuffiness on the obverse limits the grade; the reverse only has a few minor marks. Amazingly, NGC has only graded six examples finer (7/07). (#7242)

Creamy MS63 1896-O Morgan Dollar

2793 1896-O MS63 NGC. Exhibiting creamy luster and a coating of attractive, pinkish-gray coloration over both sides, this Select Mint State example also displays some lovely gold, terra cotta, and mint-green iridescence near the borders. With few marks, and showing typical weakness on the hair detail just above Liberty's ear, this piece seems appropriately graded at the current level. Exceedingly scarce any finer, with a mere 15 coins presently certified above MS63, by NGC (8/07). (#7242)

Select 1896-S Morgan Dollar

2794 1896-S MS63 ANACS. The mintmark is repunched northeast. Splashes of jade-green and golden-rose grace the peripheries of this thoroughly lustrous and nicely struck better date dollar. The cheek displays a few faint grazes, but the eye appeal is irrefutable. The mintage of the 1896-S is only half that of the 1896, but the 1896 is perhaps 20 times more common in Mint State, probably because silver dollars readily circulated in the West. (#7244)

Desirable 1896-S Dollar, MS64

2795 1896-S MS64 PCGS. The 1896-S is very desirable in all Mint State grades. The typical example is apt to be in the MS60 to MS63 range. Vibrant luster adorns the essentially untoned surfaces of this near-Gem, and an attentive strike brings out good detail on most of the design elements. A handful of obverse marks define the grade. *From The Arnold & Harriet Collection, Part Two.* (#7244)

Frosted MS64 1896-S Dollar

2796 1896-S MS64 PCGS. Much scarcer than its mintage of 5 million pieces indicates, at least half that number are believed to have been melted under the Pittman Act. This is a brilliant coin that has thick, frosted mint luster. A few minor abrasions and luster grazes account for the grade, as well as slight softness of strike in the centers. (#7244)

2797 1897 MS65 Deep Mirror Prooflike PCGS. Delightful deep mirrors enliven each side of this Gem with frosty devices, silvery on the obverse and with pale-copper and steel-blue iridescence on the reverse. A seldom-seen issue in Deep Mirror Prooflike, one of only 23 so graded at PCGS, with two finer (8/07). (#97247)

2798 1897-O MS60 NGC. Light golden hues visit this lustrous and conditionally scarce New Orleans dollar. The centers are typically brought up, but the reverse is unabraded. In a prior generation holder. (#7248)

2799 1897-O MS61 NGC. A generally appealing example of this later O-mint issue, well-defined with pleasing luster and a number of wispy abrasions. Hazy cream, orange, and silver-gray patina graces the margins, with splashes of deeper color at the obverse rims. (#7248)

2800 1897-O MS62 PCGS. Both sides of this well struck O-mint piece exhibit vibrant luster, though that of the untoned reverse is slightly stronger. A touch of milky patina visits the obverse, which displays a number of light, scattered abrasions. One of just over 4 million examples coined. (#7248)

2801 1897-O MS62 PCGS. An underrated and difficult coin to find in the finer Mint State grades. The present piece shows only a few light contact marks consistent with an MS62 grade, although apparently held back by the somewhat lackluster surfaces. (#7248)

Conditionally Elusive 1897-O Morgan Dollar MS63

2802 **1897-O MS63 NGC.** A light layer of creamy, opaque pinkish-gray coloration over each side is imbued with lovely underlying accents of steel-blue. The design elements are sharply struck throughout, including the hair detail above Liberty's ear and the eagle's breast feathers. This is a surprisingly scarce issue at the Select Mint State level, despite its original mintage of just over four million coins. (#7248)

2803 **1897-S MS66 PCGS.** This is a visually stunning Premium Gem that combines utterly brilliant, snow-white surfaces with effulgent, coruscating mint frost and great surface preservation. A few trivial marks become evident under magnification, but none of them are distracting. An outstanding example of this popular issue from the San Francisco Mint. (#7250)

2804 **1897-S MS66 PCGS.** A remarkably frosty silver dollar with booming cartwheel luster and just a bit of peripheral toning on the otherwise brilliant-white surfaces. Well struck and remarkably preserved, with a few minute marks in the reverse fields. (#7250)

2805 **1897-S MS66 Prooflike NGC.** Though the 1897-S is not particularly scarce with prooflike fields (as about 20% of the certified population is so classified), such pieces are elusive in better-than-Gem grades. This moderately reflective piece is predominantly silver-gray with only faint haze and a tiny spot of violet toning near the L in PLURIBUS. Census: 19 in 66 Prooflike, 2 finer (8/07). (#7251)

2806 **1898 MS66 PCGS.** A pleasingly detailed P-mint dollar from the late 19th century that offers strong luster beneath soft silver-gray patina. Carefully preserved with excellent eye appeal. PCGS has graded 24 finer representatives (8/07). (#7252)

2807 **1898 MS66 PCGS.** An amazing piece, the designs are boldly rendered and the surfaces are fully brilliant with frosty white luster. PCGS has only certified 24 finer examples (8/07). (#7252)

Condition Scarcity 1898 Dollar, MS67

2808 **1898 MS67 PCGS.** The 1898 is readily available in the various Mint State grades, save for the MS67 level of preservation, in which only 35 examples have been certified by PCGS and NGC, and none finer. Coruscating luster adorns nearly untoned surfaces that have been well cared for. All of the design elements are well brought up. Population: 0 in 67, 0 finer . (#7252)

2809 **1898 MS65 Deep Mirror Prooflike PCGS.** Deeply mirrored and fully brilliant, this is an elusive issue in Gem deep mirror prooflike quality as evidenced by the PCGS population. Population: 59 in 65, 12 finer (8/07). (#97253)

2810 **1898-O MS67 NGC.** Thoroughly lustrous with a crisp strike. Devoid of both toning and marks with a freshness that reinforces this piece's Superb Gem status. An outstanding example from this available O-mint Morgan dollar issue. NGC has graded just one numerically finer piece (8/07). (#7254)

2811 **1898-O MS66 Prooflike PCGS.** Brilliant and sharply struck throughout, with flashy prooflike mirrors in the fields. An exceptionally pleasing example of this otherwise common late-date O-mint dollar, and very scarce as such with only 42 other pieces so graded, and just one finer in Prooflike condition at PCGS (7/07). (#7255)

2812 **1898-S MS64 PCGS.** A frosty near-Gem with hints of gold toning along the borders. An ideal grade for the date, perhaps the best combination of price and quality. (#7256)

2813 **1898-S MS64 NGC.** VAM-6. The mintmark is clearly repunched south. A lightly toned and highly lustrous silver dollar with a good strike and a few minor obverse grazes. (#7256)

2814 **1898-S MS64 PCGS.** Despite a mintage of just over 4.1 million pieces, the 1898-S proves challenging in better Mint State grades, as most examples were paid out and collectors were slow to realize the comparative lack of Choice and better pieces. This minimally marked and well struck example has only a hint of patina and flashy luster. (#7256)

2815 **1898-S MS64 PCGS.** This strongly lustrous and flashy near-Gem has excellent detail everywhere but the highest points of the hair. Lightly marked on the devices with thin, milky patina in intermittent tendrils over each side.
From The Mario Eller Collection, Part One. (#7256)

2816 **1898-S MS64 PCGS.** Beautiful orange-gold, rose-red, and apple-green dominate the borders, while the centers remain brilliant. A nicely struck near-Gem with clean fields. The mintmark is repunched south. (#7256)

2817 **1898-S MS64 PCGS.** The surfaces of this near-Gem are luminous beneath silver-gray patina that shows occasional gold and reddish-orange accents. A lovely, well-defined survivor of this later 19th century issue, which has a mintage of just over 4.1 million pieces. (#7256)

2818 **1898-S MS65 PCGS.** Highly lustrous, with semi-reflective fields and boldly struck design elements that only betray a hint of weakness on the hair detail just above Liberty's ear. Essentially untoned with a few minor field marks that keep it from being a Gem. Conditionally scarce at this grade level.
From The Arnold & Harriet Collection, Part Two. (#7256)

2819 **1898-S MS65 NGC.** Well struck with intense mint luster over untoned silver-white surfaces. The fields are flashy and semi-reflective. A few wispy marks are noted on each side. (#7256)

2820 **1898-S MS65 PCGS.** Boldly struck and brilliant with satiny fields. A delectable Gem representative of this later S-mint Morgan issue, one that becomes elusive any finer; PCGS has graded only 60 such pieces (8/07). (#7256)

2821 **1899 MS65 PCGS.** A crisply struck, faintly toned, and fully lustrous Gem of this low mintage issue. Those forming a circulated set know that the 1899 is among the more difficult Philadelphia issues, although Uncirculated pieces remain readily collectible. (#7258)

2822 **1899 MS65 NGC.** Aside from a touch of softness at the hair above the ear, this P-mint Gem is boldly impressed throughout. Strongly lustrous with silver-gray centers and a touch of gold-green toning at the margins. This issue's mintage amounted to only 330,000 pieces.
From The Mario Eller Collection, Part One. (#7258)

2823 **1899 MS65 PCGS.** This shining, satiny Gem is predominantly silver-white with small areas of charcoal patina on the reverse. Well-preserved with attractive detail, a high-end survivor from an issue of only 330,000 pieces. (#7258)

2824 **1899 MS65 PCGS.** Housed in a first-generation PCGS holder, this important Gem has fully lustrous mint frost beneath pale gray and gold toning. (#7258)

2825 **1899 MS65 NGC.** Fully struck with satiny mint luster, there are no mentionable or distracting abrasions on either side. Light, mottled golden toning is seen on the reverse. (#7258)

2826 **1899 MS65 NGC.** A large number of high grade 1899 dollars have been consigned to this auction, which present the collector with a rare opportunity to make his or her selection for a high grade set of Morgans. This piece shows light gray-golden toning over each side with the usual strong underlying mint luster. Fully struck. (#7258)

2827 **1899 MS66 NGC.** An exceptionally attractive coin whose primary draw is the smooth, satiny mint luster that covers each side. As the grade indicates, the surfaces are clean and problem-free and this is especially true of the cheek of Liberty. Mostly brilliant with an accent of golden around each side. (#7258)

2828 **1899 MS66 NGC.** Bright and lustrous with even, light golden toning over each side. A popular, late-date issue. (#7258)

2829 **1899 MS66 NGC.** As with most examples of this popular issue, the mint luster is satiny and races around each side as the coin is tilted beneath a light. Sharply struck, each side is brilliant except for light golden accents around the margins. (#7258)

2830 **1899 MS65 Prooflike NGC.** A semi-scarce date that has always been popular because of its low circulation strike mintage of 333,000 pieces. High-grade Prooflike examples are even more desirable. A sharply struck, well preserved coin with reddish-gold peripheral toning that is deeper on the reverse. Census: 19 in 65 Prooflike, 1 finer (7/07). (#7259)

2831 **1899-S MS64 PCGS.** A highly lustrous near-Gem with frosty silver luster. Both sides have a thin veil of champagne toning with hints of smoky gold at the upper obverse. (#7262)

2832 **1899-S MS64 PCGS.** Whispers of dolphin-gray patina grace the shining surfaces of this later S-mint Morgan, surprisingly well-preserved for the grade with more luster grazes than actual marks. One of under 2.6 million pieces struck, a number that reflects the repeal of silver purchase provisions that inflated previous totals. (#7262)

2833 **1899-S MS65 PCGS.** With a mintage of under 2.6 million pieces, the 1899-S is hardly as ubiquitous as earlier S-mint issues, though Gems are available. This well-defined and lustrous example is largely silver-gray with a touch of milky patina over the obverse. If not for an abrasion at Liberty's forehead, this piece could have achieved an even finer grade. (#7262)

Lustrous 1899-S Dollar, MS66

2834 **1899-S MS66 NGC.** The NGC/PCGS population data show most certified 1899-S dollars to be in the MS63 to MS64 range. The numbers drop significantly in MS65, as well as in Premium Gem and finer. This well struck MS66 coin exhibits bright luster exuding from untoned surfaces. A few minor obverse marks do not detract. Census: 21 in 66, 1 finer (7/07).
From The Arnold & Harriet Collection, Part Two. (#7262)

2835 **1900 MS66 NGC.** This Premium Gem is awash in potent luster, and possesses well preserved, untoned surfaces. Well struck, with partial definition showing in the hair at Liberty's ear. (#7264)

Impressive 1900-O Dollar, MS67

2836 **1900-O MS67 NGC.** The 1900-O dollar is plentiful in Mint State, as evidenced by the thousands of examples certified by NGC and PCGS through the MS65 level of preservation. The certified population takes a noticeable drop in Premium Gem, and again in MS67, where about 80 coins have been so graded. To date, neither service has seen any finer. Whispers of light tan color make occasional visits to the radiantly lustrous, impeccably preserved surfaces of this example. An impressive strike leaves good definition on the design features, including the hair at Liberty's ear. Census: 53 in 67, 0 finer (8/07). (#7266)

Pleasing 1900-O Superb Gem Dollar

2837 **1900-O MS67 NGC.** Well struck with rich, deep rainbow toning over portions of the obverse, and a bright, satiny, reverse toned at the peripheries, where a few faint surface marks reside. The expertly preserved surfaces are virtually distraction-free, and only the slightest weakness is noted on the eagle's breast. A simply fabulous Superb Gem. Census: 53 in 67, 0 finer (8/07). (#7266)

2838 **1900-O/CC MS63 NGC.** VAM-11. A Top 100 Variety. This sharply struck and lightly toned Select overmintmarked dollar has a beautifully preserved reverse. The obverse has only minor marks consistent with the grade. (#7268)

2839 **1900-O/CC MS63 PCGS.** VAM-8. A Top 100 Variety. Sharply defined with satiny silver surfaces, this splendid piece has splashes of gold and heather toning on the obverse, light champagne on the reverse. The overmintmark feature is bold. (#7268)

2840 **1900-O/CC MS64 PCGS.** VAM-11. A Top 100 Variety. The beginnings of a die crack appear below Liberty's hair at the lower right. A solidly struck, essentially untoned, and flashy representative of this turn-of-the-century overmintmarked issue, lightly marked and housed in a green label holder. (#7268)

2841 **1900-O/CC MS64 NGC.** VAM-12. A Top 100 Variety. There are six different die pairs for the 1900-O/CC, but VAM-12 shows more of the CC than the others. This well struck near-Gem has effusive luster and only a hint of golden toning. The reverse is well preserved, and the obverse is also smooth.
From The Laguna Niguel Collection, Part Two. (#7268)

2842 **1900-O/CC MS64 NGC.** VAM-8B. A Top 100 Variety. Designated as VAM-8A on the NGC insert. VAM-8A is a late state of VAM-8 with die rust near the mintmark. VAM-8B has bold clash marks along Liberty's profile. A lustrous and creamy near-Gem with minor central incompleteness of strike. (#7268)

2843 **1900-O/CC MS64 PCGS.** VAM-11. A Top 100 Variety. The usual O/CC VAM, identified by the diagonal die crack above the final obverse star. This exactingly struck near-Gem has vibrant luster and light honey toning. (#7268)

2844 **1900-O/CC MS64 NGC.** VAM-12. A Top 100 Variety. One of the boldest of the 1900-O/CC overmintmark varieties, with the feature visible to a sharp unaided eye. This Choice and well struck example is essentially untoned with few marks overall, though a handful of flaws appear on the cheek.
From The Mario Eller Collection, Part One. (#7268)

2845 **1900-O/CC MS64 PCGS.** VAM-11. A Top 100 Variety. This O/CC mintmark variety shows a die crack diagnostic below the portrait on the obverse. This shining near-Gem has uncommonly strong detail for the grade and a measure of gold-tinged haze over parts of the fields. (#7268)

Lustrous 1900-O/CC Gem Dollar, VAM-11

2846 **1900-O/CC MS65 PCGS.** VAM-11. A Top 100 Variety. The fine die crack from the hair above the last three stars helps to attribute the variety, and the crack embedded in the wreath at the bowknot confirms the later die state. This MS65 coin is a radiantly lustrous, untoned specimen that exhibits a sharp strike. A few minute marks are noted on the obverse.
From The Arnold & Harriet Collection, Part Two. (#7268)

Radiant 1900-O/CC Dollar, MS65, VAM-8

2847 **1900-O/CC MS65 PCGS.** VAM-8. A Top 100 Variety. A die scratch is visible in the base of the T in LIBERTY, but no die chip is seen in the G of GOD. Radiantly lustrous surfaces display faint hints of light tan under magnification, along with sharply struck design elements. Some inoffensive grade-consistent marks are noted on the obverse. Housed in a green label holder. (#7268)

Bright 1900-O/CC Gem Dollar, VAM-11

2848 **1900-O/CC MS65 PCGS.** VAM-11. A Top 100 Variety. The incipient stage of a die crack occurs above the final three stars. This earlier die state example does not have a crack on the branch above the bowknot. Well struck, with bright luster, and just an occasional wisp of barely discernible olive-green color. A couple of grade-consistent marks are not bothersome. (#7268)

2849 **1900-S MS65 PCGS.** This is a frosty Gem example of this turn-of-the-century San Francisco Mint issue. Virtually untoned, except for mere hints of pastel color over the centers, with generally good striking definition, save for a bit of typical softness just above Liberty's ear.
From The Arnold & Harriet Collection, Part Two. (#7270)

2850 **1901 AU58 PCGS.** Dove-gray toning covers the satiny surfaces that display typical softness over the centers, and a few noticeable but small abrasions. This issue becomes a rare key date in higher Mint State grades, and is considerably more affordable in AU. (#7272)

2851 **1901 AU58 PCGS.** Silver-gray surfaces exhibit wisps of light gold, and retain a good amount of luster. Somewhat better struck than typical for the issue, as evidenced by partially definition in the hair at Liberty's ear. There are no significant marks to be reported. (#7272)

2852 **1901 AU58 NGC.** Silver-gray surfaces retain considerable luster, and display sharply impressed design elements. A few light circulation marks are noted on the obverse. (#7272)

Challenging MS61 1901 Morgan

2853 **1901 MS61 NGC.** A highly regarded conditional rarity in Mint State, despite a seemingly plentiful mintage of nearly 7 million pieces. This well struck, lightly abraded example has a thin layer of toning over the strongly lustrous surfaces. Splashes of gunmetal toning accent the eagle. (#7272)

Key Date 1901 Morgan Dollar MS61

2854 1901 MS61 PCGS. This satiny example of the key date 1901 dollar displays light-gray surfaces that are enlivened by shimmering golden highlights on each side. The design features are well produced, and distinct doubling is noted on the hair detail just above Liberty's ear. This appealing Mint State piece is certified in an early PCGS holder, with a light-green label. (#7272)

Attractive MS61 Key Date 1901 Dollar

2855 1901 MS61 NGC. This is a highly attractive example of the key date 1901 Morgan dollar for the grade. Well struck throughout, with typical as struck flatness on the eagle's breast feathers, characteristic of a new reverse hub. A coating of cream-gray patina blankets the reverse, while deep multicolored iridescence adorns the obverse, where prooflike fields are very noticeable. Small, scattered marks limit the grade. (#7272)

Coveted Mint State 1901 Morgan Dollar MS62

2856 1901 MS62 PCGS. According to Dave Bowers (1993): "Of all Philadelphia Mint business strike dollars, excepting the spectral 1895, the 1901 is the rarest in Mint State." This example exhibits bright, satiny luster and essentially untoned surfaces that possess a normal number of small abrasions, for the grade. In an early-generation PCGS holder. (#7272)

Condition Scarcity 1901 Dollar, MS63

2857 1901 MS63 PCGS. The 1901 Morgan dollar, with a mintage of 6,962,000 circulation strikes, is plentiful in circulated grades, and even pieces in the lower Mint State range of MS60 to MS62 are readily obtainable. Higher condition examples, however, are difficult to locate. David Bowers, in his *Silver Dollars & Trade Dollars of the United States*, estimates that about 100 to 200 MS63 coins are known, perhaps 10 to 20 near-Gems, and maybe two to four MS65 pieces. Bowers' estimates are more or less in line with PCGS/NGC population data.

    The present Select examples displays bright, lustrous surfaces with a concentration of light tan-gold color at the margins. A solid strike translates into sharp definition on the design elements, including fairly good detail in the hair strands over Liberty's ear. A handful of minute obverse marks preclude a higher grade.
From The Arnold & Harriet Collection, Part Two. (#7272)

Appealing 1901 Select Dollar

2858 1901 MS63 PCGS. Discussing the 1901 in his 1993 Silver and Trade dollar reference work, David Bowers says: "Most Mint State 1901 dollars are poorly struck and have inadequate luster. A coin that is MS60 to MS62 from a technical standpoint, can be dull and unattractive. As if this were not enough, most show unsightly bagmarks." The author continues: "... higher grade Mint State dollars exist but are exceedingly rare. The typical specialist in silver dollars will often find that years elapse between stocking coins in as high as MS63 grade. Forget about MS64 and MS65."

Light gray patina rests over the pleasantly lustrous surfaces of the MS63 example in this lot, and the design elements have received a well directed strike; only the breast feathers are soft. A few minute obverse marks determine the grade. Nice overall eye appeal for the grade designation. (#7272)

2859 1901-O MS66 PCGS. White, highly lustrous surfaces with a few inconsequential grazes on the left border of the cheek. The design features are well struck throughout. (#7274)

2860 1901-O MS66 NGC. An impressive Premium Gem with fully brilliant and frosty mint luster. Just a touch of design weakness is evident over Liberty's ear as nearly always. Only 11 finer examples are NGC certified. (#7274)

2861 1901-S MS63 NGC. Well struck, satiny, and essentially untoned, with creamy luster and a nice cartwheel shimmer on both sides. A typical number of minor abrasions are noted for the Select Mint State grade level. (#7276)

2862 1901-S MS63 NGC. A well struck, highly lustrous representative of this later S-mint Morgan dollar, mostly silver-gray with areas of peach patina. Light, scattered abrasions are evident on the obverse, though the reverse is clean for the grade. (#7276)

2863 1901-S MS64 NGC. This is an amazing near-Gem representative of this elusive date with only 89 finer pieces certified by NGC. Both sides have full cartwheel luster with considerable silver-white color, ringed by peripheral gold and iridescent toning, especially on the obverse. (#7276)

2864 1901-S MS64 PCGS. Boldly struck with effulgent mint frost and lightly abraded surfaces that reveal a few faint splashes of gold toning on the otherwise stone-white features. A scarcer San Francisco Mint issue at any Mint State grade level. (#7276)

2865 1901-S MS64 NGC. A strongly lustrous and well-defined near-Gem from the dawn of the 20th century, delicately toned with few marks. The 1901-S, once considered an essentially unavailable issue, remains challenging but accessible today. (#7276)

2866 1901-S MS64 NGC. An appealing turn-of-the-century S-mint piece that exhibits frosty-white surfaces with few marks. Well-defined with no evidence of the roller marks that often appear on Morgan dollars. (#7276)

2867 1901-S MS64 ANACS. Splashes of lilac and cerulean toning are visible on both sides of this sharply detailed and highly lustrous example. Scattered marks are hidden and not immediately obvious. (#7276)

2868 1901-S MS64 PCGS. One of the more challenging 20th century S-mint Morgans in Choice, the 1901-S is represented here by a predominantly silver-gray example that exhibits blushes of gold and rose. Well struck with excellent eye appeal. (#7276)

Scarce 1901-S Gem Dollar

2869 1901-S MS65 PCGS. The 1901-S is fairly scarce within the context of Morgan dollars from this mint at the turn of the century. This MS65 example reveals a dusting of golden-gray patina resting on highly lustrous surfaces. The strike, while short of full, is clearly superior to the vast majority of '01-S Dollars, and the few minute contact marks are consistent with the grade designation. We note a small spot between the P in PLURIBUS and Liberty's brow. Still, a solid Gem example of this desirable late date S-mint. Housed in a green-label holder.
From The Arnold & Harriet Collection, Part Two. (#7276)

2870 1902 MS66 PCGS. The 1902 Morgan is common in the lower levels of Uncirculated, but is elusive as a Premium Gem. Faint wisps of gold color visit lustrous surfaces, and the design elements are suitably brought up. (#7278)

2871 1902 MS66 PCGS. A character-laden Premium Gem with dappled coppery-orange and blue-green toning over minimally abraded surfaces. A truly gorgeous Morgan dollar from the Philadelphia Mint. (#7278)

2872 1902 MS66 PCGS. Brilliant silver surfaces and frosty luster on both sides provide excellent eye appeal. An important Premium Gem with only 18 finer examples certified by PCGS. (#7278)

2873 1902-S MS64 PCGS. High lustrous with dazzling cartwheel radiance in the fields, this near-Gem dollar reveals well struck design motifs and smoky plum toning near the peripheries that nicely frames the untoned centers. A few scattered milling marks limit the grade. (#7282)

2874 1902-S MS64 NGC. A lovely Choice piece, well struck with powerful luster and bands of blue and reddish-orange patina at the periphery. Like the other S-mint Morgan issues of the 20th century, the 1902-S becomes elusive in better grades. (#7282)

2875 **1902-S MS64 NGC.** Dabs of light gold-tan and purple gravitate to the margins of this highly lustrous near-Gem. Nicely struck, with minimal marks. (#7282)

2876 **1902-S MS64 NGC.** Strong luster, above-average detail, and a touch of pink and violet patina on the obverse are the prime attractions for this lovely S-mint near-Gem. A few small, scattered marks on Liberty's cheek preclude a finer grade. (#7282)

2877 **1902-S MS64 PCGS.** Well struck with flashy luster, a couple of small brown spots on the otherwise untoned obverse surfaces, and an interesting planchet flaw that resides near and beneath the ED of UNITED on the left reverse rim. Overall, an interesting mintmarked 20th century Morgan. (#7282)

2878 **1902-S MS64 NGC.** A highly appealing near-Gem with frosty silver luster that is ringed by wispy lilac toning. An excellent candidate for the value-conscious collector. (#7282)

2879 **1902-S MS64 PCGS.** Softly frosty luster is present on both sides of this near-Gem, beneath light ivory and pale lilac surfaces. Although not rare, the MS64 grade provides an excellent value, based on current market reports. (#7282)

2880 **1902-S MS65 PCGS.** Well struck and highly lustrous, with essentially white surfaces and a bright, satiny appearance. Free of individually noteworthy marks, with just a few minor coin-to-coin traces on each side. PCGS has only graded 29 pieces finer (7/07). *From The Arnold & Harriet Collection, Part Two.* (#7282)

2881 **1902-S MS65 NGC.** A brilliant Gem with light champagne toning on both sides. This is a scarce issue so fine. Census: 95 in 65, 8 finer (8/07). (#7282)

2882 **1903-O MS65 NGC.** The shining obverse surfaces of this O-mint Gem display subtle pink and peach accents, while the reverse is more vibrant with the colors dominant. Pleasingly detailed for the issue and attractive. (#7286)

2883 **1903-S—Cleaned—ANACS. AU50 Details.** Well struck with slightly subdued surfaces that display a bit of highpoint wear. The piece shows light gold and terra cotta coloration. A few shallow pinscratches and small marks are noted, mostly on the obverse. (#7288)

2884 **1903-S AU55 NGC.** A softly struck, lightly circulated representative of this challenging later S-mint issue, delicately gold-toned with strong remaining luster at the obverse margins and the reverse. Lightly abraded with small areas of distinct wear at the highpoints. (#7288)

Rare 1903-S Dollar, MS62

2885 **1903-S MS62 ANACS.** The 1903-S is one of the rarest Morgan Dollars in Mint State (David Bowers, 2006). The lustrous surfaces of this MS62 example display wisps of golden-tan toning clinging to the obverse margins, which is replaced by more extensive and deeper golden-tan, lavender, and cobalt-blue around the reverse borders. Generally well struck, including the hair over Liberty's ear and the eagle's breast feathers. A few small obverse abrasions limit the grade. *From The Mario Eller Collection, Part One.* (#7288)

Enticing Choice 1903-S Dollar

2886 **1903-S MS64 NGC.** Strong definition and vibrant luster are the chief elements of this lovely near-Gem's excellent eye appeal. A touch of reddish-orange patina graces the rims, but the minimally marked surfaces are otherwise untoned. The 1903-S ranks among the most challenging Morgan dollars of the 20th century, particularly in Mint State grades. NGC has graded only 49 finer representatives (8/07). (#7288)

Brilliant 1903-S Dollar, MS64

2887 **1903-S MS64 PCGS.** A scarce S-mint in the post-1900 series and always of interest to collectors in high grades. This piece shows the usual bright mint frost and it is untoned. Fully struck in all areas. The only grade-defining marks are a few light ones that are mostly seen on the obverse, and the reverse is surprisingly clean. (#7288)

Desirable 1903-S Gem Dollar

2888 **1903-S MS65 PCGS.** The 1903-S is a rare issue in the Morgan dollar series, and Mint State coins are desirable at all levels. Glowing luster embraces both faces of this well struck Gem, with sharp definition apparent throughout the design features. Whispers of golden-tan and red patination visit the obverse, while yellow-gold, red, and deep green are interspersed over the reverse. Contact marks are at a minimum, and the eye appeal is impressive. Housed in a green-label holder. *From The Arnold & Harriet Collection, Part Two.* (#7288)

Gorgeous 1903-S Dollar, MS66

2889 1903-S MS66 PCGS. The 1903-S Morgan is a scarce issue, as few people collected silver dollars when it was released. In a recent *Coins* magazine article about the '03-S, Tom LaMarre writes:

> "Back in the days of cheap prices and child labor, silver dollars circulated extensively in San Francisco. But the denomination would not catch on with collectors until decades later. What's more, there was little interest in mintmarks. The date on a coin was everything, and to most collectors it did not matter whether there was an "S" below the eagle ... or not."

This gorgeous Premium Gem is one of the few high grade survivors. Its smooth, impeccably silvery surfaces radiate intense luster, and exhibit sharply struck design elements, save for the most minor softness in the centers. A small milling mark beneath the E in STATES is only mentioned because it may help to identify the coin. Population: 38 in 66, 3 finer (8/07). (#7288)

2890 1903-S Small S VF35 ANACS. VAM-2. A Top 100 Variety. Aside from the 1921-S, only a single Small S VAM is known: the VAM-2 1903-S. The punch is presumed to be intended for Barber quarters, and given the number of Morgan dollar dies made over the years, perhaps the real surprise it that the wrong punch wasn't used more often. Lightly toned and problem-free with moderate highpoint wear. (#7306)

Pleasing 1904 Dollar, MS65

2891 1904 MS65 PCGS. Estimates of 1904 dollars melted run over 2 million coins, out of a business strike mintage of 2,788,000 pieces. Moreover, surviving examples are apt to be less than desirable. David Bowers, in this regard, says: "Most coins seen today are poorly to indifferently struck and with poor luster—all in all, rather sorry looking." The specimen in this lot, a solid MS65, exhibits very pleasing luster, and a melange of beautiful sky-blue, gray, golden-tan, and soft violet patination. A well directed strike leaves sharp definition on the motifs, save for minor softness in the centers. Close examination reveals no marks worthy of individual mention. Overall, a simply gorgeous '04!
From The Arnold & Harriet Collection, Part Two. (#7290)

Scarce Gem 1904 Morgan Dollar

2892 1904 MS65 PCGS. VAM-3, R.3. The 1 in the date has a short vertical spike protruding up from the right side of the base. 4 is doubled at the bottom of both crossbars. Bowers (2005) decries the quality of this issue in his *Guide Book of Morgan Silver Dollars*, but this Gem example, if not overwhelmingly lustrous, shows better than average striking quality and clean, well preserved surfaces. PCGS has graded just 13 pieces finer (8/07). (#7290)

2893 1904-O MS66 PCGS. A satiny Premium Gem with slightly reflective fields beneath intense green, gold, and iridescent toning on both sides. (#7292)

Scarce MS67 Prooflike 1904-O Dollar

2894 1904-O MS67 Prooflike NGC. This flashy Superb Gem is brilliant throughout with flashy fields and moderately contrasting mint luster over the devices. The strike is exacting, and the preservation is exceptional. No 1904-O dollars have been certified in MS68 or finer grades by either NGC or PCGS. Census: 2 in 67 Prooflike, 0 finer (8/07). (#7293)

Vibrant 1904-S Morgan Dollar, MS62

2895 1904-S MS62 PCGS. An attractive piece from the final S-mint issue before the denomination's 17-year hiatus. Only a touch of softness is present on the obverse highpoints, and the surfaces offer pleasing detail elsewhere. Strongly lustrous with scattered cloud-gray haze in the fields and a blush of peach at the upper obverse that adds color to the coin. (#7294)

Impressive 1904-S Dollar, MS65

2896 1904-S MS65 PCGS. The 1904-S Gem in this lot displays dazzling luster and just a few wisps of light gold color that shows up under magnification. The design elements are sharply impressed, including good clarity on the eagle's breast feathers and partial definition in the hair at Liberty's ear. Both sides possess a satiny finish, and a few minor marks and luster grazes that preclude an even higher grade. David Bowers, (2005) calls this issue one of the keys in the series. *From The Arnold & Harriet Collection, Part Two.* (#7294)

Key-Date 1904-S Gem Dollar

2897 1904-S MS65 NGC. This sparkling 1904-S representative is untoned save for golden-orange color at the margins and has only a few wispy, well scattered contact marks. Lustrous surfaces exhibit sharply struck design elements, save for minor softness in the hair at Liberty's ear. The '04-S is one of the key issues in the Morgan dollar series. Census: 26 in 65, 6 finer (8/07). (#7294)

Conditionally Scarce Gem 1904-S Morgan Dollar

2898 1904-S MS65 PCGS. In his silver dollar *Encyclopedia*, published in 1993, Bowers estimated that only 200 to 400 hundred examples of this San Francisco Mint issue still survived in Gem condition or better. That estimate seems conservative almost fifteen years later, as a mere 146 coins have been certified at or above MS65, by NGC and PCGS combined (including possible resubmissions). This piece is intensely lustrous and boldly struck, with slight weakness on the central design elements and few surface marks. An area of charcoal-gray color is noted near the center of the obverse. (#7294)

2899 1921-D MS66 PCGS. Grayish golden-brown color covers both sides of this Premium Gem. The underlying surfaces have full satin brilliance. PCGS has certified five finer pieces (8/07). (#7298)

2900 1921-S MS65 NGC. A brilliant and lustrous example of this mintmarked final-year issue. The wreath is soft opposite Liberty's cap, but the centers have pleasing sharpness, and the only apparent abrasion is limited to the field above the eagle's head. (#7300)

PROOF MORGAN DOLLARS

Select Proof 1879 Morgan Dollar

2901 1879 PR63 PCGS. Delicate almond-gold toning visits the margins, while the centers are brilliant. Crisply struck with only minor incompleteness on the hair above the ear. The devices are lightly frosted. Careful examination beneath a loupe locates the occasional unimportant field hairline. Housed in a first generation holder. (#7314)

Outstanding 1879 Dollar, PR66

2902 1879 PR66 NGC. Ex: Eliasberg. Subdued violet and gray patina adorns the obverse, while deep cobalt-blue and purple coloration fills the reverse fields. While David Bowers (2005) contends that most 1879 proof dollars "... are of low contrast," the sharply impressed motifs of this example stand out against the reflective fields. A couple of minor obverse marks do not detract in the least from the coin's outstanding eye appeal. Census: 30 in 66, 22 finer (8/07). (#7314)

2903 1882—Cleaned—ANACS. PR60 Details. The needle-sharp strike and glassy fields confirm status as a proof. Pale straw-gold toning visits cloudy but hairline-free surfaces. A few light gray spots are present, the most apparent on the rim above the first U in PLURIBUS. (#7317)

Attractive PR63 Cameo 1882 Morgan Dollar

2904 1882 PR63 Cameo NGC. A pleasing proof type coin whose appearance far exceeds the stated grade. There are no obvious or detracting blemishes on either side, just a few faint hairlines account for the grade. The fields are deeply reflective and the devices have a significant amount of mint frost, which accounts for the Cameo designation. Essentially a brilliant coin. (#87317)

Fully Detailed 1884 Dollar, PR61 Cameo

2905 1884 PR61 Cameo PCGS. The 1884 is one of the more popular dates in the proof series with most of the dollars from this year well produced. This piece shows pinpoint striking definition in the centers on each side. The surfaces are generally brilliant with a light accent of golden-brown around the obverse periphery. The devices are noticeably frosted which provides a cameo effect on both obverse and reverse. (#87319)

Elusive 1885 Select Proof Deep Cameo Dollar

2906 1885 PR63 Deep Cameo ANACS. The 1885 proof Morgan is not known for exhibiting cameo contrast, and Deep Cameos are virtually unobtainable. Two of the grading services—PCGS and NGC—for example, have seen a mere three Deep Cameos in all grades. The motifs of the ANACS-graded PR63 Deep Cameo in this lot appear to float over deeply mirrored, watery fields, and the impressively struck devices further enhance the overall appeal. The surfaces are essentially untoned, save for wisps of light gold color at the obverse periphery. A few inoffensive handling marks are all that stand in the way of a higher grade for this lovely proof. (#97320)

Choice Proof 1886 Morgan

2907 **1886 PR64 NGC.** VAM-15. Breen-5587. The date is repunched south, a feature most apparent beneath the flag of the 1. This prominently mirrored and exactingly struck near-Gem offers consistent medium caramel-gold patina. The piece appears pristine to the unaided eye, and a loupe reveals only trivial imperfections. A mere 886 proofs were produced. (#7321)

Fully Detailed 1887 Morgan Dollar, PR64

2908 **1887 PR64 NGC.** One of the more popular dates for proof type purposes in the Morgan dollar series. This is a well-produced date, struck before the weak strikes from the early 1890s. The fragile, glassy mirrors show a few light hairlines on the obverse, and the reverse appears to have been struck from a slightly granular planchet. Pinpoint striking details and brilliant throughout. (#7322)

2909 **1888 PR62 NGC.** The obverse is blue-green and violet with a hint of champagne, while the reverse has a cloud-gray center with the colors of the obverse at the margins. Boldly impressed with distinct reflectivity, though scattered hairlines and pinpoint contact preclude a finer grade. Still, a pleasing example of this 19th century silver proof issue. (#7323)

Repunched Date PR64 1888 Morgan Dollar

2910 **1888 PR64 NGC.** Breen-5600, "Very rare." The date is repunched left, most visible on the 1. Delicate almond-gold and champagne-rose shades enrich this flashy and unblemished Choice proof Morgan. The breast feathers are needle-sharp, and the remainder of the design is also full aside from minor incompleteness on the hair above the ear. Only 832 proofs were struck. (#7323)

Near-Gem Proof 1888 Morgan Dollar

2911 **1888 PR64 NGC.** Crisply struck overall, if a tad weak on the hair detail just above Liberty's ear. Minor cloudiness on each side, and a few faint hairlines on the obverse further limit the technical grade of the piece. Bowers (2005) notes that this issue was poorly produced, actually prompting coin dealer Harlan P. Smith to file a formal complaint with the Mint. (#7323)

Choice Proof 1894 Morgan Dollar

2912 **1894 PR64 PCGS.** A lovely proof with sharp details throughout, this piece exhibits faint cameo contrast although it has not been designated as such. Both sides have light champagne toning over fully mirrored fields and satiny devices. An important date with proofs offering an affordable option, given the rarity of similar quality business strikes. (#7329)

Gorgeous Premium Gem Proof 1894 Dollar

2913 **1894 PR66 NGC.** Both sides are cloaked in rich purple-violet, electric-blue, and sea-green toning that is likely the result of decades of storage in a paper envelope. Glittering mirrored reflectivity has no trouble penetrating the layers of color, and the underlying surfaces appear to be of impeccable quality. Fully struck and truly gorgeous. Census: 38 in 66, 37 finer (8/07). (#7329)

2914 1895 PR61 PCGS. Perhaps more so than any similar issue, the possibly mythic business strike Philadelphia Morgan dollars from 1895 have inspired their share of wishful thinking. As Roger W. Burdette stated in his July 3, 2006 article *Philly 1895 Morgan dollars*, "Rumors persist of circulation-quality Philadelphia Mint 1895 Morgan silver dollars in one collection or another. Detailed stories have been published about these coins and their secretive owners. But in the end, no genuine circulation-quality 1895 Morgan dollar has ever been examined by multiple experts or clearly certified as real."

Among the more interesting urban legends about such a discovery appears in Breen's *Encyclopedia of United States and Colonial Proof Coins*. In that 1977 work, he wrote: "Rumors that a Chicago underworld syndicate turned up a sack about 1960 have remained unverified, not even one specimen showing up." He dismissed this rumor with the lucid observation, "Underworld characters seldom bother to wait 16+ years to take their profits. Had even one such coin been released, it would have been front page news."

Three decades have passed, and still no business strike 1895 dollars have materialized. In lieu of such pieces, collectors pursue proofs such as the present specimen. Delicate silver-gray patina with a touch of violet graces the moderately reflective surfaces of this sharply struck piece. Though the fields exhibit a number of hairlines in the fields and on the devices, the coin retains significant eye appeal. An interesting piece from this prized issue of only 880 specimens.

From The Beau Clerc Collection. (#7330)

2915 1895 PR62 PCGS. In many ways, the market for the proof Morgan dollars of 1895 was underdeveloped for some years. In 1977, Walter Breen reported in his *Encyclopedia of United States and Colonial Proof Coins* that then contemporaneous auction records showed prices between $6,000 and $8,500, sizable for the time but incredibly low by today's standards. Wayne Miller, in his *The Morgan and Peace Dollar Textbook*, wrote in 1982 that as recently as the 1970s, many collectors skipped the 1895 as an expensive luxury, but the bullish coin market, with its rising prices across the Morgan series, changed the game: "The increasing difficulty of assembling a gem set of Morgan dollars has made such a project challenging to wealthy collectors, who do not consider the price of an 1895 proof to be prohibitive. The price of this date has therefore risen as the popularity of the Morgan dollar series has increased."

Even though attitudes toward the 1895 Morgan dollar have changed, the fact remains that few collectors of Morgan dollars ever obtain an example of the 1895 proof, which makes the presence of two specimens in The Beau Clerc Collection all the more extraordinary. This gold-inflected silver-gray piece displays excellent detail and strongly reflective fields. While the obverse shows minimal contrast, the reverse displays a modest cameo effect. Appealing despite the hairlines and occasional contact marks that populate the fields, and a desirable example of this most famous proof Morgan dollar issue.
From The Beau Clerc Collection. (#7330)

Beautifully Toned PR67 1896 Morgan Dollar

2916 **1896 PR67 NGC.** The 1896 proof dollar is among the best produced of all Morgans, along with the 1882 and 1898. The mintage of 762 pieces, and the high quality of survivors translates into the use of this date for those assembling a proof type set of 19th century U.S. coins. This piece is undoubtedly destined for such a high grade type set. The fields display unfathomable depth of mirrored reflectivity. There is also a significant amount of mint frost over the devices, which sets up a moderate (but unacknowledged by PCGS) contrast on each side. This is significant because the coin is draped in rich layers of cobalt blue and lavender toning. The surfaces are extraordinarily well preserved with no hairlines or noticeable contact marks. A couple of lint marks are located in the left obverse field, but magnification is necessary to see them. Census: 19 in 67, 6 finer (8/07). (#7331)

Exuberantly Toned 1899 Morgan PR68

2917 **1899 PR68 NGC.** A multi-color beauty with arcs of gold, blue-green, and mauve-rose on each side. The strike is just slightly shy of absolute on the hair above the ear, but the design details are otherwise exacting, with the eagle's breast feathers particularly impressive. This pristine specimen delivers an unmatchable combination of eye appeal and preservation. A scant 846 proofs were issued, a lower mintage than the famous 1895 dollar. The associated business strike mintage of 330,000 pieces is among the lowest from the Philadelphia Mint, although Uncirculated examples are much more available than proofs. Census: 4 in 68, 1 finer (8/07). (#7334)

Popular 1921 Zerbe Morgan Dollar, PR66

2918 **1921 Zerbe PR66 NGC.** While not of the same quality as the Chapman proofs of 1921, those struck for Farran Zerbe are much more available; some estimate as many as 200 pieces may have been produced. The diagnostic die scratch above the second U in UNUM is faintly visible under magnification, and, as reassuring as a diagnostic like that may be, it is really not necessary to confirm this coin's proof status. The surfaces are bright and highly lustrous. As on all Zerbes, there is a bit of cartwheel intermixed with the reflectivity in the proof fields. Delicate lilac patina embraces both obverse and reverse, but it is so light that at arm's-length the coin actually appears brilliant. A shallow blemish above Liberty's eye and another on the nose can be used to pedigree this specimen in the future. Census: 7 in 66, 1 finer (8/07). (#7341)

PEACE DOLLARS

2919 1921 MS64 PCGS. Splashes of autumn-brown toning are particularly prominent across the reverse. A satiny and impressively preserved near-Gem denied an even finer grade by a faint graze on the cheekbone. Still, a great example of this high-relief first-year issue. (#7356)

2920 1921 MS64 PCGS. Speckles of cobalt-blue, gold-tan, and lavender patina swirl around the borders of this near-Gem high relief Peace dollar, well-defined save for the usual highpoint softness. A few minute marks scattered about the lustrous surfaces define the grade. (#7356)

2921 1921 MS64 PCGS. Golden-gray patina rests on the highly lustrous surfaces of this near-Gem. Generally well struck, save for softness in the centers. A few minor marks limit the grade. (#7356)

2922 1921 MS64 NGC. Ice-blue and straw-gold hues embrace this coruscating near-Gem. Marks are refreshingly inconsequential, and only the characteristic inexactness of strike at the centers stands in the way of a finer grade. (#7356)

2923 1921 MS64 PCGS. The debut issue for the Peace dollar consisted of just over a million high-relief pieces. This silver-gray near-Gem displays strong luster and pleasing overall detail, though the central highpoints show a measure of softness as almost always. A great choice for the type or date collector. (#7356)

2924 1921 MS64 NGC. The 1921 Peace dollar, first in the series, is always popular for its special high relief, reminiscent of the earlier High Relief double eagles. Both sides have highly lustrous mint frost with brilliant silver surfaces. Slight central weakness is typical of nearly every known example. (#7356)

2925 1921 MS64 PCGS. Pastel ice-blue and caramel-gold grace this lustrous and carefully preserved high relief Peace dollar. The hair above the ear lacks absolute detail, but the strike is good for the issue. Housed in a green label holder. (#7356)

2926 1921 MS64 NGC. This shimmering near-Gem offers slightly above-average detail and pleasing luster. Gold and tan patina with a touch of milky haze graces the surfaces of this first-year piece. (#7356)

2927 1921 MS64 NGC. A predominantly silver-gray Choice representative, well-defined for this first-year issue with delicate lemon-gold tints on each side. Both sides exhibit pleasing luster and few marks for the grade. (#7356)

2928 1921 MS64 NGC. Blushes of tan-gold confirm the originality of this satiny and impressive near-Gem. Marks are inconsequential, and the centers have above average sharpness for this high relief date. (#7356)

2929 1921 MS64 ANACS. Splashes of pastel rose and blue toning enhance the above average design definition and brilliant silver luster of this key-date Peace dollar. (#7356)

2930 1921 MS64 PCGS. Much better struck than the usual 1921 Peace dollar, which normally (but not for the present piece) is quite mushy in the centers. This is a satiny cream-gray near-Gem, uncommonly free from contact, although a few tiny freckles of aqua and russet color are scattered across the two sides. In a green label holder. (#7356)

2931 1921 MS65 PCGS. Loops and whorls of russet and violet patina adorn this first-year Gem example. The centers are softly struck, as usual, but the devices are extraordinarily clean. (#7356)

Luxuriously Toned 1922 Peace Dollar MS66

2932 1922 MS66 PCGS. Both sides are gorgeously toned. The obverse has powder-blue, lemon, and rose-red bands that encompass the light golden-brown center. The reverse is even more colorful, adorned with apple-green, violet-red, and honey shades. Highly lustrous and well struck with smooth fields. (#7357)

Sparkling Superb Gem 1922 Dollar

2933 1922 MS67 NGC. The reverse is dusky chestnut-gray with a peripheral arc of sea-green and ruby toning. The obverse is light pearl-gray aside from a trace of golden-russet near the rim. A well preserved Peace dollar that benefits from a good strike and dazzling luster. As common as the 1922 is, it unexpectedly emerges as a rarity in the MS67 grade. Census: 10 in 67, 0 finer (7/07). (#7357)

2934 1922 AU53 PCGS. VAM-1F. A Top 50 Variety. This is the so-called Field Break variety, which shows a prominent die break in the reverse field just before the eagle's breast. This variety is one of 10 or 12 significant die breaks known for the 1922 issue, the undoubted result of the enormous mintage of more than 51 million silver dollars in this year. This piece offers silver-gold surfaces that are still somewhat lustrous, with a few dark copper-colored spots scattered about. (#133736)

2935 1922-D MS66 ICG. Solidly struck with flashy luster beneath a thin layer of intermittent cloud-gray haze. A thin die crack laces together the peripheral elements of the carefully preserved obverse. (#7358)

2936 1923-D MS65 PCGS. This gleaming D-mint Gem offers powerful luster and minimal patina alongside above-average detail. An enticing example of this issue, available in MS65 but elusive any finer. (#7361)

2937 1923-D MS65 PCGS. A brilliant and eminently appealing D-mint Peace dollar with impressive detail on the strands of Liberty's hair. A handful of faint marks on each side are entirely consistent with the grade. (#7361)

2938 1923-D MS65 NGC. This splendidly toned Gem offers streaks of mauve, gold, olive, and powder-blue. Satiny and well preserved with well struck motifs and several interesting obverse die cracks. (#7361)

2939 1923-S MS65 ANACS. A band of dusky gold toning crosses the centers of each side, but the majority of this suitably struck silver dollar remains untoned. Booming cartwheel luster sweeps the surfaces, which are well preserved aside from a few faint obverse grazes. The 1923-S has a high mintage, but is surprisingly difficult to locate as a Gem. (#7362)

2940 1924-S MS64 PCGS. This is an attractive, highly lustrous near-Gem that is essentially untoned. The surfaces have an intensely granular texture which is very unusual, for a Peace dollar, and may indicate die erosion. Scattered minor blemishes are consistent with the assigned grade. (#7364)

2941 1924-S MS64 PCGS. The hallmark of this near-Gem is the intensity of the frosty mint luster that covers both sides. The untoned, snow-white surfaces exhibit boldly struck design motifs. A few wispy blemishes and milky spots limit the grade. Housed in a green label holder. (#7364)

2942 1924-S MS64 PCGS. Milky tan toning crosses the centers of this shimmering and nicely struck near-Gem. Impressively unabraded for the designated grade. (#7364)

Exceptional 1924-S Gem Dollar

2943 1924-S MS65 ANACS. David Bowers, in his 2006 Silver and Trade dollar reference book, writes of the 1924-S that "Mint State pieces are usually seen bagmarked." The current Gem falls entirely outside of this profile. Its frosty surfaces possess dazzling luster and are impeccably preserved. Only in the upper left reverse quadrant can a few inoffensive luster grazes be observed. Moreover, slivers of pastel rainbow color concentrate at the obverse margins, and meander through portions of the reverse. Unbelievable technical quality and aesthetic appeal! (#7364)

Sharply Struck MS65 1924-S Peace Dollar

2944 1924-S MS65 NGC. The 1924-S is a well-respected strike rarity among S-mint Peace dollars. This is an especially well-detailed example that has essentially complete definition on the central hair of Liberty as well as the bottom row of feathers on the eagle's wing. Original surfaces, much of each side is still brilliant with occasional reddish-russet toning scattered about and deepening around the margins. (#7364)

2945 1925-S MS64 PCGS. A mix of rose, sky-blue, and olive-green patina rests on the lustrous surfaces of this near-Gem S-mint Peace dollar, complementing well struck design elements. A few minute obverse marks define the grade. (#7366)

2946 1925-S MS64 PCGS. A well struck near-Gem that displays pleasing luster and a delicate veil of cloud-gray patina over each side. Small dots of gold and reddish-bronze patina appear near the margins of this lower-mintage S-mint piece. (#7366)

2947 1925-S MS64 PCGS. While the shining silver-gray obverse shows only a thin layer of haze, the reverse displays lovely golden patina overall with faint mint-green accents above the eagle's head. Well struck with great eye appeal. (#7366)

2948 1925-S MS64 PCGS. Although the central design elements are weak on both sides, this is a delightful piece with highly lustrous silver-white surfaces. Hints of speckled gold show on the obverse. A condition rarity, PCGS has only certified 36 finer Gems. (#7366)

2949 1925-S MS64 PCGS. At arm's length, this shining S-mint Peace dollar presents as silver-white, though closer examination shows a touch of haze around the devices. Well-defined with few marks. PCGS has certified 37 finer examples (8/07). (#7366)

2950 1925-S MS64 PCGS. Intense mint frost shimmers over each side of this brilliant, snow-white example. The design elements are boldly rendered, as scattered small abrasions limit the grade. In a green label holder. (#7366)

2951 1925-S MS64 NGC. A well struck and strongly lustrous near-Gem representative of this S-mint Peace issue, minimally marked for the grade with excellent visual appeal. Light wisps of golden-tan toning grace the lower obverse, while the reverse is comparatively untoned. (#7366)

Satiny Gem 1925-S Peace Dollar

2952 1925-S MS65 NGC. Satin surfaces exhibit brilliant silver luster and excellent sharpness, slightly weak only at the central obverse. The grade is limited by a single faint hairline on Liberty's cheek. Slight roughness in the obverse field remains from the original planchet surface. Like several other issues, the 1925-S is an important condition rarity in the Peace dollar series, common enough in lower Mint State grade levels but scarce in Choice Mint State and rare in Gem Mint State. NGC and PCGS have graded less than 100 MS65 examples and none finer. Census: 51 in 65, 0 finer (8/07). (#7366)

2953 1926-D MS65 PCGS. A strongly lustrous Gem that offers wonderful obverse detail and tremendous eye appeal. A handful of luster grazes and faint marks on each side of this D-mint dollar are consistent with the grade. (#7368)

2954 1926-D MS65 ICG. Strongly lustrous and predominantly silver-white with splashes of thin, milky patina over each side. A boldly impressed and appealing representative of this mid-date D-mint issue. (#7368)

2955 1926-D MS66 PCGS. Boldly impressed with vibrant luster and splashes of pastel yellow and sky-blue toning. Attractive with a slightly hazy appearance on the obverse. A small mark is noted on Liberty's chin, and a dramatic die crack crosses Liberty's neck and links the lower hair and the last three words of IN GOD WE TRUST. PCGS has graded only eight finer examples (8/07). (#7368)

2956 1926-S MS65 PCGS. A solidly struck and immensely lustrous silver-white Gem representative of this mid-date S-mint issue, one with a mintage just shy of 7 million pieces. Carefully preserved with amazing eye appeal. (#7369)

2957 1926-S MS65 PCGS. This solidly struck, carefully preserved S-mint piece comes from a mintage of just under 7 million pieces. The surfaces are practically brilliant with only a touch of gold on the vibrant obverse. (#7369)

2958 1927-D MS64 PCGS. A solidly struck example of this D-mint Peace dollar, the last example of that denomination struck at that Mint until 1934. The lustrous surfaces offer hazy gold-gray patina with dabs of gunmetal and tan at the margins. (#7371)

2959 1927-D MS64 PCGS. The 1927-D was the last issue before the Denver Mint's seven-year hiatus from the denomination. This well-defined near-Gem is frosty and essentially untoned with few marks for the grade. (#7371)

2960 1927-S MS64 PCGS. Boldly struck with just a bit of the usual softness noted over the centers. The silver-gray surfaces are illuminated by fulsome luster. A handful of small marks and a couple of shallow luster grazes preclude the Gem grade assessment. An appealing example of this scarce semi-key date, rare any finer. (#7372)

2961 1927-S MS64 PCGS. Solidly struck with excellent luster and a vibrant appearance. Minimally marked for the grade with only a few faint patches of milky patina evident at the periphery. A lovely example from this issue of 866,000 pieces. (#7372)

2962 1927-S MS64 ANACS. Pleasing detail and flashy luster greatly enhance the overall eye appeal of this S-mint Peace dollar. Minimally marked with splashes of golden-tan and green patina, most of which appear at the margins. (#7372)

Scarce 1927-S Dollar, MS65

2963 1927-S MS65 NGC. The 1927-S is a scarce issue that has been considered a semi-key almost since it was struck. Gems are rarely available with most survivors in the circulated and MS60-62 grade range. This is a sharply defined example that has smooth, satiny mint luster that flows over each side virtually uninterrupted by coin-to-coin contact. Pastel olive-green color shows up under magnification. Census: 67 in 65, 1 finer (8/07). (#7372)

2964 1928 MS62 NGC. Deep lavender and dove-gray envelop this satiny key date dollar. The fields and devices appear unmarked beneath the blanket of toning. Encased in a former generation holder. (#7373)

2965 1928 MS63 PCGS. Well struck with lovely satin luster and slight wisps of gold and sky-blue color over the primarily silver-gray surfaces. A small brown spot is noted just beneath the W in WE. An attractive near-Gem example of this low mintage key date. (#7373)

2966 1928 MS64 PCGS. A solidly struck example of this prominent Philadelphia key that exhibits vibrant luster and a touch of golden patina. A handful of wispy abrasions in the fields and on the neck are the only obstacles to an even finer grade. (#7373)

2967 1928 MS64 PCGS. Thick heather and smoky gray toning hide the frosty luster of this near-Gem. The surfaces are exceptional for the grade, and the design motifs are bold. (#7373)

2968 1928 MS64 PCGS. An assertively struck key date Choice Peace dollar with booming luster and undisturbed surfaces. Faint gold and sky-blue toning denies full brilliance. Encased in an old green label holder. (#7373)

2969 1928 MS64 PCGS. Boldly struck with highly lustrous, untoned silver surfaces that exhibit semi-reflective fields and few imperfections on either side. One of the key dates to the Peace dollar series. (#7373)

2970 1928 MS64 PCGS. Pastel lemon and steel-blue invigorate this satiny low mintage dollar. Crisply struck except for the right-side margins. The fields are well preserved. (#7373)

2971 1928 MS64 PCGS. Dusky golden-brown toning subdues the satiny luster of this key-date coin. The surfaces are undoubtedly original, with no evidence that it has ever been cleaned. (#7373)

2972 1928 MS64 PCGS. A splendid specimen with sharp design features and frosty silver luster beneath light gray color that is accented by hints of gold and iridescence. (#7373)

2973 1928 MS64 PCGS. A fully original example with faint heather color over ivory luster. Sharp design elements accompany pristine surfaces. (#7373)

2974 1928 MS64 PCGS. Natural silver-gray color over frosty silver luster. Sharply struck and highly attractive, and a desirable grade for collectors seeking quality and affordability. (#7373)

2975 1928 MS64 PCGS. This attractive dollar is a borderline Gem with frosty luster and ivory surfaces accented by hints of champagne and pale lilac toning. It is unusual to have an opportunity like this, the chance to bid on multiple 1928 Peace dollars, greatly improving the chance to finish a set. (#7373)

2976 1928 MS64 PCGS. It appears that an original roll of these coins recently surfaced, given the number of similar MS64 coins in this sale. This example may have been an "end piece" with rich lavender toning over the ivory surfaces. (#7373)

2977 1928 MS64 PCGS. Long considered a key to the series, we are pleased to offer an impressive selection of 1928 Peace dollars in this sale, more than half a roll. The brilliant satin surfaces of this example are graced by subtle champagne toning, with only a few widely scattered surface marks. (#7373)

Popular 1928 Dollar, MS65

2978 1928 MS65 ANACS. The 360,649-piece mintage of the 1928 dollar is the lowest in the Peace dollar series, except for the 1922 High relief. This makes it a favorite for collectors. The lustrous surfaces of the present Gem display hints of gold-tan color, and have benefited from an impressive strike. A few trivial marks scattered about are consistent with the grade. (#7373)

2979 1928-S MS64 PCGS. The smoky mauve-gray toning is modified by dappled champagne, russet, and olive coloration over both sides. Boldly struck with typical softness noted at the junction of the eagle's wing and right (facing) leg. A lustrous and minimally abraded near-Gem example. (#7374)

2980 1928-S MS64 PCGS. Though overshadowed by its P-mint counterpart through most grades, in near-Gem and better, the 1928-S commands a substantial premium over the 1928 key. This luminous Choice example displays cloud-gray patina overall with freckles of nutmeg-brown in the obverse fields. (#7374)

2981 1928-S MS64 PCGS. Faint traces of pale gold toning are evident on the highly lustrous silver surfaces of this important Peace dollar. The strike is above average and the surfaces have few abrasions. Despite a large population of nearly 1,500 coins in MS64, PCGS has only graded 47 finer coins. (#7374)

2982 1928-S MS64 PCGS. VAM-4. Hints of gold toning visit this highly lustrous and clean-cheeked Choice Peace dollar. Brightness on the base of Liberty's neck precludes a finer grade. (#7374)

2983 1928-S MS64 PCGS. Well struck and frosty with minimal patina and few abrasions, though marks are present at the chin and around the mottos. An attractive example of an issue that becomes conditionally elusive as a Gem. (#7374)

2984 1928-S MS64 PCGS. VAM-4. TRVST is lightly die doubled. This near-Gem 1928-S is better struck than usually seen on the issue. Radiantly lustrous surfaces see wisps of faint gold-tan color. Minor marks collectively fail to distract. (#7374)

Condition Scarcity 1928-S Gem Dollar Popular VAM-3 Doubled Die Obverse

2985 1928-S MS65 ANACS. Doubled Die Obverse. VAM-3. Top 50 Variety. Doubling is seen on the TRU of TRUST. The 1928-S is a scarce, semi-key issue with only 1.632 million pieces produced. *Numismatic News* staff writer Paul Green, writing in the April 6, 2004 issue, says: "The 1928-S ... was not saved, due in part to being compared to the lower-mintage 1928 (360,649 pieces). Moreover, with the Great Depression arriving, some that were saved were probably spent."

This Gem displays sharply struck design features, much more so than is commonly seen on this issue. Intense luster radiates from both sides, and a layer of golden-gray color exhibits blushes of pale violet. Well preserved for the grade designation. (#7374)

2986 1934 MS65 PCGS. A decisively struck and shining silver-white Gem from the short-lived revival of the Peace dollar design. Both sides offer a remarkably clean appearance and show only a handful of stray marks. (#7375)

2987 **1934 MS65 PCGS.** The return of the Peace dollar in 1934 was met with minimal fanfare, and Philadelphia struck under a million pieces for the year. This strongly lustrous Gem is predominantly silver-gray with a horizontal band of golden-tan across the center of the obverse. (#7375)

2988 **1934 MS65 PCGS.** Well struck with amazingly clean pearl-gray surfaces that reveal a slight degree of speckled russet patina under magnification. Because they were generally stored in mint bags containing 1,000 coins, it is unusual to find a Peace dollar with nearly unmarked surfaces, such as this one. A lovely, satiny Gem from the final year of the series.
From The Arnold & Harriet Collection, Part Two. (#7375)

2989 **1934 MS65 PCGS.** Booming luster sweeps this exactingly struck and lightly toned gray-gold Gem. Minor contact on the cheekbone is of little import. Housed in an old green label holder. (#7375)

2990 **1934 MS65 PCGS.** A brilliant and well struck Gem that has flashy luster and virtually pristine fields. The cheek is also extremely clean, and gives the coin excellent eye appeal. (#7375)

2991 **1934 MS65 PCGS.** Satiny and fully struck with exceptionally clean surfaces. A brilliant example of this scarce, late-date Peace dollar. (#7375)

Impressive 1934 Peace Dollar, MS66

2992 **1934 MS66 PCGS.** A distinctive Premium Gem, approaching the finest available quality for this date. PCGS has only certified three finer pieces (8/07). This one has satiny silver luster beneath lilac and gold toning with lighter splashes on each side, including lemon-yellow color on the reverse. (#7375)

2993 **1934-D MS64 PCGS.** Micro D. A crisply struck and lightly abraded piece with potent luster and an alert strike. Hints of gold and powder-blue toning only add to the eye appeal. (#7376)

2994 **1934-D MS64 PCGS.** Micro D. Blazing luster brightens this assertively struck representative. Gentle gold toning confirms the originality. The reverse is well preserved, while faint contact on the portrait and minor marks at 2 o'clock decide the grade. (#7376)

2995 **1934-D MS64 PCGS.** Micro D. A well struck near-Gem with delicate steel-blue and apricot toning. Luster sweeps the impeccably preserved fields and devices. A worthy example of this lower mintage issue. (#7376)

2996 **1934-D MS64 PCGS.** Micro D. Faint pearl-gray and chestnut patina visits this shimmering and sharply impressed Choice Peace dollar. Occasional minor marks fail to significantly detract. (#7376)

2997 **1934-S AU58 PCGS.** This key date Borderline Uncirculated Peace dollar is richly patinated in dove-gray and yellow shades. Cartwheel sheen is unbroken albeit diminished. Small distributed marks are appropriate for the grade. In a green label holder. (#7377)

2998 **1934-S MS60 ANACS.** The dusky rose-gold patina that appears to the left and right yields to forest-green at the central bands. Well-defined and lustrous with no trace of wear, though the obverse devices host a number of abrasions. Still, a pleasing example of this later S-mint Peace issue. (#7377)

Satiny Key 1934-S Dollar MS62

2999 **1934-S MS62 NGC.** Ivory-gray and pale rose-pink tints confirm the originality of this satiny and sharply struck representative. Small marks are present, but these are unimportant for the designated grade. The 1934-S circulated to a greater extent than other low mintage Peace dollar issues, perhaps because six years had passed since the prior S-mint dollar, the 1928-S. (#7377)

Noteworthy Near-Gem 1934-S Dollar

3000 **1934-S MS64 NGC.** A frosty blast-white example of this challenging later S-mint Peace issue, essentially untoned with above-average detail on Liberty's often-weak hair. The obverse is surprisingly clean for the grade, and the reverse devices show only a few shallow abrasions. A lovely representative from a mintage of just over a million pieces. (#7377)

3001 **1935-S MS65 PCGS.** Three lines beneath ONE. The rich gunmetal-gray toning is interspersed with glimpses of tawny-gold. Creamy luster rolls unencumbered across this undisturbed Gem. Certified in a green label holder. (#7379)

3002 **1935-S MS65 PCGS.** Three rays below ONE. A lightly toned and thoroughly lustrous Gem from the final San Francisco issue of this popular series. The hair above the ear is shows minor incompleteness, but the strike near the borders is exemplary. (#7379)

SACAGAWEA DOLLAR

3003 **2000-P Goodacre MS68 PCGS.** Sculptor Glenna Goodacre designed the obverse of the Sacagawea dollar, and for her efforts, received 5,000 special finish 2000-P Sacagawea dollars. The finish is glossy and prooflike with no cameo contrast. This is a quality representative, flawless save for a tiny pre-finish depression above the second U in PLURIBUS. (#99584)

End of Session Four

SESSION FIVE

Live, Internet, and Mail Bid Signature Auction #446
Friday, September 28, 2007, 6:30 PM PT, Lots 3004-4167
Long Beach, California

A 15% Buyer's Premium ($9 minimum) Will Be Added To All Lots

Visit HA.com to view full-color images and bid.

PATTERNS

Rare 1850 Annular Cent Pattern
Judd-124g, PR65

3004 **1850 One Cent, Judd-124g, Pollock-143, R.8, PR65 PCGS.** Davis-67a, AW-138. Uniface pattern struck on an unperforated annular (ring) planchet. The obverse has CENT above and 1850 below, with stars flanking. The reverse has dentils around the reverse border, but no lettering or motifs. Struck in nickel or copper-nickel with a plain edge. Less than a half dozen pieces are known of this rarity. This piece and the Eliasberg coin both exhibit a die crack through the top of the T in CENT, which may be common to all known specimens. The surfaces are remarkably clean, especially considering the open fields on the obverse and the unstruck reverse. Pale gray-lilac patina covers each side. (#11534)

1850 Three Cent Silver Pattern, Judd-125 Original, PR63

3005 **1850 Three Cent Silver, Judd-125 Original, Pollock-147, R.4, PR63 PCGS.** Similar in design to the famous Judd-67 gold dollar pattern from 1836; however, the date has been moved to the obverse below the cap, and the denomination within the palm frond is expressed with a large Roman numeral III. Struck in silver with a plain edge. Bright and lightly hairlined, the surfaces are light golden-brown with an occasional dab of deep blue around the margins.
From The Beau Clerc Collection. (#11536)

Select Proof Judd-161 1854 Cent

3006 **1854 One Cent, Judd-161 Original, Pollock-187, R.4, PR63 Brown PCGS.** Similar to the contemporary Mature Head large cent, but there are no stars, the reverse wreath is smaller, and the diameter is a few millimeters smaller. Struck in bronze with a plain edge. A precisely struck and nearly unabraded example toned in dusky olive and mauve shades. The obverse dentils are doubled between 6 and 9 o'clock, suggesting the collar die slipped slightly between strikes. (#11663)

Large-Size 1855 Flying Eagle Cent Pattern
Judd-167, PR61 Brown

3007 **1855 Flying Eagle Cent, Judd-167 Original, Pollock-193, R.5, PR61 Brown NGC.** A Flying Eagle cent pattern in large format, featuring a hooked-neck eagle, slanting 5s on the obverse, and ONE CENT in the center of the reverse surrounded by a thick laurel wreath similar to that of a large cent. Struck in copper with a plain edge. The Brown designation seems a bit severe on this piece as significant portions of original mint red surround the devices on each side. Die clashed, there are numerous small contact marks on each side that account for the technical grade but none are worthy of individual mention. (#11709)

Mid-Sized 1855 Flying Eagle Cent
PR63 Brown, Judd-168

3008 **1855 Flying Eagle Cent, Judd-168 Original, Pollock-193, R.4, PR63 Brown PCGS.** The obverse shows a hook-neck eagle surrounded by thirteen stars with the date below. The reverse is similar in design to the Large Cent, but the wreath is smaller. Struck in bronze with a plain edge. A needle-sharp specimen with deep powder-blue and mahogany-brown toning. A few faint hairlines determine the grade. (#11720)

3009 **1858 Indian Cent, Judd-208, Pollock-259, Snow-PT28, R.1, AU50 ANACS.** The well-known transitional pattern for the issued 1859 Indian cent. The centered date variant with five leaf clusters on the wreath. Struck in copper-nickel with a plain edge. A briefly circulated tan-toned piece with clean fields aside from a thin mark beneath CENT. (#11884)

Gem 1859 Indian Cent with Shield Reverse, Judd-228

3010 **1859 Indian Cent, Judd-228, Pollock-272, Snow-PT4, R.1, MS65 PCGS.** A popular transitional pattern with the Indian head obverse of 1859 and the shield reverse of 1860. Struck in copper-nickel with a plain edge. This impressive Gem is unabraded, and the strike is sharp save for the upper half of the shield. The obverse has cartwheel luster, while the reverse is semi-prooflike. (#11932)

1859 Half Dollar Pattern, Judd-245, PR64
'Perfect Ribbon' Reverse

3011 **1859 Half Dollar, Judd-245, Pollock-301, 303, Low R.6, PR64 NGC.** The obverse features the "French Head" of Liberty facing right. A large eagle with a heraldic shield dominates the reverse. The eagle clutches a ribbon in its beak, and the claws grasp an olive branch and three long arrows. The "Perfect Ribbon" subvariety is characterized by four vertical lines in the shield, seven tail feathers, pointed left (observer's right) wingtip, and full leaf above the A in HALF. Struck in silver with a reeded edge. Light hairlines are covered with deep, mottled multicolored toning. (#11988)

IN GOD WE TRUST 1863 Seated Dollar
Judd-346, PR63 Red and Brown

3012 **1863 Dollar, Judd-346, Pollock-418, Low R.7, PR63 Red and Brown PCGS.** A regular issue 1863 Seated Liberty obverse die is muled with a regular issue Motto reverse die. Struck in copper with a reeded edge. Per uspatterns.com, "These and the other "with motto" patterns of this date and also 1864 and possibly 1865 are actually restrikes made circa 1869 and into the early 1870s and were offered with restrikes of the other denominations in complete sets." This fully struck specimen is ruby-red and orange with glimpses of olive toning. Each side has a few minute carbon flecks, visible beneath a loupe. Seated dollar patterns are invariably rare, and remain highly popular. (#70508)

PR63 Red 1865 Indian Cent, Judd-403

3013 **1865 Indian Cent, Judd-403, Pollock-471, High R.7, PR63 Red PCGS.** Snow-PT1a. Struck from regular issue Plain 5 dies, but in copper (instead of bronze) with a plain edge. Thick and thin planchet varieties are known, but the encapsulation makes it difficult to ascertain the thickness. A needle-sharp specimen with radiant orange fields, save for some mottled rose and russet patina on the left obverse. Housed in an old green label holder. (#80579)

Choice Red 1865 Rays Shield Nickel, Judd-417

3014 **1865 Shield Five Cents, Judd-417, Pollock-489, Low R.7, PR64 Red NGC.** This transitional pattern presents the Rays Shield nickel as issued for circulation in 1866, but the date is 1865. Struck in copper with a plain edge. A satiny brick-red and olive near-Gem with a precise strike and only minor carbon. Census: 1 in 64 Red, 1 finer (8/07). (#80599)

Select 1865 Five Dollar, Judd-446

3015 **1865 Five Dollar, Judd-446, Pollock-518, High R.6, PR63 Brown NGC.** A transitional pattern, with the obverse featuring the regular Liberty Head or Coronet Head design. The reverse is also similar to the regular 1865 issue, except for the scroll above the eagle that reads IN GOD WE TRUST. Struck in copper with a reeded edge. The reverse of the present example appears to still be about 30% mint red, with the balance magenta and brown. The obverse shows some iridescent blue, green, and magenta. Well struck and attractive despite spots on the upper arrowhead and the reverse rim at 9 o'clock. (#60633)

1868 Cent Pattern, Judd-608, PR64

3016 **1868 One Cent, Judd-608, Pollock-673, R.4, PR64 NGC.** On the obverse, Liberty is wearing a coronet inscribed LIBERTY. Around, the legend UNITED STATES OF AMERICA and below, the date. The reverse has a large Roman numeral I enclosed within a wreath of wheat, corn, tobacco, and cotton. Struck in nickel with a plain edge. This is Pollock's centered date variety, that can be secondarily attributed by the Y in LIBERTY positioned further from the hair. Nicely mirrored with a faint overlay of frost on the devices. Each side shows streaky golden-rose toning.
From The Beau Clerc Collection. (#60820)

Choice 1869 Standard Silver Quarter, Judd-723

3017 **1869 Standard Silver Quarter Dollar, Judd-723, Pollock-804, Low R.7, PR64 Brown PCGS.** Liberty wears a cap ornamented with three stars. A ribbon across Liberty's shoulder is inscribed LIBERTY. Struck in copper with a reeded edge. Both sides have fully mirrored surfaces beneath intense blue, green, and gold toning. A few pinpoint flecks and minor planchet granularity are all that limits the grade. Housed in an old green label holder. (#60950)

1869 Standard Silver Quarter, Judd-727 PR67 ★ Cameo, Beautifully Toned

3018 **1869 Standard Silver Quarter Dollar, Judd-727, Pollock-808, R.5, PR67 ★ Cameo NGC.** Liberty's hair is bound, and she wears a diadem. The obverse exergue displays IN GOD WE TRUST within a scroll. A small oak and laurel wreath crowds the centrally placed 25 CENTS. STANDARD SILVER and the date complete the reverse legends. Struck in silver with a reeded edge. An exactingly struck Superb Gem with beautiful ocean-blue, ruby-red, and gold toning. (#60954)

PR62 1869 Standard Silver Quarter Judd-728

3019 **1869 Standard Silver Quarter Dollar, Judd-728, Pollock-809, High R.6, PR62 PCGS.** On the obverse, Liberty wears a diadem inscribed LIBERTY with her hair tied in a bun facing right. IN GOD WE TRUST resides on a scroll below. On the reverse, the denomination 25 CENTS is centered in a wreath of oak and laurel leaves with STANDARD SILVER above and the date below. Struck in silver with a plain edge. A well struck and only faintly toned specimen with wispy hairlines on both fields. (#60955)

Standard Silver 1869 Half Dollar Pattern
Judd-743, PR63

3020 1869 Standard Silver Half Dollar, Judd-743, Pollock-824, High R.6, PR63 PCGS. A bust of Liberty faces right and wears a cap ornamented with large stars. A ribbon inscribed LIBERTY rests on her shoulder. IN GOD WE TRUST resides within a scroll below, and UNITED STATES OF AMERICA encircles her head. On the reverse, STANDARD SILVER is centered above the familiar wreath of cotton and corn. 50 CENTS is placed within the wreath, and the date is located beneath. William Barber's initial B is recut above the L in LIBERTY, which is also recut, and somewhat softly struck. Struck in silver with a plain edge. Much brilliance is seen on each side along with golden-brown and blue toning. (#60971)

Brilliant PR65 1870 Standard Silver Dime Pattern
Judd-843

3021 1870 Standard Silver Ten Cents, Judd-843, Pollock-942, Low R.6, PR65 NGC. The obverse has a head of Liberty with a diadem in her hair and a scroll beneath the bust rather than the date. The reverse is simply laid out with 10 CENTS in the center, surrounded by a wreath of cotton and corn with STANDARD above. Struck in silver with a reeded edge. This is a brilliant example with lovely surfaces. The obverse has a pebbly surface and appears to have been struck from rusted dies.
From The Beau Clerc Collection. (#61087)

Judd-1276 1873 Trade Dollar PR50 Details

3022 1873 Trade Dollar, Judd-1276, Pollock-1418, R.4—Whizzed—ANACS. PR50 Details. A simpler design for the Trade dollar than the adopted issue, with a small head of Liberty facing left set amid a large, open field with 13 stars at the margin. The reverse has the required legends mostly set in the middle of that side, surrounded by an olive wreath, and UNITED STATES OF AMERICA at the upper periphery. Struck in silver with a reeded edge. The present piece is hairlined and slightly glossy with faint wear above the ear and on the forehead curls.
From The Beau Clerc Collection. (#61561)

Toned 1873 Trade Dollar Pattern
Judd-1276, PR65

3023 1873 Trade Dollar, Judd-1276, Pollock-1418, R.5, PR65 NGC. A distinctive Trade dollar pattern with a small head of Liberty facing left set amid a large, open field with 13 stars at the margin. The reverse has the required legends mostly set in the middle of that side, surrounded by an olive wreath, and UNITED STATES OF AMERICA at the upper periphery. Struck in silver with a reeded edge. Nicely reflective, the surfaces are gray-lilac over each side with deeper peripheral color. (#61561)

1873 Silver Trade Dollar Pattern, Judd-1310, PR55

3024 1873 Trade Dollar, Judd-1310, Pollock-1453, R.4, PR55 PCGS. A Trade dollar design struck in the year of its regular issue debut that shows Liberty seated on the obverse wearing an Indian headdress, Liberty pole and cap in her right hand, left hand resting on a globe, and conjoined flags behind. The reverse has a small eagle in the upper half with the weight and fineness below and the statutory legends on scrolls both above and below. Struck in silver with a reeded edge. Slight friction is seen over each side. One can only speculate how this came to be. Was it carried as a pocket piece, or did several people actually use this as currency? The light gray surfaces show an accent of deeper gray around the devices and within the recesses of the design.
From The Beau Clerc Collection. (#61596)

Deeply Mirrored PR61 1873 Trade Dollar Pattern
Judd-1310

3025 1873 Trade Dollar, Judd-1310, Pollock-1453, R.4, PR61 NGC. A second example of this popular Trade dollar pattern. This is one of the designs that was sold by the Mint in six-piece sets for $30. The sets were made in silver with both plain and reeded edges, copper, and aluminum. Struck in silver with a reeded edge, the fields on this piece show exceptionally deep mirrored reflectivity, especially for a coin in this grade. Lightly hairlined with a few contact marks. Pale patina is seen over each side.
From The Beau Clerc Collection. (#61596)

PR62 1873 Trade Dollar, Judd-1310

3026 1873 Trade Dollar, Judd-1310, Pollock-1453, R.4, PR62 NGC. A Trade dollar design struck in the year of its regular issue debut that shows Liberty seated on the obverse wearing an Indian headdress, Liberty pole and cap in her right hand, left hand resting on a globe, and conjoined flags behind. The reverse has a small eagle in the upper half with the weight and fineness below and the statutory legends on scrolls both above and below. Struck in silver with a reeded edge. This is one of the designs that was sold by the Mint in six-piece sets for $30. The sets were made in silver with both plain and reeded edges, copper, and aluminum. This is a mostly brilliant example that shows a bit of light toning around the margins. Moderately hairlined. (#61596)

Brown PR65 1873 Trade Dollar Pattern
Judd-1324

3027 1873 Trade Dollar, Judd-1324, Pollock-1467, Low R.7, PR65 Brown PCGS. The obverse is virtually identical to the adopted design, but the reverse shows a small eagle with spread wings and billowing scroll in its beak. Struck in copper with a reeded edge. One of about 10 pieces known of this pattern, this is one of the finest examples certified. The even brown patina that covers each side has a subtle underlying oil-slick iridescence. Trade dollar patterns are a highly collectible area in the pattern series and they offer a wide variety of designs and compositions. This is a lovely example of this important off-metal pattern.
From The Beau Clerc Collection. (#61610)

Popular 1875 Twenty Cent Pattern
Judd-1407, PR64 Cameo

3028 1875 Judd-1407, Pollock-1550, Low R.6, PR64 Cameo PCGS. The obverse is nearly identical to the adopted design, but LIBERTY is incused rather than raised as on the regular issue coins. The reverse is recognized as the popular 1/5 OF A DOLLAR design. Struck in silver with a plain edge. Just over a dozen pieces are believed known today in silver. This is a lovely example that shows stark contrast between the deeply mirrored fields and frosted devices. Intricately detailed. The fields show a few light marks that account for the less-than-Gem grade. (#61714)

Silver 1879 Morgan Half Dollar
Judd-1599, PR62

3029 **1879 Morgan Half Dollar, Judd-1599, Pollock-1794, High R.6, PR62 PCGS.** The obverse is dominated by a portrait of Liberty nearly identical to that on the Morgan dollar, but appropriately reduced in size for the half dollar denomination. The peripheral inscription E PLURIBUS UNUM and the accompanied stars differ in placement from the Morgan dollar. The reverse features an eagle with partially spread wings, holding an olive branch in the right talon and a trio of arrows in its left claws. IN GOD WE TRUST is widely spaced below, along with the denomination and UNITED STATES OF AMERICA. Struck in silver with a reeded edge. The centers are softly struck, as is generally characteristic of this pattern issue. Approximately 12-15 pieces are believed known in silver and also in copper of this design. The devices have a hint of gold color and offer good cameo contrast with the fields, although this attribute is not recorded on the older 'green label' PCGS holder.
Ex: Superior, 5/1994, lot 1202, where it realized $4,950. (#61977)

PR62 Cameo 1879 Morgan Dollar, Judd-1613

3030 **1879 Morgan Dollar, Judd-1613, Pollock-1809, Low R.7, PR62 Cameo NGC.** The obverse is of the adopted Morgan dollar design, but the reverse shows an erect eagle with raised wings set lower in the field. The legend IN GOD WE TRUST is widely spaced. Struck in silver with a reeded edge. The brilliant surfaces are deeply mirrored with flashy mint luster over the devices. Lightly hairlined, but this coin really presents well for the grade and, in fact, appears nicer than the stated grade.
Ex: Greater New York Sale (Paramount, 4/77), lot 190; Central States Signature (Heritage, 5/03), lot 7136. (#61991)

Near-Mint 1879 Goloid Dollar in Silver, Judd-1627

3031 **1879 Goloid Metric Dollar, Judd-1627, Pollock-1823, R.5, PR58 NGC.** William Barber's design for the Goloid Metric dollar with a large head of Liberty facing left and LIBERTY on a wide ribbon around her head. The reverse is laid out with the proposed alloy in the center, surrounded by a circle of 38 stars. Struck in silver with a reeded edge. Medium blue-green and tan-brown toning graces this lightly abraded specimen, which displays slight friction on the hair above the ear. (#62005)

Mostly Red Gem 1880 Coiled Hair Goloid Metric Dollar, Judd-1655

3032 1880 Goloid Metric Dollar, Judd-1655, Pollock-1855, R.7, PR65 Red and Brown PCGS. A head of Liberty with her hair braided and coiled at the back of her head faces left. A band inscribed LIBERTY encircles her hair. There are 13 stars at the border, 7 left and 6 right. The inscription 15.3 - G. 236.7 - S. 28 - C. 14 GRAMS is centered within a circle of 38 stars on the reverse. The legend UNITED STATES OF AMERICA and the denomination GOLOID METRIC DOLLAR are above the circle, and the motto DEO EST GLORIA and 100 CENTS are below. The reverse is one of very few patterns to express the denomination in two different ways. Struck in copper with a reeded edge. Only a dozen examples are known of this rare pattern. This is a lovely piece whose original red surfaces show just the slightest mellowing of brown patina. The fields are bright and reflective, the devices display a noticeable overlay of mint frost. An outstanding example of the popular Coiled Hair design. (#61655)

PR67 1884 "Holey" Five Cent Piece, Judd-1724

3034 1884 Five Cents, Judd-1724, Pollock-1934, Low R.6, PR67 PCGS. The centers have a mint-made octagon-shaped perforation. The obverse has FIVE CENTS in large letters, the words separated by two identical Federal shields. The reverse squeezes in 13 stars, the date, and UNITED STATES OF AMERICA. "Holey" cent patterns were also struck in 1884, although Judd classifies the date side as the obverse for those varieties (Judd-1721 through 1723). Struck in nickel with a plain edge. Listed as Low R.6 in the ninth edition of Judd, but perhaps rarer, since our records indicate only one other Signature auction appearance within the past 15 years. Light chestnut-gold toning enriches the undisturbed fields and devices. Precisely struck, and certified in a green label holder. Population: 7 in 67, 0 finer (8/07). (#62154)

PR67 1883 Liberty Nickel, Judd-1710

3033 1883 Liberty Head Five Cents, Judd-1710, Pollock-1914, R.5, PR67 NGC. This Liberty nickel pattern has stars along the reverse border, and UNITED STATES OF AMERICA is across the obverse margin. The prominent V is replaced by the central legend 50 N/50 C, referring to a proposed copper-nickel alloy. The T in CENTS is repunched north. Struck in nickel with a plain edge. A well struck, brilliant, and flashy Superb Gem. Among the finest known. Census: 2 in 67, 0 finer (8/07). (#62127)

1896 Charles Barber Nickel Pattern
Judd-1770, PR64 Cameo

3035 **1896 Five Cents, Judd-1770, Pollock-1987, Low R.6, PR64 Cameo NGC.** A choice example of this popular, late date Charles Barber pattern. The 1896 nickel patterns are a series that needs to be studied by a dedicated collector. Apparently quite a bit of experimentation went into these coins as pieces are known struck in standard coin nickel and at least six varieties of German silver, according to the USPatterns.com website. This piece has bright, sparkling surfaces with deeply reflective fields that accent the frosted devices. Each side has an overlay of light lime-green, yellow, and rose toning that adds even more to the eye appeal of this lovely piece. (#62224)

1964 INCO 'Dime' Pattern, MS63, Pollock-5335

3036 **1964 Reeded Edge "Dime" Pattern, Unlisted in Judd, Pollock-5335, Unknown Rarity, MS63 NGC.** 2.24 gms. Struck by International Nickel Company. Mislabeled on the insert as Pollock-5353, an obvious transposition of the last two digits as the 5353 is a quarter pattern. The obverse features a bust of Dr. Paul D. Merica and the reverse features his laboratory where the pieces were struck. The design was created by Gilroy Roberts and the hubs were created by the Medallic Art Company. Struck in 95% nickel, 5% silicon on a permalloy core of 79% nickel, 16% iron and 5% molybdenum. Mostly brilliant, some striking weakness is seen at the top of the digits in the date.

1964 INCO Plain Edge 'Quarter' Pollock-5340, MS64

3037 **1964 Plain Edge "Quarter" Pattern, Unlisted in Judd, Pollock-5340, Unknown Rarity, MS64 NGC.** Pollock's Type Two, with large bust and laboratory as the central motifs. 83.6 gn. No indication of alloy on the field in front of the face, or on the NGC insert, but the piece appears nickel despite light tan toning. In 1964, the rising price of silver forced the Mint to change the composition of dimes, quarters, and halves. INCO tested the suitability for coinage of various nickel-based alloys.

1964 INCO 'Quarter' Pattern
Pollock-5365, MS62

3038 **1964 Reeded Edge "Quarter" Pattern, Unlisted in Judd, Pollock-5365, R.6, MS62 NGC.** Type Two. 5.61 gms. Struck by International Nickel Company. The obverse features a bust of Dr. Paul D. Merica and the reverse features his laboratory where the pieces were struck. The design was created by Gilroy Roberts and the hubs were created by the Medallic Art Company. Struck in copper-nickel on a copper core with a reeded edge. Bright surfaces are overlaid with pale lilac toning.

1964 Type Three INCO 'Quarter'
MS66, Pollock-5380

3039 **1964 Reeded Edge "Quarter" Pattern, Unlisted in Judd, Pollock-5380, R.5-6, MS66 NGC.** Type Three. 5.62 gms. Struck by International Nickel Company, and produced by General Numismatics in April 1965, which later became the Franklin Mint. The obverse bust of Dr. Paul D. Merica is set in the obverse field so it does not overlap the peripheral lettering. According to Don Taxay these pieces are composed of nickel-silicon and have a reeded edge. Flashy and lightly toned throughout with no obvious abrasions. The Type Three pieces are much better designed than the Type Two patterns. The fields are also suggestive of a proof, and may be as close as INCO came to producing proof coinage.

Undated (1964) DuPont 'Quarter' Pattern
Pollock-5391, MS64

3040 **Undated (1964) Plain Edge DuPont "Quarter" Pattern, Unlisted in Judd, Pollock-5391, R.2-3, MS64 NGC.** 5.87 gms. This metallurgical trial was produced by DuPont in 1964. They were one of several companies the U.S. Mint commissioned to find a suitable alloy replacement for silver. The obverse is of Benjamin Franklin and the reverse shows the DuPont emblem with the inscription "This token made from explosion bonded 'Detaclad.'" Detaclad is a patented process for laminating 75% copper, 25% nickel to a copper core. Plain edge. A flashy, nearly abrasion-free example with just a trace of golden toning around the devices.

Interesting Three-Piece 1964 INCO Pattern Set
All Three Pieces Struck in the Same Alloy

3041 1964 Three-Piece INCO Set of Patterns. Included are: **1964 INCO "dime," Pollock-5335, Unknown Rarity, MS64 ANACS,** struck in 95% nickel, 5% silicon on a permalloy core, with a plain edge, bright and sharply struck for the issue with just a trace of hazy toning; **1964 INCO "quarter," Pollock-5340, Unknown Rarity, MS63 ANACS,** Type Two, struck in a composition of 95% nickel, 5% silicon, with a permalloy core and a plain edge, exceptionally bright, dazzling surfaces and just a bit of light toning on each side; and a **1964 INCO "half dollar," Pollock-5375, R.7 (?), MS65 ANACS,** struck in 95% nickel, 5% silicon on a permalloy core, with a plain edge, a bright, splendidly preserved example and almost completely brilliant. (Total: 3 pieces)

3042 Private "1876 $100 Gold Union" Ultra Cameo Gem Proof NGC. Five ounces of 999 Fine gold. Struck by the private New York Mint in 2005. The designs are based on sketches by Mint engraver George T. Morgan for a proposed $100 gold coin. One of the first 300 struck, although the actual mintage is unknown. A cherry-wood presentation case is included.

CALIFORNIA FRACTIONAL GOLD

3043 1856 Liberty Octagonal 25 Cents, BG-107, Low R.4, MS65 PCGS. This satiny green-gold Gem is nearly void of marks, and the strike is good with only minor blending of detail in the centers. A popular Period One variety. Population: 4 in 65, 0 finer (7/07). (#10376)

3044 1854 Liberty Octagonal 25 Cents, BG-109, High R.5, MS65 NGC. The present Gem is tied for the honor of finest certified with a single MS65 PCGS example (as of 7/07). This sharply struck and lustrous honey-gold octagonal quarter has only a few faint reverse field grazes and a solitary, pinpoint spot near the 1 in the date. (#10378)

3045 Undated Liberty Round 25 Cents, BG-203, R.6, MS61 NGC. A pleasing example of this very scarce issue. Bright yellow-gold surfaces display well struck devices, except for softness in the O of DOLLAR. A small strikethrough is noted in the upper left obverse field. (#10388)

3046 1854 Liberty Round 25 Cents, BG-216, R.6, MS61 NGC. A much better Period One variety with satiny and smooth peach-gold surfaces. The peripheries show minor laminations, but the strike is bold despite the appearance given by the lightly engraved reverse design. (#10401)

3047 Undated Liberty Round 25 Cents, BG-223, Low R.4, MS65 Prooflike NGC. Bright yellow-gold surfaces yield pleasing field-motif contrast, and are well preserved. Sharply struck, with die polish lines in the obverse fields. Die State I, confirmed by the lowest inner left berry being visible though weak. Census: 1 in 65 Prooflike, 0 finer (7/07). (#10408)

3048 1855 Liberty Round 25 Cents, BG-226A, R.5, MS63 NGC. Misattributed as BG-227 on the NGC insert. Die State II with "broken" nose. Similar to BG-227, but there are eight pearls on the coronet instead of nine, and the stars lack repunching. Well struck, untoned, and slightly wavy, as made. NGC has graded three examples of BG-226A (not counting this piece) with the single finest as MS63 (8/07). (#10417)

3049 1855 Liberty Round 25 Cents, BG-227, R.6, MS61 PCGS. A prooflike green-gold representative of this rare Period One variety. The fields are reflective, and only lightly abraded for the grade. The well struck portrait draws some metal from the central reverse letters. In an old green label holder. (#10412)

3050 1853 Liberty Octagonal 50 Cents, BG-301, Low R.7—Holed—NCS. AU Details. The first example of this challenging issue offered by Heritage, the example offered here has a dusky orange-gold appearance with minor wear on the well-defined devices and still-lustrous fields. A suspension hole just grazes the top of Liberty's coronet. (#10416)

3051 1852 Liberty Round 50 Cents, BG-401, R.3, MS65 PCGS. An original olive-gold Gem with smooth surfaces and exceptional eye appeal. Only the berry right of the 2 lacks a full impression. Encased in an old green label holder. Population: 3 in 65, 0 finer (8/07). (#10437)

1854 Large Eagle Octagonal Dollar AU58, BG-504

3052 1854 Large Eagle Octagonal 1 Dollar, BG-504, Low R.5, AU58 NGC. This is among the most famous varieties within the California Small Denomination Gold series. BG-504 is the sole variety featured on the cover of the second edition of the standard Breen-Gillio reference. Although any Period One octagonal dollar variety is popular, BG-504 is particularly so since it copies the eagle and shield motif from the Humbert fifty dollar slugs of the era. A well struck and dusky olive-gold piece, smooth aside from minor granularity on the upper left obverse field. Census: 2 in 58, 0 finer (8/07). (#10481)

Prooflike Gem BG-508 1854 Octagonal Dollar

3053 **1854 Liberty Octagonal 1 Dollar, BG-508, High R.4, MS65 Prooflike NGC.** A remarkable Gem example of this popular Period One gold dollar. Well struck aside from the low relief date, and the flashy fields are refreshingly clean. As of (7/07), NGC has certified ten examples of BG-508, with the present piece as the single finest. (#10485)

3054 **1854 Liberty Octagonal 1 Dollar, BG-510, Low R.5, AU58 PCGS.** Splashes of golden-brown toning grace the lighter greenish-gold fields. Modestly reflective despite minor friction on the highpoints that precludes a Mint State grade. Population: 11 in 58, 14 finer (8/07). (#10487)

Choice 1853 Octagonal Dollar BG-518

3055 **1853 Liberty Octagonal 1 Dollar, BG-518, R.5, MS64 NGC.** A satiny yellow-gold near-Gem with mark-free surfaces. The left obverse field is slightly wavy, as made. The DERI legend on the reverse exergue refers to M. Deriberpie, listed with the occupation 'engraver' in James M. Parker's 1852-53 San Francisco directory. The single finest among only three pieces certified as BG-518 by NGC (7/07). (#10495)

3056 **1853 Liberty Octagonal 1 Dollar, BG-519, Low R.4, AU50 NGC.** Die State II with ascending reverse die crack. Perhaps briefly a pocket piece, since the partly lustrous surfaces lack the abrasions seen on circulating gold coins. The edge is slightly irregular at 9 o'clock, perhaps as made. (#10496)

3057 **1853 Liberty Octagonal 1 Dollar, BG-519, Low R.4, AU58 PCGS.** Luster brightens the design elements of this radiant and unmarked near-Mint example. Crisply struck, attractive, and desirable as a Period One octagonal dollar type coin. (#10496)

3058 **1853 Liberty Octagonal 1 Dollar, BG-519, Low R.4, AU58 PCGS.** This apricot-gold representative features boldly struck centers and unblemished fields. The left reverse border retains a few encapsulated green fibers. Housed in an old green label holder. Population: 25 in 58, 47 finer (8/07). (#10496)

3059 **1853 Liberty Octagonal 1 Dollar, BG-519, Low R.4, MS62 PCGS.** A gleaming yellow-gold representative of this octagonal fractional issue, well-defined with a measure of reflectivity. Faint, scattered marks in the fields and on the devices preclude a Select or better grade. Population: 24 in 62, 11 finer (8/07). (#10496)

Rare BG-525 1853 Octagonal Dollar MS63

3060 **1853 Liberty Octagonal 1 Dollar, BG-525, High R.6, MS63 NGC.** This rare Period One octagonal dollar variety is many times scarcer than the usually encountered Deriberpe marriage, BG-519. The close 53 in the date and the star near the bust tip are diagnostic. Well struck and carefully preserved. Slightly wavy, as made. Presently the only BG-525 certified by NGC (7/07). (#10502)

3061 **1853 Liberty Octagonal 1 Dollar, BG-530, R.2, AU58 PCGS.** A boldly struck example with smooth green-gold fields and a hair-thin vertical mark on the portrait. The reverse is slightly concave, as made. (#10507)

3062 **1853 Liberty Octagonal 1 Dollar, BG-530, R.2, MS63 NGC.** A smooth semi-prooflike octagonal dollar with striated fields from die polishing. A handsomely engraved Period One variety that is available in AU grades, but becomes very scarce in problem-free Mint State. Census: 4 in 63, 2 finer (7/07). (#10507)

Superb Gem 1871 Octagonal Quarter BG-715

3063 **1871 Liberty Octagonal 25 Cents, BG-715, Low R.6, MS67 NGC.** This immaculate Superb Gem has wonderfully smooth green-gold surfaces. Only minor incompleteness of strike on the hair and ribbon loop denies an even finer grade. Presently the only example of BG-715 certified by NGC (7/07). (#10542)

3064 **1872 Washington Octagonal 25 Cents, BG-722, Low R.4—Improperly Cleaned—NCS. Unc. Details.** The portrait and reverse field are hairlined, but this well struck example is otherwise pleasing. A popular California Small Denomination gold type. (#10549)

MS63 1872 Washington Quarter, BG-722

3065 **1872 Washington Octagonal 25 Cents, BG-722, Low R.4, MS63 ICG.** An orange and yellow-gold representative of the popular Washington type. The flashy fields appear well preserved. A tiny mint-made planchet flaw at 9 o'clock is of little concern. A faint die crack bisects the reverse die above CAL. (#10549)

Choice 1872 Washington Quarter BG-722

3066 **1872 Washington Octagonal 25 Cents, BG-722, Low R.4, MS64 PCGS.** This is an attractive near-Gem with yellow-gold fields imbued with tinges of light green. The lustrous surfaces exhibit evenly struck design elements that are solidly defined. The coin shows a medallic alignment, and the upper borders are wavy, as ejected from the die. Housed in a green label holder. (#10549)

Mint State 1872 Washington Quarter BG-723

3067 **1872 Washington Octagonal 25 Cents, BG-723, Low R.6, MS60 PCGS.** An originally toned example with rich orange-gold centers framed by sea-green margins. Evenly struck and semi-prooflike with pleasing surfaces for the grade. A couple of minor retained laminations bookend the denominator. Encased in an old green label holder. (#10550)

3068 **1864 Liberty Octagonal 25 Cents, BG-735, R.4, MS63 PCGS.** This awkwardly engraved variety has an overlong bust tip, and the stars are irregularly shaped. Evenly struck with attractive gold toning and flashy fields. In an old green label holder. Population: 9 in 63, 2 finer (8/07). (#10562)

3069 **1871 Liberty Octagonal 25 Cents, BG-765, R.3, MS64 Prooflike NGC.** A flashy and bright example. The strike is a bit soft on portions of the reverse, but the portrait is crisp, and only light slide marks are evident. A curious halo, which seems as made, surrounds the coronet. (#710592)

3070 **1875 Indian Octagonal 25 Cents, BG-784, High R.5, MS65 Prooflike NGC.** A charming and unabraded Gem with the usual headdress "ghosts" (as made) near the DO in DOLLAR. A few central reverse letters lack an absolute strike. The only example of BG-784 certified by NGC, as of (7/07). (#710611)

3071 **1872/1 Indian Octagonal 25 Cents, BG-790, R.3, MS64 Prooflike NGC.** The mirrored fields contrast with the radiant devices. A few minute strike-throughs and a hint of striking incompleteness are all that limit the grade. (#710617)

MS66 Prooflike 1873 Octagonal Quarter BG-793

3072 **1873 Indian Octagonal 25 Cents, BG-793, R.5, MS66 Prooflike NGC.** A penetrating strike and exceptionally unabraded fields confirm the lofty Premium Gem grade. The wreath and portrait exhibit mild cameo contrast. Slightly wavy, as produced. One of only three examples of the variety certified by NGC (7/07). (#710620)

3073 **1876 Indian Octagonal 25 Cents, BG-799C, High R.4, MS64 PCGS.** A prominently mirrored near-Gem with refreshingly smooth fields and an exacting strike. In an old green label holder. Population: 23 in 64, 14 finer (8/07). (#10629)

3074 **1878/6 Indian Octagonal 25 Cents, BG-799G, R.5, MS64 PCGS.** Flashy fields and an even strike ensure the quality of this charming example. From the same dies used to strike BG-799F, but the engraver has crudely reworked the final digit in the date. Struck from rotated dies. Population: 17 in 64, 7 finer (7/07). (#10633)

3075 **1880 Indian Octagonal 25 Cents, BG-799K, R.6, MS65 Prooflike NGC.** This impressive Gem has decidedly reflective fields, and the devices are impeccably struck. Undisturbed aside from a tiny obverse spot near 9 o'clock. NGC has certified only two examples as BG-799K, with the present lot as the single finest (7/07). (#710637)

3076 **1868 Indian Octagonal 25 Cents, BG-799T, High R.5, MS65 Prooflike NGC.** This flashy Gem is well preserved, and the strike is crisp despite minor incompleteness on the O in DOLLAR. NGC has certified just two pieces as BG-799T, both as MS65 (7/07). (#710646)

Prooflike Near-Mint BG-799AA 1881 Quarter

3077 **1881 Indian Octagonal 25 Cents, BG-799AA, R.7 AU58 Prooflike NGC.** Small letters in DOLLAR CAL identify this extremely rare Breen-Gillio variety. The central reverse is softly struck, but the only evidence of non-numismatic handling are the faint hairlines on both sides. The only example of BG-799AA certified by NGC (7/07). (#710653)

Choice 1872 Washington Round Quarter, BG-818

3078 1872 Washington Round 25 Cents, BG-818, Low R.4, MS64 PCGS. A flashy green-gold near-Gem with exemplary preservation. The reverse center has a couple of lightly impressed letters, but the remainder of the devices are bold. Within the California small denomination gold series, the Washington type is a popular change of pace from the usual parade of Indian and Liberty heads. Encased in an old green label holder. Population: 31 in 64, 25 finer (8/07). (#10679)

3079 1871 Liberty Round 25 Cents, BG-839, Low R.4, MS63 Prooflike NGC. A gleaming sun-gold example that offers pleasing detail and modestly abraded surfaces. An interesting representative of this scarce issue, one that shows a single slender die crack from the right branch of the wreath. Census: 5 in 63 Prooflike, 1 finer (8/07). (#10700)

3080 1876 Indian Round 25 Cents, BG-849, High R.5, MS64 NGC. A well-defined yellow-gold example from this elusive centennial-dated issue, moderately reflective with areas of haze. This attractive piece is the single finest example graded by NGC (8/07). (#10710)

3081 1871 Liberty Round 25 Cents, BG-865, R.5, MS64 PCGS. Bright and highly lustrous, with semi-prooflike fields and minor die rust noted on both sides. Several of the obverse stars and reverse letters are recut, and faint die clash marks are noted in the fields. A shallow pinscratch resides directly above the AR in DOLLAR. Population: 5 in 64, 0 finer (8/07). (#10726)

3082 1870 Goofy Head Round 25 Cents, BG-867, R.4, MS63 PCGS. The various "Goofy Head" Breen-Gillio varieties have a common but unknown maker. This flashy and boldly struck sun-gold example has a few faint hairlines, but no marks are visible to the unaided eye. Population: 16 in 63, 9 finer (7/07). (#10728)

3083 1878/6 Indian Round 25 Cents, BG-884, High R.5, AU58 PCGS. From the same die pair as BG-881, but the maker has crudely changed the 6 in the date into an 8. The lustrous lemon-gold and aquamarine surfaces are faintly hairlined. Housed in an old green label holder. (#10745)

3084 1872 Liberty Octagonal 50 Cents, BG-913, R.4, MS64 PCGS. Bright lemon-gold color and prominently mirrored fields announce the quality of this beautifully preserved near-Gem. Certified in an older generation holder. Population: 19 in 64, 18 finer (7/07). (#10771)

1873 Liberty Octagonal 50 Cent, BG-915
MS66, Tied for Finest

3085 1873 Liberty Octagonal 50 Cents, BG-915, Low R.4, MS66 NGC. Crisp canary-yellow surfaces on each side show a remarkable lack of contact. The obverse shows light clash marks, and the reverse shows a bit of die rust, but a decent strike makes all reverse legends readable, although F in HALF and A in DOLLAR are faint. Census: 3 in 66, 0 finer (8/07). (#10773)

3086 1871 Liberty Octagonal 50 Cents, BG-924, R.3, MS65 Prooflike NGC. A gleaming example of this octagonal half issue, well-defined with immensely reflective fields. Appealing with carefully preserved surfaces. Census: 1 in 65 Prooflike, 1 finer (7/07). (#710782)

3087 1876/6876 Indian Octagonal 50 Cents, BG-935, R.5, MS64 PCGS. The plate coin to the second edition of Breen-Gillio. Lovely sun-gold toning graces this smooth near-Gem. The centers are well struck, while the borders show minor blending of detail. *Ex: Jay Roe Collection (Bowers and Merena, 9/03), lot 417.* (#10793)

3088 1870 Goofy Head Octagonal 50 Cents, BG-936, Low R.5, MS63 PCGS. A gleaming yellow-gold representative of the popular Goofy Head variety, well-defined with solid visual appeal. A handful of faint, scattered marks affect the surfaces. Population: 5 in 63, 1 finer (7/07). (#10794)

3089 1870 Goofy Head Octagonal 50 Cents, BG-936, Low R.5, MS63 NGC. Though the fields are strongly mirrored on this Goofy Head piece, NGC has not awarded it a Prooflike designation. This well-defined yellow-gold representative shows scattered, minor flaws that have little impact on its overall visual appeal. Census: 1 in 63, 1 finer (8/07). (#10794)

3090 1876 Indian Octagonal 50 Cents, BG-949, R.4, MS65 Prooflike NGC. A beautiful canary-gold octagonal half that boasts prominently mirrored fields and an unabraded appearance. A few letters in DOLLAR lack full detail, but the strike is generally crisp. (#710807)

1876 Octagonal Half, BG-951
MS66 Deep Mirror Prooflike

3091 1876 Indian Octagonal 50 Cents, BG-951, High R.5, MS66 Deep Mirror Prooflike NGC. Highly reflective fields and precisely struck motifs proclaim the quality of this well preserved Premium Gem. Similar in appearance to BG-950, but the denticles are longer and touch the date digits. As of (7/07), the present piece is the only example of BG-951 certified as Deep Mirror Prooflike by NGC. (#710809)

High R.4 1859 Liberty Round 50 Cent
MS66 Prooflike, BG-1002

3092 **1859 Liberty Round 50 Cents, BG-1002, High R.4, MS66 Prooflike NGC.** Die State II, obverse rusted and shattered. Pebbly die rust shows around much of the obverse, while a small raised planchet flake is noted before the bust truncation. Massive die breaks and bulging appear in the area above the coronet and through the nearby stars. The obverse die failure is undoubtedly the explanation for the scarcity of this issue in higher grades. The finest certified at NGC (8/07). (#710831)

3093 **1871 Liberty Round 50 Cents, BG-1011, R.2, MS66 PCGS.** A pristine Premium Gem whose prooflike yellow-gold fields also exhibit light peach toning. The strike is inexact on the base of the wreath and the top of the bust. Population: 10 in 66, 0 finer (8/07). (#10840)

3094 **1876 Liberty Round 50 Cents, High R.6, BG-1039A MS63 NGC.** This medal turn California small denomination gold piece is softly struck on the denominator and the A in DOLLAR, but the flashy fields are carefully preserved. Presently the only example of BG-1039A certified by NGC (7/07). (#10954)

Impressive Deep Prooflike MS66
1874/3 Indian Half Dollar, BG-1052

3095 **1874/3 Indian Round 50 Cents, BG-1052, High R.4, MS66 Deep Prooflike NGC.** State I. A magnificent, deeply mirrored example with watery, reflective fields and heavily contrasting, frosted devices. As expected from this die state, the underdigit is plain as well as the die scratch that joins star 3 to the chin. Bright yellow-gold color with no mentionable defects on this superior example. (#10881)

Exemplary 1874/3 Indian Round Half, BG-1052, MS66

3096 **1874/3 Indian Round 50 Cents, BG-1052, High R.4, MS66 PCGS.** This exquisitely preserved, gleaming yellow-gold example shows exceptional reflectivity in the fields and crisp detail on the contrasting portrait. Plainly overdated with a distinctive die scratch that links the third star and the effigy's chin. The single finest example of the BG-1052 certified by PCGS (8/07). (#10881)

3097 **1875/3 Indian Round 50 Cents, BG-1058, R.3, MS63 PCGS.** The rich canary-gold fields are flashy, and the well struck portrait and stars display glimpses of lilac toning. Impressive for the designated grade, despite a few light hairlines. (#10887)

3098 **1881 Indian Round 50 Cents, BG-1069, High R.4, MS64 Deep Mirror Prooflike NGC.** The icy devices display obvious cameo contrast with the glassy fields. The strike is crisp save for a couple of soft areas near the LAR in DOLLAR. A dramatic example of this collectible Period Two variety. (#710898)

Select 1860 Octagonal Dollar BG-1102

3099 **1860 Liberty Octagonal 1 Dollar, BG-1102, R.4, MS63 Prooflike NGC.** Die State II with a diagonal bisecting obverse die crack. A boldly struck piece whose reflective fields are smooth aside from a few trivial hairlines. The 0 in the date is widely repunched. Census: 1 in 63 Prooflike, 2 finer (7/07). (#710913)

3100 **1868 Liberty Octagonal 1 Dollar, BG-1105, High R.4, MS62 Prooflike NGC.** A nicely mirrored green-gold representative. The centers show the expected blending of detail, and the fields are faintly hairlined. (#710916)

3101 **1869 Liberty Octagonal 1 Dollar, BG-1106, High R.4, MS61 NGC.** Die State I with a partial initial G beneath the portrait. The centers are soft, as always for the variety. Lightly hairlined with minor granularity near the N in final A in CALIFORNIA. (#10917)

3102 **1869 Liberty Octagonal 1 Dollar, BG-1106, High R.4, MS64 Prooflike NGC.** A prominently mirrored near-Gem with radiant fields and pleasing eye appeal. The LL in DOLLAR is legible, better definition than is usual for this indifferently struck variety. Census: 2 in 64 PL, 1 finer as 65 DPL (7/07). (#710917)

1875 Indian Octagonal Dollar
MS64 Prooflike, BG-1124

3103 **1875 Indian Octagonal 1 Dollar, BG-1125, Low R.5, MS64 Prooflike NGC.** Well struck and free of significant marks, this splendidly reflective example displays light green-gold color and a couple of minor lintmarks on the upper obverse field. The reverse die exhibits a network of branching cracks. Census: 2 in 64 Prooflike, 1 finer as MS67 DPL (7/07). (#710936)

Only Gem Prooflike BG-1127 1875 Octagonal
Indian 1 Dollar at NGC

3104 **1875 Indian Octagonal 1 Dollar, BG-1127, R.4, MS65 Prooflike NGC.** Deeply reflective orange-yellow fields on each side, with DOLLAR fully readable and better struck than normal. A small spot of copper toning is noted on the reverse. The finest BG-1127 certified Prooflike by several grade points (three, to be precise) at NGC or PCGS (8/07), as well as the only MS65 at NGC. (#710938)

Prooflike MS64 1876/5 Octagonal Dollar BG-1128

3105 **1876/5 Indian Octagonal 1 Dollar, BG-1128, R.5, MS64 Prooflike NGC.** From the same dies as BG-1127, but the 5 in the date is awkwardly altered by the coiner into a 6. This charming near-Gem has pleasing cameo contrast between the radiant motifs and the glassy fields. A few trivial hairlines determine the grade. Census: 1 in 64 Prooflike, 2 finer (7/07). (#710939)

3106 **1876/5 Indian Octagonal 1 Dollar, BG-1129, R.4 MS62 PCGS.** Orange and lime patina invigorates this well struck and unmarked octagonal dollar. Retained laminations are noted near star 10, the R in DOLLAR, and the O in GOLD. In an older green label holder. Population: 26 in 62, 27 finer (8/07). (#10940)

3107 **1876/5 Indian Octagonal 1 Dollar, BG-1129, R.4 MS63 Prooflike NGC.** The same dies as BG-1128, but the denticles were re-engraved (by the maker) and are now long and tooth-like. The fields display pleasing reflectivity, and although the strike is not full in the centers, the preservation is impressive for the assigned grade. (#10940)

3108 **1876/5 Indian Octagonal 1 Dollar, BG-1129, R.4, MS63 Deep Mirror Prooflike NGC.** Mirrored fields and frosty devices ensure the attraction of this unmarked octagonal dollar. The centers are suitably struck, and the fields have a few small to tiny strike-throughs. Census: 1 in 63 DPL, 1 finer (7/07). (#710940)

Prooflike Near-Mint 1871 Round Dollar BG-1201

3109 **1871 Liberty Round 1 Dollar, BG-1201, High R.6, AU58 Prooflike NGC.** A rare Period Two round dollar with only a hint of wear on the portrait and wreath. The fields are only faintly marked, and retain much mint flash. Struck with medal turn. NGC has certified just three examples of BG-1201, and the present piece is the only one with a Prooflike designation (7/07). (#10946)

BG-1203 1870 Round Dollar XF45

3110 **1870 Liberty Round 1 Dollar, BG-1203, Low R.5, XF45 PCGS.** This representative has minimal marks and only a trace of friction. The devices are softly struck, which affects its third party grade, although substantial prooflike luster remains. Certified in an old green label holder. (#10948)

3111 **1871 Liberty Round 1 Dollar, BG-1204, High R.5, MS64 PCGS.** Robert B. Gray bought the jewelry manufacturing business of Antoine Louis Nouizillet in 1858 or 1859, including all of his dies, hubs, and punches. After making some trials from the old dies Gray sank new punches, signified by the initial G below the bust truncation. Gray in turn sold the business in 1871 to the Levison brothers, Jacob and Herman, who operated it as the California Jewelry Company.

This late-period Gray piece shows brilliant prooflike yellow-gold surfaces that show just a few tiny flecks on the planchet, likely as made. The OLL in DOLLAR and the loop of the bow beneath are faint but distinguishable. This lovely piece is the single finest graded at PCGS (8/07). (#10949)

BG-1207 1872 Round Dollar AU55

3112 **1872 Indian Round 1 Dollar, BG-1207, R.4, AU55 PCGS.** A mildly prooflike representative with lightly abraded fields from brief non-numismatic handling. Only eight varieties of Period Two round dollars were struck, which focuses type demand for problem-free examples. BG-1207 shares the same obverse as the well known BG-1208 Token Reverse variety. Certified in an old green label holder. (#10952)

MS63 Prooflike 1872 Indian Dollar BG-1207

3113 **1872 Indian Round 1 Dollar, BG-1207, R.4, MS63 Prooflike NGC.** The penultimate Period Two variety, from the same obverse die as the famous BG-1208 Token variety. Sharply struck except for the 87 in the date. Minor marks near the final obverse star and the reverse center dot are appropriate for the grade. Struck with close to medal turn. (#710952)

GOLD DOLLARS

3114 **1849 No L—Defective Planchet (Obverse)—MS62 PCGS.** Though not noted on the holder, the widely repunched star below the tip of the bust identifies this piece as the elusive No L variety. The vivid rose-tinged orange-gold surfaces of this warmly lustrous piece show a mint-green planchet flaw just above the truncation of the portrait. (#7501)

3115 **1849 Open Wreath MS62 NGC.** Large head, with L. Bright satiny luster illuminates the lime-gold surfaces. Faint die clash marks are noted in the left obverse field, close to Liberty's face. The design details are well stuck, and there are only a few superficial marks on each side of the coin. (#7502)

3116 **1849 Open Wreath MS62 NGC.** A delicate and delightful green-gold representative of the one-year Open Wreath design. Crisply struck and lustrous with a number of wispy, yet grade-defining abrasions in the obverse fields. (#7502)

3117 **1849 Open Wreath MS63 PCGS.** Large head, with L. A radiant and well struck example of this shortly struck gold dollar subtype. Faint marks are noted below the hairbun, but the overall preservation is impressive. (#7502)

3118 1850 MS62 NGC. 1850 gold dollars are scarcer in high grades than their mintage of nearly 500,000 pieces might indicate. This MS62 coin displays soft luster and brassy-gold color, along with well impressed design elements. A few handling marks are not worthy of individual mention. (#7509)

3119 1851 MS64 PCGS. The Philadelphia Mint coined an unprecedented quantity of gold in the early 1850s, including many examples of the newly created gold dollar denomination. This sharply struck Choice example has frosty, subtly lustrous butter-yellow surfaces that show few marks for the grade. (#7513)

3120 1851-C—Scratched, Cleaned—ANACS. XF45 Details. Variety 5-E. This Charlotte gold piece is slightly bright, and the lower left obverse field has a few faint curving pinscratches. Highpoint wear is less than implied by the average strike. (#7514)

3121 1851-C AU53 PCGS. Variety 5-E. This well struck Charlotte gold dollar has the sharpness of an AU58 example, but marks are noted near the coronet tip, cheekbone, and ear. The reverse is abraded near the ST in STATES and the CA in AMERICA. (#7514)

Fully Struck AU58 1851-C Gold Dollar

3122 1851-C AU58 NGC. Variety 4-D. The 1851-C gold dollar is a common issue by Charlotte standards and can be found in a wide range of grades, including the occasional Uncirculated coin. This piece represents good value as it is just at the threshold of Mint State with most of the detail and mint luster of an Uncirculated piece. Fully struck on each side, the green-gold surfaces show no mentionable abrasions on either side. (#7514)

Desirable 1851-D Gold Dollar, MS62

3123 1851-D MS62 NGC. Variety 3-D. The sharp details and lustrous green-gold surfaces of this satiny Mint State piece capture the eye. Although it is considered the second most common Dahlonega gold dollar, less than 10,000 coins were minted, and mint state survivors remain conditionally rare. Census: 24 in 62, 11 finer (8/07). (#7515)

3124 1853 MS64 PCGS. The luminous obverse is wheat-gold, while the yellow-gold reverse shows slightly stronger luster. The pleasingly detailed portrait is carefully preserved, though faint marks are present in the fields. An attractive Type One gold dollar. (#7521)

Conditionally Scarce 1853-C Gold Dollar MS62

3125 1853-C MS62 PCGS. Variety 8-I. This Charlotte Mint issue was notoriously poorly produced, and examples exhibit some of the striking anomalies more commonly seen on pieces of California fractional gold. This example is bright and semi-prooflike, with attractive green-gold coloration over both sides. The central reverse details are somewhat mushy, as usual. The fields display a granular, orange-peel texture, and are rather "wavy", especially on the obverse. The luster quality is unmistakably that of a Mint State coin, however. Population: 9 in 62, 3 finer (8/07). (#7522)

Radiant 1853-D Gold Dollar MS62

3126 1853-D MS62 PCGS. Variety 5-G, the only known variety for this date. An impressive example of this scarce Dahlonega Mint issue, this piece has partially reflective surfaces with rich green and orange-gold surfaces. The devices are a trifle weak in the centers, as usual for this issue. The mintage of this date was a mere 6,583 coins, and only a fraction of those have survived. The 1853-D is particularly rare in Mint State. PCGS has certified 83 examples of this issue in all grades, but just 11 of those have been certified as MS60 or finer. Population: 2 in 62, 6 finer (2/07). (#7523)

3127 1853-O MS61 NGC. The issue of choice for most New Orleans gold type collectors, the 1853-O is readily available in the marketplace, though finding an attractive example can present a challenge. This lovely butter-yellow representative has strong central detail and pleasing luster, though faint, wispy abrasions are present in the fields. (#7524)

3128 1853-O MS62 PCGS. This pleasingly detailed, strongly lustrous representative shows yellow-gold centers with slightly deeper rings of color at the margins. Faint abrasions are present in the fields. An attractive representative of this popular, comparatively available New Orleans gold dollar issue. (#7524)

3129 1854 Type Two AU58 NGC. Pleasingly lustrous with just a trace of friction on Liberty's hair detail that keeps it from a Mint State holder. The khaki-gold surfaces display normal clash marks on each side, but few blemishes. A small rim abrasion is noted near 9 o'clock on the obverse of this appealing type coin. (#7531)

3130 1854 Type Two AU58 PCGS. A touch of friction affects the highpoints of this well-defined first-year Type Two gold dollar, luminous with dusky wheat-gold surfaces. Under magnification, wispy abrasions appear in the fields. (#7531)

3131 1854 Type Two AU58 PCGS. A luminous butter-yellow example of this popular Type Two type issue, well struck and pleasing with few marks. A hint of highpoint friction bars the way to a Mint State grade. (#7531)

3132 1854 Type Two AU58 PCGS. A hint of friction appears on the devices of this first-year Type Two gold dollar. This flaw has surprisingly little impact on the coin's visual appeal, as the luster remains strong and the wheat-gold surfaces show few marks. (#7531)

3133 1854 Type Two MS61 NGC. The luminous orange-gold surfaces of this first-year Type Two dollar show hints of rose at the margins. A well struck type piece, pleasing despite numerous wispy abrasions. (#7531)

Lovely 1854 Type Two Gold Dollar, MS62

3134 1854 Type Two MS62 NGC. James B. Longacre's revised design for the gold dollar shows different accessories on the portrait, though the Type One and Type Two faces show a strong similarity to each other (and to Longacre's prime classical inspiration, the *Venus Accroupie*.) This luminous and well struck example has lightly abraded, yet pleasing butter-yellow and amber-gold surfaces. (#7531)

1854 Type Two Gold Dollar MS62

3135 1854 Type Two MS62 PCGS. Moderate die rust near the obverse periphery fails to lower the eye appeal of this lustrous, boldly struck representative. Several shallow pinscratches are observed on the obverse, limiting the grade. The Type Two gold dollar and the three dollar gold piece, both introduced in 1854, share the same wreath design. (#7531)

Frosty 1854 Type Two Gold Dollar, MS63

3136 1854 Type Two MS63 PCGS. Because the Small Indian head design was only minted from 1854 to 1856, it is considered an important type issue, resulting in heightened demand. The Philadelphia Mint coined about 1.5 million of these coins in 1854 and 1855, a substantial decrease from earlier years. From 1849 through 1853, the average annual production in Philadelphia was about 2 million gold dollars per year.

Frosty surfaces and highly lustrous yellow-gold are evident on both sides of this lovely Mint State piece. Hints of pale orange and wispy blue toning are visible on both sides. The strike is sharp, and nearly full at the centers, atypical for the design. (#7531)

3137 **1855 AU58 NGC.** Second year of the short-lived Type Two gold dollar. This lightly circulated piece is well defined, save for softness in portions of Liberty's hair. Nice luster is retained on the yellow-gold surfaces. Relatively well preserved, with just a few minor contact marks and pinscratches in the left (facing) obverse field. (#7532)

3138 **1855 AU58 PCGS.** Only a hint of friction appears on the well struck devices. This shining second-year Type Two piece has yellow-gold and lemon surfaces with small, scattered abrasions, including one at the RT of LIBERTY. (#7532)

Pleasing 1855 Gold Dollar, MS62

3139 **1855 MS62 PCGS.** Both sides of this Type Two gold dollar display soft luster and rich peach-gold patination imbued with traces of mint-green and apricot. The design elements are quite sharp save for some softness in portion's of Liberty's hair and on the top part of the 8 in the date; all of the letters in LIBERTY are sharp. Clash marks are visible on each side, and most of the Indian's profile is clear on the reverse. A few scattered marks are noted on both obverse and reverse. A lovely piece for the type or date collector. (#7532)

1855 Type Two Gold Dollar MS62

3140 **1855 MS62 NGC.** Crisply struck with pleasing definition on the date and Liberty's forehead curls. Type Two gold dollars were struck only in 1854 and 1855, aside from a tiny San Francisco production in 1856. Since there was a shortage of silver coins in circulation, gold dollars saw heavy use in commerce, and Mint State survivors are scarce relative to present demand. (#7532)

Lustrous 1855 Near-Gem Gold Dollar

3141 **1855 MS64 PCGS.** The 1855 gold dollar is available without difficulty in all grades up through MS63. In his volume I of reference works to United States federal gold coinage, Paul Taglione says of higher grade pieces that they are "quite rare from an *availability rarity* viewpoint if not necessarily from an *absolute rarity* one. In point of fact, it is one of the most demanded of all gold dollars but it stakes claim to absolute rarity only at the Mint State 65 or better level ... ."

Ebullient luster issues from both sides of this near-Gem specimen, and a well directed strike imparts sharp definition to the design elements, except for the usual weakness in the top part of the 8 in the date. A few minor handling marks in the fields of the peach-gold surfaces define the grade. (#7532)

1855-O Gold Dollar, AU55

3142 **1855-O AU55 NGC.** Luster resides in the recesses of this Choice AU New Orleans Mint issue. Yellow-gold patination is imbued with hints of light tan, and sharp definition is noted on the design elements, except for the usual softness in the 8 of the date. This is a moderately rare date, from a mintage of 55,000 pieces. (#7535)

3143 1856 Slanted 5 MS64 PCGS. Satiny luster enhances both sides of this well struck representative. Uncommonly appealing for the grade with above-average preservation, and a great candidate for one's gold type set. Population: 65 in 64, 24 finer (7/07). (#7540)

Attractive 1856-D Gold Dollar, AU58

3144 1856-D AU58 PCGS. Variety 8-K. All 1,460 1856-D gold dollars were struck from a single die pair in May 1856, and fewer than 100 examples are believed to be extant (Douglas Winter, 2003). This apricot-gold Borderline Uncirculated example is crisply struck for the issue, as only the U in UNITED, the O in DOLLAR, and the 5 in the date display softness. Light clash marks are noted near Liberty's profile, but the surfaces are only faintly marked. Luster illuminates the legends and devices. A significant opportunity for the Southern gold specialist. Population: 12 in 58, 7 finer (8/07). (#7543)

3145 1858 MS63 NGC. Deep copper-gold patina over lustrous surfaces that are virtually free of bothersome marks. An appealing Select example of this conditionally scarce issue. Census: 18 in 63, 11 finer (7/07). (#7548)

Conditionally Rare 1858 Gold Dollar, MS65

3146 1858 MS65 NGC. A no-questions Gem, both sides are satiny and free of individually distracting bagmarks. The strike is also free of criticism, and the otherwise yellow-gold color assumes a subtle pink tint in select areas over both the obverse and the reverse. About 20 degrees of clockwise die rotation is noted. Census: 5 in 65, 2 finer (8/07). (#7548)

Scarce 1858-S Gold Dollar, MS61

3147 1858-S MS61 PCGS. 1858-S gold dollars are scarce in all grades, as the limited mintage of 10,000 pieces might suggest. Rich orange-gold patina adheres to partially prooflike fields on this MS61 example, and most of the design elements have benefited from a sharp strike. Wispy handling marks visible under magnification define the grade. Population: 5 in 61, 4 finer (7/07). (#7550)

Exceptional MS65 1859 Gold Dollar

3148 1859 MS65 PCGS. As noted (surely by Walter Breen) in New Netherlands 49th Auction: "The date on this dollar has wide, flat figures as seen upon the Half Dime, and totally unlike those found on the Charlotte, Dahlonega, and San Francisco coins of the year." This is a wonderful example of this scarcer early Type Three P-mint gold dollar. The mint luster is bright and frosted, and the striking details are fully brought up in all areas. The light reddish-gold surfaces do not show any mentionable defects. Population: 15 in 65, 8 finer (8/07). (#7551)

Scarce 1860-S Gold Dollar, MS61

3149 1860-S MS61 NGC. A scarce S-mint gold dollar. Only 13,000 pieces were produced, and probably no more than 125-140 individual coins are known today. Only a few dozen coins have been certified in mint condition. This is an attractive piece that has bright, semi-prooflike fields. Sharply struck, there are numerous small to medium sized abrasions on the obverse that account for the grade. Census: 17 in 61, 14 finer (8/07). (#7557)

3150 1861 MS63 NGC. This Civil War-era gold dollar issue had an ample mintage of over half a million pieces, and the economic conditions that encouraged hoarding of precious metals resulted in a number of high-grade survivors. This Select yellow-gold example has strong detail and vibrant luster with only a handful of scattered marks. (#7558)

Desirable 1861 Gold Dollar, MS66

3151 1861 MS66 NGC. A flashy Premium Gem, with frosty and brilliant light yellow surfaces, this piece ranks near the top of the Census for the date. The opportunity to bid on an MS66 or finer example of this date seldom appears. Highly desirable, not only for its exceptional aesthetic appeal, but also for technical considerations. Both sides have multiple sets of heavy clash marks. Census: 7 in 66, 2 finer (8/07). (#7558)

3152 1862 MS64 PCGS. Both sides of this yellow-gold example are awash in potent luster and exquisitely struck save for slight weakness on the C in AMERICA. Planchet lines are present at the upper right reverse, but these do not affect the grade of this lovely Choice piece. (#7560)

Gorgeous 1862 Gem Gold Dollar

3153 1862 MS65 PCGS. With a mintage of more than 1 million coins, the 1862 gold dollar is one of the most common dates of the series. Perusal of the PCGS/NGC population data indicates that several hundred Mint State examples have been certified through MS64. The date becomes somewhat more difficult in MS65 and finer grades. The Gem specimen in this lot displays gorgeous greenish-gold patina residing over scintillating luster, and a well executed strike imparts crisp and even definition over the design elements. The surfaces are minimally marked for an MS65. Population: 69 in 65, 27 finer (8/07). (#7560)

3154 1864 AU58 NGC. Just a trace of friction affects the highpoints of this still-shining butter-yellow gold dollar. Sharply struck with excellent eye appeal. Most of the 5,900 examples of this issue did not circulate, as the Civil War drove most precious metal coinage out of circulation. Census: 10 in 58, 55 finer (8/07). (#7563)

Elusive 1865 Gold Dollar, MS61

3155 1865 MS61 NGC. The 1865 gold dollar touts one of the lowest mintages of the type (3,725 circulation strikes). The date is rare in all grades; indeed, only about 70 examples ranging from XF to Mint State have been seen by NGC and PCGS combined. Partially prooflike fields on this MS61 example yield noticeable contrast with the motifs, especially on the obverse. Well struck, and revealing an even distribution of light handling marks. (#7564)

3156 1867 MS62 PCGS. Pleasing orange-gold patina bathes each side of this sharply impressed gold dollar. A mild cameo-like appearance between the lightly frosted motifs and somewhat prooflike fields results when the coin is viewed at various angles. A few wispy handling marks do not distract. This piece clearly shows the word LIBERTY imposed on the reverse between the wreath and date, the result of die clashing. A very sharp coin for the grade. Population: 13 in 62, 23 finer (8/07). (#7566)

3157 1868 MS62 Prooflike NGC. This needle-sharp example closely resembles a proof. The fields are flashy, and only the borders display cartwheel sheen. Each side has a few trivial hairlines that limit the grade but not the eye appeal. Census: 2 in 62 Prooflike, 2 finer (8/07). (#77567)

3158 1871 MS61 PCGS. The surfaces of this enticing gold dollar are surprisingly clean for the grade assigned. A well-defined example of this low-mintage issue that offers swirling luster and sun-gold accents on the peach-inflected surfaces. (#7571)

3159 1871 MS64 PCGS. Lustrous surfaces show a mix of orange-gold and lime-green patina, and a couple of light grade-defining marks on the reverse. Well struck, except for softness in the 8 of the date. Population: 16 in 64, 24 finer (7/07). (#7571)

3160 **1873 Open 3 MS63 PCGS.** A crisply struck Select example with vibrant luster, this Open 3 gold dollar has predominantly sun-gold surfaces with green-gold accents in the fields. Housed in a green label holder. (#7573)

3161 **1873 Open 3 MS63 PCGS.** Vibrant luster and radiant sun-gold surfaces confirm the quality of this Type Three gold dollar. Only the C in AMERICA lacks an exacting strike. Certified in an old green label holder. (#7573)

3162 **1873 Open 3 MS64 PCGS.** A strongly lustrous yellow-gold example that shows the later Open 3 logotype. Both sides show pleasing detail overall, though the knot of the wreath and the corresponding area of Liberty's headdress show slight softness. (#7573)

3163 **1873 Open 3 MS63 Prooflike NGC.** A carefully preserved and nicely mirrored canary-gold piece. Only the C in AMERICA lacks sharp definition. This issue is rarely seen in Prooflike condition, as attested to by the NGC population data. Census: 7 in 63 Prooflike, 0 finer (7/07). 3 (#77573)

Appealing 1873 Closed 3 Gold Dollar, MS62

3164 **1873 Closed 3 MS62 NGC.** Jeff Garrett and Ron Guth, in their gold coins encyclopedia reference, write: "The 1873 Close 3 is a very scarce coin in all grades and is, in fact, one of the rarest Type 3 gold dollars." This yellow-gold MS62 example yields prooflike fields that establish marked contrast with the design elements. Indeed, a gold-on-black appearance is evident when the piece is observed from a direct angle. Well struck, save for the usual softness in LIBERTY. Great overall appeal for the grade designation, despite some minor handling marks. (#7574)

3165 **1879 MS62 NGC.** The 1879 has a mintage of just 3,000 business strikes and 30 proofs. Philadelphia-area dealers apparently set a number of pieces aside, but the issue is undeniably scarce. This smooth example is well struck save for the ER in LIBERTY. Luster dominates the borders and devices.
From The Diemer L. Fife Collection. (#7580)

Outstanding 1880 Gold Dollar, MS68

3166 **1880 MS68 PCGS.** The 1880 gold dollar, despite the minuscule mintage of 1,600 pieces, has a high survival rate, as evidenced by the certification of several coins by PCGS and NGC. This MS68 example displays variegated apricot and lime-green patina, along with dazzling luster. A well executed strike emboldens the design elements of the immaculately preserved surfaces. Population: 23 in 68, 1 finer (8/07). (#7581)

Stellar 1885 Gold Dollar, MS68

3167 **1885 MS68 NGC.** The 1885, despite having a higher mintage than some of the later gold dollar issues, presents a greater challenge in the finer Mint State grades. The discerning date collector would find it impossible to find a better example than this incredible MS68 piece. The strike is crisp, and the butter-yellow surfaces have vibrant luster on this simply breathtaking representative, one that is practically flawless, even under magnification. Census: 3 in 68, 0 finer (8/07). (#7586)

3168 **1889 MS64 NGC.** A lovely Choice representative from the final year of the gold dollar, butter-yellow with tiny sun-gold accents. This luminous and boldly struck example is one of just 29,000 pieces minted. (#7590)

3169 **1889 MS65 NGC.** Bold detail and astonishing eye appeal are the hallmarks of this enticing Gem. The carefully preserved yellow-gold surfaces offer vibrant luster. A great example from the final year of issue. (#7590)

3170 **1889 MS64 Prooflike NGC.** A flashy and meticulously struck near-Gem with beautifully smooth fields and devices. The ER in LIBERTY is weak, as made from a lapped obverse die. Census: 5 in 64 Prooflike, 11 finer (8/07). (#77590)

Flashy 1889 Gold Dollar, MS66 Prooflike

3171 **1889 MS66 Prooflike NGC.** A flashy and beautifully smooth Premium Gem with meticulously struck devices and imposing eye appeal. These attributes are augmented by pronounced contrast between the prooflike fields and frosted motifs, as well as impeccably preserved surfaces. The reverse border has a slender peripheral die crack, which suggests that the dies were removed from service and lapped, then restored before striking the present piece. Census: 2 in 66 Prooflike, 6 finer (7/07). (#77590)

PR65 ★ Ultra Cameo 1876 Gold Dollar

3172 1876 PR65 ★ Ultra Cameo NGC. NGC has awarded a Star designation to only two proof 1876 gold dollars. It is easy to see why the present piece has received such an honor, since the eye appeal is exceptional. The motifs are glowing with frost, and display unimprovable contrast with the glassy fields. Each side has a couple of subtle roller marks, as struck, and the field east of the prominent 1 is unreflective, as made. Essentially pristine, and the appearance is the same today as it was when first made during the Centennial, 130 years ago. Only 45 proofs were struck. (#97626)

3173 1881 PR66 Deep Cameo PCGS. This is a rare issue in proof grades, regardless of the numerical level. The mintage was only 87 coins, and less than half of those are thought to have survived today (Paul Taglione, 1986). Many deceptive prooflike examples exist, and there are no distinguishing characteristics, thus certification is imperative. According to David Akers (1975), true proofs have a small unfinished area near the D on the reverse, but even this diagnostic is not conclusive. For example, the present piece does not show any evidence of this unfinished die work, yet the mirrored surfaces and sharp strike clearly indicate its proof status. The devices are frosty and lustrous, and both sides of this Premium Gem exhibit light yellow-gold color. Population: 4 in 66 Deep Cameo, 0 finer (8/07). (#97631)

Impressive 1882 Gold Dollar, PR64 Deep Cameo

3174 **1882 PR64 Deep Cameo PCGS.** Jeff Garrett and Ron Guth (2006) write of the 1882 proof gold dollar: "This date marks the first year that true proof gold dollars are actually available without too much difficulty." The authors' contention notwithstanding, Deep Cameo specimens, such as the near-Gem in this lot, are challenging. A gold-on-black appearance reaches out to the viewer, and the sharply struck design elements add extra appeal. Truly an impressive coin. Population: 3 in 64 Deep Cameo, 4 finer (8/07). (#97632)

Pleasing PR63 Cameo 1883 Gold Dollar

3175 **1883 PR63 Cameo NGC.** The mintage for proof 1883 gold dollars was 207 pieces, but of that number only 100-125 examples are believed known today. There are many prooflike 1883 dollars that, in the past, have been confused with proofs. David Akers summed up the difference best: "true proofs can be identified by their characteristic orange-peel surface." This coin has that textured, crinkled appearance in the fields. The fields are also deeply mirrored and the devices display a significant overlay of mint frost that yield a strong cameo contrast. A few stray field marks account for the grade of this lovely gold dollar. Census: 3 in 63 Cameo, 26 finer (8/07). (#87633)

Popular 1887 Gold Dollar, PR64 Cameo

3176 **1887 PR64 Cameo PCGS.** Mintages of proof gold dollars reached substantial levels, with over 1,000 coined each year from 1884 to 1889. In 1887, the mintage was 1,043 proofs. Those mintages gave contemporary collectors an opportunity to acquire a gold proof at a modest price level, when most could not afford more than a dollar or two per coin for their collections. Similarly, enough survive today that 21st century collectors have the same opportunity. This piece has delightful lemon-yellow color with traces of orange toning, especially on the reverse. Population: 6 in 64, 14 finer (8/07). (#87637)

EARLY QUARTER EAGLES

Scarce 1821 Quarter Eagle, AU58

3177 **1821 AU58 PCGS.** Quarter eagles began with the 1796 No Stars, followed by the 1796-1807 Stars, then the one-year 1808 Capped Bust Left. Then production ceased until 1821 with the debut of the Capped Head Left (1821-1834). Yet the diameter and device sizes changed in 1829, making the 1821-1827 a unique and scarce sub-type unto itself. Among these various types, diameters changed. Diameter began at 20 mm, moved to 18.5 mm in 1821, and finally 18.2 mm in 1829. Changing the thickness kept the denomination at its authorized weight. The first examples were proofs and since so few business strikes were coined after the proofs, nearly all have reflective surfaces.

The Act of June 28th, 1834 reduced the quarter eagle's weight from 67.5 grains to 64.5 grains, which resulted in melting many earlier versions including an unknown number of the 6,448 pieces struck in 1821.

This is truly a scarce type coin with only 40 coins certified in all grades at both PCGS and NGC. This specimen clearly belongs near center-stage in any early type gold collection. The fields are predictably prooflike and the devices are well defined. The only mentionable marks are a scratch near the obverse rim at 2 o'clock and a diagonal mark on the upper portion of Liberty's portrait. Bright yellow-gold color, as usual. (#7662)

AU55 Details 1830 Quarter Eagle

3178 **1830—Tooled, Cleaned—ANACS. AU55 Details.** Breen-6133, BD-1, R.4. Only one die variety of 1830 Quarter Eagles is known, and it is distinguished by the recut left upright of the I in AMERICA. The field near the profile and beneath the scroll has faint swirling marks, the obverse field is bright from a mild polishing, and the lower reverse field has patches of hairlines. Nevertheless, a sharp example of this challenging Capped Head date. A lintmark from the inner point of the tenth star identifies the present piece. (#7670)

Rare XF Details 1833 Quarter Eagle

3179 **1833—Repaired, Whizzed—ANACS. XF45 Details.** Breen-6136, BD-1, R.5. The reverse field is repaired beneath the scroll, and the obverse field has a bright, swirled surface from whizzing. The eagle's wings retain mint luster. The only dies for this rare date, which generally appears at auction only a couple of times per year. (#7673)

CLASSIC QUARTER EAGLES

3180 **1834 Classic AU55 PCGS.** Breen-6138, Small Head, R.2. This precisely struck gold type coin has ample glowing luster for the grade, and marks are minimal save for a straight thin line on the reverse near 2 o'clock. (#7692)

Mint State 1834 Classic Quarter Eagle

3181 **1834 Classic MS60 NGC.** Breen's Small Head variety, the most plentiful of four die varieties for this issue. Although "only" MS60, this example has a sharp strike with above average central details on both sides. The surfaces are attractive green-gold with reflective fields. A lovely type coin to represent the new Classic Head design introduced in the summer of 1834. (#7692)

1834 Classic Two and a Half MS61

3182 **1834 Classic MS61 NGC.** Breen-6138, Small Head, R.2. Well struck for the type, and the yellow-gold surfaces are refreshingly unabraded. Bright luster illuminates the stars, legends, eagle, and hair. The 1834 Classic quarter eagle and half eagle were the first gold issues to extensively circulate. PCGS has certified examples in grades as low as Good 4. (#7692)

Attractive AU58 1835 Classic Quarter Eagle

3183 **1835 AU58 NGC.** McCloskey-1, R.2. This is the usually seen variety for this date with the AM in AMERICA widely spaced. Generally not located in near-Mint condition, this exceptional coin has much of the original luster remaining. The fields are bright and semi-prooflike. Excellent orange and yellow-gold color. A couple of field marks are located on the reverse. (#7693)

Handsome MS62 1836 Quarter Eagle

3184 **1836 Script 8 MS62 PCGS.** Head of 1835, Breen-6143, McCloskey-H, R.4. A scarce variety noted for a widely spaced TAT in STATES and a trio of die cracks that intersect within the hair above the Liberty's ear. An unblemished orange-gold representative with minor incompleteness of strike in the centers. (#7694)

Script 8 1836 Two and a Half, MS62

3185 **1836 Script 8 MS62 PCGS.** Head of 1835, Breen-6143, McCloskey-D, R.2. This late die state coin shows a rim-to-rim die crack on the obverse that begins above star 6 and terminates between stars 12 and 13. Always scarce in mint condition, this is an especially lustrous example. Softly defined on the hair curls, as usual, only slight abrasions account for the grade. (#7694)

3186 **1838—Improperly Cleaned—NCS. AU Details.** Only one pair of dies is known for this scarce and underappreciated issue. Careful rotation beneath a light reveals patches of hairlines, but the strike is sharp and wear is minimal. Each side has one or two noticeable marks. (#7696)

Well Defined 1838 Quarter Eagle, AU55

3187 **1838 AU55 PCGS.** Breen-6146, R.2. The 1838 Philadelphia mintage of 47,030 pieces was apparently coined by a single pair of dies. This yellow-gold Choice AU specimen displays a greenish cast, and is visited by splashes of reddish-gold. Sharp definition is apparent on the design features, and a few light circulation marks are noted on each side. (#7696)

AU Definition 1838-C Two and a Half

3188 **1838-C—Improperly Cleaned—NCS. AU Details.** Only a single die pair is known for this difficult introductory Charlotte issue. This is unsurprising given the tiny emission of 7,880 pieces, the lowest in the Classic quarter eagle series. This crisply struck example has little actual wear, but the fields are cloudy from hairlines. (#7697)

Unc Details 1838-C Quarter Eagle

3189 **1838-C—Improperly Cleaned—NCS. Unc Details.** Breen-6147, Variety 1-A, R.3. Heavy repunching shows on all known examples of the issue, from a mintmark punch that was first entered too low. The fields are lightly hairlined, but the strike is bold and, despite the NCS caveat, the piece retains much appeal. A die crack at 10 o'clock on the reverse rim runs over the eagle's left (facing) wing. (#7697)

Mint State Details 1838-C Quarter Eagle

3190 **1838-C—Genuine—NCS.** Variety 1-A. This is an ungraded coin that we grade MS60 Details, incorrectly certified by NCS as a 1938-C! The C mintmark is boldly repunched, as always, and the yellow-orange surfaces show little in the way of distraction save for a couple of minor abrasions through the last two digits of the date. A few scattered ticks fleck the surfaces, but the strike is generous and much appeal remains. (#7697)

3191 **1839/8—Scratched, Cleaned—ANACS. AU Details, Net XF45.** Recut 9 or 39/8, depending on one's point of view. Yellow-gold surfaces display traces of luster, along with faint hairlines under magnification. A shallow vertical scratch is visible in the hair on Liberty's neck, and a couple of short pinscratches occur on the reverse. The design elements are sharply defined. The cleaning and scratches are really not all that bad. (#7698)

Impressive AU53 1839-O Two and a Half

3192 **1839-O AU53 PCGS.** High Date, Wide Fraction, Breen-6152, McCloskey-A, R.3. Although only 17,781 pieces were struck, two die marriages are known for this very scarce Classic Head issue. Luster dominates the peripheries and devices, and the strike is consistent. Unblemished given the grade. Essential for a New Orleans type set, and encased in a green label holder. (#7701)

Gorgeous 1839-O Quarter Eagle, AU58

3193 1839-O AU58 PCGS. High Date, Wide Fraction, Breen-6152, McCloskey-A, R.3. Nearly full luster with frosty light yellow surfaces and only a trace of wear on the hair curls and the eagle's feathers. A desirable piece at this grade level, affordable yet nice. Population: 21 in 58, 22 finer (8/07). (#7701).

LIBERTY QUARTER EAGLES

Conditionally Rare 1840-O Quarter Eagle MS60

3194 1840-O MS60 NGC. Small Mintmark. Typically softly struck for the issue, especially on Liberty's hair and the eagle's left (facing) leg. Pleasing satiny luster and lime-gold coloration occur over both sides. "This date is seldom offered and must be considered rare in any grade", according to Jeff Garrett and Ron Guth (2006). Census: 4 in 60, 12 finer (8/07). (#7720).

Rare AU 1842-C Two and a Half

3195 1842-C AU50 PCGS. Variety 3-B. A nicely struck khaki-gold example of this rare Charlotte quarter eagle issue. A mere 6,729 pieces were struck, and few if any were set aside for numismatic consideration until several decades later. The slightly glossy surfaces are surprisingly void of marks. Population: 5 in 50, 14 finer (7/07). (#7724).

Important 1842-D Quarter Eagle, MS61

3196 1842-D MS61 NGC. Variety 3-F. Only one die marriage is known for the issue, hardly a surprise since a mere 4,643 pieces were struck. This example was an early emission from the dies, since repunching is apparent beneath the bases of the 18 in the date. The strike is pleasantly sharp, with only unimportant softness noted on the shield lines and the curl beneath the ear. Minor, shallow, and mint-made planchet flaws are present near star 12, above the eagle's left (facing) shoulder and head, and beside the R in AMERICA. The borders display bright cartwheel luster, while the fields are mildly prooflike. The surfaces are remarkably free of identifiable marks. Census: 4 in 61, 1 finer (8/07). (#7725).

3197 1842-O XF45 NGC. Writing in 1992, Doug Winter said that the 1842-O quarter eagle "always shows a very weak strike." The present example is not an exception to this observation, and the design details are quite mushy, especially on the eagle. Additional elements of circulation wear and numerous tiny field marks are consistent with the XF grade level. (#7726).

3198 1843 AU50 PCGS. The obverse displays yellow-gold color with blushes of apricot, while the latter color dominates the reverse. Both faces possess generous amounts of luster, and sharp, even definition is visible on the design features. A couple of minute contact marks on the obverse are consistent with the grade. Great overall eye appeal. (#7727).

3199 1843 AU55 ANACS. Peach-gold surfaces retain luster in the recesses, and a well directed strike has left sharp definition on the design elements of this Choice AU quarter eagle. A few minor marks scattered about are not detracting. A challenging issue in this grade, and a true rarity in Mint State. (#7727).

3200 **1843 AU58 NGC.** Well struck with light greenish color and glints of golden luster remaining near the borders. Wispy hairlines are observed in the fields, and a pinscratch is noted just behind Liberty's hair bun that passes between obverse stars 10 and 11, and almost to the rim. Extremely scarce in Mint State. Census: 43 in 58, 17 finer (8/07). (#7727)

3201 **1843-C Large Date, Plain 4—Scratched, Cleaned—ANACS. AU50 Details.** Variety 5-D. Peripheral design details are precisely defined, although the centers are typically struck. Subdued by a chemical cleaning, and a few hair-thin scratches cross the portrait. (#7728)

Series-Key 1843-C Quarter Eagle, AU55

3202 **1843-C Small Date, Crosslet 4 AU55 NGC.** Variety 4-C. The 1843-C Small Date is the lowest mintage Charlotte Mint quarter eagle, and it is significantly scarcer than its Large Date counterpart. As usually seen with this variety, a bold die crack connects the bust tip to the rim, and the nearby field is swollen, courtesy of a failing obverse die. Of the 50-60 coins believed known of this major rarity, only 10-12 AU pieces are estimated to still exist. This slightly glossy example has substantial luster and a couple of moderate marks on the portrait. The obverse is nicely struck while the eagle's center is typically soft. (#7729)

3203 **1843-D Small D—Scratched, Cleaned—ANACS. XF45 Details.** Variety 4-F. A die crack crosses the right border of the first S in STATES. Hairlines appear on the reverse once it is rotated just so, and the obverse is also slightly bright. The cheek and neck have several tiny marks. (#7730)

1843-D Small D Quarter Eagle, AU55

3204 **1843-D Small D AU55 PCGS.** Variety 4-D. The more common small mintmark variety. Traces of luster reside in the recesses of this Choice AU specimen. Peach-gold surfaces display well impressed design features, save for the usual softness on the eagle's neck. A few small marks are located over each side. (#7730)

Rare 1843-O Large Date Quarter Eagle, MS61

3205 **1843-O Large Date, Plain 4 MS61 PCGS.** Liberty's neck is heavily rusted and the mintmark is sharply doubled, both characteristics of this rare and important variety. Most gold specialists agree that only about a dozen Mint State pieces are known. This specimen is fully lustrous with frosty yellow surfaces and sharp design details. A few scattered marks are visible, but the eye appeal is much higher than expected for the grade. Population: 4 in 61, 2 finer (8/07). (#7732)

3206 **1844-D—Improperly Cleaned—NCS. VF Details.** Variety 5-H. Despite the comparatively low mintage of 17,332 pieces, this Dahlonega issue is accessible to many collectors. This unnaturally luminous butter-yellow example exhibits moderate wear overall and faint hairlines in the fields. Still, an affordable representative of Dahlonega gold. (#7736)

Glowing Choice AU 1844-D Quarter Eagle

3207 **1844-D AU55 NGC.** Variety 5-H. While the 1844-D quarter eagle has a mintage of only 17,332 pieces, it is more available in better circulated grades than the production might suggest. This softly radiant yellow-orange piece is well struck overall, though the hair above the ear shows a touch of softness. Scattered abrasions are present in the fields, and a more significant vertical abrasion affects the curl at the center of Liberty's neck. (#7736)

Desirable 1846 AU58 Quarter Eagle

3208 **1846 AU58 NGC.** That fewer than 20 1846 quarter eagles have been graded as Mint State by NGC and PCGS (and none higher than MS63) indicates high-end AU coins, such as the one in this lot, are the finest most collectors can hope to acquire. Yellow-gold surfaces laced with mint-green tints retain a generous amount of luster, and are quite clean for the grade. Sharp definition adorns the design elements, save for the usual softness in the eagle's right (left facing) leg. (#7740)

Overlooked 1846 Two and a Half, AU58

3209 **1846 AU58 PCGS.** The 1846 is an overlooked date among early Coronet quarter eagles. Only 21,598 pieces were struck and few examples were set aside in high grades. Uncirculated pieces are rare indeed, and this pleasing AU58 is about as fine as most collectors will encounter. The surfaces are a bit lackluster, but there are no obvious or detracting abrasions on either side. Sharply defined except, of course, on the eagle's left (facing) leg. Population: 2 in 58, 8 finer (8/07). (#7740)

Lustrous 1846-D Quarter Eagle AU58

3210 **1846-D AU58 NGC.** Variety 7-J. This radiant canary-gold near-Mint example has a few glimpses of rose-red toning. Mint luster is virtually full, and although the centers show the expected moderate incompleteness of strike, actual wear is minimal. A few hair-thin marks near the right-side stars are inconspicuous to the eye. Census: 49 in 58, 13 finer (8/07). (#7742)

Condition Rarity 1847 Quarter Eagle, MS62

3211 **1847 MS62 PCGS.** The 1847 quarter eagle, with a mintage close to 30,000 pieces, is a rare issue in Mint State. Indeed, only about 30 or so examples have rated Mint State by PCGS and NGC, all but one between MS60 and MS63. Rich peach-gold surfaces with pleasing luster are seen on this sharply struck MS62 specimen. A few minor handling marks define the grade. (#7744)

Conditionally Rare 1848 Quarter Eagle MS62

3212 **1848 MS62 NGC.** Boldly struck, save for typical partial weakness on the eagle's neck and left (facing) leg feathers, this pleasing Mint State quarter eagle is lustrous and bright, with wheat-gold and lime-green coloration over both sides. Wispy hairlines and a couple of small abrasions limit the grade. A low-mintage issue; rare in Mint State. Census: 5 in 62, 3 finer (8/07). (#7748)

3213 **1848-C—Scratched, Cleaned—ANACS. XF45 Details.** Variety 9-F. This mid-date Charlotte issue had a low mintage of just 16,788 pieces, and the issue is challenging in AU and better grades. This briefly circulated mustard-gold example displays suspicious luminosity and shows a scratch from Liberty's lips to 9 o'clock on the obverse rim. (#7750)

3214 **1849 AU50 NGC.** An attractive example of this quarter eagle issue of 23,294 pieces, struck in the last year before Philadelphia would receive large quantities of gold from California. Solidly struck with light, even wear and scattered marks on the luminous orange-gold surfaces. (#7752)

Desirable MS62 1849 Two and a Half

3215 **1849 MS62 PCGS.** The 1849 is an unheralded rarity in Mint State, primarily due to its tiny mintage of 23,294 pieces. Far more 1849 gold dollars were struck, since they were needed in commerce to replace hoarded silver coinage. This clean and mildly prooflike example has minor incompleteness of strike on the eagle's leg, and the fields have the expected moderate marks. Population: 4 in 62, 6 finer (8/07). (#7752)

Low Mintage AU55 1849-D Quarter Eagle

3216 1849-D AU55 NGC. Variety 11-M. This is the High Date variant and the more frequently seen of the two varieties. The 1849-D is one of the scarcest D-mint quarter eagles from the 1840s. Of the 10,945 pieces struck, only 115-135 are believed extant today in all grades, the majority of which are VF-XF. This piece is generally well struck, except on the neck of the eagle, and the surfaces display rich reddish patina around the devices. A couple of field marks are located on the obverse. (#7754)

Bright 1850-C Quarter Eagle, AU50, Variety 12-G

3217 1850-C AU50 PCGS. Variety 12-G. Two different reverse dies were used for the coinage of 1850-C quarter eagles. The mintmark is centered over the digit 1 in the fraction on this variety with reverse G. The other reverse has the mintmark centered over the top of the fraction bar. Variety 12-G is slightly more common. Traces of luster reside in the recesses of this bright peach-gold specimen. Well defined, except for softness in the eagle's legs. A couple of hair-thin marks are noted on the obverse. (#7756)

3218 1851-O AU53 ANACS. Breen-6214. The date is repunched southwest. This example has green-gold centers with peripheral ruby-red patina. The eagle's neck and legs are typically defined, and faint hairlines are present. (#7762)

3219 1851-O AU53 NGC. Breen-6214. The date is repunched southwest. An original straw-gold example with an impressively unabraded appearance. The obverse is well struck for the issue, while the eagle's neck and leg show typical blending of detail. (#7762)

3220 1851-O AU55 ANACS. Breen-6214. All four digits in the date are clearly repunched southwest. A good strike for New Orleans quarter eagles of the era, although the eagle's legs and claws show blending of detail. This clean example has few marks and significant glowing luster. (#7762)

3221 1852 MS62 PCGS. A subtly lustrous butter-yellow representative of this quarter eagle issue, one struck during the heyday of the California gold rush. Minimally marked overall, though abrasions are noted in the right obverse field. (#7763)

3222 1852 MS63 PCGS. A pleasing representative from an issue that had its mintage swelled by the gold rush in California. Crisply struck with gleaming, moderately reflective yellow-gold surfaces that show a number of wispy, yet grade-defining abrasions. Population: 55 in 63, 41 finer (8/07). (#7763)

Scarce 1852-C Quarter Eagle AU55

3223 1852-C AU55 NGC. Variety 14-I. A scarce low mintage issue of only 9,772 pieces. This minimally worn example displays light greenish coloration and satiny surfaces that show very few marks of any kind. As usual, the central details are rather indistinct, especially on the eagle. Census: 18 in 55, 30 finer (8/07). (#7764)

3224 1853 MS64 PCGS. Despite a generous mintage of over 1.4 million pieces that was fueled by the California Gold Rush, Mint State examples of the 1853 quarter eagle are elusive. This boldly impressed yellow-orange piece offers strong luster and carefully preserved surfaces. PCGS has graded just five coins finer (8/07). (#7767)

3225 1854-O AU58 PCGS. Unlike many examples of this issue, the near-Mint example offered here has solid detail overall, though the peripheral regions have a sunken appearance. A touch of friction is noted on the highpoints of this radiant straw-gold coin. Population: 19 in 58, 17 finer (7/07). (#7772)

MS60 Details 1855-C Two and a Half

3226 1855-C—Cleaned—ANACS. MS60 Details. Variety 16-I. This low mintage Charlotte gold piece has nary a trace of wear, and the strike is above average, particularly on the portrait. Both fields are hairlined, and a thin strike-through is present above the eagle's head. The reverse is clashed near the eagle's wings, and a die break hugs the lower reverse rim. (#7775)

1857-O Quarter Eagle, AU58
Last O-Mint Quarter Eagle

3227 1857-O AU58 NGC. An example from the last year of quarter eagle production at the New Orleans Mint, made at a time when collecting coins by mintmark was all but unknown: That practice would not take hold until the 1893 of Augustus Heaton's seminal *Mint Marks* reference. Accordingly 1857-O quarter eagles, produced to the extent of only 34,000 pieces, are rare and elusive in Mint State. This piece boasts a bold strike on the obverse, with some reverse weakness on the left (facing) eagle's wing. The orange-gold surfaces show only scant evidence of circulation. (#7784)

Scarce 1858 Select Quarter Eagle

3228 1858 MS63 PCGS. Mint State 1858 quarter eagles are scarce at all levels of preservation. Indeed, PCGS and NGC have graded fewer than 100 Uncirculated examples. Attractive variegated yellow and reddish-gold patina covers both faces of this Select example, complementing lustrous surfaces that exhibit well impressed design elements, save for minor softness in the eagle's leg feathers. A handful of minute marks define the grade. (#7786)

3229 1859 Old Reverse, Type One AU58 NGC. Although the mintage of 39,364 pieces ensures that any 1859 quarter eagle is scarce, the Type One, with large arrowheads, is considerably more difficult than the small arrowheads Type Two. Lustrous orange-gold borders frame the smooth olive-gold fields. Census: 32 in 58, 33 finer (8/07). (#97788)

3230 1860-S AU55 PCGS. Lightly worn with vivid golden color over most of the surfaces and hints of maroon and sky-blue patina near the right portion of the obverse margins. A conditionally scarce issue in any grade above XF. Population: 8 in 55, 20 finer (7/07). (#7793)

3231 1865-S XF45 PCGS. The khaki-gold surfaces are attractively clean on both sides. Moderate wear has occurred across the central devices, but a surprising degree of luster is noted for the grade. Softly struck, as usual. Population: 8 in 45, 22 finer (8/07). (#7802)

3232 1866-S AU53 NGC. Though the 1866-S quarter eagle's mintage greatly eclipses that of its Philadelphia counterpart, its total production falls below 40,000 pieces. This briefly circulated, dusky amber-gold piece shows significant remaining luster in the fields. Census: 17 in 53, 44 finer (8/07). (#7804)

3233 1868 AU50 ANACS. A solidly struck, briefly circulated example of this low-mintage post-war issue. The still-lustrous yellow-orange surfaces show a number of light abrasions that partly define the grade. (#7807)

3234 1868 AU58 NGC. The 1868 is rare in Mint State, from a scant mintage of just 3,625 pieces. This near-Mint example has a pleasingly smooth appearance, with lovely lime and pastel peach accents on each side. It is well struck with only minor highpoint friction and a few tiny marks that appear under magnification. Census: 66 in 58, 19 finer (7/07). (#7807)

3235 1868-S AU55 PCGS. Yellow-gold surfaces display luster in the recesses of this Choice AU specimen. Well struck, except for minor weakness in the eagle's leg feathers. Both faces are relatively clean. (#7808)

3236 1869 AU58 NGC. Ample semi-prooflikeness remains evident in the fields of this khaki-colored near-Mint representative. Wispy hairlines are noted on each side, and a couple of pinscratches are evident in the left reverse field. A scarce, low mintage date that becomes even more challenging in Mint State. Census: 42 in 58, 19 finer (7/07). (#7809)

3237 1869-S AU58 NGC. A well-defined yellow-gold representative of this earlier S-mint quarter eagle, strongly lustrous with only a trace of highpoint friction. One of just 29,500 pieces for the issue. NGC has graded only 16 Mint State examples (8/07). (#7810)

3238 1870-S AU50 PCGS. Boldly struck with minimal highpoint wear and attractive dark-khaki and reddish patina. Only trivial marks and a few wispy hairlines are observed on either side. A low mintage date, scarce at any grade level. Population: 13 in 50, 26 finer (8/07). (#7812)

3239 1871 AU58 PCGS. A modestly reflective gold-orange example that has a hint of highpoint friction. Suitably struck and one of just 5,350 pieces coined. Population: 7 in 58, 23 finer (8/07). (#7813)

3240 1872-S AU55 NGC. The '72-S quarter eagle is decidedly scarce at the Choice AU grade level. This coin has a slight degree of luster remaining, and there are noticeable hairlines in the fields. The surfaces are only slightly abraded, and light khaki-gold color is noted on both sides. Census: 27 in 55, 51 finer (7/07). (#7816)

3241 1873 Open 3 MS64 PCGS. After complaints about the Mint issuing pieces that appeared to be dated 1878 in 1873, the Open 3 logotype went into production. This Choice piece is an attractive example that shows a clear difference between the second and fourth digits. Crisply detailed with lovely luster and few marks on its amber-gold surfaces. (#7817)

3242 1873 Closed 3 MS63 PCGS. Philadelphia coined just 55,200 quarter eagles before the change to the more readable Open 3 logotype. This shining yellow-orange piece displays excellent luster and strong overall detail. Minimally marked for the grade. (#7818)

3243 1873 Closed 3 MS63 PCGS. Well-defined with partly frosty, partly satiny surfaces. The apricot-gold of the fields yields to slightly deeper color on the devices. A lightly abraded, yet pleasing example of the earlier Closed 3 variant. (#7818)

3244 1873-S AU58 NGC. This lemon-gold S-mint quarter eagle gleams despite a touch of highpoint friction on the well struck devices. An enticing representative of this challenging issue, which has a mintage of just 27,000 pieces. (#7820)

3245 1873-S AU58 NGC. Hints of green grace the vibrant sun-gold surfaces of this well struck quarter eagle. Minimally marked, though minor friction is evident on the highpoints on each side. Like all 1873-S quarter eagles, this piece comes from the Closed 3 logotype. Census: 52 in 58, 25 finer (8/07). (#7820)

3246 1874 AU58 PCGS. This is a pleasing near-Mint quarter eagle, with lovely apricot-gold and rose patina and lightly worn surfaces that seem close to Mint State. A few wispy marks are noted on each side. A low mintage issue of just 3,940 business strikes. Population: 9 in 58, 16 finer (7/07). (#7821)

Gleaming 1874 Quarter Eagle, MS61

3247 1874 MS61 PCGS. The modestly reflective sun-gold surfaces show two small copper spots on the obverse rim, one near 4 o'clock and the other just below the first star to the left. Crisply struck and appealing despite a number of wispy abrasions and a line of more significant marks that appears to the left of Liberty's neck. Overall, a high-end survivor from this issue of only 3,920 pieces. Population: 4 in 61, 10 finer (8/07). (#7821)

Fascinating 1875-S Quarter Eagle, MS61

3248 1875-S MS61 NGC. This piece displays satiny luster with attractive brassy-gold color. A few light, scattered abrasions are noted on each side, though a number of these are wispy and the overall eye appeal is suggestive of a finer grade. A pleasing example of this low-mintage issue, which originally consisted of 11,600 pieces. Census: 20 in 61, 8 finer (8/07). (#7823)

Rare Mint State 1875-S Quarter Eagle MS62

3249 1875-S MS62 NGC. Bright satiny luster shines over each side of this scarce San Francisco Mint product. The wheat-gold toning is quite attractive. The design elements are boldly struck, and there are only superficial marks that limit the grade. A scarce low-mintage issue that becomes rare in Mint State. Census: 7 in 62, 1 finer (8/07). (#7823)

3250 1878 MS64 NGC. Intense luster and well-preserved yellow-gold surfaces combine for elegant eye appeal on this lovely post-centennial quarter eagle. Solidly struck with minor luster grazes on the portrait. (#7828)

3251 1878 MS64 PCGS. Soft mint frost and pleasing honey-gold and sunset-orange color are hallmarks of this near-Gem quarter eagle. Well struck with few marks, although a faint abrasion appears at the lower right obverse. A pleasing example of this mid-date Liberty quarter eagle. (#7828)

3252 1880 MS62 PCGS. Lustrous and well struck, with semi-prooflike fields and rich coloration. Several small abrasions are noted on Liberty's cheek and in the fields, preventing a higher grade. A scarce, low mintage issue with only 2,960 pieces produced. Population: 9 in 62, 17 finer (7/07). (#7832)

Singular 1882 Quarter Eagle, MS62 Deep Prooflike

3253 1882 MS62 Deep Prooflike NGC. Reflective surfaces are typical for Mint State examples of the 1882 quarter eagle, an artifact of its tiny mintage of only 4,000 pieces. Still, it is difficult to imagine another piece with the reflectivity of this amazing example. Boldly impressed devices protrude from lightly abraded fields that offer mirror-like intensity, even from a distance. The *only* 1882 quarter eagle certified as Deep Prooflike by NGC, and immensely desirable as such (8/07).

AU58 Sharpness 1885 Quarter Eagle

3254 1885—Altered Surfaces—ANACS. AU58 Details. The 1885 quarter eagle has a mintage of just 800 business strikes and 87 proofs. These mintages are similar to the 1885 double eagle, which sells for approximately ten times the price of its smaller denomination counterpart. This exactingly struck example has only a whisper of friction on the wingtips, eyebrow, and the hair above the ear. The obverse field has been lightly oiled to suggest full luster. The obverse rim has a small spot at 5 o'clock. (#7837)

3255 1886 MS61 Prooflike NGC. Though many examples from this issue of 4,000 pieces show a measure of reflectivity, few have the mirrorlike fields of this flashy honey-gold quarter eagle. Boldly impressed with myriad shallow abrasions that account for the grade. Census: 3 in 61 Prooflike, 2 finer (8/07). (#77838)

3256 1889 MS64 PCGS. Apricot-gold surfaces are imbued with traces of light green, and radiate pleasing luster. A few minute marks keep this well struck coin from full Gem status. Population: 39 in 64, 6 finer (7/07). (#7841)

3257 1891 MS63 PCGS. A flashy peach-gold piece with clean surfaces and a penetrating strike. Prominently die doubled on AMERICA and other right-side design elements, as always on this underappreciated business strike issue. One of only 10,960 pieces coined. (#7843)

3258 1895 MS63 PCGS. This is an attractive Select Mint State example, with bright satiny luster and even straw-gold toning. A couple of small red-orange alloy spots are observed near the reverse periphery, one of which fills the center of "D" in the denomination. A scarce low mintage issue of a mere 6,000 pieces. (#7847)

Elusive Premium Gem 1895 Quarter Eagle

3259 1895 MS66 PCGS. The 1895 quarter eagle had a low mintage of just 6,000 pieces. A fair number of those have survived in Mint State, but mostly in grades of MS60 through MS64. Only 10 have been graded as Premium Gems by PCGS, and none finer, as of (8/07). This example is bright and highly lustrous, with pleasing apricot, lime-green, and reddish coloration. The devices are well struck and surface blemishes are minimal. (#7847)

3260 1896 MS64 PCGS. An original apricot-gold near-Gem that has a needle-sharp strike and the overall appearance of a higher grade. A few minuscule flecks of dark debris reside in design recesses. Encapsulated in a green label holder. (#7848)

3261 1899 MS65 PCGS. A meticulously struck and highly lustrous peach and lime-gold Gem with an exceptionally mark-free reverse. From a low mintage of 27,200 pieces. Housed in an old green label holder. (#7851)

3262 1903 MS63 Prooflike NGC. Exquisitely struck design elements display pleasing contrast with Prooflike fields on this Select quarter eagle. A few wispy handling marks visible under high magnification define the grade. Difficult to obtain in Prooflike condition. Census: 2 in 63 Prooflike, 2 finer (7/07). (#77855)

3263 1904 MS66 NGC. Intense mint luster and lovely apricot-gold and peach toning occur over the flashy surfaces of this sharply struck quarter eagle. Blemish-free with a couple of tiny alloy spots noted on each side. (#7856)

3264 1905 MS64 NGC. An excellent selection for the type collector. This near-Gem, solidly struck with swirling luster, offers delightful wheat-gold and lemon-gold surfaces with a hint of caramel. (#7857)

Ebullient Gem 1905 Quarter Eagle

3265 1905 MS65 PCGS. Mint-green borders encompass the canary-gold centers. This penetratingly struck Gem has vibrant luster and an essentially immaculate reverse. The obverse displays only minimal grazes. A meritorious gold type coin, encapsulated in a green label holder. (#7857)

3266 1907 MS64 NGC. The surfaces of this luminous orange-gold example show subtly lighter shadings on the obverse. Well-defined with excellent eye appeal and only a handful of inoffensive marks. *From The Mario Eller Collection, Part One.* (#7859)

3267 1907 MS66 ★ NGC. The lemon-gold surfaces of this boldly impressed piece display distinctive, radiant luster. An uncommonly fine final-year representative that could find a home in an elite type or date set. (#7859)

PROOF LIBERTY QUARTER EAGLES

Rare 1865 Quarter Eagle
PR63 Deep Cameo

3268 1865 PR63 Deep Cameo PCGS. A few tiny contact marks and faint abrasions are visible in the fields of this pleasing proof. Exceptional contrast on both sides with rich orange color create a high degree of aesthetic appeal. Only 25 proof quarter eagles were coined, and probably just half survive today.

The Smithsonian Institution has a Proof 64 Deep Cameo example that was coined in a medal turn alignment, opposite of the standard coin turn. Most auction catalogs do not indicate the die alignment, although this example is coin turn, thus both alignments were used for proofs.

In addition to the Smithsonian coin and this specimen, others known include the Bass, Trompeter, Eliasberg, Garrett, and Norweb specimens. (#97891)

Radiant Choice Proof 1896 Quarter Eagle

3269 1896 PR64 PCGS. A pinpoint-sharp specimen with flashy fields and rich peach-gold toning. The field above the eagle's head is slightly glossy, but surfaces are nearly unabraded. Encapsulated in an old green label holder. Just 132 proofs were struck. Population: 13 in 64, 14 finer (7/07). (#7922)

1902 Quarter Eagle, PR62

3270 1902 PR62 PCGS. Only 193 proofs were struck of the 1902 quarter eagle. If one can estimate survivorship from the number certified (always a tricky proposition), most of those coins are still extant. This coin is typical of proofs struck from 1902-1904; that is, they were produced with no (or little) contrast between the fields and devices. This piece actually does show a faint bit of contrast on the reverse. The surfaces are bright and light hairlines account for the grade. (#7928)

Deeply Mirrored PR64 1904 Quarter Eagle

3271 1904 PR64 PCGS. Even though the mintage was only 170 pieces with no more than 100 surviving, proofs from 1904 are actually considered a "common" date among late-date Liberty quarter eagles. This is a lovely, brightly reflective example that has rich, reddish tinted orange-gold surfaces. The fields are deeply mirrored and the devices show just a bit of mint frost. Population: 9 in 64, 25 finer (8/07). (#7930)

INDIAN QUARTER EAGLES

3272 1908 MS64 PCGS. Both sides of this solidly struck first-year Pratt quarter eagle offer vibrant luster, and the sun-gold surfaces show only inconsequential marks. Choice and highly appealing. (#7939)

3273 1909 MS63 PCGS. Greenish-gold patina rests on lustrous surfaces, and a well executed strike brings out good detail on the design elements. Some light handling marks are visible in the fields. (#7940)

3274 1909 MS63 NGC. Peach-gold surfaces display traces of light-green color and vibrant luster, and are remarkably well preserved for the grade. A bold strike occurs on the design features. A highly attractive coin for the grade. (#7940)

3275 1910 MS63 NGC. Struck to the extent of 492,000 pieces, the 1910 quarter eagle has shown a good survival rate and is easily found in the lower grades of Mint State. This example is bright and satiny, with nice honey-gold and reddish coloration. A few tiny surface marks are barely discernible with the aid of a magnifier. (#7941)

Delightfully Toned 1910 Quarter Eagle, MS64

3276 1910 MS64 PCGS. Something in the surface treatment of these mattelike Indian Head coins produces the lovely khaki-gold and hazel-gray coloration that is so infrequently found on other earlier series. So it is with this delightful near-Gem, which shows fine-grained golden-orange coloration and tinges of bluish-gray on the lower obverse. The surfaces are distraction-free, save for the usual stray tick or two on the Indian's cheek and obverse field. (#7941)

3277 1911-D—Mount Removed—NCS. AU Details. The BER in LIBERTY is re-engraved, as is the DOLL in DOLLARS, which is opposite. The Indian's face has a thin diagonal pinscratch. The mintmark is faint but unmistakable. Lightly cleaned as well, but a bold example of this low mintage key. (#7943)

Choice AU 1911-D Two and a Half

3278 1911-D AU55 NGC. The mintmark is well outlined if not bold on this key-date example, with further proof coming in the form of the wire rim always seen on the right obverse rim. This greenish-gold example offers delightful luster, with scant wear limited to the highpoints and only a couple of tiny abrasions. (#7943)

AU58 Details 1911-D Quarter Eagle

3279 1911-D—Scratched, Cleaned—ANACS. AU58 Details. The devices are lustrous, although the cheekbone displays faint friction. The Denver mintmark is sharp. The field near the chin has a couple of thin, closely spaced scratches, a pinscratch is concealed within the headdress, and the left reverse field shows a few hairlines. (#7943)

Radiant Near-Mint 1911-D Quarter Eagle

3280 1911-D AU58 NGC. A briefly circulated lemon-gold representative of this oft-trumpeted Indian quarter eagle key, solidly struck with modestly reflective fields. The obverse surfaces show few marks, and only a hint of friction affects each side. An attractive piece with the look of a Mint State example, available for a fraction of the price. (#7943)

Gleaming 1911-D Quarter Eagle, MS61

3281 1911-D MS61 NGC. The 1911-D has the lowest mintage of any Indian quarter eagle issue by far, though its desirability has led to a high certified population and frequent auction appearances, which can distort collectors' perceptions of this desirable key. The shining surfaces of this example are predominantly sun-gold with a touch of canary-yellow on the reverse. Solidly detailed with a bold mintmark, though the obverse shows light, grade-defining abrasions in the fields. (#7943)

Desirable 1911-D Quarter Eagle, MS62

3282 1911-D MS62 NGC. The 1911-D is a noteworthy key for the Indian quarter eagle series, not only for its status as the lowest-mintage issue but for the distance between its production and that of the next-lowest issue. With just 55,680 pieces struck, the 1911-D has a mintage less than one-quarter that of the 1914, a sizable gap.

This subtly lustrous example's lightly abraded surfaces are a particularly vibrant shade of butter-yellow. The devices are boldly impressed, even the three pendants on the obverse, and the overall eye appeal is substantial for the grade. Numismatists who are beginning a date set often are encouraged to purchase the key date first, and for the well-heeled collector interested in the series, this 1911-D quarter eagle would make an excellent cornerstone. (#7943)

Key 1911-D Quarter Eagle, MS62

3283 1911-D MS62 NGC. After "buy the book before the coin," one of the most frequently dispensed pieces of numismatic advice is "buy the key dates first." The logic is that the most challenging issues are the ones most likely to appreciate in value, and that purchasing the most elusive coins first can avoid a common pitfall: the nearly-completed set that stays unfinished because the key date in the grade the collector wants is priced out of reach.

For the collector wishing to buy the key first and set the tone for his or her future set (or the one who took the opposite route), this 1911-D is a strong candidate. The sun-gold surfaces are luminous with a touch of satin, and the devices are well-defined. Light abrasions on and near the portrait account for the grade, though the overall visual appeal is strong. (#7943)

Key-Date 1911-D Weak D, AU53

3284 1911-D Weak D AU53 PCGS. The PCGS insert indicating a "Weak D" mintmark is an understatement! It is not discernible even with a loupe. Fortunately, the ANA Authentication Bureau, in the November 1996 issue of *The Numismatist*, illustrates other diagnostics of this key date. According to the Bureau: "The reverse of genuine specimens is characterized by two areas of die polish. The first—a single scratch—is situated in the deepest recess of the outer edge of the eagle's beak. The second area ... can be found in the recess just to the left of the arrowheads. There you will find several vertical die scratches." Both of these diagnostics are visible under high magnification on this AU53 example, the first (outer edge of the beak), being most apparent. Peach-gold color adorns both sides, and aside from light highpoint wear, the design elements are sharply defined. A few minor marks are not worthy of individual mention. (#7954)

1911-D Weak D Two and a Half, AU53

3285 1911-D Weak D AU53 NGC. The outlines of the D mintmark are barely distinguishable and, of course, of tantamount importance to collectors as the key date of the series. Further confirmation is provided by the wire rim always seen on the right obverse. Both sides show considerable luster, with brownish-gold highlights. (#7954)

3286 1912 MS63 NGC. The surfaces of this Select Mint State quarter eagle display pleasing khaki-gold color, with champagne accents noted in the reverse fields and near the periphery. A few trivial blemishes are found on each side. (#7944)

3287 1912 MS63 NGC. The lime-green and peach surfaces are illuminated by full satin luster. The design elements are well executed. A mere handful of trivial nicks are noted on each side, making the MS63 grade seem conservative. (#7944)

3288 1913 MS64 PCGS. This near-Gem exhibits shining luster and pleasing detail. The vibrant yellow-gold surfaces show small splashes of orange, particularly near the center of the obverse. An attractive example of this P-mint quarter eagle. (#7945)

3289 1914 MS61 NGC. A satiny example with an unblemished obverse and a few concealed marks on the reverse field. A low mintage Indian quarter eagle that becomes desirable in Mint State. (#7946)

3290 **1914 MS62 NGC.** The satiny orange-gold surfaces of this unworn piece show fewer notable marks than usual for the grade assigned. A pleasing, comparatively affordable example of this lower-mintage Indian quarter eagle issue. (#7946)

3291 **1914 MS62 NGC.** After the widely known 1911-D issue, the 1914 is the second most challenging of the Indian quarter eagles, with a mintage of only 240,000 pieces. This crisply struck sun-gold piece displays faint abrasions and considerable radiance. (#7946)

3292 **1914 MS62 PCGS.** The sun-gold obverse contrasts with the luminous reverse, which shows slightly deeper color. A solidly struck and appealing example of this Wilson-era quarter eagle issue. (#7946)

Attractive 1914 Quarter Eagle, MS63

3293 **1914 MS63 NGC.** The 1914 quarter eagle is considered the second most challenging Indian quarter eagle by many, particularly in XF and better grades. This well-defined Select example offers uncommonly high visual appeal. The fields, lemon-gold with a touch of green, have uncommonly strong luster. While both sides show grade-defining marks, these are typically pinpoint flaws, and the obverse is the superior side. An enticing example for the date collector. (#7946)

Colorful, Lustrous MS64 1914 Two and a Half

3294 **1914 MS64 PCGS.** The production of quarter eagles in this first year of World War I was a generous 240,000 coins, and pieces are widely available up to the MS63 grade level. This piece offers softly glowing luster over the antique-gold surfaces, which reveal a single nick beneath the Indian's chin as one of the few mentionable distractions. PCGS has certified only 46 coins finer (8/07). (#7946)

3295 **1914-D MS63 PCGS.** A boldly impressed lemon-gold example of this D-mint quarter eagle issue, Select with uncommonly vibrant luster. Faint, scattered abrasions in the fields account for the grade. (#7947)

3296 **1914-D MS63 NGC.** Bright luster issues from peach-gold colored surfaces that show a splash or two of apricot on the reverse. Well struck, with just a few minor marks. (#7947)

Delightful MS64 1914-D Quarter Eagle

3297 **1914-D MS64 PCGS.** A delightful khaki-gold and hazel-gray piece, near to a Gem grade and displaying scant evidence of contact. The strike is somewhat soft on the lower headdress feathers, but this is otherwise an appealing example of this fairly available issue, and one that is seldom seen in a finer grade. PCGS has certified only 36 pieces finer (8/07). (#7947)

Sharply Struck 1914-D Near-Gem Quarter Eagle

3298 **1914-D MS64 PCGS.** Brassy-gold surfaces display hints of light tan, along with pleasing luster. The strike on this near-Gem is above average, as the eagle's shoulder and leg feathers are much better defined than typically seen on the issue. We note a few unobtrusive handling marks, as well as a couple of tiny green specks. (#7947)

3299 **1915 MS63 NGC.** This Select quarter eagle exhibits attractive honey-gold patina imprinted with traces of light tan. The design elements are in receipt of an attentive strike, as relatively strong delineation occurs in the Indian's hair and headdress and on the eagle's plumage. A few minute handling marks prevent a higher grade. (#7948)

3300 **1915 MS64 PCGS.** A lustrous apricot-gold near-Gem with smooth fields and only a hint of an incomplete strike on the crevices of the lowest headdress feather. The last of the Philadelphia issues until 1926. (#7948)

3301 **1925-D MS64 NGC.** This near-Gem possesses an excellent strike on both sides, each of which gives off soft luster from apricot-gold surfaces that are imbued with traces of light green. A few minor marks in the raised exposed fields limit the grade. (#7949)

3302 **1925-D MS64 PCGS.** Much of this Roaring Twenties D-mint quarter eagle is sun-gold with elements of orange, while parts of each side are mint-green. Pleasingly detailed overall with vibrant luster, few marks, and excellent eye appeal. (#7949)

3303 **1925-D MS64 PCGS.** Sharp design elements and surprising mint frost are the main draws of this enticing yellow-gold near-Gem. A delightful example of this popular Roaring Twenties issue. (#7949)

3304 **1925-D MS64 NGC.** Uncommonly clean for the grade with enticing luster and shimmering amber-gold surfaces. A well-defined example from the issue that marked the return of the denomination after a decade-long hiatus. (#7949)

Exuberant 1925-D Two and Half MS65

3305 **1925-D MS65 PCGS.** The 1925-D is one of only three Denver Mint issues in the Indian quarter eagle series. The other two coins are the 1914-D and the key-date 1911-D. With a mintage of 578,000 coins, the 1925-D quarter eagle is considered a common coin in all grades with the exception of Gem and finer. To illustrate this point, PCGS has graded a mere 28 pieces finer than MS65 and none have graded higher than MS66. Nonetheless, the 1925-D quarter eagle is obtainable in Gem condition with a bit of patience and, as such, is popular with collectors as a type coin. This is a fully struck example that is highly lustrous and covered with rich red-gold patina. (#7949)

3306 **1926 MS64 PCGS.** A satiny almond-gold piece that has dusky apricot toning and only minor blending of detail within the headdress. Gold coins had left circulation by 1926, but quarter eagles were requested by banks to meet souvenir demand. (#7950)

3307 **1926 MS64 PCGS.** This Choice sun-gold representative has uncommonly strong luster for the issue and an obverse that approaches Gem quality. Well-defined with a graze present behind the eagle's head. A pleasing piece from the first P-mint quarter eagle issue in over a decade. (#7950)

3308 **1926 MS64 NGC.** A luminous apricot-gold representative of this Roaring Twenties quarter eagle issue, well-defined overall with excellent eye appeal for the grade. If not for a faint flaw on the cheek, this piece could make a claim for Gem status. (#7950)

3309 **1926 MS64 NGC.** Pleasing detail and shining straw-gold surfaces enhance the visual appeal of this appealingly preserved Choice quarter eagle. A lovely example from the first Philadelphia issue of the denomination since 1915. (#7950)

3310 **1926 MS64 NGC.** The lemon-gold surfaces of this Roaring Twenties quarter eagle are pleasingly preserved for the grade. A well-defined representative that has soft, swirling luster on the obverse and a slightly more metallic appearance on the reverse. (#7950)

Undisturbed 1926 Two and a Half MS65

3311 **1926 MS65 PCGS.** This satiny gold type coin features original khaki-gold toning, and the strike is crisp with only minor blending of detail on the lowest headdress plume. Philadelphia Mint Quarter eagle and eagle production resumed in 1926 after an 11-year gap. Housed in a green label holder. (#7950)

3312 **1927 MS64 PCGS.** A yellow-orange later Indian quarter eagle that displays uncommonly strong luster on both sides. Minimally marked with excellent overall detail, though the lowest pendant on the Indian's necklace is a touch soft. One of 388,000 pieces coined. (#7951)

3313 **1929 MS64 PCGS.** Highly lustrous with minor marks in the obverse fields. This solidly struck wheat-gold near-Gem has delicate honey-colored highlights on each side. A pleasing example from the final year of the denomination. (#7953)

Condition Scarcity 1929 Gem Quarter Eagle

3314 **1929 MS65 PCGS.** Despite the generous mintage of more than one-half million pieces, the 1929 quarter eagle is surprisingly difficult to locate in full Gem level of preservation. This MS65 specimen possesses nice luster and well struck devices. The peach-gold surfaces reveal just a few minor grade-consistent handling marks. (#7953)

High-End PR64 1909
'Roman Finish' Quarter Eagle

3315 1909 PR64 NGC. The so-called "Roman Finish" proofs of 1909 and 1910 are widely misunderstood, almost a hundred years after their manufacture. The matte proofs that were released in 1908 proved unpopular, and the mint sought to appease the collecting public. In 1909 and 1910, instead of finishing the coins with a sandblast surface, they struck proofs with special dies on special planchets, but with no sandblasting after striking. In other words, from untreated planchets. The result was a product that was even more unpopular with contemporary collectors than the matte finish. Proofs from these years were easily confused with business strikes. The detail, of course, is profoundly sharper than seen on any business strike. Most Roman Finish proofs have a bright yellow-gold surface but some, like this coin, have taken on a deeper, reddish hue. The recesses of the design show a lovely, contrasting lilac color. The surfaces do not show any mentionable or even noticeable "shiny spots" or contact marks. A faint line encircles the rims, probably a result of ejection from the dies. The 1909 is the scarcest proof issue from the 1908-1915 series. Of the 139 pieces struck only 55-65 are believed known today in all grades. (#7958)

3316 1854—Cleaned—ANACS. AU53 Details. A well struck, lightly worn example of this first-year odd-denomination gold issue. A number of parallel hairlines appear in the straw-gold fields, though the margins retain a semblance of original luster. (#7969)

3317 1854 AU55 NGC. Light but distinct wear appears on the uppermost areas of the devices on each side of this well struck Choice AU piece. An attractive example of this first-year issue, yellow-orange with ample remaining luster. (#7969)

3318 1854 AU55 PCGS. A still-lustrous first-year piece that shows light but distinct wear at the highpoints of the portrait. Few marks are present on the wheat-gold surfaces, and the coin would make an excellent addition to a similarly graded type or date set. (#7969)

Uncirculated 1854 Three Dollar

3319 1854 MS61 PCGS. This lustrous gold type coin has rich orange toning, and is clean for the grade aside from moderate contact on the left-side cotton leaves. The introductory 1854 is popular as a single-year type, since DOLLARS is in much larger letters on the 1855 and later dates. (#7969)

First-Year-Of-Issue 1854 Three Dollar, MS62

3320 1854 MS62 NGC. The first year of issue for the three dollar gold series. This MS62 specimen displays lustrous brassy-gold surfaces tinted with hints of light tan, and the design elements are well impressed throughout. Light grease streaks are visible in the right obverse, and both sides are clashmarked. A few wispy obverse marks are noted. (#7969)

Lustrous 1854 Select Three Dollar

3321 **1854 MS63 NGC.** While it is a commonplace to lump the 1854 in the same category as the 1878 and 1874, it is in circulated grades and the lower grades of Mint State that this applies. In MS63, this is an uncommon item. This coin exhibits rich mint luster, bright yellow-gold color, a good strike, and is just a few inconsequential marks away from an even higher grade. (#7969)

1854-O Three Dollar Gold AU Details

3322 **1854-O—Mount Removed—NCS. AU Details.** Well detailed with light khaki-gold coloration and semi-reflective fields. Wispy hairlines are noted on each side, along with a large abrasion below the mintmark, where a jewelry mount was removed. An affordable example of the only three dollar gold issue from the New Orleans Mint. (#7971)

Elusive 1854-O Three Dollar AU53

3323 **1854-O AU53 PCGS.** Liberty's hair and the corn stalks show moderate wear, but luster glints from the devices, particularly the plums and LIBERTY. The date is slightly soft, as is it opposite the relatively high relief portrait. Unlike many '54-O examples, no planchet flaws or strike-throughs are present. Population: 42 in 53, 50 finer (8/07). (#7971)

Choice AU 1854-O Three Dollar

3324 **1854-O AU55 PCGS.** Light highpoint friction limits the grade but not the eye appeal. No marks require singular mention. As is often the case for this solitary New Orleans issue, the obverse field near the border has a few shallow and inconspicuous mint-made strike-throughs. Housed in a green label holder. (#7971)

Splendid 1855 Three, MS64

Glowing 1855 Three Dollar, MS64

3325 **1855 MS64 PCGS.** Nearly Gem quality, this brilliant three has frosty yellow luster with hints of pale orange toning. The plumes of the headdress and the ribbon bow at the bottom of the wreath are both weakly defined. Although the mintage of 50,555 coins is third highest in the entire series, examples seldom appear in the better Mint State grades. Dave Bowers writes that "enough 1855 threes survive that examples are available in just about any desired grade up through and including lower Mint State ranges. However, coin for coin the 1855 is much more elusive than the 1854. Choice coins MS63 or finer are rare, and only a few true Gems are known." Population: 18 in 64, 4 finer (8/07). (#7972)

3326 **1855 MS64 PCGS.** The 1855 three dollar, coming off of a mintage of 50,555 circulation strikes, is available through the MS62 level of preservation. Select examples are more challenging, near-Gems quite scarce, and Gem-quality pieces are extremely rare.

The near-Gem coin presented in this lot displays glowing luster radiating from peach-gold surfaces that are imbued with traces of mint-green. A well executed strike brings out sharp detail on the design features, save for minor softness on the bowknot. A few minor obverse ticks preclude full Gem classification. Population: 17 in 64, 4 finer (8/07). (#7972)

3327 **1856 XF40 ANACS.** The mintage of three dollar gold pieces at Philadelphia fell from the six-figure mintage of 1854 to just 26,010 examples in 1856. This lightly worn amber-gold example offers glints of luster at the margins and slightly deeper color near the devices. (#7974)

3328 **1856—Scratched—ANACS. AU55 Details.** A boldly struck example with minor highpoint wear and bountiful butter-gold luster. A long-ago authenticity test has left a small X on the field near the profile, and close study locates a number of faint marks concealed within the hair. (#7974)

3329 1856 AU55 PCGS. Just two years after the denomination made its debut with a six-figure mintage, Philadelphia struck only 26,010 three dollar gold pieces. This still-shining amber-gold piece shows a measure of light wear on Liberty's upper hair and the feathers, with a similar effect on the wreath. (#7974)

3330 1856-S VF25 NGC. Medium S. A collectible branch mint three dollar gold piece. The olive-gold surfaces are surprisingly unabraded, and although Liberty's hair is worn, all legends are bold. (#7975)

Elusive 1856-S MS61 Three Dollar

3331 1856-S MS61 NGC. The typically encountered '56-S three dollar coin is apt to grade VF or XF, reflecting the fact that these coins circulated extensively in the channels of commerce. David Bowers, in his *United States $3 Gold Pieces* book, estimates that only 10 to 15 Mint State examples are extant. NGC and PCGS have graded nearly 30 Uncirculated specimens, some of which are likely to be resubmissions.

The yellow-gold surfaces of this MS61 example display a nearly unbroken luster flow. A sharp strike manifests itself in strong definition on the design elements, save for the usual softness in some of the curls of Liberty's hair. Some light handling marks are scattered over each side. Census: 8 in 61, 11 finer (8/07). (#7975)

Well Struck 1857 Three Dollar, MS62

3332 1857 MS62 NGC. With a mintage of 20,891 pieces, the 1857 three dollar certainly cannot be classed as a common issue. However, fewer than a hundred pieces are believed known today in the various grades of Uncirculated. Coins in the MS62 category, such as this one, are the most frequently encountered, and probably represent the best value. The reddish-gold surfaces show a number of small abrasions on each side that account for the grade. An attentive strike brings out sharp definition on the design elements. Census: 32 in 62, 19 finer (8/07). (#7976)

3333 1858—Scratched—NCS. AU Details. This briefly circulated golden-brown better date three dollar gold piece has a series of wispy pinscratches on the cheek, and further pinscratches are found near OF, behind the bust, and on the reverse border near 1, 5, and 6 o'clock. A scant 2,133 business strikes were struck. (#7978)

3334 1860—Improperly Cleaned—NCS. Unc. Details. The fields are hairlined, but this boldly struck representative exhibits bright luster throughout the legends and design crevices. Only 7,036 business strikes were coined. (#7980)

Challenging 1860 Three Dollar, MS62

3335 1860 MS62 NGC. The 1860 three dollar, with a circulation strike mintage of 7,036 pieces, is difficult to locate in Mint State. Attractive apricot-gold color adorns both faces, each of which exhibits sharply impressed design elements. The luster flow is generally uninterrupted by the tiny handling marks evenly scattered over each side. Census: 15 in 62, 19 finer (7/07). (#7980)

Noteworthy 1862 Three Dollar Gold, MS61

3336 1862 MS61 NGC. A high-end survivor from this Civil War odd-denomination issue, which has a mintage of just 5,750 business strikes. The yellow-orange piece offered here is luminous with pleasing detail, though the fields show myriad scattered abrasions that contribute to the grade. Census: 15 in 61, 28 finer (8/07). (#7983)

Elusive 1862 Select Three Dollar

3337 1862 MS63 PCGS. David Bowers, in his three dollar gold reference book, says the 1862 issue is very elusive in all grades, and estimates 30 to 40 Mint State coins to be extant. Peach-gold surfaces display partially prooflike fields, especially on the reverse. A sharp strike is seen throughout, and a handful of minute marks define the grade. Population: 8 in 63, 16 finer (8/07). (#7983)

3338 1864—Cleaned—ANACS. AU55 Details. A bright example with faintly hairlined fields. The date is lightly repunched. An elusive Civil War date with a low mintage of 2,630 pieces. (#7985)

Challenging 1864 Three Dollar MS62

3339 1864 MS62 NGC. This Civil War three dollar gold piece is from a low mintage of 2,824 coins. Luster dominates protected areas, and the surfaces are splendidly void of marks. The 18 in the date is repunched. A good value relative to comparatively plentiful dates, such as the 1878. Census: 7 in 62, 13 finer (7/07). (#7985)

Low-Mintage 1868 Three Dollar, MS62

3340 1868 MS62 NGC. The low-mintage 1868 three dollar (4,850 circulation strikes) is found mostly in circulated grades, and has perhaps fewer than 100 pieces in Mint State, mostly MS60 to MS62. Peach and yellow-gold lustrous surfaces exhibit sharply struck motifs. A few obverse handling marks preclude a higher grade. Census: 24 in 62, 15 finer (8/07).
From The Diemer L. Fife Collection. (#7989)

Rare 1870 Three Dollar, MS61

3341 1870 MS61 NGC. The 1870 three dollar (3,500 business strikes), is rare in all grades, but especially so in Mint State. To date, NGC and NGC have certified 55 Uncirculated examples, none above MS64! Semi-prooflike surfaces on this MS61 specimen yield peach-gold patina with light green tints, along with well brought up design elements. Numerous light handling marks account for the grade. Census: 13 in 61, 9 finer (8/07). (#7991)

Desirable 1872 Three, AU55

3342 1872 AU55 NGC. An elusive date, often one of the last issues obtained by specialists who collect the three dollar gold pieces. Delightful honey-gold surfaces exhibit considerable reflectivity in the fields. Light wear is consistent with the grade, and the aesthetic appeal is excellent. (#7994)

3343 1874—Cleaned—ANACS. AU53 Details. This lightly hairlined chestnut-gold type coin continues to exhibit flashy luster from selected areas. An interesting strike-through is found on the reverse near 10 o'clock. (#7998)

3344 1874—Cleaned—ANACS. MS60 Details. This unworn type piece is pleasingly detailed overall, though the knot of the bow shows slight softness and roughness. The unnaturally reflective yellow-gold surfaces show numerous faint flaws. (#7998)

Pleasing 1874 Three Dollar, MS62

3345 1874 MS62 NGC. The 1874 three dollar piece, with a mintage of 41,800 circulation strikes, is plentiful today, with a relatively high number of the certified population in the AU and Mint State grade categories. A well directed strike sharpens the design elements, save for the usual softness on some of the hair curls and the bowknot. Bright luster exudes from brassy-gold surfaces that reveal some wispy handling marks under magnification. A pleasing coin overall. (#7998)

Lustrous 1874 Select Three Dollar

3346 1874 MS63 NGC. With a mintage of 41,800 bushiness strikes, the 1874 three dollar is relatively plentiful today. This Select representative displays glowing luster and well impressed design features, except for the usual softness on the bowknot. A scattering of light ticks limits the grade. (#7998)

3347 1878—Reverse Cleaned—ANACS. MS60 Details. A piece that displays beautifully, this well struck type example has swirling luster and pleasing wheat-gold obverse surfaces. By contrast, the mustard-gold fields of the reverse are dulled from cleaning. (#8000)

Shining 1878 Three Dollar Gold, MS62

3348 1878 MS62 PCGS. The shining surfaces of this predominantly lemon-gold example display elements of pale emerald. Well-defined with no trace of wear, though the fields show a number of luster grazes and a few more significant abrasions. Nonetheless, a desirable representative of this ever-popular odd-denomination type issue. (#8000)

Sharp 1878 Three Dollar, MS64

3349 1878 MS64 PCGS. Rich yellow and orange-gold patina is laced with mint-green, and lays over highly lustrous surfaces. A well directed strike leaves strong impressions on the design features, which reveal a degree of contrast with the semi-prooflike fields. Both sides are generally well preserved. (#8000)

Radiant 1878 Three Dollar, MS64

3350 1878 MS64 PCGS. Jeff Garrett and Ron Guth (2006) write that the 1878 three dollar is the most common date of the series. The several thousand pieces certified by PCGS and NGC tends to corroborate the authors' contention. Radiant luster exudes from apricot-gold surfaces of this near-Gem example, and a well directed strike brings about sharp definition on the motifs, save for the usually-seen soft lower wreath. Some minor handling marks define the grade. (#8000)

Enticing Near-Mint 1879 Three Dollar Gold

3351 **1879 AU58 ANACS.** From a tiny issue of 3,000 pieces comes this attractive, briefly circulated golden beauty. The fields show warm luster and an attractive blend of yellow-gold and orange, the latter more prevalent on the obverse. The central devices are boldly impressed with just a trace of friction on the highpoints. A delightful example that offers more visual appeal than a number of Mint State representatives. (#8001)

Low Mintage 1879 Three Dollar MS61

3352 **1879 MS61 PCGS.** Although it had a 36-year history, the three-dollar denomination never really caught on like other gold denominations. Only ten issues saw an annual production exceeding 10,000 coins. This makes for a challenging series today. In 1879, for example, just 3,000 business strikes were produced. This is a gorgeous example for the grade with rich orange-gold color and satiny luster. The fields are lightly reflective on both sides with hints of cameo contrast. Housed in a green label holder. (#8001)

3353 **1882—Damaged—NCS. AU Details.** Lightly bent from a dull, depressed mark above the 3 in the denomination. Considerable luster brightens the lettering despite moderate wear on the wreath and portrait. A mere 1,500 business strikes were issued, along with 76 proofs. (#8004)

Lovely Prooflike 1883 Three Dollar, AU58

3354 **1883 AU58 NGC.** Although a small hoard of these coins was found in the late 1930s and another in the 1960s, this extremely low-mintage date remains difficult to find today. Just 900 business strikes and 89 proofs were coined. This is a lovely prooflike example with excellent eye appeal. The surfaces are vivid greenish-gold with attractive lilac toning at the upper obverse. Census: 22 in 58, 55 finer (10/05). (#8005)

3355 **1886 AU55 ICG.** The three dollar gold denomination continued its death spiral through the 1880s, and in 1886, the business strike mintage was just 1,000 pieces. This Choice AU example shows reflective yellow-orange surfaces with minor highpoint wear and a degree of haze in the fields. Minimally marked and pleasing. (#8008)

3356 **1886—Cleaned—ANACS. AU58 Details.** Only slight wear is present on Liberty's curls, but the semi-prooflike fields are faintly hairlined. Still a collectible souvenir of this ultra-low mintage issue. A mere 1,000 business strikes were coined. (#8008)

MS62 Prooflike 1886 Three Dollar

3357 **1886 MS62 Prooflike NGC.** Three dollar gold pieces from near the series' end—1889—are frequently found with prooflike surfaces, as the mintages were so small that the prooflike characteristics remained in the die past the end of striking. Furthermore, in many years including this one, the business strikes were manufactured from the same die used for the proofs. This piece—from an emission of 1,000 coins—offers deep orange-gold coloration with lighter yellow-gold in the protected areas around the periphery. Some light field chatter on each side precludes a finer grade, but considerable eye appeal is present. Census: 9 in 62 Prooflike, 2 finer (8/07). (#78008)

Pleasing 1888 Three Dollar, AU58

3358 1888 AU58 NGC. This high-end AU three dollar piece displays pleasing field-motif contrast, and is sharply struck, except for minor softness in the leaves left of the bowknot. Reddish-gold patina bathes both sides, each of which reveals ample luster and just a few minor circulation marks. Very pleasing in all respects. (#8010)

Lustrous and Colorful MS64 1888 Three Dollar

3359 1888 MS64 PCGS. The three dollar series abounds with low mintages, and many of those coins have not survived. While the mint struck only 5000 business strikes in 1888, enough of them remain today in Mint State condition so that their price is equal to coins from 1874 or 1878, which had substantially larger mintages. Thus, type collectors can obtain a much scarcer coin for the same price as a more common coin from these years. This piece displays thick mint luster and each side has alternating areas of rose and lilac patina. Sharply defined. (#8010)

Elusive 1889 MS61 Three Dollar

3360 1889 MS61 PCGS. Coming from a mintage of 2,300 business strikes, 1889 three dollar Mint State coins are elusive (David Bowers, *United States $3 Gold Pieces*). This MS61 example offers deep tangerine-gold surfaces, with good luster, and is sharply struck. Some faint hairlines and minute contact marks account for the grade. Certified in a green-label holder. (#8011)

Sharply Struck 1889 Three Dollar, MS62

3361 1889 MS62 NGC. This MS62 three dollar gold specimen yields a relatively high degree of field-motif contrast when it is tilted beneath a light source. The design elements have benefited from a sharp strike, and the yellow-gold surfaces reveal a few minute contact marks scattered about. A hair-thin mark is visible on Liberty's neck. *From The Diemer L. Fife Collection.* (#8011)

Attractive 1889 Three Dollar, MS64

3362 1889 MS64 PCGS. In this last year of the three dollar gold denomination, the mintage fell to 2,300 coins. Jeff Garrett and Ron Guth (2006), however, write that: "... a high percentage of the coins survived, mostly in Mint State, reflective of the increase in the number of collectors in America and the demand for the series." Luster dances about the apricot-gold and greenish tinted surfaces of this near-Gem example, and the design elements are strongly impressed. Minute obverse handling marks preclude full Gem classification. Population: 43 in 64, 35 finer (8/07). (#8011)

Cameo Proof 1871 Three, PR63

3363 **1871 PR63 Cameo NGC.** Although 30 proofs were minted, few have survived. Although Dave Bowers estimated 15 to 20 known proofs, we believe the true number of survivors may be around 10 coins, including the Eliasberg PR65, the Trompeter PR64, The Smithsonian Institution PR64 Cameo, the Bass Collection proof, the Garrett Collection proof, and the Norweb impaired proof. Few other auction records exist, and only 18 submissions to NGC and PCGS have been certified. This lovely Cameo proof has excellent contrast with rich greenish-gold surfaces and deeply mirrored fields. A few scattered marks can be seen on each side. Census: 3 in 63, 0 finer (8/07). (#88034)

3364 **1886 PR64 Cameo NGC.** Discussing the 1886 three dollar piece in his *United States $3 Gold Pieces* book, David Bowers writes: "Proofs were made in the largest quantity to date in the series and are therefore easy to find, with market appearances being fairly frequent." Bowers estimates 80 to 100 of these coins are extant today.

The near-Gem Cameo specimen in this lot displays a striking gold-on-black appearance when the coin is observed from a direct overhead angle. A solid strike emboldens all of the design features, and both sides are covered with rich apricot-gold. The reverse is rotated about 30 degrees counterclockwise. A few inoffensive slidemarks on the cheek and handling marks in the fields preclude full Gem status. Nonetheless, this coin projects great technical quality and aesthetic appeal. Census: 36 in 64 Cameo, 17 finer (8/07). (#88050)

Exquisite PR66 Cameo 1879 Flowing Hair Stella

3365 **1879 Flowing Hair, Judd-1635, Pollock-1833, R.3, PR66 Cameo NGC.** The successful introduction of a more unlikely coin is difficult to conceive. The 1879- and 1880-dated four dollar gold coins, or stellas, were a pet project of the Hon. John Adam Kasson (1822-1910) of Des Moines, Iowa, "envoy extraordinary and minister plenipotentiary" to Austria-Hungary from 1877 to 1881. Kasson's international background in the multicultural Hapsburg empire undoubtedly played a large role in his proposal for an international coin. (Kasson would later, in 1884 and 1885, serve as foreign minister to Germany. His record also includes various terms as U.S. Representative from Iowa between 1867 and 1884, as well as his 1878 attempt to enlist U.S. support for equal rights for various underprivileged classes of society in Romania and Serbia).

It helped that Kasson was the former chairman of the House Committee on Coinage, Weights, and Measures. At the beginning of 1879 Kasson, through his ally Alexander H. Stephens, then-chairman of the same committee, contacted Treasury Secretary John Sherman, asking that the Mint supply pattern pieces:

> *Will you please have a specimen or specimens, say five, of this coin struck? The obverse design similar to that of a double eagle = 6G. .3S. .7C., 7 grams — 1879.*
>
> *The reverse — "United States of America. Four Dollars. E pluribus unum. Deo est gloria," and a large star emblazoned, in the words, 'One stella, 400 cents' ... .*
>
> *All over the world this will show the intrinsic measure and value of the coin, and exhibit its remarkable adaptation to use as an international coin.* (Pollock, *United States Patterns and Related Issues*).

A chief aim of Kasson was to recommend international coinage that would assist Americans in foreign trade and travel, by alleviating inconveniences in making transactions in various currencies. The proposed four dollar coin would approximate the value of eight Austrian (and Dutch) florins, of 20 French francs, of 20 Italian lire, and of 20 Spanish pesetas.

But facilitating international travel was not Kasson's sole purpose. Kasson was closely connected with Western silver mining interests in the United States and their congressional allies, including Reps. Richard P. "Silver Dick" Bland and William Darrah Kelley, all of whom were highly desirous to see expanded domestic and international uses of silver. Kasson's proposal included a "quintuple stella" or twenty dollar gold piece, along with the stella, both of which were to be in "metric gold," and a silver dollar made of Dr. Wheeler Hubbell's "goloid" alloy—silver with about 4% gold content. Mint personnel also abetted Kasson's cause, remembering his help in overcoming objections in 1864 to introduction of the bronze cent.

And so was born the most unlikely of numismatic curiosities: a four dollar coin with a five-pointed star, with six nominal grams of gold and a seventh of alloy, not exactly worth eight florins. A fatal flaw was that the *value of the stella was not precisely that of any of those international measures,* so that transactions made in stellas would require change to be made. Another flaw is that the above-mentioned foreign currencies, just as today's, fluctuate against one another. With no fixed reference point (other than the nameplate value of four U.S. dollars and its content, purportedly six grams of alloyed gold), the stella offered no particular advantage in international commerce over the half eagle or any other U.S. gold coin.

Breen's *Complete Encyclopedia* lists "originals" without planchet striations, but comments that none have been offered in many years. Pollock lists two different metallic compositions—one of standard 90% gold/10% alloy, and another so-called "metric alloy" consisting of 6/7ths gold, 1/7 alloy. Some researchers have professed their belief that the "original" 1879 Flowing Hair patterns were struck in the metric alloy, with the larger number of restrikes of standard composition. The Pollock pattern reference under the "1879 metric dollar" says, "Tom DeLorey notes that 'the term 'metric alloy' refers to the awkward alloy necessary to make a coin of 25 grams, the weight of a French 5 francs, rather than an alloy that was 'metric' or base 10 in nature." Presumably the stella, purportedly an even 7 grams in weight, also was considered "metric," as were the quintuple stella and the "metric goloid" dollars, all supposedly struck in even gram weights.

Despite all the hullabaloo about metric coinage, it is highly doubtful that these proposed stellas were ever struck on anything other than the standard 90/10 gold coinage planchets. The planchet striations seen on all known gold stellas serve as virtual confirmation that the stella planchets, almost the same diameter as a half eagle, were produced by rolling out planchet stock 80% of the thickness of a half eagle planchet. The striations or "roller marks" in the center highpoints remained unstruck, due to the planchet thinness.

The four dollar stella is one of the most desirable of U.S. coins, and is featured in Garrett and Guth's *The 100 Greatest U.S. Coins.* The "original" mintage of the 1879 Flowing Hair stellas was supplemented, likely in 1880, by "restrikes." As far as is known, the so-called originals and restrikes are indistinguishable one from another—although the originals are reputed to lack die striations, and/or to feature the "metric" alloy—and the total mintage is estimated variously from 425 to as high as 800 pieces. The present PR66 Cameo piece is one of 20 pieces so graded at NGC, with eight Cameo pieces finer. Adding the PCGS Cameo pieces brings the total to 27 coins at both services, with 10 pieces finer (10/06). This is a spectacular, deeply mirrored coin that shows a significant amount of mint frost over the devices, which yields strong cameo contrast. The surfaces are a rich orange-gold, and there are no noticeable contact marks on either side of this remarkable specimen. One of the most attractive and eye appealing stellas extant of this curious and widely sought-after issue. (#88057)

1799 Large Stars Reverse, XF Details
BD-5, High R.5 Half Eagle

3366 1799 Large Stars Reverse—Improperly Cleaned—NCS. XF Details. BD-5, High R.5. The variety is confirmed by a wide date with the last 9 recut on the lower right, the left foot of the last A in AMERICA touching the claw, with the right foot touching the branch. John Dannreuther and Harry Bass, Jr., in their early U.S. gold coin reference book, estimate 25 to 35 known of this variety. Yellow-gold surfaces reveal fine hairlines under magnification. Generally well struck, with no significant contact marks. Some light adjustment marks are noted along the right border. Prospective bidders should not be intimidated by the light cleaning. (#98081)

AU55 Sharpness 1800 Half Eagle, BD-4

3367 1800—Cleaned—ANACS. AU55 Details. BD-4, R.4. The M in AMERICA is widely repunched. From early dies with no sign of the eventual cud above the IT in UNITED. The portrait has only faint friction, and the moderate hairlines cannot deny the eye appeal. The reverse has inconspicuous adjustment marks at its center and on cloud 7. (#8082)

Choice AU 1802/1 Five Dollar, BD-8

3368 1802/1 AU55 PCGS. Breen-6440, BD-8, R.4. A middle die state with several die cracks (but no cuds) throughout UNITED. This well struck overdated half eagle is lustrous for the designated grade, and has only a whisper of friction on the eagle's cheek and Liberty's drapery. A thin mark is noted beneath the Y in LIBERTY. Certified in a green label holder. (#8083)

Attractive BD-8 1802/1 Five Dollar MS62

3369 1802/1 MS62 PCGS. Breen-6440, BD-8, R.4. The terminal die state for the variety with a prominent die break, or cud, above the T in UNITED. The strike is generally sharp, since any softness is apparent only the left shield border, the ST in STATES, and the cloud beneath the A in STATES. Adjustment marks are limited to a few faint lines on the lower right obverse. The devices are unabraded, and it takes patient evaluation with a loupe to find a few thin marks on the obverse field near the stars. All 1802-dated half eagles are overdates, struck from two different obverse dies paired with seven reverses. One of the reverse dies was used with both obverses, for a total of eight varieties, all of which are R.4 or higher. (#8083)

Scarce BD-4 1803/2 Five Dollar MS63

3370 1803/2 MS63 PCGS. Breen-6441, BD-4, R.4. The only 1803-dated variety with a perfect T in LIBERTY. The usual die state with several peripheral obverse die cracks and a reverse die crack from 4 to 10 o'clock that wanders across the eagle's wings and shield. Light adjustment marks are noted on the reverse, but are largely relegated to the borders. The strike is precise save for minor weakness near the left shield border. Luster is uniform throughout the fields and devices, and apricot toning across the reverse border confirms the originality. A few unimportant field grazes fail to distract or threaten the designated grade. (#8084)

Mint State BD-2 1804 Five Dollar

3371 1804 Small 8 MS60 PCGS. Breen-6443, BD-2, High R.4. The obverse has a bisecting crack from 12 to 6 o'clock, and the reverse has radial cracks at 3 and 10 o'clock that join within the eagle's shield. The T in UNITED is repunched, with the initial T punch perfect. The other Ts in the reverse legend have a missing right foot. This suggests the T punch became defective while repunching the T in UNITED.

This sun-gold early half eagle has pleasing luster and a consistently crisp strike. The central obverse exhibits a few unimportant marks, but the overall look is surprisingly unblemished for the MS60 grade. Certified in a green label holder. (#8085)

Sharp 1806 Half Eagle, Round Top 6, AU58 Details

3372 1806 Round Top 6, 7x6 Stars—Cleaned—ANACS. AU58 Details. Breen-6448, BD-6, R.2. The variety is attributed by the knobbed 6, 7 stars left and 6 right on the obverse, small letters A's in AMERICA. Yellow-gold surfaces display wisps of light tan, and are lightly hairlined. Well centered design elements are sharply impressed. No adjustment or significant abrasions are evident, though we mention a couple of inoffensive hair-thin marks in the lower right obverse field for complete accuracy. All in all, nice overall eye appeal, despite the ANACS disclaimer. (#8089)

Rare AU Details BD-2 1806 Five Dollar

3373 1806 Pointed Top 6, 8x5 Stars—Damaged—NCS. AU Details.
Pointed Top 6, 8x5 Stars, Breen-6445, BD-2, High R.5. This rare variety early eagle has plentiful luster, but the centers are softly struck and the central reverse has a few parallel roller marks, as made. Exposed areas of the design show numerous individually minuscule marks, perhaps from loose storage in a frequently accessed shelf or case. (#8090)

Choice AU Sharpness 1807 Bust Left Half Eagle, BD-8

3374 1807 Bust Left—Cleaned—ANACS. AU55 Details. Breen-6453, BD-8, R.2. The 1807 Bust Left half eagle is among the most common of the type, produced from 1807 until 1812. This die marriage, BD-8, is the more common of the two varieties, with the bottom tip of the arrow feather pointing to the tip of the flag in the 5. Despite the ANACS caveat, much appeal remains on the green-gold surfaces of this lightly circulated example. The surfaces are a bit hairlined, and some undistracting adjustment marks appear near the rims on each side. (#8101)

1810 Small Date, Tall 5 Half Eagle AU53, BD-1

3375 1810 Small Date, Tall 5 AU53 NGC. Breen-6462, BD-1, High R.3. The Small Date, Tall 5 variety is considerably scarcer than the Large Date, Large 5 variety (BD-4), yet both trade at similar levels, due to strong type demand for John Reich's Capped Bust Left. A briefly circulated piece with copious luster and light straw-gold toning. Minor marks on the cheek and above the arrowheads are faded with time. (#8106)

Splendid MS63 1810 Large Date
Large 5 Half Eagle, BD-4

3376 1810 Large Date, Large 5 MS63 NGC. Breen-6459, BD-4, R.2. A simply splendid example of this early gold type coin, the most available of the Capped Bust Left series that ran from 1807 through 1812. Garrett and Guth point out that this date is one of the few of the type that can be found—for a price—in grades as high as MS66. This more-reasonable piece offers lustrous, relatively pristine greenish-gold surfaces. Only a few minuscule signs of contact preclude an even finer grade, but this piece nonetheless offers significant appeal at a reasonable cost of acquisition. Census: 30 in 63, 34 finer (8/07). (#8108)

AU Sharpness BD-2 1811 Half Eagle

3377 **1811 Small 5—Scratched, Cleaned—ANACS. AU Details, Net XF40.** Breen-6464, BD-2, R.3. A crisply struck and lightly circulated olive-gold piece that has faint adjustment marks at 11 o'clock. Wispy hairlines are on both sides but more prominent on the obverse. Two lengthy pinscratches intersect on the cheek, and the left obverse field has a large wavy pinscratch. (#8109)

AU Details 1811 Small 5 Half Eagle, BD-2

3378 **1811 Small 5—Improperly Cleaned—NCS. AU Details.** Breen-6464, BD-2, R.3. Luster glimmers from the borders and devices of this unblemished example. The reverse has faint roller marks near 5 and 11 o'clock, as produced. The green-gold color is suspicious, and the lightly granular surfaces are moderately hairlined. (#8109)

Lovely MS63 BD-1 1812 Five Dollar

3379 **1812 MS63 PCGS.** Wide 5D, Breen-6466, BD-1, R.3. Final year of the Capped Bust Left type and one of the most frequently encountered dates of the type as well. In Breen's monograph on early half eagles from the early 1960s, he speculated that "probably many coins delivered in 1813 were from 1812 dies." While this has not yet been proven to be the case, it would explain the perceived disparity in availability between the two dates that Breen noted at that time. Since then, however, that disparity has narrowed, and today the two dates have nearly identical availability.

The striking details on the obverse of this piece are especially sharp, and the reverse shows only the slightest softness of highpoint definition. Excellent mint luster and minimally abraded. A few adjustment marks were not struck out of the planchet on the highpoint of Liberty's cheek and end of the bust. The green-gold color shows a light overlay of reddish patina. A wonderful type coin. (#8112)

3380 **1812 MS63 NGC.** Breen-6466, BD-1, R.3. There are two varieties of the 1812 half eagle, both of which have the same obverse. The BD-1 has the reverse feather tip positioned over the right edge of the flag of the 5, and a very widely spaced 5 D, the D wholly under the branch (BD-2, the close 5 D has the D mostly under the feather).

    Greenish-gold patina adorns both sides of this Select example that exhibits sharply struck devices. The borders and interstices of the design elements offer the most effusive luster. A few minor handling marks are not out of context with the grade designation. Quite an attractive piece overall. (#8112)

3381 **1813 MS60 NGC.** Breen-6467, BD-1, R.2. An impressive piece, fully Mint State, with excellent green-gold luster and faint splashes of pale orange toning. This piece represents the first year of issue for the slightly modified design by John Reich, patterned after his previous Capped Head design. Mint State examples of this date are common enough in the lower grades, but difficult to find at the higher grades. Many circulated pieces also survive from the 95,428 coin mintage. As a first-year type coin, the 1813 Capped Head five is always in demand by type and date collectors. (#8116)

Attractive, Lustrous MS64 1813 Half Eagle, BD-1

3382 **1813 MS64 NGC.** BD-1, R.2. The first S in STATES is over the right side of the E in the motto. The 1813 half eagle is the first year of a new type and, like most-first-year issues, it appears to have been saved for posterity by collectors and noncollectors alike. In *Guide Book* terminology, this is the Capped Head to Left, Large Diameter, Bold Relief type (or subtype, since the Bold Relief subtype only lasted through 1815).

Although this type showed considerably increased mintages from the previous Capped Bust to Left half eagles of 1807-1812, the Capped Head to Left half eagles were also much more hoarded and melted than the previous type, as John Dannreuther points out in his indispensable *Early U.S. Gold Coin Varieties*. Most survivors of the later type are in the higher circulated grades or Uncirculated, whereas the earlier coins often show considerable wear. Dannreuther says, "Because there were relatively few gold coins in circulation stateside from 1812 onward, and none were seen after 1821 until the introduction of the lighter gold coins after July 21, 1834, this is expected. As mentioned, this type is many times rarer than those coins of 1812 and prior. Those coins of 1813 are the only available date of this type, those of 1814 through 1820 are scarce to ultra rare, while those of 1821 through 1829 are almost all rare or exceedingly rare. Those coins used in international commerce for goods and services were mostly melted. Only those few coins hoarded domestically and not melted after the weight change in 1834 are the examples we have to collect today, plus the few coins plucked from foreign sources."

We accordingly have an interesting situation in the present 1813 half eagle, as a high-grade (near-Gem) example one of the most available issues in one of the most difficult and elusive of all U.S. coin series; in other words, the quintessential type coin. The BD-1 is also the only readily available *variety* for the type. This coin offers brilliant luster emanating from the greenish-gold surfaces, which are remarkably attractive and distraction-free. A couple of minuscule ticks appear in the lower right obverse field, and both sides show some old clash marks, but the overall appearance is strictly in concordance with the near-Gem grade. This coin is almost certainly destined to fill some long-empty hole in a high-grade 19th century type set. (#8116)

Very Rare 1831 Half Eagle
Small 5D, BD-1, XF Details

3383 1831—Scratched, Improperly Cleaned—NCS. XF Details. Small
5D, Breen-6493, BD-1, High R.6. Perhaps no series in numismatics is
more difficult than the Capped Head Left half eagle. The 1813, 1818,
and 1820 are available in numbers sufficient to satisfy type demand,
but the remainder of the dates range from rare to non-collectible.
The 1831 can be acquired with great patience, unlike the 1822 (three
known), 1825/4 (two known), 1828/7 (five known), and 1832 12 Stars
(five known). This example is subdued by a chemical cleaning, and a
few brief pinscratches are noted beneath the right (facing) wing. The
upper left obverse field has a pair of strike-throughs, and the obverse
rim near 4:30 is slightly uneven. Numismatists should not overlook
the present opportunity, since a year or two may pass before another
example reaches the marketplace. (#8153)

CLASSIC HALF EAGLES

3384 1834 Plain 4—Cleaned—ANACS. XF45 Details. First Head,
Breen-6501, McCloskey 3-B, R.2. The devices are bold and lustrous,
but this first-year Classic five is a bit bright, and the upper reverse
field is abraded. (#8171)

3385 1834 Plain 4 AU55 PCGS. Second Head, Breen-6502, McCloskey
2-A, R.2. The 4 in the date is triple punched, with a script 8, the
eagle has a tongue, and the 5 in the denomination is halfway under
the fletchings. Apricot-gold surfaces yield well defined motifs and a
few minor abrasions over each side. (#8171)

3386 1834 Plain 4 AU55 NGC. Second Head, Breen-6502, McCloskey
2-A, R.2. While the curls just below Liberty's ribbon show softness,
the devices exhibit only a hint of actual wear, and the ample
remaining luster of the radiant yellow-gold fields confirms the grade.
Minimally marked and appealing. (#8171)

Sharp AU58 1834 Classic Head Five

3387 1834 Plain 4 AU58 NGC. First Head, Breen-6501, McCloskey
3-B, R.2. Later than the usual die state, with a "Scarface" die crack
beneath Liberty's eye. Sharply struck for the type, and the borders
and devices are bathed in luster. Uncommonly smooth despite a
couple of faint marks on the portrait near the chin. (#8171)

Near-Mint 1834 Classic Five

3388 1834 Plain 4 AU58 NGC. First Head, Breen-6501, McCloskey 3-B,
R.2. Slight friction is noted on Liberty's tresses, but golden-brown
luster shimmers from the borders, hair, plumage, and shield. There
are no consequential marks. A reduction in the weight of gold coins
in 1834 finally allowed them to circulate instead of getting exported.
(#8171)

3389 **1836 AU50 PCGS.** Small Head, Large Date, Breen-6508, McCloskey 5-D, R.3. This green-gold example has the unscrubbed "dirty gold" appearance desired by experienced gold collectors. The fields are surprisingly unabraded, and the portrait has only minor contact on the nose and jaw. (#8174)

3390 **1836 AU55 ICG.** Breen-6510, Third Head, McCloskey 3-C, R.2. Ample bright luster illuminates the devices and legends. Well struck for the type. Several small roundish marks are mostly relegated to the borders. (#8174)

3391 **1837 XF45 ICG.** Large Date, Large 5, Breen-6512, McCloskey 2-B, R.3. Primarily light tan-gold with some deeper toning along the reverse margin. Each side has a few marks near the dentils, but the fields and devices are smooth. (#8175)

Small Date 1837 Five Dollar, AU58

3392 **1837 AU58 NGC.** Small Date, Breen-6513, McCloskey 3-C, R.4. Luster fills the borders and devices of this pleasing Borderline Uncirculated representative. Although it currently commands a meager premium, the 1837 is significantly scarcer than the 1834 through 1836 dates, and provides good value to the knowledgeable gold type collector. (#8175)

3393 **1838 AU55 NGC.** Large Arrows, Small 5, Breen-6514, McCloskey 1-A, R.2. The D in the denomination has its vertical bar to the left of the terminus of the olive stem. A briefly circulated and well-defined example, yellow-gold with a touch of green. Light, scattered abrasions appear across the still-lustrous surfaces. (#8176)

LIBERTY HALF EAGLES

3394 **1839—Sea Salvaged—ANACS. Unc. Details. Net AU50.** The major devices are well struck, and no wear is present, but the surfaces are subdued and minutely granular from long-term exposure to seawater. A single-year design subtype, since the sleepy-eyed portrait of Liberty would be replaced by a more alert rendition in 1840. (#8191)

3395 **1840 Narrow Mill AU58 PCGS.** This is a pleasing near-Mint example with considerable luster and pleasing green-gold coloration. Highpoint wear is minimal, and only trivial abrasions are scattered over each side. Population: 14 in 58, 13 finer (7/07). (#8194)

3396 **1840 Broad Mill AU58 PCGS.** Well struck aside from the curl below the ear. The obverse is pleasantly unabraded, while the reverse field exhibits hair-thin marks. Population: 14 in 58, 13 finer (8/07). (#8194)

3397 **1840 Broad Mill AU58 NGC.** The wide rim feature is undesignated on the NGC holder. Nicely struck with minor softness on the eagle's neck and Liberty's lovelock. The appearance is original, and there are no offensive marks. (#8194)

Sharp 1840-D Five Dollar, VF35
Scarce 4-C Small D Variety

3398 **1840-D Small D VF35 NGC.** Variety 4-C. The Small Mintmark variety with diagnostic die crack extending from the arrow feather to the D. Scarcer than the Tall D variety. Douglas Winter, in his Dahlonega Mint gold coins reference, says "This variety appears to be rare." Peach-gold surfaces on this VF35 example reveal hints of luster in some of the protected areas. Nice detail, and a minimum of contact marks. (#8199)

1840-O Narrow Mill Five Dollar, AU58

3399 **1840-O Narrow Mill AU58 NGC.** The Narrow Mill is the more common of the two varieties. This high-end About Uncirculated New Orleans Mint specimen possesses ample luster residing on peach-gold, minimally abraded surfaces. A sharp strike translates into good definition on the design elements, except for the usually seen softness in the centers. (#8200)

3400 **1840-O Narrow Mill MS63 NGC.** One of the most abused adjectives in numismatics is the word "rare." When dealing with popular coins, like a 1909-S VDB Lincoln cent, it is immediately clear to collectors that such an issue is only rare relative to the other dates in the series, yet in reality thousands of examples have been certified in Uncirculated grades. In all fairness, there are a handful of 1909-S VDB cents that are indeed rare, with "handful" being the operative term. Those examples truly deserving of this adjective are ones that stand far and above any other specimens in terms of state of preservation and aesthetic qualities. Enter the current coin. This 1840-O half eagle transcends the word rare, being one of the finest known examples in existence. More specifically, it is ranked as the third finest known to Doug Winter in his seminal treatise on the subject, *Gold Coins of the New Orleans Mint* (2006).

This piece is of the Narrow Mill type and exhibits raised die lines at IB in LIBERTY. It is identified as Variety Two by Winter. There are a few inconsequential abrasions in the unprotected fields, completely commensurate with the grade assigned by NGC over a decade ago. Unusual are the surfaces displaying vivacious luster and an above average strike that is typically absent on 1840-O fives. The rich, yellow-gold coloration on both sides gracefully transitions to reddish-gold at the peripheries. This is a superb specimen in every sense of the word.

Experts agree that a total of less than 200 1840-O half eagles exist in all grades. The combined totals of the NGC *Census Report* and the PCGS *Population Report* suggest an even lower survival rate, especially when taking into consideration the trend of coins being submitted more than once in pursuit of a higher grade designation. The coin in this lot ranks in the upper echelon of known examples. To enthusiasts of New Orleans gold coinage, this piece represents a nearly insurmountable high grade, and to purveyors of southern gold the current specimen is recognized as one the few Select Uncirculated 1840-O five dollars extant. As of (8/07) NGC has graded two examples in MS63, with just one finer.

Ex: Auction '88, lot 1910; Tangible Investments of America (Stack's, 5/95), lot 438; Louisiana collection; Doug Winter; Midwestern collection; Chicago Collection (Heritage, 8/1998), lot 7633. (#8200)

1841-D Five Dollar, AU58
Variety 5-B, Tall D

3401 1841-D Tall D AU58 NGC. Variety 5-B. While not indicated on the NGC insert, this is the Tall D variety, that Douglas Winter, in his Dahlonega Mint gold coins reference, says" "This is a rare and important variety which deserves to sell for a significant premium over variety 5-D (the Small Mintmark)." PCGS reports having graded nine "Medium" (Tall) D mintmark pieces, only one of which is finer than this NGC-graded piece. This AU58 example retains ample luster on peach-gold surfaces that are minimally abraded. Sharply struck throughout. (#98204)

AU53 Sharpness 1842-C Half Eagle

3402 1842-C Large Date—Cleaned—ANACS. AU53 Details. Variety 5-C. A bright, glossy, and hairlined representative of this difficult variety. Possibly repaired on the portrait and left obverse field. A scratch is noted above the eagle's right (facing) wing. Luster glimmers from the recesses of the devices. (#8209)

Pleasing 1842-O Half Eagle, VF30

3403 1842-O VF30 NGC. A moderately circulated, yet attractive representative of this challenging earlier New Orleans issue, which appears infrequently on the market; Garrett and Guth (2006) draw a comparison to the 1842-D Large Date, Large Letters variant, noting that the latter sells at auction with significantly greater frequency. The still-luminous orange-gold surfaces show a measure of the central softness that characterizes most examples, though the fields and devices are free of significant distractions. (#8212)

3404 1843-O Small Letters—Repaired, Rim Damaged, Cleaned—ANACS. AU55 Details. Well-defined with only minor wear, though the yellow-gold surfaces show suspiciously uniform luster. Faint evidence of rim damage is visible, particularly on the reverse, and the reverse fields exhibit areas of disturbed texture resulting from repairs. (#8217)

Scarce AU 1844-D Five Dollar

3405 1844-D AU50 PCGS. A Winter-unlisted variety that pairs his H reverse with a different obverse than his 11. The date is a bit farther to the left, and the last 4 in the date is centered between the truncation of the bust and the denticles. The surfaces are bright and yellow-gold in color with numerous small abrasions over each side. Population: 17 in 50, 57 finer (8/07). (#8221)

3406 1845-D—Damaged—ANACS. XF40 Details. Variety 12-I. This richly detailed if slightly bright Dahlonega has a small but relatively deep circular dig on Liberty's cheek. Luster still beckons from protected areas. (#8224)

Uncirculated Details 1846-C Five

3407 1846-C—Improperly Cleaned—NCS. Unc. Details. Variety 8-E. An early die state that clearly shows the repunching on the base of the 1. The eagle's neck and Liberty's lovelock lack absolute detail, but the strike is above average for a Charlotte Mint product. There is no indication of wear, and no abrasions are evident apart from the patches of hairlines found on both sides. (#8227)

3408 1847 AU58 PCGS. Although it is one of the most common No Motto half eagles due to its large mintage of nearly 1 million pieces, survivors in Mint State is nonetheless scarce. Much luster remains on the amber-gold surfaces, which show few distractions save for minor strike weakness on the eagle. (#8231)

Exceptional 1847 Five Dollar, MS63

3409 1847 MS63 PCGS. One of the more frequently encountered No Motto half eagles and often used as a type coin. This piece displays exceptionally strong mint luster, especially for a coin of this age. The fields are semi-reflective with a generous mixture of mint frost. Sharply struck throughout. The surfaces display rich orange-gold color and there are no obvious or detracting blemishes present. Population: 19 in 63, 6 finer (8/07). (#8231)

3410 1847-D VF30 NGC. Variety 17-I. This Dahlonega five dollar piece retains considerable detail on the eagle's shield and left (facing) wing. A trio of hair-thin parallel marks are noted above the RT in LIBERTY. (#8234)

Rare 1847-O Half Eagle XF45 Details

3411 1847-O—Damaged, Polished—ANACS. XF45 Details. Per Winter, the 1847-O is the rarest New Orleans Mint half eagle, both overall and in high grades. Only 12,000 pieces were struck, and Winter estimates that only 40 to 50 pieces are known. The present boldly detailed example is bright and glossy from polishing, and has obverse edge marks at 3 and 6 o'clock. (#8235)

Appealing 1849-C Half Eagle AU58

3412 1849-C AU58 NGC. Variety 12-F. Despite being scarce at all grade levels, the 1849-C issue is probably the most relatively available of all Charlotte Mint half eagles from the 1840s. The current near-Mint example is reasonably well struck for a Charlotte Mint product, even if typically weak on some of the design's central highpoints. Some satiny mint luster remains evident, as the piece also displays light wear and a few trivial abrasions. Census: 21 in 58, 30 finer (8/07). (#8241)

3413 1849-D XF40 NGC. Variety 22-N. The still-luminous orange-gold surfaces of this mid-date Dahlonega piece show even, light to moderate wear over each side. The fields and devices exhibit a number of scattered abrasions, including one that affects the 8 and 4 of the date. (#8242)

Bold 1850-C Five Dollar AU58

3414 1850-C AU58 NGC. Variety 15-F. An early die state with only faint die cracks near the FI in FIVE. This area eventually develops a prominent retained die break. This clean example is well struck save for minor incompleteness on the eagle's neck feathers. Liberty's cheek is a bit glossy, and faint marks are noted above the eagle's head. (#8244)

Original Choice XF 1850-D Five

3415 1850-D XF45 NGC. Variety 24-P, although it should be noted that Winter's reverses O and P are different states of the same die. This undipped "dirty gold" example will be of great interest to those in search of original examples. A lightly abraded golden-brown example with a slightly above average strike. (#8245)

3416 1851 AU58 NGC. A crisply struck and eminently appealing near-Mint representative of this earlier Coronet half eagle issue, yellow-orange with faint, scattered abrasions. Elusive in Mint State, with just 61 such pieces graded by NGC (8/07). (#8246)

Very Rare Variety 17-F 1851-C Five-XF45

3417 1851-C XF45 PCGS. This is the extremely rare die marriage listed as Variety 17-G in the Winter standard reference. The "G" designation is inaccurate, since the reverse differs from the usual 16-G variety. The mintmark is much lower in the field and rests above the V instead of the E. It is the F reverse from 1849, with a radial die crack near the U in UNITED. The obverse die shows the second 1 in the date slightly higher, virtually touching the bust. There is **no** punchmark on the lobe of Liberty's ear, unlike 16-G. The base of the first 1 in the date is repunched northwest. A search of Heritage Permanent Auction Archives, which images dozens of '51-C fives, failed to locate another example from these dies.

The present piece retains its "original skin." Golden-tan patination bathes the borders. The borders are sharply struck, while Liberty's curls and the fletchings show some incompleteness of strike. An important opportunity for the specialist. (#8247)

Choice AU 1851-O Five

3418 1851-O AU55 NGC. This No Motto O-mint five is refreshingly unabraded aside from a faint thin vertical mark near the profile. Liberty's curls and the eagle's neck and fletchings lack a full strike, but peripheral elements such as the stars and dentils are boldly brought up. A mere 41,000 pieces were struck, and unimpaired survivors are scarce. Census: 12 in 55, 24 finer (7/07). (#8249)

3419 1852 MS61 PCGS. The 1852 is one of the few No Motto half eagles that is occasionally available in Mint State. This example is slightly subdued, but is generally well struck and free of severe marks. (#8250)

Scarce 1852 Five Dollar, MS62

3420 1852 MS62 PCGS. The mintage of nearly 574,000 pieces in 1852 is one of the highest for the Liberty Head No Motto type five dollar. While the date is fairly common in circulated grades, Jeff Garrett and Ron Guth (2006) say "Mint State coins are scarce, and there are probably fewer than 150 pieces known at that level." Soft luster emanates from the green-gold surfaces of this MS62 specimen. Sharply struck, and showing just a few minute handling marks. Population: 50 in 62, 31 finer (8/07). (#8250)

3421 1852-C XF45 NGC. Variety 18-H. This green-gold Charlotte Mint five has subdued, moderately abraded surfaces. Liberty's curls and the eagle's neck are typically brought up, yet the wings and borders have pleasing definition for the grade. (#8251)

Lovely 1852-C Half Eagle, AU50

3422 1852-C AU50 NGC. Variety 18-H. The 1 in the date is nearly merged with the bust. Though the 1852-C is one of the more available half eagles from Charlotte, finding attractive pieces with an aura of originality becomes harder with time. The lightly circulated example offered here has dusky orange-gold surfaces with luminous peripheries. The fields show a few scattered abrasions and the central devices exhibit typical softness, but the coin retains excellent overall visual appeal. A strong candidate for the collector of branch mint gold. (#8251)

Sharply Struck 1854 Five Dollar, MS62

3423 1854 MS62 NGC. Most of the known 1854 half eagles fall within the Extremely Fine to About Uncirculated grade range. The lustrous surfaces of this yellow-gold MS62 example are imbued with light tan, and exhibit sharply struck design elements. Wispy handling marks in the fields define the grade. What may be either a toning or a light grease streak is visible in the upper left obverse. Census: 19 in 62, 15 finer (8/07). (#8256)

Lustrous MS64 1854 Five Dollar
A Notable Condition Rarity From the 1850s

3424 1854 MS64 NGC. Specialists will surely appreciate this coin for the condition rarity that it is. The mintage of 160,675 pieces really does not give one an indication of the rarity of this date in AU and Uncirculated grades. Probably less than 200 pieces are extant today in the various grades of AU. But it is in mint condition that the 1854 really shines as a condition rarity. Fewer than 100 pieces are known in all Uncirculated grades. At the MS64 level, this is one of only seven coins certified by both of the major services, and none are finer (8/07). The surfaces are softly frosted and there are only the smallest abrasions present, none of which are worthy of mention. Sharply struck, except of course on the eagle's neck, as always seen on half eagles from this era. (#8256)

3425 1854-C Weak C VF35 NGC. Variety 22-I. The scarcely discernible mintmark on the reverse is diagnostic for this prominent Charlotte variety. This pleasing Choice VF example has dusky yellow-orange surfaces and few marks aside from a shallow depression on the chin. (#98257)

3426 1855-D Large D—Ex-Jewelry, Cleaned—ANACS. XF40 Details. Variety 32-AA. This lower mintage Dahlonega half eagle is glossy from cleaning, and solder remnants are noted near the obverse border at 3, 6, and 11 o'clock. (#8263)

Rare Near-Mint 1856-S Five Dollar

3427 1856-S AU58 PCGS. Large S. Two different mintmark sizes are known for the 1856-S three dollar piece, half eagle, and eagle. The present problem-free example has substantial bright luster and an above average strike. No marks are consequential. An opportunity for the devoted specialist. Population: 11 in 58, 3 finer (7/07). (#8270)

Scarce 1857 Five Dollar, MS62

3428 1857 MS62 PCGS. Even though 98,188 pieces were struck of the 1857, it was not widely saved at the time of issue. Similarly, it is often an overlooked date by all but the most serious 19th century gold specialists. In spite of the MS62 grade, the main attraction of this coin is its outstanding mint luster. The luster is thick and softly frosted, the same one would expect on a Gem coin. A few small abrasions are peppered over each side, which account for the grade. Sharply and evenly defined on each side. Population: 14 in 62, 15 finer (8/07). (#8271)

Lustrous 1857-C Half Eagle, AU58

3429 1857-C AU58 PCGS. Variety 25-J. The surfaces of this near-Mint example exhibit significant luster around the margins. Sharply struck, as usually seen. Lightly abraded, and as such this is an atypical example. The only mentionable marks are a shallow scratch above the eagle's left (facing) wing and a planchet lamination on the eagle's neck. Rich reddish-gold color. Just outside the Condition Census for the issue. (#8272)

3430 1857-S AU50 NGC. The 1857-S saw heavy use in commerce, and most survivors are well circulated, according to Garrett and Guth (2006). This brassy-gold example is one of the few survivors in high grade. Excellent definition shows on the motifs, and both sides are minimally abraded. Census: 9 in 50, 57 finer (7/07). (#8275)

Conditionally Scarce 1857-S Half Eagle MS61

3431 1857-S MS61 NGC. This low mintage issue saw heavy use in the West Coast channels of commerce, and remains scarce today at every grade level. Just 16 examples have been certified in Mint State, by NGC and PCGS combined, and several of those were "survivors" of the *S.S. Central America* shipwreck. This piece is well struck with somewhat muted luster and variegated lime-gold and pink-rose coloration. Surface marks are not excessive for the grade. (#8275)

3432 1861 MS61 NGC. Some prooflike tendencies are noted on the honey-gold surfaces of this Civil War era five dollar piece. Generally well defined, save for minor softness in portions of Liberty's hair. Faint handling marks in the fields show up under magnification. (#8288)

3433 1861 MS61 PCGS. In the first year of the Civil War, Philadelphia struck 688,084 half eagles, though that conflict drastically reduced the number of transactions conducted with precious-metal coins. This lustrous lemon-gold piece has strong obverse detail, though the eagle's neck lacks detail. Scattered abrasions account for the grade. (#8288)

Challenging 1861-S Half Eagle AU55

3434 1861-S AU55 NGC. This appealing Choice AU half eagle is well struck on most design features, except for the eagle's arrow fletchings and right (facing) talons. Even highpoint wear is noted on both sides. The light greenish coloration is augmented by considerable amounts of reddish mint luster for the grade. This issue is a formidable rarity at all grade levels. Census: 5 in 55, 8 finer (8/07). (#8291)

Elusive Civil War-Era 1862 Five Dollar, AU58

3435 1862 AU58 PCGS. Moderate scattered field abrasions appear on the lustrous yellow-gold surfaces of this low-mintage Civil War issue, produced to the extent of only 4,465 pieces. A wedge of smoke-gold patina appears on the reverse from the eagle's head upward toward 11 o'clock. The federal government had ceased to pay out gold coins by 1862, leading to drastically reduced mintages. While most later dates in the long-running Liberty Head series are fairly obtainable, earlier dates such as this rare issue are extremely elusive and see ceaseless collector demand. Population: 2 in 58, 1 finer (8/07). (#8292)

Sumptuous 1864 Half Eagle, MS61

3436 1864 MS61 PCGS. By 1864, the Civil War had left an indelible imprint on the future of American coins and currency. One of the major consequences was the hoarding of precious metal, and the Union government had little bullion to mint in the East. The half eagle production for 1864, for example, amounted to just 4,100 pieces. That issue is one in a string of low-mintage P-mint issues from 1862 to 1872.

This attractive yellow-orange example offers vibrant luster and exquisite detail. The reverse shows a splash of rose in the fields. Though the surfaces show a number of marks and wispy abrasions, the piece is unworn and retains strong visual appeal. An excellent representative for the discerning date collector. Tied for the finest certified by either NGC or PCGS (8/07). (#8296)

Low Mintage AU50 1868 Five Dollar

3437 1868 AU50 NGC. A scarce issue from a low mintage of 5,700 coins, all struck in mid-January 1868 and apparently all from one pair of dies. A second die pair was utilized for the few proofs that were struck the following month. Pale pinkish-yellow gold with traces of luster in the protected areas, and hints of greenish coloration on both sides. The surfaces are moderately abraded. (#8315)

Scarce 1868-S Five Dollar, AU50

3438 1868-S AU50 NGC. The 1868-S was a much-needed issue on the west coast in the late 1860s. The 52,000 pieces produced were almost all used in the channels of commerce and only three coins have been certified to date (8/07) in mint condition. This coin shows light friction over the highpoints. Weakly struck, as usual, in the centers. A surprising amount of mint luster remains for a coin in this grade. Attractive pinkish-rose patina is seen over each side. (#8316)

Coveted 1870-CC Five Dollar AG3

3439 1870-CC AG3 PCGS. As is also the case for the double eagle and eagle, the first-year 1870-CC is the rarest Carson City half eagle. Mintages were slightly lower in 1873 and 1876, but more examples of those dates have survived, probably because they circulated additional years in the Western frontier. This golden-brown example has a bold date and mintmark. About half of the letters in UNITED, AMERICA, and FIVE D are worn into the rim. (#8320)

Lovely AU 1870-S Half Eagle

3440 1870-S AU50 NGC. Although the surfaces are typically abraded for the issue, this is a pleasing example with considerable satiny luster remaining visible, and with medium green-gold color. The reverse exhibits a few more significant flaws above and behind the eagle's neck and head. This scarce S-mint issue has a mintage of just 17,000 coins, and since nearly all entered Western commerce, survivors are elusive, especially in better grades. (#8321)

Rare Choice AU 1870-S Half Eagle

3441 1870-S AU55 NGC. Boldly struck, save for flatness on the eagle's neck, with slight wear on the highpoints and substantial bits of red-orange luster still evident near the devices. Hairlines and small abrasions are noted on both sides. According to Garrett and Guth (2006): "The 1870-S half eagle is found only in circulated condition and usually well worn at that. There are no known examples of the date in Mint State." Census: 10 in 55, 3 finer (8/07). (#8321)

Conditionally Rare 1871-CC Five Dollar, AU55

3442 1871-CC AU55 PCGS. Variety 1-A, which employs the same reverse die as on the 1870-CC. Beautifully lustrous yellow-gold surfaces are the hallmark of this Choice AU half eagle, one of nearly 21,000 pieces struck in the second year of the Carson City Mint. Although this issue is seen more often than any other CC issue from 1870 to 1873, pieces are nonetheless rare in any grade, and the average example is only about Choice XF or so. This coin is well struck, even though light softness appears in the usual areas. Light clash marks show on each side, and a few light abrasions are consistent with the Choice AU grade assessed. Population: 9 in 55, 5 finer (8/07). (#8323)

3443 1871-S XF40 PCGS. The date is lightly repunched south, visible on all four digits. Since only 25,000 pieces were struck, the entire issue likely shares the characteristic. The curls and eagle's neck are typically brought up, but sharpness elsewhere is consistent with a finer grade. A bright mark is noted near star 4. Certified in a green label holder. Population: 10 in 40, 41 finer (8/07). (#8324)

Lustrous 1872-S Half Eagle
One of Three Mint State Examples

3444 1872-S MS61 NGC. Jeff Garrett and Ron Guth (2006) write that the 1872-S half eagle is a very rare issue in any grade. The NGC/PCGS population figures confirm this, and indicate that most survivors seem to be in the Extremely Fine to About Uncirculated grade range. A mere three Mint State pieces have been seen, all MS61 NGC-graded.

Lustrous brassy-gold surfaces abound on this Uncirculated example, and the semi-prooflike fields highlight the motifs. An attentive strike brings out sharp definition on the design elements, save for minor softness in the arrow feathers and the eagle's neck feathers. Light, inoffensive handling marks evenly scattered about preclude a higher grade. (#8327)

3445 1873 Closed 3 MS62 NGC. A solidly struck example with luminous sun-gold and peach surfaces that show light, scattered abrasions. The Closed 3 logotype, evident on the present piece, was criticized as confusing and replaced later in the year by the Open 3. Census: 21 in 62, 7 finer (8/07). (#8329)

3446 1873 Closed 3 MS62 PCGS. This lustrous Mint State piece is held back from a finer grade by the presence of some moderate field abrasions that are largely confined to the obverse. The amber-gold coloration is a plus, along with the somewhat prooflike reverse. Population: 16 in 62, 15 finer (8/07). (#8329)

3447 1873 Open 3 MS62 PCGS. A beautiful orange-red example of this low mintage and conditionally rare Philadelphia issue. The luster is a bit subdued, but the portrait and reverse field are unblemished. Population: 9 in 62, 18 finer (8/07). (#8328)

3448 1878-S MS62 NGC. Pleasingly detailed with vibrant luster, an attractive 19th century S-mint half eagle. The shining lemon-gold surfaces show a number of wispy abrasions that account for the grade. (#8347)

3449 1879 MS63 PCGS. A frosty yellow-gold Select example of this Hayes-era issue, exquisitely detailed in the centers with faint, scattered abrasions. Eminently appealing. Population: 24 in 63, 9 finer (8/07). (#8348)

Rare Choice 1879 Half Eagle

3450 1879 MS64 PCGS. This is a significant opportunity for the advanced Liberty half eagle collector, as Choice and Gem examples of the date are almost never encountered. This example is sharply struck with fully brilliant gold surfaces and only a few minor abrasions, consistent with the grade. The reverse is well preserved. Population: 5 in 64, 4 finer (7/07). (#8348)

3451 1879-CC VF35 PCGS. A mere 17,281 pieces were produced of this Carson City issue, and survivors are scarce at any grade level. This example displays typical softness of definition on the eagle's neck and wing feathers. The design's highpoints are typically worn for the grade, but surface blemishes are minimal. An appealing Choice VF example with surprisingly deep rose-gold coloration. (#8349)

Appealing AU50 1879-CC Five Dollar

3452 1879-CC AU50 PCGS. Although half eagles were the "little sisters" of gold coinage throughout much of U.S. numismatic history, generally produced in much smaller quantities than their larger siblings, in 1879 Carson City managed to manufacture a respectable amount of five dollar pieces, 17,281, making it the third-largest mintage of the 1870s and a larger emission than the eagles and double eagles combined. This example offers only a passable strike, but there are no singular abrasions and the surfaces, with mellow orange-gold coloration, show considerable luster remaining and lots of eye appeal. A couple of tiny, undistracting planchet laminations near star 13. Population: 11 in 50, 33 finer (8/07). (#8349)

3453 1880 MS64 NGC. The lustrous surfaces show yellow-gold color imbued with faint accents of rose. The striking details are fully brought up on the obverse, and show only slight softness on the eagle's neck on the reverse. Surface marks are minimal. (#8351)

Highly Lustrous Gem 1880 Half Eagle

3454 1880 MS65 PCGS. The high-mintage 1880 five dollar, with a mintage over 3 million pieces, is common in all grades except near-Gem and finer. Dazzling luster bathes apricot-gold surfaces of the Gem presented in this lot. Well preserved and generally sharply struck. Population: 8 in 65, 1 finer (8/07). (#8351)

3455 1880-S MS63 Prooflike NGC. This sharply struck half eagle has medium salmon-pink toning, and only one relevant mark, above the olive branch, is found on the suitably reflective fields. Scarce in Prooflike condition, with none graded above MS63 by NGC. Census: 6 in 63 Prooflike, 0 finer in Prooflike (7/07). (#78353)

3456 1881 MS64 NGC. A lovely Choice representative of this available 19th century half eagle issue, well-defined and frosty with few marks for the grade. The surfaces are predominantly amber-gold with peach and sun-gold accents. (#8354)

Exceptionally Lustrous MS66 1881 Five Dollar

3457 **1881 MS66 NGC.** While considered one of the most available dates in the entire five dollar series, the herd definitely thins out at the MS66 level. Only 11 other pieces have been so graded by NGC with one finer, and PCGS has not certified any at this level (8/07). This is an amazingly lustrous coin. The surfaces are nearly devoid of abrasions of any size. Fully struck also, but to underscore the coin's strongest feature: the mint frost on this coin must be seen to be believed and fully appreciated. (#8354)

3458 **1881/0 MS61 PCGS.** FS-301, formerly FS-005. This shining sun-gold piece exhibits distinct orange elements on both sides. Well-defined with the right side of the underdigit plain under magnification, though myriad shallow abrasions affect the surfaces. Population: 7 in 61, 27 finer (8/07). (#8355)

Vibrant Gem 1881-S Half Eagle

3459 **1881-S MS65 PCGS.** The single finest 1881-S half eagle graded by PCGS (8/07), this radiant exemplar displays enticing apricot-gold surfaces with a few tiny alloy flecks on the obverse. The strike is crisp, and the overall preservation more than meets the high standards of the grade. Only a few faint luster grazes in the fields preclude an even loftier designation. An outstanding survivor from a mintage of under a million pieces. (#8357)

Outstanding Gem 1882 Five Dollar Gold

3460 **1882 MS65 PCGS.** This vibrant exemplar, tied for the finest certified by PCGS (8/07), should appeal to even the most discerning of date collectors. Peach and straw accents enliven the yellow-gold surfaces, as does the coin's swirling luster. A handful of pinpoint marks lie scattered across the surfaces, but the crisply detailed portrait is well-preserved overall, and the minuscule flaws are entirely consistent with the grade. (#8358)

Vibrant 1882 Five Dollar MS65

3461 **1882 MS65 NGC.** Lustrous and penetratingly struck with a clean reverse and only minor obverse grazes. Rim crumbling, unusual for the series, is present on the obverse between 12 and 2 o'clock. The high mintage 1882 is plentiful in typical Mint State, but emerges as a conditional rarity at the MS65 level. Census: 28 in 65, 2 finer (8/07). (#8358)

Conditionally Rare 1882 Half Eagle MS63 Prooflike

3462 **1882 MS63 Prooflike NGC.** This decidedly prooflike example displays bright honey-gold coloration and flashy mint frost. The design elements are sharply struck throughout, and there are a normal number of scattered abrasions on each side, for the grade. A readily available issue that becomes rare in Prooflike condition. Census: 2 in 63 Prooflike, 0 finer (8/07). (#78358)

Single Finest Certified 1882-CC Half Eagle

3463 1882-CC MS63 NGC. The mintage figure for the 1882-CC half eagle amounts to 82,817 coins, a plentiful amount by the standards of the era and the Carson City Mint. For comparison purposes, the previous and subsequent CC-mint half eagle emissions were 13,886 and 12,598 pieces, respectively—each less than one-sixth as much as the 1882 figure.

Why was such a relatively large number of half eagles produced at Carson City during the year? In the first place, 1881 saw the Carson City Mint presses shut down for most of the year, so that the following year looks overlarge in comparison, and in the second place there were modest increases in gold yields from the nearby Comstock Lode that translated into increased gold coinage. Rusty Goe's *The Mint on Carson Street* notes that most of the 1882-CC half eagles found their way outside of Nevada, and those remaining nearby circulated extensively, leading to a large supply today in Fine to AU. Goe says "Uncirculated specimens, though existing in lower quantities, are more available than any pre-1890-CC date."

Although found fairly often in circulated condition, most 1882-CC half eagles average only AU or so, and the population drops precipitously in Mint State. While there are about three dozen Mint State 1882-CC half eagles at both services combined, as of (8/07) this is *the only MS63 example of the date certified at either NGC or PCGS, and there are none finer.* Jeff Garrett and Ron Guth note that many of the high-grade examples of this date are quite bagmarked, and that appealing examples are rare.

The present example is thus a pleasant surprise on many counts, as it offers extremely pleasing appeal and surfaces that are quite pristine for the grade and mint. The straw-gold surfaces show few distracting contact marks, either large or small, and the bold strike is an added bonus. Radiant luster cascades from each side, and a couple of tiny dark toning spots fail to dampen the appeal. (#8359)

3464 1883-S MS62 PCGS. Sharply struck and intensely lustrous, with alluring yellow-gold and rose toning that turns to mint-green near the periphery. Numerous small abrasions define the grade. A conditionally elusive issue in Mint State. Population: 30 in 62, 14 finer (8/07). (#8363)

Low Mintage Choice 1883-S Half Eagle

3465 1883-S MS64 PCGS. This is one of the more underrated issues in the Liberty half eagle series. As the population data reveals, the date is at least scarce in all grades, and virtually unobtainable in the better grades of Mint State. This near-Gem displays excellent luster and apricot-gold patination that takes on a slightly deeper shade around the margins. All of the design features are well executed. Population: 3 in 64, 0 finer (7/07). (#8363)

3466 1885-S MS64 PCGS. The San Francisco Mint's high production of multiple-dollar denominations continued even after California's gold stocks were largely exhausted. This shining apricot-gold and orange-gold piece offers pleasing detail overall and smooth surfaces. (#8368)

3467 1886-S MS64 NGC. A well struck and beautifully preserved near-Gem with sweeping luster and medium peach color. The mintmark is lightly repunched. (#8370)

Attractive 1886-S Five Dollar MS65

3468 1886-S MS65 PCGS. The San Francisco Mint struck no double eagles in this year—the only such gap from 1854 to 1911—but it made up for it with the mintage of more than 3.26 million half eagles, plus a considerable number of eagles. Because of indifferent shipping and storage near the time of production, PCGS has certified only seven coins in MS65, with none finer (7/07). This example shows a bold if not full strike, with ebullient luster over the peach-gold surfaces, and there are relatively few post-strike impairments. (#8370)

Select 1888-S Half Eagle, Tied for Finest-Graded

3469 1888-S MS63 PCGS. Highly lustrous, with alluring rose-gold coloration, and scattered minor blemishes that restrict the grade. The obverse stars are softly struck, but most of the other design elements are boldly reproduced. Despite a mintage of nearly 294,000 pieces, the 1888-S half eagle is scarce in Mint State, and none have been graded above MS63 by either of the major services. Population: 6 in 63, 0 finer (8/07). (#8373)

3470 1890-CC AU58 PCGS. A hint of highpoint friction affects the sharply struck devices, but the apricot-gold fields still shine. Small dots of copper alloy are present on the portrait and the right obverse rim. An attractive example of this comparatively available Carson City half eagle issue, an excellent choice for the type collector. (#8376)

Impressive 1890-CC Five Dollar MS63

3471 1890-CC MS63 PCGS. The Carson City Mint in 1890 made its first half eagles since 1885, a total of 53,800 coins, and CC-mint issues starting with this date are collectible in high grade. This piece boasts instant eye appeal, a combination of the bold sunset-orange coloration and the radiant luster. Surface abrasions are minimal for the grade, and the strike is bold, save for some softness on the eagle's neck. Certified in a green-label holder. Population: 23 in 63, 30 finer (7/07). (#8376)

3472 1891 MS62 NGC. Warm, dusky pumpkin-orange surfaces give this later 19th century half eagle a distinctive appearance. Solidly struck with numerous light abrasions and a touch of peach at the margins. (#8377)

3473 1891-CC MS61 PCGS. Boldly struck and lustrous, with light coloration and scattered superficial marks that are relatively few in number. The most readily available Carson City half eagle issue, but examples are scarce above the MS62 grade level. (#8378)

Nifty 1891-CC Five Dollar MS63

3474 1891-CC MS63 PCGS. A lovely orange-gold Carson City gold type coin that boasts vivid luster and only moderate field grazes. Well struck and attractive. The 1891-CC is more available than its mintage of 208,000 pieces suggests, but most examples grade between AU55 and MS62, and PCGS has certified only a single piece above MS64 (7/07). (#8378)

3475 1892-CC AU58 NGC. The luster is nearly full and the mint-green and peach coloration is very attractive. Well struck design elements show minimal wear, and both sides are dotted with tiny field marks. One of just 82,968 pieces produced. (#8380)

3476 1893 MS64 PCGS. An alertly struck pumpkin-gold piece that benefits from an especially smooth reverse. Faint obverse grazes are only visible beneath a glass. (#8383)

3477 1893-CC AU58 NGC. This example is boldly struck, and only the slightest degree of wear is evident over the highpoints. There are a few wispy hairlines and tiny contact marks on each side. Final year of issue for the Carson City Mint, and always a popular choice for type purposes. (#8384)

3478 1893-O MS62 PCGS. The shining surfaces of this pleasingly detailed, lightly abraded O-mint half eagle are yellow-gold with distinct orange elements. Highly appealing with distinctly above-average visual appeal. PCGS has graded only eight finer examples (8/07). (#8385)

MS63 1894-O Five Dollar
Tied For Finest Certified

3479 1894-O MS63 NGC. Although the New Orleans Mint struck several ten dollar issues after 1894, the 1894-O was the final half eagle from the Southern facility aside from the rare 1909-O. The 1894-O is also rare, with less than half the mintage of the 1909-O, but demand is less because the length of the Liberty five series deters most collectors. When found, the 1894-O typically grades AU55 to MS61. However, the present superior example has pleasing luster and surprisingly few marks. The cheek is particularly smooth. The borders are well struck, although the curls near the ear are slightly soft, as are the claws and fletchings. Census: 2 in 63, 0 finer (8/07). (#8388)

3480 1894-S AU55 PCGS. Ex: Bass Collection. This is a highly attractive Choice AU example from the San Francisco Mint. Only traces of wear are noted on the well struck devices, and a great deal of luster remains evident. Numerous small contact marks are observed on each side of the coin. A scarce, low mintage issue of only 55,900 pieces. (#8389)

Lovely Gem 1895 Half Eagle

3481 1895 MS65 NGC. This lustrous and highly appealing apricot-gold example shows a hint of frost in the fields and on the boldly impressed devices. The portrait is clean, though a mark and scattered luster grazes are present in the fields. Still, these flaws are minor and entirely appropriate for the Gem designation. NGC has graded only eight finer pieces (8/07). (#8390)

Seldom-Seen Mint State 1895-S Five Dollar

3482 1895-S MS61 NGC. The lower Mint State grade is apparently attributed to a couple of reeding marks on the cheek and left obverse field, but the deep reddish-orange coloration and bold strike nonetheless imbue this coin with significant eye appeal and make it high-end for the assigned grade. Seldom seen in Mint State, as most examples of the emission entered circulation. (#8391)

3483 1896-S MS64 PCGS. The 1896-S is scarce in all grades, and is even more difficult to locate in Mint State than suggested by its low mintage of 155,400 pieces. A solitary MS67 example has been certified by PCGS, but most mere mortals can only aspire to own one of the four MS64 pieces encapsulated by NGC or PCGS. The present well struck near-Gem has canary-gold toning and an exceptionally preserved reverse. (#8393)

3484 1898 MS64 ★ NGC. A penetrating strike and flashy mint luster ensure the charm of this pale peach-gold near-Gem. Only lightly abraded. As of (7/07), no other business strike 1898 has a star designation, which presumably was awarded for its semi-prooflike fields. (#8396)

1898 Liberty Five MS65

3485 1898 MS65 NGC. This meticulously struck Gem has lovely apricot and green-gold toning. Careful rotation reveals a few wispy field grazes, but the quality is vastly superior to the typically abraded Mint State examples usually encountered. Very scarce as a Gem relative to common dates such as the 1901-S. Census: 22 in 65, 8 finer (8/07). (#8396)

3486 1900 MS64 PCGS. Sharply struck with hints of peach, orange, and honey color against a backdrop of yellow-gold. The strongly lustrous surfaces of this piece, a representative from the final 19th century half eagle issue from Philadelphia, display light, scattered marks in the reverse fields that account for the grade. (#8400)

3487 1900 MS64 PCGS. With slightly over 1.4 million pieces struck, this turn-of-the-century issue is popular with type collectors. Crisply struck and frosty with a hint of reddish-tan on the peach-gold surfaces. (#8400)

3488 1900 MS64 PCGS. An appealing Choice gold type coin with vigorous honey-gold luster and an exacting strike. The portrait is impressively unabraded, and the reverse is also exemplary. (#8400)

Immaculate MS67 1901 Five Dollar

3489 1901 MS67 NGC. A common date and readily available in Uncirculated grades. However, the 1901, like any gold type coin, is only occasionally offered for sale in Superb condition. This, of course, is because the metal itself is so soft that it is easily abraded by even the slightest contact with other coins. Which means, high grade gold had to have been cared for even more carefully than other coinage metals. This piece has lovely, softly frosted mint luster and rich reddish color over each side. Fully struck as well. Census: 13 in 67, 0 finer (8/07). (#8402)

3490 1901-S MS64 PCGS. A satiny and enticing near-Gem from the dawn of the 20th century, apricot-gold with elements of peach. The detail is bold overall, though the slightest hint of softness visits the lowest curl on Liberty's neck. (#8404)

3491 1902 MS64 NGC. Boldly struck and lustrous, with pleasing khaki-gold coloration and a few pinpoint-sized marks and shallow luster grazes that limit the grade. According to Ron Guth and Jeff Garrett (2006): "This may be an underrated date whose scarcity will someday be appreciated." Census: 89 in 64, 17 finer (7/07). (#8405)

3492 1903-S MS64 PCGS. A decisively struck and shining peach-gold and yellow-gold representative of this S-mint issue, carefully preserved with only pinpoint marks. This piece has excellent visual appeal for the grade. (#8408)

3493 1903-S MS64 NGC. This boldly impressed and satiny Choice piece offers warm yellow-orange surfaces with only faint, incidental marks. A delectable representative of this early 20th century S-mint issue. (#8408)

3494 1903-S MS64 NGC. Crisply struck with delicate peach accents against the apricot-gold of the shining surfaces. This lovely 20th century Liberty half eagle has excellent eye appeal and only a handful of wispy marks, though these are enough to preclude a finer grade. (#8408)

3495 1904-S MS62 NGC. Well struck with scintillating luster and lovely honey-gold and rose toning. Scattered small marks and one moderate abrasion, just above F in FIVE, are grade-limiting factors. An elusive issue at all levels of Mint State. Census: 22 in 62, 16 finer (7/07). (#8410)

3496 1906 MS64 PCGS. Orange and green-gold luster shimmers across this crisply struck Liberty five. The reverse is well preserved, and the obverse has only moderate grazes. (#8413)

3497 1907 MS63 NGC. A pleasing Select example of the penultimate P-mint Liberty half eagle issue, a solidly struck sun-gold example with pleasing luster. The fields and the solidly struck devices are clean for the grade. (#8416)

3498 1907-D MS63 PCGS. A crisply struck apricot-gold example from the second and final year of Denver Mint Liberty five dollar production. Clean for the grade despite a few marks on the left obverse. Housed in a first generation holder. (#8417)

3499 1907-D MS64 PCGS. The last Liberty half eagle issue produced at Denver, the 1907-D has an ample mintage of 888,000 pieces, though anything finer than this near-Gem proves elusive. Solidly struck with satiny yellow-gold surfaces that show elements of orange and green. (#8417)

Finest Certified 1907-D Liberty Half Eagle, MS67

3500 1907-D MS67 PCGS. An interesting variety, the mintmark is punched far to the left of center, below centered below the first talon in the eagle's claw left of the feather tip, and leaning sharply to the left as well.

This specimen is an amazing Superb Gem, the only such piece ever certified by PCGS with none finer. Both sides have pristine surfaces with highly lustrous mint frost and rich yellow luster. Coined in the second year of Denver Mint production and representing excellent quality control for such a young facility. Only one collector in the Set Registry program can own such a remarkable coin. (#8417)

PROOF LIBERTY HALF EAGLES

Rare 1890 Five, PR61 Cameo

3501 1890 PR61 Cameo PCGS. Careless handling accounts for the grade on this nonetheless-appealing piece, with numerous but not particularly heavy contact marks in the obverse fields and on Liberty's face. The surfaces are a deep reddish-gold. Garrett and Guth posit that there are only 20 to 25 pieces known of this rare proof issue, produced to the extent of only 88 recorded pieces. (#88485)

Premium Gem Cameo Proof 1895 Half Eagle

3502 1895 PR66 Cameo PCGS. An amazing Cameo proof, the obverse has rich honey-gold color with lighter yellow color and pale blue toning on the reverse. The devices have nearly complete mint frost, contrasting nicely with the deeply mirrored and watery fields, with the typical appearance found on 19th century proof gold coins. Exceptional surfaces are free of any significant contact marks, making pedigree tracking nearly impossible.

Nearly all 1895 proofs, like most other gold proofs of the 19th century, have cameo contrast. Usually associated with the earliest strikes from new dies, the low mintage of proof gold pieces virtually guaranteed that all examples were lovely cameo proofs. For those few dies that eventually lost the ability to produce cameo proofs, resurfacing involved acid etching the die to recreate the frosted devices, with polishing to renew the deeply mirrored fields.

Only about 20 to 25 proofs of this issue are known today, mostly in lower grades. Garrett and Guth comment that "most of the coins seen are graded PR64, with Gem examples being extremely rare." Among the survivors from a mintage of 81 proofs are two specimens in the Smithsonian Institution and an example in the American Numismatic Society. In all grades and designations, PCGS has certified 19 proof 1895 half eagles, including a single PR66 Deep Cameo, the only piece better than this one. Population: 1 in 66 Cameo, 0 finer (8/07). (#88490)

Choice Proof 1899 Five Dollar

3503 1899 PR64 PCGS. While the production of business strike half eagles, both in Philadelphia and at the San Francisco facility, reached significant numbers as the 19th century drew to a close, its proof half eagle counterpart is seldom offered. Even the official mintage of just 99 pieces fails to convey the rarity of the issue. This specimen is almost certainly the same piece offered in our 1996 ANA Sale, a coin that was then uncertified, but now resides in a PCGS holder. The deep, glassy mirrors are tinged in reddish patina and display appreciable contrast between fields and devices. A cluster of tiny blemishes to the left of the date and beneath the eagle's beak will identify any future market appearances. Population: 15 in 64, 2 finer (7/07). (#8494)

Elusive PR63 1904 Half Eagle

3504 1904 PR63 PCGS. Garrett and Guth point out that this issue is the "rarest from 1900 to 1907" in proof, with the lowest population numbers and the fewest number of coins appearing at auction from the time period. They note, further, that many pieces of the issue entered circulation, as impaired proofs are not uncommon. This piece displays lovely orange-gold mellowing of the surfaces on each side, and while the surfaces appear perfect to this cataloger's eyes, under a 10x loupe minuscule signs of contact appear. It is nonetheless extremely appealing, and an elusive issue to boot. Population: 4 in 63, 17 finer (8/07). (#8499)

Enticing Gem 1908 Half Eagle

3505 **1908 MS65 PCGS.** While the Saint-Gaudens designs of 1907 echoed the coins of ancient Greece, Bela Lyon Pratt's concept for the quarter eagle and half eagle reflected the influence of another past civilization, Egypt. The sunken devices, reminiscent of the incuse relief carvings found at temples and in tombs, created an effectively flat plane on both sides, as the highest points of the portrait and eagle are flush with the field.

The Pratt design offered little to no protection for the surfaces, however, and the half eagles in particular often show numerous abrasions. Even the 1908, saved in limited quantities for its novelty, is infrequently found above Choice. This MS65 piece offers shining yellow-orange surfaces with slightly paler color at the margins. Solidly struck and carefully preserved with the exquisite obverse deserving particular mention. A visually appealing example that displays beautifully.

From The Jim O'Neal Collection of Indian Half Eagles. (#8510)

Top-Flight Gem 1908-D Indian Head Five
Among the Finest Certified

3506 1908-D MS65 PCGS. There are numerous connections between noted sculptors-coin designers Augustus Saint-Gaudens, Bela Lyon Pratt, Saint-Gaudens assistant Henry Hering, and Yale University in New Haven, Connecticut. Saint-Gaudens, of course, achieved renown both as a sculptor and designer of the double eagle and eagle coins that bear his name. Bela Lyon Pratt (1867-1917), designer of the incused Indian Head quarter eagle and half eagles, was a Norwich, Connecticut, native who began study at age 16 at the Yale School of Fine Arts. At age 19 he entered the Art Students League in New York, where Saint-Gaudens taught. On Saint-Gaudens' recommendation Pratt studied at Paris' École des Beaux-Arts, returning to the United States in 1892. He was appointed Professor of Sculpture at the Boston Museum School of Fine Arts in 1894. Pratt was awarded a Bachelor of Fine Arts degree from Yale in 1899. (A note in Roger Burdette's seminal *Renaissance of American Coinage 1905-1908* notes that "Pratt was not one of Augustus' assistants, and may have considered The Saint more of a competitor than mentor." Nonetheless, the Yale website identifies Pratt as Saint-Gaudens "former assistant.")

Yale's famous statue of Revolutionary War hero-martyr Nathan Hale, which stands on the Old Campus outside of Connecticut Hall where Hale slept as a Yale student, is a Bela Lyon Pratt design. The alumni donors who commissioned the statue were unable to afford Saint-Gaudens' fee, so they turned to Pratt for the design. In Yale's Memorial Hall (part of Woolsey Hall), a memorial to the Yale graduates who gave their lives in the Civil War is graced by four statues, "Peace, Devotion, Memory, and Courage," designed by Saint-Gaudens' assistant Henry Hering. According to the Yale site, "Dynamic crevices and profound shadows temper the rigid austerity of the cold marble bodies, connecting this monument stylistically to the work of Hering's mentor, the celebrated turn-of-the-century American sculptor Augustus Saint-Gaudens."

When the novel, incused Indian Head-design quarter eagles and half eagles made their debut in 1908, no less prominent a numismatist than Samuel H. Chapman fired off a pointed criticism of the design to President Roosevelt, objecting to— among other things—the eagle, the Indian's portrait, and the incuse design. Roosevelt sent the objections on to his friend William Sturgis Bigelow, whose impetus for the incuse coinage led to his hiring Pratt to model the designs. Bigelow refuted the objections point by point, to which Chapman provided a rebuttal, but in any case the gold coinage proceeded, although little loved at the time.

Despite a plentiful mintage of 148,000 coins, the 1908-D is a difficult issue to obtain in Gem grade. Most survivors average MS62 or thereabouts. In MS65, the present example is one of only eight pieces so graded at PCGS, with an added four at NGC (7/07). This lovely coin offers primarily antique-gold, mattelike surfaces imbued with tinges of greenish-gold. Both sides are exceptionally distraction-free, with a few trivial contact marks on the reverse noted at E PLURIBUS UNUM. A delectable first-year Gem of this popular issue, suited for a top-flight gold collection.

From The Jim O'Neal Collection of Indian Half Eagles. (#8511)

Amazing 1908-S Half Eagle, MS66

3507 1908-S MS66 PCGS. The Indian half eagle design was first struck in 1908, with three Mints coining the denomination: Philadelphia, Denver, and San Francisco. Of the three, San Francisco had the lowest mintage at 82,000 pieces, the third-lowest production for any issue in the series. Between the small output for the S-mint pieces and the more frequent use of gold coins on the West Coast compared to the East Coast, it is little wonder that the 1908-S Indian half eagle's population trails that of its P-mint counterpart in grades through MS66. This attractive, well struck sun-gold representative offers soft, shimmering luster with a hint of satin. The delightfully preserved surfaces show only the tiniest of flaws, with luster grazes outnumbering actual marks by a considerable margin. An amazing representative for the discerning date collector. Population: 13 in 66, 8 finer (7/07).

From The Jim O'Neal Collection of Indian Half Eagles. (#8512)

Wonderful Gem 1909 Half Eagle

3508 1909 MS65 PCGS. By 1909, any novelty value that the Indian Head half eagle design once had was gone. Yet production went up compared to 1908, with 627,060 pieces struck, while the actual domestic commercial use for the coins was flat on the East Coast. Thus, many examples stayed in bank vaults or were shipped overseas, and today, the 1909 ranks as one of the most available issues in MS65, though it is not the most common.

This delightful Gem offers strong detail overall and powerful luster. The wheat-gold surfaces show only a handful of insignificant flaws that are entirely consistent with the assigned grade. An excellent selection for the type collector who seeks a slightly better date. PCGS has certified just six finer representatives (7/07).

From The Jim O'Neal Collection of Indian Half Eagles. (#8513)

Appealing 1909-D Half Eagle, MS64

3509 1909-D MS64 PCGS. Jeff Garrett and Ron Guth (2006) call the 1909-D half eagle "... the most common date of the series and available in most Mint State grades, including Gem condition." Indeed, PCGS and NGC have certified several thousand pieces through MS64, while roughly 140 Gems have been seen, and fewer than 10 Premium Gems. This MS64 example displays rich orange-gold color and vibrant luster, and exquisite strike definition is apparent on the design elements. A few trivial marks on each side prevent a higher grade. Excellent technical quality and aesthetic appeal for the designated grade.

From The Jim O'Neal Collection of Indian Half Eagles. (#8514)

Outstanding MS63 1909-O Indian Head Half Eagle

3510 1909-O MS63 PCGS. Ex: Cherny Collection. Variety One: The mintmark is weakly impressed and shows doubling on its left side. In 1909 the New Orleans Mint, not having struck a half eagle since 1894 nor a gold coin of any other denomination since 1906, struck a small quantity of half eagles: 34,200 pieces to be precise, making the issue the only O-mint Indian Head half eagle. That was not only the last gasp of the New Orleans Mint, whose fate had been sealed for several years since the new Denver Mint came online in 1906, but it was also the last O-mint gold coinage. The paltry mintage of 34,200 1909-O half eagles must have appeared especially insignificant next to the gargantuan emission of half eagles in 1909 from the Denver Mint, amounting to more than *3.4 million* examples!

Although it is conditionally rare and one of several issues in the series that are elusive in the higher Mint State grades, the 1909-O thus bears a special allure "due to its status as a one-year type," as Douglas Winter puts it in *Gold Coins of the New Orleans Mint: 1839-1909*. The issue appears to have gone directly into circulation with little notice or fanfare, as the typical piece encountered today grades just AU or Choice AU.

In MS63 grade, the present lot is one of only seven examples so graded at PCGS, with 13 finer, while NGC has graded six pieces in MS63, with 16 finer (7/07). As always, those population figures are almost certainly artificially augmented by resubmissions, in the case of this key-date issue likely multiple ones.

While most 1909-Os seem to have rather unattractive patination, the MS63 coin that we offer here displays outstanding color characteristics—a blend of pretty orange-gold and mint-green. The luster is also pleasing, again unusual for the issue. Strike can be a problem on Mint State coins, especially on the lower feathers of the headdress and on the eagle's legs. The present coin is above average in those areas as well. The only hint of minor softness occurs on the mintmark, which is typical for the variety, and on the eagle's shoulder, but even there, all feather detail is visible. A few minute marks on the Indian's cheek and on the raised, exposed fields, especially on the reverse, preclude an even higher grade. Overall, a great representative of this key date.

From The Jim O'Neal Collection of Indian Half Eagles. (#8515)

Rare 1909-S Near-Gem Five Dollar

3511 1909-S MS64 PCGS. This is a sharply struck example, as are most, and it exhibits beautiful deep orange-gold color with frosty luster. David Akers has estimated that fewer than 20 pieces exist in MS64 or better grades, and current population data seems to support his words, written 20 years ago: "The 1909-S is one of the four or five rarest issues of the series. Among San Francisco Mint issues it is virtually on a par with the 1915-S and is far more rare than the lower mintages 1908-S. Mint State examples at any level are rare and in the high Mint State grades, i.e. MS-64 or better, there are probably fewer than 20 specimens in all." Population: 16 in 64, 4 finer (7/07).

From The Jim O'Neal Collection of Indian Half Eagles. (#8516)

Lovely Gem 1910 Indian Half Eagle
None Finer at PCGS

3512 1910 MS65 PCGS. Gold gurus Jeff Garrett and Ron Guth note that they consider the 1910 issue "an available date in Gem grades for this series." The last three words of warning are key to understanding the statement, however, as pieces in MS65 are a full order of magnitude rarer than MS64 pieces, according to the current combined NGC/PCGS population data. While it is true that Gem 1910s are more available, according to Garrett-Guth, than 15 of the 24 issues in the series, it is equally true that Gems of whatever stripe are the subject of intense demand by type and date collectors alike.

This piece is one of 17 Gems of the issue so certified at PCGS, and there are none finer at that service. NGC has certified 21 pieces in MS65, with two coins finer (7/07). The surfaces offer striking eye appeal, with a combination of deep sunset orange-red in the fields complementing tinges of azure-hazel on the highpoints. Brilliant luster emerges unimpeded from both sides, which show none but the most trivial contact marks away from the focal areas. Simply lovely!

From The Jim O'Neal Collection of Indian Half Eagles. (#8517)

High-End MS64 1910-D Indian Five

3513 1910-D MS64 PCGS. Fortunately for the many connoisseurs of this series, the 1910-D is an issue that is both well produced and frequently encountered in Mint State, all the way up to the rarefied levels above MS65, although those pieces are of course few and far between. The heightened availability and quality of the issue, like so many 20th century gold coins, are due to repatriations of high quality coins from overseas. This piece offers lustrous, delightful orange-gold surfaces tinged with azure and gray on the highpoints. While a few tiny contact marks on the reverse appear to account for the grade, the piece nonetheless appears quite high-end and appealing. Population: 26 in 64, 10 finer (7/07).

From The Jim O'Neal Collection of Indian Half Eagles. (#8518)

Exuberant, Lustrous MS64 1910-S Indian Head Half Eagle Only Four Finer at PCGS

Terrific Gem 1911 Half Eagle

3514 1910-S MS64 PCGS. Although somewhat more than 300 *certification events* in Mint State are documented between NGC and PCGS combined, the population of the 1910-S issue at the Gem level thins out drastically. As of this writing there are only six pieces in MS65 at both services combined, a situation that exerts added pressure on high-end near-Gems such as the present coin. This coin's brilliant luster is its chief attribute, bright and gleaming, and seemingly more often found on a Liberty Head coin than on an Indian Head piece. The surfaces are intensely satiny and a light yellow-gold, also atypical for the series. Although examination with a loupe reveals a few trivial contact marks on the reverse, the only mentionable abrasion is a small nick in the left obverse field, directly before the Indian's nose. Even it is minute and mentioned only for strict accuracy. The exuberant luster and unbounded eye appeal more than compensate! Population: 17 in 64, 4 finer (7/07).
From The Jim O'Neal Collection of Indian Half Eagles. (#8519)

3515 1911 MS65 PCGS. The 1911 sported a comparatively high mintage for the Indian half eagle series, with the third-highest production at the time, behind only the 1909-D and 1911-S. Compared to its S-mint counterpart, however, the 1911 has a better survival rate, particularly in Mint State grades. As a consequence, the P-mint issue is comparatively more available and more affordable, though loftier levels of preservation remain challenging.

Garrett and Guth (2006) note that "(most of) the 1911 half eagles are found with minor weakness on the headdress feathers and with average luster." The strike of this piece, however, is bold throughout, and the emerald-accented lemon-gold surfaces display vibrant luster. The devices and fields are equally well-preserved. This issue is scarce in Gem and practically impossible to acquire in better condition; PCGS has certified only one finer representative (7/07).
From The Jim O'Neal Collection of Indian Half Eagles. (#8520)

Sharp, Splendid 1911-D Half Eagle, MS64

3516 **1911-D MS64 PCGS.** Although it is perhaps less often trumpeted than its smaller cousin—and certainly far less often encountered in Mint State—the 1911-D Indian Head half eagle is even more a key to its series in Mint State (along with the 1909-O) than the 1911-D quarter eagle is to that series. The two major grading services have certified more than 3,000 1911-D quarter eagles in Mint State (including duplications), yet *the number of 1911-D half eagles certified as Mint State is less than one-tenth as much:* 241 pieces as of 7/07, again counting resubmissions.

Despite the larger mintage of the half eagle—72,500 pieces compared to 55,680 coins of the quarter eagle—it appears to have been saved in much smaller quantities, and/or melted in much larger ones. According to the Garrett-Guth *Gold Encyclopedia,* about half of the 1911-D quarter eagles that appeared at auction from 1991-2005 were Mint State, but only one-sixth of the 1911-D half eagles were Uncirculated. This fact is unsurprising when one stops to consider how much buying power five dollars had in pre-World War I America; even if the low mintage was known, many people simply could not afford to tie up five dollars permanently.

Of course, in the higher Mint State levels, the comparisons are even more profound: While NGC and PCGS combined have certified more than 615 1911-D quarter eagles in MS64, with 85 pieces finer, for the 1911-D half eagle the combined MS64 population is 23 coins, with only five finer (7/07). Assuming a reasonable figure for resubmissions, it thus appears likely that there are not many more than 15 or so separate *pieces* at both services that merit a near-Gem ranking. At PCGS, this coin is one of 12 pieces so certified, and only two coins at that service surpass it, both MS65s.

The present MS64 example boasts pleasing khaki-gold surfaces with a splendid strike that is its foremost attribute, although the luster is excellent and there are relatively few abrasions for the grade. A couple of tiny ticks are noted on the Indian's cheek that are grade-consistent, and a couple of small marks appear in the left obverse field and on the reverse around IN GOD WE TRUST, but they are completely undistracting and fail to detract from the enormous appeal of this charming and elusive specimen. This coin truly represents a rare opportunity for the Indian Head half eagle collector.

From The Jim O'Neal Collection of Indian Half Eagles. (#8521)

Scarce 1911-S Half Eagle, MS64

Pleasing Gem 1912 Indian Five
None Finer at PCGS

3517 1911-S MS64 PCGS. The 1911-S half eagle, despite its rather generous mintage of 1,416,000 pieces, is scarce in all Mint State grades, though perhaps slightly less so in the MS60 to MS62 range. Its scarcity elevates dramatically above that level, with about 180 MS63 to MS66 coins having been seen by PCGS and NGC. This near-Gem example displays beautiful orange-gold and lime-green patina over well frosted surfaces, and a sharp strike imparts good definition to the design features, including the mintmark. Kept from potential Gem status by a few minute facial marks. Population: 18 in 64, 8 finer (7/07).
From The Jim O'Neal Collection of Indian Half Eagles. (#8522)

3518 1912 MS65 PCGS. Fortunately for collectors of this series, the P-mint issues of 1911, 1912, and 1913 share similarities in mintages, survivorship, and production quality that make them not only numerically available for a price in Gem condition, but aesthetically pleasing when they are encountered in such condition. Their overall good production characteristics include generally sharp strikes and abundant eye appeal, with surfaces that are usually yellow-gold with a hint of green. The present piece offers a more golden-orange color that is especially pleasing, with generous luster over the mattelike surfaces and a remarkable absence of singular abrasions. Population: 41 in 65, 0 finer (7/07).
From The Jim O'Neal Collection of Indian Half Eagles. (#8523)

3519 1912-S MS64 PCGS. The S-mintmarked Indian Head quarter eagles from 1912 through 1915 are among the most elusive issues in this series loaded with difficult issues, although one cannot exclude the 1909-O, 1911-D, and the famous 1929 from that list. Garrett and Guth typecast the 1912-S as a "one of the classic rarities" of the series. As of (7/07), PCGS has certified a mere 20 pieces as MS64, with a single MS65 coin finer. There are a few light abrasions on the exposed Indian's cheek and in the field nearby that account for the grade, but the luster is generous over the orange-gold surfaces. The mintmark is weak, as nearly always on this issue. The reverse appears high-end for the grade, and the strike elsewhere is pleasingly bold for this issue that is normally seen weakly struck. It is doubtful that a more pleasing piece could be found, even with extensive searching, making this another significant opportunity for some forthright bidder.

From The Jim O'Neal Collection of Indian Half Eagles. (#8524)

3520 1913 MS65 PCGS. The color is a delight on this stunning Gem Indian Head half eagle, ranging from the predominant deep orange-red to pinkish-gold on some of the obverse highpoints. The reverse, with its considerably more open fields, blends in dollops of hazel-gray in the exposed areas. The 1913 is another popular P-mint for collectors seeking a Gem of the Indian Head type, due to its combination of good strike and appealing luster. Such is the case here, with a remarkable paucity of mentionable abrasions complementing the bold impression and generous luster emanating from the deeply colored surfaces. Although PCGS has seen 48 certification events of this issue, only a single piece has surpassed it at that service—one MS66—while NGC has seen six coins at that level (7/07).

From The Jim O'Neal Collection of Indian Half Eagles. (#8525)

Exceptional 1913-S Five Dollar, MS64

3521 **1913-S MS64 PCGS.** The 1913-S five dollar carries with it a reputation of poor quality. In his *A Handbook of 20th-Century United State Gold Coins, 1907-1933*, David Akers writes of this issue: "The strike is typically only average to good and the mintmark is usually very weak and little more than a shapeless 'blob.' Problems near the border indicate die deterioration and the luster is nearly always sub-par."

Akers' comments have little or no application to the near-Gem that we offer in this lot. First of all, the mintmark is bold and clearly defined. Second, the overall strike is sharp, including that on all of the peripheral elements. Excellent definition is also apparent on the eagle's plumage and on most of the feathers of the headdress. Finally, the luster is anything but "subpar;" indeed, it is bright and invigorates the apricot-gold surfaces that are laced with hints of light green. A few inoffensive handling marks in the raised, exposed fields just barely preclude an even higher grade. Population: 14 in 64, 2 finer (7/07).

From The Jim O'Neal Collection of Indian Half Eagles. (#8526)

Bold, Lustrous MS63 1914 Five Dollar

3522 **1914 MS63 PCGS.** A few small abrasions on each side preclude a finer grade for this piece, notably on the Indian's cheek and the left obverse field nearby. The exposed reverse also shows a few abrasions, including a scrape through the first A in AMERICA. The bold luster and attractive honey-gold surfaces, however, are partial compensation.

From The Jim O'Neal Collection of Indian Half Eagles. (#8527)

Stunning 1914-D Indian Five, MS66
Tied for Finest of the Issue

3523 **1914-D MS66 PCGS.** The present coin is among the standout specimens in this fine consignment, as one of only two MS66 pieces of the 1914-D issue certified at PCGS (7/07). NGC has also certified a single coin MS66. One could easily make the case that this coin is among the handful of finest Indian Head half eagles of the entire type, as PCGS has, including the inevitable resubmissions, certified 55 coins in this lofty Premium Gem grade.

Although not a San Francisco Mint product, the 1914-D is nonetheless a scarcer issue among the Indian Head half eagle series, with a skimpy mintage of 247,000 pieces. In 2006, gold pundits Jeff Garrett and Ron Guth noted that this issue "is a scarcer date, and is frequently found well struck even on the feather tips and eagle's chest and wings. The surfaces are less granular and more lustrous than seen on many dates of this series. In terms of rarity, this date is available in most grades up to MS-64, but the populations fall off drastically at the gem MS-65 level, as seen on most dates. For this date and mint, a total of 20 coins have been graded as MS-65 ... . This places the issues (sic) just ahead of the 1914 Philadelphia issue in terms of rarity in gem, as the 14th scarcest."

This coin offers so many superlative attributes that one hesitates to single one out to the detriment of the others. The surfaces are remarkably free of even the most picayune abrasions, from the exposed open fields on the reverse to the highpoints of the Indian's cheek on the obverse. Neither there nor in the left obverse field nearby—the focal points of the obverse—are there any abrasions above the microscopic sort. The color is a pleasing moderate honey-gold laced with tinges of mint-green, with generous luster and a bold strike. A small planchet flaw appears underneath OF on the reverse, but as a prestrike anomaly it does not affect the grade. More importantly, it fails to affect the enormous appeal of this stunning piece. Population: 2 in 66, 0 finer (7/07).

From The Jim O'Neal Collection of Indian Half Eagles. (#8528)

3524 **1914-S MS64 PCGS.** The later S-mint Indian Head half eagles constitute some of the best-known rarities in a series replete with difficult and seldom-seen issues. The 1916-S is fairly available, due to a hoard of a few hundred original pieces that was squirreled away at the time of issue, but the 1912-S through 1915-S coins are all elusive in Mint State. Even among those difficult S-mint issues, the 1914-S has earned the title of key to the Indian Head half eagle set in Mint State, according to Garrett and Guth. While a Heritage cataloger a few Signature auctions ago wrote, "The '14-S is the only contender capable of taking on the 1911-D half eagle for top rarity honors among 20th century gold issues," Garrett and Guth are less equivocal on the issue: "Most examples of the 1914-S half eagle are found with well-struck devices, but the luster tends to be muted and the eye appeal challenged. Lacking the mint-imparted glow of many other issues, the 1914-S issue is, therefore, very difficult to find above the grade of MS-63. In fact, a single coin has been graded as MS-65 by NGC, with none seen that high or higher by PCGS or ANACS. Even in MS-64 grades, this date is rarer than many other issues in MS-65, with the 1914-S boasting a mere eight coins graded as high as MS-64. Thus, the 1914-S has earned its place as the most difficult and rarest issue of the series to find in MS-64 or higher grades. This date should be considered the key date to the series."

This specimen displays hallmark gritty surfaces, but it also offers bright and frosty luster, the comments above from Garrett and Guth notwithstanding. The coloration is an attractive antique copper-gold, and a few wispy bagmarks account for the near-Gem grade. The mintmark is clearly discernible, and the overall strike is above average. The eye appeal is quite attractive for the issue. Any U.S. gold specialist should pay close attention to this seldom-seen offering. PCGS has encapsulated seven examples in MS64 with none finer; NGC reports a lone MS65 example (7/07).

From The Jim O'Neal Collection of Indian Half Eagles. (#8529)

Vibrant 1915 Gem Five Dollar

3525 1915 MS65 PCGS. The 1915 half eagle, coming from a mintage of 588,000 business strikes, can be obtained with relatively little difficulty through MS63. The PCGS/NGC population drops somewhat in near-Gem, and the two services have seen fewer than 70 coins in MS65, and none finer.

Vibrant luster adorns both sides of the MS65 coin in the present lot. This is complemented by attractive peach-gold color that is imbued with traces of light green, as well as by an impressive strike that brings out sharp definition on the design features. A couple of grade-consistent obverse marks do not detract from the coin's overall outstanding eye appeal. Population: 35 in 65, 0 finer (7/07).
From The Jim O'Neal Collection of Indian Half Eagles. (#8530)

Gorgeous 1915-S Five Dollar, MS64

3526 1915-S MS64 PCGS. The relatively low mintage 1915-S half eagle (164,000 pieces) is elusive in all grades, particularly so in Mint State, where approximately 280 coins are reported by PCGS and NGC. These two services combined have seen just 18 near-Gems, and a solitary piece finer.

Both sides of the MS64 example in this lot are awash with potent luster, and display a rich blend of apricot-gold and mint-green color. A well executed strike results in sharp definition on the design features, including the Indian's hair and feathers in the headdress, and the eagle's plumage. A few minor marks keep from full Gem status, but a gorgeous specimen nevertheless. Population: 9 in 64, 0 finer (7/07).
From The Jim O'Neal Collection of Indian Half Eagles. (#8531)

Elusive 1916-S Gem Five Dollar

3527 1916-S MS65 PCGS. Advanced collectors of Indian Head half eagles seldom have an opportunity to acquire such a high-grade example of this date, as relatively few Gem-quality pieces are known; PCGS/NGC population reports indicate 16 MS65 coins have been certified, and five pieces finer (MS66s). This MS65 specimen has rich orange and rose colored gold surfaces with frosty luster. It is well struck with sharp obverse and reverse details throughout. A rather large hoard of these coins was discovered a number of years ago, but nearly all pieces from that hoard were at the lowest Mint State grade levels, and contained no MS64 or MS65 coins (David Akers, 1988). *From The Jim O'Neal Collection of Indian Half Eagles.* (#8532)

Bright 1929 Half Eagle, MS64

3528 1929 MS64 PCGS. The 1929 coinage of half eagles resumed after a 13-year hiatus. This issue is rare in all Mint State grades. Moreover, David Akers, in his 20th-century United States gold coins reference book, says "... the majority of Uncirculated specimens are quite heavily bagmarked, thereby falling into the MS60 to MS62 category."

This near-Gem specimen exhibits brassy-gold surfaces with touches of apricot, along with bright luster. A solid strike emboldens the design features, with no areas revealing hints of weakness. The coin possesses just a few minute contact marks that prevent the achievement of full Gem classification. An exceptional example of this difficult issue. *From The Jim O'Neal Collection of Indian Half Eagles.* (#8533)

ADDITIONAL INDIAN HALF EAGLES

3529 1908 MS62 PCGS. Apricot-gold patina laced with traces of light green enriches both sides of this half eagle. Well struck, except for weakness on the eagle's shoulder. The surfaces possess soft luster, and reveal a few minor handling marks. (#8510)

3530 1908 MS62 NGC. This well struck example from the first year of issue displays luminous, lightly abraded orange-gold surfaces. A touch of rose is noted at the lower truncation of the portrait. (#8510)

3531 1908 MS62 PCGS. The outer regions of this shining first-year half eagle are predominantly orange-gold, while the centers show substantial sun-gold elements. A well-defined piece that shows a number of wispy abrasions in the fields. (#8510)

3532 1908 MS63 PCGS. The luminous orange-gold surfaces of this Select piece show faint glimmers of yellow at the margins. A pleasingly detailed first-year representative that exhibits mild, scattered abrasions. (#8510)

Luminous Choice 1908 Indian Half Eagle

3533 1908 MS64 PCGS. The glowing surfaces of this near-Gem are an attractive blend of yellow-orange and peach. Pleasingly detailed with an uncommonly clean obverse, though the reverse displays several pinpoint marks in the fields. The Pratt quarter eagle and half eagle designs debuted to a mixed reception in 1908, though the design has gained widespread numismatic and artistic acceptance in the years since its passing from circulation. (#8510)

Splendid MS64 1908 Indian Five

3534 1908 MS64 PCGS. A splendid first-year example of this novel recessed relief design. The orange-red surfaces shimmer with luster, and the strike is exacting, even with the intricacies of the headdress. Well preserved despite an unimportant reed mark beneath OF, and an excellent candidate for a quality gold type set. (#8510)

3535 1908-D MS63 PCGS. The centers of this exceptionally lustrous D-mint half eagle are lemon-gold, while the margins range from rich orange-gold to mint-green. A solidly struck first-year example that shows only faint abrasions. (#8511)

Noteworthy Choice 1908-D Half Eagle

3536 1908-D MS64 NGC. A gorgeous yellow-orange representative of this mintmarked first-year issue, well-defined with splashes of deeper color at the obverse periphery. Minimally marked with pleasing luster and excellent visual appeal. Like the vast majority of Indian Head half eagle issues, the 1908-D is highly elusive in better condition; NGC has graded just four finer examples (8/07). *From The Diemer L. Fife Collection.* (#8511)

3537 1908-S MS62 PCGS. A well-struck and luminous orange-gold representative of the lowest-mintage Indian half eagle issue from 1908. Small abrasions pepper the portrait and the nearby fields. (#8512)

1908-S Indian Half Eagle, MS64

3538 1908-S MS64 PCGS. While a legitimately scarce issue, the 1908-S is actually more plentiful than the other S-mint Indian half eagles in higher grades. This piece has the soft, frosted appearance seen on so many 1908-S fives, and the strike is sharp throughout. There are no singularly mentionable abrasions on either side. Attractive tan-golden luster overlies the surfaces. (#8512)

Attractive 1909 Indian Head Half Eagle MS63

3539 1909 MS63 NGC. Boldly defined and highly lustrous, this Select example's lightly marked surfaces are seemingly close to a higher grade designation. Reddish-gold color shines from the devices, while the fields are imbued with an attractive greenish-khaki tint. A favorite issue of type collectors. (#8513)

3540 1909-D MS62 PCGS. The strongly lustrous surfaces of this type Indian half eagle are an appealing blend of lemon-gold and sun-gold. Well-defined overall with faint, scattered abrasions that preclude a Select grade. (#8514)

3541 1909-D MS62 NGC. A pleasing example of this populous Denver half eagle issue, well-defined overall with luminous yellow-orange surfaces. Light, scattered abrasions account for the grade. (#8514)

3542 1909-D MS62 PCGS. A well-defined example of this popular Indian half eagle type issue, predominantly orange-gold with glints of yellow near the devices. Light, scattered abrasions on each side account for the grade. (#8514)

3543 1909-D MS62 PCGS. The luminous apricot-gold surfaces exhibit elements of orange. An unworn example of this ever-present Indian half eagle issue that shows pleasing central detail, though the lowest pendant is soft and both sides display a number of abrasions. Still, suitable for a similarly graded type set. (#8514)

3544 1909-D MS63 PCGS. Zones of yellow-orange mingle with areas of mint-green on this well struck Indian half eagle. A distinctive Select example of this popular type issue with above-average luster. (#8514)

3545 1909-D MS63 NGC. Even honey-gold toning is illuminated by intense mint frost on the reverse, while the obverse has a more satiny appearance. Boldly struck with a sharply defined mintmark, and a few stray field abrasions that limit the grade. A pleasing Select Mint State specimen. (#8514)

3546 1909-D MS63 ICG. Well struck and lustrous, with an unblemished obverse and a small number of scattered blemishes on the reverse. The design elements, including the mintmark, are sharply impressed. An ideal choice for type purposes. (#8514)

3547 1909-D MS63 ICG. Boldly struck with a bright satiny finish and attractive honey-gold coloration. A few grade-limiting marks are noted in the reverse fields. This issue's easy availability at grade levels up to MS64 make it a popular target for type collectors. (#8514)

3548 1909-D MS63 ICG. A well struck example of this widely collected Indian half eagle type issue, predominantly yellow-orange with apricot accents on the lustrous obverse. Faint, scattered abrasions define the grade. (#8514)

Sharp 1909-D Five Dollar, MS64

3549 1909-D MS64 NGC. This common date issue is available in most Mint State grades through MS64, as evidenced by the thousands of pieces certified by NGC and PCGS. This near-Gem specimen displays a sharp strike throughout, along with peach-gold luster that gives off a faint greenish cast. A few minute marks on each side define the grade. (#8514)

Near-Gem 1909-D Indian Five

3550 1909-D MS64 PCGS. Soft, attractive luster is the most noteworthy feature of this lovely example. The well struck devices are pleasingly preserved, as are the fields. Although the 1909-D is the most plentiful issue of the series, quality Mint State coins are under strong demand from type collectors. Conditionally elusive any finer, with just 86 such pieces graded by PCGS (8/07). (#8514)

Attractive 1909-D Indian Head Five Dollar MS64

3551 1909-D MS64 ANACS. The surfaces are a lovely red-gold, with hints of hazel near the peripheries. This issue is surprisingly scarce in the higher Mint State grades, considering its easy availability in lower grades. This is a robustly struck and essentially problem-free example, with a better-than-average appearance for the grade. (#8514)

Popular 1909-O Half Eagle, XF45

3552 1909-O XF45 NGC. An always-popular issue as the key date in the Indian Head half eagle series as well as the last O-mint gold (and the only New Orleans gold produced in the 20th century). While the numerical grade in terms of wear appears technically correct, in terms of luster the surfaces suggest an AU rating. (#8515)

Mint State 1909-O Indian Five

3553 1909-O MS60 NGC. The '09-O five appeals to many with its historical and numismatic significance. Struck during the final year of operation at the New Orleans Mint before that facility permanently stopped the coining presses, it is also the only Indian gold coin of any denomination struck in Louisiana. The mintage of just 34,200 coins and the release of most or all into circulation means that few have survived in Mint State grades. This piece has light yellow color with full mint brilliance and splashes of deeper rose toning on both sides. The mintmark is clear and sharp, a further important consideration when seeking an example of this issue. (#8515)

3554 1910 MS62 NGC. Bright peach-gold surfaces display well struck design elements, except for minor softness on the eagle's shoulder. We note a few trivial marks on each side. (#8517)

3555 1910 MS62 ANACS. Boldly struck with lovely red-gold surfaces that show soft, pleasing luster. Light, scattered abrasions and a handful of longer flaws appear on each side of this Pratt-designed half eagle. (#8517)

3556 1910-D MS62 PCGS. The heavy production of 1909-D half eagles led to a surfeit of the coins, and in 1910, Denver struck only 193,600 examples of that denomination. This lustrous and well-defined example, wheat-gold with elements of orange, has scattered abrasions that account for the grade. (#8518)

3557 1911 MS62 PCGS. Boldly impressed with subtly lustrous, lightly abraded orange-gold surfaces. An unworn and desirable representative of this earlier Indian Head half eagle issue. (#8520)

3558 1911 MS62 NGC. This attractive type piece shows better-than-average luster and excellent detail. The lightly abraded sun-gold surfaces show a number of faint marks and a handful of significant abrasions. (#8520)

Nice Near-Gem 1911 Half Eagle

3559 1911 MS64 PCGS. A nice piece for a type set, with softly lustrous greenish-gold surfaces and a representative of one of the more frequently encountered issues in the series. Such pieces are much more pricey one grade point finer, and many collectors accordingly turn to near-Gems such as the present example to fill that empty hole in their set. (#8520)

3560 1911-D AU55 ANACS. The 1911-D Half Eagle is a scarce date from a low mintage of just 72,500 coins. Slight wear is evident on the high points of this bright almond-gold example. The fields are moderately abraded. (#8521)

Pleasing Select Mint State 1912 Indian Half Eagle

3561 1912 MS63 NGC. Rich rose-gold coloration adorns both sides of this matte-like example. A pleasing Mint State specimen with boldly struck design elements and a few minor marks that keep the piece from receiving an even finer grade. A desirable type coin at the Select Uncirculated grade level. (#8523)

3562 1913 MS62 PCGS. The fields have a dusky orange appearance, while the centers have lighter yellow-gold color. This mid-date P-mint piece shows a number of shallow field abrasions that preclude a finer grade. (#8525)

Attractive 1913 Five Dollar, MS64

3563 **1913 MS64 NGC.** A substantial number of high-end About Uncirculated and lower-level Mint State coins are known of the 1913 five dollar. Nice near-Gem and Gem examples are also obtainable. Attractive luster graces the yellow-gold surfaces of this MS64 specimen. Well defined, with a few minute grade-defining marks. (#8525)

Lustrous Select Mint State 1914 Indian Head Half Eagle

3564 **1914 MS63 NGC.** The luster is stronger and more frosty than ordinarily seen on any Indian Head half eagle issue. This piece displays even khaki-gold coloration over each side. The obverse is blemish-free, while a few wispy marks are evident on the reverse fields, and near the reverse motto. This date has the lowest mintage of any Philadelphia Mint issue, for the type. (#8527)

Appealing 1914-S Half Eagle, MS62

3565 **1914-S MS62 PCGS.** The peach-gold surfaces on this 1914-S five dollar have above-average luster, and the design features are generally bold. Under magnification, numerous faint marks are observed on the raised, exposed fields, especially those at the upper obverse and reverse. Still, a pleasing example of this mintmarked issue, difficult to locate in the better Mint State grades. PCGS has graded 23 finer pieces (8/07). (#8529)

Sharp 1915 Near-Gem Half Eagle

3566 **1915 MS64 NGC.** The 1915 is one of the more attractive issues of the Indian Head five dollar series (Jeff Garrett and Ron Guth, 2006), and this near-Gem specimen is no exception. Its highly lustrous surfaces yield peach-gold color tinged with light green, and the design elements are well defined. A few minor handling marks in the raised fields, especially those of the reverse, limit the grade. (#8530)

Popular Choice 1915 Half Eagle

3567 **1915 MS64 NGC.** This shimmering caramel-gold near-Gem has a sharp strike with nearly absolute definition within the Indian's headdress. The few small marks that are present are unworthy of further elaboration. The last of the Philadelphia Mint issues until 1929, since gold coins little circulated on the East Coast by 1915. (#8530)

Captivating MS64 1915 Half Eagle

3568 **1915 MS64 PCGS.** The half eagles of 1915 would be the last examples of that denomination struck at Philadelphia until 1929, and while the issue is more generally available than others in the series, finding an attractive example can prove challenging. This pleasingly detailed near-Gem has clean sun-gold surfaces and above-average detail and luster. Two faint, parallel marks on the Indian's jaw are the only significant bar to an even finer grade. PCGS has graded 36 pieces finer (8/07). (#8530)

3569 **1916-S MS61 NGC.** A boldly impressed and slightly brassy example of the penultimate half eagle issue intended for circulation. Though the piece has a clean appearance at arm's length, closer inspection reveals a number of wispy, grade-defining abrasions. (#8532)

Impressive 1795 Small Eagle Ten, AU50, BD-1

3570 1795 13 Leaves AU50 PCGS. Breen-6830, Taraszka-1, BD-1, High R.3. It is always an interesting pursuit to seek the origins of coinage designs. As a small part of a much larger article in *Coin World*, March 1, 1999, Richard Giedroyc wrote of the reverse design:

> "The Small Eagle reverse appearing on the coins of 1795 to 1797 is believed to have been adapted from a first century B.C. Roman onyx cameo in the Kunshistorisches Museum. The position of the eagle is different on the museum cameo, although the palm branch and circular wreath accompanying the eagle on the U.S. coin is strikingly similar to the design on the cameo."

Only 5,583 pieces were struck of this design type. But then, there was little demand for the ten dollar denomination in the channels of commerce. In 1795 Philadelphia, the average laborer earned ten dollars for two weeks wages for a six-day workweek. As a result, there was minimal need for such a high-denomination gold coin.

This particular coin is pleasing overall with just the slightest friction over the highpoints. The striking details are well defined overall with strong detailing on Liberty's hair and the eagle's wings. There are no mentionable or distracting abrasions, and each side shows a strong reddish accent of patina around the devices with the remainder of the coin retaining its original greenish-gold color. Rarely found finer, this is a splendid, high grade example of this popular, first-year design type. (#8551)

3571 **1797 Large Eagle AU55 NGC.** Breen-6834, Taraszka-8, BD-2, High R.4. In their *Early U.S. Gold Coin Varieties* (2006), Harry W. Bass, Jr. and John Dannreuther identify this variety as being the first of the Large Eagle tens struck. Of the 1797 eagles bearing the Large Eagle reverse, one obverse die (Bass-Dannreuther 2) was married to three reverse dies (Bass-Dannreuther A, B, and C) to create three distinct varieties. This variety and BD-4 are very scarce in absolute terms, with the other variety, BD-3, legitimately rare with fewer than 50 examples known in all grades. As a point of clarification, the 1797 BD-1 variety is of the Small Eagle type. It is fascinating that the emission sequence observed by researcher Anthony Taraszka, and confirmed in the Bass-Dannreuther reference, puts the other two varieties of this date and type as struck after both of the 1798/7 tens. Striking coins in a year with dies dated either earlier or later was common practice in the formative years of our first Mint. Unfortunately, it was also standard procedure to record the amount of coins struck in a calendar year, regardless of the dates on the actual coins delivered. Thankfully, researchers such as Taraszka, Bass, and Dannreuther have compiled an emission sequence for this and other series by meticulously studying the die states of all known varieties. Data garnered from such investigations allows for more accurate mintage figures to be ascertained.

The Large, or Heraldic, Eagle design was based on the Great Seal of the United States and debuted on the 1796 quarter eagles. It replaced the Small Eagle design that many disliked due to its resemblance to a scrawny chicken. Breen and other past researchers have credited Robert Scot as the lone creator of the Large Eagle design. However, current research suggests that John Smith Garner and Robert Scot both designed Heraldic Eagle punches for the early U.S. gold issues. By 1799 Scot's design became the standard for the eagle series and was employed until the final year of production in 1804 (Bass-Dannreuther, 2006). The coin in this lot features one of Garner's three reverse designs and is easily identifiable by the eagle's long, thin neck. As of (8/07), NGC has graded 24 1797 Large Eagle tens at the AU55 level. The surfaces retain generous portions of mint luster and there is a significant presence of reddish patina on each side. Sharply defined throughout with no obvious or mentionable marks on the obverse or reverse. Population: 34 in 55, 57 finer (8/07). (#8559)

3572 **1799 Small Stars Obverse—Repaired, Whizzed, Rim Filed—ANACS. AU50 Details.** Breen-6840, Taraszka-20, BD-8, R.5. This variety is characterized by the leaf on the reverse that touches the I in AMERICA rather than pointing to the space between the I and C, and the date is spaced 1 7 9 9. The surfaces show obvious signs of whizzing, and the 'Repaired' disclaimer by ANACS apparently refers to an irregularity in the field above the arrow points on the reverse. Well defined for the grade. (#98562)

1799 Ten Dollar Small Stars Obverse
AU55 Details BD-8, R.5

3573 **1799 Small Stars Obverse—Cleaned, Rim Damage—ANACS. AU55 Details.** Irregular Date, Small Stars, Breen-6840, Taraszka-20, BD-8, R.5. This scarce variety is attributed by the 17 of the date tilted far right, the 7 higher than the 1, reverse star 12 touching upper beak and also the scroll with two points. John Dannreuther and Harry Bass, in their book *Early U.S. Gold Varieties*, estimate 45 to 55 examples of this variety to be known. Bright reddish-gold surfaces are lightly hairlined, and the rim damage at 3 o'clock on the obverse is hardly noticeable within the holder. The design elements are well struck, and there is an even distribution of minute marks over the obverse. Overall, the impairments are not all that bad. (#98562)

Well Worn BD-1 1800 Eagle

3574 **1800—Damaged—ANACS. VG8 Details.** Breen-6842, Taraszka-23, BD-1, High R.3. Here is a chance to buy an early eagle at an affordable price. Green-gold color with extensive wear. A couple rim bumps and minor punctures are evident on the surfaces, perhaps repaired to remove an old mount. (#8563)

AU53 Sharpness 1800 Eagle, BD-1

3575 **1800—Cleaned—ANACS. AU53 Details.** Breen-6842, Taraszka-23, BD-1, High R.3. A middle die state with die cracks atop LIBERTY and bold clashmarks above the A in STATES. The only dies for this low mintage date. This example is bright from a gentle polishing, and subtle tooling is noted above the R in LIBERTY. A few faint mint-made adjustment marks cross the shield, but wear is generally limited to the top of the cap, the drapery, and the eagle's cheekbone. The 1800 provides good value relative to the more available 1799 and 1801. (#8563)

Well Defined 1800 Ten Dollar, AU55 Details, BD-1

3576 **1800—Ex-Jewelry—ANACS. AU55 Details.** Breen-6842, Taraszka-23, BD-1, High R.3. A single die pair is known. This piece is an intermediate die state with die cracks atop LIBERTY. Peach-gold surfaces exhibit blushes of apricot around the borders, and well defined design elements. Evidence of moderate jewelry damage is visible in some of the rim areas. (#8563)

XF Details 1801 Ten Dollar, BD-2

3577 **1801—Improperly Cleaned—NCS. XF Details.** Breen-6843, Taraszka-25, BD-2, R.2. Luster beckons from Liberty's hair and the eagle's plumage, but the yellow-green surfaces are slightly bright and minutely granular. Marks are generally limited to a few minor rim dings and a peripheral abrasion over the STA in STATES. An opportunity to acquire a sharp example of this eagerly pursued early large gold type. (#8564)

1801 Eagle, XF Details, BD-2

3578 **1801—Ex-Jewelry, Tooled—ANACS. XF Details.** Breen-6843, Taraszka-25, BD-2, R.2. Star 8 has two points to the cap, star 13 almost touches the bust, and the eagle's upper beak just about touches star right below its beak. Well defined motifs, and bright yellow-gold surfaces with an overall greenish cast. Metal has been scooped out in the field below the bust, possibly to remove solder, or in an attempted puncture. (#8564)

3579 **1801—Damaged—NCS. AU Details.** Breen-6843, Taraszka-25, BD-2, R.2. The reverse rim has a small ding at 6:30, and the rim appears flat at 5:30, although the obverse rim opposite is unaffected. Liberty's cap and drapery have only a hint of highpoint wear. The reverse field is moderately prooflike and perhaps slightly bright. The obverse has scattered small marks, while the reverse is generally smooth. Despite minor problems, many collectors would jump at the chance to obtain a partly lustrous example of this large and scarce early gold type. (#8564)

3580 **1801 AU55 PCGS.** Breen-6843, Taraszka-25, BD-2, R.2. The common 1801 eagle variety with star 8 close to the Liberty cap, this is an excellent candidate for a type collection. Both sides have rich green-gold color and sharp design motifs, with only a few faint surface marks and insignificant hairlines that are expected for the grade. The impression is well-centered with full borders on both sides. A tiny obverse rim bruise at 11 o'clock is hidden by the PCGS holder. Just a trace of rub appears on the obverse, but the reverse appears to be full Mint State.
From The Diemer L. Fife Collection. (#8564)

3581 **1801 MS63 NGC.** Breen-6843, Taraszka-25, BD-2, R.2. One of two varieties of the year. This Wide Date variant is distinctly different from its Close Date counterpart. More than 40 years ago, Walter Breen listed the differences in his monograph on the ten dollar series. "First 1 practically touching curl well to left of the usual position; first star high, presenting only one point to the curl and that one at a moderate distance ... L away from cap; Y free of adjacent star ... there are several spine-like vertical marks on the cap just above the hair, evidently clash marks from vertical stripes on the shield."

The 1801 has a larger survival rate than other early tens, leading one to conclude that a hoard or two may have existed at one time. In addition to higher numbers in all grades, there are also more Uncirculated examples of this date known than other early tens. A significant number of Mint State 1801 tens are extant today, making this the logical choice for many high grade gold type sets. That being said, there are relatively few MS63 or finer 1801 tens that are known today. Only 77 coins have been certified by the two major services in this grade with 68 pieces finer (8/07). This is a particularly attractive coin. The mint luster is bright and the fields display a semi-reflective gleam on each side. The striking details are full, something that can be said about few early tens. Liberty's hair details are completely defined as are the feathers on the eagle's breast just above the shield. There are a few small abrasions scattered over each side, but none are worthy of individual mention. Rich yellow-gold color. (#8564)

Handsome Uncirculated
BD-3 1803 Ten Dollar

3582 1803 Small Stars Reverse MS60 NGC. Breen-6844, Taraszka-28, BD-3, R.4. This impressive apricot-gold representative is surprisingly free from abrasions, and the strike is crisp aside from the eagle's left (facing) claw. The centers are unusually well brought up, particularly the breast feathers and the hair near the ear. The obverse has light peripheral adjustment marks, as produced, but the eye appeal is exceptional for the grade. Clash marks from the curls surround the eagle's beak. The reverse side of the holder has a vertical mark that appears in the images without any effect on the coin itself. An opportunity for the alert early gold specialist. (#8565)

LIBERTY EAGLES

Luminous VF 1838 Eagle

3583 1838 VF20 NGC. The warm honey-gold surfaces of this moderately circulated piece remain surprisingly luminous. Faint, scattered abrasions affect both sides, and a rim bruise is noted near 10 o'clock on the reverse rim. Still, a pleasing example of this noteworthy issue, the first eagle struck for commerce since 1804, with a mintage of just 7,200 pieces. Census: 1 in 20, 33 finer (8/07). (#8575)

Attractive 1838 Ten Dollar, XF40

3584 1838 XF40 PCGS. The 1838 is significant for at least three reasons. It has a very low mintage of 7,200 pieces. It is the first ten dollar date since 1804. It is one of only two dates of the Large Letters subtype. The present piece has a noticeable amount of remaining luster, and the strike is decent despite a few flat stars. A few marks are noted in the field near the eagle's head. Encapsulated in a green label holder. Population: 6 in 40, 33 finer (8/07). (#8575)

Rare Choice AU 1838 Ten Dollar

3585 **1838 AU55 NGC.** The 1838 is significant as the first ten dollar piece issued since 1804. It is also quite rare, since only 7,200 pieces were struck and most of those were melted long ago. It is much scarcer than the 1839 Large Letters, the only other issue of this underappreciated design subtype. Liberty leans forward, has a sweeping curl over the ear, and her truncation is strongly curved. The eagle's beak is open. As he did with the Matron head cents of 1839, Gobrecht modified the type until satisfied with the design, which continued unchanged for years afterward.

This is a sharply struck and radiant butter-gold piece that has pleasing extent of remaining luster, particularly near the eagle's neck. Distributed small to moderate marks are unobtrusive for the grade. Census: 4 in 55, 8 finer (8/07). (#8575)

1839 Ten Dollar, Type of 1838, VF35

3586 **1839 Type of 1838, Large Letters VF35 PCGS.** Mislabeled on the insert as a Type of 1840. This is definitely a Type of 1838 with its distinctly different hair style. Scarce in all grades, and generally not found finer than the present coin. This piece shows even wear over the highpoints and attractive orange-gold color that deepens slightly around the margins. (#8576)

1839 Ten Dollar, Type of 1838, Large Letters, AU53

3587 **1839 Type of 1838, Large Letters AU53 PCGS.** The Type of 1838, with a smaller portrait than the subsequent Type of 1840, is most easily identified by the rear bust truncation above star 13. Listed as 1839/8 on the PCGS holder, with traces of the outer circles of the underdigit 8 peeking out from the right side of the prominent 9. Yellow-gold surfaces display traces of luster in the protected areas, and are lightly abraded. Good design detail throughout, except for weakness in the star centers. (#8576)

Enticing Choice XF 1839 Eagle, Type of 1840, Small Letters

3588 **1839 Type of 1840, Small Letters XF45 ANACS.** With a mintage of slightly less than half of its Large Letters counterpart, the Type of 1840 is more elusive in all grades. The most striking detail about this piece is not its striking detail, though it has plenty of that in spite of light wear, but its still-lustrous surfaces, which are deep pumpkin-orange with copper-influenced rose and violet accents at the stars, date, shield, and peripheral reverse lettering. Overall, a desirable, lightly circulated example of this elusive type. (#8580)

Shining 1841 Eagle, MS60

3589 1841 MS60 NGC. Like the other early Coronet eagle issues, the 1841 is a condition rarity in strict Mint State. Though heavily abraded, this well-defined orange-gold piece shows no trace of wear. A small alloy spot appears at the top of the bun of hair, and reflectivity is evident at the margins. Census: 3 in 60, 8 finer (8/07). (#8582)

Choice AU 1842 Large Date Ten

3590 1842 Large Date AU55 NGC. The more available of the two 1842 logotype varieties, but a scarce item in any grade, since the mintage of 81,507 pieces is shared with the Small Date. The Guide Book breaks down the production into 18,623 Small Date and 62,884 Large Date pieces, but the actual difference in rarity suggests a more even mintage distribution. A sharply struck piece with plentiful luster and a few moderate reverse field marks. Census: 5 in 55, 9 finer (7/07). (#8584)

3591 1842 Small Date AU53 NGC. A partly lustrous and typically abraded straw-gold No Motto eagle. The obverse rim has a small nick at 3 o'clock. The *Guide Book* reports a mintage of only 18,623 pieces, only a handful of which remain in Mint State. Census: 24 in 53, 45 finer (7/07). (#8585)

Borderline Uncirculated 1843 Eagle

3592 1843 AU58 NGC. Breen-6861, his "very rare" triple-punched date. *Coin World's Coin Values* separately lists a Doubled Date variety, which is unpriced above AU50. Traces of misplaced dates are visible on Liberty's neck. This sharply struck example has dazzling peripheral luster, and is minimally abraded save for a faint straight line between the right (facing) wing and the upper arrow. Census: 12 in 58, 2 finer (7/07). (#8588)

Pleasing 1844-O Gold Eagle AU58 NGC

3593 1844-O AU58 NGC. While a relatively common coin in VF and even XF condition, the '44-O gold eagle is a condition scarcity in AU, and is very rare in Mint State. The current specimen displays bright greenish-gold surfaces, with nice luster retained in the recessed areas. The design elements exhibit excellent definition, except for weakness in the hair over Liberty's ear. A few small contact marks scattered over each side do not distract. Census: 42 in 58, 5 finer (8/07). (#8591)

Interesting 1845 Eagle, Unc Details

3594 1845—Graffiti—NCS. Unc Details. This crisply struck, if lightly abraded earlier Coronet eagle has no trace of wear, and the yellow-gold surfaces show strong reflectivity. The obverse fields have cursive letters that spell out "Emma" and the initials "ESB," while the reverse has an X scratched above the eagle's head. An intriguing piece that hints at an enduring story. (#8592)

1846/5-O Ten Dollar AU50

3595 1846/5-O AU50 NGC. Certified as a Normal Date variety by NGC, but the present lot is the variety listed in the *Guide Book* as an 1846-O 6 Over 5. The mintmark is centered between the EN in TEN. The various varieties of 1846-O eagles divide a low mintage of 81,780 pieces. This boldly defined example has medium green-gold toning and glimmers of remaining luster. Distributed marks include minor edge nicks near 1:30 on each side. (#8596)

3596 1847-O AU55 NGC. The lightly abraded surfaces display traces of luster in the protected areas, and the solidly struck devices show faint wear. An interesting example of this available New Orleans eagle, possible the most available of that Mint's antebellum gold issues. (#8598)

3597 1847-O AU58 NGC. Ex: *S.S. Republic.* Breen-6881. Listed on the NGC holder as "Doubled 1," although the base of the 8 also shows recutting. A well struck piece that has glimmers of remaining luster. (#8598)

Important Mint State 1847-O Eagle

3598 1847-O MS60 NGC. Although the date is a high mintage issue and commonly seen in nearly all grades below Mint State, examples are seldom encountered finer. NGC has certified just 17 pieces in all Mint State grades, for example. This delightful green-gold example is weak at the central obverse. Census: 1 in 60, 16 finer (8/07). (#8598)

Clean Choice AU 1848-O Ten

3599 1848-O AU55 NGC. A clean straw-gold example with only a single identifying mark, found beneath the T in UNITED. Pockets of luster illuminate design elements. The deeply hubbed stars have soft centers, but the eagle's wings and neck are precisely detailed. A scarce New Orleans issue. Census: 17 in 55, 20 finer (8/07). (#8600)

3600 1849 AU58 NGC. A modestly reflective yellow-orange example, well struck with a measure of friction on the devices. Though each side shows a number of scattered marks, these have little individual impact on the coin's eye appeal. An intriguing memento from the California Gold Rush years. (#8601)

3601 1849 AU58 PCGS. An attractive and crisply struck apricot-gold representative with ample remaining luster. The fields display only minor marks when viewed beneath a loupe. Population: 18 in 58, 35 finer (7/07). (#8601)

MS61 1849 No Motto Ten

3602 1849 MS61 NGC. All No Motto eagles are rare in Mint State, including the 1849. The strike is typical on Liberty's curls and the left shield border, but the extent of bright luster is satisfactory for the grade, and field marks are individually minor save for a horizontal pinscratch above the date. Census: 14 in 61, 29 finer (8/07). (#8601)

3603 1850 Large Date AU58 NGC. Minor friction appears on the well struck devices of this near-Mint example. Only moderately abraded for a briefly circulated No Motto eagle. Census: 49 in 58, 21 finer (7/07). (#8603)

Challenging 1850-O Eagle, AU50

3604 1850-O AU50 PCGS. The 1850-O ten dollar is usually seen in circulated condition, rarely above Extremely Fine, and almost never in Mint State (Jeff Garrett and Ron Guth, 2006). Peach-gold patina with hints of light green bathes both sides of this AU50 example, and traces of luster reside in the protected areas. Generally well defined, save for softness in some of the star centers. A few minor marks are not detractive. Housed in a green-label holder. Population: 13 in 50, 10 finer (7/07). (#8605)

3605 1851 AU58 NGC. Circulated examples of the 1851 ten dollar are available through AU50, after which the rarity increases dramatically. Well struck, with yellow-gold surfaces that are lightly abraded. Luster resides in the recesses of both sides. Census: 34 in 58, 19 finer (8/07). (#8606)

3606 1853 AU58 NGC. A band of luster fills the borders of this original near-Mint No Motto ten. Crisply struck, and attractive overall despite a few moderate marks on the upper reverse field. (#8610)

Choice AU 1854-O Small Date Ten

3607 **1854-O Small Date AU55 NGC.** Incorrectly designated as a Large Date on the NGC holder. Breen believed the Large Date was rarer, but Heritage auction records demonstrate there is only marginal difference in rarity between the two logotypes, which are identically priced in the 2008 *Guide Book*. Both varieties are scarce, since the combined mintage is just 52,500 pieces. This partly lustrous example lacks mentionable marks, and has an interesting die break within the hair above the ear. (#8614)

3608 **1854-S XF45 PCGS.** The 1854-S eagle is the first coin of this denomination struck at the San Francisco Mint. This Choice XF specimen displays attractive honey-gold patina, and traces of luster in the recesses. The design features have benefited from a sharp strike, further enhancing the coin's overall appeal. We note a couple of inoffensive milling marks on Liberty's neck. (#8615)

3609 **1854-S AU53 NGC.** A briefly circulated eagle from the first year of operation for the San Francisco Mint, lightly abraded overall with delicately green-tinted yellow-gold surfaces and pleasing central detail. An attractive piece and a tangible link to the heady days of the California Gold Rush. (#8615)

3610 **1861-S XF45 NGC.** Despite more than tripling the previous year's production, in 1861, San Francisco struck only 15,500 eagles. This lightly circulated, well struck honey-orange example shows faint, scattered abrasions. Luminous and appealing. Census: 15 in 45, 57 finer (8/07). (#8634)

3611 **1862 AU55 NGC.** This low mintage Civil War eagle is a bit scarcer than the '57-O twenty, yet it trades for one-third the price. Substantial bright luster remains. Liberty's cheek is abraded. Census: 14 in 55, 17 finer (8/07). (#8635)

Rare Choice AU 1865 Ten Dollar

3612 **1865 AU55 NGC.** Since gold coins failed to circulate in 1865 except in the far West, ten dollar production was limited that year to 25 proofs and 3,980 business strikes. The latter were ignored by collectors of the day. NGC has certified just 28 pieces in all grades, with a solitary MS60 as the single finest. The present moderately abraded example displays substantial subtle luster. The obverse center shows some incompleteness of strike. From the historic year of 1865, when the Civil War ended and reconstruction began. Census: 4 in 55, 4 finer (8/07). (#8641)

3613 **1867—Repaired, Improperly Cleaned—NCS. XF Details.** The 1867 is one of many rare Philadelphia Mint issues from 1863 to 1877. Just 3,090 pieces were struck, and NGC and PCGS combined have certified only about 100 examples. This glossy survivor shows subtle tooling beneath the left (facing) wing and above the right wingtip. (#8651)

Formidable Choice AU 1871 Ten

3614 **1871 AU55 NGC.** The 1871 is a formidable sleeper with a mintage of just 1,790 pieces. None of those were set aside by collectors until the 20th century. NGC has certified only 40 pieces in all grades, about one per six months of the firm's existence. A well struck and moderately abraded example with luster about the stars, legends, and devices. Census: 13 in 55, 7 finer (7/07). (#8660)

Luminous 1871-CC Eagle, AU Sharpness

3615 **1871-CC—Genuine—NCS.** Though the holder describes the piece merely as "Genuine," the devices have pleasing sharpness and only a hint of actual wear, for an approximately AU details grade. The luminous pink-gold and apricot surfaces show numerous hairlines from a past cleaning, and the portrait and obverse fields show a handful of small abrasions. Still, a collectible example of this desirable issue early Carson City issue. (#8661)

Amazing 1872-S Eagle, AU55

3616 **1872-S AU55 NGC.** This surprisingly lustrous yellow-gold piece appears even finer at arm's length, though closer inspection reveals minor but distinct wear on the highpoints. The crisply struck devices and partly reflective fields display scattered abrasions. This issue of 17,300 pieces is found predominantly in lower grades, with Choice AU representatives conditionally rare. Census: 21 in 55, 12 finer (8/07). (#8665)

3617 **1875-CC AU55 NGC.** Two Mints, Philadelphia and Carson City, struck eagles in 1875. In most years, the Philadelphia issue would have a much higher mintage than that of the Carson City pieces. The situation in 1875, however, was an extraordinary reversal of the norm, and for all gold denominations below the double eagle, Philadelphia's production was negligible. Just 100 examples of the P-mint issue were struck, compared with 7,715 coins from Carson City. Of course, any insinuation that this issue is common would be far from correct.

Like a number of other 1870s eagle issues, the 1875-CC eagle is scarce in any grade and a condition rarity even in XF grades. Garrett and Guth (2006) corroborate this assessment: "Very Fine and low-end Extremely Fine examples are the best that most collectors can hope to obtain, as the rarity and prices increase dramatically up through AU58." The opportunity to acquire a Choice AU example such as the present piece comes infrequently; in fact, Heritage has sold only one other example at this grade level and no finer representatives.

The dusky yellow-orange surfaces of this coin show a number of fine abrasions. A small dig is noted below Liberty's eye, and a spot of rub appears to the left of the eagle's neck. Such flaws, however, are consistent with the grade, and the luminous fields are pleasing. The devices offer above-average definition, particularly on the hair framing Liberty's face and the eagle's feathers. A noteworthy candidate for the Carson City gold enthusiast. Census: 3 in 55, 3 finer (7/07). (#8673)

Low-Mintage 1876-CC Eagle, XF Details

3618 1876-CC—Repaired, Improperly Cleaned—NCS. XF Details. This Carson City issue from the centennial year has an official mintage of just 4,696 pieces, and certified populations project a survival rate as low as 3%. This lightly worn piece displays luminous orange-gold surfaces that show significant hairlines from a past cleaning. Softly struck with an area of conspicuous smoothing at Liberty's forehead. (#8675)

Ultra-Low Mintage XF45 1877 Ten

3619 1877 XF45 ICG. There are no proof-only dates in the Liberty eagle series, unlike the other gold denominations. But many Philadelphia ten dollar issues from the 1860s and 1870s have tiny mintages. Chief among those are the 1873, 1875, and 1877, each of which had productions of fewer than 1,000 pieces. This moderately circulated example retains prooflike luster in protected areas, and the only noticeable mark is relegated to the field beneath the right scroll end. (#8677)

Boldly Detailed VF25 1877-CC Ten

3620 1877-CC VF25 PCGS. This orange-gold rare date Carson City ten is certainly to be of interest to specialists of the legendary Western facility. The eagle's wings are surprisingly detailed for the grade, and some mint luster remains. The fields are smooth, but a couple of marks on the face require mention. Only 3,332 pieces were struck. Certified in a green label holder. (#8678)

3621 1878 MS62 NGC. Between a low survival rate in Mint State and a small original mintage of just 73,700 pieces, the 1878 eagle is elusive in higher grades. This luminous peach-gold and orange-gold example shows pleasing detail and luster, though a number of faint ticks are present on the surfaces. Census: 23 in 62, 23 finer (8/07). (#8680)

3622 1879 MS62 PCGS. This better date Liberty ten is crisply struck and lacks the obtrusive abrasions often encountered on MS62 examples of the type. Luster is particularly effusive near the borders and across the eagle. Population: 51 in 62, 40 finer (8/07). (#8683)

3623 1879-S MS61 PCGS. An attractive example of this conditionally scarce issue. Luster extends into the open fields, and the strike is penetrating. There are no detracting marks. Population: 20 in 61, 20 finer (7/07). (#8686)

3624 1879-S MS61 NGC. A moderately scarce date, with the typical example falling into the AU50 to AU58 grade range, and only a few dozen examples certified in Mint State. Peach-gold surfaces exhibit sharply struck design elements on this MS61 specimen, and the most potent luster occurs in the areas around and the interstices of the design elements. Tiny marks evenly scattered about define the grade. (#8686)

3625 1880 MS62 PCGS. Although the 1880 has a fairly high mintage, examples are scarcer at the MS62 level than some later, much lower mintage issues, such as the 1891-CC. This example has a suitable luster, a good strike, and a clean reverse. (#8687)

Bright AU58 1881-CC Ten Dollar

3626 1881-CC AU58 PCGS. Variety 1-A. Later die state with thin die cracks through the bottom of 881 in the date trailing off into the denticles on the right. A common CC ten and often used for type purposes, but not often found finer than near-Mint. This is an attractive piece that is missing just a bit of luster in the open areas of the fields; otherwise, the devices are surrounded by bright mint frost. Well struck, there are numerous small abrasions present on each side, but none are worthy of individual mention. (#8692)

Scarce 1882-CC Eagle XF45

3627 1882-CC XF45 PCGS. This is a scarce, low mintage Carson City issue. The current Choice XF example displays lightly worn surfaces that have few marks on either side. There is considerable luster on this piece, for the grade. Only 6,764 pieces were produced, and survivors are scarce to rare at any level of preservation. (#8696)

3628 1882-S MS62 PCGS. Well struck and highly lustrous, with appealing apricot-gold and rose toning. There are no severe abrasions, just a number of trivial contact marks across each side. Conditionally scarce at this grade level, and rare any finer. Population: 58 in 62, 10 finer (7/07). (#8698)

3629 1882-S MS62 NGC. A crisply struck representative of this lower mintage and conditionally scarce issue. Fully lustrous, and the reverse is well preserved. Census: 70 in 62, 21 finer (8/07). (#8698)

3630 1883 MS63 ICG. A lustrous and lightly abraded apricot-gold eagle with a crisp strike. Unlike the P-mint eagles of 1880 to 1882, the 1883 poses a challenge in Select and better grades. (#8699)

3631 1884-S MS62 PCGS. This lustrous and attractive representative has good eye appeal for the MS62 level. A scarcer date that can be found in AU58 to MS61, but challenging any finer. Population: 43 in 62, 4 finer (8/07). (#8705)

3632 1885-S MS62 PCGS. Lustrous and lightly abraded with exquisite design detail. An obverse strike-through at 5:30 is of little consequence. (#8707)

3633 1885-S MS62 PCGS. This boldly impressed scarcer date Liberty ten has vibrant luster and distributed minor to moderate marks. (#8707)

3634 1886-S MS62 NGC. Pleasing for the grade, since the shimmering luster is unbroken and individual marks are unimportant. A sharply struck piece with good value relative to the MS63 level. (#8709)

3635 1888-S MS63 PCGS. Vibrant mint frost shimmers over both sides of this Select eagle, well-defined save for minor softness on some of the obverse stars, the mintmark, and the lower parts of the eagle. A lovely, flashy straw-gold representative with faint, scattered abrasions consistent with the grade. Challenging any finer, with just three such pieces graded by PCGS (8/07). (#8714)

3636 1889 AU55 NGC. Close to Mint State, and the surfaces are unperturbed aside from inconspicuous scuffs in the field beneath the hair bun. The 1889 has long been targeted by speculators, due to a compellingly low production of only 4,440 pieces. (#8715)

3637 1889-S MS63 PCGS. An attractive example of this S-mint eagle issue, solidly struck with rich sun-gold surfaces. Lustrous with light, scattered abrasions. PCGS has graded just 13 pieces finer (7/07). (#8716)

3638 1889-S MS63 PCGS. Variegated peach-gold and mint-green patina rests on lustrous surfaces that yield well impressed design elements. A few minute marks account for the grade. (#8716)

3639 1890 MS62 PCGS. A luminous and enticing apricot-gold representative of this lower-mintage Philadelphia eagle issue. Well struck with a number of minor abrasions that account for the grade. PCGS has graded 16 finer pieces (8/07). (#8717)

3640 1890-CC AU53 PCGS. An evenly struck apricot-gold Carson City ten with extensive and bright peripheral luster. The devices also offer substantial luster. Only 17,500 pieces were struck. (#8718)

3641 1890-CC AU58 NGC. This shining wheat-gold piece displays pale apricot accents and minor alloy at the margins and near the portrait. Lightly abraded overall with pleasing central detail and a hint of friction on the highpoints. One of only 17,500 pieces coined. (#8718)

Low Mintage MS62 1890-CC Ten

3642 1890-CC MS62 NGC. Unencumbered cartwheel luster bathes this exactingly struck representative. Minor marks are distributed, but none are individually relevant. IN GOD WE TRUST is lightly die doubled, likely the case for all examples of this much better date. Only 17,500 pieces were struck. Census: 34 in 62, 12 finer (7/07). (#8718)

3643 1891-CC AU58 NGC. The normal mintmark variety, which is probably scarcer than the Breen-7035 RPM. The hair above the ear has a hint of friction, but this Carson City type coin has considerable luster and no obvious marks. (#8720)

3644 1891-CC MS62 PCGS. Breen-7035. The popular variety with a clearly repunched mintmark. This Carson City ten has booming, unbroken luster and a decisive strike. The reverse is surprisingly unabraded for the grade, while the obverse displays the expected number of tiny marks and a whisper of struck-in grease between the IB in LIBERTY. (#8720)

3645 1891-CC MS62 NGC. The most available Carson City eagle in Mint State, thanks in part to a mintage that reached six figures. The lightly abraded, highly lustrous surfaces are yellow-gold with a trace of green. A sharply struck and undeniably attractive example of this popular issue. (#8720)

3646 1891-CC MS62 NGC. Vibrant luster and an exacting strike ensure the eye appeal of this moderately abraded piece. The 1891-CC is the only readily available CC-mint ten in Mint State. (#8720)

3647 1892-CC AU50 ANACS. By and large, the Carson City eagle issues of the 1890s are more affordable than their earlier counterparts, and the 1892-CC is no exception. This still-lustrous lemon-gold example shows pleasing peripheral detail and faint, scattered marks. Minor highpoint wear affects the softly struck devices. (#8722)

3648 1892-CC AU58 NGC. Mint luster is nearly full. Original, unmarked, and attractive. IN GOD WE TRUST and STATES are die doubled, characteristic of this scarce Carson City issue. Significantly scarcer than its 1891-CC predecessor. (#8722)

3649 1892-CC AU58 NGC. A sharp example with substantial orange-gold luster and surprisingly few bagmarks. The upper reverse legends are die doubled north. Only 40,000 pieces were struck for this penultimate Carson City eagle issue. (#8722)

3650 1893 MS64 PCGS. Unencumbered luster and a sharp strike affirm the quality of this clean-cheeked near-Gem. The reverse is well preserved, and the obverse field has only a few moderate grazes. (#8725)

3651 1893 MS62 Prooflike NGC. Hints of green and orange grace the lemon-gold surfaces of this solidly struck Philadelphia eagle. The fields retain strong reflectivity despite a number of abrasions. Census: 30 in 62 Prooflike, 12 finer (8/07). (#78725)

3652 1893-S MS62 PCGS. Complete cartwheel luster exudes from peach-gold surfaces that display sharply struck design elements. The portrait and reverse field are typically abraded. Jeff Garret and Ron Guth (2006) write: "Although the 1893-S eagle is considerably rarer than the 1893-S silver dollar, a smaller audience for the former means that it sells for a fraction of the price of the latter." (#8728)

Lustrous Select 1894-O Ten

3653 1894-O MS63 NGC. Like all New Orleans eagles from the 1890s, the 1894-O is collectible in Mint State, but becomes very scarce in MS62. MS63 examples are rare, and under strong demand from Southern gold specialists. This fully lustrous piece lacks mentionable marks, and the strike is also precise. Census: 14 in 63, 2 finer (7/07). (#8730)

3654 1894-S AU55 PCGS. Ample luster remains on the brassy-gold surfaces that show wisps of tan patina. The design elements are sharply struck, and a few minor abrasions are noted over each side. Population: 17 in 55, 18 finer (7/07). (#8731)

Low Mintage MS60 1894-S Ten Dollar

3655 1894-S MS60 NGC. 1890s San Francisco eagle mintages bottomed out in 1894, with a tiny production of 25,000 pieces. Double eagles were the preferred S-mint gold denomination that year, with a mintage of more than 1 million pieces. This precisely struck example is only lightly abraded for the grade, and has full luster on the reverse. The base of the 1 is repunched. (#8731)

3656 1895 MS62 Prooflike NGC. Gorgeous yellow-gold color complements sharply struck design elements on this bright ten dollar piece, and pronounced field-motif contrast is evident when the coin is rotated under a light source. A scattering of tiny marks and luster grazes preclude a higher grade, nevertheless, this MS62 example exudes considerable eye appeal. Census: 6 in 62 Prooflike, 0 finer (7/07). (#78732)

3657 1899 MS64 NGC. The 899 in the date is lightly recut inside the upper loops. This almond-gold near-Gem has good luster and an exacting strike. A few faint field grazes correspond with the grade. (#8742)

Lustrous 1899 Ten Dollar MS65

3658 1899 MS65 NGC. Scintillating luster and a precise strike combine with clean surfaces to confirm the quality of this attractive Liberty gold type coin. The light apricot toning is consistent throughout. Faint die cracks connect the tops of UNITED and AMERICA. NGC has certified only 19 pieces finer (8/07). (#8742)

3659 1899-S MS62 PCGS. This thoroughly lustrous representative has the overall look of a finer grade, although a slight color change is found on the portrait highpoints. (#8744)

Terrific Choice 1900-S Eagle

3660 1900-S MS64 PCGS. Though the 1900-S commands little premium over type in moderately circulated grades, like other lower-mintage branch mint issues that experienced heavy circulation, it commands a substantial price in Select and better grades. The immensely appealing near-Gem offered here ranks among the finest examples known today. The portrait and stars on the obverse are bold, and the eagle exhibits crisp detail. The shining surfaces are predominantly yellow-orange, though a few tiny copper dots appear near the devices and an area of peach is present around the word OF on the reverse. While the coin's overall appearance is clean, a few pinpoint marks on the cheek and grazes in the nearby fields preclude a finer grade. Population: 2 in 64, 1 finer (8/07). (#8746)

3661 1901 MS63 PCGS. A lustrous orange and olive-gold example of popular Liberty type. The reverse on its own appears to merit a much higher grade, and the obverse is smooth aside from a few faint hairlines. Encapsulated in a green label holder. (#8747)

3662 1901 MS64 NGC. This vibrantly lustrous canary-gold near-Gem is crisply impressed and has a well preserved obverse field. A quality representative of the gold type. (#8747)

3663 1901 MS64 NGC. Blazing luster illuminates this well struck and attractive olive-gold Liberty type coin. The reverse is beautifully preserved, and no obverse marks require individual mention. In a prior generation holder. (#8747)

Lustrous MS63 1901-O Eagle

3664 1901-O MS63 PCGS. This issue ranks among just five New Orleans gold coins issued during the 20th century. The only others are the 1903-O, 04-O, and 06-O eagles, and the 1909-O half eagle. Frosty luster brings out the rich orange-gold color of this piece, with sharp design details on both sides. Few similar or finer examples have been certified by PCGS. Population: 42 in 63, 11 finer (8/07). (#8748)

3665 1901-S MS63 NGC. Breen-7075. The base of the 19 is repunched. An attentively struck gold type coin with a well preserved reverse and a few distributed minor marks on the left obverse field. (#8749)

3666 1901-S MS64 NGC. A precisely struck and highly lustrous type representative that boasts a minimally abraded reverse and only minor obverse grazes. The colors are typically of an original 20th century gold coin, with pumpkin-gold centers and green-gold peripheries. (#8749)

3667 1901-S MS64 NGC. This impressive gold type coin has small but interesting strike-throughs (as made) near star 6 and the first A in AMERICA. Lustrous and smooth with green-gold toning and a penetrating strike. (#8749)

3668 1901-S MS64 NGC. Sharply struck throughout, with pleasing, glowing luster. Tan-gold surfaces display faint traces of light green, and reveal just a few minor grade-defining marks. (#8749)

3669 1901-S MS64 NGC. Dazzling luster emanates from both sides of this near-Gem S-mint coin, and rich yellow-gold patination is laced with traces of light tan. A few minute obverse marks preclude full Gem classification. (#8749)

Spectacular MS65 ★ 1901-S Ten Dollar

3670 1901-S MS65 ★ NGC. The star designation represents superior eye appeal for the grade, and that is immediately obvious when one views this piece. The fields appear to have been struck either from polished dies or the planchet was polished prior to striking. The obverse is fully prooflike and the reverse is just a bit less so. Star 13 is the only area that prevents a full strike designation. The warm, orange-gold surfaces show a few minor marks, which seem unjustly magnified in importance by the bright prooflike fields. One of only two pieces given the ★ designation at the MS65 level with five other ★ coins in MS66 and 67 grades (8/07). (#8749)

3671 1901-S MS63 Prooflike NGC. Although the 1901-S is a type coin, it is scarce with prooflike fields. This flashy and well struck ten dollar piece has moderate field marks, but the eye appeal is uncontested. Census: 9 in 63 Prooflike, 1 finer (7/07). (#78749)

3672 1902 MS62 Prooflike NGC. Apparently the first 1902 to receive a Prooflike designation, since the (8/07) NGC Census shows no such pieces. Precisely struck and surprisingly clean for the grade. A low mintage date. (#78750)

3673 1902-S MS64 NGC. This precisely struck Liberty ten has vivacious luster and honey-gold shadings. A hair-thin vertical mark near the eye is all that limits the grade. The present auction provides an uncommon opportunity to choose between multiple quality examples of the 1902-S. (#8751)

3674 1902-S MS64 NGC. Energetic luster invigorates this pale peach and olive near-Gem. Intricately struck, and high end for the grade due to its paucity of marks. The reverse border has a small strike-through at 2 o'clock. (#8751)

3675 1902-S MS64 NGC. Lime and apricot toning graces the generally smooth surfaces. Dazzling luster and an attentive strike further ensure the eye appeal. A meritorious candidate for the type collector who wants a scarcer date than the 1901-S. (#8751)

3676 1902-S MS64 NGC. This Liberty gold type coin provides vibrant luster and generally smooth fields. The cheek has a few moderate marks. Well struck save for stars 6 and 7. (#8751)

Scarce Near-Gem 1903 Ten Dollar

3677 1903 MS64 PCGS. This lustrous scarcer date eagle has the first glance appearance of a higher grade, although thorough evaluation beneath a loupe locates a few trivial obverse hairlines. Despite its 20th century Philadelphia Mint origin, a lower mintage issue seldom seen above the MS63 level. Population: 40 in 64, 1 finer (7/07). (#8752)

3678 1903-O MS62 PCGS. This boldly struck O-mint ten has lime-green borders and honey-gold centers. The reverse is surprisingly smooth, while the obverse shows a few moderate marks on the portrait. (#8753)

Select 1903-O Ten, Ex: Bass

3679 1903-O MS63 PCGS. Ex: Bass. The 1903-O is collectible in Mint State, but the typical Uncirculated example is heavily abraded or has subdued luster. The present sharply struck piece, however, has full luster and generally smooth surfaces. Only a slender nick above the eye merits mention. Population: 74 in 63, 9 finer (7/07). (#8753)

3680 1905 MS63 NGC. A mix of apricot-gold and mint-green color bathes lustrous surfaces, complementing sharply struck design elements. Scattered contact marks and scuffs account for the grade. (#8757)

3681 1905-S MS61 NGC. Satin luster is unbroken by the various tiny marks that correspond to the grade. Traditionally, the most difficult 20th-century issue of the type to locate in Mint State, although the 1900-S (if it is considered 20th-century) is also challenging. Census: 57 in 61, 22 finer (7/07). (#8758)

3682 1906-D MS64 NGC. This beautiful near-Gem features a powerful strike and undiminished cartwheel sheen. Refreshingly unabraded, and from the initial year of production at the Denver Mint. (#8760)

Amazing MS66 1906-D Eagle

3683 1906-D MS66 NGC. Amazing quality for this date, approaching the finest known. In fact, a single finer piece is graded by NGC, and no better ones are certified by PCGS. The design elements are full and crisp, with impressive honey-gold color and frosty luster. During the first year of operation, the Denver Mint coined 981,000 eagles, and nearly all of the survivors are lower grade than this specimen. Census: 1 in 66, 1 finer (8/07). (#8760)

3684 1906-O MS62 NGC. The final New Orleans ten dollar issue becomes very scarce at the MS62 level. This well struck piece has surprisingly few consequential marks, and its luster is comprehensive. Census: 59 in 62, 42 finer (8/07). (#8761)

3685 1907 MS63 ANACS. Well defined with the sole exception of star 13. Thoroughly lustrous, and highly attractive for the grade. 1907 was the last stand for this long-lived type. (#8763)

3686 1907 MS64 PCGS. The orange-gold and apricot-gold surfaces of this lovely near-Gem offer pleasing luster with a hint of frost. Faint, scattered marks on each side preclude a finer grade. A delightful representative from the final Liberty eagle issue. (#8763)

Challenging 1907-D Near-Gem Ten Dollar

3687 1907-D MS64 NGC. Most certified Mint State 1907-D examples are at the low end of the grading scale. Near-Gems, such as the specimen in the present lot, can be challenging, and Gems are rare. Lustrous peach-gold surfaces exhibit sharply struck design elements. A few minute obverse marks define the grade. Census: 50 in 64, 6 finer (7/07). (#8764)

PROOF LIBERTY EAGLES

Cameo 1891 Eagle, PR63

3688 1891 PR63 Cameo NGC. This piece would have garnered a full Gem or finer grade except it has a thin scratch in the obverse field. Otherwise, both sides are virtually perfect. It is fully brilliant with pristine, mirrored fields that surround frosty and sharply defined devices. Exceptional contrast, nearly in the Ultra Cameo category. Only about 15 to 20 proofs of this issue survive from a mintage of 48 coins. The existing population includes two Deep Cameo pieces in the Smithsonian Institution. Other known proofs include the Eliasberg-Bass coin, and the Trompeter, Garrett, Pittman, and Carter specimens. (#88831)

Rare Proof 1892 Ten Dollar

3689 **1892 PR61 PCGS.** The *Guide Book* reports a proof mintage of 72 pieces, but perhaps only half of that number have survived. PCGS has certified 23 pieces in all grades, four in circulated condition, with an unknown number of resubmissions over the past 21 years. This is a flashy example with moderate field hairlines and a hint of striking softness at the centers. Cameo contrast is obvious, but undesignated since the specimen resides in a green label holder. Population: 3 in 61, 10 finer (8/07). (#8832)

INDIAN EAGLES

3690 **1907 No Periods MS62 NGC.** Rich apricot-rose and lime toning covers the satiny, nicely preserved surfaces of this first-year example. The boldly rendered design motifs exhibit minimal weakness on the headdress. This piece would make an excellent No Motto type representative. (#8852)

3691 **1907 No Periods MS62 PCGS.** Rich apricot-gold patination graces both sides of this Indian Head ten dollar gold piece, and is complemented by sharply struck devices. Some minor marks on the cheek and neck cause this otherwise gorgeous specimen to fall just short of the next highest grade. (#8852)

Superior Choice 1907 No Periods Indian Ten

3692 **1907 No Periods MS64 NGC.** A boldly impressed and radiant Choice No Motto type coin with vibrant luster and beautifully unperturbed surfaces. This lot provides an excellent balance between quality and affordability. The fields above the date and near the reverse border exhibit significant die wear, as made and unusual for the series. (#8852)

Magnificent Gem 1907 No Periods Eagle

3693 **1907 No Periods MS65 NGC.** An immensely appealing representative of this short-lived type, well-detailed overall with vibrant sun-gold surfaces and intense luster. Unlike lower-graded examples of the same issue, this piece shows only a few tiny flaws in the fields, and the devices are carefully preserved as well. As with all Saint-Gaudens eagles, the 1907 No Periods is challenging in Gem. An excellent candidate for the similarly graded type or date set. (#8852)

Delightfully Toned 1907 No Periods Ten, MS66 ★

3694 **1907 No Periods MS66 ★ NGC.** Charles Barber, not exactly an admirer of designer Augustus Saint-Gaudens, fiddled with his design posthumously to create the circulation issue, removing the periods or triangular stops. The Star designation is aptly earned, with gorgeous alternating areas of mint-green and pinkish-gold scattered throughout both sides of this pristine piece. Although the 1907 No Periods is one of the most available dates in the series in Gem grade or higher, this coin is nonetheless quite memorable, and could be the starting point for a phenomenally beautiful date run or type coin assemblage of delectably toned gold. Census: 3 in 66 ★, 20 finer (8/07). (#8852)

3695 1908 Motto MS62 PCGS. A shining lemon-gold example from the first issue following the Congressionally mandated addition of IN GOD WE TRUST to the Saint-Gaudens coinage designs. Solidly struck with vibrant luster, though both the fields and devices show a number of abrasions. (#8859)

Luminous, Low Mintage 1908-S Ten MS63

3696 1908-S MS63 NGC. The '08-S has a mintage of just 59,850 pieces, and since San Francisco gold coins circulated to some extent in 1908, the majority of survivors are in XF and AU grades. Pleasing Select examples are both elusive and desirable. This lustrous and alertly struck Indian ten is remarkably smooth except for a faded, thin mark on the field near the chin. (#8861)

3697 1909-D MS61 NGC. Vibrant luster graces the straw-gold and sun-gold surfaces of this earlier With Motto Saint-Gaudens eagle. Well struck with myriad shallow abrasions that account for the grade. *From The Diemer L. Fife Collection.* (#8863)

3698 1909-D MS62 PCGS. Despite a hefty production of half eagles for the year, Denver produced only 121,540 eagles in 1909. This satiny and well struck piece has muted antique-gold surfaces that show a number of wispy abrasions. (#8863)

3699 1909-S MS62 PCGS. The satiny orange-yellow surfaces are largely free of marks, as are the well struck obverse devices. If not for a scrape on the eagle's wing, this coin might have received a higher grade. Nonetheless, this S-mint ten displays beautifully. (#8864)

3700 1910 MS63 NGC. This is a highly attractive Select Mint State example that exhibits the fine grain surface textures that are typical for this early issue. The effulgent mint luster is especially rich on the reverse, and both sides are adorned with pleasing honey-gold coloration. A couple of small abrasions are noted on Liberty's cheek. (#8865)

Scarce 1910 Indian Ten, MS64

3701 1910 MS64 PCGS. Like many Saint-Gaudens eagle issues, the 1910 becomes elusive in Choice and finer grades. The piece offered here has a pleasing level of detail and soft, satiny luster. The green-gold surfaces are well-preserved with no marks worthy of individual mention. An attractive example of this moderate-mintage Philadelphia issue. (#8865)

3702 1910-D MS63 PCGS. Boldly struck with matte-like surfaces and shimmering luster. The orange-gold coloration is most attractive. A few trivial marks are noted in the reverse fields. (#8866)

3703 1910-D MS63 NGC. A radiant Select representative of this populous Denver eagle issue, well-defined overall with lightly abraded yellow-gold fields. Subtle canary accents visit the devices. (#8866)

3704 1910-D MS64 PCGS. Rich orange and olive shades endow this lustrous and suitably struck near-Gem. Despite a plentiful production, the 1910-D is tougher than expected in better Uncirculated grades, and its combined certified population is much smaller than that of any generally accepted Saint-Gaudens eagle type issue. (#8866)

Opulent Gem 1910-D Eagle

3705 1910-D MS65 NGC. The most available of the branch mint issues, the 1910-D is possible to acquire even in Gem, though anything finer presents a challenge. The wheat-gold piece offered here is slightly satiny on the obverse, though the reverse has stronger luster. Carefully preserved with excellent visual appeal and none of the softness that often appears on the peripheral elements. (#8866)

3706 1911 MS63 NGC. A sun-gold Select example that offers strong luster juxtaposed against the slight granularity of the surfaces. Both sides have a clean appearance, though faint, scattered abrasions account for the grade. (#8868)

Captivating 1911 Indian Head Ten Dollar MS64

3707 1911 MS64 PCGS. Few Indian Head eagles possess the eye appeal of this near-Gem. The fully brilliant surfaces display matte-like fields and dazzling, intense mint frost over both obverse and reverse. The design features are boldly struck, and there are just a handful of grade-limiting marks, all of them trivial, on each side. (#8868)

3708 1911-D AU55 PCGS. With just 30,100 pieces struck, the 1911-D eagle is one of the lowest-mintage regular issues of the 20th century. This lightly circulated, still-lustrous example has butter-yellow surfaces with a few faint alloy streaks. Minimally marked and pleasing for the grade. (#8869)

3709 1912 MS62 NGC. This shining amber-gold piece exhibits a bit of satin on each side, though the reverse has a greater level of that element. Well-defined overall with light, scattered abrasions that combine to limit the grade. (#8871)

3710 1912 MS63 NGC. Both sides of this straw-gold Select eagle exhibit vibrant luster. Lightly abraded on the chin with excellent peripheral detail and a solidly struck eagle, though the hair over the ear displays a touch of softness. (#8871)

3711 1912 MS63 NGC. An exuberantly lustrous example of this available issue, with brilliant orange-gold surfaces that show a couple of light abrasions precluding a finer grade. Nonetheless attractive, and providing a good price:aesthetic balance. (#8871)

Gorgeous 1912 Indian Ten, MS66

3712 1912 MS66 PCGS. The 1912 eagle, with a mintage of just over 400,000 pieces, has a reputation as one of the more available issues in the Saint-Gaudens series. While not present in such quantities as the 1926 or 1932, Garrett and Guth (2006) state that enough "were coined and saved to satisfy collector demand." While this holds true even for Gems, anything finer is a condition rarity.

The surfaces of this immensely appealing Premium Gem are yellow-orange with a touch of peach at the upper right obverse. Aside from a touch of softness at the hair below the headband, the minimally marked devices have strong detail, and the glowing fields have a slightly satiny appearance. One of just nine pieces so graded by PCGS, with just two finer across both major services (8/07). (#8871)

Exceptional MS66 1912 Ten Indian

3713 1912 MS66 NGC. Among Philadelphia Mint ten Indians, the 1912 is one of the more frequently encountered. It is also often used as a type coin. However, there is a sharp drop-off from MS64 to 65 (388 vs. 69 coins graded), and even more precipitously from MS65 to MS66 with only 27 pieces certified by the two services combined (8/07). While this issue is known for frosted, granular surfaces this piece seems to have received an extra dose of each. The mint frost seen here is comparable to that on S-mint gold, and each side has a pronounced, large-grain texture. Magnification reveals a couple of shallow marks on the face of the Indian—seemingly the only abrasions present on this magnificent coin. The bright yellow-gold surfaces have just the slightest accent of reddish patina. (#8871)

3714 1912-S AU58 ANACS. Still lustrous with noticeable highpoint wear on both sides, and several moderate abrasions on the reverse. This issue is scarce in Mint State, like all S-mint Indian Head gold eagles. (#8872)

3715 1913 MS62 NGC. A well struck and softly lustrous piece with enticing canary-gold surfaces that show a number of small, wispy abrasions. This Philadelphia issue has a mintage of under half a million pieces (8/07). (#8873)

3716 1913 MS64 PCGS. Both sides of this lemon-gold near-Gem offer effusive luster, and the solidly struck devices show only the faintest of marks. The reverse margins and the eagle's rear leg show small crimson alloy spots. An attractive example from an issue that is available in Choice, but less so than the two main type issues. (#8873)

3717 1913 MS64 NGC. A well struck example that offers warm luster and luminous orange-gold and green-gold surfaces. Only a few faint ticks on the devices and in the fields keep this lovely P-mint piece from an even finer grade. (#8873)

Extraordinary MS66 1913 Ten Dollar

3718 **1913 MS66 PCGS.** Only moderately scarce when compared to other P-mint ten Indians, this piece is certainly a distinguished survivor. A small group of about 20 high grade 1913 tens were found a number of years ago in Niagara Falls, New York. They were found behind the bar-back in an old tavern and removed by the contractors. A couple of near-perfect examples are known that are not from this hoard, but we are uncertain of the origin of this piece.

Only one coin has been certified as finer by the two major grading services. That particular coin was sold in our offering of the Steven Duckor Collection and it realized $126,500. The highwater mark for an MS66 was in our 2007 FUN Auction and that coin brought $32,200. To date (8/07) only 22 coins have been certified in MS66 grade (12 at PCGS and 10 at NGC). These pieces realistically represent 14-17 coins once resubmissions are factored out.

The surfaces of this piece has a fine granularity and are extraordinarily bright and radiant. Like the Duckor coin, this piece has mint luster that is bright and frosted and is suggestive of an S-mint coin. The color is yellow-gold with just the slightest hint of reddish patina. The only marks that are noticeable (with magnification) are located on the reverse on the upper tail feathers and in the field above the M in UNUM. Fully struck in all areas. Simply amazing quality and one of the finest P-mint tens available. (#8873)

3719 **1913-S—Cleaned—ANACS. AU Details. Net XF45.** A bit bright due to a wipe from a jewelry cloth, but luster beckons from protected areas. Only 66,000 pieces were struck for this conditionally rare branch mint issue. (#8874)

Lustrous Near-Gem 1914-D Eagle

3720 **1914-D MS64 PCGS.** Scattered surface marks limit the grade of this condition rarity, with only a few higher quality pieces known. PCGS has only graded 25 Gems (8/07). Design definition is bold and the luster is brilliant, with frosty yellow surfaces and attractive rose toning. (#8876)

3721 **1914-S MS61 PCGS.** Bright peach-gold surfaces reveal light handling marks scattered over each side. Fairly well defined, except for minor softness on the eagle's shoulder. (#8877)

3722 **1915 MS63 NGC.** A strongly lustrous sun-gold Select example of this Philadelphia issue, the last eagle struck at that Mint until 1926. Both sides of this well struck piece show scattered abrasions, including a mark at the hair superimposed over Liberty's ear. (#8878)

Lovely 1915 Ten Dollar, MS64

3723 **1915 MS64 NGC.** Many of the 151,000 ten dollar gold pieces resided for decades in European banks (Jeff Garrett and Ron Guth, 2006), helping to account for their relatively abundant numbers today. Bright brassy-gold surfaces abound on this radiantly lustrous near-Gem, and sharp definition is apparent on the design elements. A few inconsequential marks preclude full Gem status. An excellent high-grade type coin. (#8878)

3724 **1916-S AU58 ANACS.** Well-defined overall with ample luster on the butter-yellow surfaces and only a touch of friction. A minimally marked and pleasing example from the last eagle issue before its four-year hiatus, which was spurred by the Great War. (#8880)

3725 **1926 MS64 PCGS.** Invigorating luster embraces the peach-gold faces of this near-Gem ten dollar piece, and a well directed strike brings out nice definition on the motifs. The grade is defined by a few small marks on each side. (#8882)

3726 **1926 MS64 PCGS.** The butter-yellow surfaces of this lovely type eagle offer hints of emerald on the obverse. A boldly impressed and pleasing representative that has strong luster. (#8882)

3727 **1926 MS64 NGC.** This lustrous near-Gem displays yellow-gold color tinted with light tan. Sharply struck, and possessing just a few minute marks. (#8882)

3728 **1926 MS64 PCGS.** Bright, effulgent luster radiates from the rose-gold surfaces. The design details are sharply produced throughout. A modicum of small abrasions confirm the near-Gem grade level. (#8882)

3729 **1926 MS64 NGC.** A pleasing near-Gem with only minor luster grazes on the softly lustrous yellow-gold surfaces. One of the few issues in the Indian eagle series that is affordable in near-Gem condition, the 1926 is a strong candidate for the type collector. (#8882)

Frosty Gem 1926 Indian Eagle

3730 **1926 MS65 PCGS.** Housed in an older green-label PCGS holder, this Gem is fully brilliant with frosty yellow-gold luster and splendid surfaces. The 1926 and 1932 Indian eagles are the most common dates in the series, and are often chosen for type collections. However, just eight finer quality pieces are PCGS certified, limiting the availability of this date. (#8882)

3731 **1932 MS63 NGC.** The highest-mintage eagle issue, the 1932 was minted on the cusp of Franklin Roosevelt's gold recall and the subsequent demise of that metal as a circulating medium in the United States. This well-defined example has swirling luster and a pleasing antique-gold appearance. Light, scattered abrasions are noted on the devices and in the fields. (#8884)

3732 **1932 MS64 PCGS.** Vibrant luster and above-average detail contribute heavily to the strong eye appeal of this Choice yellow-gold example. Minimally marked overall and a pleasing type coin. (#8884)

3733 **1932 MS64 NGC.** A flashy and well struck yellow-gold example, an attractive Choice selection for the type collector. If not for a handful of faint abrasions to the left of the date and around the eagle, this piece would be a Gem. (#8884)

3734 **1932 MS64 PCGS.** This orange-gold Choice piece has elements of butter-yellow in the obverse fields. Solidly struck with excellent luster and few marks, a wonderful selection for the type collector. (#8884)

3735 **1932 MS64 PCGS.** The luminous yellow-gold surfaces of this Saint-Gaudens eagle type piece have an alluring blend of frost and satin. Well struck with few marks overall and a thin alloy streak that passes through the G of GOD. (#8884)

3736 **1932 MS64 NGC.** The lemon-gold and sun-gold fields have strong luster and a touch of haze that is suggestive of long-term storage. Solidly struck with just a few too many marks for a finer grade, but a pleasing type piece nonetheless. (#8884)

3737 **1932 MS64 NGC.** Excellent eye appeal is the dominant mode for crisply struck sun-gold example. Well struck with vibrant luster and mint-green accents in the fields. A delightful type piece. (#8884)

3738 **1932 MS64 NGC.** A well struck and enticing butter-yellow representative of this quintessential type issue, shining with minimally marked fields. A few faint flaws on the portrait preclude a Gem designation. (#8884)

3739 **1932 MS64 PCGS.** An immensely lustrous type piece, this well struck Saint-Gaudens eagle has pleasing detail overall and just a few too many marks to qualify for Gem status. Highly attractive for the grade. (#8884)

3740 1932 MS64 PCGS. A strongly lustrous near-Gem representative of this ubiquitous type issue, partly green-gold with elements of yellow and even orange. Pleasingly detailed overall with a touch of frost on the obverse. (#8884)

3741 1932 MS64 PCGS. A wonderful yellow-gold example of this readily collectible Saint-Gaudens eagle issue, well-defined with excellent visual appeal. The devices are clean, though the area to the left of the date shows a luster scrape and accompanying marks. (#8884)

3742 1932 MS64 NGC. A frosty butter-yellow and peach-gold near-Gem, this Indian eagle hails from the high-mintage 1932 issue, struck just one year before the moratorium on American gold coinage. The surfaces show mostly luster grazes with only a few marks of any importance. (#8884)

3743 1932 MS64 NGC. Though the apricot-gold surfaces show a number of luster grazes, they display few actual marks. A well-defined and pleasing Saint-Gaudens eagle that would make an excellent addition to a type set. (#8884)

Superlative 1932 Indian Eagle, MS66

3744 1932 MS66 NGC. A sensational example with brilliant and highly lustrous mint frost. The surfaces are virtually perfect and the honey-gold color is delightful. While Premium Gems are rather easy to locate, given a little patience, finer quality examples are almost impossible to find. NGC and PCGS have combined to grade just eight coins above this one. (#8884)

LIBERTY DOUBLE EAGLES

3745 1850 XF45 PCGS. Traces of luster grace the orange-gold peripheries of this early P-mint double eagle. Well struck with few marks overall, though a heavier abrasion is noted between the second and third stars on the obverse. (#8902)

S.S. Central America 1850 Twenty AU50

3746 1850 AU50 NGC. *Ex: S.S. Republic.* This straw-gold double eagle retains glimpses of its initial luster, and the subdued surfaces are only lightly abraded, accounting for light circulation. Minutely granular near obverse star 6. Most of the twenties from the SSCA were struck at San Francisco; the present piece is an exception. (#8902)

AU 1850 Twenty Dollar

3747 1850 AU50 NGC. Luster brightens the shield, rays, legends, coronet, and stars. Well defined with minor wear on Liberty's hair and cheek. A minor reverse rim ding is noted at 12:30, and the fields and portrait display the expected number of small marks. The earliest collectible date of the denomination. (#8902)

1850 Double Eagle, AU50

3748 1850 AU50 NGC. Generally good design detail, with semi-bright yellow-gold surfaces that are lightly abraded. A light obverse rim bruise is noted at 8 o'clock. A very popular date as the first year of the regular issue for the type and denomination. Mint State examples of this issue are rare (Jeff Garrett and Ron Guth, 2006). (#8902)

XF 1850-O Twenty Dollar

3749 1850-O XF40 NGC. The 1850-O is historically significant as the first New Orleans double eagle issue, and it is more difficult to locate than the 1851-O, the usually encountered O-mint date. This apricot-gold example displays luster within design crevices, especially on the reverse, and there are no obtrusive marks. (#8903)

3750 1851 XF45 PCGS. Extensively, but not heavily abraded, with nearly enough luster to qualify as an AU. Only slightly worn, and showing very deep coloration. A scarcer issue. (#8904)

3751 1851 AU53 NGC. This early date orange-gold double eagle displays glimmers of luster near protected regions, and there are no noteworthy marks for the AU53 level. (#8904)

3752 1851 AU55 PCGS. This yellow-orange piece has pleasing peripheral detail, though the portrait shows a measure of softness on the hair. A lightly abraded, briefly circulated, yet luminous and pleasing example of this second-year double eagle issue. (#8904)

Scarce 1851-O Twenty Dollar, AU50

3753 **1851-O AU50 PCGS.** The 1851-O double eagle was struck to the tune of 315,000 pieces, and most of the survivors grade Very Fine or Extremely Fine. Scarce in AU, and quite rare in Mint State. The AU50 coin in this lot displays bright brassy-gold surfaces that retain luster in the protected areas. Relatively sharp definition is apparent on the design elements, and the marks seen on both sides are minor. (#8905)

Pleasing AU53 1851-O Twenty

3754 **1851-O AU53 NGC.** The mintage of 315,000 coins was struck from nine pairs of dies, and as a result there is wide variance in striking quality for this issue. This particular coin is slightly soft over the highpoints on each side, indicating evenly worn dies on both obverse and reverse. There are no mentionable or detracting abrasions on either side of this attractive green-gold O-mint Type One twenty. (#8905)

Choice AU 1851-O Twenty

3755 **1851-O AU55 NGC.** The eagle's wingtips and Liberty's hair are slightly darkened from brief circulation, but bountiful yellow-gold luster shines from all protected areas of the design. Abrasions are present, but are individually unimportant save for a thin mark between obverse stars 5 and 6. (#8905)

3756 **1852 AU58 ANACS.** Peach-gold surfaces retain generous luster, and exhibit well defined motifs. A few marks are evenly distributed, not unexpected for a large, heavy gold coin that has seen limited circulation. (#8906)

Vibrant Near-Mint 1852-O Double Eagle From the *S.S. Republic*

3757 **1852-O AU58 NGC.** The loss of the *S.S. Republic*, one of the most significant American maritime disasters in the years just after the end of the Civil War, was not that ship's first encounter with a hurricane. In October 1864, the vessel, then the *U.S.S. Mobile*, was damaged in a storm near the border between Texas and Mexico. The Union government considered repairs too costly, and after its sale at auction, it sailed as a passenger ship and cargo transport between New York and New Orleans, and it was on this route that a second hurricane overwhelmed it.

With the route it traveled, it is unsurprising that double eagles from New Orleans were among the coins recovered in the excavation of the wreck. This desirable double eagle combines the cachet of New Orleans gold with one of the most desirable treasure pedigrees of modern times. The sun-gold surfaces offer distinct reflectivity on each side, an atypical but known finish for the issue. The obverse fields show numerous abrasions, though the well struck portrait displays only minor friction. Of the 17 examples of this issue certified by NGC and pedigreed to the *S.S. Republic*, only one has received a finer grade (8/07). The coin comes with an informative, still shrink-wrapped DVD in an attractive brass-accented wooden case with book-style slipcover. (#8907)

3758 1853—Repaired, Cleaned—ANACS. AU55 Details. Generally well defined, with apricot-gold surfaces that reveal fine hairlines under magnification. Some smoothing has taken place on portions of Liberty's portrait and in the adjacent fields, apparently to remove pockmarks, several of which are still visible in Liberty's hair. Possibly a sea recovery piece. (#8908)

Luminous 1853-O Double Eagle, AU53

3759 1853-O AU53 NGC. Though the New Orleans Mint was the prime beneficiary of the California gold shipped to government facilities in earlier years, 1854 saw the opening of San Francisco as an official Mint, and the supply of gold to the Crescent City dried up. This well struck and softly lustrous orange-gold example hearkens back to New Orleans' boom times, though the briefly circulated surfaces show a number of abrasions. (#8910)

Lustrous 1853-O Double Eagle, AU55

3760 1853-O AU55 NGC. Although quite a few pieces have been certified in various AU grades, this issue is a condition rarity with just six coins certified as Mint State. At the start of the California Gold Rush, the New Orleans Mint was the closest operating mint to California. From 1850 through 1852, New Orleans coined 646,000 double eagles, representing 625,000 ounces of pure gold. Today, with gold at $660 per ounce, that is over 400 million dollars worth of gold.

In 1853, with higher production of private gold coinage in California, the New Orleans mintage dropped to 71,000 coins, and in 1854, when the San Francisco Mint opened, New Orleans gold coinage almost disappeared entirely, as only 13,000 double eagles were coined from 1854 to 1856.

This piece is a splendid Choice AU coin with nearly full green-gold luster, accented by subliminal rose toning. The appearance is familiar to those who are cognizant of California gold pieces. Census: 38 in 55, 38 finer (8/07). (#8910)

3761 1854 Large Date AU53 NGC. A still-lustrous orange-gold example from the more elusive Large Date variety, characterized by thinner, taller numerals than the usual Small Date logotype. Highly appealing despite the scattered abrasions that affect the fields and the lightly worn devices. (#98911)

1854-S Double Eagle, Uncirculated Details

3762 **1854-S—Improperly Cleaned—NCS. Unc Details.** Well struck and highly lustrous, with rich lime-gold coloration and matte-like surface textures. A handful of minor abrasions are noted on the upper obverse. A couple of spindly die cracks (as struck) extend across the lower reverse. Somewhat brighter than expected, from improper cleaning. (#8913)

3763 **1855 XF45 PCGS.** Luster outlines the design elements of this tan-gold Liberty twenty. Distributed moderate marks are appropriate for the denomination and grade. (#8914)

3764 **1855-S AU55 NGC.** Well struck and luminous with traces of orange evident on the honey-gold surfaces. Just a touch of wear appears on the highpoints of this lightly abraded S-mint double eagle. (#8916)

Near Mint 1855-S Twenty

3765 **1855-S AU58 NGC.** Ex: *S.S. Republic*. Small S. A mint worker has patched the crossbar of the A in STATES, which was broken on the working hub. A partly lustrous Type One example with a clean reverse and a moderately abraded obverse. Only the second year of production for the San Francisco Mint, which was struggling to coin the quantities of double eagles needed for West Coast commerce. (#8916)

Delightful 1855-S Double Eagle, AU58

3766 **1855-S AU58 PCGS.** Ex: *S.S. Central America*. Variety 14E, Bold S. This coin should experience considerable attention as it crosses the auction block. Only a trace of wear prevents a Mint State grade, and it is certainly possible that a different numismatic observer might call it MS60 or even finer. The surfaces are fully brilliant with frosty yellow-gold luster and minimal marks. Population: 36 in 58, 15 finer (8/07). (#8916)

Choice AU 1856-S SSCA Twenty

3767 **1856-S Full Serif, Broken A AU55 PCGS.** Ex: *S.S. Central America*. SSCA 5111. This pleasing Type One double eagle is pedigreed to Davy Jones' locker, where it resided between 1857 and 1988. Yellow gold with occasional orange blushes. Luster is nearly full, but the wingtips and eyebrow display friction. Housed in a gold label holder. (#70010)

Interesting Near-Mint 1856-S Twenty

3768 **1856-S AU58 NGC.** Discovery of the *S.S. Central America* treasure has turned the 1856-S double eagle into a common date among Type One twenties. This example has a look entirely unlike those from the treasure, suggesting that it may be a scarce pre-treasure example that survived through the normal channels of commerce and numismatics. Light wear and frosty green-gold color are visible with nearly complete luster. The usual tiny surface marks and rim bumps are evident. (#8919)

Select SSCA 1856-S Twenty Dollar

3769   1856-S Full Serif, Right S MS63 PCGS. Ex: *S.S. Central America*. Variety-17D. SSCA 6078. The *S.S. Central America* provided collectors with thousands of nice Mint State Type Two twenties, but most of those were dated 1857-S. PCGS has certified a total of 70 MS63 1856-S twenties, compared to 830 1857-S pieces in that grade. The difference becomes even more pronounced in higher grades. PCGS numismatists nonetheless were able to identify several different '56-S die varieties, including 17D, the Full Serif, Right S. Only seven examples of 17D are certified by PCGS, with the finest as MS61. For some reason, the present piece is unlisted in the 17D PCGS population. It is well struck and thoroughly lustrous. There is no discoloration, or any other evidence that it spend more than a century on the Atlantic Ocean floor. Smooth aside from a cluster of faint marks within the reverse circle of stars. Housed in a gold label holder. (#70017)

Difficult 1857 Double Eagle, AU58

3770   1857 AU58 NGC. The 1857 double eagle is most often found in Very Fine or Extremely Fine condition. High-end About Uncirculated examples, such as the piece in this lot, are more difficult to acquire, and Mint State coins are elusive. Ample luster resides on the peach-gold surfaces of this sharply struck specimen. A few light marks are scattered over each side. (#8920)

Scarce 1857 Double Eagle, MS61

3771   1857 MS61 NGC. The 1857 double eagle is scarce in Mint State; NGC and PCGS combined have seen only about 70 Uncirculated examples. A well executed strike brings out good definition on this MS61 coin. Its peach-gold surfaces exhibit the most potent luster in the areas around, and in the interstices of, the design elements. Numerous tiny marks are evenly scattered over both sides. Census: 12 in 61, 14 finer (7/07). (#8920)

3772   1857-S AU55 NGC. Ex: *S.S. Republic*. This reverse die is unrecorded in Robert Evans' July 2000 *Numismatist* article, presumably because it was struck too late in 1857 to participate in the September 1857 *S.S. Central America* shipwreck. The mintmark has an unusually small lower serif (referred to as an "Inverted S" by NGC, although the mintmark could have been unevenly entered instead) and is located far right and too close to the letter N. The E in AMERICA has a broken upper crossbar. The coin itself is partly lustrous and refreshingly unabraded. (#8922)

Vibrant Select 1857-S Double Eagle
From the *S.S. Central America*

3773   1857-S MS63 PCGS. Variety 20B, Bold S. Ex: *S.S. Central America*, SSCA 4531. This exquisitely detailed Select example still shines on the sesquicentennial of the sinking of the ill-fated *Central America*. The sun-gold fields and straw-gold devices are largely clean, though a cluster of small marks is noted to the right of the date. (#8922)

3774 1857-S Bold S MS63 PCGS. Ex: *S.S. Central America*. Variety 20B. SSCA 0900. Blazing luster radiates from both sides of this Select survivor from the *S.S. Central America*. A powerful strike leaves excellent definition over the design elements. Peach-gold surfaces display occasional traces of apricot, and just a few minute grade-defining marks. Housed in a gold-label PCGS holder. (#70001)

Scarce 1859 Twenty Dollar, AU53

3775 1859 AU53 PCGS. Much scarcer than the mintage of 43,597 pieces would indicate, the 1859 is also a particularly rare item in high grade with the average specimen only grading VF30. This is one of the finer pieces known. There is very little to separate this coin from one that is technically Uncirculated. The luster sparkles on each side, and the medium yellow-gold color abounds overall. Sharply struck with myriad detracting abrasions overall. (#8926)

Choice AU 1859-S Twenty

3776 1859-S AU55 NGC. Ex: *S.S. Republic*. Lustrous for the designated grade, particularly on the reverse which has essentially full luster. Liberty's hair and the wingtips have only a hint of wear. Marks are minimal for a lightly circulated double eagle. A splendid souvenir of a famous treasure ship, second in importance only to the *S.S. Central America*. (#8928)

1859-S Twenty Dollar, AU58

3777 1859-S AU58 NGC. The 1859-S double eagle, with a mintage of over 600,000 pieces, is readily available through Extremely Fine, and can be located in About Uncirculated with some searching and patience. Mint State coins are rare. This AU58 specimen retains a good amount of luster on the peach-gold surfaces. Well struck, with just a few minute marks. Census: 97 in 58, 22 finer (8/07). (#8928)

Well Struck 1860-S Double Eagle, AU58

3778 1860-S AU58 NGC. The appealing greenish-gold surfaces are remarkably free of abrasions for a pre-Civil War S-mint double eagle. Scrutiny under a glass does reveals a few grade-consistent surface impairments, but only a small dig on Liberty's neck requires singular mention. Much luster remains, and the strike is impressively robust. NGC has graded only 22 examples finer (8/07). (#8931)

3779 1861 AU58 PCGS. A subtly lustrous example with luminous antique-gold surfaces and pillowy detail on the portrait. Philadelphia struck nearly 3 million double eagles during this Civil War year. (#8932)

Well Defined 1861 Double Eagle, MS61

3780 1861 MS61 NGC. Jeff Garrett and Ron Guth (2006) write that "The large mintage (nearly 3 million pieces), the highest of any double eagle until 1904, makes the 1861 a common issue in most grades." Brassy-gold surfaces of this MS61 coin exhibit good luster and sharply defined design elements. Minor luster grazes scattered about help account for the grade.
From The Diemer L. Fife Collection. (#8932)

Appealing 1861 Twenty Dollar MS62

3781 1861 MS62 NGC. The fields are uncommonly smooth for the grade, although extensive scrutiny with a loupe locates some inconspicuous marks on the cheek. The recovery of the *S.S. Republic* has made the 1861 affordable in Mint State, but examples remain scarce relative to demand, partly because of its Civil War date. (#8932)

Ex: S.S. *Republic* 1861-S Double Eagle AU53

3782 1861-S AU53 NGC. Ex: *S.S. Republic.* This better date Liberty twenty displays copious reverse luster, and the obverse retains luster within the hair, stars, coronet, and date. The left obverse has a few faded abrasions, and a strong glass locates minor granularity. Despite recent shipwreck recoveries, the 1861-S remains very rare in Mint State. (#8935)

Borderline Uncirculated 1861-S Twenty

3783 1861-S AU58 NGC. Luster is especially extensive on the reverse of this conditionally scarce S-mint No Motto twenty. Highpoint wear is minimal, and although moderate marks are present on the cheek and beneath the hair bun, the eye appeal is uncontested. NGC has encapsulated just 14 pieces finer (7/07). (#8935)

Scarce 1862 Twenty, XF45

3784 1862 XF45 NGC. A scarce Civil War issue, many of the 92,098 pieces struck were shipped to Europe where paper money was not welcome, as pointed out in Bowers' reference on this denomination. This coin was handled, however, as it shows even wear over the highpoints and numerous abrasions in the fields. Deep reddish color is seen over each side. (#8937)

3785 1862-S AU50 NGC. Light, even wear appears across the well struck devices. The yellow-gold and green-gold fields retain ample luster, and the lightly abraded piece has excellent eye appeal overall. A pleasing representative of this Civil War-era double eagle issue. (#8938)

Choice AU 1862-S Twenty

3786 1862-S AU55 NGC. Considerable luster brightens this originally toned straw-gold example. The obverse has noticeable marks above the portrait and within the hair, but the surfaces are otherwise only moderately abraded. By the second year of the Civil War, all U.S. coins were hoarded except in the far West, where silver and gold continued to circulate. (#8938)

1862-S Twenty, AU55

3787 1862-S AU55 PCGS. While minted in substantial numbers, the 1862-S twenty is surprisingly difficult at all grade levels and downright scarce in AU. It is well struck with only traces of highpoint wear and surprisingly intense luster for the grade. A few moderate marks are noted on the left obverse. Population: 31 in 55, 46 finer (8/07). (#8938)

Lustrous AU58 1862-S Twenty

3788 **1862-S AU58 NGC.** The 1862-S has traditionally been considered one of the scarcer Type Two twenties. However, several higher grade examples were found in the salvage operations on the *S.S. Republic,* thus increasing the availability of this issue. This piece shows just the slightest break in the mint luster in the fields and over the cheek of Liberty. Sharply struck throughout. There are a number of small, but individually insignificant abrasions on each side. (#8938)

Borderline Uncirculated 1862-S Twenty

3789 **1862-S AU58 NGC.** Ex: *S.S. Republic.* The 86 in the date is lightly repunched. This well struck representative has luster across the open fields, and no consequential marks are present. The Civil War affected the West to a much lesser extent than the North or South. By 1862, all silver and gold coins vanished except in the far West, where paper money was refused in commerce. (#8938)

Desirable 1863-S Twenty Dollar, AU58

3790 **1863-S AU58 NGC.** Glowing peach luster dominates protected areas, while the cheek and fields are olive-gray. A few moderate marks on the portrait are typical for these large denomination gold coins. The *S.S. Republic* and *Brother Jonathan* shipwrecks have reduced the rarity of the 1863-S in recent years, but near-Mint pieces are still desired by the many builders of Liberty twenty sets. (#8940)

Attractive 1863-S Twenty AU58

3791 **1863-S AU58 NGC.** Ex: *S.S. Republic.* Large S. This sun-gold near-Mint double eagle has considerable ebullient luster, and only a whisper of friction is noted on the wingtips. The portrait and obverse field display occasional moderate marks, but the reverse is impressively unabraded. (#8940)

Scarce Choice AU 1864-S Twenty

3792 **1864-S AU55 NGC.** This partially lustrous representative possesses original mustard-gold toning, which suggests it belonged to the numismatic community prior to the recovery of the *S.S. Brother Jonathan* and *S.S. Republic* shipwrecks. Luster glows from the legends, stars, rays, wings, shield, and hair. UNUM is typically struck, and a few marks are distributed, as appropriate for the grade. (#8942)

Near-Mint 1864-S Double Eagle

3793 **1864-S AU58 NGC.** Ex: *S.S. Republic.* An impressive example with virtually complete luster, and marks are inconsequential for the grade. The bright surfaces are nicely struck save for some blending of detail on the arrowheads and right-side scroll. 1864 was the year of the *Brother Jonathan* shipwreck, which like the *S.S. Republic* provided a number of '64-S twenties. (#8942)

3794 1865 MS65 NGC. This is the final Type One Philadelphia Mint double eagle issue, and, until recently, the 1865 was a truly scarce item in Mint State. In 2002, writing in "An Insider's Guide to Collecting Type I Double Eagles", Douglas Winter and Adam Crum estimated the number of Mint State survivors at 12 to 15 pieces. In July of 2003, however, the wreck of the *S.S. Republic* was discovered, two hundred miles off the coast of Georgia. More than 17,000 coins, valued at hundreds of millions of dollars, were recovered from the *Republic*, and, to date, 307 of those pieces have been identified as 1865s, and certified by NGC in grades ranging from AU58 to MS66. All but nine of those examples have been assigned Mint State grades. Obviously, this event represents a sea change in the overall status of the 1865 issue. It should be noted, however, that only 21 of the *S.S. Republic* coins have been graded at MS65, with a single MS66 ★ atop NGC's *Census Report* (8/07).

The currently offered Gem example is a sharply struck double eagle with brilliant, light yellow-gold color and exceptional mixed luster, mostly frosty on the obverse, but with a pleasing satiny sheen on the reverse. The surfaces are well preserved, and, while the obverse fields and central device have a few faint luster grazes and nicks that are consistent with the grade, these hardly detract at all from this coin's splendid overall eye appeal. The obverse is covered with fine diagonal die polish lines, slanting down to the right, while the reverse has a few such lines, slanting down to the left, that are visible above the eagle's head and within the shield. The obverse has a slanting die line extending through the upper part of star 4, and into the field. The reverse has several spidery die cracks that reside mainly near the upper reverse legends and near the eagle's wing tips. A small milky area, directly to the right of obverse star 4, may represent a faint fingertip remnant from long ago, but is not worthy of much concern.

All in all, we would have to classify this piece as a remarkably clean and attractive example, and we highly recommend it for consideration to potential bidders who are interested in finding that one special piece, either as a type representative or to fill a previously near-impossible role as a Gem specimen of this Civil War date. (#8943)

Satiny MS61 1865-S Twenty

3795 1865-S MS61 NGC. A satiny and surprisingly unabraded Mint State No Motto twenty. The obverse border has an occasional trace of struck-in grease, as made, but the overall eye appeal is superior for the grade. The reverse die is virtually shattered by a network of peripheral cracks and a small rim die break at 7:30. (#8944)

United States Branch Mint, San Francisco

Low-Mintage 1866-S No Motto Twenty Dollar, XF45

3796 1866-S No Motto XF45 NGC. Douglas Winter and Adam Crum, in their 2002 *An Insider's Guide to Collecting Type I Double Eagles,* write that:

"Approximately 12,000 1866-S double eagles were struck with the Type I reverse in February, prior to instructions from Philadelphia were received to change over to the new Type II reverse. This is an unheralded but very scarce issue that is actually among the rarest Liberty Head double eagles of any type in higher grades. It is also an interesting transitional coin that represents the only dual issue Liberty Head double eagle."

The peach-gold surfaces of this Choice XF example are imbued with hints of light tan, and display traces of luster in some of the recesses. The strike is comparatively strong for the issue, and the few minute marks scattered about are not out of line with the grade designation. Census: 47 in 45, 59 finer (8/07). (#8945)

3797 1866-S No Motto AU55 NGC. Recorded mintage figures of U.S. coins are sometimes meaningless. The 1866-S No Motto twenty is considered the second rarest of the S-mint double eagles, despite a reported mintage of 120,000 pieces, according to Dave Bowers in his *A Guide Book of Double Eagle Gold Coins* (2004). Actually, the recorded mintage figure for this coin has been the subject of debate for many years. The 2008 edition of *A Guide Book of United States Coins* documents the mintage of this issue at 12,000 pieces. The 1997 *Guide Book* qualifies the mintage of 12,000 coins as being only an estimate. Older versions of the same reference simply leave the mintage line blank. It is important to note that past and present researchers, including R.W. Julian most recently, have confirmed through a review of actual documentation in the *National Archives* that the San Francisco Mint did indeed strike 120,000 1866-S No Motto double eagles. It is apparent that someone, somewhere along the line, concluded that the 120,000 figure must be a typographical error and a zero was dropped.

Now that we have concluded that 120,000 1866-S No Motto twenties were struck, we must take on the next mystery: where did they go? Leading authorities unequivocally agree that only 200 or so of this issue exists in all grades combined. Were they melted? That is one plausible answer, especially considering that the 1866-S double eagle is a transitional date; the No Motto version is a Type One and the With Motto issue is a Type Two. Breen (1988) points out that six obverse dies were shipped to the San Francisco Mint in November of 1865 to be used with old reverse dies. The new With Motto reverse dies were then shipped four months later. Perhaps it was decided that all 1866 double eagles released for circulation should include the new With Motto design and the No Motto pieces were melted, considering that all 1866 Philadelphia double eagles were of the new Type Two design. Whatever the fate of the 1866-S No Motto twenties, it is a fact that a least some were released into circulation. We also know that even fewer, if any at all, were pulled from circulation and saved in high grade. The NGC *Census Report* confirms this fact, as only one piece has been graded as MS60 with none finer (8/07). The story is the same with the PCGS *Population Report*. Ample luster remains on this Choice AU specimen, which exhibits bright orange-gold coloration and is only moderately abraded. Census: 17 in 55, 4 finer (8/07). (#8945)

3798 **1866-S Motto AU53 NGC.** A well struck and luminous yellow-orange representative of this early With Motto issue, lightly abraded overall with minor highpoint wear. While the two cent piece displayed IN GOD WE TRUST as early as 1864, 1866 saw the motto's near-universal adoption across denominations. (#8950)

3799 **1867—Obverse Scratched—NCS. Unc. Details.** The left obverse field has two clusters of pinscratches, near the mouth and forehead. This is a semi-prooflike example with a bold strike and flashy fields. The reverse is attractively preserved. (#8951)

3800 **1868-S AU55 NGC.** This well struck post-war S-mint double eagle is predominantly yellow-gold with hints of mint-green in the still-lustrous fields. Appealing despite the numerous light, scattered abrasions and minor highpoint wear that account for the grade. (#8954)

3801 **1869 AU53 PCGS.** A briefly circulated sun-gold and amber example of this post-war issue, well-defined overall with a touch of alloy streakiness at the lower obverse. Appealing despite the presence of faint, scattered abrasions on both sides. PCGS has certified 64 finer examples (8/07). (#8955)

Frosty AU55 1869 Double Eagle

3802 **1869 AU55 NGC.** Frosty light yellow surfaces have full luster except for a trace of rub that is limited to the highest points of the design. The usual scattered surface marks are evident on both sides, but all are individually insignificant. Hints of pink color add to the eye appeal of this desirable piece. (#8955)

Elusive Choice AU 1869 Double Eagle

3803 **1869 AU55 NGC.** The deep green-gold color of this Choice AU example is complemented by peach peripheral accents on each side. The coin is well struck and only shows a modest degree of wear on the design's highest points. This issue is considered scarce in AU condition, and it becomes extremely challenging in Mint State. (#8955)

3804 **1870-S AU53 NGC.** This issue is scarce in high grades, and the typical survivor grades around VF to XF. This AU example is lustrous and well detailed, with numerous small marks and hairlines and moderate highpoint wear that seems typical for the assigned grade level. (#8959)

3805 **1870-S AU55 NGC.** Despite light wear on the devices, the surfaces of this Choice AU S-mint piece show a modicum of reflectivity. An attractive yellow-gold example that shows faint, scattered abrasions. (#8959)

Scarce 1871-CC Twenty, XF45

3806 **1871-CC XF45 PCGS.** Variety 1-A. Only 17,387 pieces were struck of this semi-key issue, most of which are located (when located) in VF-XF grades. A couple of dozen AU examples are known and there are even a few Mint State pieces at the top of the Condition Census, which is quite a different grade positioning from the 1870-CC where there are no Uncirculated pieces known and only nine AUs certified. This is a bright yellow-gold example that has even wear over the highpoints. Numerous small abrasions are peppered over each side, but the only ones worthy of mention are located in the left obverse field. (#8961)

AU Details 1871-CC Twenty Dollar

3807 **1871-CC—Whizzed—NCS. AU Details.** This rare date, low mintage example has Mint State sharpness on the reverse. The obverse has been whizzed, and both sides are hairlined. Nonetheless desirable, since branch mint gold authority Douglas Winter states the 1871-CC is the second rarest Carson City issue within the double eagle denomination, trailing only the famous 1870-CC. (#8961)

3808 **1871-S AU50 ANACS.** The base of an errant 1 is located west of the base of 7. Pockets of luster glimmer when this typically abraded piece is rotated beneath a light. The obverse rim has a few small spots (#8962)

3809 **1871-S AU55 NGC.** Minor repunching is noted left of the base of the 7. Ample glowing luster illuminates protected areas. Less abraded than is usual for a lightly circulated double eagle, although the rims have a few inconsequential marks. (#8962)

3810 **1872 AU55 NGC.** The yellow-orange surfaces of this briefly circulated Philadelphia double eagle retain considerable luster. Well struck with a number of faint, scattered abrasions on the obverse, though the reverse is comparatively clean. (#8963)

Rarely Encountered Uncirculated 1872-S Twenty

3811 **1872-S MS61 NGC.** One of the more frequently seen Type Two twenties, the 1872-S is occasionally encountered in the various AU grades but it is rare in mint condition. How rare? Only 10 pieces have been certified by both services in finer condition than this piece. The surfaces show full mint luster and are obviously frosted. Sharply struck. Each side shows the usual number of abrasions expected from a gold coin in this grade and the only larger, and therefore mentionable ones, are located in the right obverse field. A rare opportunity for the gold collector. (#8965)

3812 **1873 Open 3 AU58 NGC.** Vibrant luster and an assertive strike add to the appeal of this moderately abraded and essentially friction-free example. Encased in a prior generation holder. (#8967)

3813 **1873 Open 3 AU58 NGC.** Though a touch of friction visits the highpoints of this well struck piece, the green-gold surfaces retain the vast majority of their original luster. Faint, scattered abrasions visit the fields. An attractive representative of this later logotype. (#8967)

3814 **1873 Open 3 MS61 PCGS.** A satiny, unworn wheat-gold example that shows faint hints of green at the margins. This Open 3 coin offers excellent peripheral detail with only a touch of central softness, though a number of wispy abrasions preclude a better grade. (#8967)

3815 **1873 Open 3 MS61 PCGS.** The Open 3 logotype proved to be a success, as the final digit is much more readable than for the Closed 3 variant. This vibrant yellow-gold example has a flashy obverse and a shining reverse. Well struck with numerous luster grazes and abrasions, though the eye appeal remains strong. (#8967)

3816 **1873 Open 3 MS61 NGC.** The yellow-gold fields show numerous grade-defining abrasions, though the well struck devices are comparatively unaffected. An area of malachite-green copper spotting appears at the upper right rays on the reverse. (#8967)

3817 **1873 Open 3 MS62 NGC.** A well struck sun-gold example with pleasing luster, struck from the later Open 3 logotype with its distinct final digit. Numerous scattered marks and a few more significant abrasions define the grade. (#8967)

3818 **1873 Open 3 MS62 PCGS.** Frosty and well struck, this apricot-gold piece hails from the slightly more populous Open 3 variant. Wispy abrasions on the portrait and grazes in the fields account for the grade. A distinctive cobalt-blue patch appears at the left obverse rim. (#8967)

Popular 1873-S Closed 3 Twenty MS61

3819 **1873-S Closed 3 MS61 NGC.** This lustrous orange-gold Type Two twenty has a good strike apart from the two stars beneath the ST in TRUST. The reverse is impressively unabraded, and although the obverse has its quota of small marks, none poses an individual distraction. The Closed 3 variety is more obtainable than its Open 3 counterpart, since dies with the updated logotype took their time to arrive from Philadelphia cross-country to San Francisco. (#8969)

3820 1873-S Open 3 AU50 PCGS. The mintage of 1,040,600 pieces was split between the Closed (or Close) 3 and Open 3 varieties, of which the Open 3 is scarcer. (The Smithsonian Institution lacks an example of either variety.) This piece offers deep, mellow orange-gold coloration with considerable luster remaining. (#8979)

3821 1874 MS60 NGC. A well struck wheat-gold example that shows lovely luster and no trace of wear. Despite the myriad abrasions that define the grade, this P-mint double eagle retains significant eye appeal. (#8970)

3822 1874-CC XF45 NGC. Honey-gold color bathes both sides of this Carson City issue. Generally well defined, and with the normal scattering of small circulation marks. (#8971)

Bright AU55 1874-CC Twenty

3823 1874-CC AU55 PCGS. The 1874-CC has a surprisingly large mintage of 115,085 pieces. This is surprising after the low output from 1870 through 1873. Survivors are eagerly sought after by collectors who need a Carson City Type Two for type sets, but there is a relatively low upper limit for such pieces as the finest coins certified are MS62. The surfaces on this piece are bright and lustrous, as one would expect from a CC twenty, but show the usual heavy abrasions on the obverse. (#8971)

3824 1874-S AU58 PCGS. This S-mint twenty dollar retains a generous amount of luster on its apricot-gold surfaces, and the design elements are well impressed. Some small abrasions are scattered over each side. (#8972)

1874-S Double Eagle, MS61

3825 1874-S MS61 NGC. Of the nearly 750 1874-S double eagles certified by NGC and PCGS as Mint State, the vast majority grade MS60 or MS61; no coins are finer than MS63. This MS61 example displays well impressed design features, and honey-gold surfaces whose luster flow is somewhat interrupted by small contact marks scattered about. (#8972)

3826 1875 MS62 PCGS. Both sides of this double eagle offer rich luster and vibrant butter-yellow surfaces. Light to moderate abrasions pepper the well struck devices and fields, yet the overall eye appeal is better than the grade might suggest. (#8973)

3827 1875-CC AU55 PCGS. This earlier Carson City double eagle issue has an unusually high mintage for the series and a significant survival rate, two factors that contribute to its popularity with type collectors. This briefly circulated, softly struck Type Two example retains much of its original luster. Assorted marks, including a line of reed marks, affect the yellow-gold surfaces. (#8974)

Attractive, Semi-Prooflike 1875-CC Twenty, MS62

3828 1875-CC MS62 NGC. While one of the more frequently encountered CC twenties, and especially from the 1870s, the 1875-CC has added appeal as a Type Two. This bolsters both the demand and price for this issue far beyond its availability as a CC type coin. This is an exceptionally pleasing example that has bright, semi-prooflike fields and a stronger strike than usually seen on Type Two twenties. A lustrous, medium orange-gold coin with only small abrasions scattered about. (#8974)

3829 1876-CC XF45 NGC. The 1876-CC is one of the more available Carson City double eagle issues, particularly in VF and XF grades. This lightly worn, luminous yellow-orange piece shows significant remaining luster at the reverse periphery. Well struck with light abrasions that pepper each side. (#8977)

3830 1876-CC—Reverse Cleaned—ANACS. AU53 Details. An unusually designated piece, well struck with pleasing yellow-gold obverse surfaces. The reverse exhibits slightly different coloration and disturbed luster. Both sides display areas of deep copper alloy on and around the central devices (perhaps the original motivation for the cleaning?) Still an interesting representative of this Carson City issue. (#8977)

Well Struck AU55 1876-CC Double Eagle

3831 **1876-CC AU55 PCGS.** Peach-gold patination is imbued with traces of mint-green, and luster resides in the recesses of this choice AU Carson City issue. It possesses a better-than-average strike for the date, as the radial lines in most of the stars are crisp. A few minor marks scattered over both sides are consistent with what would be expected for a coin seeing limited circulation. (#8977)

Uncirculated 1876-CC Twenty

3832 **1876-CC MS60 NGC.** The 1876-CC is available in XF and AU grades, but Mint State examples are scarce, and the issue becomes prohibitively rare above the MS62 level. This piece has luminous luster and a surprisingly mark-free reverse. The obverse is only moderately abraded aside from the field near star 4 and a pinscratch to the R in LIBERTY. (#8977)

3833 **1876-S MS62 NGC.** The fields are well-preserved, and the few faint abrasions evident on the devices are minor for the grade. A strongly lustrous and pleasingly detailed yellow-gold example from the centennial year. (#8978)

3834 **1876-S MS62 PCGS.** A popular issue on several different counts: as a representative of the U.S. Centennial year; as the last of the Type Two double eagles; and for type sets as one of the most plentiful mintages in the Type Two series. Despite the large emission of nearly 1.6 million pieces, high-end pieces such as this delightful and lustrous MS62 piece are always in demand. The surfaces boast pretty apricot-gold coloration, a strong strike, good eye appeal, and a few light abrasions that parallel the grade. Some nice strike doubling is noted on TWENTY, as a bonus. (#8978)

3835 **1877 MS61 NGC.** Exuberant mint frost gives this piece a flashy, dazzling appearance. The devices are well struck throughout, but moderate obverse bagmarks prevent a higher grade designation. (#8982)

3836 **1877-CC XF45 NGC.** The initial Type Three Carson City double eagle issue, the 1877-CC has a mintage of 42,565 pieces. Despite this low figure, a number of repatriated pieces have entered the market, and the issue rates as one of the more available for the series. This luminous and well struck orange-gold piece has light, even wear and scattered marks across the surfaces. Slightly deeper color appears around the devices. (#8983)

Bright 1877-CC Double Eagle, AU53

3837 **1877-CC AU53 NGC.** This is the first issue of the Type 3 design struck at the Carson City Mint. A bright, brassy-gold AU53 coin with traces of luster in the recessed areas. The design elements are well defined, save for some light wear on the highpoints. A few minute ticks do not disturb. (#8983)

3838 **1877-CC MS62 PCGS.** In recent decades, many 1877-CC double eagles have found their way back into the United States from old, overseas holdings. On the surface, the recovery of long lost specimens of this elusive issue sounds like great news for collectors. In reality, it is bitter-sweet as the vast majority of the repatriated 1877-CC twenties are circulated examples or, at the very least, too heavily abraded to be deemed Mint State. Large gold pieces that are transported in canvas bags over thousands of miles could only be negatively impacted in terms of condition. The NGC *Census Report* and the PCGS *Population Report* paint a clear picture on the absolute rarity of this issue in Mint State grades, as neither service has graded a single example beyond the MS62 level, and the combined number of coins graded as MS62 total only 15 pieces (8/07). One can safely assume that the collective 15 MS62 examples reported by NGC and PCGS is artificially high; the direct result of the same coin being submitted more than once in order to achieve a higher grade opinion.

Doug Winter in his *Gold Coins of the Old West, the Carson City Mint 1870-1893* shares his observations: "This issue is generally found in Very Fine and Extremely Fine grades. About Uncirculated 1877-CC double eagles are somewhat scarce and most survivors in this grade are no better than average quality AU50s. High-end About Uncirculated pieces are quite scarce, while fully Mint State coins are very rare." Breen, Garrett-Guth, and Bowers, in their respective writings on this series, echo Winter's sentiments. The current example is rare, not only as a date, but more importantly as a conditionally challenging issue. This is a remarkably lustrous coin with flashy, semi-prooflike fields. The peripheries have taken on a deeper red patina and there are a couple of grease stains (as struck) close to star 13. Sharply defined throughout, there are a few small abrasions on the obverse but almost none on the reverse. Census: 7 in 62, 0 finer (8/07). (#8983)

3839 1877-S MS61 PCGS. This solidly struck S-mint double eagle is predominantly yellow-gold with splashes of orange at the upper right obverse. Strongly lustrous with numerous grade-defining abrasions on and around the portrait. (#8984)

3840 1877-S MS61 PCGS. Jeff Garrett and Ron Guth (2006) indicate that large numbers of this issue have returned to the States from European and South American countries, most of them being heavily abraded. While this MS61 peach-gold specimen possesses some minute grade-defining marks, it exudes nice luster and displays sharply struck design elements. Actually quite an appealing coin for the grade designation. (#8984)

3841 1878 MS61 PCGS. While the hazy yellow-orange obverse has strong rotational luster, the reverse is distinctly reflective. Well-defined with scattered abrasions overall and pleasing detail save for the lower obverse stars. (#8985)

3842 1878 MS61 PCGS. This crisply struck P-mint double eagle has vibrantly lustrous yellow-gold surfaces that show subtle pink and green accents. While the reverse is comparatively clean, the obverse shows myriad grade-defining marks and a handful of more significant abrasions near the date. (#8985)

Flashy 1878 Twenty Dollar, MS61

3843 1878 MS61 PCGS. A great deal of "flash" greets the observer of this double eagle, which is somewhat unusual for an MS61. The vibrant peach-gold surfaces display considerable field-motif contrast, and the design elements are the recipient of a well executed strike. The piece has its share of evenly distributed ticks, but these are greatly overshadowed by the aforementioned attributes. (#8985)

3844 1878 MS62 PCGS. The butter-yellow fields of this boldly impressed double eagle show a measure of reflectivity. Scattered abrasions are present on both sides of this slightly hazy piece. (#8985)

3845 1878 MS62 PCGS. An attractive example of this early Type Three double eagle issue, well-defined in the centers with pleasing luster. Only a touch of softness is present at the yellow-orange margins of this lightly abraded piece. (#8985)

3846 1878 MS62 PCGS. Peach and yellow gold patination is imbued with hints of light tan, and sharply defined motifs are noted on both sides. Lustrous surfaces reveal some light marks, especially on the obverse. This issue is plentiful through MS61, but the numbers fall off in MS62, and even more significantly in MS63. (#8985)

Low Mintage 1879-CC Double Eagle XF45

3847 1879-CC XF45 NGC. Semi-prooflike luster brightens the stars and legends of this nicely struck and moderately worn example. Carson City double eagle production dwindled from 138,441 pieces in 1876 to 10,708 pieces in 1879. None were struck in 1880 and 1881. Comstock lode bullion was either diminishing, or shipped directly to San Francisco for coining. (#8989)

Minuscule Mintage 1879-O Twenty Dollar, XF40

3848 1879-O XF40 NGC. The 1879-O double eagle comes with a minuscule mintage of 2,325 pieces. Jeff Garrett and Ron Guth (2006), in their U.S. gold coin reference, contend that fewer than 150 examples are known today. NGC and PCGS combined have certified about 130 specimens in all grades.

Honey-gold patina imbued with traces of light tan covers both sides of this XF40 example, each of which display traces of luster in the recesses. Sharp definition characterizes the design features, except for wear on the highpoints. Light contact marks are evenly distributed on the surfaces, none of which are individually noteworthy. (#8990)

3849 1879-S AU58 NGC. This briefly circulated near-Mint piece offers ample remaining luster and excellent detail. A number of shallow abrasions are present on each side of this yellow-gold S-mint double eagle. (#8991)

3850 1879-S AU58 NGC. A semi-prooflike Borderline Uncirculated piece that has copious luster and only the expected number of moderate field marks. (#8991)

Finest Certified 1879-S Twenty, MS64

3851 **1879-S MS64 PCGS.** While the 1879-S as a date is not generally thought of as rare, like a long list of Liberty Head double eagles in high grade, it is conditionally quite elusive. Unlike most Liberty Head double eagles, however, it is rare in any Mint State grade. The issue in the past has been underrated, due to its large emission exceeding 1.2 million pieces, but *in grades above MS62 the issue is surpassingly rare. The present example is the single highest graded of the issue at either NGC or PCGS, and it is the finest by two grade points that we have ever had the privilege of offering.*

The current NGC and PCGS population data eloquently tell the story: While NGC has certified 36 pieces in MS62, there is not a single piece graded MS63, much less one in MS64. (Even the 1897-S's sibling, the famously rare 1879-O double eagle with a mintage of 2,325 pieces, shows one example graded MS63 at NGC.) PCGS has certified 45 examples of the 1879-S in MS62, yet there are only three specimens certified MS63 (or—as always—one piece submitted three times). Finally, in MS64, the present example is the only one so certified.

Once considered a common Type Three double eagle, the 1879-S in recent years has seen a burgeoning awareness of its true rarity in the numismatic marketplace. Heritage has offered a total of only 11 MS62 examples of the 1879-S in the past dozen or so years. While in the mid-1990s the selling price was only slightly higher than generic pieces, 10 years later the average price for an MS62 had increased fifteenfold. In 2004's *Type Three Double Eagles 1877-1907*, the authors made the following observations: "The 1879-S Double Eagle can be located in any circulated grade without much difficulty although nice About Uncirculated coins are not nearly as common as their current price level would indicate. This is a scarce date in Uncirculated with a great majority of the known specimens grading Mint State-60. It becomes rare in Mint State-61 and any 1879-S Double Eagle grading Mint State-62 or better is very rare."

Bowers' *Guide Book of Double Eagles* probably understates the elusiveness of the issue in MS62 by saying, "The 1879-S is another easy winner in the double eagle sweepstakes—with examples being readily available in just about any grade desired from VF to MS-62. Higher level coins are in another category, however, and are very elusive." Of course, on the latter point he is absolutely correct.

The latest (and most encyclopedic) gold coin reference available, Jeff Garrett and Ron Guth's *Encyclopedia of U.S. Gold Coins 1795-1933*, offers the following comments: "Although the mintage for the 1879 New Orleans issue was tiny, the San Francisco Mint produced an abundant number of coins. Many were shipped overseas for international trade. Large numbers have returned in recent decades. Most are just Extremely Fine or About Uncirculated, and the issue is actually scarce in Mint State. In choice condition the 1879-S double eagle is very rare. Some high-grade examples seen are partially prooflike. Amazingly, two NGC MS-62 examples sold for more than $29,000 each in early 2005."

The present example boasts a bold strike, with full radial details seen on each peripheral star, and none of the mentionable weakness so often seen on the highpoints of Liberty's hair. The surfaces offer intense luster over medium orange-gold surfaces that show a hint of reflectivity in the fields. For such a large gold coin, the surfaces are remarkably free of all but a few smallish abrasions that are consistent with the near-Gem grade level. This beautiful and rare coin is bound to catch the attention of Registry Set collectors and connoisseurs of the finest rare-date gold. Population: 1 in 64; there are none finer (8/07). (#8991)

3852 1881-S MS62 PCGS. At the time of its release, apparently no examples of the 1881-S were set aside by numismatists. Mint State examples exist, but were indifferently stored as bullion or bank reserves. The issue is nearly unobtainable in MS63 or finer grades, and many astute collectors instead seek a high-end MS62 example. This lustrous and evenly struck example has a few scattered bagmarks, but is pleasing for the grade overall. (#8995)

3853 1882-CC XF45 PCGS. A lightly circulated and radiant lemon-gold example of this available mid-date Carson City double eagle issue, well struck with a number of scattered abrasions. A noteworthy example that retains significant eye appeal despite its flaws. (#8997)

Well Struck 1882-CC Double Eagle, AU55

3854 1882-CC AU55 NGC. Traces of luster reside within the recesses of the yellow-gold surfaces of this Choice AU Carson City example, and an attentive strike brings out sharp definition on the design elements. A few minute marks are scattered about, including a couple of rim bruises, but these are fewer and less severe than typically found on the issue (Douglas Winter, 2001). (#8997)

3855 1882-S MS62 PCGS. Although this date is readily available in MS62 and lower grades, good luck finding a nicer one! PCGS (8/07) has only graded 30 pieces in the higher grade tiers, and those coins seldom appear for sale. This honey-gold example has a few scattered surface marks as expected, with reflective or mirrored fields. (#8998)

3856 1883-CC XF45 NGC. With a mintage of just under 60,000 pieces and a sizable survival rate, the 1883-CC double eagle is one of the most readily collectible pre-1890 issues of Carson City gold. This well struck and luminous yellow-orange representative displays faint, scattered flaws and a measure of haze over the surfaces. (#8999)

3857 1883-CC AU55 PCGS. Light, even wear affects the highpoints of this radiant, modestly reflective yellow-gold piece. A mildly abraded representative of this mid-date issue, one of the more affordable Carson City double eagle issues in better grades. (#8999)

3858 1883-S MS62 PCGS. The small, squat S mintmark. Peach-gold surfaces exhibit bright luster, and reveal scattered minute obverse marks. An attentive strike brings out good definition on the design elements. (#9000)

3859 1883-S MS62 PCGS. The scarce Tall, clearly defined S mintmark. Orange-gold patina rests over lustrous surfaces that are imbued with hints of light green, and a well directed strike brings out good definition on the design elements. A few small marks are scattered over the obverse, and what appear to be minuscule pieces of dirt are visible around the ICA of AMERICA. (#9000)

3860 1883-S MS62 PCGS. An interesting example for the collector of 19th century gold. The well-defined devices and luminous fields are predominantly yellow-orange, though some alloy spots are present in the right obverse field. Still, a pleasing S-mint piece. (#9000)

3861 1883-S MS62 PCGS. A crisply struck yellow-orange example of this higher-mintage S-mint piece, luminous with a number of faint ticks on the devices. While Mint State examples of this issue are available, Select and better pieces present a significant challenge. (#9000)

3862 1883-S MS62 NGC. The lemon-gold and orange surfaces of this S-mint double eagle offer delightful luster, and the strike is solid. A number of light to moderate abrasions on each side preclude a finer grade. (#9000)

3863 1883-S MS62 PCGS. Jeff Garrett and Ron Guth (2006) indicate that the San Francisco double eagles of this period were carelessly handled in overseas trade, and are consequently heavily bagmarked. This well struck MS62 example displays soft luster and pronounced field-motif contrast on the reverse. While possessing some scuffs and light marks, this specimen is not "heavily" bagmarked. (#9000)

Lustrous 1883-S Select Twenty Dollar

3864 1883-S MS63 PCGS. Brass-gold color is visible in the centers of this Select double eagle, while a lime gold hue can be seen in the low points and peripheries. Well struck, as is usual for this date, which is generally considered obtainable only in grades up to MS62. The surfaces are fully lustrous and show a minimum of distracting marks. Fewer than 15 pieces have been certified finer, all MS64s. (#9000)

Near-Mint 1884-CC Double Eagle

3865 1884-CC AU58 NGC. An original Borderline Uncirculated example with nearly complete mint luster. The obverse field has its share of moderate marks, but the portrait and the reverse are unexpectedly smooth. The '90-CC is the most available Carson City twenty in the AU58 grade, yet the '84-CC trades for close to the same price. (#9001)

Attractive MS61 1884-CC Twenty

3866 1884-CC MS61 PCGS. A median rarity in the Carson City series with Uncirculated examples occasionally available. This is an attractive, fully frosted that shows numerous small abrasions, most of which are peppered across the obverse. Sharply defined throughout, which is an important consideration on this issue as many are weakly struck on the obverse. Rich orange-gold color. (#9001)

3867 1884-S MS61 PCGS. In 1884, the Mints' combined output of double eagles fell below a million pieces, though San Francisco produced the lion's share. This satiny and solidly struck apricot-gold piece displays a number of grade-defining abrasions on the portrait and in the fields. (#9002)

3868 1884-S MS62 PCGS. This is a pleasing example of this San Francisco issue that shows flashy cartwheel luster and pretty lime-green and peach toning. A few marks and luster grazes are noticeable on the obverse. (#9002)

3869 1884-S MS61 Prooflike NGC. Both sides of this straw-gold S-mint double eagle show excellent reflectivity, though the obverse is more flashy than the reverse. Crisply struck with myriad light, scattered abrasions that account for the grade. Census: 3 in 61 Prooflike, 2 finer (8/07). (#79002)

3870 1885-S MS62 PCGS. A lustrous and attractive example with fewer than the usual number of marks for the MS62 level. The upper loop of the mintmark is lightly repunched. (#9005)

3871 1885-S MS62 PCGS. This sharply struck S-mint representative displays nice luster on yellow-gold surfaces that have a greenish cast. A few light grazes and ticks are not disturbing. Actually, a rather pleasing coin for the grade. (#9005)

Pleasing Select 1885-S Twenty

3872 1885-S MS63 PCGS. Like many of its brethren, this piece is a condition rarity with satiny luster and crimson-gold color. The surfaces have scattered marks as expected for the grade. Despite an adequately large mintage, few high quality pieces have survived as most went into circulation at the time of issue. PCGS has only examined 29 finer examples of this date (7/07). (#9005)

Bright MS62 1887-S Twenty

3873 1887-S MS62 PCGS. The 1887-S is a lower mintage S-mint twenty with only 283,000 pieces produced. The MS62 level is generally the finest grade available (and affordable) for most collectors. Only 71 pieces have been certified by the two major services in MS63 with four finer (one of which is an MS65). This is a sharply struck example with bright yellow-gold surfaces. Numerous small abrasions are scattered over the obverse but few are seen on the reverse. (#9007)

3874 1888 MS60 NGC. The 1888, while readily available in circulated grades, becomes elusive in Mint State. This luminous orange-gold example is well-defined and retains a measure of eye appeal despite a number of considerable abrasions. (#9008)

3875 1888-S MS62 PCGS. Dynamic luster sweeps this impressively unblemished Type Three twenty. A good value relative to a typical MS63 piece. (#9009)

Tied for Finest 1889 Twenty, MS63

3876 1889 MS63 PCGS. The grading services have never graded an 1889 twenty any finer than this piece. For the connoisseur, this is tied with few others as the finest available example. The surfaces have a few scattered marks that are consistent with the grade. Rich yellow-gold luster and brilliant mint frost is enhanced by subtle rose toning and a few splashes of darker color. The opportunity to actually acquire an MS63 representative seldom appears. It has been nearly two years since the last PCGS MS63 piece offered at auction. In fact, this is only the fourth similar example we have offered in the past eight years. Population: 13 in 63, 0 finer (8/07). (#9010)

3877 1889-S MS62 PCGS. A lustrous yellow-gold example with a solitary tiny blue spot on the shield. There are a few small marks on the jaw and near the profile, but overall, the surfaces are clean for the designated grade. (#9012)

Subtly Patinated 1889-S Twenty, MS64
One of the Finest Known

3878 1889-S MS64 PCGS. Two quotes explain the rarity and ultimate high price this piece will fetch at auction. The first is from Doug Winter's book:

"A few small hoards of 1889-S Double Eagles have entered the market from overseas sources. Nearly all of the coins from these groups were heavily bagmarked and graded between About Uncirculated-58 and Mint State-62."

The second quote is from Bowers' book on double eagles:

"The formula for San Francisco Mint double eagles of the 1880s holds true for this, the concluding year: examples are readily available in circulated grades and in Mint State from 60 to 62. *Any higher grade coin is rare, curiously so.*" (Emphasis ours).

The MS64 grade level is the finest the 1889-S twenty can be found in. And at that level, only 12 coins have been so graded by both services. This is an exceptionally attractive example whose eye appeal carries it beyond the technical grade assigned by PCGS. The fields are bright with a glint of semi-reflectivity, and each side has subtle shadings of rose and lilac patina. Fully struck with no mentionable abrasions. Population: 8 in 64, 0 finer (8/07). (#9012)

3879 1890-CC VF35 NGC. An interesting piece that appears to possess a significant amount of remaining luster, yet the portrait has moderate wear. The sun-gold surfaces are attractively unabraded. The scarcer reverse without die doubling on TWENTY and PLURIBUS. (#9014)

Popular 1890-CC Twenty Dollar, AU58

3880 1890-CC AU58 NGC. The yellow-gold surfaces of this popular Carson City issue representative retain considerable luster, and have benefited from an attentive strike. A few minute marks, especially on the obverse, are consistent with a large gold coin that has seen some circulation. (#9014)

3881 1891-S MS63 PCGS. Well struck and lustrous with satiny orange-gold surfaces. Minor marks and luster grazes on Liberty's cheek and in the nearby fields preclude a finer grade. Still, a pleasing example of this available S-mint double eagle issue from the late 19th century. (#9018)

Pleasing AU58 1892-CC Twenty Dollar

3882 1892-CC AU58 NGC. The penultimate issue in the Carson City series, and an issue that is relatively available in XF and AU. The 1892-CC is also a well-produced date that usually shows a strong strike and good luster. Unlike most examples, this coin does not have the deep, heavy abrasions that are usually seen. Bright and lustrous, the fields show slight reflectivity, with medium orange-gold color overall. (#9020)

Bright, Semi-Prooflike MS61 1892-CC Twenty

3883 1892-CC MS61 PCGS. While numerous XF-AU coins have surfaced over the past dozen or so years, few solid Uncirculated examples were a part of the hoards that were dispersed. This is a lovely '92-CC whose eye appeal far surpasses the mental image one has of an MS61. The striking details show pinpoint definition on each side. The fields are bright and close to a Prooflike designation on the PCGS insert. Minimally abraded also, this is a coin that should be considered by a collector who is open to buying an even higher graded 1892-CC—the eye appeal is just that strong. (#9020)

Vibrant Select 1892-S Twenty

3884 1892-S MS63 PCGS. Many 1892-S double eagles, along with other San Francisco twenty dollar issues of the era, were shipped to Europe or South America for international trade (Jeff Garrett and Ron Guth, 2006), making this date readily available in all but the highest Mint State grades. This Select example exhibits elegant yellow-gold color with a faint green cast, and pleasing luster. A sharp strike emboldens the design features. A few faint abrasions on the obverse account for the grade. (#9021)

Important 1893-CC Double Eagle, MS62

3885 1893-CC MS62 PCGS. For Carson City coinage specialists, this is an excellent opportunity to acquire the final double eagle, and a Mint State coin at that. The coin is brilliant with attractive yellow color, the fields are slightly reflective, and the surfaces have few scattered surface marks consistent with the grade. Sharp design features complete this pretty picture. We are certain the connoisseur will be delighted with this example. While lower Mint State grades are seen with some frequency, the population figures reveal only a few that have been graded MS62, and very few finer. Less than one example per year exceeds this quality in the PCGS grading room. Population: 74 in 62, 17 finer (8/07). (#9023)

3886 **1893-S MS63 PCGS.** A sharply struck representative of an issue that fell just shy of a million pieces, largely sun-gold with elements of honey. Select with strong luster and pleasing eye appeal despite light abrasions on the devices. (#9024)

3887 **1894 MS63 NGC.** Boldly impressed with slightly hazy yellow-orange surfaces that show surprisingly flashy luster. A pleasing Select representative of this later 19th century double eagle. (#9025)

3888 **1894-S MS62 PCGS.** The intense, coruscant luster over both sides of this dazzling coin would be considered outstanding and highly desirable on a double eagle from any series or date. The well struck design elements are fully evident, along with lovely honey-gold coloration. A number of small to moderate bagmarks define the grade. (#9026)

3889 **1895 MS62 NGC.** This crisply detailed and shining apricot-gold example shows delicate green accents in the fields. The fields of this late 19th century double eagle show more luster grazes than actual marks, though wispy abrasions are present on Liberty's cheek. (#9027)

3890 **1895 MS63 PCGS.** This crisply struck and shining Select piece exhibits faint pink accents on the yellow-gold obverse. The reverse shows a long alloy streak that stretches from the lower left reverse rim to the upper right. Nevertheless, this Philadelphia double eagle displays attractively. (#9027)

3891 **1895 MS61 Prooflike NGC.** This suitably struck Liberty twenty has flashy fields and the expected number of small to moderate marks. The 1895 is plentiful in typical Mint State, but prooflike pieces are highly elusive. Census: 7 in 61, 17 finer (8/07). (#79027)

3892 **1895 MS62 Prooflike NGC.** A crisply struck and distinctly reflective yellow-gold representative of this higher-mintage P-mint issue, appealing despite light to moderate abrasions overall. Census: 13 in 62 Prooflike, 4 finer (8/07). (#79027)

3893 **1895-S MS63 PCGS.** This radiantly lustrous '95-S Select double eagle is just a few unobtrusive wispy marks from a higher grade. Pretty peach-gold coloration is laced with hints of lime-green, and is complemented by sharply impressed design elements. (#9028)

3894 **1897 MS63 PCGS.** A sharply struck 19th century example that displays flashy luster and above-average eye appeal for the grade. The yellow-orange obverse has few abrasions of significance, though both sides show grazes. (#9031)

3895 **1897 MS63 PCGS.** Luster rolls unencumbered across the moderately abraded olive-gold surfaces. The 1897 is nearly unobtainable as a Gem. PCGS has only certified one piece as MS65, with none finer. Housed in a green label holder. (#9031)

3896 **1897 MS64 PCGS.** Among PCGS-certified pieces, this near-Gem is second only to the singular MS65 example offered by Heritage in the Milwaukee ANA sale (8/07). The satiny peach-gold surfaces host pleasingly detailed, minimally marked devices. (#9031)

3897 **1897-S MS63 PCGS.** Well struck and highly lustrous, with semi-reflective fields and appealing green-gold and rose toning. A slight degree of scuffiness on Liberty's cheek, and in the adjacent field area, precludes a higher grade assessment. (#9032)

3898 **1897-S MS63 PCGS.** A Select green-gold example of this high-mintage San Francisco issue, well-defined overall with few marks for the grade. Softly lustrous with a rim bruise visible below the 7 in the date. (#9032)

3899 **1897-S MS63 Prooflike NGC.** Boldly impressed with strong reflectivity on both sides. This late 19th century S-mint double eagle has light, scattered abrasions on the devices and in the yellow-gold fields. Census: 7 in 63 Prooflike, 1 finer (8/07). (#79032)

Select 1898 Twenty Dollar

3900 **1898 MS63 PCGS.** The orange-gold devices are framed with lighter yellow-gold toning. Dazzling luster sweeps the relatively smooth fields, and the cheek displays only minor grazes. A better date with a low mintage of 170,395 pieces. Its S-mint counterpart has a production of more than 2.5 million pieces. PCGS has certified only seven examples finer (5/07). (#9033)

3901 **1898-S MS63 NGC.** Splendid luster and lovely peach-gold coloration are the hallmarks of this Select Mint State example. Boldly struck and free of any severe marks. This issue is in constant demand from type collectors. (#9034)

3902 **1898-S MS63 PCGS.** Lustrous and well struck, with apricot-gold, rose, and lime-green toning and few marks. An attractive type coin and a good value at this grade level. (#9034)

3903 **1898-S MS64 PCGS.** Booming luster and a bold strike combine with a clean reverse for attractive eye appeal. A charming khaki-gold 19th century type coin. The base of the 9 is lightly repunched. (#9034)

3904 **1898-S MS64 PCGS.** Ebullient luster and original green-gold toning confirm the appeal of this boldly impressed example. The right-side reverse denticles display a few marks. The base of the 89 in the date shows recutting, and AMERICA is lightly die doubled north. (#9034)

3905 **1898-S MS64 PCGS.** A green-gold near-Gem with enervating luster and pleasing preservation. Liberty's portrait is impressively unabraded. The date is lightly repunched southwest, visible on the base of the 89. (#9034)

3906 **1898-S MS64 PCGS.** Precisely struck and lustrous with blended lime and straw-gold shadings. The preservation is exemplary save for a few marks near the mouth. Light reverse die doubling is localized to the tops of OF AMERICA. (#9034)

3907 **1898-S MS64 PCGS.** This near-Gem exhibits gorgeous apricot-gold color that shows a glimpse or two of green on the reverse. The design features are boldly struck, and just a few minor scuffs prevent a higher grade. An attractive example of this higher-mintage West Coast issue. (#9034)

3908 **1898-S MS64 PCGS.** A vibrant orange-gold near-Gem that offers bold central detail, though the stars are a touch soft. Strongly lustrous with more luster grazes than actual marks on the surfaces. (#9034)

Handsome Gem 1898-S Twenty

3909 **1898-S MS65 PCGS.** A thoroughly lustrous green-gold Gem with a clean portrait and minimally abraded fields. Only a minuscule percentage of '98-S twenties can compete with the preservation of the present piece. The 89 in the date is lightly recut. Population: 68 in 65, 2 finer (8/07). (#9034)

Attractively Patinated MS65 1898-S Twenty

3910 **1898-S MS65 PCGS.** The 1898-S is the most frequently seen S-mint twenty with a date from the 19th century. As such, it is in constant demand by type collectors. This is a lovely Gem example that shows the thick mint luster that is usually seen on S-mint gold. Sharply defined throughout with a subtle mixture of rose and lilac patina. Population: 68 in 65, 2 finer (8/07). (#9034)

3911 **1898-S MS63 Prooflike NGC.** The moderately abraded fields provide noticeable reflectivity. Minute die doubling is present on the reverse, visible above the F in OF and the MER in AMERICA. Census: 10 in 63 Prooflike, 1 finer (8/07). (#79034)

3912 **1899 MS64 PCGS.** A handsome near-Gem with smooth fields and devices. Vibrant luster illuminates the boldly struck motifs. Difficult to secure any finer. (#9035)

3913 **1899-S MS62 PCGS.** Flashy luster graces this well struck twenty. The reverse is splendidly preserved, and the obverse is attractive despite some brightness on the nose. (#9036)

3914 **1899-S MS63 PCGS.** Boldly impressed with flashy luster and radiant wheat-gold surfaces. While both sides show faint abrasions, the piece has strong visual appeal for the grade. An attractive example of this turn-of-the-century S-mint issue. (#9036)

3915 **1899-S MS63 PCGS.** Rich honey-gold color is visible on both sides of this highly lustrous piece, with splashes of deep olive toning on the high points. All of the design elements are well brought up. A few minute obverse marks define the grade. (#9036)

Lustrous 1899-S Double Eagle, MS64

3916 **1899-S MS64 PCGS.** Glowing luster emanates from the peach-gold surfaces tinted with lime-green. The strike is sharp, and none of the few minute marks scattered about are worthy of individual mention. Large numbers of the '99-S are known through the MS63 grade level, but the population drops precipitously in MS64. (#9036)

Scintillating 1899-S Double Eagle, MS62 Prooflike

3917 **1899-S MS62 Prooflike NGC.** With just over 2 million examples struck, the 1899-S has an appreciable population of certified Prooflike pieces, though such coins represent only a tiny fraction of the original mintage. This gleaming yellow-gold piece exhibits excellent reflectivity on each side and crisp detail, though the obverse shows a number of scattered abrasions that account for the grade. Census: 5 in 62 Prooflike, 7 finer (8/07). (#79036)

Prooflike Select 1899-S Double Eagle

3918 **1899-S MS63 Prooflike NGC.** Impressively reflective fields confirm the Prooflike designation, and scarce as such despite a mintage of more than 2 million pieces. A boldly struck yellow-gold twenty with moderately abraded fields and an inconspicuous graze on the cheek. Census: 5 in 63 Prooflike, 2 finer (7/07). (#79036)

3919 **1900 MS64 PCGS.** This turn-of-the-century near-Gem offers exacting detail and soft, pleasing luster. The surfaces are predominantly yellow-orange with soft peach accents at the margins. (#9037)

3920 **1900 MS64 NGC.** A lovely representative of this turn-of-the-century issue, solidly struck with vibrant luster and a hint of satin. The glowing orange-gold surfaces show a number of luster grazes but few actual marks. (#9037)

3921 **1900 MS64 PCGS.** The strongly lustrous surfaces and solidly struck devices range from green-gold to yellow-gold. An attractive Choice example from the final P-mint double eagle issue of the 19th century. (#9037)

3922 1900 MS64 PCGS. Decisively struck with flashy luster and an uncommonly clean appearance for the grade. The minimally marked obverse is yellow-orange, while the reverse is closer to orange-gold. A lovely example from the final P-mint double eagle issue of the 19th century. (#9037)

3923 1900 MS64 PCGS. This decisively struck example from the last year of the 19th century exhibits scintillating luster and generally well-preserved yellow-gold surfaces. The fields show no marks worthy of individual mention, though the flaws' combined effect precludes a better grade. (#9037)

3924 1900 MS64 ANACS. Dazzling luster emanates from peach-gold surfaces tinted with hints of light tan. Sharply struck throughout, further enhancing this near-Gem's eye appeal. A few minute marks preclude a higher grade. (#9037)

3925 1900 MS64 PCGS. Exquisite detail and delightful, frosty luster characterize the obverse of this yellow-orange near-Gem, while the reverse shows more typical luster. A lovely example of this later Liberty double eagle issue. (#9037)

3926 1900 MS64 PCGS. A vibrant yellow-gold piece from the close of the 19th century, crisply struck in the centers with canary accents. Strongly lustrous with only scattered, inoffensive marks, though these combine to preclude Gem status. (#9037)

3927 1900 MS64 PCGS. The pale yellow-gold surfaces of this shining near-Gem show faint green accents. This solidly struck Philadelphia double eagle shows a number of grade-defining marks, including one on the ear. Difficult any finer, as PCGS has graded just 54 finer examples (8/07). (#9037)

3928 1900 MS63 Prooflike NGC. A flashy Select example with a few inconspicuous marks near Liberty's jaw. Well struck aside from the centers of a few obverse stars. NGC has certified only four 1900 twenties as Prooflike, with the present piece as the single finest among those (7/07). (#79037)

3929 1901 MS64 NGC. This lustrous honey-gold near-Gem is meticulously struck and carefully preserved. A few unimportant rose-russet freckles are noted. A popular lower mintage issue, encased in a prior generation holder. (#9039)

3930 1901 MS64 PCGS. A softly lustrous orange-gold example of this turn-of-the-century issue, boldly impressed with excellent visual appeal. A touch of cloudiness visits the minimally marked obverse surfaces. (#9039)

3931 1901 MS64 PCGS. While this turn-of-the-century issue has a much lower mintage than the more famous type issues for Liberty double eagles, it is available for only a tiny premium over those ubiquitous dates. This shining apricot-gold piece is highly appealing despite a graze on Liberty's cheek and small marks that pepper each side. (#9039)

Challenging MS63 1901-S Double Eagle

3932 1901-S MS63 PCGS. A thoroughly lustrous sun-gold Select Type Three twenty that boasts an even strike and a well preserved reverse. A few light obverse grazes are fewer than expected of the grade. The 1901-S is plentiful in grades through MS62, but since John H. Clapp may have been the only one setting aside high grade branch mint gold coins in 1901, few have survived in Select Uncirculated condition. (#9040)

3933 1902 MS60 NGC. The 1902 has a mintage of only 31,140 pieces, and it has long been a target for hoarders and speculators. This crisply struck green-gold representative has good luster, and is generally smooth despite a minor obverse rim mark at 5 o'clock. *From The Diemer L. Fife Collection.* (#9041)

3934 1902-S MS62 PCGS. Highly lustrous with a flashy cartwheel sheen and well struck design elements. Bright honey-rose coloration adorns both sides. Moderately bagmarked, as usual for the grade. (#9042)

3935 1903 MS63 PCGS. A strongly lustrous, boldly impressed representative of this early 20th century double eagle issue, one that has a significantly lower mintage than its 1904 counterparts, yet commands only a modest premium. Sharply struck with shining yellow-orange fields and light, grade-defining abrasions on the hair behind the coronet. (#9043)

3936 1903 MS64 PCGS. This early 20th century double eagle issue came just one year before the mammoth mintage of 1904. Only light grazes appear in the straw-gold fields of this highly lustrous near-Gem, and the cheek is clean. (#9043)

3937 1903 MS64 PCGS. Fully struck with strong mint luster and appealing straw-gold surfaces. Small marks and luster grazes account for the grade of this lovely later Liberty double eagle. (#9043)

3938 1903 MS64 NGC. This charming and carefully preserved Choice Liberty twenty exudes ebullient cartwheel luster, and all devices are evenly impressed. (#9043)

3939 1903 MS64 PCGS. When common date pieces are discussed, the 1904 double eagle is first to be mentioned, although this 1903 issue is also plentiful, and a good choice for type purposes. This sharply struck example has frosty surfaces with traces of pink color over brilliant yellow luster. (#9043)

Prooflike MS62 1903 Double Eagle

3940 1903 MS62 Prooflike NGC. Exceptionally well struck design features are highlighted by moderately reflective fields. Attractive pale almond-gold toning graces both sides. The reverse is well preserved, while the obverse has the expected marks on the cheek and left obverse field. Census: 3 in 62 Prooflike, 5 finer (7/07). (#79043)

3941 1903-S MS64 PCGS. This lovely 20th century double eagle is exquisitely struck with highly lustrous peach-gold surfaces that sport tinges of light green. A few minute obverse marks account for the grade. The 1903-S has a mintage of under a million pieces, compared to the over 5 million produced at that Mint the next year. PCGS has graded only eight finer representatives (8/07). (#9044)

3942 1904 MS63 NGC. A shining yellow-gold example of this ubiquitous issue, sharply struck with slight haze over the lightly abraded surfaces. The overall quality approaches Choice, but falls just shy. (#9045)

3943 1904 MS63 PCGS. Warm luster and enticing apricot-gold surfaces are the prime draws of this lightly abraded, yet pleasing type piece. Solidly struck with a splash of peach at the lower CA of AMERICA. (#9045)

3944 1904 MS64 PCGS. A decisively struck yellow-gold representative that shows slightly deeper peach and orange at the peripheries. Both sides offer flashy luster and surprisingly few marks for the grade. A lovely type piece. (#9045)

3945 **1904 MS64 PCGS.** A sharply struck and uncommonly attractive near-Gem representative of this ever-popular Liberty type issue. Gleaming with a touch of haze in the fields and faint, grade-defining marks on the devices. (#9045)

3946 **1904 MS64 PCGS.** Both sides of this flashy yellow-gold Choice piece exhibit a measure of reflectivity. Crisply defined with two small, yet grade-limiting abrasions present on Liberty's cheek. Still, an excellent candidate for the type collector. (#9045)

3947 **1904 MS64 NGC.** Well-defined overall with excellent luster and strong visual appeal, this type near-Gem is yellow-orange with a touch of haze in the fields. Minor, scattered marks account for the grade. (#9045)

3948 **1904 MS64 PCGS.** Boldly impressed with elements of satiny luster on the obverse, though the orange-gold reverse offers flashier luster. An attractive type piece with a distinctive appearance. (#9045)

3949 **1904 MS64 PCGS.** A sharply struck and enticing orange-gold representative of this ever-present double eagle issue, one of the highest-mintage coins of the early 20th century. Faint, scattered marks preclude a finer grade. (#9045)

3950 **1904 MS64 PCGS.** A well executed strike leaves sharp definition on the motifs of this highly lustrous near-Gem. Some minor obverse contact marks and scuffs define the grade. (#9045)

3951 **1904 MS64 PCGS.** A pleasing near-Gem that exudes potent luster from its peach-gold surfaces. The design features are well impressed throughout, and a few minute, grade-consistent marks are visible over each side. (#9045)

3952 **1904 MS64 PCGS.** Radiant luster adorns both sides of this sharply struck double eagle. Peach-gold surfaces are imbued with traces of light green, and reveal two or three notable scratches along the upper left scroll and eagle's wing. (#9045)

3953 **1904 MS64 PCGS.** A strongly lustrous sun-gold representative of this ubiquitous double eagle issue, boldly struck and highly appealing. A handful of wispy marks on Liberty's cheek are the only bar to a finer grade. (#9045)

3954 **1904 MS64 PCGS.** A decisively struck and appealing yellow-gold example, minimally marked with attractive luster. A great representative of this ever-popular Liberty double eagle issue. (#9045)

3955 **1904 MS64 PCGS.** An eye-catching exemplar of this noted type issue, boldly impressed with powerful luster on both sides. The sun-gold obverse contrasts with the lighter lemon-gold reverse. (#9045)

3956 **1904 MS64 PCGS.** A frosty green-gold and yellow-gold representative of the quintessential Liberty double eagle type issue, solidly struck with few marks on the obverse. A handful of scattered abrasions on the reverse account for the grade. (#9045)

3957 **1904 MS64 PCGS.** A pleasing apricot-gold near-Gem, with sharply delineated motifs. Radiantly lustrous surfaces are minimally abraded. (#9045)

3958 **1904 MS64 PCGS.** A solidly struck and dusky yellow-orange example of this ubiquitous issue, offered here in Choice condition. Softly lustrous with solid eye appeal and few marks. (#9045)

3959 **1904 MS64 PCGS.** Though the attractive yellow-gold surfaces of this near-Gem show a few too many marks for a finer grade, the overall eye appeal is strong nonetheless. Strongly lustrous with excellent detail. (#9045)

3960 **1904 MS64 PCGS.** This yellow-orange Liberty type double eagle shows pleasing detail overall, though the luster is a touch subdued. A few wispy abrasions in the obverse fields account for the grade. (#9045)

3961 **1904 MS64 PCGS.** A boldly impressed Choice example of this popular type issue, yellow-orange with slightly subdued luster. A cherry-red copper spot to the right of the date adds character to the piece. (#9045)

3962 **1904 MS64 PCGS.** This crisply detailed near-Gem is predominantly yellow-gold with a touch of apricot. Pleasing for the grade with excellent central detail, a great example of this popular type issue. (#9045)

Shining Gem 1904 Double Eagle

3963 **1904 MS65 PCGS.** Vibrant luster graces the carefully preserved surfaces, which showcase an enticing blend of lemon-gold, peach, and orange. The strike is crisp, and the overall visual appeal is strong. A delightful representative of this ubiquitous issue, one clearly finer than the Choice representatives found more often on the market. (#9045)

Sharp 1904 MS65 Double Eagle

3964 **1904 MS65 NGC.** Effusive luster exudes from both sides of this Gem twenty dollar, and an attentive strike leaves sharp definition on the design features. A noticeable mark is visible at the obverse margin a little clockwise of 12 o'clock. This issue is sought after by type collectors due to its high availability in the better Mint State grades. (#9045)

Flashy 1904 Gem Twenty Dollar

3965 **1904 MS65 PCGS.** Jeff Garrett and Ron Guth (2006) say of the 1904 double eagle that it "... is by far the most common date of the series." PCGS/NGC population data would certainly corroborate this, as tens of thousands have been certified. The orange-gold surfaces of this flashy Gem yield dazzling luster, and exhibit sharply struck design elements. Both faces are devoid of significant marks. This is a wonderful high-grade type example. (#9045)

Delightful Gem 1904 Double Eagle

3966 1904 MS65 NGC. While Choice representatives of this high-population issue are ubiquitous in the marketplace, Gems are considerably less available. This carefully preserved representative, butter-yellow with hints of green and peach at the margins, exhibits warm luster and excellent visual appeal. A strong candidate for a similarly graded type or date set. (#9045)

Phenomenal 1904 Double Eagle, MS66

3967 1904 MS66 PCGS. (Gargantuan, enormous, prodigious, monumental), pick which adjectives you will to describe the mintage of 1904 double eagles—and many others as well spring to the tongue (and pen). Between the San Francisco and Philadelphia mints, they managed to produce nearly 11.5 million coins, an amount of gold that in today's dollars would be valued at nearly *7.4 billion dollars!* Philadelphia edged out San Francisco by about a 6:5 ratio in terms of pieces produced. Despite those (massive) mintages, the population becomes quite rarefied in grades above Gem Mint State: As of (8/07), PCGS has certified only two coins finer than the present piece, one of 124 in MS66. This piece boasts fully struck surfaces on both sides, with lovely orange-gold coloration and lustrous radiance. Certified in an old-style PCGS green-label holder. (#9045)

Top Ranked MS66 1904 Double Eagle

3968 1904 MS66 PCGS. There are type coins and then there are archetypal type coins, those that represent the ultimate in the coiner's art and produced in sufficiently plentiful quantities to stand for the best and brightest of the various U.S. coin series. Such coins would include the Morgan dollars from 1879-S to 1882-S, the 1908 No Motto Saint-Gaudens twenty, the 1932 ten dollar Indian, and the 1904 Liberty Head double eagle, of course. With more than 6 million examples manufactured in 1904 at Philadelphia alone, this issue is the zenith of the Liberty Head double eagle. Pieces can be found in all grades up through MS66. The present coin is nonetheless at the top rank of surviving members, with deep sunset-orange patination untroubled by even the most minuscule distraction. Pieces in finer grade are few and far between. (#9045)

3969 1904 MS62 Prooflike NGC. Both sides of this vibrant sun-gold example show distinct reflectivity. The fields show myriad shallow marks, while the sharply struck portrait of Liberty shows a number of abrasions. Appealing despite its flaws and an interesting choice for the type collector. (#79045)

3970 1904 MS63 Prooflike NGC. Rich orange-gold patina complements exquisitely struck design elements, yielding sharp eye appeal for the numerical grade. Kept from near-Gem by a handful of minute obverse marks. (#79045)

3971 1904-S MS64 PCGS. The sun-gold obverse displays satiny textures, while the green-tinged reverse exhibits stronger luster. Both sides show excellent central detail, and the overall eye appeal of this type near-Gem is grand. (#9046)

3972 1904-S MS64 PCGS. Crisply struck with satiny yellow-gold surfaces that offer apricot accents. The fields and devices show only a handful of scattered marks. The 1904-S has one of the highest mintages of any double eagle issue, as does its Philadelphia counterpart. (#9046)

3973 **1905 MS61 ICG.** Philadelphia's high production of double eagles in 1904 led to saturation, and for the next year, that Mint struck only 58,919 pieces. This unworn yellow-gold representative has strong detail, though the surfaces host myriad abrasions. (#9047)

Terrific Choice 1905-S Double Eagle

3974 **1905-S MS64 PCGS.** Despite a mintage of over 1.8 million pieces, the 1905-S presents a challenge in better Mint State grades; Garrett and Guth (2006) describes the issue as "quite scarce" in Choice, with examples of higher quality "rarely seen." This shining near-Gem displays vibrant luster and minimally marked wheat-gold surfaces with vivid sun-yellow accents. The crisply detailed portrait is particularly clean. PCGS has graded only seven finer pieces (8/07). (#9048)

3975 **1906 MS62 PCGS.** Exquisite strike definition is apparent on the design elements of this MS62 double eagle. Lustrous yellow-gold surfaces are tinted with light green and tan, and are just barely kept from a Select grade by a handful of relatively light contact marks. The 1906 Philadelphia issue becomes somewhat more elusive in finer levels of preservation. (#9049)

Near-Gem 1906-S Liberty Twenty

3976 **1906-S MS64 PCGS.** This lustrous and impressively smooth Choice Liberty twenty has a good strike with only minor blending on the hair southwest of the Y in LIBERTY, which is also indistinct on business strikes of the type. An occasional minute aqua fleck is noted, but the overall look is that of a finer grade. But it is exceptionally difficult to locate an MS65, since PCGS and NGC combined have certified only seven such pieces (8/07). (#9051)

Lovely MS64 1907-D Liberty Twenty

3977 **1907-D MS64 PCGS.** The second of just two D-mint Liberty double eagle issues, the 1907-D had a sizable mintage, though its production did not exceed a million pieces. This well-defined and slightly satiny near-Gem has pleasing antique-gold surfaces with faint lavender accents. (#9053)

Choice 1907-D Liberty Twenty

3978 **1907-D MS64 PCGS.** A luminous peach-gold near-Gem that has glimpses of lime near the rims. The reverse is splendidly smooth, and the obverse has only unimportant surface imperfections. Unlike its Philadelphia Mint counterpart, Denver only struck the Liberty type in 1907. Encased in a green label holder. (#9053)

3979 **1907-S MS62 PCGS.** This vibrantly lustrous representative is from the last year of the Liberty Head double eagle design. The pronounced honey-rose coloration is decidedly attractive. An appealing coin for final-year type purposes. (#9054)

3980 **1907-S MS63 PCGS.** Glowing luster emanates from apricot-gold surfaces that exhibit well defined design elements. A few minuscule marks define the grade. (#9054)

Apricot-Tinted MS64 1907-S Liberty Twenty

3981 **1907-S MS64 NGC.** An apricot-tinted Choice Liberty twenty from the final year of the long-running type. The strike is precise, and marks are individually inconsequential. The base of the 7 in the date is lightly repunched. As of (8/07), NGC and PCGS combined have certified just 13 pieces finer. (#9054)

Wonderful Near-Gem 1907-S Double Eagle

3982 **1907-S MS64 PCGS.** Though this final-year mintmarked Liberty issue has a substantial mintage of over 2.1 million pieces, few representatives offer better preservation or visual appeal than this lovely Choice double eagle. The well-defined devices project from peach-accented yellow-gold fields that exhibit lively luster. A pair of shallow abrasions on the cheek and assorted other marks account for the grade. PCGS has graded just two coins finer (8/07). (#9054)

PROOF LIBERTY DOUBLE EAGLE

Rare PR58 1906 Twenty Dollar

3983 **1906 PR58 PCGS.** Wispy field marks confirm brief non-numismatic handling, but the honey-gold fields retain nearly all of their initial mirrored flash. A low mintage date, with only 94 proofs struck in addition to just 69,596 business strikes. Housed in a green label holder. Population: 2 in 58, 33 finer (8/07). (#9122)

HIGH RELIEF DOUBLE EAGLES

AU58 Details 1907 High Relief Twenty

3984 **1907 High Relief, Wire Rim—Repaired, Cleaned—ANACS. AU58 Details.** The ER in AMERICA are inconspicuously tooled, and the piece is a bit bright from a light cleaning, but even the experienced numismatist might miss these defects. Liberty's knee and chest display faint friction, but the fields and devices shimmer with satin luster. (#9135)

Eagerly Pursued 1907 High Relief Twenty
Wire Rim, Uncirculated Details

3985 **1907 High Relief, Wire Rim—Altered Surface—NCS. Unc. Details.** This collectible High Relief twenty is a bit bright and may be lightly coated with a clear oil. The obverse is satiny, the reverse is lustrous, and both sides are nearly free from abrasions. Sharply struck with the usual hint of flatness on the Liberty's raised knee. (#9135)

Select Mint State MCMVII High Relief

3986 **1907 High Relief, Wire Rim MS63 PCGS.** A lovely and original pumpkin-gold representative of this American numismatic classic. The satiny fields are refreshingly smooth, and in fact there are fewer marks than on the typical MS65-graded 1924 double eagle. The strike is precise, even on the high points such as Liberty's raised knee and the upper edge of the eagle's front wing. Although higher-graded examples are always available on the market, the present piece is a wonderful compromise between quality and affordability. Certified in a green label holder. (#9135)

Impressive MCMVII High Relief MS64

3987 1907 High Relief, Wire Rim MS64 NGC. The year 2007 is the centennial of Augustus Saint-Gaudens' world-famous MCMVII high relief. The extremely rare ultra high reliefs are out of reach for all but the most deep-pocketed collectors, but a high relief is obtainable by the advanced collector. The historical importance of the low mintage high relief was identified early on by numismatists, and most survivors grade between AU55 or finer. But many pieces show flatness on Liberty's raised knee, and other examples exhibit faint scuffs or even abrasions from handling before they reached a collector's hand. The present gently shimmering representative is well struck, even on the knee, and the obverse on its own is sufficiently clean that it threatens a finer grade. The reverse has only faint peripheral marks at 2:30. (#9135)

Flat Rim 1907 High Relief, Unc. Details

3988 1907 High Relief, Flat Rim—Reverse Scratched—NCS. Unc. Details. This satiny yellow-gold Saint-Gaudens High Relief has a small cluster of closely-spaced pinscratches above the sun, probably from an attempt to efface a now-absent spot. The obverse field has a couple of faint grazes. A splendidly struck example of this world-famous low mintage gold type. (#9136)

PROOF HIGH RELIEF DOUBLE EAGLE

Brilliant PR63 1907 High Relief

3989 1907 High Relief PR63 NGC. This Wire Rim piece, certified by NGC as a proof, has all of the required characteristics for such a determination. The strike is bold and sharp, the fields are satiny, and the die polishing lines in the obverse and reverse fields are crisp, flowing up onto the wide borders on each side. The die polishing lines are visible to some extent on al High Relief double eagles, but they are especially bold on the proofs, most prominent between the rays in the left obverse field. Both sides of this example have satiny yellow-gold luster tending toward green, with traces of additional rose toning. (#9132)

SAINT-GAUDENS DOUBLE EAGLES

3990 1907 Arabic Numerals MS62 PCGS. This final version of the 1907 Saint-Gaudens double eagle was only arrived at after the High Relief and Ultra High Relief designs were found to be impractical for the production of business strikes. This example is boldly detailed with soft mint frost and appealing orange-gold coloration. Moderate bagmarks limit the grade.
From The Laguna Niguel Collection, Part Two. (#9141)

3991 1907 Arabic Numerals MS63 PCGS. A nicely struck apricot-gold example that exhibits only the expected number of minor marks. This green label holder coin is accompanied by a certificate of authenticity that states the piece is from the Jefferson Coin & Bullion 1907 "Saint" (sic) hoard. (#9141)

3992 1907 Arabic Numerals MS63 PCGS. A powerful strike leaves sharp definition on the design elements of this Select twenty dollar, including Liberty's face, fingers, and toes, the panes of the Capitol building, and the eagle's plumage. A handful of light marks accounts for the grade. (#9141)

3993 1907 Arabic Numerals MS63 NGC. Sun-gold outer sections and lemon-gold centers show equally strong luster on this lowered-relief first-year piece. Well struck with shallow, scattered abrasions that account for the grade. (#9141)

3994 1907 Arabic Numerals MS63 NGC. This first-year type coin has radiant sun-gold luster, and the strike on the Capitol building is razor-sharp. Generally smooth, but a shiny mark is present near the base of the olive branch. Encapsulated in a former generation holder. (#9141)

3995 1907 Arabic Numerals MS64 PCGS. A delightful mixture of apricot, rose, and mint-green coloration adorns the highly lustrous surfaces of this alluring near-Gem. It is well struck, with a few minor field marks on the obverse that preclude a finer grade designation. From the first year of the Saint-Gaudens double eagle series. (#9141)

3996 1907 Arabic Numerals MS64 PCGS. Lovely lime-green and pastel rose coloration adorns the shimmering surfaces of this first-year example. Boldly struck overall, with a handful of grade-limiting abrasions noted on the obverse and very few marks whatsoever on the reverse. (#9141)

3997 1907 Arabic Numerals MS64 PCGS. This Choice first-year double eagle has predominantly sun-gold surfaces with elements of green-gold in the fields. Well struck with more grazes than actual marks. (#9141)

3998 1907 Arabic Numerals MS64 PCGS. Delicate green-gold and sun-gold shades grace this lovely Choice example. A pleasingly detailed example from the first of just two Philadelphia No Motto issues. (#9141)

3999 1907 Arabic Numerals MS64 PCGS. The sun-gold surfaces of this first-year low-relief example show traces of straw-gold at the lower reverse. Well-defined with a clean appearance, though Liberty's legs and the nearby fields show a few too many marks for a higher grade. (#9141)

4000 1907 Arabic Numerals MS64 PCGS. This lustrous and solidly struck near-Gem shows a measure of alloy discoloration at Liberty's knee and her upper gown. The obverse shows few marks, though several abrasions are present below the eagle on the reverse. (#9141)

4001 1908 No Motto MS64 NGC, Short Rays Obverse, crisply struck and clean for the designated grade; and a **1999 reproduction of a 1934 tribute medal** to Augustus Saint-Gaudens from the maker of the original medal, the Medallic Art Company, the rectangular medal is gold plated fine silver and weighs 133.5 gms. (Total: 2 items) (#9142)

4002 1908 No Motto MS65 PCGS. Long Rays Obverse. This khaki-gold Gem provides vibrant luster and pleasantly unperturbed surfaces. The strike is crisp despite the usually seen minor bluntness on the eagle's leg. (#9142)

4003 1908 No Motto MS65 NGC. Both the strike and the vibrancy of the luster are decidedly finer on this Gem than on the typical 1908 No Motto twenty. Rich coloration and minimal surface marks increase the appeal. (#9142)

4004 1908 No Motto MS65 NGC. Long Rays obverse. Dynamic sun-gold luster sweeps this exactingly struck Gem. Well preserved aside from a thin mark concealed within the wings. Housed in an older generation holder. (#9142)

4005 1908 No Motto MS66 PCGS. Short Rays obverse. This green-gold Premium Gem has a good strike and well preserved devices. The fields exhibit only faint grazes. The strike is razor-sharp on the Capitol building, and the eagle's leg is only slightly soft. (#9142)

4006 1908 No Motto, Wells Fargo Nevada MS66 PCGS. Short Rays Obverse. This shimmering butter-gold Premium Gem is well struck aside from only minor incompleteness of strike on the eagle's leg. An attractive representative from this famous single-issue hoard. (#99142)

4007 1908-D No Motto MS64 PCGS. Long Rays Obverse. This satiny near-Gem exhibits fine grain surface textures and pleasing pastel coloration. The design features are boldly, if not fully struck, and most of the grade-limiting marks are very superficial. (#9143)

4008 1908-D No Motto MS64 PCGS. While this issue's Philadelphia counterpart was minted in quantity, the 1908-D No Motto double eagle's production was comparatively modest. This well struck near-Gem shows a measure of haze over the lustrous apricot-gold surfaces. (#9143)

4009 1908 Motto MS62 NGC. A well struck and satiny example of the first Philadelphia Motto issue, yellow-orange with slightly hazy fields. The devices and the nearby regions show scattered abrasions and a number of luster grazes. (#9147)

4010 1908 Motto MS63 PCGS. Following a Congressional mandate in 1908, the Mint placed IN GOD WE TRUST on the reverse of the eagle and double eagle designs by Augustus Saint-Gaudens. This Motto double eagle has pleasing detail and subtly lustrous, lightly abraded yellow-orange surfaces. (#9147)

4011 1908 Motto MS63 PCGS. Exquisitely struck, with lustrous peach-gold surfaces. A few minor ticks evenly scattered about preclude a higher grade. The motto IN GOD WE TRUST was added late in 1908. (#9147)

1908 Motto Double Eagle MS64

4012 1908 Motto MS64 PCGS. The rich orange centers are bounded by green-gold shades. This nicely struck and lightly abraded example features unencumbered satin luster. While the No Motto 1908 is common, the Motto variety is scarce, since only 156,258 pieces were struck. Interestingly, 1908 proofs are the Motto variety, which suggests they were struck relatively late in the year. (#9147)

Lovely Near-Gem 1908 Motto Double Eagle

4013 1908 Motto MS64 PCGS. In contrast to the No Motto version struck earlier in the year, the 1908 Motto pieces have a much lower mintage of 156,200 pieces and a significantly worse survival rate in better Mint State grades. A touch of haze visits the strongly lustrous yellow-orange surfaces of this near-Gem, which shows a handful of minor, yet grade-defining marks on the well struck devices. PCGS has graded 50 finer examples (8/07). (#9147)

4014 1908-D Motto MS64 PCGS. This canary-gold Choice Saint-Gaudens twenty features good luster and pleasing preservation. The strike is precise on Liberty's face, as well as on the Capitol building. (#9148)

4015 1908-D Motto MS64 NGC. The satiny apricot-gold surfaces show a touch of emerald at the margins. Though the 1908-D is the most available of the first-year motto issues, it was not saved in quantity, and attractive near-Gem and better pieces are more elusive than one might think. (#9148)

Gem 1908-D With Motto Twenty

4016 1908-D Motto MS65 PCGS. Although the mintage of 349,500 coins seems considerable, this issue is an important condition rarity in the Saint-Gaudens series with just 25 finer pieces certified by PCGS (8/07). The surfaces exhibit muted mint frost with brilliant yellow and orange-gold color, accented by hints of pink. (#9148)

Scarce 1908-S Saint-Gaudens AU53

4017 1908-S AU53 NGC. A scarce date in the Saint-Gaudens series with a tiny mintage of only 22,000 pieces. This coin is a moderately worn example with light greenish-gold and reddish patina. Only small contact marks are seen on either side. A substantial degree of mint luster remains evident, for the grade. (#9149)

Low Mintage 1908-S Double Eagle AU55

4018 1908-S AU55 NGC. One could probably win a bar bet — at a major coin convention, at least — by challenging a numismatist to come up with the lowest mintage date of the normal relief Saint-Gaudens double eagle series. Despite the numerous major rarities in the series, the answer would be this coin, the 1908-S, whose total issue amounted to only 22,000 pieces. In part, this is evidence of how little mintage figures correspond with true rarity, but in the case of this date, it would probably be safe to say that it is less likely to be encountered in hoard quantity in the future. Unlike many Saint-Gaudens double eagles, the 1908-S is more often found circulated than not, and such is the case with this reddish-gold coin, which displays light wear along Liberty's forehead, breast, and right (facing) leg, as well as on the eagle's breast and wing. A good deal of mint luster is evident in the recessed areas of the design. (#9149)

4019 1908-S—Cleaned—ANACS. AU58 Details. Just 22,000 pieces were struck for this popular and elusive issue. This example has a pair of minor rim bruises on the obverse at 7:30, and careful rotation reveals light hairlines. (#9149)

Smooth Choice 1909 Twenty Dollar

4020 1909 MS64 PCGS. This lower mintage issue is divided into two varieties of nearly equal scarcity, the normal date and the 1909/8 overdate. The normal date is surprisingly scarce as a near-Gem, and Gems are sufficiently rare that they are out of reach for most collectors. The present piece is fully struck with unusual detail on the face, Capitol building, and branch hand. Contact marks are also absent, uncommon for a large denomination gold coin. This satiny near-Gem is well worthy of personal examination by the alert bidder. (#9150)

4021 1909/8 AU58 NGC. An attractive, briefly circulated representative of this distinctive double eagle overdate, the only one for the Saint-Gaudens series and the last for the denomination. This well struck sun-gold piece still shines and shows few marks, though a hint of friction appears on the highpoints. (#9151)

4022 1909/8 MS61 NGC. A flashy representative of this popular overdate. Well struck, with peach-gold, lightly abraded surfaces. (#9151)

Popular 1909/8 Twenty Dollar MS62

4023 1909/8 MS62 PCGS. An obvious overdate variety that shows the lower curve of the underdigit 8 above and to the southeast of the base of the 9. A satiny yellow-gold double eagle with a good strike and imposing eye appeal. Marks are surprisingly few for the MS62 level, although faded abrasions are present near the stem of the olive branch. (#9151)

Bold 1909/8 Twenty Dollar MS62

4024 1909/8 MS62 PCGS. The most prominent overdate of the double eagle denomination. The lower left curve of the 8 is unmistakable, and the variety has appeared in the Guide Book since its 1946 inception. This lustrous and suitably struck piece has the number of small marks associated with the MS62 level, but there is no individually mentionable contact. (#9151)

Impressive 1909/8 Double Eagle, MS64

4025 1909/8 MS64 PCGS. Only about 80,000 of these overdate double eagles were originally coined, according to conventional wisdom. Although Mint records do not track the coinage of individual die pairs, the overdate and normal date varieties seem to be equal in overall availability. Since 161,282 double eagles were struck in Philadelphia during the year, it seems that about half that total is the mintage for each variety. Gems are extremely rare, and Choice Mint State coins like this piece are the best that can be obtained without a high level of patience and a strong numismatic budget. The surfaces of this near-Gem are brilliant with frosty luster and rich orange-gold color. Population: 77 in 64, 17 finer (8/07). (#9151)

Scarce 1909-D Twenty, MS64

4026 1909-D MS64 PCGS. For at least 20 years the 1909-D has been an overlooked issue among early Saints. In an interview with a local paper in 1978, Steve Ivy listed the 1909-D as a coin to buy for long-term investment. It still remains a good buy today when one considers the availability and price of other dates and mintmarks in the series. Only one hoard of any note has been discovered and distributed over the past 30 years, that of several hundred pieces and found in 1983, most of which graded MS63 or less.

This is a remarkably clean coin whose satiny mint luster shows a lovely interplay of pale rose and lilac patina. Fully struck throughout. (#9152)

4027 1909-S MS64 PCGS. Attractive apricot-gold and mint-green colors intermingle over the radiantly lustrous surfaces of this near-Gem, and an exquisite strike emboldens the design features. Just a few trivial marks away from full Gem. (#9153)

4028 1909-S MS65 PCGS. The wheat-gold surfaces of this well-defined Gem shine beneath a measure of haze. Despite a sizable mintage, this earlier S-mint Saint-Gaudens double eagle is difficult to find any finer; PCGS has graded just seven such examples (8/07). (#9153)

4029 1910 MS64 PCGS. Well-defined with strong luster that has a degree of satin. The yellow-orange surfaces have only light marks, though these combine to preclude a finer grade. Still, an attractive example of this early With Motto issue. (#9154)

4030 1910-D MS64 NGC. Both sides are pleasing for the grade, though the obverse shows just a few too many marks for the piece to qualify as a Gem. A well-defined Denver double eagle, this sun-gold example shows a measure of haze over the highly lustrous fields. (#9155)

4031 **1910-S MS64 PCGS.** The San Francisco Mint struck numerous Saint-Gaudens double eagle issues, all of the With Motto variety. This Choice example hails from the third such issue, well-defined with satiny apricot-gold surfaces and a single copper spot in the left obverse field. (#9156)

4032 **1911 MS63 NGC.** Both sides of this well-defined early With Motto double eagle show warm, appealing luster. Vivid sun-gold and orange-gold surfaces show few abrasions for the grade. (#9157)

4033 **1911 MS63 PCGS.** This is a gorgeous Select Mint State specimen, with fine grain surfaces that exhibit rose-gold coloration and shining, satiny luster. The piece is well struck and nicely preserved, with a handful of small abrasions on the obverse and a shallow luster graze on the lower reverse, beneath GOD WE. (#9157)

Desirable Choice 1911 Double Eagle

4034 **1911 MS64 NGC.** Though this Philadelphia issue of under 200,000 pieces commands little premium through the lowest levels of Mint State, Select and better pieces are more challenging and priced accordingly. Faint green accents visit the lustrous surfaces of this yellow-gold example, well-defined with solid eye appeal. NGC has graded 55 finer pieces (8/07). (#9157)

4035 **1911-D MS65 PCGS.** The satiny surfaces of this D-mint double eagle display lovely peach and mint-green accents and crisply defined motifs. Carefully preserved with two tiny allow spots visible at Liberty's upper gown. (#9158)

4036 **1911-D MS65 NGC.** FS-501, formerly FS-1911.5. Breen-7383. The mintmark is broadly repunched. This example projects the bright, intense luster that one always hopes to see on a Gem, along with rich honey-gold coloration and few surface disturbances. Perhaps the most popular repunched mintmark variety in the Saint-Gaudens double eagle series. (#9158)

4037 **1911-D MS65 PCGS.** A shining yellow-orange Gem representative of this earlier issue, one of the more available Saint-Gaudens double eagles from Denver. Well struck with only a few minor, isolated flaws that are entirely consistent with the grade assigned. (#9158)

4038 **1911-D/D MS65 PCGS.** FS-501. The mintmark is clearly repunched west, and is likely the best-known repunched mintmark variety within the Saint-Gaudens series. A satiny Gem with a well preserved reverse field. (#9158)

4039 **1911-D MS66 NGC.** Sharply struck throughout with rich, satiny luster. This subtly granular yellow-gold and green-gold Premium Gem offers excellent visual appeal for this D-mint issue. (#9158)

4040 **1911-S MS63 NGC.** The lustrous, carefully preserved surfaces display fine grain textures in the fields. Yellow-gold and rose coloration adorns both sides. The design elements are well struck throughout. (#9159)

4041 **1911-S MS64 PCGS.** A well-defined and subtly lustrous sun-gold example of this earlier S-mint Saint-Gaudens double eagle, one that shows few marks on the devices. A few faint digs are present to the left of Liberty. (#9159)

4042 **1911-S MS64 PCGS.** Satiny and bright, with straw-gold and rose coloration over each side, this near-Gem example displays boldly struck design details and a normal number of scattered abrasions for the grade. A relatively available issue at this level which quickly becomes scarce any finer. (#9159)

4043 **1911-S MS64 PCGS.** The design elements are boldly rendered on both sides, and the satiny surfaces exhibit fine grain field textures. An attractive and lightly marked near-Gem. (#9159)

4044 **1911-S MS64 PCGS.** A well directed strike brings out strong definition on this near-Gem S-mint twenty dollar. Somewhat grainy surfaces yield pleasing luster and honey-gold color. (#9159)

4045 **1911-S MS64 PCGS.** The satiny mustard-gold surfaces of this Choice Saint-Gaudens double eagle display faint olive accents. Well struck and pleasing with a few faint abrasions on the knees. The 1911-S is one of several readily available issues of the time available today, thanks to a number of repatriated hoards. (#9159)

4046 **1911-S MS64 PCGS.** The 1911-S has one of the highest survival rates for any S-mint Saint-Gaudens double eagle issue, with hoard sources both domestic and abroad (from Latin America in particular). This well struck, lightly marked sun-gold piece has pleasing luster and solid eye appeal. (#9159)

4047 **1911-S MS64 PCGS.** A satiny yellow-gold example of this heavily repatriated issue, well-defined overall with excellent visual appeal. Light, scattered marks that affect the central devices preclude an even finer grade. (#9159)

4048 **1911-S MS64 PCGS.** Rich satiny luster gives the matte-like surfaces a pleasingly vibrant sheen. Boldly struck with infrequent abrasions and a couple of tiny obverse alloy spots. (#9159)

Enticing Gem 1911-S Double Eagle

4049 **1911-S MS65 PCGS.** The softly lustrous yellow-orange surfaces of this attractive Gem have faint elements of sun-gold in the fields. The central devices exhibit strong detail, and the overall eye appeal is strong. While the 1911-S is one of the more available Saint-Gaudens issues, finding an attractive piece can take time, and anything finer is a condition rarity; PCGS has graded just 23 such coins (8/07). (#9159)

Conditionally Elusive MS66 1911-S Twenty

4050 1911-S MS66 NGC. A conditionally elusive coin, the 1911-S is widely available in the lower Mint State grades. NGC has certified several thousand examples in MS62, MS63, and MS64. In MS65, however, only 249 Gems are graded, and in MS66 the number drops to 36, with one (an MS66 ★ piece) finer. This may be surprising, given the generous original mintage of more than three-quarters of a million pieces, and little evidence of the wholesale meltings that would afflict many later issues in the series. The present piece offers orange-gold, untroubled surfaces with excellent luster and premium appeal. Census: 35 in 66, 0 finer (8/07). (#9159)

4051 1912 MS63 NGC. This softly lustrous sun-gold Select piece comes from a mintage of only 149,750 pieces. Well struck with a hazy obverse and light, scattered abrasions on the devices of that side. (#9160)

4052 1912 MS63 PCGS. This predominantly orange-gold P-mint double eagle exhibits unusual coloration. A sizable violet alloy spot appears above and to the left of Liberty's branch, and similarly colored accents grace the highpoints of both sides. Lustrous and well strike with scattered, grade-defining abrasions. (#9160)

4053 1912 MS63 PCGS. Vibrant luster and pleasing overall detail are the prime draws of this lovely wheat-gold piece, one that has better visual appeal than its grade might suggest. This low-mintage issue was exported in quantity, and its survival rate is above-average as a consequence. (#9160)

Lustrous Near-Gem 1912 Saint-Gaudens

4054 1912 MS64 PCGS. Technically, the 1912 double eagle is a new type created by the addition of two stars placed below the date near the oak leaves. This was done to represent the addition of New Mexico and Arizona to the Union. Apricot-gold luster radiates from both sides of this near-Gem, and a well executed strike defines the design elements. Scattered light marks limit the grade. (#9160)

Popular MS63 1913 Double Eagle

4055 1913 MS63 PCGS. A satiny olive-gold Saint-Gaudens with refreshingly smooth fields and only minor flatness on Liberty's knee. The eye appeal is pleasing for the MS63 grade. The 1913 is popular because of its mintage of 168,780 pieces, a fraction of the high water mark for the series, the 8.8 million emission of the 1928. (#9161)

Select 1913 Double Eagle

4056 1913 MS63 PCGS. A satiny, nicely struck, and original green-gold example. As expected of the grade, the fields display faint grazes and a couple of pinpoint spots, but there are no singularly relevant marks. The Philadelphia Mint issues between 1911 and 1915 are popular because of their relatively low mintages.
From The Diemer L. Fife Collection. (#9161)

4057 1913-D MS64 PCGS. This crisply struck Denver Mint twenty has vibrant luster and radiant olive-gold surfaces. A good value relative to the MS65 grade. (#9162)

4058 1913-D MS64 PCGS. This 48-star D-mint double eagle has a luminous apricot-gold obverse and a sun-gold reverse with more vibrant luster. Well-defined overall with faint, scattered marks that account for the grade. (#9162)

Conditionally Rare 1913-D Double Eagle, MS65

4059 1913-D MS65 PCGS. A remarkable pinkish-gold Gem with fully brilliant and frosty mint luster on both sides. The devices are remarkably well-struck. For the one-a-year collector, the 1913-D double eagle is the only issue that can be easily found in Gem quality, but just four finer coins are certified by PCGS (8/07). (#9162)

Scarce MS62 1913-S Saint-Gaudens Twenty

4060 1913-S MS62 PCGS. The 1913-S has an enticingly low mintage of 34,000 pieces, and many collectors and speculators have set aside of number of examples. This lustrous and attractively preserved representative has a good strike, with any softness limited to the Capitol building and UNITED. (#9163)

Low Mintage 1913-S Select Twenty Dollar

4061 1913-S MS63 PCGS. The 1913-S double eagle comes with a rather paltry mintage of 34,000 pieces. Yet a large number were apparently saved, as they are available in Mint State grades below MS65 (Jeff Garrett and Ron Guth, 2006). Lustrous surfaces of this Select example display adequately struck devices for the issue, and are lightly marked. Free of the copper-spots that typically plague this date. (#9163)

Lustrous 1913-S Double Eagle, MS63

4062 1913-S MS63 PCGS. Jeff Garrett and Ron Guth (2006) write that: "Quality control slipped a bit for this San Francisco issue, with many coins showing copper spots from improperly mixed alloys." The lustrous yellow-gold surfaces of this Select example reveal no such spots. Moreover, the strike is better than usually seen on the issue. A few minute handling marks define the grade. *From The Diemer L. Fife Collection.* (#9163)

Attractive 1913-S Double Eagle, MS64

4063 1913-S MS64 PCGS. Few issues illustrate the topsy-turvy nature of Saint-Gaudens double eagles as the 1913-S; while the total mintage amounted to just 34,000 pieces, the overall survival rate is high, though attractive near-Gem and better pieces can be challenging. This yellow-orange piece shows a pair of small copper spots, one on Liberty's upper gown and the other at the base of her torch. Well struck with soft but pleasing luster. PCGS has certified only 20 coins finer (8/07). (#9163)

Shining 1913-S Double Eagle, MS64

4064 1913-S MS64 NGC. This lower-mintage issue is popular, but finding an attractive piece can prove challenging, as most examples show a soft strike. The sun-gold piece offered here displays above-average detail, and the immensely lustrous surfaces show only light, scattered marks that are consistent with the grade. An appealing survivor from this issue of just 34,000 coins. (#9163)

4065 1913-S MS65 PCGS. Of the 52 different Saint-Gaudens double eagle issues, the 1913-S has the third lowest recorded mintage of coins at just 34,000 pieces. Only the 1907 High Relief and the 1908-S can boast of lower mintage figures. Fortunately for collectors of this series, many coins were saved and examples, at least in ordinary grades, are available for only a slight premium. However, advanced collectors who seek the finest specimens for their collections are not so lucky, as Gem examples of this popular issue are very rare. NGC and PCGS have graded a combined total of only 26 MS65 1913-S twenties with one finer, a lone MS66 at PCGS (8/07). And how many of the 26 Gem pieces were submitted two, three, or even four times in pursuit of an MS66 holder?

Sloppy workmanship is one factor responsible for the lack of high grade examples of this date. Garrett and Guth explain in their *Encyclopedia of U.S. Gold Coins*: "Quality control slipped a bit for this San Francisco issue, with many coins showing copper spots from improperly mixed alloys. The strikes also tend to be a challenge. With time and care, fully struck MS64 coins can be obtained, but in Gem MS65 grades, this date is very rare indeed." Breen (1988) notes that many of the Uncirculated 1913-S double eagles extant came from French bank hoards in the mid-1950s, but most of them display "extensive bag marks." The Smithsonian Institution's finest specimen grades MS63, further illustrating the conditional rarity of this issue.

This is a fully detailed example that has bright, satiny mint luster. There are no obvious or distracting marks on either side of this low mintage, condition rarity in the Saint-Gaudens series. Population: 19 in 65, 1 finer (8/07). (#9163)

Challenging Select 1914 Twenty

4066 1914 MS63 NGC. This shimmering yellow-gold Saint-Gaudens twenty has a bold strike and only moderate obverse marks. Liberty's chest and raised knee exhibit honey and steel-blue toning. A favorite issue for speculators, due to its low mintage of 95,250 pieces, the smallest production of any Philadelphia Motto date. (#9164)

Scarce 1914 Double Eagle MS63

4067 1914 MS63 PCGS. Dusky antique-gold surfaces showcase soft, pleasing luster. This well struck example is appealing despite scattered grade-defining abrasions. The Philadelphia mintages between 1911 and 1915 are fewer than 200,000 pieces for each date, but only the 1914 has a mintage below the 100,000 plateau. (#9164)

Sharply Struck 1914 Select Double Eagle

4068 1914 MS63 PCGS. Satiny surfaces display a pastel peach-gold color with a greenish cast. Sharply struck, as evidenced by crisp definition in Liberty's fingers and toes, the Capitol dome, and the eagle's plumage. A mark on Liberty's torso and a couple on the eagle preclude a higher grade. (#9164)

4069 1914-D MS64 NGC. This Choice D-mint double eagle offers vibrant yellow-gold surfaces with small glints of paler canary color. Well-defined with light, scattered marks and a handful of grade-defining abrasions. (#9165)

4070 1914-D MS65 NGC. A well directed strike leaves sharp definition on the motifs, complemented by radiant luster and rich rose-gold patina. A few minute surface marks are consistent with the Gem grade designation. (#9165)

4071 1914-S MS65 PCGS. With a mintage just shy of 1.5 million pieces, the 1914-S is neither the rarest nor the most common Saint-Gaudens double eagle issue, though overseas hoards have preserved numerous examples. This Gem, largely sun-gold with glints of wheat in the fields, has strong luster and pleasing detail. (#9166)

4072 1915 MS63 PCGS. A luminous green-gold Select representative of this earlier P-mint Saint-Gaudens issue, well struck with a handful of shallow abrasions on the devices on each side. The 1915 is available in Mint State, though its mintage of just over 150,000 pieces is low compared to many issues. (#9167)

4073 1915-S MS65 PCGS. This piece shows the clean fields, rich coloration, and unimpeded luster of a true Gem. The design elements are crisply struck throughout, and the surfaces reveal few marks, as expected. David Akers (1988) calls this "... one of the most common of the early issues," but notes that Gems are "certainly scarce." (#9168)

4074 1915-S MS65 PCGS. Peach-gold surfaces display the typical satiny luster, and benefit from a solid strike. Well preserved surfaces complement the foregoing attributes, adding to the coin's pleasing eye appeal. One of the most common dates in the Saint-Gaudens series, and desirable for type purposes. (#9168)

4075 1915-S MS65 PCGS. A softly lustrous Gem representative of this available S-mint issue, yellow-gold with mint-green accents in the fields. This well struck piece shows a few faint marks, though these are consistent with the grade assigned. (#9168)

4076 1916-S MS64 PCGS. The 1916-S double eagles would be the last pieces of the denomination struck for four years, as World War I and its immediate aftermath chilled the demand for what had become an international trade coin. This Choice and well struck yellow-gold piece displays excellent luster and only a handful of marks. (#9169)

4077 1920 MS63 PCGS. Generally well struck, with orange-gold patina and radiant luster. Most of the design elements are well brought up. (#9170)

4078 1922 MS64 PCGS. This well struck and strongly lustrous Philadelphia near-Gem has hazy apricot-gold surfaces that display faint alloy spots near Liberty's waist. Housed in a first-generation PCGS holder. (#9173)

4079 1922 MS64 PCGS. A canary-gold Choice type coin with potent luster and relatively clean surfaces. Well struck save for slight incompleteness on the eagle's breast. (#9173)

4080 1922 MS65 NGC. The surfaces of this delightfully preserved Gem are predominantly wheat-gold with glints of lighter straw. A solidly detailed P-mint piece that shows a thin die crack through the letters of LIBERTY and along the right rim. (#9173)

4081 **1922 MS65 PCGS.** While the 1922 is available in Gem, anything finer is a condition rarity. This carefully preserved apricot-gold example, strongly lustrous with a hint of satin on the solidly struck obverse devices, offers plenty of eye appeal. (#9173)

4082 **1922 MS65 PCGS.** The strongly lustrous sun-gold surfaces of this Philadelphia double eagle are carefully preserved, particularly the well-defined devices. A small violet copper spot appears below the eagle's neck. Though this issue is available in Gem, it is surprisingly rare any finer; PCGS has graded just seven finer representatives (8/07). (#9173)

4083 **1922 MS65 PCGS.** This Gem showcases lovely green-gold surfaces with abundant cartwheel luster. The strike is crisp, although the reverse shows a few light abrasions below the eagle. An attractive example of this overlooked issue, conditionally rare any finer, with just seven such pieces graded by PCGS (7/07). (#9173)

4084 **1922 MS65 PCGS.** A slightly better date in Gem condition, and this representative has strong luster, a good strike, and bold visual appeal. The peach-inflected surfaces show just a few minor flaws, and with only seven higher-graded pieces at PCGS (8/07), it is rare any finer. (#9173)

Gem 1923 Saint-Gaudens Twenty

4085 **1923 MS65 NGC.** The 1923, like the 1927 and similar dates, had a high survival rate in overseas hoards. Yet only a small fraction of the original mintage survives in Gem today. The present example offers attractive luster and largely mark-free yellow-gold surfaces with glints of apricot. Tied for the finest certified by NGC (7/07). (#9175)

Lustrous Gem 1923 Double Eagle, MS65

4086 **1923 MS65 PCGS.** An impressive Gem with rich orange-gold luster and scattered darker toning spots on each side. Both sides have frosty luster and excellent eye appeal. An easy date to locate in Gem quality, but not any finer. Just three better ones have been certified by PCGS, and only one by NGC (8/07). (#9175)

4087 **1923-D MS65 PCGS.** This lovely Gem is awash with luster, complemented by sharply struck devices. Peach-gold surfaces display hints of olive-green. The only mentionable marks occur in the area of the eagle's neck, and these do not detract from the overall appeal. (#9176)

4088 **1923-D MS66 PCGS.** The carefully preserved yellow-orange surfaces of this Premium Gem show lovely luster, and the strike is solid. A lovely representative of the last generally available D-mint double eagle. (#9176)

4089 **1924 MS65 PCGS.** The shining surfaces of this Gem are predominantly sun-gold with subtle emerald accents. A minimally marked and attractive representative of this ubiquitous later Saint-Gaudens issue. (#9177)

4090 **1924 MS65 PCGS.** Sharply struck with satiny luster and pleasing mint-green, gold and rose toning. A few trivial blemishes on each side are consistent with the grade. An enticing Gem representative of this noted type issue. (#9177)

4091 **1924 MS65 PCGS.** The luminous peach-gold and apricot-gold surfaces of this type Gem show faint dots of deeper copper alloy. Carefully preserved with only a few faint marks in the fields. (#9177)

4092 **1924 MS65 PCGS.** Lovely peach patina ensures the eye appeal of this lustrous gold type coin. The fields are uncommonly smooth, and the devices are also exceptionally unabraded. Housed in a first generation holder. (#9177)

4093 **1924 MS65 PCGS.** The smooth, richly frosted surfaces are temptingly close to an even higher grade. Beautifully colored in reddish-gold and orange-gold shades that must be seen to be fully appreciated. Certified in an old green label holder. (#9177)

4094 **1924 MS65 PCGS.** Delicate green-gold tints grace the otherwise sun-yellow surfaces of this type Gem. Solidly struck with a pleasing appearance and few marks in the fields on each side. (#9177)

4095 **1924 MS65 NGC.** A strongly lustrous and well-defined example of this well-known type issue, predominantly yellow-gold with copper accents. Both sides show a measure of alloy spotting, with dots of green at Liberty's feet, the upper reverse periphery, and just below the eagle's beak. (#9177)

4096 **1924 MS65 PCGS.** This well struck and softly lustrous type Gem is amber-gold with a hint of honey. A few isolated grazes appear in the fields, but these flaws are consistent with the grade. (#9177)

4097 **1924 MS65 PCGS.** Scarcely any marks appear in this type Gem's yellow-gold and apricot-gold fields, though a single flaw is noted on Liberty's knee. Well struck with an alloy spot present on the eagle's near wing. (#9177)

4098 **1924 MS66 PCGS.** The intense satiny glow over both sides of this impressive piece illuminates the lovely, variegated toning scheme of apricot and lime-green. The design motifs are boldly rendered, and only a few of the details are slightly weak. A well preserved Premium Gem with no surface marks of any consequence. (#9177)

4099 **1924 MS66 NGC.** A nicely preserved representative of this ever-popular type issue, well struck with luster that is strong, if not flashy. The yellow-gold surfaces have elements of peach and lemon. (#9177)

4100 1924 MS66 NGC. This noteworthy type piece has rich lemon-gold surfaces, and the strike is exacting save for the stars near the Capitol building. The fields are beautifully smooth. Interesting clash marks are noted beneath DOLLARS. (#9177)

4101 1924 MS66 PCGS. Radiant luster adorns each side of this peach-gold twenty, and all of the design elements are well brought up. Minimally abraded for the grade level, and a visually enticing Premium Gem example. (#9177)

4102 1924 MS66 PCGS. Attractive yellow-gold surfaces are imbued with traces of khaki, and exhibit pleasing luster. A powerful strike emboldens the design features that display excellent definition on Liberty's face, fingers, and toes. Both sides are wonderfully preserved. (#9177)

Captivating 1924-D Double Eagle, MS62

4103 1924-D MS62 PCGS. Though all three active Mints struck Saint-Gaudens double eagles in the millions, only those of Philadelphia are readily available today; the vast majority of mintmarked pieces never left the United States and were melted in the 1930s. This peach-tinged apricot-gold example is an exception. This strongly lustrous and well struck piece shows few marks on the reverse, though Liberty's legs exhibit a number of abrasions. (#9178)

Desirable 1924-D Double Eagle, MS63

4104 1924-D MS63 PCGS. Despite a substantial mintage of over 3 million pieces, the 1924-D is one of the less available Saint-Gaudens issues on the market, a victim of the gold recall and mass melting spurred by the policies of President Roosevelt. The yellow-orange surfaces of this luminous Select survivor show an arc of deeper carrot color at the upper obverse rim. Light, scattered abrasions in the fields and on Liberty's legs preclude a finer grade. (#9178)

Noteworthy Near-Gem 1924-D Double Eagle

4105 1924-D MS64 PCGS. The rich yellow-orange surfaces of this enticing Choice example offer spectacular luster, which is just one element of this piece's incredible visual appeal. The strike is solid, and the coin's overall surface quality is tantalizingly close to the Gem level, with a single flaw at Liberty's waist the only bar to a finer grade.

Despite a sizable mintage in excess of 3 million pieces, the 1924-D was not preserved in quantity, as its P-mint counterpart was; rather, the 1924-D double eagles largely stayed within the United States, and the vast majority were melted after Franklin D. Roosevelt's gold recall. This issue is conditionally rare any finer, with just nine such pieces certified by PCGS (8/07). (#9178)

Eye-Appealing 1924-D Saint, MS64

4106 1924-D MS64 PCGS. Despite the enormous mintage for a Saint-Gaudens double eagle exceeding 3 million pieces, most examples were subsequently melted during the gold recall of the 1930s, and most of the survivors today are those fortunate enough to be shipped overseas. Bold luster radiates from the orange-gold surfaces of this delightful example, which shows a bold strike from the typical dies that are worn around the rims, a characteristic of the issue. More importantly, only a few stray nicks and scrapes appear on the surfaces, making this a good choice for a date set, with excellent eye appeal, at a fraction of the price of a Gem coin. (#9178)

Mint State Details 1924-S Double Eagle

4107 1924-S—Obverse Scratched—ANACS. MS60 Details. Faint scratches in the right obverse field prevent an unqualified grade for this brilliant yellow gold example. Without the scratches, it would probably grade MS63 or possibly even MS64. The strike is typical with some weakness on each side, and with a beveled reverse rim. (#9179)

Upper-End MS64 1924-S Twenty
An Important Absolute and Condition Rarity

4108 1924-S MS64 PCGS. One of the legendary rarities in the Saint-Gaudens series, the 1924-S was apparently one of the most heavily melted issues as very few coins are known today. Only a few scattered pieces have been found since 1953 in Europe, and no sizeable hoards have been reported. The mint luster is thick and heavily frosted with greenish-gold and orange hues. Sharply defined in all areas, the surfaces are remarkably clean with no mentionable abrasions or alloy spots. Fewer than 200 coins have been seen at both PCGS and NGC in MS64 (minus the usual resubmissions). An MS64 1924-S is the finest coin most collectors will have an opportunity to own. Above that, only 22 coins have been graded. As such, this is a coin that should be carefully inspected by the advanced collector. (#9179)

Choice XF 1925-D Twenty

4109 **1925-D XF45 PCGS.** Nearly 3 million 1925-D double eagles were struck, but only a fraction of the production escaped Treasury vaults prior to the FDR gold recall. The 1925-D is very scarce in Mint State, but it is extremely rare below the AU55 grade. PCGS has certified only two such pieces, the present lot and an AU50. (#9181)

Scarce 1925-D Twenty, MS63

4110 **1925-D MS63 PCGS.** The 1925-D is one of several mintmarked, semi-key issues from the 1920s in the Saint-Gaudens series. It is scarce in all grades, but rarely encountered finer than MS63-64. As usually seen, the striking details on this piece are strongly brought up on each side. The mint luster is uncommonly thick and frosted for a Denver product, but this is consistent with other 1925-D twenties seen and is a trait that is generally found on this issue. A number of small, but individually insignificant abrasions are scattered over each side, which account for the grade. Bright pink-gold color. (#9181)

Radiant 1925-D Double Eagle, MS63

4111 **1925-D MS63 PCGS.** The overarching theme of decimated mintages among later Saint-Gaudens double eagle issues affects the 1925-D. Garrett and Guth (2006) note that "the seemingly large mintage was virtually eliminated." This Select piece is an attractive sun-gold survivor, strongly lustrous with pleasing detail and few marks overall, though two parallel abrasions are present to the right of Liberty's branch. (#9181)

Frosty 1925-D Saint-Gaudens, MS64

4112 **1925-D MS64 PCGS.** This piece ranks as a personal favorite on the present cataloger's list of personal favorites in this sale, a combination of the lovely sunset-orange surfaces with tinges of hazel-gray, the frosty, mattelike surfaces, and a relative paucity of mentionable distractions, large or small. The strike is sharp but less than full, and the often-seen die crack through the eagle's beak and the left periphery is noted. Another high-mintage issue made rare by the subsequent meltings of the 1930s, when most of the mintage was obliterated. As of this writing (8/07), PCGS has certified only six coins finer: four MS65s and two MS66s. (#9181)

4113 **1926 MS65 NGC.** Well struck and highly lustrous, with beautiful peach and lime-green coloration and a lovely satiny sheen across each side. A few stray marks are noted, but they are not excessive for this Gem double eagle.
From The Laguna Niguel Collection, Part Two. (#9183)

4114 **1926 MS65 PCGS.** Lime margins and caramel-gold centers confirm the originality of this lustrous Gem. A small planchet flaw (as made) is found below the DO in DOLLARS. Encased in a first generation holder. (#9183)

Sharp MS64 1926-S Saint-Gaudens Twenty

4115 1926-S MS64 PCGS. The appearance of several hoards over the past 50 years has relegated this former rarity to the more affordable range of mintmarked Saints struck in the 1920s. This is an uncommonly fine MS64 example that is close to Gem classification. The surfaces are bright and satiny with no mentionable abrasions on either side. Sharply struck throughout. (#9185)

4116 1927 MS63 PCGS. A lovely Select Mint State double eagle with great luster and beautiful peach and lime-green coloration. A few minor abrasions limit the grade. An excellent coin for type purposes. Housed in a green label PCGS holder. (#9186)

4117 1927 MS65 PCGS. A beautifully toned example with olive-green margins surrounding peach-tinted centers. Smooth save for a mark on the left (facing) leg. Faint fingerprints are noted at 4:30 on the obverse and 12 o'clock on the reverse. (#9186)

4118 1927 MS65 PCGS. Pleasing luster adorns the peach-gold surfaces of this Saint-Gaudens twenty dollar. The well executed strike is evident in the delineation on the Capitol dome, Liberty's facial features, fingers, and toes, and the eagle's plumage. (#9186)

4119 1927 MS65 PCGS. Blazing luster exudes from apricot-gold surfaces that have a faint greenish cast. The design elements are well impressed, including the fingers on Liberty's hand holding the branch, and on the eagle's plumage. Well preserved throughout. One of the most available issues of the series. (#9186)

4120 1927 MS65 PCGS. From one of the better-produced issues in the Saint-Gaudens series, this Gem presents boldly struck design elements and pleasing luster that highlights the lovely mint-green and rose-gold coloration. A few small marks are noted that do not seem excessive for the grade. (#9186)

4121 1927 MS65 PCGS. A well struck and shining yellow-orange piece that exhibits distinct carrot accents in the fields. Though a mark is present on Liberty's shin, the coin's overall eye appeal is consistent with the Gem designation. (#9186)

4122 1927 MS65 PCGS. This boldly impressed example possesses vibrant cartwheel sheen. A few small marks are concealed on the eagle. Housed in a green label holder. (#9186)

4123 1927 MS65 NGC. Both sides of this Gem are awash in luster, and have received an attentive strike. Apricot-gold surfaces are minimally abraded. (#9186)

4124 1927 MS66 PCGS. Though the 1927 has a mintage of under 3 million pieces, its comparatively high survival rate in Mint State has made it popular with type collectors. This yellow-orange Premium Gem offers strong detail and vibrant luster. PCGS has graded only 12 finer examples (8/07). (#9186)

4125 1927 MS66 NGC. A hint of frost on each side distinguishes this lovely sun-yellow Saint-Gaudens example. A solidly defined and uncommonly well-preserved type piece for the collector of 20th century gold. (#9186)

4126 1927 MS66 NGC. Unusually deep orange-gold coloration is highlighted by intense satiny luster on each side of this impressive Premium Gem. An uncommonly attractive example of this common date double eagle. Likely destined for a type collection with emphasis on eye appeal. This issue becomes extremely elusive above MS66. (#9186)

4127 1927 MS66 NGC. The undeniable eye appeal of this Premium Gem would be difficult to improve upon. It is well struck with shimmering mint frost and beautiful golden-rose and mint-green toning across each side. Surface marks are minimal. The 1927 Saint-Gaudens is widely known as one of the most common dates in the series, but examples with this level of visual allure are scarce. (#9186)

4128 1927 MS66 PCGS. Shimmering luster, sharp detail, and clean surfaces make this pink-gold Premium Gem example exceptionally appealing. An excellent selection for the type collector. PCGS has graded only 12 finer representatives (8/07). (#9186)

4129 1927 MS66 PCGS. A touch of haze visits the upper obverse of this yellow-gold and apricot Premium Gem. An attractive type piece that sports vibrant luster and excellent detail that feed the coin's amazing eye appeal. (#9186)

Gorgeous 1927 Saint-Gaudens, MS67

4130 1927 MS67 NGC. This is a gorgeous Superb Gem with sharply defined obverse and reverse design motifs and fully lustrous orange-gold surfaces. The 1927 double eagle is a common date, although the Superb Gem MS67 grade represents the finest available quality. None have ever received a higher grade. Census: 38 in 67, 0 finer (8/07). (#9186)

Notable 1927-S Double Eagle, MS64

4131 1927-S MS64 PCGS. The Great Recall of 1933-1934, when President Franklin D. Roosevelt ordered the United States off of the gold standard, resulted in massive meltings of Saint-Gaudens double eagles. Some of the most beautiful coins ever minted were systematically converted from works of art into mundane gold bars, many of which are still stored in government vaults at Fort Knox, Kentucky. The later dates in the series were most affected by the meltings, as many were still in government possession at the time of the recall. As such, numerous recorded mintage figures of gold coins struck during the 1920s and 1930s are completely useless when trying to ascertain the rarity of a particular issue. Ironically, it was Franklin Roosevelt's fifth cousin, President Theodore Roosevelt, who commissioned Augustus Saint-Gaudens to create new designs for our country's circulating gold coinage.

Breen suggested that only 15 examples of the 1927-S twenty were in existence when he published his landmark *Complete Encyclopedia* in 1988. That number seems ridiculously low based on our knowledge of this issue today. However, it may not have been too far off when Breen was researching Saint-Gaudens double eagles for inclusion in his seminal reference. Apparently more examples have been repatriated from European holdings since then. Yet even today the survival rate for this date is very low. In *The Coinage of August Saint-Gaudens* (Ivy Press, 2006) the authors comment of this rare issue: "The key status of the 1927-S is based on absolute rarity rather than conditional rarity. In all grades, there are probably only 160-170 pieces extant today, but curiously, two-thirds of the pieces known are Uncirculated." As with all '27-S Saints we have handled, the mint luster is thick and frosted. The bright surfaces have a noticeable overlay of reddish patina that deepens even more around the margins. Fully struck. There are a few scattered marks on each side, none of individual note, that keep this coin from an MS65 grade. Population: 5 in 64, 8 finer (8/07). (#9188)

4132 **1928 MS65 PCGS.** The 1928 is the highest-mintage double eagle issue and the last readily collectible one as well, though the melting that affected later dates also reduced its population. A shining and well-defined yellow-orange Gem, this well-preserved piece would fit well in a similarly graded type or date set. (#9189)

4133 **1928 MS66 PCGS.** Boldly struck with good definition on Liberty's face, fingers, and toes. The eagle is also crisply detailed. Highly lustrous with exquisite lime and peach-gold coloration, this Premium Gem has outstanding eye appeal. A small mark on Liberty's abdomen precludes an even loftier grade designation. (#9189)

4134 **1928 MS66 NGC.** Mint-green and peach coloration attractively adorns each side of this well struck, highly lustrous Premium Gem. Surface blemishes are nearly nonexistent. A small, dark reddish-brown spot is noted beneath Liberty's left (facing) breast. (#9189)

4135 **1928 MS66 PCGS.** Highly lustrous peach-gold surfaces are laced with tints of light green, and the design elements are sharply delineated. A few minor ticks may have precluded an even finer grade. A truly superior Premium Gem! (#9189)

4136 **1928 MS66 PCGS.** Shimmering mint luster over surfaces adorned with lovely, light peach-gold and pastel rose coloration ensures the splendid eye appeal of this Premium Gem. The design elements are well struck, and both sides of the piece are minimally marked. (#9189)

4137 **1928 MS66 PCGS.** Both sides of this shining double eagle are butter-yellow with a touch of orange. A well-defined representative from the highest-mintage issue for the denomination, though subsequent melting sharply reduced its available population. (#9189)

4138 **1928 MS66 PCGS.** Well struck on Liberty's face and fingers, and on all of the eagle's wing and breast feathers. This Premium Gem is highly lustrous and highly attractive, displaying pastel colors of peach and lime-green and minimal surface marks. A bit of olive-drab verdigris is noted on the lower left reverse rim, near 7 o'clock. (#9189)

TERRITORIAL GOLD

4139 **Baldwin & Co. 'Restrike' Deep Cameo Proof PCGS.** A 906 Fine Justh & Hunter ingot was the source alloy for this unusual relic medal, struck by the Royal Canadian Mint. The ingot, in turn, came from the 1857 S.S. *Central America* shipwreck. Dated 1857/O but struck in 2002. The surfaces are nearly flawless. The presentation faux book, fact sheet, and certificate of authenticity are included with the lot. (#10028)

4140 **Baldwin & Co. 'Restrike' Deep Cameo Proof PCGS.** Dated 1857/O, but struck in 2002 by the Royal Canadian Mint. The source for the 906 Fine alloy was a Justh & Hunter ingot recovered from the S.S. *Central America* shipwreck. An immaculate example with exemplary cameo contrast. A certificate of authenticity, fact sheet, and faux book accompany. (#10028)

4141 **Baldwin & Co. 'Restrike' Deep Cameo Proof PCGS.** This interesting relic medal was struck by the Royal Canadian Mint from gold alloy taken from a Justh & Hunter ingot, which in turn was recovered from the treasure ship S.S. *Central America*. Dated 1857/O, the 1850 was the date of the genuine Baldwin "Horseman" ten, and 1857 was the year of the SSCA shipwreck. Fully struck and essentially perfect. The presentation box, fact sheet, and certificate of authenticity accompany. (#10028)

4142 **Baldwin & Co. 'Restrike' Deep Cameo Proof PCGS.** A modern copy of the legendary Baldwin 'Horseman' Territorial Ten Dollar issue. Essentially pristine, and the contrast between the devices and field is unimprovable. Dated 1857/O on the obverse, and 2002 on the reverse. A relic medal whose source bullion was a Justh & Hunter ingot from the S.S. *Central America* shipwreck. Counterstamped JUSTH & HUNTER/4220 on the reverse. (#10028)

4143 **Baldwin & Co. 'Restrike' Deep Cameo Proof PCGS.** A lightly toned example with pleasing cameo contrast. Perfect save for a tiny lintmark beneath the E in CENTRAL. A .916 fine Justh & Hunter ingot, recovered from the cargo of the S.S. *Central America*, provided the source gold bullion. (#10028)

4144 **Baldwin & Co. 'Restrike' Deep Cameo Proof PCGS.** Exemplary contrast and seamless mirrored fields confirm the quality of this interesting relic medal. Struck in 2002 from a Justh & Hunter ingot retrieved from the 1857 S.S. *Central America* shipwreck. Since no coin designs are known for assayers Justh & Hunter, the famous 1850 Baldwin & Co. Vaquero motifs were used instead. (#10028)

4145 **Baldwin & Co. 'Restrike' Deep Cameo Proof PCGS.** Unsold Justh & Hunter ingots recovered from the S.S. *Central America* were melted to supply the gold for this "restrike" issue. The designs are inspired by the 1850 Baldwin ten dollar piece, although the 0 is overdated with 7 to signify the date of the SSCA shipwreck. (#10028)

4146 **Baldwin & Co. 'Restrike' Deep Cameo Proof PCGS.** The famous 1850 Baldwin 'Horseman' Territorial ten dollar issue serves as the design inspiration for this 2002 restrike. Kuner's name appears on the obverse, since he engraved the original 1850 dies. He would likely repudiate the reverse, however, since the additional S.S. CENTRAL AMERICA legend has small mistakes, such as a widely spaced ICA and several unbalanced and misaligned letters. (#10028)

Splendid N Reversed C. Bechtler Dollar MS62

4147 **(1837-42) C. Bechtler Dollar, N Reversed MS62 NGC.** K-4, R.4. A pleasing and highly attractive example of this popular and memorable Bechtler variety. Recessed areas are canary-gold, while the fields are sky-gray and pale orange. Abrasions are primarily trivial, the sole exception is a brief, thin mark between the CA in CAROLINA. A minor and mostly retained lamination (as produced) passes across the R in CAROLINA. Listed on page 349 of the 2008 *Guide Book*. Census: 5 in 62, 3 finer (7/07). (#10055)

Mint State C. Bechtler Five Dollar, K-20

4148 (1837-42) C. Bechtler Five Dollar, 134G, With Star MS61 NGC. K-20, R.4. A yellow-gold example with pale lime patina across the open fields. Flashes of luster and an even strike ensure the eye appeal. As expected of the MS61 grade, a few wispy marks are present, some above the 1 in 134. Struck from widely rotated dies, and listed on page 350 of the 2008 *Guide Book*. As a denomination, Bechtler five dollar pieces are significantly scarcer than Bechtler gold dollars. Bullion customers probably preferred payment in gold dollars, since higher denominations would have been cumbersome in commerce. Census: 10 in 61, 0 finer (7/07). (#10097)

XF40 Details 1860 Clark, Gruber Half Eagle

4149 1860 Clark, Gruber & Co. Five Dollar—Cleaned—ANACS. XF40 Details. K-2, R.4. Unlike the 1860 ten and twenty dollar Clark, Gruber & Co. denominations, the five dollar pieces closely imitate the designs of their Federal counterparts. The fields are a bit glossy from a cleaning, and the lower obverse has several pinpoint marks, but luster emerges from protected areas. Listed on page 366 of the 2008 *Guide Book*. (#10136)

AU 1853 Assay Office Twenty

4150 1853 Assay Office Twenty Dollar, 900 Thous. AU50 NGC. K-18, R.2. This is one of the most available of all Territorial gold coins issued in California. As such, it is an excellent candidate for the collector who wants a single representative of Gold Rush coinage. This example clearly shows the 900 punched over 880. A deep, thin mark crosses the E in AMERICA, and the obverse has a rim ding at 8 o'clock. Substantial luster remains. Splashes of pale orange add to the eye appeal. Listed on page 355 of the 2008 *Guide Book*. (#10013)

1854 Twenty Dollar Kellogg & Co, AU58, K-2

4151 1854 Kellogg & Co. Twenty Dollar AU58 NGC. K-2, R.4. This is the variety with long arrows that have arrowheads that touch or nearly touch the inner curve of the scroll at the lower right. This high-end AU coin is fully original with some olive-gold patina in the fields and over the raised features. Nicely defined in the centers with scattered small abrasions and a few heavier ones on Liberty's cheek. Listed on page 363 of the 2008 *Guide Book*. (#10222)

Scarce Variety 1855 Kellogg & Co Twenty Dollar AU Details

4152 1855 Kellogg & Co.—Repaired—NCS. AU Details. K-3c, R.5. This Short Arrows die marriage is unlisted in the Kagin reference. The O in CO is buried in the hair, as on Kagin-3b, but the date is set further to the left. This boldly detailed example appears to have been harshly cleaned, and Liberty's cheek and neck have been smoothed. Faint tooling marks are also noted near the bust truncation, with the aid of a magnifier. Listed on page 363 of the 2008 *Guide Book*. (#10225)

Proof Restrike 1855 Kellogg & Co. Fifty

4153 **1855 Kellogg & Co. Fifty Dollar Restrike Gem Proof PCGS.** Struck on August 25, 2001, with a proof mintage on that date of 128 pieces. Struck at the Presidio on gold alloy removed from ingots recovered from the *S.S. Central America.* The boldly struck devices exhibit cameo contrast with the unabraded surfaces. A couple of faint pale-gray spots in the field near the portrait deny perfection. PCGS holder has minor scuffs. (#10228)

Imposing Kellogg Fifty Dollar Proof Restrike

4154 **1855 Kellogg & Co. Fifty Dollar Restrike Gem Proof PCGS.** Coined on August 26, 2001, from a proof mintage of 200 pieces on that date. A flawless example of this popular relic medal issue. The 887 thousands fine gold bullion within the medal came from unsold large Kellogg & Humbert ingots recovered from the *S.S. Central America.* The fields display faint parallel striations, as made from the die preparation. (#10228)

Scarce Restrike Proof Kellogg Fifty Dollar

4155 **1855 Kellogg & Co. Fifty Dollar Restrike Gem Proof PCGS.** Struck August 28, 2001, with a tiny proof mintage of 50 pieces. This is the second lowest production of any date, behind only the 8/24 proof mintage of 25 pieces. This interesting relic medal was struck on a former San Francisco Mint coin press, and its gold alloy came from *S.S. Central America* Kellogg & Humbert ingots. Included with the lot is the canary-gold box of issue with its certificate of authenticity, mauve brochure, and glass-enclosed metal frame. (#10228)

Popular Restrike Gem Proof 1855 Kellogg $50

4156 **1855 Kellogg & Co. Fifty Dollar Restrike Gem Proof PCGS.** Struck on August 29, 2001. The proof mintage for that date was 93 pieces. Virtually immaculate aside from a pair of faint reeding marks on the reverse. Included with the lot is a yellow box from the California Historical Society, a certificate of authenticity, a brochure, and a presentation case complete with velvet inset, glass panel, metal frame, and screwdriver.

Restrike Gem Proof 1855 Kellogg Fifty

4157 **1855 Kellogg & Co. Fifty Dollar Restrike Gem Proof PCGS.** Struck August 31, 2001. The mintage for that date was 483 pieces. Essentially as struck, although the exterior of the PCGS holder has a few faint hairlines. Included with the lot is the gold-colored presentation case from the California Historical Society, a purple informative pamphlet, a certificate of authenticity, and the glass frame and velvet case. No screwdriver is included. (#10228)

Nifty Restrike Proof 1855 Kellogg Fifty

4158 **1855 Kellogg & Co. Fifty Dollar Restrike Gem Proof PCGS.** This relic medal was struck on September 7, 2001, from a mintage of 223 proofs with that date. Made from unsold melted-down Kellogg & Humbert ingots recovered from the *S.S. Central America.* Struck at the Presidio near San Francisco. The gold presentation box, brochure, certificate of authenticity, screwdriver, and frame are all included, along with a copy of the 2002 55th Edition of *A Guide Book of United States Coins,* marked "*S.S. Central America* Special Edition" on the front cover, in Mint condition. (#10228)

Exemplary Restrike Proof Kellogg Fifty Dollar

4159 **1855 Kellogg & Co. Fifty Dollar Restrike Gem Proof PCGS.** Minted September 7, 2001, from 887 Fine gold reclaimed from melted down Kellogg & Humbert ingots recovered from the legendary *S.S. Central America* shipwreck. A flawless example with impressive contrast between the intricate devices and the glassy fields. The gold-colored box, purple brochure, certificate of authenticity, screwdriver, and steel, glass, and velvet frame all accompany the lot. (#10228)

Popular Restrike Kellogg Fifty Dollar Proof

4160 **1855 Kellogg & Co. Fifty Dollar Restrike Gem Proof PCGS.** Struck on the 144th anniversary of the sinking of the famous *S.S. Central America* treasure ship, September 12, 2001. The proof mintage for that date was 587 pieces. This interesting relic medal issue was coined from melted down Kellogg & Humbert gold bars recovered from the shipwreck. (#10228)

Immaculate Restrike Proof Kellogg & Co. Fifty

4161 **1855 Kellogg & Co. Fifty Dollar Restrike Gem Proof PCGS.** Struck on Sept. 12, 2001, with a proof mintage of 587 pieces. This was the 144th anniversary of the sinking of the *S.S. Central America*. A scarce and popular relic medal that contains nearly 2.5 ounces of gold, whose source was melted down Kellogg & Humbert ingots recovered from the SSCA shipwreck. No box or certificate accompanies the lot. The coin itself is immaculate, although the PCGS holder has a few faint marks. (#10228)

Impressive 36.40-Ounce Kellogg & Humbert Gold Ingot Ex: *Central America*

4162 **Kellogg & Humbert Gold Ingot.** A disaster such as the sinking of a ship focuses the attention of people on what is truly important, life itself. It also brings out the best and worst in people. A passage from *America's Lost Treasure* is of interest and was written later by one of the survivors, William Chase:

> "Some of the men unbuckled their gold-stuffed belts and flung their hard-earned treasure upon the deck to lighten their weight. Chase claimed that he could easily have picked up thousands of dollars, if he thought he had a chance of reaching safety with this treasure. Shortly before eight o'clock, the *Central America*, with its decks now awash, was rapidly filling with water and sinking lower into the sea. In a dinner conversation earlier in the voyage Captain Herndon had told the Eastons that if his ship were ever to go down, he would go with it. Now, having done everything he could to save the women and children, and wondering if he could have done anything different to avoid the imminent tragedy, Captain Herndon retired to his quarters. Stoic and proud, he returned to the wheelhouse wearing his full-dress uniform."

Of the gold ingots that slipped to the bottom of the sea 150 years ago, the most plentiful were those from the well-respected firm of Kellogg & Humbert. More than 400 of these ingots were recovered in 1988. In spite of its considerable heft, the present piece is actually one of the smaller ingots recovered. The smallest from Kellogg & Humbert was 5.71 ounces and the largest weighed an amazing 933.94 ounces! At the time the *Central America* sunk, this particular ingot was valued at $620.77.

The ingot is 52 mm tall, 41 mm wide, and 30 mm deep. The top side reads: No 1028/36.40 OZ/825 FINE/$620.77. The individual ingot number is repeated at the top of the back side. The company imprint is neatly impressed on the right side. Two assay chips are out of opposing corners, as always. Bright overall with no traces of the rust that is often seen on these ingots.

Affordable 1849 Moffat Five Dollar, XF Details

4163 **1849 Moffat & Co. Five Dollar—Mount Removed—NCS. XF Details.** K-4a, R.4. A thick die crack across the tops of the central letters in the denomination distinguishes the variety. This glossy lemon-gold territorial piece has scattered abrasions and light, even wear across the devices. Evidence of a former mount is visible near 12 o'clock on the obverse rim, and the reverse shows a pinscratch below the eagle's beak. Still, an affordable example of this popular territorial issue. (#10240)

Desirable 1849 Moffat Ten, XF40

4164 **1849 Moffat & Co. Ten Dollar, "Ten Dol." XF40 NGC.** K-6a, High R.5. The first coins issued by the private firm of Moffat & Company were 1849-dated Ten Dollar gold pieces. At the time of their production, Moffat & Company was the only private minter located in San Francisco besides Norris, Gregg, & Norris, and this denomination does not usually appear much finer than this. This is an unusually attractive coin for the grade with even overall wear and plenty of bold definition remaining in the more protected areas of the design. The number of abrasions is not excessive, and the color is a rich, original, green-gold shade. A perfect candidate for inclusion in a circulated Territorial gold type set that requires a representation of Moffat & Company coinage. Listed on page 352 of the current 2008 *Guide Book*. (#10246)

Scarce VF25 1849 Moffat & Co. Ten

4165 **1849 Moffat & Co. Ten Dollar, "Ten D." VF25 PCGS.** K-5, R.5. K-5 and K-5a appear to be the same variety, with no difference seen in the size of the reverse letters. This green-gold representative has pleasing sharpness on the eagle, while the portrait shows the expected amount of wear. Only lightly abraded. Listed on page 352 of the 2008 *Guide Book*. Population: 5 in 25, 28 finer (7/07). (#10249)

4166 **Uncertified Gold Pinch.** 22.57 gms. of gold flakes or dust. The flakes are yellow-tan. The source of the gold pinch is unknown. *From The Diemer L. Fife Collection.*

4167 **Montana Placer Gold Nugget.** Weight: 18.98 grams. Size: 25 x 17 x 1.1 mm. Rich yellow-gold color with traces of quartz or other impurities. Our consigner states that this nugget was found in Montana. *From The Diemer L. Fife Collection.*

End of Auction